# Contemporary Perspectives on the Psychology of Attitudes

The attitude concept has long formed an indispensable construct in social psychology. In this volume, internationally renowned contributors review contemporary developments in research and theory to capture the current metamorphosis of this central concept.

This collection of the latest developments in the field provides a scholarly and accessible overview of the study of attitudes and examines the implications for its position as a paradigm of social psychological understanding. The book is divided into three parts. Part I addresses the structural and behavioral properties of attitudes including the affective-cognitive structure of attitudes, the nature of attitude ambivalence and intention–behavior relations. Part II focuses on representational and transformational processes, such as meta-cognitive attitudinal processes, the role of implicit and explicit attitudinal processes, cultural influences and attitude change. In Part III the editors draw together these contemporary perspectives and elaborate on their impact for future theorizing and research into attitudes.

Empirically supported throughout, this collection represents a timely integration of the burgeoning range of approaches to attitude research. It will be of interest to social psychologists, sociologists, political scientists and researchers with an interest in attitudinal phenomena.

**Geoffrey Haddock** and **Gregory R. Maio** are established researchers in the field of attitudes and social cognition. They are both members of the Social Psychology Research Group at Cardiff University.

# Contemporary Perspectives on the Psychology of Attitudes

**Edited by**
**Geoffrey Haddock and Gregory R. Maio**

 Psychology Press
Taylor & Francis Group
HOVE AND NEW YORK

First published 2004 by Psychology Press
27 Church Road, Hove, East Sussex, BN3 2FA

Simultaneously published in the USA and Canada
by Psychology Press Inc
270 Madison Avenue, New York, NY 10016

*Psychology Press is a part of the Taylor and Francis Group*

Copyright © 2004 Psychology Press

Typeset in Times by RefineCatch Limited, Bungay, Suffolk
Printed and bound in Great Britain by
TJ International Ltd, Padstow, Cornwall

Cover design by Sandra Heath

This publication has been produced with paper manufactured to strict
environmental standards and with pulp derived from sustainable
forests.

*British Library Cataloguing in Publication Data*
A catalogue record for this book is available from the British Library

*Library of Congress Cataloging-in-Publication Data*
   Contemporary perspectives on the psychology of attitudes :
   the Cardiff Symposium / edited by Geoffrey Haddock & Gregory R.
   Maio.
       p. cm.
   Includes bibliographical references and index.
   ISBN 1-84169-326-X (hbk)
       1. Attitude (Psychology)–Congress. I. Haddock, Geoffrey. II. Maio,
   Gregory R.
   BF327.C66 2004                                     2004000162
   152.4–dc22

ISBN 1-84169-326-X

# Contents

## 13 The role of exemplar stability in attitude consistency and attitude change

CHARLES G. LORD

## 14 Putting Humpty together again: Attitude organization from a connectionist perspective

J. RICHARD EISER

# Tables

# Figures

# Contributors

**Christopher J. Armitage**, Department of Psychology, University of Sheffield, Sheffield S10 2TP, UK

**Karin Arnold**, School of Psychology, Cardiff University, PO Box 901, Cardiff CF10 3YG, UK

**Richard P. Bagozzi**, Jesse H. Jones Graduate School of Management, PO Box 2932, Rice University, Houston, TX 77252, USA

**Tilmann Betsch**, Department of Psychology, University of Erfurt, Nordhäuser Strasse 63, 99089 Erfurt, Germany

**Steven J. Breckler**, Executive Director for Science, American Psychological Association, 750 First Street NE, Washington, DC 20002-4242, USA

**Pablo Briñol**, Universidad Autonoma de Madrid, Departamento de Psicologia Social, Carretera de Comenar, Km. 15, 28049 Madrid, Spain

**Mark Conner**, School of Psychology, University of Leeds, Leeds LS2 9JT, UK

**J. Richard Eiser**, Department of Psychology, University of Sheffield, Sheffield S10 2TP, UK

**Hans-Peter Erb**, University of Jena, Institute of Psychology, Department of Social Psychology, Humboldtstr. 26, D-07743 Jena, Germany

**Victoria M. Esses**, Department of Psychology, University of Western Ontario, London, Ontario N6A 5C2, Canada

**Ayelet Fishbach**, Department of Psychology, University of Maryland—College Park, College Park, Maryland 20742, USA

**Geoffrey Haddock**, School of Psychology, PO Box 901, Cardiff University, Cardiff CF10 3YG, UK

**Etsuko Hoshino-Browne**, Department of Psychology, University of Waterloo, 200 University Avenue West, Waterloo, Ontario N2L 3G1, Canada

**Thomas L. H. Huskinson**, School of Psychology, PO Box 901, Cardiff University, Cardiff CF10 3YG, UK

**Karen Jordens**, Vrije Universiteit Brussel, Department of Psychology, Pleinlaan-2, B-1050 Brussels, Belgium

**Arie W. Kruglanski**, Department of Psychology, University of Maryland— College Park, College Park, Maryland 20742, USA

**Howard Lavine**, Department of Political Science, State University of New York at Stony Brook, Stony Brook, NY 11794–4392, USA

**Charles G. Lord**, Department of Psychology, Texas Christian University, Fort Worth, TX 76129, USA

**Gregory R. Maio**, School of Psychology, PO Box 901, Cardiff University, Cardiff CF10 3YG, UK

**Lucia Mannetti**, Dipartimento di Psicologia dei Processi, di Sviluppo e Socializzazione, Via dei Marsi 78, I-00815, Roma, Italy

**James M. Olson**, Department of Psychology, University of Western Ontario, London, Ontario N6A 5C2, Canada

**Sheina Orbell**, Department of Psychology, University of Essex, Wivenhoe Park, Colchester CO4 3SQ, UK

**Frank van Overwalle**, Vrije Universiteit Brussel, Department of Psychology, Pleinlaan-2, B-1050 Brussels, Belgium

**Marco Perugini**, Department of Psychology, University of Essex, Wivenhoe Park, Colchester CO4 3SQ, UK

**Richard E. Petty**, Department of Psychology, Ohio State University, 1885 Neil Avenue Mall, Columbus, OH 43210–1222, USA

**Antonio Pierro**, Dipartimento di Psicologia dei Processi, di Sviluppo e Socializzazione, Via dei Marsi 78, I-00815, Roma, Italy

**Henning Plessner**, Institut für Psychologie, Universität Heidelberg, Hauptstr. 47–51, D-69117 Heidelberg, Germany

**Elke Schallies**, Institut für Psychologie, Universität Heidelberg, Hauptstr. 47–51, D-69117 Heidelberg, Germany

**Yaacov Schul**, Department of Psychology, Hebrew University, Jerusalem, Israel

**Paschal Sheeran**, Department of Psychology, University of Sheffield, Sheffield, S10 2TP, UK

**Steven J. Spencer**, Department of Psychology, University of Waterloo, 200 University Avenue West, Waterloo, Ontario, N2L 3G1, Canada

**David Trafimow**, Department of Psychology, Box 3452, New Mexico State University, Las Cruce, NM 88003, USA

**Patrick T. Vargas**, Department of Advertising, 103 Gregory Hall, University of Illinois, Urbana IL 61801, USA

**Adam S. Zanna**, Department of Psychology, University of Waterloo, 200 University Avenue West, Waterloo, Ontario N2L 3G1, Canada

**Mark P. Zanna**, Department of Psychology, University of Waterloo, 200 University Avenue West, Waterloo, Ontario N2L 3G1, Canada

# Introduction and overview

*Geoffrey Haddock and*
*Gregory R. Maio*

Attitudes refer to our overall evaluations of objects. For example, both of us like the Toronto Maple Leafs hockey team and dislike the music of R.E.O. Speedwagon. Over the past 75 years, social psychologists have devoted considerable attention to the empirical study of attitudes. Indeed, attitudes research has always been at the core of social psychology, and it is fair to say that we have discovered a great deal about the attitude concept. For example, we have learned that attitudes can serve different psychological needs. While some attitudes might reflect our underlying values, others help us behave in ways appropriate to important reference groups. Similarly, we have learned that attitudes can be derived from affective information (e.g., feelings about an object), cognitive information (e.g., beliefs associated with an object), and behavioral information (e.g., past experiences with an object). Third, we have learned that attitudes often predict behavior, and have specified when this correspondence is most likely to occur. Fourth, we have also learned a great deal about how attitudes can be changed. The thoroughly comprehensive and scholarly text by Eagly and Chaiken (1993) is testimony to the myriad of developments that have taken place within the attitudes literature.

That said, the attitude concept is undergoing somewhat of a metamorphosis. Although much past research reflects the traditional notion that attitudes are simple tendencies to like or dislike attitude objects, contemporary research has begun to adopt more complex perspectives. For example, recent advances on the mental structure of attitudes have suggested that attitudes (and their components) might not always be simply positive or negative, but may subsume both positivity and negativity (e.g., Cacioppo & Berntson, 1994). Second, contemporary research on the psychological needs served by attitudes has greatly extended the classic models proposed by Katz, Smith, and colleagues over 40 years ago, allowing us to better understand the reasons we hold attitudes (e.g., Maio & Olson, 2000). Third, recent research on the concept of attitude strength has documented that strong and weak attitudes are associated with many different outcomes (e.g., Petty & Krosnick, 1995). As a final example, methodological advances have allowed researchers to consider with greater precision the existence and implications of possessing implicit (e.g., non-conscious) and explicit (e.g., conscious) attitudes (e.g., Fazio, Jackson, Dunton, & Williams, 1995; Greenwald, McGhee, & Schwartz, 1998). Although these (and numerous other) advances have generated a myriad of novel questions surrounding the nature of attitudes, it seemed to us that there was a real need to integrate the many different components of this research.

In July 2000, more than two dozen researchers from around the world gathered at the Gregynog Estate in the picturesque hills of mid-Wales for a meeting on the psychology on attitudes, jointly sponsored by the European Association of Experimental Social Psychology and the University of Wales. The primary objective of the meeting was to integrate recent advances in knowledge regarding the mental structure of attitudes, the motivations underlying attitudes, and the relation between attitudes and behavior. The meeting was an unequivocal success and led us to consider the possibility of producing an edited volume that would bring together numerous recent developments within contemporary attitudes research. Toward that aim, this book contains chapters by most of the contributors to the Gregynog meeting, as well as contributions we invited after the meeting.

The volume itself is divided into three parts. Part I of the volume is titled "Attitudes, Attitude Properties, and Behavior." This section focuses upon structural and behavioral properties of attitudes, and deals with issues such as the affective-cognitive structure of attitudes, the nature of attitude ambivalence, and the behavioral implications of attitudes. After considerable discussion, we ended up drawing the rather awkward conclusion that our own contributions, as minimal as they may be, help set the stage for the remaining chapters that focus on structural and behavioral properties of attitudes. In Chapter 1, Gregory R. Maio, Victoria M. Esses, Karin Arnold, and James M. Olson propose that the effects of affective, cognitive, and behavioral information on attitudes depend upon individuals' motivational goals. As well as describing their function–structure model, they demonstrate how individual differences in the need to approach or avoid affective experiences play a role in attitude formation and attitude change. In Chapter 2, Geoffrey Haddock and Thomas L. H. Huskinson describe research suggesting that there are chronic differences across individuals in the degree to which attitudes are derived from affective and cognitive information. They provide evidence that such differences exist, are associated with attitude-relevant individual difference measures, and have implications for persuasion and attitude accessibility. In Chapter 3, David Trafimow and Paschal Sheeran discuss whether it is sensible to partition attitudes into affective and cognitive components. They state that such a partition is sensible and argue that cognition is translated into affect before it can influence behavior. Different strands of evidence are presented in support of this proposal. In Chapter 4, Steven J. Breckler introduces the concept of attitude ambivalence and compares different formulae that have been developed to measure this construct. He then proceeds to describe the concept of "multivalence" and considers how this concept can be assessed. In Chapter 5, Howard Lavine discusses the role of ambivalence in political attitudes. He presents a theoretical argument that links ambivalence toward American presidential candidates to electoral decision making, showing that ambivalence is associated with a variety of outcomes. In addition, he argues that political ambivalence does not only exist at the level of specific politicians, but also occurs at the more abstract left–right dimension. In Chapter 6, Christopher J. Armitage and Mark Conner discuss how attitude ambivalence moderates the attitude–behavior relation. They introduce research demonstrating that non-ambivalent attitudes are more predictive of subsequent behavioral intentions and behavior. In Chapter 7, Sheina Orbell continues the emphasis on behavioral consequences of attitudes by demonstrating that positive intentions are not necessarily translated into behavior. She then discusses how the consideration of self-regulatory processes can serve to initiate or maintain goal-directed behavior. In Chapter 8, Marco Perugini and Richard P. Bagozzi conclude Part I of the book by discussing the importance of automatic and reasoned processes in predicting behavior. They argue that intentions play a key role in predicting behavior, and introduce two models that incorporate the role of automatic, emotional, motivational, and means-end processes in enhancing the prediction of intentions and behavior.

Part II of the book is titled "Attitude Awareness, Attitude Representations, and Change." This section focuses upon representational and transformational processes of attitudes, and deals with issues such as meta-cognitive attitudinal processes, implicit and explicit attitudinal processes, the representation and organization of attitudes, cultural influences, and attitude change processes. In Chapter 9, Pablo Briñol and Richard E. Petty consider the role of meta-cognitive processes in attitude change. They argue that in order for a message to elicit meaningful attitude change, recipients of the message should not only generate thoughts that agree with the message, but they must also have confidence in the validity of their thoughts. In Chapter 10, Yaacov Schul reviews evidence regarding how individuals process and cope with invalid messages. He argues that we are poor detectors of deception and that we can prepare for invalid messages by either increasing or decreasing message processing. In Chapter 11, Tilmann Betsch, Henning Plessner, and Elke Schallies introduce the value-account model of attitude formation. Their model asserts that implicit and explicit attitude formation involve different mechanisms of information integration, with implicit attitude formation guided by a principle of summation and explicit attitude formation guided by a principle of averaging. In Chapter 12, Patrick T. Vargas also discusses the role of implicit and explicit components of attitudinal phenomena. He considers how the correspondence principle (Ajzen & Fishbein, 1977) and the theory of transfer appropriate processing (Roediger, 1990) can be applied to the study of attitudes and behavior, and uses these models as a framework to show how implicit and explicit attitudes are differentially predictive of different types of behavior. In Chapter 13, Charles G. Lord discusses the role of exemplar stability in attitude consistency and attitude change. Based upon attitude representation theory (Lord & Lepper, 1999), he demonstrates that the consistency of an individual's subjective representation of an attitude object predicts the degree to which the favorability of their attitude remains stable over time. In Chapter 14, J. Richard Eiser considers the issue of how attitudes are cognitively organized and represented. Using a connectionist framework, he illustrates how attitude organization is built via learned associations, concluding that attitudes should be conceptualized as dynamic systems that evolve over time. In Chapter 15, Karen Jordens and Frank Van Overwalle also advance a connectionist framework to analyze processes of attitude representation and change. They argue that attitudes can be learned or changed with little awareness or mental effort, and propose a connectionist perspective on attitude formation and cognitive dissonance. In Chapter 16, Etsuko Hoshino-Browne, Adam S. Zanna, Steven J. Spencer, and Mark P. Zanna present a historical perspective of cross-cultural research on attitude-relevant constructs. They assert that while some psychological processes are thought to be consistent across cultures, the operation of these processes is a function of culture. Evidence in support of this proposal is presented, using the concept of cognitive dissonance. In Chapter 17, Arie W. Kruglanski, Ayelet Fishbach, Hans-Peter Erb, Antonio Pierro, and Lucia Mannetti describe the unimodel theory of persuasion. Based on the premise that persuasion is best conceptualized as a special case of judgment formation, Kruglanski and colleagues demonstrate how the unimodel both accounts for other findings in the persuasion literature and asks novel questions that set it apart from dual-process models of persuasion (e.g., Chaiken, Liberman, & Eagly, 1989; Petty & Cacioppo, 1986).

Following the individual contributions, in Part III we conclude the volume by highlighting and integrating theoretical issues raised within contemporary attitudes research (Chapter 18). Furthermore, we consider some of the issues that we believe are likely to stimulate attitudes research in the future.

## Acknowledgments

Finally, our introduction would be incomplete without thanking those individuals and organizations that provided assistance throughout this project. First, we wish to the European Association of Experimental Social Psychology, the University of Wales, and the Psychology Departments of Cardiff University, the University of Bristol, and the University of Exeter, all of whom provided financial support for the Gregynog meeting. Second, we wish to thank Paul Dukes, Lucy Farr, Ruben Hale, Claire Lipscomb, Susan Rudkin, and Kathryn Russel from Psychology Press; they have been helpful and patient through all stages of the project. Third, we wish to thank Mark Zanna, Norbert Schwarz, Jim Olson, Vicki Esses, and Clive Seligman, all of whom nurtured our interest in the study of attitudes. Finally, and certainly not least, we are grateful to Margaret Newson and Audra, Kestrel, and Gabriella Maio for the support and understanding they provided throughout this project.

# References

Ajzen, I., & Fishbein, M. (1977). Attitude-behavior relations: A theoretical analysis and review of empirical research. *Psychological Bulletin, 84,* 888–918.

Cacioppo, J. T., & Berntson, G. G. (1994). Relationship between attitudes and evaluative space: A critical review, with emphasis on the separability of positive and negative substrates. *Psychological Bulletin, 115,* 401–423.

Chaiken, S., Liberman, A., & Eagly, A. H. (1989). Heuristic and systematic processing within and beyond the persuasion context. In J. S. Uleman & J. A. Bargh (Eds.), *Unintended thought* (pp. 212–252). New York: Guilford Press.

Eagly, A. H., & Chaiken, S. (1993). *The psychology of attitudes.* Fort Worth, TX: Harcourt Brace Jovanovich.

Fazio, R. H., Jackson, J. R., Dunton, B. C., & Williams, C. J. (1995). Variability in automatic activation as an unobtrusive measure of racial attitudes: A bona fide pipeline? *Journal of Personality and Social Psychology, 69,* 1013–1027.

Greenwald, A. G., McGhee, D. E., & Schwartz, J. K. (1998). Measuring individual differences in implicit cognition: The implicit association test. *Journal of Personality and Social Psychology, 74,* 1464–1480.

Lord, C. G., & Lepper, M. R. (1999). Attitude representation theory. In M. P. Zanna (Ed.), *Advances in Experimental Social Psychology* (Vol. 31, pp. 265–343). San Diego, CA: Academic Press.

Maio, G. R., & Olson, J. M. (Eds.) (2000). *Why we evaluate: Functions of attitudes.* Mahwah, NJ: Lawrence Erlbaum Associates, Inc.

Petty, R. E., & Cacioppo, J. T. (1986). The elaboration likelihood model of persuasion. In L. Berkowitz (Ed.), *Advances in experimental social psychology* (Vol. 19, pp. 123–205). San Diego, CA: Academic Press.

Petty, R. E., & Krosnick, J. A. (Eds.) (1995). *Attitude strength: Antecedents and consequences.* Hillsdale, NJ: Lawrence Erlbaum Associates, Inc.

Roediger, H. L. (1990). Implicit memory: Retention without remembering. *American Psychologist, 45,* 1043–1056.

# Part I

# Attitudes, attitude properties, and behavior

# 1 The function–structure model of attitudes

## Incorporating the need for affect

*Gregory R. Maio, Victoria M. Esses,*
*Karin H. Arnold and James M. Olson*

## Introduction

Why do I like the Toronto Maple Leafs so much? This question occurs often to the first author and many other fans of this ice hockey team, especially during losing streaks. No doubt similar questions occur to millions of sport fans worldwide, all of whom spend abundant time and money watching a collection of grown men or women kick, throw, or shoot a spheroidal object across a delineated terrain under a complex system of rules. It could be suggested that fans' favorability toward their teams arises because of their beliefs, feelings, and past experiences regarding the teams. People may like particular sports teams because the teams' players appear to have good personal and athletic attributes, the teams make us feel good, and people may have many fond memories of seeing the team perform live on outings with mom or dad.

This explanation is difficult to reconcile, however, with observations that some teams consist of disreputable characters who have no history with the region for which they play, some teams retain a high fan base despite losing with torrid frequency (e.g., the Toronto Maple Leafs in the 1980s), and many "bandwagon" fans have little or no prior experiences with the teams. It may not be possible to explain fans' positive attitudes toward their teams simply by looking at their beliefs, feelings, and past behaviors regarding the teams; other factors must moderate the effects of these attitude components.

The present chapter proposes that, in general, the effects of beliefs, feelings, and past behaviors on attitudes depend on salient motivational goals. We begin by outlining a model of attitudes that explicitly considers the motivations that guide attitudes, in addition to the beliefs, feelings, and behaviors that influence attitudes. We then focus on one new motivation that may play an important role in attitude formation and change: the need for affect.

## The function–structure model

According to the three-component model of attitudes (see Zanna & Rempel, 1988), attitudes express beliefs, feelings, and past behaviors regarding the attitude object. For example, a young man might have a positive evaluation of a colorful polyester Hawaiian shirt because he believes that the shirt looks good on him (cognitive component) and the shirt reminds him of fun times in the tropics (emotional component). In addition, through self-perception processes (Bem, 1972; Olson, 1990, 1992), he might decide that he must like the shirt because he can recall that his coworkers had no trouble convincing him that he should wear a similar shirt to important business functions (behavioral component). On the basis of these beliefs, feelings, and past behaviors, he might form a general positive attitude toward the conspicuous item. In general, people who have positive attitudes toward an attitude object should often possess beliefs, feelings, and behaviors that are favorable toward the object, whereas people have negative attitudes toward an attitude object should often possess beliefs, feelings, and behaviors that express unfavorability toward the object (see Eagly & Chaiken, 1993).

Nonetheless, people's beliefs, feelings, and behavior toward an object can sometimes differ in their valence and, therefore, in their implications for their overall attitude. For example, the young man in our example may feel uncomfortable in the polyester fabric of the vivid Hawaiian shirt, despite his other positive beliefs and emotions. Research on the valence of people's attitude-relevant beliefs, feelings, and behaviors has provided evidence that they are empirically distinct. For instance, some researchers have asked participants to list their beliefs, emotions, and behaviors regarding an attitude object and to rate the valence of each response (Esses & Maio, 2002; Haddock & Zanna, 1998). Results have generally indicated low to moderate correlations between the components of attitudes toward a large variety of issues, objects, and behaviors (e.g., birth control, blood donation, microwaves; Breckler & Wiggins, 1989; Crites, Fabrigar, & Petty, 1994; Esses & Maio, 2002; Haddock & Zanna, 1998; Trafimow & Sheeran, 1998). Consistent with these low relations, attitude-relevant feelings and beliefs are also clustered separately in memory (Trafimow & Sheeran, 1998).

Researchers have found that some attitudes are uniquely related to feelings about the attitude object, whereas other attitudes are uniquely related to beliefs about the attitude object. For example, feelings are particularly strong predictors of attitudes toward blood donation (Breckler & Wiggins, 1989), intellectual pursuits (e.g., literature, math; Crites et al., 1994), smoking (Trafimow & Sheeran, 1998), condom use (de Wit, Victoir, & Van den Bergh, 1997), deaf people (Kiger, 1997), politicians (see Glaser & Salovey, 1998, for a review), and alcohol and marijuana use in frequent users of these drugs (Simons & Carey, 1998). In contrast, beliefs are strong predictors of reactions to persuasive messages (Breckler & Wiggins, 1991) and attitudes toward a variety of controversial issues (e.g., capital punishment, legalized abortion, nuclear weapons; Breckler & Wiggins, 1989; Crites et al., 1994). All of these unique relations support the distinction between the cognitive and affective components of attitudes. No prior theory, however, predicts *when* one component will more strongly influence attitudes than the other components.

This issue is important because the relative predictive power of different components can vary, even for similar attitude objects. For example, although researchers have found that affect is a stronger predictor than cognition of attitudes toward most minority groups (Esses, Haddock, & Zanna, 1993; Haddock, Zanna, & Esses, 1993; Jackson, Hodge, Gerard, Ingram, Ervin, & Sheppard, 1996; Kiger, 1997; Stangor, Sullivan, & Ford, 1991), cognition can also be a stronger predictor than affect of attitudes toward some minority groups (Esses et al., 1993). In general, the relative weighting of these sources of information can vary across individuals and attitude objects (e.g., Eagly, Mladinic, & Otto, 1994; Esses et al., 1993; Haddock et al., 1993; Haddock & Huskinson, Chapter 2 this volume; Trafimow & Sheeran, Chapter 3 this volume).

We propose that motivational goals exert a fundamental influence on the dominance of particular attitude components. We have previously labeled this conceptualization the *function–structure model* of attitudes (FSM; Maio & Olson, 2000a). As shown in Figure 1.1, this model proposes that salient motivations influence the weighting of information within each attitude component. Certain goals might be salient because they are chronically or temporarily accessible for some individuals. For example, the attitude object may be associated in memory with a particular motive (e.g., Shavitt, 1990), causing the motive to be chronically accessible when the object is present. Alternatively, temporary features of the immediate situation may be associated in memory with a particular motive (e.g., Young, Thomsen, Borgida, Sullivan, & Aldrich, 1991). For instance, the presence of credit card logos or money might activate utilitarian motivations to pursue wealth, and this motive might be particularly strong in a person who is surrounded by others wearing expensive clothing.

The effect of the salient goals on the weighting of each component should depend on the extent to which the components contain information that is particularly relevant to the goals. Consider again our Hawaiian shirt example. If the man who is thinking about the shirt is experiencing a need to impress others, then his belief that the shirt suits him should have a large impact on

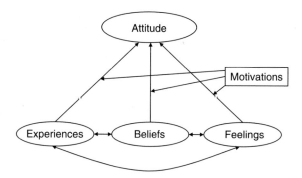

*Figure 1.1* The function–structure model of attitudes: motivations moderate the effects of beliefs, feelings, and experiences on attitudes.

his current attitude. In contrast, if he has stronger pecuniary concerns, his belief that the shirt was inexpensive should be weighted most heavily. Alternatively, if he is experiencing a strong need to feel comfortable and relaxed, then his attitude should be influenced heavily by the discomfort evoked by the polyester fabric. In sum, salient motivations should affect the weights assigned to various beliefs, feelings, and past experiences, and these components should, in turn, affect the current overall attitude to the object.

What are the types of motivation that may be influential? Seminal theories of attitude function (Katz, 1960; Smith, Bruner, & White, 1956) provide some clues about potentially influential motivations. Smith et al. (1956) suggested that attitudes can serve object-appraisal, social-adjustment, and/or externalization functions. The object-appraisal function encompasses the ability of attitudes to summarize the positive and negative characteristics of objects in our environment. In other words, attitudes enable people to approach things that are beneficial for them and avoid things that are harmful to them. The social-adjustment function is served by attitudes that help us identify with well-regarded individuals and dissociate from disliked individuals. For example, people often like and purchase styles of clothing that are worn by celebrities. The externalization function is served by attitudes that defend the self against internal conflict. For instance, a poor squash player might grow to dislike the game because it threatens his or her self-esteem.

In a separate program of research, Katz (1960) proposed that attitudes may serve knowledge and utilitarian functions, which are similar to Smith et al.'s (1956) object-appraisal function. Specifically, the knowledge function reflects the ability of attitudes to summarize information about objects in the environment, and the utilitarian function exists in attitudes that maximize rewards and minimize punishments obtained from objects in the environment. Katz also proposed that attitudes may serve an ego-defensive function. This function is similar to Smith et al.'s externalization function, because both functions involve protecting self-esteem. Finally, Katz suggested the existence of a value-expressive function, which exists in attitudes that express the self-concept and central values (Rokeach, 1973; Schwartz, 1992). For example, some people favor cycling to work because they value health.

It is possible, however, to distinguish between motives that are fulfilled by particular attitude positions versus motives that are fulfilled by holding attitudes per se. This point is illustrated by Smith et al.'s (1956, p. 41) description of the object-appraisal attitude function:

> Attitudes aid us in classifying for action the objects of the environment, and they make appropriate response tendencies available for coping with these objects. This feature is a basis for holding attitudes in general as well as any particular array of attitudes. In it lies the function served by holding attitudes per se.

This description emphasizes that *all* strong attitudes simplify interaction with the environment, regardless of whether the attitudes are negative or positive. For example, people who definitely like *or* dislike MG sports cars should have less difficulty deciding whether to purchase one of these vehicles than people who have no strong prior attitude toward them. In contrast, other attitude functions explain why people form a negative versus positive attitude. For example, the social-adjustive function explains why people like clothing that is popular, whereas they dislike clothing that is unpopular. That is, the negativity or positivity of attitudes toward clothing depends on whether the clothing fulfils social-adjustive concerns.

These seminal models of attitude function do not provide a comprehensive list of functions, however, because they propose overlapping functions and neglect other important functions (Maio & Olson, 2000a). The overlap is shown by the fact that the value-expressive function can encompass utilitarian motives, because contemporary models of values recognize that social values can serve many goals, some of which are utilitarian in nature (e.g., achievement, enjoying life; Schwartz, 1992). Moreover, persuasive messages that target different utilitarian values have different effects on participants' subsequent attitudes (Maio & Olson, 2000b). Consequently, the existing classes of attitude function can be further subdivided. Furthermore, research in and outside of the social psychology literature has identified motivations that are not considered at all in current models of attitude function, such as a need for consistency (Cialdini, Trost, & Newsom, 1995) and the need for dominance (Murray, 1938, 1951).

Rather than use a limited taxonomy of motivations, the FSM is open to a wide range of motivations, which may be reflected in prior taxonomies of human motivations (e.g., Murray, 1938) and values (e.g., Schwartz, 1992). Motivations for forming attitudes in general have been particularly neglected in past theorizing. Smith et al.'s (1956) object-appraisal function (which subsumes the knowledge and utilitarian functions described by Katz), has been the only motivation that has been theoretically and empirically linked to the formation of attitudes per se (Eagly & Chaiken, 1993; Herek, 1986; Olson & Zanna, 1993; see also Katz's, 1960 knowledge function). The importance of the object-appraisal motive is supported by data showing that people respond faster to attitude objects for which they have highly accessible (i.e., easy to retrieve) attitudes (Fazio, 1995, 2000). These data support the notion that attitudes facilitate responding to attitude objects, at least when the attitudes themselves are accessible. Participants are also more likely to form or maintain attitudes in situations that elicit a high need for closure than a low need for closure (Kruglanski, Webster, & Klem, 1993; Thompson, Kruglanski, & Spiegel, 2000). This finding is consistent with the role of the object-appraisal motivation, because the need for closure is a need for "a definite answer on some topic, *any* answer as opposed to confusion and ambiguity" (Kruglanski, 1989, p. 14). Attitudes are capable of providing such "answers." Therefore, they should be formed and protected when people make decisions about attitude objects.

The object-appraisal function does not provide a complete account of the motives served by attitude formation, however. This function explains how attitudes simplify the cognitive processing of attitude objects, but it does not completely explain the intensity of people's affective reactions to attitude objects. In theory, attitudes could direct people's thoughts and behaviors in a manner that is devoid of feeling. For example, when people try to decide whether they should vote for a specific politician, they could simply recall an abstract, emotionless evaluation indicating varying degrees of unfavorability or favorability toward the politician. This recalled evaluation could direct their vote without the elicitation of strong negative or positive feelings. Attitudes *are* accompanied by affective reactions, however (e.g., Cacioppo & Petty, 1979; Dijker, Kok, & Koomen, 1996; see also Olson & Fazio, 2001), and the psychological function of these reactions should be addressed.

The FSM proposes that there is an additional motive that can help explain attitude formation. Specifically, people may have a built-in need to experience emotions, and attitudes can help fulfil this need. This hypothesis is partly based on Zajonc's (1980) proposal that the experience of affect is a basic process and that affective reactions give meaning to the world around us. Affect serves many functions, such as keeping us aroused, helping us communicate with others, and providing motivational impetus to our behavior. Affect may even elicit its own unique system for information processing (Epstein, 1998). Consequently, the experience of emotions may be intrinsically satisfying (Maio & Esses, 2001), and people may form attitudes as a means of experiencing and expressing emotions.

In addition, however, people's attitude positions may be influenced by individual differences in and situational determinants of their need for cognitive simplicity and their need for affect. For example, people may adopt attitude positions that enable them to maintain the simplest perspective (Webster & Krugklanski, 1994). If a message presents simple information in favor of one point of view (e.g., favorable to censorship) and complex information in favor of an alternate point of view (e.g., unfavorable to censorship), people who are experiencing a need for cognitive simplicity might be more likely to adopt the attitude associated with the simple information.

Similarly, because people who are high in the need for affect should seek and enjoy affective stimulation, their attitude positions might be influenced more strongly by affective information (e.g., taste of a product) than by more cognitive, factual information (e.g., nutritional value of a product). Among people who are high in the need for affect, attitudes toward an object might be more favorable if a message describing the object is accompanied by positive affective stimuli (e.g., attractive models) than if the message contains positive information but no emotional value.

In sum, the FSM proposes that attitude positions are influenced by beliefs, feelings, and past experiences regarding the attitude object, and that the impact of these attitude components depends on salient motivations. In addition, the model proposes that the formation of attitudes in general fulfills a need for cognitive simplicity *and* a need for affect, which may also influence attitudinal positions. To date, most of the research on this model has focused on the role of the need for affect, because this variable is a new and potentially important motive. We focus on this need for the remainder of the chapter.

## The need for affect

Before addressing the relation between the need for affect and attitudinal processes, it is important to consider the conceptual properties of this need in more detail. The need for affect is simply the general motivation of people to approach or avoid situations and activities that are emotion inducing for themselves and others. This need includes the desire to experience and understand the emotions of oneself and others, and it subsumes the belief that emotions are useful for shaping judgments and behavior (Maio & Esses, 2001).

By postulating this variable, we are assuming that people differ in the extent to which they pursue a variety of affective experiences, which may vary in their clarity, intensity, quality, specificity, stability, and valence. Of course, people should nonetheless desire some affective states (e.g., clear moods, positive emotions) more than others (e.g., obscure moods, negative emotions). The notion of a need for affect is consistent with such preferences, but further suggests that there are also meaningful differences in the pursuit of affect in general, regardless of the extent to which some emotions are preferred over others.

Supporting this hypothesis, considerable theory and research indicate that people seek a broad range of emotional experiences (Jung, 1970; Salovey & Mayer, 1990; see also Tomkins, 1962, 1963). In addition, many individual difference measures of emotional experience share this focus on a variety of emotions (e.g., Booth-Butterfield & Booth-Butterfield, 1990; King & Emmons, 1990; Kring, Smith, & Neale, 1994; Larsen & Diener, 1987), including some earlier preliminary attempts to examine a need for emotional experiences (Raman, Chattopadhyay, & Hoyer, 1995; Sojka & Giese, 1997). Thus, it is interesting to quantify and investigate the extent to which people seek emotions in general, while also examining potential antecedents and consequences of this need.

Our attempts to examine this variable have distinguished between the tendency to approach emotions and the tendency to avoid them. At first glance, these motivations might seem to be exact opposites. However, researchers have found that, in general, approach and avoidance motivations are at least somewhat distinct (e.g., Hull, 1952; Lewin, 1951; Miller, 1959; see also Higgins, 1997). In particular, attitudes research increasingly supports the notion that liking an attitude object is not the opposite of disliking an attitude object (Cacioppo, Gardner, & Berntson, 1997). Although people who like an attitude object (e.g., a beverage) tend not to dislike it, people can sometimes both like and dislike an attitude object (e.g., Kaplan, 1972; Maio, Bell, & Esses, 1996; Thompson, Zanna, & Griffin, 1995). Similarly, the motivations to approach emotions and to avoid emotions should be negatively related, making it meaningful to examine the net inclination to approach vs. avoid emotions. Nevertheless, the existence of a negative relation does not preclude examining both motivations separately, especially if these motivations are only weakly negatively related. In fact, it is important to examine both motivations because they might have some distinct correlates (see Maio & Esses, 2001, for a more detailed discussion of this possibility).

Examinations of the need for affect can also focus on both individual differences in the need for affect and situational determinants of the need for affect. Regarding individual differences, a variety of factors may lead to stable differences in the need for affect. For example, some people may experience chronically high levels of negative affect because of stressful life events or other individual differences (e.g., low coping ability). These frequent experiences of negative emotions may reduce people's desire to experience any emotions. In contrast, other people may have a strong sense of psychological security that enables them to pursue emotions. At the same time, temporary situational circumstances should influence the need for affect. For example, a person who has recently experienced an intense emotional experience should feel a need to come down from the highs and lows, temporarily reducing the person's inclination to experience affect. Alternatively, after hearing evidence that emotions are beneficial, a person should form a positive attitude toward affective experiences and seek them out. Because of the potential for individual differences and situational malleability, our research has developed both an individual differences measure of the need for affect and experimental manipulations of this need. Below, we briefly review the general evidence regarding these approaches, before turning to applications of these approaches in the context of attitudes.

### Individual difference approach

We first developed an individual differences measure of the need for affect, called the Need for Affect Questionnaire (Maio & Esses, 2001). To begin developing this measure, we asked 355 participants to complete 60 different items to assess their need for affect. Exploratory factor analyses and item analyses revealed that these items subsumed distinct and internally consistent emotion approach and emotion avoidance dimensions. The 60 items were then reduced to 26 items, with 13 items assessing the tendency to approach affect (e.g., "I feel that I need to experience strong emotions regularly," "I like to dwell on my emotions") and 13 items assessing the tendency to avoid affect ("If I reflect on my past, I see that I tend to be afraid of feeling emotions," "I would prefer not to experience either the lows or highs of emotion") In the second stage, confirmatory factor analyses further supported the two-factor model, while revealing a moderate, significant negative correlation between the two latent factors ($r = -.48$). In addition, we found that the scale possessed good test–retest reliability over a two month period ($r = .85$).

Given the moderate negative relation between emotion approach and emotion avoidance, our principal analyses of scores from this scale separately consider the total need for affect (approach minus avoidance; i.e., avoidance items reverse scored), the emotion approach dimension, and the emotion avoidance dimension. This strategy is justified by the fact that the emotion approach dimension and the emotion avoidance dimension occasionally exhibit distinct correlates (Maio & Esses, 2001). Nevertheless, for the issues examined in this chapter, many of the conclusions obtained from the emotion approach and emotion avoidance subscales are similar to the conclusions that would be derived from the total need for affect.

It is therefore important that there is evidence for the construct validity of the total need for affect. As expected, the total need for affect is related to a number of individual differences in cognitive processes, emotional processes, and dimensions of personality, in the expected directions (Maio & Esses, 2001). For example, there were significant positive correlations between the need for affect and affect intensity (the tendency to experience strong emotions; Larsen & Diener, 1987), sensation seeking (Zuckerman, 1994), and affective orientation (awareness and use of emotions in communication; Booth-Butterfield & Booth-Butterfield, 1990), whereas there were significant negative correlations with ambivalence over emotional expressiveness (tendency to feel torn about expressing emotions; King & Emmons, 1990) and alexithymia (difficulties describing, experiencing, and analyzing feelings; Taylor, Ryan, & Bagby, 1985). In addition, the need for affect was negatively correlated with the need for closure (a preference for clarity and order and an avoidance of uncertainty; Webster & Kruglanski, 1994) and the personal need for structure (the tendency to prefer structured situations to unstructured situations; Neuberg & Newsom, 1993; Thompson, Naccarato, & Parker, 1989), while being positively correlated with the need for cognition (Cacioppo, Petty, & Kao, 1984), which reflects the tendency to engage in and enjoy effortful thought. Importantly, however, the need for affect is only moderately related to these other individual differences, supporting the hypothesis that the need for affect is distinct from these variables.

Our individual differences measure also possesses predictive validity (Maio & Esses, 2001). For example, in one study, we tested whether people who are high in the need for affect are more inclined to view films that are emotionally involving. In this study, 116 participants completed the Need for Affect Questionnaire and some filler surveys. The participants then rated their willingness to view film clips that would be shown in a subsequent laboratory session. Two of the films were described as possessing neither happy nor sad content, whereas two other films were described as possessing both happy and sad content. We expected that the tendency to prefer films that were happy and sad over nonemotional films would be greater for participants who are high in the need for affect than for participants who are low in the need for affect. As predicted, the relative preference for the emotional films was greater among participants who were high in the need for affect than among participants who were low in the need for affect.

The need for affect also predicts involvement in a real-life, emotion-inducing situation, even when the situation elicits negative emotions. For example, in one study, British participants were asked to complete an open-ended questionnaire assessing their cognitive, affective, and behavioral reactions to the death of Princess Diana, approximately three months following her death (Maio & Esses, 2001). We then calculated the number of cognitions, emotions, and behaviors that were reported by each person. Our hypothesis was that participants who were high in the need for affect would be more motivated to think about her death, react emotionally to her death, and perform behaviors relevant to her death because such reactions would help participants experience, contemplate, and create relevant emotions. As expected, participants who were high in the need for affect reported more emotions, behaviors, and cognitions experienced after the death of Princess Diana than did participants who were low in this need.

In sum, the individual differences measure of the need for affect possesses substantial coherence, test–retest reliability, construct validity, and predictive validity. Given these attributes, the measure provides a useful means of examining the need for affect in a variety of contexts.

### Situational approach

Because the need for affect is analogous to an attitude toward emotion, this "attitude" should be malleable. Of course, a common technique for changing attitudes utilizes persuasive messages. Thus, to manipulate the need for affect, people could be given messages that support or refute the value of emotional experiences. Participants who receive a pro-emotion message should subsequently exhibit a stronger inclination to pursue emotions than participants who receive an anti-emotion message.

This technique has been adopted in our research (Maio, Esses, Ashton, Watt, & Kennedy, 2001). First, we developed an essay that was either anti-emotion or pro-emotion (Maio et al., 2001). The essay included four paragraphs describing negative or positive consequences of high emotionality. The anti-emotion essay suggested that highly emotional people are less likely than unemotional people to be free from schizophrenia, avoid divorce, experience work success, show logical aptitude, and possess high life satisfaction. The pro-emotion essay used virtually identical wording, except that this essay claimed that highly emotional people are *more* likely to experience these positive outcomes and abilities. Participants were asked to summarize and elaborate these essays, as part of an alleged study of reading comprehension.

In an ostensibly different study, participants then completed (a) a thought-listing measure of their reactions to a distressing essay describing a real-life massacre and (b) scales assessing their inclination to view a novel emotional or unemotional film. As expected, participants who received the pro-emotion essay subsequently exhibited more emotional reactions to the description of the massacre. The manipulation did not influence cognitive responses to the description of the massacre. In addition, as expected, participants exhibited a greater interest in viewing the emotional film after receiving a pro-emotion message than after receiving an anti-emotion message. Thus, participants' preferences for affective experiences were at least temporarily altered.

### *Summary*

To date, our research has developed an individual differences measure of the need for affect and a persuasive message manipulating this need. As described below, most of our studies have used the individual differences measure to examine the role of the need for affect in attitudinal processes. This research has also employed the manipulation to test a mechanism for the operation of the need for affect in one attitudinal process (formation of extreme attitudes). We hope to eventually use the manipulation (and other manipulations) to help triangulate the causal mechanisms for other attitudinal processes.

## Implications for attitudinal processes

We have examined the role of the need for affect in three attitudinal processes: the formation of extreme attitudes, responses to fear-inducing messages, and reactions to affective versus cognitive messages. The examination of attitude extremity tests the FSM's predictions about the role of the need for affect in the formation of attitudes per se, whereas examining reactions to messages (e.g., fear-inducing messages) tests the FSM's predictions about the role of the need for affect in the formulation of attitudinal positions.

### *Attitude extremity*

The fulfillment of the need for affect is an important function of attitudes. People who are high in the need for affect should be more likely to spontaneously form attitudes than people who are low in this need. Moreover, people who are high in the need for affect should be more likely to possess *extreme* attitudes, because extreme attitudes are particularly likely to be accompanied by strong emotions. To test this hypothesis, we conducted a study that measured participants' need for affect and their attitudes toward 30 controversial issues (Maio & Esses, 2001), which were modelled after the issues used in a previous study (Maio, Roese, Seligman, & Katz, 1996). The controversial issues included abortion, censorship, euthanasia, genetic engineering research, and violent television programming. Participants rated their attitudes toward each issue using a 9-point scale from –4 (extremely unfavorable) to 4 (extremely favorable), and attitude extremity for each item was determined by calculating the absolute value of the difference between participants' responses and zero (see Wegener, Downing, Krosnick, & Petty, 1995). We then averaged each participant's attitude extremity across items.

The study also included a measure of the need to evaluate, which is the tendency to form evaluations of objects, ideas, and people in one's environment. Past research has indicated that people who are high in the need to evaluate are less likely to express neutral attitudes than people who are low in this trait (Jarvis & Petty, 1996). Given this evidence, we wished to test whether any observed relation between the need for affect and attitude extremity would be independent of the relation between the need to evaluate and attitude extremity. We expected that the need for affect and the need to evaluate would predict attitude extremity independently, because our prior research found that the need for affect and the need to evaluate were not significantly related.

As expected, attitude extremity was significantly correlated with the need for affect and the need to evaluate. Specifically, participants who possessed higher levels of either need indicated more extreme attitudes than did participants who were low in the needs. In addition, a regression analysis that included both individual differences variables as simultaneous predictors of attitude extremity revealed unique effects of the need for affect and the need to evaluate, with the need for affect accounting for a greater proportion of variance.

These encouraging results raised an interesting issue: Does the relation between the need for affect and attitude extremity occur because the need for affect influences how people retrieve and report their attitudes or because the need for affect influences the original formation of the attitudes? In other words, did our participants who possessed a high need for affect simply report extreme attitudes regardless of their previously experienced beliefs, feelings, and behaviors, or did their responses reflect that a high need for affect had previously guided them toward the pursuit of extreme positive and negative beliefs, feelings, and behaviors?

The mechanism for the influence of the need for affect may depend on the nature of the attitude object. If the attitude object is relatively new or unfamiliar, then an individual might express his or her need for affect by reporting an extreme attitude, without necessarily having a strong basis for doing so. On the other hand, if people have had many opportunities to learn about the attitude object, then people who possess a high need for affect may have pursued and utilized emotionally valenced information to form an extreme attitude.

We expected that our study of attitude extremity tapped the latter process of attitude formation, because the study examined attitudes toward controversial issues (e.g., abortion, censorship) that participants had likely considered previously. Consequently, people who were high in the need for affect were able to draw upon their previously stored attitude-relevant beliefs, feelings, and behaviors, which should have been relatively extreme in valence. There would have been no need to exaggerate the extremity of these beliefs, feelings, and behaviors in the attitude report itself.

This reasoning can be tested by manipulating the need for affect immediately prior to measuring attitudes toward the controversial issues. If the need for affect influenced prior attitude formation processes for the controversial, familiar topics, then the manipulation should not significantly influence participants' subsequent attitude extremity for these issues. Maio et al. (2001) tested this explanation by experimentally manipulating the need for affect and then measuring participants' attitudes toward the 30 controversial issues that had previously been examined using the Need for Affect Scale (Maio & Esses, 2001). Results indicated no significant effect of the manipulation on the extremity of participants' attitudes toward the controversial issues, despite the aforementioned significant effects of the manipulation on emotional reactions to a massacre and choice of emotional film. That is, in this study, the manipulation influenced participants' subsequent experience and choice of emotions, but did not cause greater extremity in attitudes toward previously encountered, controversial issues. Thus, it is likely that the attitude extremity responses were a manifestation of past associations with the controversial issues and not a result of reporting more extreme attitudes than actually existed.

In sum, people who are high in the need for affect tend to possess more extreme attitudes toward controversial issues, and this tendency seems to be the outcome of processes during attitude formation. That is, people who are high in this need may be more likely to approach and utilize negative and positive emotional information while forming and maintaining their attitudes. Future research should further test this hypothesis by examining the effect of the need for affect manipulation on the utilization of information during the formation of novel attitudes. If our reasoning is correct, people who are high in the need for affect should form stronger evaluative reactions to information about new attitude objects, leading to more extreme attitudes.

### Reactions to fear-inducing messages

In addition to influencing attitude formation, the need for affect should influence how people respond to persuasive messages that attempt to change their pre-existing attitudes. Individuals who are high in the need for affect should seek and mentally rehearse persuasive messages that enable them to maintain a high amount of emotion. Indeed, as described above, people who are made to experience a high need for affect exhibit more emotional reactions to a message about a distressing incident (a real-life massacre) than people who are made to experience a low need for affect. Because such messages fulfill their need for emotional experience, people who are high in the need for affect should be more likely to rehearse the content of the messages. Moreover, if the message content is compelling, it should cause greater acceptance of the position advocated by the message.

We began to address this issue by testing whether the need for affect influences reactions to persuasive messages that induce one specific negative emotion: fear. For example, does the need for affect influence reactions to an advertisement that arouses fear by portraying the fatal consequences of care-less driving? Prior research has attempted to discover when and how fear-eliciting messages cause attitude change (e.g., Janis, 1967; Janis & Feshbach, 1953; Leventhal, 1970; Rogers, 1975, 1983). Classic attitude change theory suggested that fear-inducing messages should be influential when they moti-vate people to rehearse and accept the messages' recommendations (e.g., Hovland, Janis, & Kelley, 1953; see Ruiter, Abraham, & Kok, 2001, for a review). Theoretically, people who are high in the need for affect should find it rewarding to mentally rehearse the content of fear-inducing messages, because this rehearsal enables them to experience their fear. Moreover, people who are high in the need for affect are better able to utilize and deal with emotions (Maio & Esses, 2001), enabling them to better process the message arguments in the midst of their fear. In addition, people who are high in the need for affect are more likely to believe that emotions such as fear are useful for guiding future behavior, and thus may be more motivated to process the message arguments. All of these processes should cause people who are high in the need for affect to react more favorably to fear-eliciting messages.

To test this reasoning, we asked participants to view two compelling advertisements that were nominated for commercial advertising awards. One advertisement was a fear-eliciting video advertisement about careless driving, and the other was an affectively neutral advertisement about smoking. (The differences in affective content were established in pre-testing.) We then asked participants to rate their attitudes toward the advertisements and their inten-tions to follow the advertisements' specific recommendations. The results indicated that the need for affect was positively correlated with the favorabil-ity of participants' reactions to the fear-eliciting advertisement and with their intentions to implement the recommendations of the advertisement. In con-trast, the need for affect was not significantly correlated with participants' reactions and intentions regarding the neutral advertisement.

Overall, these results support our hypothesis that people who are high in the need for affect are more likely to rehearse and accept the content of cogent, fear-inducing messages than people who are low in the need for affect. The need for affect did not predict people's acceptance of the affectively neutral message. Thus, the effect of the need for affect occurred specifically on an emotive, fear-eliciting message.

### Reactions to affective versus cognitive messages

The relation between the need for affect and reactions to the fear-inducing message is simply one piece of evidence to support a broader hypothesis: the need for affect should cause people to accept affective messages more readily, regardless of the specific negative emotions (e.g., fear) and positive emotions (e.g., happiness) that the messages elicit. Although this hypothesis is consistent with the relation between the need for affect and reactions to fear-eliciting messages, the role of the need for affect in reactions to positive affective messages must also be explored.

To address this goal, we designed an experiment that exposed participants to affective messages that elicited either negative or positive emotions. Additional participants were exposed to dry, cognitive messages that conveyed negative or positive beliefs about the message topic. To maintain experimental control over the messages, we wanted each message to target the same issue, for which participants would have no prior experience. We utilized messages previously designed and used by Fabrigar and Petty (1999), which negatively or positively described a fictitious animal, lemphurs, and emphasized either emotional information about these creatures or factual, cognitive information. The emotional message provided vivid descriptions of a lemphur brutally hunting and attacking a swimmer (negative emotional message) or frolicking with the swimmer (positive emotional message). In contrast, the cognitive message gave positive factual information about lemphurs (e.g., they are intelligent) or negative factual information (e.g., they have an unpredictable temperament). As in our experiment examining effects of fear-inducing messages, we expected that both messages would be cogent, because Fabrigar and Petty (1999) explicitly designed them to be strong and obtained evidence supporting their effectiveness.

In a pre-test session, our participants completed an individual differences measure of the need for affect and an individual differences measure of the need for cognition (i.e., the tendency to seek and enjoy effortful cognitive tasks; Cacioppo et al., 1984). In the main experimental session, participants read the affective or cognitive message and then rated their attitudes toward lemphurs using semantic-differential scales. In theory, people's standing on the need for affect and the need for cognition should interact to determine their reactions to affective and cognitive messages. Specifically, individuals who are high in the need for affect and low in the need for cognition should possess more positive attitudes toward lemphurs after reading affective messages that describe these creatures positively than after reading affective messages that describe these creatures negatively, while being less strongly influenced by the valence of the cognitive messages. In contrast, people who are low in the need for affect and high in the need for cognition should possess more positive attitudes toward lemphurs after reading cognitive messages that describe these creatures positively than after reading cognitive messages that describe these creatures negatively, while being less strongly influenced by the valence of the affective messages.

To test these predictions using our data, we first created an index of the extent to which participants were high on the need for affect and low on the need for cognition. This index of affective dominance simply subtracted participants' z-score for the measure of need for cognition from their z-score for the measure of the need for affect. Thus, higher scores on this measure reflected higher need for affect and lower need for cognition (i.e., affect dominant), whereas lower scores reflected higher need for cognition and lower need for affect (i.e., cognition dominant). This variable was then entered as a predictor of post-message attitudes toward lemphurs in a regression analysis. The additional predictors were the valence of the message (negative vs. positive), the type of message (affective vs. cognitive), and the interactions among the predictors.

Results indicated that the three-way interaction between our index of affective-cognitive dominance, message valence, and message type was significant. Figure 1.2 depicts the predicted post-message attitudes of participants who were one standard deviation above or below the mean for affective-cognitive dominance. As expected, when participants' affective-cognitive dominance scores revealed high affect dominance, the participants were more favorable toward lemphurs after reading the positive affective message about these creatures than after reading the negative affective message about them. In contrast, the valence of the cognitive message exerted less of an impact on these participants' attitudes. Among participants with high cognitive dominance, positive versus negative cognitive messages elicited about the same effect on attitudes toward lemphurs as did positive versus negative affective messages. Although this equivalence of affective and cognitive messages was unexpected, this result is consistent with prior evidence that affective messages are more effective for affectively based attitudes than are cognitive messages, whereas cognitive messages are not consistently more effective at changing cognitively based attitudes (Edwards, 1990; Fabrigar & Petty, 1999). Thus, the general pattern of effects on post-message attitudes supported our hypotheses and was consistent with past evidence.

We also examined participants' post-message feelings (e.g., love, anger, disgust) and beliefs about lemphurs (e.g., useful, safe, harmful), using the same self-report scales as employed by Fabrigar and Petty (1999). As expected, participants who were high in the need for affect and low in the need for cognition exhibited more favorable feelings toward lemphurs after reading the positive affective message about these creatures than after reading the negative affective message about them. In contrast, the valence of the cognitive message exerted less of an impact on these participants' feelings. Among participants who were low in the need for affect and high in the need for cognition, the positive cognitive message elicited more positive feelings toward lemphurs than did the negative cognitive message. In contrast, the valence of the affective message exerted a weaker impact on these participants' feelings. Participants' beliefs about lemphurs were not significantly predicted by affective dominance or its interactions with message type and valence.

Additional analyses revealed that the relation between the affective-cognitive dominance index and affective responses rested mainly on participants' need for affect scores. That is, when we replaced the affective dominance

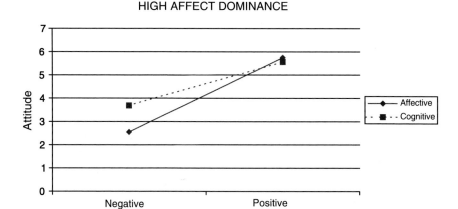

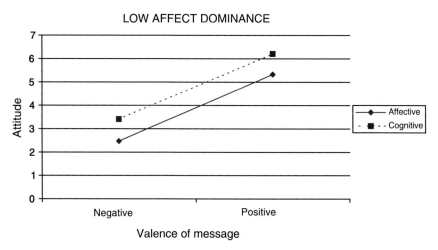

*Figure 1.2* The effects of affective and cognitive messages that are negative or positive as a function of affective dominance.

variable (i.e., need for affect – need for cognition) with the need for affect in our regression analysis, we obtained the same pattern of results as before. As expected, participants who were high in the need for affect exhibited more favorable feelings toward lemphurs after reading the positive affective message than after reading the negative affective message, whereas the valence of the cognitive message exerted less of an impact on these participants' feelings. Among participants who were low in the need for affect, the positive cognitive message elicited more positive feelings toward lemphurs than did the negative cognitive message, whereas the valence of the affective message exerted a weaker impact on these participants' feelings. Affective responses were not predicted by the need for cognition or its interactions with the other variables (i.e., valence, message type), and cognitive responses to lemphurs were not predicted by the need for affect or its interaction with the other variables.

In sum, the need for affect and the need for cognition combined to predict attitudes following the emotional and cognitive messages, such that the affect-ive messages were more influential for people who were higher in the need for affect and lower in the need for cognition. In addition, however, the need for affect uniquely influenced participants' affective responses to the message, such that the feelings of the participants who were high in the need for affect were more strongly influenced by the valence of the affective messages than by the valence of the cognitive messages. These results support the FSM's predictions about the role of the need for affect in responses to affective vs. cognitive messages.

## Directions for future research and conclusions

This chapter began by describing a model of attitudes that attempts to inte-grate current understanding of attitude function and structure. We then focused on the role of the need for affect in attitudes. We described how this need can be measured and manipulated and then examined its implications for understanding three attitudinal processes: the formation of extreme atti-tudes, reactions to fear-eliciting messages, and reactions to affective and cog-nitive persuasive messages. The research indicated that people who are high in the need for affect were more likely to form extreme attitudes, agree with the thrust of fear-eliciting messages, and yield to affective (rather than cognitive) messages. Thus, these findings provided consistent support for the importance of the need for affect as a motive in attitude formation and change.

In particular, these results support our contention that attitude function and structure interact to influence attitudes. For example, in our examination of the relation between the need for affect and reactions to affective and cognitive persuasive messages, we found that our motivational variable (i.e., the index of affective dominance) interacted with the type of information that was presented (i.e., affective vs. cognitive) to predict final attitudes. Put simply, the affective information was utilized more heavily by those people who were motivated to use and experience the emotions.

It would be worthwhile to continue examining the influence of the need for affect on the utilization of affective information. For instance, a straight-forward implication of our findings is that the attitudes of people who are high in the need for affect should be more strongly based on affective support than on cognitive support. Previously, we have noted that this unique reliance on affective information should be less pronounced when people have had ample time to form cognitions and behaviors that are consistent with their feelings (Maio & Esses, 2001). In such situations, there is sufficient opportunity for the feelings, beliefs, and behaviors to become similar over time (see Eagly & Chaiken, 1998), belying any original reliance on affective information. Nonetheless, attitudes should be more closely related to affect than cognition or past behaviors when the attitude is nascent and there has been little opportunity to integrate the feelings, beliefs, and behaviors, and some recent data are consistent with this hypothesis (see Haddock & Huskinson, Chapter 2, this volume).

In addition, it would be interesting to test whether the need for affect moderates the influence of mood on attitude change. Past research has found that people in a negative mood are more likely to carefully scrutinize persuasive messages than people in a neutral mood, whereas people who are in positive moods are more likely to utilize simple cues within the message to form their attitudes (e.g., attractiveness of the message source; Mackie & Worth, 1991; Schwarz, Bless, & Bohner, 1991). It could be argued that such mood effects should be more pronounced for people who are higher in the need for affect, because these people are more likely to rehearse and utilize their mood (see also Haddock, Zanna, & Esses, 1994). Nevertheless, we expect that the potential effects of the need for affect depend on the precise mechanism underlying the effect of mood. For example, it has been suggested that people in negative moods attempt to repair their moods (e.g., Cialdini, Darby, & Vincent, 1973; Isen, Horn, & Rosenhan, 1973), which might cause people in negative moods to engage in systematic processing of information that may improve their moods (cf. Wegener, Petty, & Smith, 1995). If this is correct, the effects of negative mood may be weaker among people who are high in the need for affect, because people who are high in the need for affect should be less perturbed by negative mood. This possibility is important because there are many theories about the mechanisms through which mood affects persuasion (Mackie & Worth, 1991; Schwarz et al., 1991; Wegener et al., 1995). Future research using the need for affect may help to untangle the relevant mechanisms.

There is also a need to examine the precise mechanism through which the need for affect directs the pursuit and experience of emotions. Bargh (1990) has suggested that motives can be activated automatically from memory and spontaneously influence people's perceptions of situations, outside of conscious awareness. We believe that the need for affect operates in this manner. People who are high in the need for affect should be more sensitive to the presence of emotional stimuli in their environment, and they may project their emotions into this environment. There are several testable implications of this reasoning. For example, researchers could test whether people who are higher in the need for affect are more distracted by emotional words in Stroop color-word detection tasks. In addition, researchers can test whether people who are high in the need for affect are more likely to infer emotional themes from the ambiguous pictures that are used in thematic apperception tests (e.g., a picture of a man sitting at a desk; Murray, 1938). Such results would indicate that people who are high in the need for affect more readily detect and project emotions in their environment. Ongoing research is examining these hypotheses.

In addition to these interesting theoretical issues, there are a number of practical implications of our findings. For instance, there are important implications of our finding that the need for affect moderates the acceptance of fear appeals. This finding has applied importance because fear messages can backfire (e.g., Janis & Feshbach, 1953), and such findings have caused many people who work in public safety to conclude that fear appeals do not work (Nell, 2002). In contrast, our results indicate that fear appeals can work, provided that they are directed at people who are high in the need for affect. Fortunately, it may be easy to find advertising spots that are likely to be seen by these individuals. For instance, many films explicitly claim to elicit positive and negative emotions. One such film was *Stepmom* (1998), which featured the advertising tagline, "Be there for the joy. Be there for the tears." Our data indicate that people who are high in the need for affect are drawn to films that promise a range of emotions. Thus, fear appeals that are inserted into advertising before or during such films may be more successful than fear appeals that are inserted in nonemotive films that attract a different audience (e.g., documentaries). Such audience-targeted marketing is already employed heavily for commercial products.

Before such practical implications are explored, however, the existing research should be bolstered by studies using different operationalizations of the need for affect and of the potential outcome variables (e.g., message processing). To date, our research has relied primarily on our individual differences measure. In the long run, we hope to replicate all of our findings with varying manipulations of the need for affect. Such efforts would help to ensure that this construct has been properly triangulated, and provide a greater measure of confidence for any practical applications.

In sum, the FSM attempts to articulate the potential ways in which psychological motivations may affect the weighting of information within attitudes. According to this model, information that is relevant to chronically or temporarily salient motivations is weighted more heavily in the computation of attitudes. This chapter describes how one novel motivation, the need for affect, plays a role in these processes. Put simply, individuals who are high in the need for affect are more strongly influenced by affective information about attitude objects, and these people are more likely to form extreme attitudes. Not only do these results have many theoretical and practical implications, but they also reaffirm the importance of examining the role of motivational processes in attitude formation and change. Our model predicts that the potential role of attitude-relevant motivations is complex, partly because many relevant motivations exist. Yet, researchers have focused on only a small set of motivations. We hope that a more diverse array of motivations will be examined in future research, with the aim of identifying common and unique mechanisms through which the motives influence attitude formation and change.

# References

Bargh, J. A. (1990). Auto-motives: Preconscious determinants of social interaction. In E. T. Higgins & R. M. Sorrentino (Eds.), *Handbook of motivation and cognition: Foundations of social behavior* (Vol. 2, pp. 93–130). New York: Guilford Press.

Bem, D. J. (1972). Self-perception theory. In L. Berkowitz (Ed.), *Advances in experimental social psychology* (Vol. 6, pp. 1–62). San Diego, CA: Academic Press.

Booth-Butterfield, M., & Booth-Butterfield, S. (1990). Conceptualizing affect as information in communication production. *Human Communication Research, 16,* 451–476.

Breckler, S.J., & Wiggins, E. C. (1989). Scales for the measurement of attitudes toward blood donation. *Transfusion, 29,* 401–404.

Breckler, S. J., & Wiggins, E. C. (1991). Cognitive responses in persuasion: Affective and evaluative determinants. *Journal of Experimental Social Psychology, 27,* 180–200.

Cacioppo, J. T., Gardner, W. L., & Berntson, G. G. (1997). Beyond bipolar conceptualizations and measures: The case of attitudes and evaluative space. *Personality and Social Psychology Review, 1,* 3–25.

Cacioppo, J. T., & Petty, R. E. (1979). Attitudes and cognitive response: An electrophysiological approach. *Journal of Personality and Social Psychology, 37,* 2181–2199.

Cacioppo, J. T., Petty, R. E., & Kao, C. F. (1984). The efficient assessment of need for cognition. *Journal of Personality Assessment, 48,* 306–307.

Cialdini, R. B., Darby, B., & Vincent, J. (1973). Transgression and altruism: A case for hedonism. *Journal of Experimental Social Psychology, 9,* 502–516.

Cialdini, R. B., Trost, M. R., & Newsom, J. T. (1995). Preference for consistency: The development of a valid measure and the discovery of surprising behavioral implications. *Journal of Personality and Social Psychology, 69,* 318–328.

Crites, S. L., Fabrigar, L. R., & Petty, R. E. (1994). Measuring the affective and cognitive properties of attitudes: Conceptual and methodological issues. *Personality and Social Psychology Bulletin, 20,* 619–634.

de Wit, R., Victoir, A., & Van den Bergh, O. (1997). "My mind's made up by the way that I feel": Affect, cognition and intention in the structure of attitudes toward condom use. *Health Education Research, 12,* 15–24.

Dijker A. J., Kok G., & Koomen, W. (1996). Emotional-reactions to people with aids. *Journal of Applied Social Psychology, 26,* 731–748.

Eagly, A., & Chaiken, S. (1993). *The psychology of attitudes.* Fort Worth, TX: Harcourt Brace Jovanovich.

Eagly, A. H., & Chaiken, S. (1998). Attitude structure and function. In D. T. Gilbert, S. T. Fiske, & G. Lindzey (Eds.), *The handbook of social psychology.* New York: McGraw-Hill.

Eagly, A., Mladinic, A,, & Otto, S. (1994). Cognitive and affective bases of attitudes toward social groups and social policies. *Journal of Experimental Social Psychology, 30,* 13–137.

Edwards, K. (1990). The interplay of affect and cognition in attitude formation and change. *Journal of Personality and Social Psychology, 59,* 202–216.

Epstein, S. (1998). Cognitive-experiential self-theory. In D. F. Barone, M. Hersen, & V. B. Van Hasselt (Eds.), *Advanced personality* (pp. 211–238). New York: Plenum Press.

Esses, V. M., Haddock, G., & Zanna, M. P. (1993). Values, stereotypes, and emotions as determinants of intergroup attitudes. In D. M. Mackie & D. L. Hamilton (Eds.), *Affect, cognition, and stereotyping: Interactive processes in group perception* (pp. 137–166). New York: Academic Press.

Esses, V. M., & Maio, G. R. (2002). Expanding the assessment of attitude components and structure: The benefits of open-ended measures. In W. Stroebe & M. Hewstone (Eds.), *European review of social psychology* (Vol. 12, pp. 71–102). Chichester, UK: Wiley.

Fabrigar, L. R., & Petty, R. E. (1999). The role of affective and cognitive bases of attitudes in susceptibility to affectively and cognitively based persuasion. *Personality and Social Psychology Bulletin, 25*, 363–381.

Fazio, R. H. (1995). Attitudes as object-evaluation associations: Determinants, consequences, and correlates of attitude accessibility. In R. E. Petty and J. A. Krosnick (Eds.), *Attitude strength: Antecedents and consequences* (pp. 247–252). Mahwah, NJ: Lawrence Erlbaum Associates, Inc.

Fazio, R. H. (2000). Accessible attitudes as tools for object appraisal: Their costs and benefits. In G. R. Maio & J. M. Olson (Eds.), *Why we evaluate: Functions of attitudes* (pp. 1–36). Mahwah, NJ: Lawrence Erlbaum Associates, Inc.

Glaser, J., & Salovey, P. (1998). Affect in electoral politics. *Personality and Social Psychology Review, 2*, 156–172.

Haddock, G., & Zanna, M. P. (1998). On the use of open-ended measures to assess attitudinal components. *British Journal of Social Psychology, 37*, 129–149.

Haddock, G., Zanna, M. P., & Esses, V. M. (1993). Assessing the structure of prejudicial attitudes: The case of attitudes toward homosexuals. *Journal of Personality and Social Psychology, 65*, 1105–1118.

Haddock, G., Zanna, M. P., & Esses, V. M. (1994). Mood and the expression of intergroup attitudes: The moderating role of affect intensity. *European Journal of Social Psychology, 24*, 189–205.

Herek, G. M. (1986). The instrumentality of attitudes: Toward a neofunctional theory. *Journal of Social Issues, 42*, 99–114.

Higgins, E. T. (1997). Beyond pleasure and pain. *American Psychologist, 52*, 1280–1300.

Hovland, C. I., Janis, I. L., & Kelley, H. H. (1953). *Communication and persuasion: Psychological studies of opinion change.* New Haven, CT: Yale University Press.

Hull, C. L. (1952). *A behavior system: An introduction to behavior theory concerning the individual organism.* New Haven, CT: Yale University Press.

Isen, A. M., Horn, N., & Rosenhan, D. L. (1973). Effects of success and failure on children's generosity. *Journal of Personality and Social Psychology, 27*, 239–247.

Jackson, L. A., Hodge, C. N., Gerard, D. A., Ingram, J. M., Ervin, K. S., & Sheppard, L. A. (1996). Cognition, affect, and behavior in the prediction of group attitudes. *Personality and Social Psychology Bulletin, 22*, 306–316.

Janis, I. L. (1967). Effects of fear arousal on attitude change: Recent developments in theory and experimental research. In L. Berkowitz (Ed.), *Advances in experimental social psychology* (Vol. 3, pp. 166–224). San Diego, CA: Academic Press.

Janis, I., & Feshbach, S. (1953). Effects of fear-arousing communications. *Journal of Abnormal and Social Psychology, 48*, 78–92.

Jarvis, W. B. G., & Petty, R. E. (1996). The need to evaluate. *Journal of Personality and Social Psychology, 70*, 172–194.

Jung, C. G. (1970). *The development of personality.* Princeton, NJ: Princeton University Press.

Kaplan, K. L. (1972). On the ambivalence-indifference problem in attitude theory and measurement: A suggested modification of the semantic differential technique. *Psychological Bulletin, 77*, 361–372.

Katz, D. (1960). The functional approach to the study of attitudes. *Public Opinion Quarterly, 24*, 163–204.

Kiger, G. (1997). The structure of attitudes toward persons who are deaf: Emotions, values, and stereotypes. *Journal of Psychology, 13*, 554–560.

King, L. A., & Emmons, R. A. (1990). Conflict over emotional expression: Psychological and physical correlates. *Journal of Personality and Social Psychology, 58*, 864–877.

Kring, A. M., Smith, D. A., & Neale, J. M. (1994). Individual differences in dispositional expressiveness: The development and validation of the Emotional Expressivity Scale. *Journal of Personality and Social Psychology, 66*, 934–949.

Kruglanski, A. W. (1989). *Lay epistemics and human knowledge: Cognitive and motivational bases.* New York: Plenum Press.

Kruglanski, A. W., Webster, D. M., & Klem, A. (1993). Motivated resistance and openness to persuasion in the presence or absence of prior information. *Journal of Personality and Social Psychology, 65*, 861–876.

Larsen, R. J., & Diener, E. (1987). Affect intensity as an individual difference characteristic: A review. *Journal of Research in Personality, 21*, 1–39.

Leventhal, H. (1970). Findings and theory in the study of fear communications. In L. Berkowitz (Ed.), *Advances in experimental social psychology* (Vol. 5, pp. 119–187). New York: Academic Press.

Lewin, K. (1951). *Field theory in social science.* New York: Harper.

Mackie, D. M., & Worth, L. T. (1991). Feeling good, but not thinking straight: The impact of positive mood on persuasion. In J. P. Forgas (Ed.), *Social cognition and judgment* (pp. 201–219). New York: Pergamon Press.

Maio, G. R., Bell, D. W., & Esses, V. M. (1996). Ambivalence and persuasion: The processing of messages about immigrant groups. *Journal of Experimental Social Psychology, 32*, 513–536.

Maio, G. R., & Esses, V. M. (2001). The need for affect: Individual differences in the motivation to approach or avoid emotions. *Journal of Personality, 69*, 583–616.

Maio, G. R., Esses, V. M., Ashton, M. C., Watt, S. E., & Kennedy, K. (2001, June). *Reactions to positive and negative emotional stimuli: Dispositional and situational variability in the need for affect.* Paper presented at the Amsterdam Symposium: Feelings and Emotions, Amsterdam, The Netherlands.

Maio, G. R., & Olson, J. M. (2000a). Emergent themes and potential approaches to attitude function: The function-structure model of attitudes. In G. R. Maio & J. M. Olson (Eds.), *Why we evaluate: Functions of attitudes* (pp. 417–442). Mahwah, NJ: Lawrence Erlbaum Associates, Inc.

Maio, G. R., & Olson, J. M. (2000b). What *is* a value-expressive attitude? In G. R. Maio & J. M. Olson (Eds.), *Why we evaluate: Functions of attitudes* (pp. 249–270). Mahwah, NJ: Lawrence Erlbaum Associates, Inc.

Maio, G. R., Roese, N. J., Seligman, C., & Katz, A. (1996). Rankings, ratings, and the measurement of values: Evidence for the superior validity of ratings. *Basic and Applied Social Psychology, 18*, 171–181.

Miller, N. E. (1959). Liberalization of basic S-R concepts: Extensions to conflict behavior, motivation and social learning. In S. Koch (Eds.), *Psychology: A study of science, Study I* (pp. 198–292). New York: McGraw-Hill.

Murray, H. (1938). *Explorations in personality*. New York: Oxford University Press.

Murray, H. (1951). Toward a classification of interaction. In T. Parsons & E. A. Shils (Eds.), *Toward a general theory of action* (pp. 434–464). Cambridge, MA: Harvard University Press.

Nell, V. (2002). Why young men drive dangerously: Implications for injury prevention. *Current Directions in Psychological Science, 11*, 75–78.

Neuberg, S. L., & Newsom, J. T. (1993). Personal need for structure: Individual differences in the desire for simple structure. *Journal of Personality and Social Psychology, 65*, 113–131.

Olson, J. M. (1990). Self-inference processes in emotion. In J. M. Olson & M. P. Zanna (Eds.), *Self-inference processes: The Ontario symposium* (Vol. 6, pp. 17–41). Hillsdale, NJ: Lawrence Erlbaum Associates, Inc.

Olson, J. M. (1992). Self-perception of humor. Evidence for discounting and augmentation effects. *Journal of Personality and Social Psychology, 62*, 369–377.

Olson, J. M., & Zanna, M. P. (1993). Attitudes and attitude change. *Annual Review of Psychology, 44*, 117–154.

Olson, M. A., & Fazio, R. H. (2001). Implicit attitude formation through classical conditioning. *Psychological Science, 12*, 413–417.

Raman, N. V., Chattopadhyay, P., & Hoyer, W. D. (1995). Do consumers seek emotional situations: The need for emotion scale. *Advances in Consumer Research, 22*, 537–542.

Rogers, R. W. (1975). A protection motivation theory of fear appeals and attitude change. *The Journal of Psychology, 91*, 93–114.

Rogers, R. W. (1983). Cognitive and physiological processes in fear appeals and attitude change: A revised theory of protection motivation. In J. T. Cacioppo & R. E. Petty (Eds.), *Social psychophysiology: A sourcebook* (pp. 153–176). New York: Guilford Press.

Rokeach, M. (1973). *The nature of human values*. New York: Free Press.

Ruiter, R. A. C., Abraham, C., & Kok, G. (2001). Scary warnings and rational precautions: A review of the psychology of fear appeals. *Psychology and Health, 16*, 613–630.

Salovey, P., & Mayer, J. D. (1990). Emotional intelligence. *Imagination, Cognition, and Personality, 9*, 185–211.

Schwarz, N., Bless, H., & Bohner, G. (1991). Mood and persuasion: Affective states influence the processing of persuasive communications. In L. Berkowitz (Ed.), *Advances in Experimental Social Psychology* (Vol. 24, pp. 161–199). San Diego, CA: Academic Press.

Schwartz, S. H. (1992). Universals in the content and structure of values: Theoretical advances and empirical tests in 20 countries. In M. P. Zanna (Ed.), *Advances in experimental social psychology* (Vol. 25, 1–65). San Diego, CA: Academic Press.

Shavitt, S. (1990). The role of attitude objects in attitude functions. *Journal of Experimental Social Psychology, 26*, 124–148.

Simons, J., & Carey, K. B. (1998). A structural analysis of attitudes toward alcohol and marijuana use. *Personality and Social Psychology Bulletin, 24*, 727–735.

Smith, M. B., Bruner, J. S., & White, R. W. (1956). *Opinions and personality*. New York: Wiley.

Sojka, J. Z., & Giese, J. L. (1997). Thinking and/or feeling: An examination of interaction between processing styles. *Advances in Consumer Research, 24*, 438–442.

Stangor, C., Sullivan, L. A., & Ford, T. E. (1991). Affective and cognitive determinants of prejudice. *Social Cognition*, *9*, 359–380.

*Stepmom* (1998). Information retrieved from http://us.imdb.com/Title?Stepmom +(1998) on April 11, 2002.

Taylor, G. J., Ryan, D., Bagby, R. M (1985). Toward the development of a new self-report alexithymia scale. *Psychotherapy and Psychosomatics*, *44*, 191–199.

Thompson, E. P., Kruglanski, A. W., & Spiegel, S. (2000). Attitudes as knowledge structures and persuasion as a specific case of subjective knowledge acquisition. In G. R. Maio & J. M. Olson (Eds.), *Why we evaluate: Functions of attitudes* (pp. 59–96). Mahwah, NJ: Lawrence Erlbaum Associates, Inc.

Thompson, M. M., Naccarato, M. E., & Parker, K. E. (1989, June). *Assessing cognitive need: The development of the personal need for structure and personal fear of invalidity scales*. Paper presented at the annual meeting of the Canadian Psychology Association, Halifax, Nova Scotia.

Thompson, M. M., Zanna, M. P., & Griffin, D. W. (1995). Let's not be indifferent about (attitudinal) ambivalence. In R. E. Petty & J. A. Krosnick (Eds.), *Attitude strength: Antecedents and consequences* (pp. 361–386). Mahwah, NJ: Lawrence Erlbaum Associates, Inc.

Tomkins, S. S. (1962). *Affect, imagery, and consciousness: Vol. 1: The positive affects*. New York: Springer.

Tomkins, S. S. (1963). *Affect, imagery, and consciousness: Vol. 2: The negative affects*. New York: Springer.

Trafimow, D., & Sheeran, P. (1998). Some tests of the distinction between cognitive and affective beliefs. *Journal of Experimental Social Psychology*, *34*, 378–397.

Webster, D. M., & Kruglanski, A. W. (1994). Individual differences in need for cognitive closure. *Journal of Personality and Social Psychology*, *67*, 1049–1062.

Wegener, D. T., Downing, J., Krosnick, J. A., & Petty, R. E. (1995). Measures and manipulations of strength-related properties of attitudes: Current practice and future directions. In R. E. Petty and J. A. Krosnick (Eds.), *Attitude strength: Antecedents and consequences* (pp. 455–487). Mahwah, NJ: Lawrence Erlbaum Associates, Inc.

Wegener, D. T., Petty, R. E., & Smith, S. M. (1995). Positive mood can increase or decrease message scrutiny: The hedonic contingency view of mood and message processing. *Journal of Personality and Social Psychology*, *69*, 5–15.

Young, J., Thomsen, C. J., Borgida, E., Sullivan, J., & Aldrich, J. H. (1991). When self-interest makes a difference: The role of construct accessibility in political reasoning. *Journal of Experimental Social Psychology*, *27*, 271–296.

Zajonc, R. B. (1980). Feeling and thinking: Preferences need no inferences. *American Psychologist*, *35*, 151–175.

Zanna, M. P., & Rempel, J. K. (1988). Attitudes: a new look at an old concept. In D. Bar-Tal & A. W. Kruglanski (Eds.), *The social psychology of knowledge*, (pp. 315–334). Cambridge, UK: Cambridge University Press.

Zuckerman, M. (1994). *Behavioral expressions and biosocial bases of sensation seeking*. Cambridge, UK: Cambridge University Press.

# 2 Individual differences in attitude structure

*Geoffrey Haddock and*
*Thomas L. H. Huskinson*

Mankind are governed more by their feelings than by reason

Samuel Adams

We are what we think. All that we are arises with our thoughts

The Buddha

As these quotes from Samuel Adams and the Buddha attest, there are divergent opinions about the primary determinants of our actions. Whereas Adams postulated that we are governed by our feelings, the Buddha placed a greater emphasis on our thoughts. Who is correct? It seems to us that there is something to be said for both positions. On the one hand, it seems likely that some people's actions are driven primarily by their feelings and emotions. On the other hand, it seems equally likely that other individuals' actions are guided mainly by their thoughts and cognitions. If we were to assume that individuals do indeed differ in the principal determinant of their actions, one could also question whether there are differences across people in how they generally structure their attitudes and opinions about the world. Do some people possess attitudes that are consistent primarily with their feelings? Do other people possess attitudes that are consistent primarily with their beliefs? Do yet others have attitudes that are based equally upon their feelings and beliefs? These types of questions are at the heart of this chapter. To make a long story short, we believe that there are differences across people in the degree to which they possess attitudes that are consistent with their affective and cognitive responses. Furthermore, and perhaps more importantly, we believe that these differences have implications for understanding various attitude-relevant phenomena.

This chapter is structured as follows. We begin by defining the attitude concept and reviewing some past studies that have investigated how affective and cognitive information jointly predict attitudes toward individual objects. On the basis of this research, we propose that people can differ in the degree to which they possess attitudes that are evaluatively consistent with their affective and cognitive responses. Next, we describe research we have conducted that addresses this individual difference perspective. This work has sought to (a) test for the existence of these differences, (b) determine the degree to which they are associated with relevant individual difference constructs, and (c) consider some outcomes associated with these differences in attitude structure. We conclude by discussing the importance of such differences for the attitude concept and consider future research questions.

## Defining the attitude concept

Our conceptualization of the attitude concept is based upon the multicomponent model of attitude. As depicted in Figure 2.1, multicomponent models share the basic tenet that attitudes are global evaluations of stimulus objects that are derived from three sources of information: affective responses, cognitions, and behavioral information (e.g., Eagly & Chaiken, 1993; Zanna & Rempel, 1988):

- *Affective information* refers to feelings or emotions associated with an attitude object. For instance, an individual may indicate that blood donation makes him or her feel anxious and afraid.
- *Cognitive information* refers to beliefs about an attitude object. For instance, an individual may believe that British Prime Minister Tony Blair is intelligent and advocates economic policies that promote social equality.
- *Behavioral information* refers to past behaviors associated with the attitude object. For instance, an individual might possess a positive attitude toward increasing police powers as a result of having signed a petition in favor of this issue.

As one might expect, these sources of information are mutually associated, or, in the words of Eagly and Chaiken (1993, p. 201), share a "synergistic relation." That is, positive feelings are usually accompanied by positive beliefs and positive behavioral experiences. At the same time, affect, cognition, and behavior are not quantitatively redundant. A number of researchers

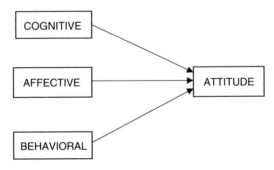

*Figure 2.1* The multicomponent model of attitude.

have concluded that these sources of information are empirically distinct, as demonstrated by studies of discriminative validity (e.g., Breckler, 1984; Crites, Fabrigar, & Petty, 1994; see Eagly & Chaiken, 1993 for a review).

## Relative importance of affective and cognitive information in predicting attitudes

The multicomponent model has led researchers to investigate the relative importance of these sources of information as predictors of individual attitudes. In accomplishing this aim, it is worth noting that the vast majority of this research has concentrated on the role of affect and cognition in guiding attitudes. In this chapter, we adopt that perspective and focus on the role of affect and cognition (although we discuss the role of behavior toward the end of the chapter).

One of the first influential studies examining the affective-cognitive structure of attitudes was reported by Abelson, Kinder, Peters, and Fiske (1982), who explored the role of affect and cognition in predicting attitudes toward American presidential candidates. In this study, participants indicated the personality traits and feelings they associated with the Democratic and Republican primary candidates in 1980, as well as reporting their attitudes toward these individuals. Abelson et al. (1982) found that affective responses associated with the presidential candidates influenced individuals' attitudes above and beyond the contribution of their beliefs about the candidates (which were also uniquely predictive of attitudes). Following from this study, subsequent research on political attitudes by Eagly, Mladinic, and Otto (1994), Granberg and Brown (1989), Haddock and Zanna (1997), and Lavine, Thomsen, Zanna, and Borgida (1998) has also demonstrated the unique importance of both affect and cognition in predicting political attitudes.

In the domain of intergroup attitudes, Esses, Haddock, and Zanna (1993 (see also Haddock & Zanna, 1993; Haddock & Zanna, 1994; Haddock, Zanna, & Esses, 1993) assessed the relative importance of affective and cognitive information in predicting prejudice. In a number of studies, these researchers found that *both* affect and cognition were important in predicting attitudes toward a variety of target outgroups, and that the relative contribution of affect and cognition differed as a function of factors such as the target group under study and individual differences in right-wing authoritarianism (RWA; Altemeyer, 1996). For instance, Esses et al. (1993) found that attitudes toward groups evaluated most favorably were best predicted by affective information, whereas attitudes toward groups evaluated most negatively were best predicted by cognitive information. In addition, affective information was found to serve as the best predictor of the attitudes expressed by low RWAs, whereas cognitive information served to best predict the attitudes of high RWAs. Other research in the domain of intergroup attitudes has also demonstrated the unique importance of both affective and cognitive information as predictors of prejudice (see e.g., Jackson, Hodge, Gerard, Ingram, Ervin, & Sheppard, 1996; Stangor, Sullivan, & Ford, 1991).

In the domain of attitudes toward social policy issues, Eagly et al. (1994, Study 2) examined the evaluative implications of both affect and cognition for attitudes toward issues such as abortion on demand, affirmative action, and welfare assistance for the poor. Using open-ended elicitation measures, Eagly and her colleagues found that cognitions were the most important predictor of attitudes, although affective responses usually contributed significantly to the prediction of attitudes.

Finally, Breckler and colleagues (e.g., Breckler, 1984; Breckler & Wiggins, 1989, 1991) explored the role of affect and cognition in the structure of attitudes toward a wide range of attitude objects. Using a number of stimuli as well as different assessment strategies (e.g., equal appearing interval scales, semantic differential scales, and thought-listing procedures), Breckler and colleagues discovered that both affective and cognitive information uniquely predicted attitudes. Furthermore, they found that the relative importance of each class of information was, to some extent, a function of the stimulus object under examination.

Overall, research assessing the affective-cognitive structure of attitudes, which has used a diverse array of response techniques and has studied a wide variety of attitude objects, has found: (a) that *both* affective and cognitive information are important in guiding attitudes, and (b) that the evaluative implications of feelings and beliefs are positively correlated. Taken together, these findings are consistent with the proposal that *individuals* can differ in the determinants of their attitudes.

## Intra-attitudinal consistency

Associated with research assessing the relative importance of affect and cognition are studies that have investigated the degree of consistency among individuals' attitudes, feelings, and beliefs about a particular attitude object. The most commonly studied form of intra-attitudinal consistency is that of evaluative-cognitive (E-C) consistency. As its label suggests, E-C consistency refers to the degree of consistency or congruence between an individual's overall evaluation of a stimulus object (i.e., their attitude) and the evaluative implications of their cognitions (i.e., their beliefs or thoughts) about the attitude object. For instance, if an individual maintains an unfavorable attitude toward IBM computers, high evaluative-cognitive consistency would imply that their beliefs about these computers are also negative.

The concept of evaluative-cognitive consistency was initially proposed by Milton Rosenberg (e.g., Rosenberg, 1956, 1968). Rosenberg discovered that there was considerable congruence between individuals' beliefs and evaluations, but acknowledged the existence of individual difference variation in evaluative-cognitive consistency, suggesting individuals' attitudes are not always associated with the evaluative implications of their beliefs. In those instances where evaluative-cognitive consistency was absent, Rosenberg (1968) stated that such attitudes were vacuous, or, in the words of Converse (1970), non-attitudes.

Rosenberg's work generated a substantial amount of research on intra-attitudinal consistency. For example, Norman (1975) extended Rosenberg's work by demonstrating that differences in evaluative-cognitive consistency were associated with the strength of the attitude–behavior relation. Norman found that individuals high in evaluative-cognitive consistency showed a more pronounced tendency to behave in accordance with their evaluations. Similarly, research by Chaiken and Baldwin (1981) and Chaiken and Yates (1985) demonstrated that high E-C consistency is associated with more organized cognitions, greater attitude polarization as a function of thought, and less susceptibility to self-perception effects.

A more recent development in this area of work is the consideration of other forms of intra-attitudinal consistency. This insight arose as a result of the recognition that affect should not be considered synonymous with attitude (Breckler, 1984; Eagly & Chaiken, 1993; Millar & Tesser, 1989; Zanna & Rempel, 1988). Based on the distinction between affect and attitude, researchers have studied other forms of structural consistency, such as evaluative-affective (E-A) consistency (i.e., the consistency between attitudes and the evaluative implications of affective responses) and affective-cognitive (A-C) consistency (i.e., the consistency between the evaluative implications of feelings and beliefs). In research that is most relevant to this chapter, Chaiken, Pomerantz, and Giner-Sorolla (1995) used the multiple intra-attitudinal consistency conceptualization to challenge Rosenberg's (1968) assumption that attitudes low in evaluative-cognitive consistency should be considered vacuous. Chaiken et al. (1995) observed that E-C consistency was not highly associated with indices of attitude strength, leading them to conclude that attitudes low in evaluative-cognitive consistency should not necessarily be considered vacuous, but rather as possibly being based primarily upon affective information. To test this proposal, Chaiken et al. (1995) asked participants to indicate their attitude, affective responses, and cognitive responses toward capital punishment. After standardizing participants' attitude, affect, and cognition scores, Chaiken et al. (1995) calculated the absolute difference between attitude and affect as well as the absolute difference between attitude and cognition. By using median splits on each of these absolute difference scores, individuals were classified into one of four groups: (a) high evaluative-affective consistency and low evaluative-cognitive consistency; (b) low evaluative-affective consistency and high evaluative-cognitive consistency; (c) high evaluative-affective consistency and high evaluative-cognitive consistency; (d) low evaluative-affective consistency and low evaluative-cognitive consistency. Chaiken and colleagues proceeded to use this 2×2 classification strategy to determine the extent to which attitudes low in *both* evaluative-cognitive consistency and evaluative-affective consistency differed from those high in either one or both forms of evaluative consistency.

They found that attitudes low in both evaluative-cognitive consistency and evaluative-affective consistency were less accessible and less stable than attitudes high in one or both forms of evaluative consistency. These findings suggest that low evaluative-cognitive consistency should not be considered synonymous with attitude vacuity. Furthermore, and of relevance to our own research, Chaiken et al.'s (1995) demonstration that individual attitudes can be primarily affect or cognition based helps provide a framework for the proposal that *individuals* can differ in the determinants of their attitudes.

## Are affective and cognitive information equally important across individuals?

The studies we have described thus far demonstrate the importance of affective and cognitive information in guiding single attitudes. One question arising from this work is whether individuals may differ in the degree to which they rely upon affective and cognitive information in structuring their opinions. Are some individuals' attitudes affect-based, while other individuals' attitudes are more cognitively consistent? Do people differ in the consistency of their attitudes, feelings, and beliefs? Although these types of questions have been posed by attitude theorists (see, for example, Zanna & Rempel, 1988), we feel that they have not received the attention they deserve. Accordingly, the aim of the research described in this chapter is to advance our understanding of possible individual differences in attitude structure.

In considering this aim, the first question that needs to be addressed is how such differences might be conceptualized. One way to assess these differences is to extend Chaiken et al.'s (1995) taxonomy from the level of a single attitude object to the level of the individual. As depicted in Figure 2.2, this framework allows for the possibility that some individuals maintain predominantly affect-based attitudes that are especially consistent with the evaluative implications of the feelings or emotions they associate with

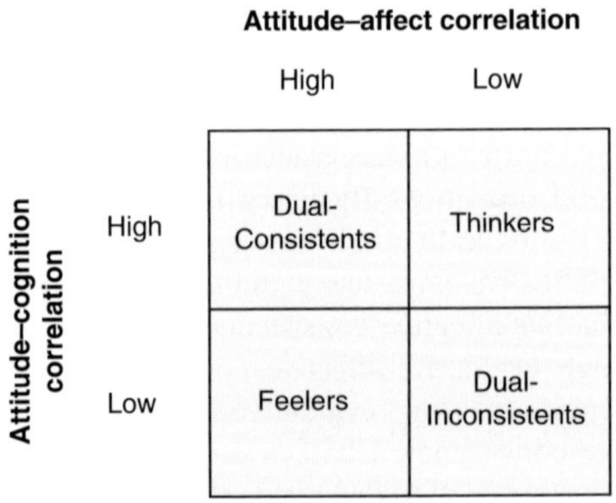

**Attitude–affect correlation**

|  | | High | Low |
|---|---|---|---|
| **Attitude–cognition correlation** | High | Dual-Consistents | Thinkers |
| | Low | Feelers | Dual-Inconsistents |

*Figure 2.2* 2×2 typology of individual differences in attitude structure (adapted from Chaiken et al. (1995).

attitude objects (i.e., "*Feeler*" type individuals), whereas others possess primarily cognition-based attitudes that are more consistent with the evaluative implications of their beliefs (i.e., "*Thinker*" type individuals). Furthermore, because of the synergistic relation between affect and cognition, some people should generally maintain attitudes that are strongly and equally based upon both affective and cognitive information (i.e., "*Dual-Consistent*" type individuals), whereas others should typically possess attitudes that are not highly consistent with either their emotions and beliefs (i.e., "*Dual-Inconsistent*" type individuals). Thus, individuals could be classified into one of four cells.

With the 2×2 taxonomy in mind, precisely *how*, quantitatively, can individuals be classified? To assess these differences, we measure individuals' attitudes, affective responses, and beliefs toward a number of stimulus objects that cover a diverse range of attitudinal phenomena. Given the presence of multiple attitude, affect, and cognition scores, these indices are used to generate attitude–affect ($r_{ea}$), attitude–cognition ($r_{ec}$), and affect–cognition ($r_{ac}$) correlations for each participant. Individuals could then be classified into one of four categories on the basis of median splits of their attitude–affect and attitude–cognition correlations. By using the 2×2 classification scheme described earlier, individuals with a high (i.e., above the median) within-person attitude–affect correlation and a low (i.e., below the median) within-person attitude–cognition correlation would be designated as *Feelers*. In contrast, individuals with a high attitude–cognition correlation and a low attitude–affect correlation would be classified as *Thinkers*. Individuals above the median on both indices would be designated as *Dual-Consistents*, whereas individuals below the median on both indices would be labeled *Dual-Inconsistents*.

## Existence of individual differences in attitude structure: Some research findings

The remaining sections of this chapter focus on studies examining the viability of this individual difference perspective to attitude structure. In doing so we introduce four studies. The first two studies were designed to show that such differences in attitude structure do indeed exist, and that they are associated with relevant individual difference constructs that have found to be relevant to the study of attitudes. The remaining two studies begin to focus on some implications of such individual differences. There, we devote our attention to understanding outcomes associated with possessing attitudes that differ in their affective and cognitive basis.

### Study 1: Demonstrating individual differences

The primary aim of our first study was to demonstrate that individuals differ in the degree to which they possess attitudes that are differentially consistent with the evaluative implications of their affective and cognitive responses. In this study (see Haddock, 1994; Haddock & Zanna, 1999, for additional details), participants completed separate measures of attitude, affective responses, and cognitive responses for each of 14 attitude objects. These objects covered a range of attitudinal domains (e.g., politics, social groups, social policies, educational concerns, gender issues). To measure attitudes, participants completed (for each object) semantic differential measures. To assess the affective and cognitive components, participants completed open-ended measures (Esses & Maio, 2002; Haddock & Zanna, 1998). On the measure of affect, participants listed the feelings they experienced with respect to the attitude object. After completing this task, they then rated the valence of each response on a five-point scale (ranging from very negative to very positive). This task was repeated for each attitude object. An affect score was computed for each object by summing the valence scores and then dividing by the number of responses. On the measure of cognition, participants listed the beliefs they associated with the attitude object. After completing this task, they then rated the valence of each response. Once again, this task was repeated for each attitude object. A cognition score was computed for each object by summing the valence scores and then dividing by the number of responses. These multiple attitude, affect, and cognition scores were then used to compute within-person correlations.

The results of this study demonstrated that there was considerable variance across individuals in the degree to which their attitudes were associated with the favorability of their affective and cognitive responses. For ease of presentation we discuss each within-person correlation in turn.

*Magnitude of the attitude–affect relation*

The mean within-person correlation between the attitude and affect scores was .57. Overall, there was a reasonably high correlation between the favorability of individuals' attitudes and the evaluative implications of their feelings. At the same time, attitude and affect were not quantitatively redundant. Across the sample, this correlation ranged from −.15 to .92, indicating that there was considerable variability across participants in the extent to which their attitudes were associated with the evaluative implications of their feelings. While some participants expressed affective responses that corresponded almost perfectly with their attitudes, others reported feelings that were orthogonal to the favorability of their overall evaluations.

*Magnitude of the attitude–cognition relation*

The mean within-person correlation between the attitude and cognition scores was .61. Overall, there was a reasonably high correlation between the favorability of individuals' attitudes and the evaluative implications of their feelings. At the same time, attitude and cognition were not quantitatively redundant. Similar to the $r_{ea}$ data, there was considerable variability in the magnitude of this relation. Across individuals, this correlation ranged from .08 to .92, indicating that there were large differences in the extent to which individuals' attitudes were associated with the evaluative implications of their beliefs. While some participants expressed cognitive responses that corresponded almost perfectly with their attitudes, others reported beliefs that were orthogonal to the favorability of their overall evaluations.

*Magnitude of the affect–cognition relation*

A third within-person correlation involved the computation of the degree of association between the evaluative implications of affective and cognitive responses. Given their synergistic relation (Eagly & Chaiken, 1993), these two types of responses were expected to be positively associated. Indeed, the mean within-person correlation between the affect and cognition scores was .56. As with the $r_{ea}$ and $r_{ec}$ findings, there was once again enormous variability in the magnitude of this relation, with individual correlations ranging from −.22 to .94.

*Classifying participants using the 2×2 strategy*

Median splits were used to classify participants as high or low on the basis of their $r_{ea}$ and $r_{ec}$ correlations. The resulting number of respondents classified in each of the four cells is displayed in the first row of Table 2.1. Given the positive correlation between affect and cognition, more participants were designated as Dual-Consistents or Dual-Inconsistents than Feelers or Thinkers. Overall, 78 participants were designated as Dual-Consistents and Dual-Inconsistents (39 in each category), whereas the remaining participants were classified as Feelers and Thinkers (15 in each category). Mean attitude–affect, attitude–cognition, and affect–cognition correlations for the four groups of participants are also presented in Table 2.1. Although by nature somewhat tautological, an examination of these $r_{ea}$, $r_{ec}$, and $r_{ac}$ correlations among the groups demonstrates the magnitude of differences across individuals in the extent to which attitudes are consistent with the evaluative implications of affective and cognitive information. For instance, Dual-Consistent participants possessed attitudes that were highly (and equally)

*Table 2.1* Mean within-person correlations: data from Haddock & Zanna (1999)

|  | Dual-Consistent | Dual-Inconsistent | Feeler | Thinker |
|---|---|---|---|---|
| N | 39 | 39 | 15 | 15 |
| $r_{ea}$ | .80 | .39 | .76 | .41 |
| $r_{ec}$ | .81 | .43 | .52 | .79 |
| $r_{ac}$ | .79 | .63 | .55 | .53 |

*Note*: N = number of participants classified within each group; $r_{ea}$ = attitude–affect correlation; $r_{ec}$ = attitude–cognition correlation; $r_{ac}$ = affect–cognition correlation.

consistent with both their affective responses ($M$ = .80) and cognitive responses ($M$ = .81). In contrast, the attitudes of Dual-Inconsistents were much less associated with their feelings ($M$ = .39) and beliefs ($M$ = .43). Finally, participants in the Feeler and Thinker groups displayed a marked asymmetry in the average magnitude of their attitude-affect and attitude-cognition correlations. Feelers possessed attitudes that were much more consistent with their affective ($M$ = .76) than cognitive ($M$ = .52) responses, whereas Thinkers possessed attitudes that were more consistent with their cognitions ($M$ = .79) than their affects ($M$ = .41).

To assess the reliability of these classifications, a separate study by Haddock (1994) assessed the degree to which classification in the 2×2 typology is consistent across sets of attitude objects. In this work, Haddock (1994) assessed attitudes, affective, and cognitive responses toward a large group of objects. A series of analyses in which attitude objects were randomly divided into sets, with separate within-person correlations being derived for each set, showed that classifications on one set of attitude objects predicted classification on a second set of attitude objects. That is, high (low) consistency among the favorability of attitudes, feelings, and beliefs for one subset of attitude objects was usually associated with high (low) consistency among a second subset of attitude objects. These findings are important, because they suggest that these structural differences are replicable across attitude objects.

Overall, the results of this study suggest that there is variation across individuals in the degree to which their attitudes are associated with the favorability of their affective and cognitive responses. For some people, feelings are more closely linked to attitudes, whereas other people have attitudes that are more linked to their beliefs. Yet others appear to have attitudes that are equally (strongly or weakly) associated with their feelings and beliefs.

### Study 2: Association with relevant individual difference constructs

A second study (Huskinson & Haddock, 2002) provides supplemental evidence regarding the proclivity of individual differences in attitude structure. This study had two primary aims. First, it was designed to provide additional evidence regarding the 2×2 attitude structure typology among a separate sample, who could be classified using different attitude objects and different measures. Second, and of greater importance, this study assessed the degree to which attitudinally relevant individual difference dimensions were associated with differences in attitude structure. Toward this goal, Huskinson and Haddock (2002) examined how the constructs of Need to Evaluate, Need for Cognition, and Need for Affect might be related to individual differences in attitude structure.

The Need to Evaluate (Jarvis & Petty, 1996) assesses differences across individuals in the desire to engage in evaluative responding. Individuals high in the Need to Evaluate have been found to respond faster to attitude questions (Jarvis & Petty, 1996) and evaluatively consistent (than inconsistent) words (Hermans, DeHouwer, & Eelen, 2001), as well as forming more spontaneous person judgments (Tormala & Petty, 2001). As applied to individual differences in attitude structure, one might expect individuals high in the Need to Evaluate to possess attitudes that are structurally consistent. On that basis, it was expected that scores on the Need to Evaluate scale would be positively correlated with each of the within-person correlations. Furthermore, in line with this prediction, it was also anticipated that Dual-Inconsistents, those individuals whose attitudes showed the least amount of consistency with their feelings and beliefs, would be lowest in the Need to Evaluate.

The Need for Affect (Maio & Esses, 2001, p. 584) assesses individual differences in "the motivation to approach or avoid emotion-inducing situations." Individual differences in the Need for Affect have been associated with an increased desire to watch emotional movies and more emotional reactions toward the death of Princess Diana (see Maio et al., Chapter 1, this volume, for a more detailed discussion). As applied to individual differences in attitude structure, we wondered whether a high Need for Affect score would be associated with higher attitude–affect within-person correlations. Similarly, we wondered whether the highest Need for Affect scores would be found among Feelers.

The Need for Cognition (Cacioppo & Petty, 1982) assesses the degree to which there exist "individual differences in people's tendency to engage in and enjoy effortful cognitive activity" (Cacioppo, Petty, Feinstein, & Jarvis, 1996, p. 197). Individual differences in the Need for Cognition are associated with numerous attitude-relevant outcomes, such as information recall, responsiveness to peripheral cues, and knowledge (see Cacioppo et al., 1996, for a review). In our research, we were interested in whether individual differences in the Need for Cognition would be associated with attitude–cognition within-person correlations, such that a high Need for Cognition would be associated with possessing attitudes that are highly consistent with the evaluative implications of one's beliefs.

To address the extent to which these individual difference constructs are associated with individual differences in attitude structure, Huskinson and Haddock (2002) had participants complete measures of attitude, affect, and cognition for multiple objects. The objects represented a range of attitudinal phenomena and included many stimuli that were not included in the study reported earlier in this chapter. In this study, attitudes, affective responses, and cognitions were all assessed using semantic differential measures (see Crites et al., 1994, for additional details about the measures of affect and cognition). In addition, participants completed the Need to Evaluate, Need for Affect, and Need for Cognition scales.

*Within-person correlations*

The mean within-person correlations found by Huskinson and Haddock (2002) are listed in Table 2.2. As in the earlier study, there was considerable

*Table 2.2* Mean within-person correlations: Data from Huskinson & Haddock (2002)

|  | Dual-Consistent | Dual-Inconsistent | Feeler | Thinker |
|---|---|---|---|---|
| N | 46 | 46 | 26 | 26 |
| $r_{ea}$ | .89 | .61 | .90 | .71 |
| $r_{ec}$ | .87 | .56 | .68 | .88 |
| $r_{ac}$ | .83 | .58 | .72 | .74 |

*Note*: N = number of participants classified within each group; $r_{ea}$ = attitude–affect correlation; $r_{ec}$ = attitude–cognition correlation; $r_{ac}$ = affect–cognition correlation.

variability in the degree to which participants' attitudes were associated with the favorability of their feelings and beliefs. Similarly, the magnitude of these correlations are comparable to those obtained by Haddock and Zanna (1999). We also found a similar distribution of individuals within the 2×2 framework to those reported by Haddock and Zanna (1999). As can be seen in Table 2.2, 32% of participants in the Huskinson and Haddock (2002) sample were classified as either Dual-Consistents or Dual-Inconsistents, with 18% apiece being classified as Feelers or Thinkers. Thus, a different sample of respondents, using different attitude objects and measures, produced comparable classification to that obtained by Haddock and Zanna (1999).

### Relationship between individual difference measures and within-person correlations

Huskinson and Haddock (2002) found that scores on the Need to Evaluate scale were significantly correlated with the magnitude of the within-person attitude–affect ($r = .19$) and attitude–cognition ($r = .16$) correlations. The correlation between the Need to Evaluate and affective-cognitive consistency was marginally significant ($r = .13$). As expected, individuals high in the Need to Evaluate possessed attitudes that were more consistent with their affective and cognitive responses. A supplemental analysis examined mean differences in the Need to Evaluate as a function of the 2×2 typology. Perhaps not surprisingly, Dual-Inconsistents possessed Need to Evaluate scores that were significantly lower than all other groups ($p < .01$). These data provide preliminary evidence that individual differences in the Need to Evaluate are associated with individual differences in attitude structure.

   The other significant correlation was that between scores on the Need for Affect scale and the within-person attitude–affect correlation ($r = .21$). As expected, individuals high in the Need for Affect also had higher correlations between the favorability of their attitudes and the evaluative implications of their affective responses. Furthermore, Feelers possessed Need for Affect scores that were higher than those of all other groups ($p < .07$). Thus, individual differences in the Need for Affect are associated with individual differences in attitude structure.

Finally, scores on the Need for Cognition scale were not correlated with the magnitude of attitude–cognition within-person correlations ($r = .00$). Indeed, Need for Cognition demonstrated no significant effects in this study.

*Summary*

Overall, the results of this study provide additional evidence regarding the viability of the individual difference approach to attitude structure. As in the study reported by Haddock and Zanna (1999), there was considerable variability across individuals in the degree to which attitudes were consistent with the evaluative implications of their affective and cognitive responses. Furthermore, this study provides initial evidence regarding how these differences are associated with attitudinally relevant individual difference dimensions. As expected, individual differences in the Need to Evaluate and the Need for Affect were correlated with individual differences in attitude structure. However, the Need for Cognition was not correlated with attitudinal consistency. The current results suggest that the tendency to engage in thoughtful processing does not necessarily lead an individual to possess attitudes that are more consistent with the favorability of their beliefs. Individuals high in the Need for Cognition think more about the world, but their attitudes do not appear to be more cognitively based.

## Outcomes associated with individual differences in attitude structure

Recently, we have turned our attention to the investigation of outcomes associated with individual differences in attitude structure. To be of utility, it is necessary to demonstrate that such individual differences have important consequences for attitudinally relevant phenomena. Of course, at the level of individual attitudes, research has already demonstrated that attitudes that vary in their affective-cognitive basis differ on a number of outcomes, such as the attitude–behavior relation (e.g., Norman, 1975), accessibility (e.g., Chaiken et al., 1995) and the susceptibility to different types of persuasive appeals (e.g., Edwards, 1990; Fabrigar & Petty, 1999). Our research has sought to extend these findings by investigating whether *individuals* themselves might differ along these important outcomes. Dual-Consistents, Dual-Inconsistents, Feelers, and Thinkers might be expected to differ in a number of ways. For example, recall Chaiken et al.'s (1995) results about the consistency of individuals' attitude toward capital punishment and the accessibility of their attitude. Extrapolating these findings, one can, for example, test whether Dual-Consistents, across attitude objects, respond to attitudinal questions more quickly than Dual-Inconsistents. Similarly, Dual-Consistents should also be expected to show more a pronounced tendency to behave in accordance in their attitudes (cf. Norman, 1975), and show an enhanced ability to process attitude-relevant information. Other outcomes might be expected among Feelers and Thinkers. These individuals should be differentially influenced by affective and cognitive appeals (cf. Edwards, 1990; Fabrigar & Petty, 1999), and may be expected to differ in their ability to process affective and cognitive information. The remainder of the chapter serves as an initial demonstration of some of the implications of individual differences in attitude structure.

### Study 3: Outcomes of Dual-Consistency versus Dual-Inconsistency

Among Dual-Consistents and Dual-Inconsistents we have investigated how individual differences in attitude structure are associated with the latency with which individuals can respond to questions about their attitudes. At the level of individual attitudes, Chaiken et al. (1995) found that individuals low in both evaluative-affective and evaluative-cognitive consistency held attitudes that were less accessible than attitudes that were highly consistent with either affect and/or cognition. Based on these findings, Huskinson and Haddock (in press) tested whether Dual-Consistents, those individuals with high correlations between both their attitudes and affects and attitudes and cognitions, would, across attitude objects, hold attitudes that were more accessible than those of Dual-Inconsistents.

In this study, students, at the beginning of the academic year, completed measures of attitude, affect, and cognition for multiple attitude objects. These objects represented a range of attitudinal stimuli, such as political issues, social groups, and consumer products. Attitudes, affective responses, and cognitive responses were assessed using semantic differential measures described by Crites et al. (1994). On the basis of their responses to these questions, participants were classified using the 2×2 typology. Approximately four months after completing the initial set of measures, individuals who were classified as either Dual-Consistents or Dual-Inconsistents returned to the lab to participate in a second study. Their task was to respond to a series of questions about a number of countries. For each country, a series of evaluative bipolar dimensions were presented on a computer screen. These dimensions represented various affective and cognitive properties of attitude (see Verplanken, Hofstee, & Janssen, 1998, for a complete list of countries and items). For each trial, participants were required to indicate, by means of a key press, which of the two possible responses best represented their perception of the country.

The results of the study revealed differences in the overall response latency between Dual-Consistents and Dual-Inconsistents. For the sake of simplicity, we combine the data across attitude objects. A mixed-model ANOVA revealed a marginally significant effect of individual type ($p = .08$). As can be seen in Figure 2.3, on both the measures of affect and cognition, Dual-Consistents provided faster responses than Dual-Inconsistents. Thus, approximately four months after having been initially classified, the speed with which participants answered affective and cognitive items about a

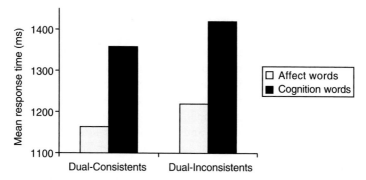

*Figure 2.3* Differences in attitude accessibility as a function of individual differences in attitude structure.

completely independent set of attitude objects varied as a function of individual differences in attitude structure.[1]

There are two primary issues raised by this study. First, the results of this study provide initial evidence regarding outcomes associated with individual differences in attitude structure. What makes these data particularly compelling is the temporal separation between the session in which participants were classified and the session in which the accessibility data were gathered. Such a demonstration offers impressive testimony regarding the stability of such differences. Second, these results may be fundamental in understanding other possible differences between the Dual-Consistent and Dual-Inconsistent groups. For example, because accessible attitudes are strong (i.e., predictive of behavior and resistant to change; see Fazio, 1995), these results support Chaiken et al.'s (1995) contention that an attitude is strong to the extent that has it has evaluatively consistent support from feelings and/or beliefs, extrapolating these differences to the level of the individual. Similarly, these results extend other findings on the antecedents of differences in accessibility (see Fazio, 1995). Our findings serve as preliminary evidence that such differences can extend to the level of chronic differences across individuals.

### Study 4: Outcomes of Feelers versus Thinkers

A recent study by Huskinson and Haddock (2004) provides initial evidence about consequences associated with the Feeler and Thinker categories. In this study, we were interested in assessing whether Feelers and Thinkers would be differentially influenced by affective versus cognitive information about a consumer product. To foreshadow, our hypothesis was that an affect-based

---

1 It is also worth noting that there was a significant main effect of word type. Similar to Verplanken et al. (1998), we found that affective terms were responded to more quickly than cognitive terms (cf. Giner-Sorolla, 2001).

appeal might be more persuasive among Feelers, whereas a cognition-based appeal might be more persuasive among Thinkers.

A number of studies have investigated how *single* attitudes that are either affectively or cognitively based are differentially susceptible to affective or cognitive appeals. For instance, Edwards (1990) tested whether the sequence in which affective and cognitive information is presented at the attitude formation stage impacts subsequent resistance to affective and cognitive appeals. In one of Edwards's studies, participants were asked to *both* sample a pleasant tasting high-energy sports drink and read positive information about the drink's benefits. The experience of tasting the beverage was considered as affective information, whereas reading about the beverage's attributes was equated with cognitive information. What is important to note that Edwards (1990) manipulated the order in which the affective and cognitive information was presented, and that the information presented first was deemed to be the basis of the participant's attitude. Immediately after having been exposed to the positive affective and cognitive information about the beverage (called "Power-Plus"), participants expressed their initial attitude toward it. At the persuasion stage of the experiment, participants were presented with additional information about the beverage. Specifically, they were given the opportunity to *both* sample the scent of the drink, as well as reading additional information about its properties. In this phase of the study, the affective and cognitive information was negative. Similar to the formation stage, participants were provided with both types of information, and the persuasive information that was provided first determined whether the appeal was affectively or cognitively based. Upon having been exposed to the negative affective and cognitive appeal, participants again reported their attitude toward Power-Plus. The results of this study demonstrated that affect-based attitudes were more likely to change in response to an affective appeal, whereas cognition-based attitudes exhibited equal change under both types of appeals (see also Edwards & von Hippel, 1995; cf. Millar & Millar, 1990).

In an attempt to rule out some alternative explanations of Edwards's (1990) results, Fabrigar and Petty (1999) also investigated the susceptibility of affective and cognitive attitudes to different types of appeals. Fabrigar and Petty were concerned that previous findings might have been due to either differences in the attribute dimensions made salient during the experiment or direct experience with the attitude object. In their research, Fabrigar and Petty (1999) were able to discount these alternative explanations. Furthermore, they demonstrated that an affective appeal was more successful in changing affect-based attitudes, whereas a cognitive appeal showed a tendency to be more successful in changing cognition-based attitudes. These results are consistent with a matching effect of attitude basis and persuasion: attitudes are more likely to change when its basis and the nature of the appeal focus on the same attitude dimension.

We were interested in extrapolating these findings to the level of individual differences. Rather than creating affective and cognitive attitudes and assessing their susceptibility to different appeals, we examined whether individuals whose attitudes are most consistent with either their feelings or beliefs would show different responsiveness to affective and cognitive information. In line with the majority of previous research (e.g., Edwards, 1990; Edwards & von Hippel, 1995; Fabrigar & Petty, 1999; cf. Millar & Millar, 1990), we predicted that an affective appeal would be most effective among Feelers, whereas a cognitive appeal might be more effective among Thinkers.

In our study, individuals who were classified as Feelers or Thinkers at the beginning of the academic year were asked to participate in a study ostensibly being jointly conducted by the Departments of Psychology and Marketing. Participants were informed that they would be evaluating a new type of beverage, a sports drink called Power-Plus. Participants were then presented with either an affective or cognitive appeal. Participants in the affect condition were given the opportunity to sample Power-Plus. After cleansing their palate, participants were given a drink that contained water with a combination of concentrated fruit squashes (resulting in a flavor that was not very familiar to our participants). The mixture had been refrigerated and was intended to have a positive taste. Participants in the cognition condition were provided with written information about the drink's taste. This appeal focused on the drink's positive taste and flavor.[2] Note that in both conditions, the information contained within the appeal was targeted at the same attribute (the drink's flavor and taste). Immediately after either tasting (or reading about the taste of) Power-Plus, participants indicated their attitude toward the beverage.

The results of the study can be summarized as follows. To begin, much to our surprise, there was a significant main effect of appeal. Overall, participants who received the cognitive information about Power-Plus, regardless of their Feeler–Thinker status, reported an overwhelmingly positive attitude about the beverage. However, of greater importance, the interaction between the Feeler–Thinker dimension and information type was significant. Simple effects analyses revealed that the affect-based appeal led to more favorable attitudes among Feelers than Thinkers, whereas the cognitive appeal produced somewhat (but not significantly) more favorable attitudes among Thinkers than Feelers. We also computed a contrast in which we compared the mean rating of Thinkers in the affect appeal condition to participants from all other groups. Given the unanticipated strength of the cognitive appeal, we tested whether Thinkers who actually tasted the beverage would provide significantly lower ratings than everyone else in the study. The results of this contrast supported this view.

The results of this study provide preliminary evidence of one outcome associated with differences between the Feeler and Thinker categories. Of

2 We wish to thank Lee Fabrigar and Rich Petty for sharing with us the materials from the Fabrigar and Petty (1999) paper.

course, these data can be linked with studies that have explored how newly created affective and cognitive attitudes are influenced by different types of appeals. Our findings correspond with results obtained by Edwards and colleagues (Edwards, 1990; Edwards & von Hippel, 1995) and Fabrigar and Petty (1999) regarding the role of matching in attitude-basis and persuasion.

## Summary and directions for future research

Philosophers, scientists, religious figures, and political leaders have long questioned the role of affect and cognition as determinants of human behavior. Within social psychology, one attempt to uncover the relative importance of feelings and beliefs has been to assess the degree to which they serve as predictors of attitude. Numerous studies have demonstrated that either affect, cognition, or both affect and cognition are significant unique predictors of attitude. Our own work in this area has tried to take a somewhat new perspective to this issue: Do people differ in the degree to which they possess attitudes that are consistent with the evaluative implications of their feelings and beliefs? The data presented in this chapter suggest that such differences exist, and, more importantly, that they are associated with important attitude-relevant outcomes. To date, we have demonstrated that (a) there is considerable variation across individuals in the extent to which they possess attitudes that are consistent with the evaluative implications of their feelings and beliefs; (b) such variation is associated with attitude-relevant individual difference constructs; and (c) variation in attitude structure corresponds with important outcomes.

We believe that these findings have important implications for our understanding of the attitude construct. The results provide strong support for the multicomponent perspective of attitude. Affective and cognitive information were associated with the favorability of individuals' attitudes. Furthermore, there was considerable variability across individuals in the extent to which the evaluative implications of their feeling and beliefs were correlated with overall evaluations. Consistent with other researchers (e.g., Breckler, 1984; Breckler & Wiggins, 1989, 1991; Eagly et al., 1994), we would argue that in order to obtain a comprehensive understanding of individuals' attitudes, it is important to assess multiple sources of information. That said, it must be pointed out that in our research, we, like most researchers, have not emphasized the behavioral component as a predictor of attitudes. As an initial step in understanding the role of behavioral information within an individual differences perspective, we are interested in pursuing whether behavioral information is particularly important in predicting attitudes among Dual-Inconsistents.

Although the data reported in this chapter are promising, it is clear that additional work is required to better understand the implications of individual differences in attitude structure. At present, we are assessing how these differences are associated with outcomes relating to information processing and the relation between attitudes and behavior. With respect to information processing, we wish to investigate whether individual differences in attitude structure influence individuals' abilities to process affective and cognitive information. In one such study, adapting the remember–know paradigm (see Gardiner, Ramponi, & Richardson-Klavehn, 2002) we are investigating whether Dual-Consistents, Dual-Inconsistents, Feelers, and Thinkers exhibit differences in the ability to encode and retrieve affective and cognitive information. Within the realm of attitudes and behavior, we seek to explore whether Dual-Consistents, across domains, show a higher association between their attitudes and behavior. We also plan to assess whether self-perception effects (see Bem, 1972) are most likely to occur among Dual-Inconsistents.

Our approach to individual differences in attitude structure should be placed in the context of other research that seeks to examine the role of feelings and beliefs. Of note, Trafimow and Sheeran (Chapter 3, this volume) have investigated the role of affect and cognition in determining attitudes. Trafimow and Sheeran postulate that cognition influences behavior only after it has been translated into affect. Of relevance to the current chapter, they question whether individuals vary in the degree to which people attach affect onto cognition. Similarly, using an approach where individuals can be classi-fied as affective or cognitive, they have demonstrated, using within-person and multiple regression analyses, that individuals differ in the degree to which their attitudes are under affective versus cognitive control. Furthermore, they have found that higher scores on a measure of conscientiousness were associ-ated with attitudes that were more consistent with individuals' cognitions. As our own research, as well as that of Trafimow and Sheeran, continues to develop, it is hoped that together they will serve to elucidate some interesting conclusions about how affective and cognitive information interact to predict attitudes and behavior.

To conclude, let us return to the beginning of the chapter. Recall that Samuel Adams, the historic American patriot (as well as someone associated with excellent beer) noted that individuals are governed more by their feelings than by reason. In contrast, the Buddha suggested that what we are arises from our thoughts. If we apply these statements to the psychology of atti-tudes, it seems to us that there is indeed something to be said for both of these positions. Some people have attitudes that are usually governed by feelings; some have attitudes that are usually derived from beliefs; and yet others have attitudes that are derived equally from affect and cognition. We believe that the individual difference can serve an informative function in increasing our understanding of the attitude concept, and we hope that a consideration of this perspective will allow attitude researchers to continue to develop pro-vocative questions about how individuals evaluate and navigate their social world.

## Acknowledgments

We thank Greg Maio for his comments on an earlier draft of this chapter. Tom Huskinson was supported by a Doctoral Fellowship from the Economic and Social Research Council.

## References

Abelson, R. P., Kinder, D. R., Peters, M. D., & Fiske, S. T. (1982). Affective and semantic components in political person perception. *Journal of Personality and Social Psychology*, *42*, 619–630.

Adams, S. Quote taken from *www.thequotationspage.com*.

Altemeyer, B. (1996). *The authoritarian specter*. Boston: Harvard University Press.

Bem, D. J. (1972). Self-perception theory. In L. Berkowitz (Ed.), *Advances in experimental social psychology* (Vol. 6, pp. 1–62). San Diego, CA: Academic Press.

Breckler, S. J. (1984). Empirical validation of affect, behavior, and cognition as distinct components of attitude. *Journal of Personality and Social Psychology*, *47*, 1191–1205.

Breckler, S. J., & Wiggins, E. C. (1989). Affect versus evaluation in the structure of attitudes. *Journal of Experimental Social Psychology*, *25*, 253–271.

Breckler, S. J., & Wiggins, E. C. (1991). Cognitive responses in persuasion: Affective and evaluative determinants. *Journal of Experimental Social Psychology*, *27*, 180–200.

Buddha. Quote taken from *www.thequotationspage.com*.

Cacioppo, J. T., & Petty, R. E. (1982). The need for cognition. *Journal of Personality and Social Psychology*, *42*, 116–131.

Cacioppo, J. T., Petty, R. E., Feinstein, J. A., & Jarvis, W. B. G. (1996). Dispositional differences in cognitive motivation: The life and times of individuals varying in need for cognition. *Psychological Bulletin*, *119*, 197–253.

Chaiken, S., & Baldwin, M. W. (1981). Affective-cognitive consistency and the effect of salient behavioral information on the self-perception of attitudes. *Journal of Personality and Social Psychology*, *41*, 1–12.

Chaiken, S., Pomerantz, E. M., & Giner-Sorolla, R. (1995). Structural consistency and attitude strength. In R. E. Petty & J. A. Krosnick (Eds.), *Attitude strength: Antecedents and consequences* (pp. 387–412). Hillsdale, NJ: Lawrence Erlbaum Associates, Inc.

Chaiken, S., & Yates, S. M. (1985). Affective-cognitive consistency and thought-induced attitude polarization. *Journal of Personality and Social Psychology*, *49*, 1470–1481.

Converse, P. E. (1970). Attitudes and non-attitudes: Continuation of a dialogue. In E. R. Tufte (Ed.), *The quantitative analysis of social problems* (pp.168–189). Reading, MA: Addison-Wesley.

Crites, S. L. Jr., Fabrigar, L. R., & Petty, R. E. (1994). Measuring the affective and cognitive properties of attitudes: Conceptual and methodological issues. *Personality and Social Psychology Bulletin*, *20*, 619–634.

Eagly, A. H., & Chaiken, S. (1993). *The psychology of attitudes*. Fort Worth, TX: Harcourt Brace Jovanovich.

Eagly, A. H., Mladinic, A., & Otto, S. (1994). Cognitive and affective bases of attitudes toward social groups and social policies. *Journal of Experimental Social Psychology*, *30*, 113–137.

Edwards, K. (1990). The interplay of affect and cognition in attitude formation and change. *Journal of Personality and Social Psychology, 59*, 202–216.

Edwards, K., & von Hippel, W. (1995). Hearts and minds: The priority of affective and cognitive factors in person perception. *Personality and Social Psychology Bulletin, 21*, 996–1011.

Esses, V. M., Haddock, G., & Zanna, M. P. (1993). Values, stereotypes, and emotions as determinants of intergroup attitudes. In D. M. Mackie & D. L. Hamilton (Eds.), *Affect, cognition and stereotyping: Interactive processes in group perception* (pp. 137–166). New York: Academic Press.

Esses, V. M., & Maio, G. R. (2002). Expanding the assessment of attitudinal components and structure: The benefits of open-ended measures. In W. Stroebe & M. Hewstone (Eds.), *European review of social psychology* (Vol. 12, pp. 71–102). Chichester, UK: Wiley.

Fabrigar, L. R., & Petty, R. E. (1999). The role of affective and cognitive bases of attitudes in susceptibility to affectively and cognitively based persuasion. *Personality and Social Psychology Bulletin, 25*, 363–381.

Fazio, R. H. (1995). Attitudes as object-evaluation associations: Determinants, consequences, and correlates of attitude accessibility. In R. E. Petty & J. A. Krosnick (Eds.), *Attitude strength: Antecedents and consequences.* Mahwah, NJ: Lawrence Erlbaum Associates, Inc.

Gardiner, J. M., Ramponi, C., & Richardson-Klavehn, A. (2002). Recognition memory and decision processes: A meta-analysis of remember, know, and guess. *Memory, 10*, 83–98.

Giner-Sorolla, R. (2001). Affectively based attitudes are not always faster: The moderating role of extremity. *Personality and Social Psychology Bulletin, 27*, 666–677.

Granberg, D., & Brown, T. A. (1995). On affect and cognition in politics. *Social Psychology Quarterly, 52*, 171–182.

Haddock, G. (1994). *Investigating the existence of individual differences in attitude structure.* Unpublished doctoral dissertation, University of Waterloo.

Haddock, G., & Zanna, M. P. (1993). Predicting prejudicial attitudes: The importance of affect, cognition, and the feeling-belief dimension. In L. McAlister & M. L. Rothschild (Eds.), *Advances in consumer research* (Vol. 20, pp. 315–318). Provo, UT: Association for Consumer Research.

Haddock, G., & Zanna, M. P. (1994). Preferring "housewives" to "feminists": Categorization and the favorability of attitudes toward women. *Psychology of Women Quarterly, 18*, 25–52.

Haddock, G., & Zanna, M. P. (1997). The impact of negative advertising on evaluations of political candidates: The 1993 Canadian federal election. *Basic and Applied Social Psychology, 19*, 205–223.

Haddock, G., & Zanna, M. P. (1998). On the use of open-ended measures to assess attitudinal components. *British Journal of Social Psychology, 37*, 129–149,

Haddock, G., & Zanna, M. P. (1999). Affect, cognition, and social attitudes. In W. Stroebe & M. Hewstone (Eds.), *European review of social psychology* (Vol. 10, pp. 75–100). Chichester, UK: Wiley.

Haddock, G., Zanna, M. P., & Esses, V. M. (1993). Assessing the structure of prejudicial attitudes: The case of attitudes toward homosexuals. *Journal of Personality and Social Psychology, 65*, 1105–1118.

Hermans, D., DeHouwer, J., & Eelen, P. (2001). A time course analysis of the affective priming effect. *Cognition and Motivation, 15*, 143–165.

Huskinson, T., & Haddock, G. (2002a). *Individual differences in attitude structure: Variance in the chronic reliance on affective and cognitive information.* Paper presented at the annual meeting of the Society of Personality and Social Psychology, Savannah, GA.

Huskinson, T., & Haddock, G. (2004). Individual differences in attitude structure: Variance in the chronic reliance on affective and cognitive information. *Journal of Experimental Social Psychology, 40,* 82–90.

Huskinson, T. L. H., & Haddock, G. (in press). Individual differences in attitude structure and the accessibility of attitudes. *Social Cognition.*

Jackson, L. A., Hodge, C. N., Gerard, D. A., Ingram, J. M., Ervin, K. S., & Sheppard, L. A. (1996). Cognition, affect, and behavior in the prediction of group attitudes. *Personality and Social Psychology Bulletin, 22,* 306–316.

Jarvis, W. B. G., & Petty, R. E. (1996). The need to evaluate. *Journal of Personality and Social Psychology, 70,* 172–194.

Lavine, H., Thomsen, C. J., Zanna, M. P., & Borgida, E. (1998). On the primacy of affect in determination of attitudes and behavior: The moderating role of affective-cognitive ambivalence. *Journal of Experimental Social Psychology, 34,* 398–421.

Maio, G. R., & Esses, V. M. (2001). The need for affect: Individual differences in the motivation to approach or avoid emotions. *Journal of Personality, 69,* 583–615.

Millar, M. G., & Millar, K. U. (1990). Attitude change as a function of attitude type and argument type. *Journal of Personality and Social Psychology, 59,* 217–228.

Millar, M. G., & Tesser, A. (1989). The effects of affective-cognitive consistency and thought on the attitude-behavior relation. *Journal of Experimental Social Psychology, 25,* 189–202.

Norman, R. (1975). Affective-cognitive consistency, attitudes, conformity, and behavior. *Journal of Personality and Social Psychology, 32,* 83–91.

Rosenberg, M. (1956). Cognitive structure and attitudinal affect. *Journal of Abnormal and Social Psychology, 53,* 367–372.

Rosenberg, M. J. (1968). Hedonism, inauthenticity, and other goals toward expansion of a consistency theory. In R. P. Abelson, E. Aronson, W. J. McGuire, T. M. Newcomb, M. J. Rosenberg, & P. H. Tannenbaum (Eds.), *Theories of cognitive consistency: A sourcebook* (pp. 73–111). Chicago: Rand McNally.

Stangor, C., Sullivan, L. A., & Ford, T. E. (1991). Affective and cognitive determinants of prejudice. *Social Cognition, 9,* 359–391.

Tormala, Z. L., & Petty, R. E. (2001). On-line versus memory-based processing: The role of "need to evaluate" in person perception. *Personality and Social Psychology Bulletin, 27,* 1599–1612.

Verplanken, B., Hofstee, G., & Janssen, H. J. W. (1998). Accessibility of affective versus cognitive components of attitudes. *European Journal of Social Psychology, 28,* 23–35.

Zanna, M. P., & Rempel, J. K. (1988). Attitudes: A new look at an old concept. In D. Bar-Tal & A. W. Kruglanski (Eds.), *The social psychology of knowledge* (pp. 315–334). Cambridge, UK: Cambridge University Press.

# 3    A theory about the translation of cognition into affect and behavior

*David Trafimow and Paschal Sheeran*

Two assumptions have dominated the social psychology of attitudes over the past century. The first assumption is that attitudes cause behaviors. The second assumption is that attitudes have both an affective and cognitive component. It follows from these two assumptions that affect and/or cognition cause behaviors. This conclusion suggests at least two questions:

1    Does it really make sense to partition attitudes into an affective and a cognitive component?
2    Even if the partition does make sense, how do these two components work together to determine behaviors?

The present chapter is an attempt to answer these questions. As is detailed in the first major section of this chapter, the available data present a reasonably solid basis for answering the first question. In contrast, there are few solid data for an answer to the second question. Nevertheless, we present a theory in the second major section that is designed to answer it.

## Affective and cognitive attitude components

The usual method for demonstrating that attitudes have an affective and a cognitive component is to provide participants with items that are presumed to be affective or cognitive. The participants respond to the items, and a factor analysis is performed on the responses. Although a good deal of early research failed to provide much support for separate affective and cognitive factors (Mann, 1959; Ostrom, 1969; Woodsmansee & Cook, 1967), more recent analyses have reversed this trend (Abelson, Kinder, Peters, & Fiske, 1982; Breckler, 1984; Breckler & Wiggins, 1989; Crites, Fabrigar, & Petty, 1994). Thus, to the extent that factor analysis is deemed to be a valid way of testing for affective and cognitive components of attitudes, it now seems clear that there is quite a bit of support for the distinction between the two components.

### The problem of interpreting factors

However, there are good reasons for questioning the validity of factor analysis for this purpose. One problem that Fishbein (1980) discussed pertains to the interpretation of the factors. He discussed a factor analysis pertaining to the behavior of "My smoking cigarettes." The first factor comprised the items "enjoyable," "satisfying," and "pleasant." The second factor comprised the items "healthy," "beneficial," "good," and "wise." There was also a third factor that need not concern us. The normal reaction would be to interpret Factor 1 as reflecting affect and Factor 2 as reflecting cognition. However, Fishbein suggested that Factor 1 could just as easily be interpreted as representing "attitude" and that Factor 2 could be interpreted as representing "health belief." Note that either interpretation provides a plausible account of the factor loadings.

Fishbein did not stop there. He pointed out that his interpretation implies two more predictions. First, if Factor 1 is actually a measure of attitude, then it should do a much better job of predicting behavioral intention than should Factor 2. Further, the influence of health beliefs should already be incorporated into one's attitude, and so the inclusion of Factor 2 along with Factor 1 should not add to the prediction of intention above and beyond the prediction engendered by Factor 1 alone. In fact, the correlation between intention and Factor 1 was .8 whereas the correlation between intention and Factor 2 was only .48. More importantly, the multiple correlation predicting intention from both Factors 1 and 2 was .8, thereby indicating that the prediction of intention was the same regardless of whether Factor 2 was included in the regression equation or not.

Although these analyses support Fishbein's interpretation, they are not necessarily inconsistent with the idea of affective and cognitive attitude components. However, Fishbein performed some additional analyses that are compatible with only one of the two interpretations. According to Fishbein's theory of reasoned action, attitudes are based on beliefs about consequences and evaluations of those consequences. Each belief about the likelihood of a consequence is multiplied by an evaluation of how good or bad it would be if the consequence actually happened, and attitudes are based on the sum of the products ($\Sigma b_i e_i$). Thus, if Factor 1 is really an attitude measure and Factor 2 is just a measure of health beliefs, then $\Sigma b_i e_i$ should be more correlated with Factor 1 than with Factor 2. In contrast, if Factor 1 is really an affective factor and Factor 2 is a cognitive factor, then $\Sigma b_i e_i$ should be more correlated with Factor 2 than with Factor 1. Consistent with Fishbein's view, and contrary to the idea of affective and cognitive attitude components, the correlation of $\Sigma b_i e_i$ with Factor 1 was greater than its correlation with Factor 2.

In sum, at least with regard to the behavior Fishbein tested, the seemingly obvious interpretation of the two factors as representing affect and cognition clearly provided a worse account of the data than did Fishbein's interpretation. We are not arguing that therefore the bifurcation of attitude into affective and cognitive components is wrong. Rather, we are arguing that factor analyses can be interpreted in a variety of ways, and it is a complicated issue to decide among potentially competing explanations. If nothing else, Fishbein's analyses demonstrate that one cannot interpret factors simply by looking at the content of the items that load on them.

### The semantic problem

Fishbein's arguments cast doubt upon the interpretation of any factor analysis in the attitude domain. As an example, consider a factor analytic study by Crites et al. (1994). These researchers found that delighted/sad and joy/sorrow load on the same factor and that useful/useless and valuable/worthless load together. Does this mean that delighted/sad and joy/sorrow compose an affective factor and that useful/useless and valuable/worthless compose a cognitive factor? We have already seen Fishbein's demonstration that an analysis of factor loadings provides an insufficient basis for interpreting factors. However, there is an additional problem. Let us be extremely specific here. Suppose a participant endorses "delighted" in response to the attitude object (whether this is a real object or a behavior does not matter here). Is this a description of how she really feels (i.e., her affect towards the object) or is it an evaluation of the attitude object (i.e., her cognition about an attribute of the object)? A plausible argument could be made either way.

At the risk of belaboring this point, we would like to conduct a thought experiment. Imagine the existence of aliens from Pluto who are extremely knowledgeable about humans, and that this knowledge includes an understanding of the English language. In addition, suppose that these aliens were completely devoid of affect. What would happen if these aliens were participants in a typical factor analytic study? Assuming that the alien participants understand English, they would know that delighted/sad and joy/sorrow are semantically similar to each other and that useful/useless and valuable/worthless are semantically similar to each other. This semantic knowledge would be reflected in their responses, and thus two factors would be obtained. If a social psychologist who was unaware that the aliens from Pluto were devoid of affect analyzed the data, he would conclude that the first factor measured the aliens' affect and that the second factor measured the aliens' cognition towards the attitude object. Clearly, then, if factor analytic evidence can be explained plausibly by the relative semantic similarity of items that load on the same factor, then it is difficult to make a strong case that such evidence provides an unambiguous method for demonstrating affective and cognitive components of attitudes.

### Other evidence for affective and cognitive attitude components

Given the problems with factor analytic evidence described above, Trafimow and Sheeran (1998) looked for another way to test the distinction between affective and cognitive attitude components. These researchers started from the traditional idea that attitudes are a function of beliefs. If we are to assume that there is an affective and a cognitive component, then where would these components come from? One possible answer is that there are different types of beliefs. Some beliefs are more affective whereas other beliefs are more cognitive. The assumption is not that any beliefs are necessarily purely affective or purely cognitive, only that some beliefs have a preponderance of affect or cognition, and could be termed "affective" or "cognitive" beliefs, respectively. Once this assumption is made, it suggests the possibility that, during the process of forming an intention, affective beliefs are compared with each other to form a more general affect toward the behavior, and cognitive beliefs are compared with each other to form a more general cognition towards the behavior. When these comparisons are made, associations are established between affective beliefs and other affective beliefs, between cognitive beliefs and other cognitive beliefs, but not between affective and cognitive beliefs.

The assumption of associations between beliefs of a similar type and a lack of associations between dissimilar types (i.e., between affective and cognitive beliefs) implies a way of testing the distinction between affective and cognitive attitude components. Suppose participants are asked to recall their beliefs. If they had previously formed associative pathways between affective beliefs and other affective beliefs, then these pathways should also be capable of being used for retrieval. Thus, after recalling a particular affective belief, the participant should be able to traverse an associative pathway to another affective belief which should result in an increased likelihood that this other affective belief will be recalled. By similar reasoning, the recall of a cognitive belief should cue the recall of another cognitive belief. The recall of cognitive beliefs after affective ones, or the recall of affective beliefs after cognitive ones, should be less likely because of a paucity of retrieval routes across the two belief types. In sum, according to Trafimow and Sheeran's *associative hypothesis*, if participants are asked to recall their beliefs about a behavior, they should tend to recall affective beliefs adjacent to each other and they should tend to recall cognitive beliefs adjacent to each other. In short, the list of beliefs should be clustered by belief type.

Trafimow and Sheeran (1998) performed five studies. The first two were factor analytic studies, and although the data supported the distinction between affective and cognitive attitude components, these studies suffered from the same problems that plagued previous factor analytic research. However, they also performed three studies based on their associative hypothesis. In the typical study, participants were presented with a list of beliefs about a behavior, though they were not told what the behavior actually was. Half of these beliefs were affective (e.g., "you may feel that performing the behavior is unpleasant") and half of them were cognitive (e.g., "it could be useful to perform the behavior"). Participants were then randomly assigned to decide whether or not they would intend to perform the behavior (experimental condition), whether or not someone else named Sarah would intend to perform the behavior (control condition 1), or to memorize the beliefs (control condition 2). According to the associative hypothesis, it is the process of forming a behavioral intention that induces people to undergo the associative process described above. In the two control conditions, where participants did not form behavioral intentions, there was no reason for them to do so. Therefore, it follows that only the participants in the experimental condition should have formed the hypothesized pattern of associations. Finally, after a short delay to clear working memory, participants in all of the conditions were asked to recall the beliefs.

Consistent with the associative hypothesis, the amount of clustering in the experimental condition was significantly greater than chance clustering, or the amount of clustering in either of the control conditions. Note that the semantic content of the beliefs was exactly the same in all three of the conditions, and so the findings cannot be explained on the basis of the semantic characteristics of the items. Of course, there are other potential objections. For example, perhaps the fact that participants were presented with the beliefs, rather than generating their own beliefs somehow caused the clustering in the experimental condition. Or, perhaps not being told what the behavior actually was caused this clustering. Or, perhaps the beliefs that the experimenters thought were affective or cognitive were not thought so by the participants. However, additional experiments showed that it was possible to obtain clustering even when: (a) participants generated their own beliefs; (b) the behavior was known to the participants; (c) when participants themselves later categorized their own responses as being affective or cognitive. It is also worth noting that the researchers tested for clustering on the basis of valence (whether the beliefs were positive versus negative) and did not obtain clustering in any of the studies. In sum, the success of the associative hypothesis provides a strong case for distinguishing between affective and cognitive attitude components.

## A theory about the translation of cognition into affect and behavior

In one way at least, the distinction between affective and cognitive attitude components presents a problem. As an example, consider the situation faced by Josephine, the heroine from Gilbert and Sullivan's famous opera *H.M.S. Pinafore*. She is in love with a poor sailor but has been offered a marriage to the First Lord of the Admiralty. She can have a difficult life as the poor wife of a poor sailor, or an easy life of glory as the wife of the lord. In Act II, she neatly summarizes the problem as one of affect versus cognition, "Oh, god of love, and god of reason, say, which of you twain shall my poor heart obey!" Josephine's problem is the focus of the theory to be presented.

### Some preliminary concepts

It is possible to argue that information processing is inherent in the very fabric of the universe, even at the level of quantum mechanics. Consider some experiments reported by the Nobel Prize winning physicist Leon Lederman (1993, pp. 177–179). Electrons are directed toward a screen with two slits that are very close to each other. Approximately half of the electrons go through each slit. Now, one of the slits is covered with lead foil. The obvious prediction is that half of the electrons should go through the uncovered slit, and half of them should bounce off the lead foil. In fact, what happens is that all of the electrons go through the uncovered slit. To quote Lederman, "How does the electron know which slit to go through?" (p. 179).

There are two reasons why physicists have decided to ignore this question. First, quantum mechanics is concerned with initial conditions (e.g., electrons are fired from a gun) and with results (e.g., an electron goes to a particular place), but not with what happens in between. Second, according to the Heisenberg uncertainty principle, any attempt to follow the electron through its path would screw up the experiment. This is because bouncing a photon off an electron (how else could we "see" the electron?) would affect its momentum or direction.

So if physicists can not tell us "how the electron knows which slit to go through," why did we bring up the issue? We certainly do not pretend to be able to beat the physicists at their own game. Our point is much more simple. We just want to establish the principle that information processing is a basic property of the universe (i.e., the electron does "know" which slit to go through), and it is not restricted to humans.

Of course, information processing is not restricted to electrons either. Plants grow towards the sun, which implies that they "know" where the sun is. Mosquitoes fly towards light, which implies that they "know" where the light is. So what does this have to do with affect and cognition? We propose that affect and cognition are different types of information processing. Affect is usually described as involving some kind of "feeling" towards something. It is also considered to have only two flavors—positive or negative (Johnston, 1999), though there can be different intensities of the two flavors. In contrast, cognition is often described as involving some kind of thought towards something. Thus, cognition is not restricted to only two flavors (see also Verplanken, Hofstee, & Janssen, 1998).

### Britain versus France in the time of Napoleon

Theoretically, if affect and cognition are different systems (or at least different networks of associations), how can a person integrate input from both of these systems to make a decision, particularly when the two sources of input are in conflict? To us, this seems analogous to the war between France under Napoleon against Britain. The difficulty in this war, for both countries, is that they had very different situations. Britain had a powerful navy whereas France had a powerful army. For Britain to attack France meant fighting on land—a battle between armies; and for France to attack Britain meant fighting in the water—a battle between navies. Thus, for the two countries to fight directly meant either that Britain had to develop an army, or that France had to develop a navy. Neither Britain's army nor France's navy were very effective for most of the war, and so the leaders of the two countries had to resort to indirect methods (e.g., the British blockaded the French in an effort to put them at an economic disadvantage and make it difficult for them to get supplies). Finally, of course, Britain did develop an army, and the Duke of Wellington beat Napoleon at Waterloo, but not until the war had gone on for 23 years! Had Britain not developed an army, the war could have gone on indefinitely.

Let us return now to affect and cognition. If affect and cognition are in conflict, and if there is to be a winner in the sense that the person forms a behavioral intention (or performs a behavior) that is consistent with either affect or cognition, then there must be a common battleground. Either the affect must somehow be translated into cognition, or the cognition must somehow be translated into affect. It is also possible that both affect and cognition are translated into something else, but we will ignore this possibility. Without a common battleground, poor Josephine would stand all day by the rail of the ship and never come to a decision! Thus, the issue before us is whether affect is somehow translated into cognition, or whether cognition is somehow translated into affect. As Josephine might have said, "Which of the twain shall it be?"

### The limbic system, the cortex, and evolution

Although we suspect that translation of affect into cognition and of cognition into affect both happen, for the purpose of forming behavioral intentions and performing behaviors, we believe that the crucial process is the translation of cognition into affect. Our reasoning stems from a consideration of the structure of the brain and of how humans evolved. There is now a good deal of evidence that affective processing depends on a region of the brain that developed during the evolution of early mammals (see Johnston, 1999 for a review). This region, the limbic system, is sandwiched between a lower, more primitive motor system (the "reptilian" brain) and a higher, "new mammalian" system that was (and is) responsible for thinking and reasoning.

What was the advantage of evolving an affective system? According to Johnston (1999), one possibility is that it gives meaning to events and facilitates learning. If environments always remained constant, learning would be quite inefficient. It would be more efficient for evolution to rely on genetically programming responses to environmental stimuli. For example, it is easy to imagine an animal without an affective system that would run from a predator. All that is necessary is for this behavior, in response to that particular predator, to be genetically programmed into the animal. However, to the extent that environments are not constant, genetic programming is insufficient. Suppose that the animal in the example is faced with a changing environment or is forced to move into a new environment. In either case, there is no opportunity for appropriate genetic programming. In this case, the animal must either learn or die. By providing the gift of meaning, affect aids learning, which increases adaptability to environmental changes, and ultimately contributes to gene propagation.

What about cognition? Our best guess here is that cognition evolved because of the social interaction that resulted from mammals (e.g., chimpanzees) living in small groups. Living in a group conferred several benefits upon its members. The group provided protection, an early warning system, and potential mates. Another advantage is that one member of the group who happened upon some food could share with another member of the group, and be the beneficiary of such sharing in a reverse situation. However, to get the maximum benefit of the group, members had to be good at social interaction. Imagine that a particular group member shares with other members but is not shared with in return. This group member is unlikely to survive and propagate genes. In contrast, a group member who is good at "deal making," whether for food, sex, or protection, would be more likely to propagate its genes to the next generation (Cosmides & Tooby, 1992). In sum, then, we believe that cognition evolved largely as an aid to the deal making that was necessary to take full advantage of the potential benefits of social interaction.

We argued earlier that for affect and cognition to "battle it out" so that one of the two can "win," either affect must be translated into cognition or cognition must be translated into affect. The foregoing comments provide two reasons to believe that cognition is translated into affect rather than the reverse. First, if an affective system evolved before a cognitive system, then this implies that a mechanism for going from affect to behavior was already in place irrespective of any issues pertaining to cognition. Thus it would be easy for evolution to attach a cognitive system as an "add-on" to an affective system that was already there. It would take a great deal more "rewiring" to detach the affective system from the motor system, attach a cognitive system to it, and then attach an affective system on to the cognitive one. However, even if our evolutionary reasoning is flawed, there is a second line of reasoning that seems to follow straightforwardly from the brain's physical structure. As we said earlier, the limbic system (affective system) is sandwiched between a more primitive motor system and the higher reasoning system. Thus, it seems much more likely that the effect of higher reasoning on behavior is mediated by the affective system, than that the effect of the affective system on behavior is mediated by the system for higher reasoning. Or, to use the terms "affect" and "cognition," our conclusion is that cognition is translated into affect rather than the reverse.

If cognition must be translated into affect before it can influence behavior, then it follows that cognition cannot directly affect behavior! Rather, it is the affect that *results from*, or is *attached to*, the cognition that matters. Returning to Josephine's problem, the implication is that Josephine has positive affect attached to marrying the poor sailor (the "god of love") and she also has affect *attached to* doing what is wise (i.e., it is not the "god of reason" that counts, it is the affect that Josephine has attached to the "god of reason"). Now Josephine is in much less of a bind. She can sum across the various relevant affects and come to a decision. More generally, we assume that this is how humans make behavioral decisions. They have affects from various sources, including cognitions, and the decision is simply the result of combining all of the affects. If the resulting sum is greater than some threshold, the person will decide in favor of the behavior; otherwise, the person will decide against it.

### Evidence consistent with the theory

We acknowledge that our theory about the translation of cognition into affect and behavior is speculative. However, evidence from three areas of research is consistent with the theory and is worth describing here. This research concerns persons with damage to the prefrontal area of the brain, the predictive validity of affect compared to cognition, and response latencies to affective versus cognitive items.

### Prefrontal damage

Damasio (1994) documented several cases of people who had suffered damage to the prefrontal area. As an example, consider a person that was identified as "Eliot" by Damasio, who had suffered a radical change in his personality after prefrontal damage caused by a tumor. In contrast to before the damage, Eliot showed enormous deficits in decision making and also tended not to react affectively to stimuli. This "correlation" between a lack of affective responding and decision-making deficits suggests the possibility that affect plays an important role in decision making. On the other hand, it is possible that the prefrontal damage caused cognitive deficits as well, and it was the cognitive deficits that were responsible for Eliot's inability to make decisions.

Damasio employed a huge number of tests of cognitive deficits, and Eliot performed consistently well. As a result of all these tests, Damasio concluded that there was no evidence of cognitive malfunctioning with respect to perceptual ability, past memory, short-term memory, new learning, language, and ability to do arithmetic. Eliot was also normal, or better than normal, when it came to attention, various tests of working memory, and a number of other cognitive functions too numerous to describe here. In sum, despite the huge efforts that were made to find cognitive deficits, no evidence for any of them was obtained. Thus, because Eliot's poor decision making could not be attributed to any cognitive deficits, Damasio concluded that it was the emotional deficit that the damage caused which was responsible for the poor decision making. Damasio's neurological theory of the connection between emotions and decision making is too complicated to discuss here (there are several systems involved, including the limbic system and prefrontal area). It is sufficient, at this point, to note the strong relationship between emotional and decision-making deficits, that are not paralleled by cognitive deficits.

### Relative importance of affect versus cognition in predicting behavior

One implication of the idea that the predictive validity of cognition depends upon the affect that is attached to that cognition is that affect should generally better predict intentions and/or behaviors than does cognition (unless the cognition induces affect). Of course, it is extremely difficult to test a general hypothesis about "most" intentions/behaviors. Nonetheless, Trafimow, Sheeran, Lombardo, Finlay, Brown, and Armitage (in press) attempted to provide such a test, as follows. The procedure involved two stages. First, a group of undergraduate participants were asked to generate behaviors at random (no reason was given for doing so). Second, participants in the main experiment completed measures of affect, cognition, and intention in relation to 14 behaviors that had been most frequently nominated during the first stage. Consistent with predictions, several analyses indicated that affect was a better predictor of intention compared to cognition: (a) the median correlation between affect and intention was significantly larger than the median correlation between cognition and intention; (b) the median beta weight for affect was significantly larger than the median beta weight for cognition; (c) the median unique variance explained in intention by affect was $R^2 = .17$ compared to only $R^2 = .03$ for cognition. A second study employed the same procedure with two modifications. We used a different measure of cognition to make sure that this had not influenced our findings, and we increased the number of behaviors that participants had to rate to $n = 19$ (see Table 3.1 for a list of behaviors). Findings were identical to our initial experiment: affect had a stronger correlation, beta weight, and explained greater variance than did cognition. In sum, although cognition may better predict certain behaviors than does affect, in general, affect is the better predictor.

### The relative accessibility of affect versus cognition

The second area of research that is consistent with our theory concerns the relative accessibility of affective versus cognitive components of attitudes. If cognition has to be translated into affect before it can influence intentions and behavior, then we would expect that response latencies to affect items would be shorter than response latencies to cognition items. A series of experiments by Verplanken et al. (1998) showed that this was indeed the case. Participants were asked to indicate how they *felt* about an attitude object (affect) and how they *thought* about that object (cognition). They were also asked to respond as quickly as possible by pressing one of two buttons to indicate whether their thoughts or feelings were *good–bad, negative–positive,*

*Table 3.1* Behaviors used in Trafimow et al. (2004), Study 2

---

*Behaviors*

---

Buy a newspaper
Eat fruit
Go to the pub
Avoid getting drunk
Attend all lectures
Avoid fast food
Read a novel
Engage in exercise
Avoid lying in bed
Avoid watching TV
See a play
Write in a journal
Do volunteer services
Meditate
Donate money to charity
Recycle
Write a letter to friend/family
Go for a walk
Clean the bathroom

---

*troublesome–excellent*, or *unfavourable–favourable* (note that participants' affective and cognitive responses were to the same items). The results of four experiments involving two attitude objects (brand names and countries) all found that participants exhibited shorter response latencies to affective compared to cognitive items. Moreover, when the data pertaining to filler affective and cognitive items were analyzed, findings were identical. Recent research (Giner-Sorolla, 2001) has confirmed these findings but noted that at least a moderately intense affect must be associated with the attitude object in order to obtain these effects. On the other hand, Giner-Sorolla (2001) did not actually test affect versus cognition directly, but rather tested attitudes that were presumed, based on some other analyses, to be affective or cognitive. Depending on how one evaluates these other analyses, it is possible to argue that Giner-Sorolla did not actually test affect and cognition. Therefore, it is not yet clear whether Verplanken et al.'s conclusion should be qualified by the Giner-Sorolla findings.

### Implications of the translation of cognition into affect

Our theory also suggests some interesting implications for a variety of issues including how people weigh short-term versus long-term considerations when making decisions, what attributions people make about moral and immoral behaviors, and whether there might be individual differences in the extent to which affect is attached to cognition.

*Short-term versus long-term considerations*

Imagine that a person who wants to lose weight is confronted with a beautiful slice of chocolate cake. One way of conceptualizing this dilemma is to assume that the person weights (no pun intended) the short-term pleasure of eating the cake against the long-term health risk—the classic problem of affect versus cognition. However, as we suggested earlier, if affect and cognition are really different systems, there would seem to be no way for either affect or cognition to win out over the other. Consequently, we would think about this a different way. Consider the cognition that it would be healthier not to eat the cake. According to the translation of cognition into affect, this cognition would get translated into *current* affect towards eating the cake. Let us be clear here. We are not talking about anticipated affect. We are talking about the current affect that is stimulated by the cognition that it would be healthier not to eat the cake. We do not deny the importance of anticipated affect, but we believe its effect is indirect. Someone might anticipate negative affect in the future because of the possibility of being unhealthy, but our position is that this anticipated affect is completely irrelevant except for one eventuality. Specifically, if anticipating negative affect in the future causes negative *current* affect, then the behavior will be less likely to be performed.

This reasoning has the benefit of also accommodating short-term cognitions. For example, suppose our hero had been trying to weigh the pleasure of eating the cake against looking like a glutton to an attractive woman who happened to be in the room at the time. According to our theorizing, the thought of enjoying the cake produces positive current affect, and the thought of looking like a glutton (and associated thoughts about not getting to have sex with this woman) produce negative current affect. If the positive affect is greater than the negative affect, the person will eat the cake; if the reverse is true, the person will not eat the cake. Again, we wish to emphasize that although a lot of considerations may play into any behavioral decision, it is the current affects engendered by these considerations that influence the behavior.

The idea that nothing affects our decisions without first being translated into current affect clarifies why it is so hard for people to diet, save money, exercise regularly, quit smoking, and, in general, provide for the long term. Long-term considerations tend not to arouse as much affect as do short-term considerations. This gives an important edge to eating the chocolate cake, buying the new car that one cannot really afford, putting off jogging for another day, having just one more cigarette, and so on. For people to overcome this "affect deficit," we believe that they must either react less affectively to short-term issues (which is probably rather unlikely), learn to attach more affect to long-term issues, or generate some countervailing short-term issues.

Interestingly, findings from Mischel's classic experiments on delay of gratification are consistent with this analysis. For example, one series of experiments examined the efficacy of several strategies that children could use to increase their waiting time and thereby obtain a treat (Mischel, Ebbeson, &

Raskoff-Zeiss, 1972). Consistent with the idea that short-term positive affect can overcome the negative affect associated with waiting for the reward, Mischel et al. found that playing with a toy or "thinking fun thoughts" were extremely effective in helping the children delay. In fact, thinking fun thoughts was more effective than playing with the toy, and was much more effective than thinking sad thoughts or thinking about the rewards (which are likely to have increased current negative affect). In sum, longer-term considerations can outweigh shorter-term considerations *if* people attach greater affect to those longer-term considerations. The trick is to endeavor to experience positive affect when we resist temptation.

*Morality*

What is the difference between a moral versus an immoral person? A moral philosopher might argue that a moral person behaves in accordance with moral principles whereas a less moral person is less driven by principles. Our theory, though not necessarily inconsistent with this answer, suggests a different way of looking at the question. Imagine two people, Joe and Sarah, who both have the opportunity to lie to gain money. Suppose that both Joe and Sarah think the following thoughts: (1) It would be good to gain a lot of money. (2) It is wrong to lie. In addition, suppose that thought 1 causes Joe to have a lot of positive affect and thought 2 causes only a slight amount of negative affect. In contrast, suppose the reverse is true for Sarah. Clearly, we would predict that Joe will tell the lie (and get the money) and Sarah will not; Joe will behave immorally and Sarah will behave morally.

Let us now generalize the above reasoning. Suppose a person attaches a great deal of positive affect to behaving in accordance with ethical principles and a great deal of negative affect to not behaving according to those principles. This person will often behave according to ethical principles and will seldom behave otherwise. People who attach less positive affect (or more negative affect) to obeying principles will do so less often. Our point is that morality ultimately comes down to where one places one's affect.

Applying this to attributions, the above theorizing suggests that people make trait attributions pertaining to morality largely on the basis of affect. To set the stage, however, we first need to consider an experiment by Trafimow and Trafimow (1999). They tested an idea derived from Kant (1991/1797) that some duties are more important than others. Perfect duties may never be violated (lying and betrayal are examples of perfect duties); one violation is sufficient for Kant to deem the person as immoral. In contrast, imperfect duties, such as the duties to be friendly, charitable, and cooperative, can be violated even by a moral person. For example, although one is never allowed to lie, it is permitted to use one's dollar to buy a pen rather than giving it to someone who is starving. Trafimow and Trafimow's experiment involved presenting scenarios involving violations of perfect and imperfect duties and eliciting trait attributions. Consistent with Kant's idea, people were more willing to make a strong trait attribution for violations of perfect than imperfect duties. For example, people made stronger trait attributions of dishonesty after the performance of a dishonest behavior than they did trait attributions of unfriendliness after the performance of an unfriendly behavior.

So why did this happen? According to our theory, participants make stronger attributions to violations of perfect compared to imperfect duties because they attach greater negative affect to violations of perfect duties. To test this idea, Trafimow, Bromgard, Finlay, and Ketelaar (2003) recently applied a misattribution paradigm. The logic was as follows. If people's strong attributions to violations of perfect duties are really driven by the strong negative affect caused by those violations, then removing the negative affect should reduce the strength of the attributions. Removing negative affect should be less important where violations of imperfect duties are concerned, because they engender less negative affect than do violations of perfect duties. Trafimow et al. (2004) did not know how to remove negative affect, but they did think of a way to induce participants to misattribute negative affect to an irrelevant stimulus. Participants were presented with a picture that had nothing to do with violations of duties and had nothing to do with affect. Half of the participants were led to believe that the picture caused negative affect whereas the other participants were not led to believe this. Subsequently, all participants were presented with violations of perfect and imperfect duties. If affect is irrelevant, and the process of making trait attributions to the various violations is a purely cognitive process, then the picture manipulation should have no effect on trait attributions. In fact, however, there was a strong interaction. Trait attributions to violations of perfect duties were much weaker in the misattribution condition than in the other condition, but there was no difference where trait attributions to violations of imperfect duties were concerned. In sum, although the findings were about morality attributions rather than moral behavior, they are certainly suggestive of the importance of affect in the morality domain. Future research could consider the extent to which affect attached to *moral norms* affects how well this variable predicts intentions and behavior (see Manstead, 2000, for a review).

### The role of individual differences

If we are correct in assuming that cognitions influence behaviors only after becoming translated into current affects, then it implies that a person's ability to attach affects onto cognitions will play a crucial role in whether their behaviors will be affected by these cognitions. Let us first consider a trivial example. Suppose people were given a gift of $1,000,000 tax free! Most of them would probably be extremely happy about it, at first, despite evidence that wealth and long-term happiness are essentially uncorrelated when participants below the poverty level are excluded from the sample (Brickman,

Coates, & Janoff-Bulman, 1978; Inglehart, 1990). The reason this is so is that people have successfully attached affect to money (presumably because money can buy things that are desired).

But people can attach affect onto many things other than money. As we discussed earlier, people can attach affect onto long-term cognitions (e.g., planning for retirement), anticipated affect (e.g., I will really feel sorry one year from now if I don't do X), and moral principles (e.g., It is wrong to be dishonest). We suspect there might be an individual differences variable here. That is, we suspect that some people might be more likely than others to attach affects onto cognitions. We will call this individual difference variable "affect attachment." All else being equal, we would expect that people who are high in affect attachment would be more likely to be influenced by cognitions that, in people low in affect attachment, would tend not to arouse much affect.

In fact, the studies by Trafimow et al. (in press) described earlier suggest that there are individual differences in the weight given to affects versus cognitions in forming behavioral intentions. Because participants completed measures of affect, cognition and intention in relation to 14 and 19 behaviors, it was possible to compute within-participants correlations between affect and intention and between cognition and intention. We then partitioned respondents according to the relative strength of these correlations. Participants for whom the affect–intention correlation was larger than the cognition–intention correlation were deemed to be under "affective control" whereas participants for whom the reverse was true were deemed to be more under "cognitive control." (Of course, we recognize that affective and cognitive control is not an "either/or" phenomenon. As Haddock and Huskinson, Chapter 2, this volume, have documented, people can be strongly or weakly influenced by either affect or cognition.) We then reran the between-participants regressions on the 14 and 19 behaviors described earlier and computed the median unique variance attributable to affect and cognition for both groups.

Although affect was generally a better predictor than cognition in the original between-participants regression analyses, there were substantial differences in the predictive validity of these variables for different subgroups. Figure 3.1 shows the percentage of variance explained in intention by affect and cognition for participants under affective and cognitive control in our first study. Consistent with expectations, affect was a significantly better predictor of intention for affectively controlled participants compared to cognitively controlled participants. Importantly, however, cognition was a significantly better predictor of intention among cognitively controlled participants compared to affectively controlled participants. When we conducted equivalent analyses in our second study involving 19 behaviors, findings were similar. In sum, the results of both studies support the idea that there are individual differences in the weights given to affect versus cognition in forming behavioral intentions. It should be noted that the within-participants analyses used to determine affective versus cognitive control were independent

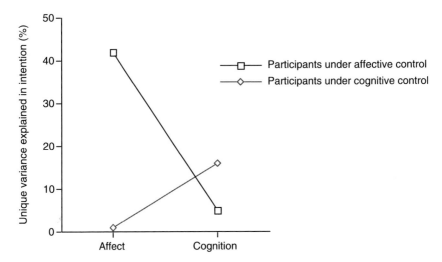

*Figure 3.1* Percentage variance explained in intention by affect and cognition for affectively controlled versus cognitively controlled participants (adapted from Trafimow et al., 2004, Study 1).

of the between-participants analyses performed on the subsamples (see Trafimow, Kiekel, & Clason, in press).[1]

There is also preliminary evidence that certain personality variables play a role in determining the relative importance of affect versus cognition in predicting intention. For example, Abraham, Sheeran, Schaalma, Brug, and de Vries (2002) measured a series of affective and cognitive beliefs presumed to influence attitudes toward blood donation. A measure of participants' *conscientiousness* was also taken. Abraham et al. hypothesized that greater conscientiousness would be associated with giving greater weight to cognition in forming one's overall attitude. A regression of attitude on affective and cognitive beliefs showed significant associations for several affective beliefs but no significant associations for any of the cognitive beliefs (a finding that is consistent with our earlier analysis of the relative importance of affect and cognition). However, when the interactions between conscientiousness and cognitive beliefs entered the regression equation at the second step, there was a significant increment in the variance explained in attitude. Simple slopes analyses indicated that greater

---

1 Trafimow et al. (in press) proved that as the number of participants and number of behaviors increases, the dependence of between-participants and within-participants analyses decreases. Ultimately, as the number of participants and number of behaviors increases to infinity, dependence drops to zero. So, the question, then, was how many participants and behaviors are necessary for reasonable independence. Trafimow et al.'s computer simulations demonstrate that the two types of analyses are "independent enough" when there are 15 participants and 15 behaviors.

conscientiousness was associated with weighting cognition more heavily during attitude formation.

Our interpretation of these findings is that conscientiousness is one correlate of affect attachment; that is, more conscientious people are likely to attach greater affect to the cognitive consequences of a behavior than are less conscientious people. For less conscientious people, current affect towards the behavior is likely to be the key determinant because they do not attach the same degree of affect to cognitive beliefs. Of course, conscientiousness is probably only one of several personality dispositions that are associated with affect attachment. Other plausible correlates include need for affect (Maio & Esses, 2001), need for cognition (Cacioppo & Petty, 1982), and sensation seeking (Zuckerman, 1994). Future research might profitably be directed towards developing a measure that captures individual differences in affect attachment in relation to short-term and long-term cognitive beliefs, moral norms, and other putatively "cognitive" predictors of behavior.

## Conclusion

This chapter examined two assumptions that have dominated social psychological research on the relations among affect, cognition, and behavior. We have shown that accumulated evidence supports the distinctiveness of affect versus cognition as components of attitudes—notwithstanding the difficulties associated with interpreting factor analytic findings. However, we also pointed out that very little attention has been paid to how affect and cognition—two different information processing systems—could work together to determine behaviors. To overcome this deficit, we have presented a theory that proposes that cognition is translated into affect to influence behavior. Our theory has been informed by consideration of evolutionary processes and brain structures, by findings from selected empirical studies, and by the potential for understanding how people weigh short- versus long-term considerations, make moral judgments, and exhibit individual differences. At the end of this chapter—as at the outset—we acknowledge that our theory is extremely speculative. However, to rephrase the gambler's maxim: If you don't speculate, you can't accumulate (knowledge).

## References

Abelson, R. P., Kinder, D. R., Peters, M. D., & Fiske, S. T. (1982). Affective and semantic components in political person perception. *Journal of Personality and Social Psychology, 42*, 619–630.

Abraham, C., Sheeran, P., Schaalma, H., Brug, H., & de Vries, N. (2002). *Conscientious as a predictor, and moderator of relationships, in the theory of reasoned action.* Manuscript in preparation. University of Sussex, UK.

Breckler, S. J. (1984). Empirical validation of affect, behavior, and cognition as distinct components of attitude. *Journal of Personality and Social Psychology, 47*, 1191–1205.

Breckler, S. J., & Wiggins, E. C. (1989). Affect versus evaluation in the structure of attitudes. *Journal of Experimental Social Psychology, 25,* 253–271.

Brickman, P., Coates, D., & Janoff-Bulman, R. J. (1978). Lottery winners and accident victims: Is happiness relative? *Journal of Personality and Social Psychology, 36,* 917–927,

Cacioppo, J. T., & Petty, R. E. (1982). The need for cognition. *Journal of Personality and Social Psychology, 42,* 116–131.

Cosmides, L., & Tooby, J. (1992). Cognitive adaptations for social exchange. In J. H. Barkow, L. Cosmides, & J. Tooby (Eds.), *The adapted mind: Evolutionary psychology and the generation of culture.* Oxford: Oxford University Press.

Crites, S. L., Fabrigar, L. R., & Petty, R. E. (1994). Measuring the affective and cognitive properties of attitudes: Conceptual and methodological issues. *Personality and Social Psychology Bulletin, 20,* 619–634.

Damasio, A. R. (1994). *Descartes' error: Emotion, reason, and the human brain.* New York: Grosset/Putnam.

Fishbein, M. (1980). Theory of reasoned action: Some applications and implications. In H. Howe & M. Page (Eds.), *Nebraska Symposium on Motivation, 1979* (pp. 65–116). Lincoln, NB: University of Nebraska Press.

Giner-Sorolla, R. (2001). Affective attitudes are not always faster: The moderating role of extremity. *Personality and Social Psychology Bulletin, 27,* 666–677.

Haddock, G., & Huskinson, T. L. H. (in press). Individual differences in attitude structure. In G. Haddock & G. R. Maio (Eds.), *Attitudes in the 21st century: The Gregynog Symposium.* Hove, UK: Psychology Press.

Inglehart, R. (1990). *Culture shift in advanced industrial society.* Princeton, NJ: Princeton University Press.

Johnston, V. S. (1999). *Why we feel: The science of emotions.* Reading, MA: Helix Books.

Kant, I. (1991). *The metaphysics of morals* (M. Gregor, Trans). Cambridge: Cambridge University Press. (Original work published 1797)

Lederman, L. (1993). *The God particle: If the universe is the answer, what is the question?* Boston: Houghton Mifflin.

Maio, G. R., & Esses, V. M. (2001). The need for affect: Individual differences in the motivation to approach or avoid emotions. *Journal of Personality, 69,* 583–615.

Mann, J. H. (1959). The relationship between cognitive, affective, and behavioral aspects of racial prejudice. *Journal of Social Psychology, 49,* 223–228.

Manstead, A. S. R. (2000). The role of moral norm in the attitude-behavior relation. In D. J. Terry & M. A. Hogg (Eds.), *Attitudes, behavior, and social context: The role of norms and group membership.* (pp. 11–30). Mahwah, NJ: Lawrence Erlbaum Associates, Inc.

Mischel, W., Ebbeson, E. B., & Raskoff-Zeiss, A. (1972). Cognitive and attentional mechanisms in delay of gratification. *Journal of Personality and Social Psychology, 21,* 204–218.

Ostrom, T. M. (1969). The relationship between the affective, behavioral and cognitive components of attitude. *Journal of Experimental Social Psychology, 5,* 12–30.

Trafimow, D., Bromgard, I. K., Finlay, K. A., & Ketelaar, T. (2004). *The role of affect in trait attributions from violations of perfect and imperfect duties.* Manuscript under review.

Trafimow, D., Kiekel, P., & Clason, D. (in press). The simultaneous consideration of between-participants and within-participants analyses in personality and social psychology: The issue of dependence. *European Journal of Social Psychology.*

Trafimow, D., & Sheeran, P. (1998). Some tests of the distinction between cognitive and affective beliefs. *Journal of Experimental Social Psychology, 34,* 378–397.

Trafimow, D., Sheeran, P., Lombardo, B., Finlay, K. A., Brown, J., & Armitage, C. J. (in press). Affective and cognitive control of persons and behaviors. *British Journal of Social Psychology.*

Trafimow, D., & Trafimow, D. (1999). Mapping imperfect and perfect duties on to hierarchically and partially restrictive trait dimensions. *Personality and Social Psychology Bulletin, 25,* 686–695.

Verplanken, B., Hofstee G., & Janssen, H. J. W. (1998). Accessibility of affective versus cognitive components of attitudes. *European Journal of Social Psychology, 28,* 23–35.

Woodmansee, J. J., & Cook, S. W. (1967). Dimensions of verbal racial attitudes: Their identification and measurement. *Journal of Personality and Social Psychology, 7,* 240–250.

Zuckerman, M. (1994). *Behavioral expression and biosocial bases of sensation-seeking.* Cambridge, UK: Cambridge University Press.

# 4 Hold still while I measure your attitude

## Assessment in the throes of ambivalence

*Steven J. Breckler*

> It will be conceded at the outset that an attitude is a complex affair which
> cannot be wholly described by any single numerical index.
>
> (Thurstone, 1928, p. 530)

The social psychology of attitude ambivalence has a bifurcated history. In 1972, Kalman Kaplan focused on the concept of ambivalence, and proposed a method for its measurement. The ensuing 20 years was a period of relative dormancy for the concept, but then a resurgence of theoretical and empirical scrutiny emerged in the early 1990s. My goal in this chapter is to summarize the extant operationalizations and conceptualizations of ambivalence, while describing limitations of these approaches. I will then describe theory and research supporting the concept of multivalence, which is a broader and more inclusive approach to interpreting conflicted attitudes.

### Brief history of ambivalence assessment

Before illustrating the need to progress beyond traditional measures of ambivalence, it is important to consider ways in which attitude ambivalence has been measured. Interest in attitude ambivalence can be traced chiefly to a long-standing concern with the interpretation of middlemost responses on bipolar rating scales (Kaplan, 1972; Klopfer & Madden, 1980; Moore, 1973). An example of the bipolar rating scale is shown in the top panel of Figure 4.1. The problem is that a midpoint rating can be interpreted in many ways—as indicating neutrality, uncertainty, indifference, or even ambivalence. A single check-mark on a single bipolar rating scale does not provide enough information to distinguish among these (and other) meanings.

One of the more interesting interpretations of a middlemost response is the possibility that it reflects ambivalence—simultaneous endorsement of both favorable and unfavorable positions. It is this interpretation that captured the interest of Kalman Kaplan, who developed a method for measuring attitude ambivalence. Kaplan (1972) proposed that bipolar scales be split at the zero-point, forming two unipolar scales. As shown in Figure 4.1, people are

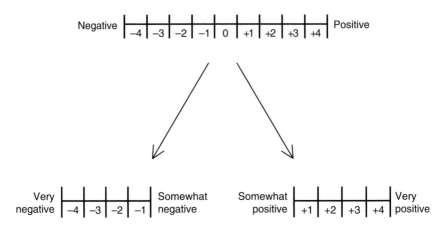

*Figure 4.1* Kaplan's (1972) procedure splits a traditional bipolar rating scale into two unipolar rating scales.

asked to make two ratings on the unipolar scales, rather than providing one rating on a single bipolar scale. One scale focuses on the positive (favorable) features, and the other on the negative (unfavorable) features of the attitude object. The two ratings can then be used to derive a numerical index of attitude ambivalence.

The index favored by Kaplan was derived by defining two components of attitude. One, called Total Affect, is computed by adding the two unipolar ratings. The other, called Polarity, is computed as the absolute value of the difference between the two unipolar ratings. For reasons that will be clear later, it is best to label the two unsigned unipolar ratings as the weaker or smaller ($A_w$) and the stronger or larger ($A_s$). Using this terminology, Kaplan defined ambivalence as:

$$A_w + A_s - |A_w - A_s|$$

In more conceptual terms, this formula maps onto the two components as:

Total Affect – Polarity

Kaplan did not appear to recognize that this index simplifies to $2 \times A_w$.

In a previous paper (Breckler, 1994), I suggested that the Kaplan (1972) index of ambivalence produces some undesirable properties. The most important is that, for any given value of $A_w$, the index remains constant across all possible values of $A_s$. The index I prefer can be traced at least to Brown and Farber (1951), who were concerned with measuring aspects of competing inhibitory and excitatory responses. Scott (1966) translated the same idea into an index of ambivalence as:

$(A_w)^2 / A_s$

To appreciate the behavior of this index, we can plot its values against the range of values that can be taken on by the weaker of the two components (i.e., $A_w$). This is done in Figure 4.2, where it can be seen that for any given value of $A_s$, ambivalence is a positively accelerating function of $A_w$.

Others have proposed variations on the same theme, deriving ambivalence indexes based on two unipolar ratings (Hass, Katz, Rizzo, Bailey, & Eisenstadt, 1991; Scott, 1966, 1969; Thompson, Zanna, & Griffin, 1995). Although good cases can be made for some of them (especially the Thompson et al. index), the differences may be relatively minor. Empirically, they tend to be very highly correlated (Breckler, 1994).

### Some drawbacks

Kaplan's procedure assumes that people are able to make sense of the split between positive and negative sides of the bipolar scale. The semantic differential tradition, which is the essence of a bipolar attitude scale, takes

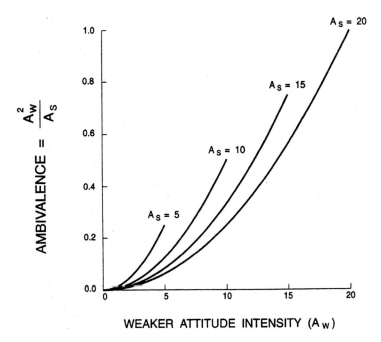

*Figure 4.2* A desirable ambivalence index as a function of weaker and stronger attitude intensities. The four curves represent different values of the stronger intensity (after Breckler, 1994). This ambivalence index was proposed by Scott (1966), and was derived from Brown and Farber (1951).

advantage of a natural organization of thought around polar opposites (positive *versus* negative, strong *versus* weak, passive *versus* active). Kaplan's procedure asks people, quite explicitly, to focus on one pole and to ignore the other. That is, it forces people to depart from the way they naturally approach judgment tasks. For example, respondents are asked to focus only on the positive aspects of their attitudes, and to ignore the negative ones. Then, with that focus in mind, they are asked to judge how positive their attitude is. The focus is then changed to just the negative aspects, ignoring the positive ones. It is not clear, however, that this is easily accomplished. Can people really hold constant one side of the bipolar continuum and focus, independently, on the other? Clearly people will complete the task when they are asked to do it. But there is little evidence that the ratings carry the intended meaning.

A second drawback is of greater theoretical importance. Splitting a bipolar scale into two unipolar scales creates two measures: one is an assessment of positivity or favorability; the other is an assessment of negativity or unfavorability. From these two assessments, we compute an index of discrepancy or discordance between them. But this is a very simple version of ambivalence, as I will elaborate below. Perhaps the most appropriate term is not ambivalence, but *bivalence*—the degree to which a person's attitude can be described simultaneously as positive and negative. The semantic opposites (positive versus negative) still drive the entire procedure; they continue to identify the only acceptable forms of conflicting or discrepant evaluations, thoughts, emotions, and behaviors.

### Generalizing the dual unipolar-rating procedure

A modification of the procedure developed by Kaplan (1972) was proposed by Norris, Larsen, and Cacioppo (2002). They introduced the idea of the *affect matrix* as a way of assessing the separate positive and negative aspects of evaluation. The idea is to create a grid in a two-dimensional table. Each axis marks five levels of either positive or negative affect, from *not at all* (positive or negative) to *extremely* (positive or negative). The result is a table with 25 cells. The respondent's task is to locate his or her positive and negative feelings by selecting one of the 25 cells. In essence, this is an alternative method for obtaining the two unipolar ratings. The difference is that (a) it does not require the cumbersome task of putting one dimension "on hold" while rating the other; (b) it focuses respondents' attention on the distinctly positive and negative aspects of their attitudes.

### Directly asking about ambivalence

The concept of ambivalence is not a difficult one to grasp. The term is used in everyday language, and common phrases capture the idea well. David Jamieson (1993) took advantage of this to create a direct assessment of ambivalence—a simultaneous ambivalence scale (SIMAS). The SIMAS scale is based on multiple generic items that people rate in terms of how well they characterize their attitude. The scale includes items that tap ambivalence between thoughts and feelings (e.g., "My head and my heart seem to be in disagreement on the issue of X") and items that tap ambivalence within thoughts and feelings (e.g., "I have strong mixed emotions both for and against X, all at the same time"). The scale has good internal consistency reliability, and relates in predictable ways to such things as conflicts in values, attitude change, and attitude–behavior relationships. By using multiple items that articulate ambivalence within and between thoughts and feelings, the SIMAS is a procedural advance over the dual unipolar-scale approach. The drawback, of course, is that it relies on people's ability to directly confront and express their own ambivalence.

### Let people express multivalence

Another set of approaches to assessing ambivalence has deep roots in the attitude measurement literature. Rather than relying on single-item, bipolar rating scales, attitudes can also be assessed by either having people list their thoughts and feelings in an open-ended way, or by indicating their agreement or disagreement with multiple attitude statements. The listed thoughts approach was demonstrated by Bell, Esses, and Maio (1996), who found that it works well in allowing people to spontaneously express both positive and negative evaluations (see Esses & Maio, 2002, for an overview).

### Traditional multi-item approaches

Another traditional attitude measurement approach is to use multi-item attitude scales. Thurstone's method of equal appearing intervals (Thurstone, 1928) or Likert's method of summated ratings (Likert, 1932) are the classic examples. This was the essence of the approach taken by Katz and Hass (1988) in their study of racial ambivalence. Although they did not use the formal methods of Thurstone or Likert, Katz and Hass did develop multi-item scales of pro-black and anti-black attitudes. They then used the scores on each scale to compute an index of attitude ambivalence.

## Prevalence of ambivalence

Conceptually, ambivalence is an interesting and provocative problem. Beyond the measurement issues, it carries significant theoretical import. Before taking on those issues, however, it is important to establish that ambivalence is more than a rare and curious phenomenon. How prevalent is it? Do people commonly experience and express ambivalence toward social attitude objects? The answers are that ambivalence is quite prevalent, and that people readily express it. I can offer two lines of evidence from my own research in support of this conclusion.

The 1992 US presidential election focused on two front-running candidates (the elder George Bush and the ultimate winner, Bill Clinton). The race also included a third significant candidate, Ross Perot. This election was interesting because many voters and political commentators expressed forms of ambivalence, especially about Bill Clinton and Ross Perot. To formally assess this assumed ambivalence, we conducted a telephone survey of 413 eligible voters in the Baltimore, Maryland area both before and after the election. Each person surveyed was asked to rate each of the three candidates on dual (positive, negative) unipolar rating scales. To make the scales amendable to a telephone survey, we used thermometer-like scales with anchors of 0 (not at all positive or not at all negative) to 100 (very positive or very negative). The ordering of scales (with respect to candidates and with respect to positivity versus negativity) was counterbalanced across respondents.

The results for ratings of Ross Perot are shown in Figure 4.3. This is a sunflower plot, in which the density of the plotted symbols reflects the number of respondents. The horizontal axis is the computed bipolar attitude (the positive rating plus the negative rating). The vertical axis is ambivalence, computed as $(A_w)^2 / A_s$. The functional limits of the index are shown by the superimposed curve, the outline of which looks something like a tree. It is readily seen that ambivalence is dispersed over the entire possible range, and that it is prevalent. Indeed, there was a very dense concentration of

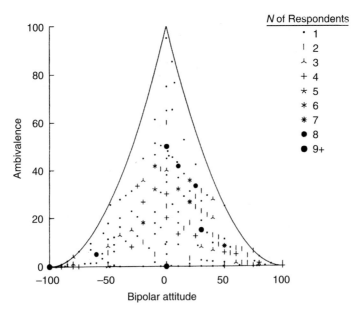

*Figure 4.3* Dispersion of attitude ambivalence toward Ross Perot during the 1992 US presidential election.

respondents who rated Ross Perot as 50 (out of 100) on both the positive and the negative unipolar scales (resulting in an ambivalence index of 50).

Another demonstration comes from a survey of 73 college students, who provided numerous attitudinal ratings of eight social and political issues (gun control laws, cigarette smoking, socialized medicine, capital punishment, sports scholarships, legalized abortion, prayer in public schools, and nuclear power). Included among the measures was a question that asked the students to select one of five descriptions that best described their attitude on each topic. The five choices (each of which was defined for the students) were: favorable, unfavorable, neutral, indifferent, or ambivalent. The percentages of students who rated themselves as either neutral, indifferent, or ambivalent on each of the eight topics are shown in Table 4.1. These percentages show that ambivalence was clearly the option of choice when one of the polarized (favorable or unfavorable) options was not selected. That is, if the students did not describe themselves as polarized in either the favorable or unfavorable direction, they were much more likely to describe themselves as ambivalent than as neutral or indifferent.

The same students also completed the Kaplan-like unipolar rating scales for each of the eight topics. Using the ambivalence index described earlier ( $(A_w)^2 / A_s$), we computed the percentage of students who showed at least some degree of ambivalence (i.e., an index value greater than zero). These percentages are also shown in Table 4.1. Once again, a substantial percentage of students showed ambivalence in their ratings. For some of the topics (nuclear power, socialized medicine, sports scholarships, capital punishment), over half of the students showed some degree of ambivalence, even if they chose not to describe themselves as "ambivalent."

It is clear from these two studies that ambivalence occurs with regularity and sometimes with high frequency. From registered voters expressing

*Table 4.1* Percentage of students who rated themselves as "ambivalent," "neutral," or "indifferent," and percentage who showed non-zero ambivalence based on their ratings on dual unipolar rating scales

| Attitude topic | Percentage identifying themselves as: | | | Percentage showing non-zero ambivalence |
|---|---|---|---|---|
| | Ambivalent | Neutral | Indifferent | |
| Legalized abortion | 11.0 | 0.0 | 0.0 | 48.0 |
| Gun control laws | 15.1 | 5.5 | 0.0 | 45.2 |
| Nuclear power | 41.1 | 12.3 | 5.5 | 86.3 |
| Socialized medicine | 32.9 | 9.6 | 4.1 | 76.7 |
| Sports scholarships | 26.0 | 9.6 | 5.5 | 65.8 |
| Cigarette smoking | 21.9 | 1.4 | 5.5 | 24.7 |
| Prayer in public schools | 12.3 | 9.6 | 9.6 | 26.0 |
| Capital punishment | 28.8 | 0.0 | 0.0 | 67.1 |

ambivalence toward political candidates, to college students describing their attitudes toward social and political issues, ambivalence is expressed often.

## From ambivalence to multivalence

Kaplan's (1972) method of using two unipolar scales has been very influential in guiding researchers' approach to assessing attitude ambivalence. This approach has been used in our own studies of the prevalence of ambivalence and other recent studies of attitude ambivalence. Examples include Armitage and Conner's (2000) analysis of attitude–behavior relationships, Jonas, Diehl, and Brömer's (1997) study of information processing, and Sparks, Conner, James, Shepherd, and Povey's (2001) study of health-related behaviors.

Although these and other studies have pursued theoretical and conceptual implications of attitude ambivalence, Kaplan himself was more concerned with solving the practical problem of disambiguating the interpretation of midpoint scale responses. The question I ultimately want to address is whether Kaplan's procedure fully captures the conceptual nuances of midpoint responses. A number of important theoretical traditions inform our understanding.

### *Bidimensional views*

Many perspectives suggest that attitudes subsume two basic latent dimensions. A positive or favorable attitude is assumed to be reflected in approaching behaviors, whereas a negative or unfavorable attitude is reflected in avoidance of the attitude object. These presumed behavioral manifestations of attitude bring to mind the approach–avoidance conflict, a classic yet mostly abandoned concept in the history of psychology. Still, it was this literature (specifically, the work of Brown & Farber, 1951) that inspired Scott (1966) to propose the first index of ambivalence as $(A_w)^2 / A_s$. In Brown and Farber's terms, $A_w$ represents the weaker excitatory or inhibitory (approach or avoidance) potential, and $A_s$ represents the stronger potential. Recently, Townsend and Busemeyer (1989; Busemeyer & Townsend, 1993) revived the idea of approach–avoidance conflicts to develop a better understanding of decision making under conditions of uncertainty.

Observable manifestations of attitudes are assumed to reflect or represent underlying latent evaluative states. The ubiquitous bipolar attitude scale carries with it a strong assumption of how those evaluative states are organized. Specifically, it assumes that evaluation of affect lies along a single continuum, and that it is not possible to experience opposite positions along it. That is, one can feel either good or bad, but not both at the same time. In contrast to the opposition created by bipolar rating scales, a number of theorists have suggested that positive and negative evaluative substrates are separable and can be served by relatively independent substrates (e.g., Cacioppo & Bernston, 1994). For example, Larsen, McGraw, and Cacioppo (2001) showed that people can be made to feel happy and sad at the same time. Thus, attitude ambivalence may reflect the simultaneous activation of distinct and separable psychological and neural substrates.

Theorists concerned with the cognitive representation of attitudes suggest that attitudes are often supported by bipolar or dual knowledge structures (Judd & Kulik, 1980; Pratkanis, 1989). Thus, whether a person supports or opposes a controversial social issue, knowledge about the issue is organized around at least two coherent and accessible schemata—one representing the supportive or favorable position, and another around the opposing or unfavorable position. Presumably, these bipolar knowledge structures are also accompanied by some kind of tag that identifies one or the other as the accepted or endorsed position. But the idea that people possess and groom at least two centers of knowledge raises the possibility that both can be tagged as the preferred position. For example, situations that prime one or the other could (at least momentarily) make that the accepted position. And situations that prime both simultaneously could heighten one's experience of ambivalence.

### *Multivalence*

These theoretical perspectives are all quite compatible with the bivalence interpretation of ambivalence—as the opposition of positive versus negative evaluations. But the concept of ambivalence can be generalized in a number of ways. One is to include attitudes that reflect multiple evaluative positions—a concept that is best captured by the term *multivalence*. According to this view, bivalence is one special case of multivalence that allows only two evaluative positions, each of which must lie on different sides of the bifurcation. Multivalence allows for endorsement of varying positive positions and varying negative positions. It more fully captures the entire range of evaluation, and can include evaluative dispersion that does not necessarily cross the boundary of positive versus negative evaluation.

The concept of multivalence is quite compatible with other theoretical perspectives on the ambivalence problem. One relates to the functional approach of understanding social attitudes (Maio & Olson, 2000). When we list the many functions of attitudes, value expression is almost always included. The idea is that attitudes provide a vehicle for expressing many important, core values such as those discussed by Rokeach (1973).

In a number of studies, Irwin Katz and Glen Hass and their colleagues have made the case that racial ambivalence is caused by an underlying evaluative discrepancy in values. For example, Katz and Hass (1988) found that endorsement of pro-black versus anti-black attitude statements can be traced to the apparent discrepancy inherent in two American core values: *individualism*, which emphasizes personal freedom, self-reliance, and the Protestant ethic versus *communalism*, which emphasizes equality, social justice, concern for others, and the ideals of humanitarianism and egalitarianism. To the extent that these two values support white Americans' attitudes toward black

Americans, simultaneous adherence to them is likely to produce racial (attitudinal) ambivalence.

Relating attitude ambivalence to discrepancy in values is interesting, because it clearly allows for the more general case of attitude multivalence. That is, the discrepancy between the values of individualism and communalism does not necessarily imply racial attitudes of *opposite* polarity. That is one possible outcome, but not the only one. Racial attitudes could have greater dispersion over the positive (or negative) ranges of evaluation as a result of value conflict, without necessarily crossing the evaluative midpoint.

The idea of attitude multivalence is also compatible with another tradition of attitude theory. It is commonly proposed that attitudes are comprised of multiple subcomponents. The tripartite model of attitude structure—which identifies affect, behavior, and cognition as distinct attitude components—has rich theoretical precedence and empirical support (Breckler, 1984). We know that the correspondence between attitude components (e.g., affect and cognition) can be relatively low, even approaching independence. This suggests a different kind of ambivalence—one reflecting a conflict between attitude components (Thompson, Zanna, & Griffin, 1995). Ambivalence might occur, for example, when a person has negative feelings (affect) toward an object, but positive beliefs (cognition). The affective-cognitive discrepancy can be thought of as a form of attitude ambivalence. It is captured well by phrases such as "My heart tells me one thing, but my mind tells me another."

The interesting thing about this form of ambivalence is that it represents the kind of conflict that occurs when comparing items or objects of fundamentally different composition. It is the kind of conflict that occurs when comparing apples and oranges. From this perspective it is not sensible to characterize attitudes as falling somewhere along a single bipolar continuum. Affect exists in one dimension, and cognition exists in another, and behavior in yet a third. The dimensions may not be orthogonal (independent), but they are clearly separable and not easily contained on any single bipolar dimension. The idea of multivalence can accommodate evaluative discrepancies among attitude components.

Finally, the idea of bipolar knowledge structures has been generalized in a way that is more compatible with multivalent attitudes. Lord and Lepper's (1999) attitude representation theory (ART) emphasizes the potential for multivalent cognitive organization of attitudes and the conditions under which different representations (of different valences) might be activated.

## Assessment of attitude multivalence

The concept of attitude ambivalence surely has precedence in these and many other theoretical traditions. The question is whether this diversity in ambivalence theory is captured well by a corresponding diversity in ambivalence measurement. The idea of multivalence complicates the assessment approach. Kaplan's dual unipolar-rating scale approach is simple and elegant. It was a logical solution to the practical problem of interpreting midscale responses. I would suggest, however, that it does not capture the conceptual richness of attitudes, because it does not allow for the assessment of multivalence. How, then, can we assess multivalence? The approach I have been pursuing is to start with traditional attitude scaling procedures that allow the expression of multivalence.

### Taking Thurstone seriously

Following the lead of Katz and Hass, and taking Thurstone's admonition seriously that attitudes are complex affairs, I have been working on a method for assessing attitude multivalence based on Thurstone's method of equal-appearing intervals (EAI). The EAI approach creates multi-statement scales, where each statement has a scale value placing it on the bipolar evaluative continuum. Respondents check the statements with which they agree, and a score is computed as the average or median scale value of the endorsed items. The construction of an EAI scale is laborious, but when done properly it produces a multi-item scale that captures a very rich and diverse array of affect, behavior, and cognition relating to an attitude topic.

In the attitude survey mentioned earlier in the chapter, we assessed students' attitudes toward eight social and political issues. For each of the eight topics, we developed an EAI scale. An example, for the topic of legalized abortion, is reproduced in Table 4.2 (where the scale items are sorted by scale values, rather than the random arrangement used with the actual scale). For each statement, respondents are asked to indicate whether they agree or disagree. Because people can select any combination of statements as reflecting their attitude, it allows them to express as much (or as little) multivalence as they like.

Traditionally, a single measure of attitude is derived from an EAI scale. It is the central tendency measure—the average scale value of statements with which the respondent indicates agreement. Of course, the average does not distinguish among very different patterns of endorsement. For example, one person may indicate agreement with items 7, 8 and 10 on the legalized abortion EAI scale, producing an average score of 4.34 (see Table 4.2). Another person may endorse items 3 and 13, which produces an average score of 4.14. In both cases, the central tendency measure indicates a near-midpoint location on the evaluative continuum. Yet these two hypothetical respondents are revealing differences in their patterns of endorsement. The first is selecting items that cluster near the evaluative midpoint, which is consistent with a pattern of neutrality or perhaps indifference. The second is selecting far more polarized statements, which is consistent with a pattern of ambivalence (simultaneously endorsing statements across the evaluative range).

We do have methods for capturing qualities of the endorsement pattern that go beyond central tendency. One in particular—the dispersion measure— offers potential for indexing ambivalence. The standard deviation, for example, can capture the evaluative range or variability of endorsed statements. The

*Table 4.2* A scale to assess attitudes toward legalization of abortion, constructed using the method of equal-appearing intervals (items have been sorted by their scale values)

| Scale items | Scale values |
| --- | --- |
| 1. The practice of abortion is equivalent to murder. | 1.06 |
| 2. For me, the decision is clear cut: outlaw abortion. | 1.20 |
| 3. Abortion is wrong. | 1.55 |
| 4. I oppose legalized abortion. | 1.92 |
| 5. The unborn fetus is never given a choice about abortion. | 3.07 |
| 6. Too many people use abortion as a method of birth control. | 3.13 |
| 7. The slight benefits of abortion do not justify it being legalized. | 3.81 |
| 8. Clinics do not give women complete information before performing abortions. | 4.00 |
| 9. We don't know when life really begins. | 5.10 |
| 10. The decision others make about abortion is their own, not mine. | 5.22 |
| 11. Abortions are acceptable only during the first trimester. | 6.07 |
| 12. There are certain instances in which abortion is necessary. | 6.36 |
| 13. Personally, I would never choose to have an abortion, but I would support someone who does. | 6.73 |
| 14. Outlawing abortion is discriminatory. | 6.92 |
| 15. If abortion is outlawed, many women will lose their lives by having unsafe abortions. | 7.67 |
| 16. Keeping abortions legal keeps them safe. | 7.73 |
| 17. Women have the right to control their own bodies. | 8.04 |
| 18. I am strongly pro-choice. | 8.54 |

larger the value of this measure, the greater is the evaluative variability of endorsed statements. The standard deviation of endorsed scale values for our first hypothetical respondent is .77, whereas the standard deviation for the second respondent is 3.66. Clearly, the standard deviation measure captures the difference in evaluative range or multivalence of endorsed statements.

The EAI-derived measure of multivalence possesses a number of desirable properties. Focusing on its psychometric properties, we administered these scales twice (with an average separation of two weeks) so that we could compute test–retest correlations. Across the eight attitude topics, the average test–retest correlation for the EAI standard deviation measure was .65. This was much better than the average test–retest correlation of .46 for the dual unipolar-scale procedure. It is also quite comparable to the average test–retest correlation of .73 for Jamieson's SIMAS scale, which was also included in the survey.

To assess construct validity, we followed the lead of Katz and Hass (1988) by also assessing the students' values. Using the method developed by Rokeach (1973), students completed a survey of 18 values, each of which was rated for its importance as a guiding principle in the student's life. Eighteen values could create conflict in numerous ways. One potential conflict is between Freedom (independence, free choice) and Salvation (a saved, eternal life) with respect to two of the attitude domains we sampled: legalized abortion and prayer in public schools. By themselves, endorsements of the importance of the two values (Freedom and Salvation) were unrelated (the correlation was .02).

Additional ratings from our students confirmed the intuition that placing high importance on the value of Freedom implies a favorable attitude toward legalized abortion, whereas placing high importance on the value of Salvation implies an unfavorable attitude toward legalized abortion. Indeed, the correlation between students' actual self-endorsements of Freedom and the average of EAI-endorsed scale values for the legalized abortion scale was .26. In contrast, the correlation between self-endorsement of Salvation and EAI attitudes was −.42. Thus, despite the relative independence in the endorsement of the two values, the implied differences in legalized abortion attitudes were found.

The central question was whether a pattern of conflicting value endorsement would be related to students' assessed ambivalence and multivalence in this attitude domain. We computed the degree of each student's conflict between these two values by using the same formula used for computing attitude ambivalence ($(A_w)^2 / A_s$). This value-conflict index was then correlated with the EAI standard deviation measure of multivalence on the legalized abortion attitude scale. This correlation was reliably greater than zero, with $r = .32$. The value-conflict index was not correlated, however, with either the bivalence index (derived from dual unipolar-rating scales) or with the SIMAS measure. Thus, the kind of evaluative dispersion indexed by the EAI approach appears to be more sensitive to value conflict than the kind of bivalence picked up by the other approaches.

Similarly, our students' ratings confirmed that placing high importance on the value of Freedom implies an unfavorable attitude toward prayer in public schools, whereas placing high importance on the value of Salvation implies a positive attitude. The correlation between self-endorsed Salvation and EAI attitude toward school prayer was .53. Although not reliably different than zero, the correlation between Freedom and attitude was in the expected direction ($r = −.14$). As we found with the legalized abortion issue, the value-conflict index was correlated with the EAI standard deviation measure of multivalence on the school prayer attitude scale. This correlation was reliably greater than zero, with $r = .35$. As with the legalized abortion issue, the value-conflict index was not correlated with either the bivalence index or the SIMAS measure of ambivalence toward school prayer.

## Summary

Interest in ambivalence theory and measurement has grown in the last four decades. Although many researchers find Kaplan's (1972) dual unipolar-rating scale approach useful, others have explored alternative ways to assess ambivalence. In large part, this represents an effort to make the measurement technology more harmonious with theoretical conceptions of ambivalence. My goal in this chapter was to draw a distinction between attitude *bivalence* and attitude *multivalence*. Multivalence is more inclusive of the broad range of conceptual nuances that underlie the ambivalence construct. The split bipolar-scale approach allows for the assessment of bivalence, but it is not as well suited for assessing multivalence. Multi-statement scales, such as the equal-appearing interval scale, are better able to capture multivalence. A small demonstration supported the efficacy of this approach.

### Note

The views and opinions expressed in this chapter do not necessarily reflect those of the US National Science Foundation.

### References

Armitage, C. J., & Conner, M. (2000). Attitudinal ambivalence: A test of three key hypotheses. *Personality and Social Psychology Bulletin, 26*, 1421–1432.

Bell, D. W., Esses, V. M., & Maio, G. R. (1996). The utility of open-ended measures to assess intergroup ambivalence. *Canadian Journal of Behavioural Science, 28*, 12–18.

Breckler, S. J. (1984). Empirical validation of affect, behavior, and cognition as distinct components of attitude. *Journal of Personality and Social Psychology, 47*, 1191–1205.

Breckler, S. J. (1994). A comparison of numerical indexes for measuring attitude ambivalence. *Educational and Psychological Measurement, 54*, 350–365.

Brown, J. S., & Farber, I. E. (1951). Emotions conceptualized as intervening variables—with suggestions toward a theory of frustration. *Psychological Bulletin, 48*, 465–495.

Busemeyer, J. R., & Townsend, J. T. (1993). Decision field theory: A dynamic-cognitive approach to decision making in uncertain environments. *Psychological Review, 100*, 432–459.

Cacioppo, J. T., & Bernston, G. G. (1994). Relationship between attitudes and evaluative space: A critical review, with emphasis on the separability of positive and negative substrates. *Psychological Bulletin, 115*, 401–423.

Esses, V. M., & Maio, G. R. (2002). Expanding the assessment of attitude components and structure: The benefits of open-ended measures. In W. Stroebe & M. Hewstone (Eds.), *European Review of Social Psychology* (Vol. 12, pp. 71–102). Chichester, UK: Wiley.

Hass, R. G., Katz, I., Rizzo, N., Bailey, J., & Eisenstadt, D. (1991). Cross-racial appraisal as related to attitude ambivalence and cognitive complexity. *Personality and Social Psychology Bulletin, 17*, 83–92.

Jamieson, D. W. (1993). *The attitude ambivalence construct : Validity, utility, and measurement*. Paper presented at a symposium on Attitudinal Ambivalence at the 101st annual meeting of the American Psychological Association, Toronto, Canada.

Jonas, K., Diehl, M., & Brömer, P. (1997). Effects of attitudinal ambivalence on information processing and attitude-intention consistency. *Journal of Experimental Social Psychology, 33*, 190–210.

Judd, C. M., & Kulik, J. A. (1980). Schematic effects of social attitudes on information processing and recall. *Journal of Personality and Social Psychology, 38*, 569–578.

Kaplan, K. J. (1972). On the ambivalence-indifference problem in attitude theory and measurement: A suggested modification of the semantic differential technique. *Psychological Bulletin, 77*, 361–372.

Katz, I., & Hass, R. G. (1988). Racial ambivalence and American value conflict: Correlational and priming studies of dual cognitive structures. *Journal of Personality and Social Psychology, 55*, 893–905.

Klopfer, F. J., & Madden, T. M. (1980). The middlemost choice on attitude items: Ambivalence, neutrality, or uncertainty? *Personality and Social Psychology Bulletin, 6*, 97–101.

Larsen, J. T., McGraw, A. P., & Cacioppo, J. T. (2001). Can people feel happy and sad at the same time? *Journal of Personality and Social Psychology, 81*, 684–696.

Likert, R. (1932). A technique for the measurement of attitudes. *Archives of Psychology, 140*, 5–53.

Lord, C. G., & Lepper, M. R. (1999). Attitude representation theory. In M. Zanna (Ed.), *Advances in Experimental Social Psychology* (Vol. 31, pp. 265–343). San Diego, CA: Academic Press.

Maio, G. R., & Olson, J. M. (2000). *Why we evaluate: Functions of attitudes.* Mahwah, NJ: Lawrence Erlbaum Associates, Inc.

Moore, M. (1973). Ambivalence in attitude measurement. *Educational and Psychological Measurement, 33*, 481–483.

Norris, C. J., Larsen, J. T., & Cacioppo, J. T. (2002). *The affect matrix: Indexing positive and negative affective processes.* Paper presented at 14th annual meeting of the American Psychological Society, New Orleans, LA.

Pratkanis, A. R. (1989). The cognitive representation of attitudes. In A. R. Pratkanis, S. J. Breckler, & A. G. Greenwald (Eds.), *Attitude structure and function* (pp. 71–98). Hillsdale, NJ: Lawrence Erlbaum Associates, Inc.

Rokeach, M. (1973). *The nature of human values.* New York: Free Press.

Scott, W. A. (1966). Measures of cognitive structure. *Multivariate Behavioral Research, 1*, 391–395.

Scott, W. A. (1969). Structure of natural cognitions. *Journal of Personality and Social Psychology, 12*, 261–278.

Sparks, P., Conner, M., James, R., Shepherd, R., & Povey, R. (2001). Ambivalence about health-related behaviors: An exploration in the domain of food choice. *British Journal of Health Psychology, 6*, 53–68.

Thompson, M. M., Zanna, M. P., & Griffin, D. W. (1995). Let's not be indifferent about (attitudinal) ambivalence. In R. E. Petty & J. A. Krosnick (Eds.), *Attitude strength: Antecedents and consequences* (pp. 361–386). Mahwah, NJ: Lawrence Erlbaum Associates, Inc.

Thurstone, L. L. (1928). Attitudes can be measured. *American Journal of Sociology, 33*, 529–554

Townsend, J. T., & Busemeyer, J. R. (1989). Approach-avoidance: Return to dynamic decision behavior. In C. Izawa (Ed.), *Current issues in cognitive processes* (pp. 107–133). Hillsdale, NJ: Lawrence Erlbaum Associates, Inc.

# 5 Attitude ambivalence in the realm of politics

*Howard Lavine*

Nearly all contemporary public opinion research rests on the assumption that sociopolitical attitudes are unidimensional and bipolar—i.e., positive, negative, or neutral evaluative responses (e.g., Eagly & Chaiken, 1993; Green & Citrin, 1994; Lodge, McGraw, & Stroh, 1989). In studies of mass belief systems and electoral behavior, for example, attitudes toward policies, candidates, and groups are typically operationalized as summary statements that range from "unfavorable," "oppose," "cold," or "negative" at one end of the continuum to "favorable," "support," "warm," or "positive," at the other. This view implies that positive attitudes are the diametric opposite of negative attitudes, such that the more one likes a political object the less one dislikes it. Unfortunately, this structural assumption masks a fundamental and readily acknowledged aspect of belief systems, namely, that individual opinions are not simply positive or negative evaluative tendencies, but instead are often simultaneously positive and negative (Alvarez & Brehm, 1995; Cacioppo, Gardner, & Berntson, 1997; Feldman & Zaller, 1992; Hochschild, 1981; Huckfeldt & Sprague, 1998; Lavine, 2001a; Lavine, Borgida, & Sullivan, 2000; Lavine, Thomsen, Zanna, & Borgida, 1998; Nelson 1999; Thompson, Zanna, & Griffin, 1995; Zaller & Feldman, 1992). That is, rather than endorsing one side of a political debate and refuting the other, individuals often embrace central elements of both sides.

Earlier models of political belief systems assumed that individuals who internalize elements of both sides of a political conflict were expressing "nonattitudes" (Converse, 1964), or that such opinions perforce reflect deficiencies in survey measurement (Achen, 1975). Analysts now believe that such complex attitudes often represent the problem of reconciling strongly held but conflicting principles and considerations simultaneously present in the political culture in order to make difficult political choices (Alvarez & Brehm, 1995; Feldman & Zaller, 1992; Huckfeldt & Sprague, 1998; Lavine, 2001a). Recent work in particular suggests that *ambivalence*—the endorsement of conflicting considerations or beliefs associated with an attitude object—is a prevalent characteristic of the public's political opinions, and that ambivalence has important consequences for political judgment and decision making. For example, policy attitudes marked by evaluative conflict are held with less certainty and are more difficult to retrieve from memory (Huckfeldt & Sprague, 1998; Lavine et al., 2000), less stable over time (Lavine, 2001a; Zaller & Feldman, 1992), and more vulnerable to persuasion than relatively one-sided (unambivalent) attitudes (Bassili, 1996). These phenomena may be diagnostic of the operation of more immediate and fundamental dynamics of ambivalence, namely that it renders the political choice process excessively difficult and unreliable (Alvarez & Brehm, 1995), and contextually dependent on whatever relevant considerations are momentarily salient (Lavine, Huff, Wagner, & Sweeney, 1998; Tourangeau, Rasinski, Bradburn & D'Andrade, 1989). For example, in their examination of abortion attitudes, Alvarez and Brehm (1995) found that respondents who highly valued both women's rights *and* religion (the primary underpinnings of *pro-choice* and *pro-life* positions, respectively) revealed considerably greater error variance in their policy choices than did respondents who valued one of these considerations to the relative exclusion of the other. It is these basic consequences of ambivalence—judgmental unreliability and context dependence—that are used in the present research to construct an argument relating ambivalence to the nature and functioning of electoral attitudes and decision-making.

Most of the work on ambivalence in political psychology is based on studies of policy issues (e.g., Alvarez & Brehm, 1995, 1997; Feldman & Zaller, 1992; Huckfeldt & Sprague, 1998; Steenbergen & Brewer, 2000; Tetlock, 1986; Zaller & Feldman, 1992). There is comparatively little work on how ambivalence toward other political entities, candidates and groups for example, might influence electoral attitudes and voting behavior (although see Lavine, 2001a; Lavine et al., 1998; Meffert, Guge, & Lodge, 2000). However, it is within an electoral context that ambivalence might be expected to exert the strongest effects. In particular, presidential campaigns provide voters with an intense flow of conflicting partisan information over a sustained period of time. It is within this context as well that individuals are most likely to devote active attention to the political arena (something that they are otherwise unlikely to do, see Delli Carpini & Keeter, 1996; Kinder, 1998). Inevitably, some of that information will cast each candidate in a favorable light, and some in an unfavorable light. Moreover, unlike issue debates, even politically quiescent individuals will collect a large amount of (inconsistent) information about the candidates, making it likely that a substantial portion of the public will react to them with at least a modicum of ambivalence (Lavine, 2001a; Lavine et al., 1998; Meffert et al., 2000; Saris & Galhofer, 2000; Zaller, 1992).

In the next section, I present a theoretical argument linking ambivalence toward presidential candidates to electoral decision making. Then, using national survey data, I show that ambivalence toward candidates is associated with a variety of consequences, including attitudinal instability, a substantial delay in the formation of behavioral (voting) intentions, a decrease in the predictive value of key attitudinal antecedents of summary candidate evaluation (i.e., personality assessments and issue proximity), and ultimately a weakening in the prediction of vote choice. These effects of ambivalence are candidate specific, and not the result of general dispositions of particular individuals to be high or low in ambivalence toward all candidates (see Newby-Clark, McGregor, & Zanna, 2002; Thompson & Zanna, 1995, for an analysis of the dispositional roots of ambivalence). Moreover, I show that the moderating effects of ambivalence are not reducible to (and are typically greater than) those of political sophistication, education, political interest, strength of partisanship, or alternative indicators of attitude strength (e.g., extremity or certainty of opinion).

I then turn to the proposition that attitudinal conflict exists not only at the level of specific attitude objects (e.g., Bill Clinton, capital punishment), but also at the more abstract and fundamental level of the left–right dimension. I situate this notion on the premise that mass political ideology can be understood at the level of root likes and dislikes toward politically salient *social groups* (Conover & Feldman, 1981; Converse, 1964; Kinder & Sanders, 1996; Sniderman & Tetlock, 1986; Sniderman, Brody, & Tetlock, 1991). Using survey data from the period of 1984 to 2000, I show that the occurrence of ideological or *group ambivalence*—holding positive feelings toward such groups as the poor, blacks, Jews, environmentalists, liberals, labor unions, *and* big business, Protestants, conservatives, whites, fundamentalist Christians, and the military—reduces the ideological consistency of voters' policy attitudes, the accuracy of their perceptions of the policy stands of presidential candidates, and the extent to which their vote choices reflect their own issue preferences. Finally, I address the descriptive and theoretical implications of ambivalence for the efficacy of mass political persuasion.

## Ambivalence and the attitude response process

Specifying how ambivalence might affect electoral judgment and decision making requires an understanding of how political opinions are typically formed and expressed. Recent studies of social cognition and public opinion have mounted strong evidence challenging the notion that citizens possess fixed attitudes in the traditional sense of the term: i.e., stable, preformed summary opinions that can be directly summoned from memory (for a recent review, see Lavine, 2001b). Instead, the evidence points to the idea that most people possess rather poorly integrated belief elements that might or might not be used to construct a summary opinion at a given time (Strack & Martin, 1987; Tourangeau, Rips, & Rasinski, 2000; Wilson & Hodges, 1992; Zaller & Feldman, 1992). According to this view, opinions are constructed on the spot on the basis of whichever considerations are recently activated or at the "top of the head" (Zaller, 1992). Thus, rather than retrieving a representative sample of beliefs, people tend to oversample from whichever beliefs are most salient or accessible at the time. When political opinions are construed in this way, *ambivalence* becomes a central construct in regulating the dynamics of political choice. The essential idea is this: when ambivalence is high, stochastic processes and systematic changes in political context can result in the retrieval of belief elements used to construct an attitude at Time 1 that differ greatly in valence from those used to construct the attitude at Time 2. Moreover, within an electoral context, ambivalence should increase voters' receptivity to partisan persuasive messages from each of the competing campaigns. According to the McGuire–Zaller model of attitude change (McGuire, 1968; Zaller, 1992), persuasion depends on the conjunctive probability that a message will be received and accepted as valid. In the political realm, reception is largely a function of political knowledge (see Zaller, 1992), whereas acceptance is a function of the extent to which the message (e.g., a TV ad, a political debate) squares with the voter's political predispositions (e.g., values, ideology, policy attitudes, party affiliation). Thus, if a message is received, and if it resonates with an internalized consideration, acceptance of the message—and thus attitude change—is facilitated (for a review of reception-yielding models, see Eagly & Chaiken, 1993). Because by definition ambivalent voters have endorsed at least some of the arguments offered by both sides of the political spectrum, the acceptance function of the persuasion model should generally be higher among ambivalent than one-sided voters.

This conceptual analysis of ambivalence has a number of important implications for mass electoral politics. First, it suggests that when ambivalence is high, candidate evaluations should be unstable over the course of a presidential campaign. Instability, in turn, should keep voters from foreclosing on a particular candidate, thus rendering them susceptible to the effects of the campaign (e.g., revelations about and mistakes made by the candidates, international conflict). In contrast, voters with comparatively one-sided candidate attitudes (e.g., many positive beliefs but few or no negative beliefs) should express relatively stable candidate attitudes as the beliefs used to construct them have similar evaluative implications. For these univalent voters, voting intentions should crystallize earlier in the campaign—perhaps before it even begins in earnest in the fall—leaving such individuals relatively impervious to the events of the campaign.

Beyond creating intra-attitudinal instability, ambivalence should weaken *inter*-attitudinal relationships. Specifically, evaluative assessments of candidate character and level of agreement with the candidates' policy preferences—two major antecedents of vote choice (see Kinder, 1998)—should exert weaker effects on overall candidate attitudes as candidate ambivalence increases. In line with the constructionist model of opinion formation described above, conflicted (ambivalent) voters with similar assessments of a candidate's character and similar policy attitudes may nevertheless hold substantially different summary opinions about the candidate to the extent that different considerations are salient for different voters when the summary evaluation is formed. This should occur as stochastic processes and systematic events in the campaign selectively prime positive considerations about a candidate for some ambivalent voters but prime negative considerations for other ambivalent voters. For example, two voters who agree with a candidate on civil rights but disagree with the candidate on economic issues should nevertheless hold discrepant summary attitudes toward the candidate if civil rights is salient to one voter but the economy is salient to the other. By contrast, one-sided (unambivalent) voters with similar policy attitudes and trait evaluations should form highly similar summary candidate evaluations, as whatever considerations are most salient have similar evaluative implications. In sum, ambivalent attitudes toward presidential candidates should be associated with difficulty and delay in the formation of crystallized voting intentions, unstable candidate opinions throughout the campaign, reduced electoral influence of character judgments and issue proximity, and a general weakening in the prediction of vote choice.

## Candidate ambivalence and electoral decision making

To examine these propositions, I rely on survey data from the National Election Study (NES) from the presidential elections of 1980 to 1996. The NES surveys are based on national probability samples of adults in the United States, with sample sizes of approximately 2000. Each of these presidential election year interviews included items assessing the extent to which the major party candidates possessed a variety of positive character traits (e.g., decent, compassionate, intelligent, moral, inspiring, cares about people like you, leadership, commands respect). In all surveys, the trait items read as follows:

> Think about [candidate]. The first phrase (or word) is [trait]. In your opinion does the phrase [trait] describe [candidate] extremely well (=1), quite well (=2), not too well (=3), or not well at all (=4)?

The trait items were recoded so that higher numbers indicated more positive assessments of candidate character. Composite character assessment scores were constructed for each candidate by averaging the trait items ($a$'s ranged from .86 in 1980 to .93 in 1984, and were highly similar across levels of ambivalence). For each election year, a comparative character assessment score was constructed by subtracting each respondent's composite score for the Democratic candidate from his or her composite score for the Republican candidate.

To assess the influence of respondents' policy attitudes on overall candidate evaluation, I constructed a single issue proximity score for each respondent in each election year by averaging all issues for which both respondent attitudes and respondent perceptions of the candidates' attitudes were available (the number of issues ranged from 4 in 1992 to 10 in 1996). The formula used to construct issue proximity was:

$$IP = \sum_{i=1}^{n} |V_{ij} - D_i| - |V_{ij} - R_i|$$

where $V_{ij}$ is voter j's position on issue i, $D_i$ is the mean perception of the Democratic candidate's position on issue i, and $R_i$ is the mean perception of the Republican candidate's position on issue i (Markus, 1982). Using respondents' mean placement of the candidates rather than each respondent's own placement helps to reduce projection (i.e., "projecting" one's own opinion onto the preferred candidate, see Alvarez & Nagler, 1995, 1998).

*Ambivalence*

There are two challenges in measuring ambivalence. The first is identifying the types of reactions that give rise to an evaluative conflict (Meffert et al., 2000; Steenbergen & Brewer, 2000). The second is the manner in which those reactions should be numerically operationalized. My concern here is with positive and negative evaluations of the candidates' character and issue preferences. The NES candidate open-ended likes/dislikes items provide a highly suitable means for assessing these aspects of candidate-centered evaluative conflict. The likes/dislikes questions ask "Is there anything in particular about [CANDIDATE] that might make you want to vote [FOR or AGAINST] him?" Four follow-up probes are provided ("Anything else?"). Respondents are thus invited to provide up to five likes and five dislikes for each of the two major party candidates.

The problem of integrating these positive and negative reactions into a numerical index requires a theory of the conditions necessary to arouse ambivalence. Behavioral conflict theorists (e.g., Mowrer, 1960) and contemporary attitude theorists (e.g., Cacioppo et al., 1997; Hass, Katz, Rizzo, Bailey, & Eisenstadt, 1991; Thompson, Zanna, & Griffin, 1995) cite two necessary and sufficient conditions for the arousal of ambivalence. First, the conflictual (positive and negative) reactions to the attitude object should be similar in magnitude. As one component becomes stronger than the other— in the present case as the number of likes and dislikes becomes unequal—the attitude should polarize toward positivity or negativity, thereby reducing ambivalence. Second, ambivalence would seem to require that the positive and negative components be of at least moderate intensity. Thus, ambivalence should be greater when voters have several positive and negative reactions to a candidate than when they have only one positive and one negative reaction. Taking these two ideas together, I construct a similarity–intensity measure of ambivalence suggested by Thompson et al. (1995). For each of the three types of *individual* candidate analyses reported below (i.e., the role of ambivalence in moderating the stability of individual candidate evaluations, and in moderating the effects of issue proximity and character assessments on individual candidate evaluations), I computed the Thompson et al.

formula for each of the two major party candidates using the candidate-centered likes/dislike counts. For the analyses involving the effects of issue proximity and character assessments on overall candidate evaluations, I computed two ambivalence scores for each candidate, one for ambivalence about the candidate's character and one for ambivalence about the candidate's perceived issue positions. Candidate *character* ambivalence scores were constructed for each respondent using the NES candidate likes/dislikes master code categories corresponding to candidate character. Candidate *issue* ambivalence scores were constructed using the candidate likes/dislikes master code categories corresponding to candidate issue positions.[1] For the stability analyses, I compute ambivalence scores for each candidate using all likes/dislikes (i.e., references to issues, character, party) for that candidate.

A variation on the Thompson et al. (1995) ambivalence formula was used in the two further meta-candidate analyses (timing of the formation of vote intention and vote choice):

$$\text{Ambivalence}_{\text{comp}} = \frac{P_R + P_D + N_R + N_D}{4} - [|P_R - P_D| + |N_R - N_D|]$$

where $P_R$ and $P_N$ represent the number of positive reactions to the Republican and Democratic candidate respectively, and $N_R$ and $N_D$ represent the number of negative reactions to the candidates. This formula is different from the Thompson et al. (1995) measure (which compares the intensity and similarity of positive and negative affect for a *single* candidate) in that it compares the overall intensity of affect toward both candidates (on the left) corrected by the extent to which the respondent's positive and negative reactions vary *between* the candidates (on the right). $P_R$, $P_N$, $N_R$, $N_D$ range from 0–5, and thus Ambivalence$_{\text{comp}}$ ranges from a low of $-7.5$ when reactions are highly polarized such that one candidate is strongly liked and the other is strongly disliked (e.g., when $P_R$ and $N_D$ are 5 and $N_R$ and $P_D$ are 0) to $+5.0$ when reactions to both candidates are highly intense and ambivalent (i.e., when all four components are 5). Thus, Ambivalence$_{\text{comp}}$ captures the extent to which respondents' feelings toward the candidates are similar or polarized, with overall ambivalence increasing as intensity of feeling toward the candidates increases.

In the analyses that follow, each of a set of control variables related to cognitive ability and attitude strength (e.g., education, political knowledge,

---

1 Candidate *character* ambivalence scores were constructed using the "Experience and Ability," "Leadership Qualities," and "Personal Qualities" NES master code categories for candidates. Candidate *issue* ambivalence scores were constructed using the "Government Management," "Government Activity/Philosophy," "Domestic Policies," and "Foreign Policies" master code categories. Finally, responses coded under the "Group Connections" category were added to both the character and issue ambivalence scores, as these responses picked up on both character- and issue-related considerations.

attitude extremity, attitude certainty, sum of open-ended likes and dislikes) was entered into regression models along with partisanship, ideology, and political interest. The candidate evaluation and time of reported crystalliza- tion of vote intention models were estimated using ordinary least-squares regression. The vote choice models were estimated using logistic regression. To facilitate comparison of the coefficients, all variables were recoded to a 0 to 1 scale. Moreover, to ease the interpretation of key interactions and to reduce multicollinearity between individual and crossproduct terms, all variables were centered about their means (Aiken & West, 1991).[2]

### *Ambivalence and the crystallization of behavioral intentions*

To assess *when* during a presidential campaign voters reported forming their voting intentions, each of the NES surveys asked "How long before the elec- tion did you decide that you were going to vote the way you did (1 = 'knew along along/from the first' to 10 = 'on election day')?" The estimated effects of ambivalence$_{comp}$, and the control variables on the reported time of crystal- lization of voting intention are shown in Table 5.1. As can be seen in the table, strong partisans and those with polarized character assessments were consist- ently more likely to form crystallized voting intentions earlier in the election campaign than weak partisans/independents and those with moderate assessments of candidate character. The expected effect of ambivalence was also significant and correctly signed in every election. As ambivalence increased, voting intentions crystallized later in the campaign. Moreover, for all but the 1980 election, ambivalence exerted the *strongest* effect of all the variables in the model. Holding the other variables at their means, the pre- dicted timing of vote intention score (across elections) at maximum ambiva- lence is 6.00 (on the 1–10 scale), corresponding to voters making up their minds five to seven weeks before the election. In contrast, at minimum levels of ambivalence, the predicted timing score is 3.85, corresponding to voters making up their minds in late July, three and half months before the election.

These results suggest that harboring both positive and negative evaluative reactions toward the candidates led a substantial proportion of voters to

2 Extremity scores are absolute differences between each rating and the scale midpoint. Items to assess the certainty of character assessments were available only in 1996. In 1996, certainty was measured with two 3-point items in which respondents were asked "How certain are you of this?" (very certain, pretty certain, not very certain) after rating the character of Dole and Clinton on the attributes "moral" and "gets things done." A single certainty score was com- puted for each candidate by averaging respondents' answers to the two items. A measure of the total number of likes/dislikes for each candidate was computed by adding the number of positive and negative reactions to that candidate. Political knowledge was assessed with items measuring recognition of and knowledge about political figures (e.g., Al Gore, Newt Gingrich, Yasser Arafat), the ideological orientation of presidential candidates and parties, and civics questions (e.g., Who nominates judges to the Federal Courts?).

*Table 5.1* Reported time of crystallization of behavioral intention as a function of ambivalence and control variables

|  | Election | | | | |
|---|---|---|---|---|---|
|  | 1980 | 1984 | 1988 | 1992 | 1996 |
| Ambivalence | .20** | .34*** | .24*** | .44*** | .44*** |
|  | (.09) | (.06) | (.06) | (.06) | (.08) |
| Education | .08 | .01 | .05 | −.03 | −.05 |
|  | (.06) | (.04) | (.04) | (.04) | (.05) |
| Information | −.11 | −.09* | −.08 | −.06 | −.05 |
|  | (.08) | (.04) | (.06) | (.04) | (.07) |
| Certainty of character assessments | — | — | — | — | .00 |
|  |  |  |  |  | (.06) |
| Strength of partisanship | −.11** | −.11** | −.12*** | −.20*** | −.26*** |
|  | (.04) | (.04) | (.04) | (.03) | (.05) |
| Strength of ideology | −.03 | −.02 | −.09*** | −.09** | −.08 |
|  | (.05) | (.04) | (.03) | (.03) | (.05) |
| Extremity of character assessments | −.53*** | −.22*** | −.20** | −.34*** | −.14 |
|  | (.07) | (.06) | (.07) | (.06) | (.08) |
| Extremity of issue proximity | −.05 | −.01 | −.14 | .01 | .19 |
|  | (.08) | (.08) | (.08) | (.03) | (.17) |
| N | 780 | 1,133 | 1,027 | 1,054 | 609 |
| $R^2$ | .23 | .19 | .21 | .19 | .23 |

*Note*: All variables are scaled from 0 to 1. Entries are unstandardized regression coefficients. Standard errors are in parentheses. $* = p < .05$; $** = p < .01$; $*** = p < .001$. Effects of political interest and total number of likes/dislikes toward the candidates not shown.

remain unforeclosed into the last stages of a campaign. This finding is consistent with the idea that ambivalence renders the behavioral choice process comparatively difficult. If indeed this is the case, ambivalent voters should also exhibit temporally unstable candidate attitudes. The next section examines this hypothesis.

### *Ambivalence and the stability of candidate attitudes*

To determine whether ambivalence toward a given candidate promoted instability in the overall evaluation of that candidate (and not toward both candidates generally), two interaction terms were constructed. For analyses involving a Democratic candidate, the first interaction term involved multiplying ambivalence scores (derived from the Thompson et al. formula) toward the Democratic candidate by the pre-election candidate evaluation scores of the Democratic candidate (*matched interaction*; e.g., ambivalence toward Clinton × evaluation of Clinton). In the second interaction term, ambivalence scores toward the Republican candidate were multiplied by the pre-election candidate evaluation scores of the Democratic candidate (*mismatched interaction*; e.g., ambivalence toward Dole × evaluation of

Clinton). For analyses involving a Republican candidate, the matched interaction term consisted of the product of ambivalence scores toward the
Republican candidate and pre-election candidate evaluation scores of
the Republican candidate. The mismatched interaction term consisted of the
product of ambivalence scores toward the Democratic candidate and pre-
election candidate evaluation scores of the Republican candidate. The dependent variable in each analysis is the post-election candidate evaluation (an
interval of approximately six weeks). The hypothesis that ambivalence pro-
motes instability is captured by a negatively signed interaction, indicating
that the positive slope of pre-election candidate evaluations on post-election
candidate evaluations will be attenuated as ambivalence increases. Importantly,
if the effect of ambivalence is candidate specific, only the *matching* interaction term in each analysis should be significant. That is, ambivalence toward one candidate should decrease evaluative stability toward that candidate
only, and not toward the other major party candidate in a given election year.

Estimates of the effects on post-election candidate evaluation are shown in
Table 5.2. As can be seen in the table, the effect of pre-election candidate
evaluation was significantly moderated by the correct (matched) candidate-
specific ambivalence term in four of five elections for Democratic candidates
(all but 1984), and in three of five elections for Republican candidates (1984,
1992, and 1996). In each of these cases, the interaction was of the correct
(negative) sign and of substantive magnitude. Moreover, only one of ten
mismatched interactions was significant (Dukakis in 1988), and their average
magnitude was a trivial −.05.

### Ambivalence, character assessments, issue proximity, and candidate attitudes

To estimate whether candidate-specific ambivalence moderated the influence
of character assessments and issue proximity on summary candidate attitudes, two separate ambivalence scores were constructed for each analysis,
one corresponding to ambivalence about the candidate's character (i.e., to
what extent does the respondent hold mixed beliefs about the candidate's
personality traits?), and the other corresponding to ambivalence about the
candidate's issue positions (i.e., to what extent does the respondent have
mixed reactions to the candidate's perceived issue positions?).

To estimate the moderating effects of ambivalence, two matched and two
mismatched interaction terms were constructed. In the first pair of terms,
candidate *character* ambivalence scores were separately multiplied by the
matched and the mismatched character assessment scores (e.g., Clinton
ambivalence × Clinton character assessment, and Dole ambivalence × Clinton
character assessment, respectively). These interaction terms test whether the
slope of the character judgment factor varies as ambivalence changes. The
prediction is that the matched (but not the mismatched) interaction terms
involving character assessments and character ambivalence will be negative,

Table 5.2 Post-election candidate evaluation as a function of pre-election candidate evaluation, ambivalence, and control variables

| | Election | | | | | | | | | |
|---|---|---|---|---|---|---|---|---|---|---|
| | 1980 | | 1984 | | 1988 | | 1992 | | 1996 | |
| | Reagan | Carter | Reagan | Mondale | Bush | Dukakis | Bush | Clinton | Dole | Clinton |
| Pre-election candidate evaluation | .56*** | .61*** | .67*** | .53*** | .52*** | .49*** | .60 | .56 | .57*** | .71*** |
| | (.02) | (.02) | (.02) | (.02) | (.02) | (.02) | (.02) | (.02) | (.02) | (.02) |
| Ambivalence (Republican) | .04 | .05 | .03 | .01 | .05 | .03 | .08*** | .08*** | -.02 | -.06** |
| | (.03) | (.03) | (.03) | (.02) | (.03) | (.03) | (.02) | (.02) | (.03) | (.02) |
| Ambivalence (Democrat) | .05 | .15*** | -.03 | -.05 | -.02 | .02 | -.01 | -.02 | -.01 | .02 |
| | (.03) | (.03) | (.03) | (.03) | (.03) | (.03) | (.03) | (.03) | (.02) | (.02) |
| Ambivalence (Republican) × pre-election candidate evaluation | -.23 | .003 | -.37*** | -.12 | -.07 | -.30** | -.25** | .11 | -.32** | -.06 |
| | (.14) | (.12) | (.09) | (.09) | (.11) | (.11) | (.08) | (.09) | (.12) | (.08) |
| Ambivalence (Democrat) × pre-election candidate evaluation | -.02 | -.45*** | .01 | -.10 | -.03 | -.36** | -.15 | -.50*** | .04 | -.21** |
| | (.11) | (.14) | (.10) | (.12) | (.11) | (.12) | (.09) | (.11) | (.10) | (.08) |
| N | 1,174 | 1,191 | 1,694 | 1,690 | 1,559 | 1,547 | 2,000 | 1,988 | 1,348 | 1,417 |
| $R^2$ | .53 | .57 | .66 | .50 | .53 | .46 | .57 | .53 | .51 | .78 |

Note: All variables are scaled from 0 to 1. Entries are unstandardized regression coefficients. Standard errors are in parentheses. $* = p < .05$; $** = p < .01$; $*** = p < .001$. Effects of party identification, political ideology, education, political knowledge, total number of likes/dislikes toward the candidates, extremity of pre-election evaluation, and certainty of character assessment not shown.

indicating that the positive slopes of character assessments on summary candidate attitudes decrease as ambivalence toward that candidate increases. In the second set of interaction terms, candidate *issue* ambivalence scores were separately multiplied by the matched and the mismatched issue proximity scores. These terms test whether the slope of the issue proximity factor varies as ambivalence changes. The prediction here is that the matched (but not the mismatched) interaction terms will be negative for Republican candidates but *positive* for Democratic candidates. This is because issue proximity is scored such that high values indicate greater agreement with the Republican candidate's issue positions. Thus, the *main effect* of issue proximity should be positive for Republican candidates and negative for Democratic candidates. If ambivalence weakens the positive issue proximity effect on Republican candidates, the interaction terms should be negative; similarly, if ambivalence weakens the negative issue proximity effect on Democratic candidates, the interaction terms should be positive. The dependent variable in the analysis is the pre-election summary candidate attitude (the NES feeling thermometer item).

Estimates of the effects on summary candidate attitude are shown in Table 5.3. As the table indicates, 8 of 10 of the matched interactions involving ambivalence about the candidate's character were significant and correctly signed (all but Reagan in 1984 and Bush in 1988), whereas only 1 of 10 of the mismatched interactions reached significance (Dole in 1996). Similarly, 5 of 10 matched interactions (and only one of the mismatched interactions) involving ambivalence about the candidate's issue positions were significant and of the correct sign (negative for Republican candidates and positive for Democratic candidates). Predicted summary candidate attitude scores (calculated at minimum and maximum levels of candidate-specific ambivalence, character assessment, and issue proximity) ranged across 89% of the scale (.07 to .96, on a scale ranging from 0 to 1) as a function of character assessments at minimum ambivalence, but ranged across only 48% of the scale (.34 to .82) at maximum ambivalence (a 46% reduction in the effect). Similarly, predicted summary candidate attitudes scores ranged across 26% of the scale (.46 to .62) as a function of issue proximity at minimum ambivalence, but were completely flat (.60 to .60) at maximum ambivalence. These analyses provide further evidence that ambivalence has important consequences for electoral decision making. Not only does it promote instability in candidate attitudes, but ambivalence also weakens the predictive utility of two prime ingredients of candidate evaluation: judgments of candidate character and agreement/ disagreement with the candidate's positions on salient campaign issues.

### Ambivalence, behavioral intention, and vote choice

The final empirical question related to ambivalence toward candidates is whether ambivalence diminishes the predictive impact of voters' summary candidate judgments (operationalized here as vote intentions; candidate

Table 5.3 Summary candidate attitudes as a function of character assessment, issue proximity, ambivalence, and control variables

| | Election | | | | | | | | | |
|---|---|---|---|---|---|---|---|---|---|---|
| | 1980 | | 1984 | | 1988 | | 1992 | | 1996 | |
| | Reagan | Carter | Reagan | Mondale | Bush | Dukakis | Bush | Clinton | Dole | Clinton |
| Character ambivalence (Republican) | .15*** (.04) | -.01 (.04) | .09* (.04) | -.13*** (.04) | .09 (.05) | .03 (.05) | .05 (.04) | .055 (.03) | .09* (.04) | -.02 (.04) |
| Character ambivalence (Democrat) | -.01 (.04) | .06 (.04) | .04 (.04) | .06 (.04) | -.01 (.04) | .09* (.04) | -.01 (.04) | .10** (.04) | -.16*** (.05) | .14** (.05) |
| Issue ambivalence (Republican) | .08* (.04) | .09* (.04) | .07** (.03) | -.04 (.03) | .09* (.04) | .07 (.04) | .11*** (.03) | -.05 (.03) | .10* (.05) | .10** (.04) |
| Issue ambivalence (Democrat) | .04 (.04) | .16*** (.04) | .05 (.03) | .02 (.04) | -.01 (.04) | .07 (.05) | -.01 (.04) | .07 (.04) | .02 (.05) | .01 (.05) |
| Character assessment | .87*** (.03) | .95*** (.03) | .80*** (.03) | .74*** (.03) | .81*** (.04) | .81*** (.04) | .79*** (.03) | .72*** (.03) | .65*** (.04) | .76*** (.03) |
| Issue proximity | .036 (.02) | -.02 (.02) | .15*** (.02) | -.16* (.03) | .10*** (.03) | -.11*** (.03) | .03 (.02) | -.037 (.02) | .10*** (.03) | -.10*** (.03) |
| Ambivalence × character assessment (Republican) | -.59** (.21) | -.04 (.20) | -.27 (.16) | -.22 (.24) | -.05 (.28) | -.22 (.35) | -.66** (.18) | .04 (.18) | -1.12*** (.23) | -.18 (.16) |
| Ambivalence × character assessment (Democrat) | .13 (.17) | -.58*** (.19) | .01 (.17) | -.58* (.26) | .02 (.20) | -.85** (.25) | -.29 (.19) | -.97*** (.21) | .55** – (.26) | .63** (.20) |
| Ambivalence × issue proximity (Republican) | -.19 (.14) | .37** (.14) | -.26* (.12) | .21 (.13) | -.22 (.15) | -.15 (.16) | -.34** (.10) | -.18 (.10) | -.27 (.17) | .14 (.16) |
| Ambivalence × issue proximity (Democrat) | -.06 (.12) | .01 (.12) | -.11 (.14) | .32* (.14) | -.11 (.18) | .36* (.18) | -.19 (.14) | .56*** (.12) | -.15 (.19) | .14 (.17) |
| N | 1,023 | 1,029 | 1,070 | 1,069 | 971 | 965 | 1,461 | 1,456 | 867 | 901 |
| $R^2$ | .63 | .69 | .66 | .66 | .64 | .59 | .65 | .63 | .61 | .80 |

Note: All variables are scaled from 0 to 1. Entries are unstandardized regression coefficients. Standard errors are in parentheses. * = $p < .05$; ** = $p < .01$; *** = $p < .001$. Effects of party identification, political ideology, education, political knowledge, total number of likes/dislikes toward the candidates, extremity of character assessment and extremity of issue proximity not shown.

evaluations produced highly similar results). The hypothesis that ambivalence weakens the connection between voting intentions (expressed in the pre-election interview) and reported vote choice is captured by a negatively signed interaction of ambivalence$_{comp}$ and vote intention (0 = intention to vote for the Democratic candidate; 1 = intention to vote for the Republican candidate) on vote choice (0 = voted for the Democrat; 1 = voted for the Republican; nonvoters excluded). The logit estimates are given in Table 5.4. As can be seen in the table, the ambivalence × vote intention interaction was significant and correctly signed in all election years. At minimum ambivalence, voters were highly likely to vote for the intended candidate (predicted probability of .96 for voters intending to vote for the Democratic candidate, and .91 for voters intending to vote for the Republican candidate). However, the correspondence between vote intention and subsequent vote choice was much weaker among voters at maximum ambivalence; here, the predicted likelihood of voting for the intended candidate was only .68 for the Democrats, and .71 for the Republicans.

## Group ambivalence and electoral decision making

In almost all work to date, ambivalence has been conceived of and measured as simultaneous positive and negative evaluation toward specific attitude objects (e.g., Bill Clinton, capital punishment). In this section, I pursue the idea that individuals may also experience a more general and abstract type of ideological conflict. What I have in mind is not, however, an ideological ambivalence in which great numbers of people simultaneously embrace the philosophical principles of liberalism and conservatism, endorsing, for example, both *laissez-faire* capitalism and broad government intervention in the economy. This would appear to take leave of a great deal of evidence that

*Table 5.4* Vote choice as a function of vote intention, ambivalence, and control variables

|  | *Election* | | | | |
|---|---|---|---|---|---|
|  | *1980* | *1984* | *1988* | *1992* | *1996* |
| Ambivalence | −3.06 | −1.08 | .81 | 3.53 | −.17 |
|  | (2.38) | (1.36) | (1.28) | (1.97) | (1.79) |
| Vote intention | 6.36*** | 5.86*** | 3.97*** | 6.49*** | 5.70*** |
|  | (.85) | (.53) | (.42) | (.66) | (.68) |
| Ambivalence × vote intention | −11.16** | −7.03** | −10.53*** | −5.94* | −8.45** |
|  | (4.86) | (2.41) | (2.39) | (3.47) | (3.47) |
| N | 540 | 780 | 675 | 861 | 589 |

*Note*: All variables are scaled from 0 to 1. Entries are logit coefficients. Standard errors are in parentheses. * = $p < .05$; ** = $p < .01$; *** = $p < .001$. Effects of party affiliation, political ideology, education, political knowledge, certainty and extremity of character assessment, extremity of issue proximity, and total number of likes/dislikes about the candidates not shown.

the American mass public is "innocent of ideology" (Kinder & Sears, 1985). Instead, consistent with work on the group-centric notion of American politics (e.g., Adorno, Frenkel-Brunswik, Levinson, & Sanford, 1950; Bobo, 1983; Conover & Feldman, 1981; Converse, 1964; Kinder & Sanders, 1996; Klingemann, 1979; Nelson, 1999; Sniderman et al., 1991; for a review, see Kinder, 1998), mass ideology—and thus ideological ambivalence—can be understood at the level of root likes and dislikes toward politically salient *social groups.*

Groups constitute an integral part of the American political landscape. The policy and electoral cleavages that divide racial, religious, and gender groups are well documented (e.g., Chaney, Alvarez, & Nagler, 1996; Kinder & Sanders, 1996; Kinder & Winter, 2001; Mendelberg, 2001). More importantly, there would appear to be strong evidence that sympathies and resentments toward salient social groups—blacks, whites, liberals, conservatives, gays, Jews, poor people, rich people, evangelical Christians—fundamentally shape citizens' political views toward a range of objects, including issues, candidates, and parties. Although most Americans would appear to be blissfully unaware of the abstract niceties of liberalism and conservatism (for a review, see Kinder, 1983), many are able work out what they stand for politically by knowing which groups they like and which they dislike (and which candidates, parties, and policies are likely to provide benefits or deprivations to specific groups; see also Conover, 1984; Conover & Feldman, 1981; Kinder & Sanders, 1996; Nelson, 1999; Sniderman et al., 1991).

The idea of *group ambivalence* is that group likes and dislikes can be ideologically compatible or in conflict with one another. Favorable attitudes toward some groups—fundamentalist Christians, the rich, big business—imply a preference for conservative candidates and the Republican party, whereas favorable attitudes toward other groups—blacks, Jews, homosexuals, feminists, the poor—imply a preference for liberal candidates and the Democratic party. Reliable political judgment and decision making should be facilitated by holding positive feelings toward one but not both sets of ideologically linked groups. However, group-level attitudinal conflicts will not be perceived universally; just as individuals can and do endorse conflicting considerations toward candidates and issues, they might also possess positive feelings toward groups spanning the political spectrum, from blacks, Jews, and feminists on the left, to fundamentalist Christians and big business on the right. In fact, there is reason to believe that group ambivalence is widespread. First, in the mass public as a whole, liking for the cognate groups "liberals" and "conservatives" is largely orthogonal (Conover & Feldman, 1981). That is, citizens do not tend to like liberals in proportion to the extent that they dislike conservatives, or vice versa. Second, ambivalence toward both issues (Feldman & Zaller, 1992) and candidates (Lavine, 2001a) appears to be quite common (see also Hochschild, 1981; Lane, 1962), suggesting the existence of a more general intrapsychic split in the political mind, one arguably rooted (at least in part) in simultaneous liking for social groups identified with the left and the right.

In the analyses that follow, I examine three potential consequences of group ambivalence. First, as political opinions appear to be strongly driven by group sympathies and resentments (e.g., Conover & Feldman, 1981; Kinder & Sanders, 1996; Sniderman et al., 1991), group ambivalent individuals—those with positive feelings toward groups associated with the political right and left—should hold less ideologically consistent policy attitudes than individuals with ideologically polarized group feelings. For example, individuals with positive affect toward liberal but not conservative identified groups should tend to hold uniformly liberal policy attitudes, whereas those with positive feelings toward groups across the political spectrum should tend to hold ideologically mixed policy opinions. Second, in addition to diminishing the organization of one's political evaluations, group ambivalence should interfere with the accuracy of one's political *perceptions*. In particular, I examine whether group ambivalence impedes *accurate* perception of the candidates' policy stands (i.e., perceiving Democratic candidates as taking liberal issues positions and Republican candidates as taking conservative issue positions). If, as many analysts have argued (e.g., Carmines & Stimson, 1989; Converse, 1962, 1964; Nie, Verba, & Petrocik, 1979; Zaller, 1992), organization in political thinking is created largely through social diffusion and the "time bundling" of issues during presidential elections—in essence, cue taking in terms of "what goes with what" from political elites—voters with ideologically polarized group evaluations should be more likely than voters with ideologically mixed group evaluations to recognize that Democratic candidates tend to hold liberal issue positions and Republican candidates tend to hold conservative issue positions. Finally, if group ambivalent individuals are both less ideologically consistent in their own attitudes and less accurate in their perceptions of the attitudes of political elites, they should be less likely to vote in the normative manner, that is, on the basis of policy issues. In particular, they should be more likely to make voting "mistakes," such that they cast votes for the candidate *farther* from rather than *nearer* to them on the issues.

National Election Studies (NES) data from the five most recent presidential elections (1984–2000) were used to examine the relations between group ambivalence on one hand, and interattitudinal consistency, perceptual accuracy, and voting mistakes, on the other. Each of these presidential election year interviews included thermometer ratings assessing feelings toward a wide variety of societal groups. The instruction in all surveys read as follows:

I'd like to get your feelings toward some of our political leaders and other people who are in the news these days. I'll read the name of a person and I'd like you to rate that person using something we call the feeling thermometer. Ratings between 50 degrees and 100 degrees mean that you feel favorable and warm toward that person. Ratings between

0 and 50 degrees mean that you don't feel favorable toward the person and that you don't care too much for that person. You would rate the person at the 50 degree mark if you don't feel particularly warm or cold toward the person. (After political leaders are rated): And still using the feeling thermometer, how would you rate the following groups.

Each election year survey contained a variety of social groups traditionally identified with the political left and the political right (see Conover & Feldman, 1981). Groups typically associated with liberal voting behavior and liberal policy preferences—Jews, feminists, blacks, gays and lesbians, labor unions, civil rights leaders, the poor—were used to construct a measure of feelings toward liberal groups, and those typically associated with conservative voting behavior and conservative policy preferences—fundamentalist Christians, big business, whites, Protestants, the military—were used to construct a measure of feelings toward conservative groups. A measure of feelings toward liberal groups was derived by averaging the thermometer scores across the liberal identified groups, and a measure of feelings toward conservative groups was derived by averaging across scores on the conservative identified groups.

Theoretically, group ambivalence should be high to the extent that feelings toward the two types of groups are similar in valence and extreme in magnitude. First, as positive feelings toward one group become stronger than the other—for example, as affect toward conservative groups becomes more positive than affect toward liberal groups—ideological group feelings become polarized, thus reducing ambivalence (Thompson et al., 1995). Second, group ambivalence should be high to the extent that feelings toward the conflicting groups are intense or extreme (i.e., deviating from the midpoint of the thermometer scale). Taking these two ideas together, ambivalence is a positive additive function of the similarity and intensity of feeling toward liberal and conservative groups. A variation on the Thompson et al. (1995) similarity-intensity index is used to measure group ambivalence:

$$\text{Group Ambivalence} = [(|G_C - 50| + |G_L - 50|)/2] - |G_C - G_L|$$

where $G_C$ and $G_L$ represent averaged feelings toward liberal and conservative groups. The term on the left (within the brackets)—the average of the two absolute values—represents the average level of evaluative extremity or intensity toward the liberal and conservative identified groups. Averaged feelings toward the two groups are subtracted from 50 (the midpoint of the feeling thermometer scale) to determine the extent to which feelings toward the groups are extreme. Higher deviation scores represent more intense group evaluations. The term on the right (i.e., $|G_C - G_L|$) represents the similarity of affect toward the two groups. Group ambivalence is high when both the intensity and similarity terms of the equation are high. High similarity can reflect either simultaneously liking or mutual hostility toward the two sets of groups. Ambivalence scores range from −50, when feelings toward one group are at zero and feelings toward the other are at 100 (i.e., 50–100 = –50), to +50, when feelings toward the two groups are both either 100 or 0 (i.e., 50–0 = 50).

To assess the ideological consistency of respondents' policy attitudes, I coded each pair of policy opinions (e.g., government services and aid to blacks) as ideologically consistent if the two opinions were on the same side of the issue on the 7-point NES policy scale (e.g., responses of 1, 2, or 3 for both policy issues, or responses of 5, 6, or 7 for both policy issues, once the items are recoded in the same ideological direction). Each pair of consistent responses was given a score of 1. A score of 0 was given to issue pairs in which one or both of the responses fell at the midpoint; if one or both of the responses were missing values; or, if the two responses were ideologically incompatible (a 1, 2, or 3 on one issue and a 5, 6, or 7 on the other issue). Thus, I am measuring the extent to which respondents held policy attitudes reflecting the same (liberal or conservative) ideological orientation. A final index of issue consistency was derived by computing the proportion of issue pairs for which each respondent held ideologically compatible policy preferences.[3]

### Group ambivalence and interattitudinal consistency

The OLS estimates of group ambivalence and several control variables on interattitudinal consistency are shown in Table 5.5. As can be seen in the table, only two variables exerted uniformly significant effects: extremity of ideology and group ambivalence, with the latter exerting much stronger effects throughout. As group ambivalence increased, the consistency of respondents' policy attitudes decreased markedly, from .38 when group ambivalence was at its minimum to .21 when ambivalence reached its maximum. The effects of the other variables were sporadically significant, small in magnitude, and of inconsistent sign.

### Group ambivalence and the accuracy of political perception

To determine whether respondents correctly located the candidates' issue positions, I measured whether or not their perceptions accorded with the mean perceived candidate location in the sample (for a similar operationalization of "correct" voter perception, see Hamill, Lodge, & Blake, 1985). Specifically, I calculated the proportion of items for which respondents located the candidate on the consensual side of the issue (i.e., the liberal side for Democratic candidates and the conservative side for Republican candidates).[4]

---

3 Respondents who failed to answer at least half of the issue items in a given election year were excluded from all analyses. This resulted in the exclusion of 6.2% of the sample across election years (rates ranged from 3.4% in 2000 to 12.2% in 1984).

4 Only items for which the mean candidate perception was less than three or greater than five on the 7-point issue scale were included in the analysis. That is, I used only policy items in which a candidate was perceived as taking a clear stand on one side of the issue. This resulted in five usable items in 1984 and 1996, four items in 1988 and 2000, and two items in 1992.

*Table 5.5* Ideological consistency of policy attitudes as a function of group ambivalence and control variables

|  | Election | | | | |
|---|---|---|---|---|---|
|  | *1984* | *1988* | *1992* | *1996* | *2000* |
| Group ambivalence | −.18*** | −.09* | −.19*** | −.31*** | −.09* |
|  | (.05) | (.05) | (.105) | (.04) | (.04) |
| Information | .01 | −.08* | .04 | −.05 | .04 |
|  | (.03) | (.04) | (.03) | (.03) | (.03) |
| Education | .03 | −.04 | .06* | .06** | .01 |
|  | (.03) | (.03) | (.03) | (.02) | (.03) |
| Extremity of party ID | .01 | .01 | .01 | .01 | .01 |
|  | (.01) | (.01) | (.01) | (.01) | (.01) |
| Extremity of ideology | .02** | .03*** | .04*** | .05*** | .04*** |
|  | (.01) | (.007) | (.008) | (.007) | (.01) |
| Political interest | .00 | −.02 | .03 | .01*** | .01* |
|  | (.02) | (.02) | (.02) | (.004) | (.004) |
| $R^2$ | .03 | .04 | .06 | .20 | .06 |

*Note*: Entries are OLS coefficients. Standard errors are in parentheses. * = $p < .05$; ** = $p < .01$; *** = $p < .001$.

For example, if the perception of Reagan's position on increased defense spending averaged 5.8 on a 7-point scale, scores of 5, 6, or 7 would be deemed correct, and scores of 1 through 4 would be deemed incorrect. Correct candidate perception scores were regressed on group ambivalence and the set of control variables in Table 5.5. OLS estimates are presented in Table 5.6. As can be seen in the table, both information (political knowledge) and group ambivalence exerted consistent effects on candidate accuracy throughout the election years. Higher levels of information and lower levels of group ambivalence were associated with higher levels of accuracy. As with interattitudinal consistency, the other variables were significant only sporadically, smaller in magnitude, and inconsistently signed. Holding the other variables at their means, predicted accuracy scores (on the 0 to 1 scale) ranged from .72 at minimum group ambivalence to .55 as group ambivalence reached its maximum.

### Group ambivalence and voting mistakes

To this point, the results indicate that the opinions of group ambivalent voters are less ideologically constrained and that their perceptions of the candidates' issue locations are less accurate than those of voters with less group ambivalent structures. The former should therefore be especially likely to make behavioral "mistakes" such that they cast votes for candidates farther from rather than nearer to them on the issues (for a conceptually similar definition of voting error, see Lau & Redlawsk, 1997). In this last empirical

*Table 5.6* Accuracy of perception of candidate issue location as a function of group ambivalence and control variables

| | Election | | | | |
|---|---|---|---|---|---|
| | *1984* | *1988* | *1992* | *1996* | *2000* |
| Group ambivalence | −.13** | −.19** | −.20** | −.19*** | −.11* |
| | (.04) | (.06) | (.07) | (.06) | (.06) |
| Information | .19*** | .10* | .28*** | .31*** | .17*** |
| | (.03) | (.04) | (.04) | (.04) | (.04) |
| Education | .19*** | .00 | .17*** | .07* | .10* |
| | (.03) | (.03) | (.04) | (.03) | (.04) |
| Extremity of party ID | .00 | .00 | .03** | .01 | .01 |
| | (.01) | (.01) | (.01) | (.01) | (.01) |
| Extremity of ideology | −.01 | .00 | .02 | .03*** | .02* |
| | (.01) | (.01) | (.012) | (.01) | (.01) |
| Political interest | −.07*** | −.03 | .03 | .01* | .03*** |
| | (.02) | (.03) | (.03) | (.005) | (.01) |
| $R^2$ | .17 | .03 | .13 | .21 | .11 |

*Note*: Entries are OLS coefficients. Standard errors are in parentheses. * = $p < .05$; ** = $p < .01$; *** = $p < .001$.

section, I examine whether group ambivalence leads to disproportionately high rates of noncorrespondence between issue preference and vote choice, thereby diminishing the rationality of voting behavior. I test this possibility by creating a binary dependent variable score such that 0 = *match* between issue proximity and vote choice (a vote for the candidate nearer to the respondent on the issues) and 1 = *mismatch* between issue proximity and vote choice (a vote for the candidate farther from the respondent on the issues). I then predicted "voting mistakes" from the variables included in the accuracy of perception model. In these analyses, I included only respondents whose issue proximity scores implied a clear preference for one of the candidates. To this end, I excluded respondents within one half of one standard deviation from the indifference point on issue proximity (i.e., the point at which the voter's issue preferences are equidistant between the two candidates).[5]

Respondents voted "correctly"—for the candidate nearer to their own issue preferences—81.44 percent of the time (mistakes ranged from a low of 13.68% in 1996 to a high of 26.03% in 1992). The logit coefficients for mistakes in vote choice are shown in Table 5.7. As can be seen in the table, only one variable in the model consistently predicted voting mistakes: group

5 The rate of voting errors is of rather little consequence among citizens with only a marginal preference for one candidate over the other on the issues. Only when a clear preference based on issue proximity exists does it make sense to regard the noncorrespondence between issue preference and vote choice a "mistake." Including these respondents in the analysis produced substantively identical results.

*Table 5.7* Mistakes in vote choice as a function of group ambivalence and control variables

| | Election | | | | |
|---|---|---|---|---|---|
| | *1984* | *1988* | *1992* | *1996* | *2000* |
| Group ambivalence | 2.87*** | 5.26*** | 3.88*** | 5.36*** | 3.61*** |
| | (.89) | (1.09) | (.65) | (1.01) | (.88) |
| Information | −.95* | −.75 | −.21 | −.02 | −1.77*** |
| | (.43) | (.70) | (.40) | (.60) | (.55) |
| Education | .08 | .19 | −.86* | −.24 | −1.49** |
| | (.13) | (.58) | (.37) | (.59) | (.57) |
| Extremity of party ID | .41 | −.37 | −1.19*** | .15 | −1.05* |
| | (.47) | (.49) | (.30) | (.52) | (.43) |
| Extremity of ideology | −1.79*** | −.86 | −.31 | −1.08 | −1.45** |
| | (.53) | (.52) | (.34) | (.59) | (.52) |
| Political interest | −1.77*** | −1.57** | .21 | −2.14 | .03 |
| | (.48) | (.52) | (.27) | (1.60) | (.51) |
| *N* | 557 | 482 | 711 | 536 | 553 |

*Note*: Entries are logit coefficients. Standard errors are in parentheses. $* = p < .05$; $** = p < .01$; $*** = p < .001$.

ambivalence. The other variables were significant exactly twice each in five elections. Moreover, the effect of group ambivalence was substantial. Across the five elections, the probability of making a voting mistake among individuals with group ambivalence scores two standard deviations below the mean of this variable (i.e., relatively univalent voters) was only .05; among voters with group ambivalence scores two standard deviations above the mean (i.e., ambivalent voters), the likelihood of such a behavioral error rose to a nontrivial .37.

Thus, holding mixed feelings toward salient social groups exerts (by far) the strongest impact on rational voting behavior, stronger again than levels of formal schooling, knowledge about politics, the extremity of political predispositions, or political interest.

## Implications and conclusions

Research conducted over the past two decades has amply shown that the power and functionality of attitudes depends on a variety of strength-related properties, such as the degree of importance accorded an attitude (Krosnick, 1988), the consistency of an attitude's underlying elements and its consistency with other attitudes (Chaiken, Pomerantz, & Giner-Sorolla, 1995; Lavine et al., 1998), its accessibility (Fazio, Chen, McDonel, & Sherman, 1982), and even its degree of heritability (Tesser, 1993). In this chapter, I attempt to make an empirical case for the role of ambivalence in regulating the occurrence of attitudinal phenomena. The analyses suggest that ambivalence has strong and wide-ranging effects in the political realm, from conditioning the ability of voters to form: (1) stable attitudes toward presidential candidates; (2) ideologically consistent policy attitudes; (3) accurate perceptions of the policy attitudes of candidates; to moderating: (1) the occurrence of behavioral "errors," or vote choices incommensurate with voters' policy preferences; (2) relations between candidate character assessments and issue proximity on one hand and overall candidate evaluations on the other; (3) relations between behavioral intentions and actual (voting) behavior. In short, attitude ambivalence reliably and strongly regulates electoral perception, evaluation, and decision making.

While the empirical case for ambivalence appears quite solid, what theoretical apparatus can be advanced to understand *why* such effects occur? At least within the realm of *political* attitudes—a normatively important realm of the social world that nevertheless ranks low on most people's interest scales (see Kinder, 1998)—researchers have cast strong doubt on the traditional assumption that people have fixed opinions on a range of matters that they can directly retrieve from memory and report as survey responses. Instead, according to Zaller and Feldman (1992, p. 579) and others, people "carry around in their heads a mix of only partially consistent considerations and ideas." Conceptually, people (on most issues) thus possess a distribution of possible attitudes depending on the valence and extremity of each available consideration and the likelihood that a given consideration will be used in constructing the opinion at a given time (see also Strack & Martin, 1987; Tourangeau et al., 2000; Wilson & Hodges, 1992). This "episodic-constructionist" theory of the nature of political attitudes accords central importance to ambivalence in contributing to the dynamics of public opinion and electoral choice. The essence of the idea is that stochastic processes create variability in the considerations used to construct an opinion at a given time. At certain times, beliefs favoring a positive attitudinal response will be ascendant in the cognitive system, and therefore given disproportionate weight in the construction of an opinion; at other times, beliefs favoring a negative attitudinal response will be ascendant. This provides a compelling explanation for why ambivalent policy attitudes are likely to be unstable, susceptible to response effects, and associated with greater error variance. As others have noted (e.g., Zaller & Feldman, 1992), it is difficult to conceive of how a response model in which attitudes are simply readouts of precomputed evaluations could account for such phenomena.

But the effects of ambivalence are likely to be precipitated by more than randomly varying cognitive contexts in which the retrieval process makes use of whatever beliefs happen to be momentarily accessible. Individuals who endorse the arguments on both sides of a political conflict (e.g., "abortion is murder" and "women should have control of their own bodies") should be systematically more vulnerable to active attempts to change their political opinions than those with comparatively univalent attitude structures. According to diverse accounts of the persuasion process (e.g., Chaiken,

Liberman, & Eagly, 1989; Chaiken et al., 1995; Lodge & Taber, 2000; Petty & Cacioppo, 1986; Zaller, 1992), individuals are often motivated to accept congenial arguments at face value but to expend considerable cognitive energy in counterarguing and refuting arguments that are attitude discrepant. By definition, ambivalent individuals possess a greater range of congenial arguments toward a given object; therefore, a political message from the political left *or* right should be more likely to resonate with a pre-existing belief among ambivalent than univalent individuals, and thus heighten message acceptance. This relative openmindedness provides an account for the finding that ambivalent voters remain behaviorally unforeclosed until the later stages of a presidential campaign, whereas univalent voters typically form their voting intentions before the fall campaign begins.

Finally, I consider the idea that ambivalence exists at a deeper level than individual attitude objects, dividing the political mind along the underlying left–right dimension. However, rather than supposing that any large proportion of citizens wrestles with the philosophical underpinnings and implications of liberalism and conservatism—that would appear to be taking leave of decades of evidence to the contrary (for reviews, see Kinder & Sears, 1985; Smith, 1980)—I argue that ideological ambivalence stems from the possession of positive feelings toward politically salient groups on both the political left and the political right. To the extent that likes and dislikes toward such groups inform a variety of other political opinions (for evidence on this point, see Brady & Sniderman, 1985; Kinder & Sanders, 1996; Sniderman et al., 1991), simultaneous liking for groups on *both* sides of the political spectrum might be expected to lead to attitudes that are less ideologically consistent (Table 5.5), perceptions that are less accurate (Table 5.6), and vote choices that are less commensurate with the individual's issue preferences (Table 5.7). The effects of group ambivalence on ideological policy constraint and issue-based voting behavior seem easily explainable in terms of the episodic-constructionist model of the attitude response process; the effects on perception require more explanation. It may be that ideological consistency mediates the effects of group ambivalence on perception. In particular, if policy consistency is created largely through social diffusion from political elites, voters with ideologically consistent issue preferences should be more likely than voters with ideologically mixed preferences to recognize that Democratic candidates tend to hold liberal issue positions and Republican candidates tend to hold conservative issue positions.

There is growing recognition that ambivalence in the political realm has significant consequences for political judgment and decision making. At the very least, ambivalence is implicated as an antecedent, consequence, or moderator of such phenomena as opinion instability, biased political reasoning, susceptibility to context effects, perceptual accuracy, and the clarity and predictability of political choice. Perhaps more importantly, recent work on attitude ambivalence has challenged Converse's (1964) longstanding thesis that attitude instability and other vagaries of public opinion can be explained by the absence of real attitudes. Instead, such vagaries appear to be the product of having too many political attitudes, with roughly as many ideas on one side of an issue as on the other.

## References

Achen, C. H. (1975). Mass political attitudes and the survey response. *American Political Science Review, 69*, 1218–1231.

Adorno, T., Frenkel-Brunswik, E., Levinson, D. J., & Sanford, N. R. (1950). *The authoritarian personality*. New York: Harper.

Aiken, L. S., & West, S. G. (1991). *Multiple regression: Testing and interpreting interactions*. Thousand Oaks, CA: Sage.

Alvarez, M. R., & Brehm, J. (1995). American ambivalence towards abortion policy: development of a heteroskedastic probit model of competing values. *American Journal of Political Science, 39*, 1055–1082.

Alvarez, M. R., & Brehm, J. (1997). Are Americans ambivalent towards racial policies? *American Journal of Political Science, 41*, 345–374.

Alvarez, M. R., & Nagler, J. (1995). Economics, issues, and the Perot candidacy: Voter choice in the 1992 presidential election. *American Journal of Political Science, 39*, 714–744.

Alvarez, M. R., & Nagler, J. (1998). Economics, entitlements, and social issues: Voter choice in the 1996 presidential election." *American Journal of Political Science, 42*, 1349–1363.

Barton, A. H., & Parsons, W. R. (1977). Measuring belief system structure. *Public Opinion Quarterly, 41*, 159–180.

Bassili, J. N. (1996). Meta-judgmental versus operational indexes of psychological attributes: The case of measures of attitude strength. *Journal of Personality and Social Psychology, 71*, 637–653.

Bobo, L. (1983). Whites' opposition to busing: Symbolic racism or realistic group conflict? *Journal of Personality and Social Psychology, 45*, 1196–1210.

Brady, H. E., & Sniderman, P. M. (1985). Attitude attribution: A group basis for political reasoning. *American Political Science Review, 79*, 1061–1078.

Breckler, S. J. (1994). A comparison of numerical indexes for Measuring attitude ambivalence. *Educational and Psychological Measurement, 54*, 350–365.

Cacioppo, J. T., Gardner, W. L., & Berntson G. G. (1997). Beyond bipolar conceptualizations and measures: The case of attitudes and evaluative space. *Personality and Social Psychology Review, 1*, 3–25.

Carmines, E., & Stimson, J. (1989). *Issue evolution: Race and the transformation of American politics*. Princeton, NJ: Princeton University Press.

Chaiken, S., Liberman, A., & Eagly, A. H. (1989). Heuristic and systematic information processing within and beyond the persuasion context. In J. S. Uleman & J. A. Bargh (Eds.), *Unintended thought* (pp. 212–252). New York: Guilford Press.

Chaiken, S., Pomerantz, & Giner-Sorolla, R. (1995). Structural consistency and attitude strength. In R. E. Petty & J. A. Krosnick (Eds.), *Attitude strength: Antecedents and consequences* (pp. 387–412). Mahwah, NJ: Lawrence Erlbaum Associates, Inc.

Chaney, C., Alvarez, M. R., & Nagler, J. (1996). *Explaining the gender gap in the 1992 U.S. Presidential Election*. Paper presented at the Annual Meeting of the Midwest Political Science Association, Chicago, IL.

Conover, P. (1984). The influence of group identifications on political perception and evaluation. *Journal of Politics, 46*, 76–785.

Conover, P., & Feldman, S. (1981). The origins and meanings of liberal/conservative self-identifications. *American Journal of Political Science, 25*, 617–645.

Converse, P. E. (1962). Information flow and the stability of partisan attitudes. *Public Opinion Quarterly, 26*, 578–599.

Converse, P. E. (1964). The nature of belief systems in mass publics. In D. E. Apter (Ed.), *Ideology and discontent* (pp. 206–261). New York: Free Press.

Delli Carpini, M. X., & Keeter, S. (1996). *What Americans know about politics and why it matters.* New Haven, CT: Yale University Press.

Eagly, A. H., & Chaiken, S. (1993). *The psychology of attitudes.* New York: Harcourt, Brace, Jovanovich.

Fazio, R. H., Chen, J., McDonel, E. C., & Sherman, S. J. (1982). Attitude accessibility, attitude–behavior consistency, and the strength of the object-evaluation association. *Journal of Experimental Social Psychology, 18*, 339–357.

Feldman, S., & Zaller, J. R. (1992). The political culture of ambivalence: Ideological responses to the welfare state. *American Journal of Political Science, 36*, 268–307.

Green, D. P., & Citrin, J. (1994). Measurement error and the structure of attitudes: Are positive and negative judgments opposite? *American Journal of Political Science, 38*, 256–281.

Hamill, R. C., Lodge, M., & Blake, F. (1985). The breadth, depth, and, utility of class, partisan, and ideological schemata. *American Journal of Political Science, 29*, 850–870.

Hass, G., Katz, I., Rizzo, N., Bailey J., & Eisenstadt, D. (1991). Cross-racial appraisal as related to attitude ambivalence and cognitive complexity. *Personality and Social Psychology Bulletin, 17*, 83–92.

Hochschild, J. L. (1981). *What's fair? American beliefs about distributive justice.* Cambridge, MA: Harvard University Press.

Huckfeldt, R., & Sprague, J. (1998). *Sources of ambivalence in public opinion: The certainty and accessibility of abortion attitudes.* Paper presented at the Annual Meeting of the International Society of Political Psychology, Montreal, Canada.

Kinder, D. R. (1983). Diversity and complexity in American public opinion. In A. Finifter (Ed.), *Political science: The state of the discipline.* Washington, DC: American Political Science Association.

Kinder, D. R. (1998). Opinion and action in the realm of politics. In D. T. Gilbert, S. T. Fiske, & G. Lindzey (Eds.), *Handbook of social psychology* (4th ed., pp. 778–867). New York: McGraw-Hill.

Kinder, D. R., & Sanders, L. M. (1996). *Divided by color.* Chicago, IL: University of Chicago Press.

Kinder, D. P., & Sears, D. O. (1985). Public opinion and political action. In G. Lindzey & E. Aronson (Eds.), *Handbook of social psychology* (3rd ed., pp. 659–782). New York: McGraw-Hill.

Kinder, D. R., & Winter, N. (2001). Exploring the racial divide: Blacks, whites, and opinion on national policy. *American Journal of Political Science, 45*, 439–453.

Klingemann, H. D. (1979). Measuring ideological conceptualizations. In S. H. Barnes & M. Kaase (Eds.), *Political action: Mass participation in five Western democracies* (pp. 215–254). Beverly Hills, CA: Sage.

Krosnick, J. A. (1988). The role of attitude importance in social evaluation: A study of policy preferences, presidential candidate evaluations, and voting behavior. *Journal of Personality and Social Psychology*, *55*, 196–210.

Lane, R. E. (1962). *Political ideology*. New York: Free Press.

Lau, R., & Redlawsk, D. (1997). Voting correctly. *American Political Science Review*, *91*, 585–598.

Lavine, H. (2001a). The electoral consequences of ambivalence toward presidential candidates. *American Journal of Political Science*, *45*, 915–929.

Lavine, H. (2001b). On-line vs. memory-based process models of political evaluation. In K. R. Monroe (Ed.), *Political psychology* (pp. 225–248). Mahwah, NJ: Lawrence Erlbaum Associates, Inc.

Lavine, H., Borgida, E., & Sullivan, J. L. (2000). On the relationship between attitude involvement and attitude accessibility: Toward a cognitive-motivational model of political information processing. *Political Psychology*, *21*, 81–106.

Lavine, H., Huff, J. W., Wagner, S. H., & Sweeney, D. (1998). The moderating influence of attitude strength on the susceptibility to context effects in attitude surveys. *Journal of Personality and Social Psychology*, *75*, 359–373.

Lavine, H., Thomsen, C. J., & Gonzales, M. H. (1997). The development of inter-attitudinal consistency: The shared consequences model. *Journal of Personality and Social Psychology*, *72*, 735–749.

Lavine, H., Thomsen, C. J., Zanna, M. P., & Borgida, E. (1998). On the primacy of affect in the determination of attitudes and behavior: The moderating influence of affective-cognitive ambivalence. *Journal of Experimental Social Psychology*, *34*, 398–421.

Lodge, M., McGraw, K. M., & Stroh, P. (1989). An impression-driven model of candidate evaluation. *American Political Science Review*, *83*, 399–420.

Lodge, M., & Taber, C. S. (2000). Three steps toward a theory of motivated reasoning. In A. Lupia, M. D. McCubbins, & S. L. Popkin (Eds.), *Elements of reason: Understanding and expanding the limits of political rationality* (pp. 183–213). New York: Cambridge University Press.

Markus, G. B. (1982). Political attitudes during an election year: A report on the 1980 NES panel study. *American Political Science Review*, *76*, 538–560.

McGuire, W. J. (1968). Personality and susceptibility to social Influence. In E. F. Borgatta & W. Lambert (Eds.), *Handbook of personality theory and research* (pp. 1130–1187). Chicago: Rand-McNally.

Meffert, M., Guge, M., & Lodge, M. (2000). Good, bad, and ambivalent: The consequences of multidimensional political attitudes. In W. E. Saris & P. Sniderman (Eds.), *The issue of belief: Essays at the intersection of nonattitudes and attitude change*. Amsterdam: University of Amsterdam Press.

Mendelberg, T. (2001). *The race card: Campaign strategy, implicit messages, and the norm of equality*. Princeton, NJ: Princeton University Press.

Mowrer, O. H. (1960). *Learning theory and behavior*. New York: Wiley.

Nelson, T. E. (1999). Group affect and attribution in social policy opinion. *Journal of Politics*, *61*, 331–362.

Newby-Clark, I. R., McGregor, I., & Zanna, M. P. (2002). Thinking and caring about cognitive inconsistency: When and for whom does attitudinal ambivalence feel uncomfortable? *Journal of Personality and Social Psychology*, *82*, 157–166.

Nie, N. H., Verba, S. S., & Petrocik, J. R. (1979). *The changing American voter*. Cambridge, MA: Harvard University Press.

Petty, R. E., & Cacioppo, J. T. (1986). The elaboration likelihood model of persuasion. In L. Berkowitz (Ed.), *Advances in experimental social psychology* (Vol. 19, pp. 123–205). San Diego, CA: Academic Press.

Saris, W. E., & Galhofer, I. (2000). The quality of survey responses: A theoretical evaluation. In W. E. Saris & P. Sniderman (Eds.), *The issue of belief: Essays at the intersection of nonattitudes and attitude change.* Amsterdam: University of Amsterdam Press.

Smith, E. R. A. N. (1980). The levels of conceptualization: False measures of ideological sophistication. *American Political Science Review, 74*, 685–696.

Sniderman, P. M., Brody, R. A., & Tetlock, P. E. (1991). *Reasoning and choice: Explorations in political psychology.* Cambridge, UK: Cambridge University Press.

Sniderman, P. M., & Saris, W. E. (2000). Introduction. In W. E. Saris & P. Sniderman (Eds.), *The issue of belief: Essays at the intersection of nonattitudes and attitude change.* Amsterdam: University of Amsterdam Press.

Sniderman, P. M., & Tetlock, P. E. (1986). Symbolic racism: Problems of motive attribution in political analysis. *Journal of Social Issues, 42*, 129–150.

Steenbergen, M., & Brewer, P. R. (2000). The not-so ambivalent public: Policy attitudes in the political culture of ambivalence. In W. E. Saris & P. Sniderman (Eds.), *The issue of belief: Essays at the intersection of nonattitudes and attitude change.* Amsterdam: University of Amsterdam Press.

Strack, F., & Martin, L. (1987). Thinking, judging, and communicating: A process account of context effects in attitude surveys. In H. Hippler, N. Schwarz & S. Sudman (Eds.), *Social information processing and survey methodology* (pp. 123–148). New York: Springer-Verlag.

Tesser, A. (1993). On the importance of heritability in psychological research: The case of attitudes. *Psychological Review, 100*, 129–142.

Tetlock, P. E. (1986). A value pluralism model of ideological reasoning. *Journal of Personality and Social Psychology, 50*, 819–827.

Thompson, M., Zanna, M. P., & Griffin, D. W. (1995). Let's not be indifferent about (attitudinal) ambivalence (pp. 361–386). In R. E. Petty & J. A. Krosnick (Eds.), *Attitude strength: Antecedents and consequences.* Hillsdale, NJ: Lawrence Erlbaum Associates, Inc.

Thompson, M. M., & Zanna, M. P. (1995). The conflict individual: Personality-based and domain-specific antecedents of ambivalent social attitudes. *Journal of Personality, 63*, 259–288.

Tourangeau, R., Rasinski, K. A., Bradburn, N., & D'Andrade, R. (1989). Belief accessibility and context effects in attitude measurement. *Journal of Experimental Social Psychology, 25*, 401–421.

Tourangeau, R., Rips, L. J., & Rasinski, K. A. (2000). *The psychology of survey response.* New York: Cambridge University Press.

Wilson, T. D., & Hodges, S. D. (1992). Attitudes as temporary constructions. In L. Martin & A. Tesser (Eds.), *The construction of social judgment* (pp. 37–65). Mahway, NJ: Lawrence Erlbaum Associates, Inc.

Zaller, J. R. (1992). *The nature and origins of mass opinion.* New York: Cambridge University Press.

Zaller, J. R., & Feldman, S. (1992). A simple theory of the survey response: Answering questions versus revealing preferences. *American Journal of Political Science, 36*, 579–616.

# 6 The effects of attitudinal ambivalence on attitude–intention–behavior relations

*Christopher J. Armitage and*
*Mark Conner*

## Introduction

Imagine the scene. It is a hot holiday and so you walk into a bar. As the air conditioning hits you, the bartender asks: "Would you like a beer?". What happens next? If we're involved in a game show such as *Candid Camera* or *You've Been Framed* hilarity ensues. If the encounter is more mundane, most models of attitude formation would suggest that we would weigh up the pros and cons of having a beer before deciding whether or not to do so. On a hot day, a beer may be cold, refreshing, mood lifting and tasty. It may also be warm, intoxicating, inappropriate and bitter. So, how do we decide what to do? If our thoughts and feelings are polarized in either the "pro" or "con/anti" direction, the prediction is straightforward: in general, people who are "pro" beer are likely to buy a beer whereas people who are "anti" beer are likely to opt for something else. However, social psychological research tells us that our attitudes are rarely so clear cut and that it is quite likely that we might think that drinking beer would be both tasty and inappropriate, and/or would make us feel both happy and guilty. Under such circumstances, it would be difficult for us to predict our own behavior from our attitude, much less the social psychologist, who is drinking quietly in the corner and observing our every move.

Aside from the fact that it would be difficult to predict our actions from our overall evaluation, this scenario throws up other issues: for example, it seems likely that we would have to engage in more systematic processing to resolve the pros and cons and to reach a decision. Similarly, what would happen if someone suggested we try a campari and soda with ice? The more conflicted we were about our beer, the more easily we might be persuaded to buy a campari and soda. By the same token: What will happen in a similar situation in the future? Presumably, if our attitude towards beer continues to be caught between two poles, it is plausible that we would have to continue to work through the pros and cons, and so form a new attitude on each separate occasion.

The scenario we outlined above is typical of many situations we face on a daily basis: "Should we eat a pie?" "Should we vote to legalize cannabis?"

"Should we attend medical checks?" It provides a summary of some of the kinds of research questions that social psychologists are interested in, namely: (a) "How well do attitudes predict behavior?" (b) "Can attitudes be changed by persuasive communications?" (c) "How do attitudes affect the way in which we view the social world?" (d) "What effect does our behavior have on our attitudes?" (Eagly, 1992). Of these four research questions, the present chapter focuses on the attitude–behavior relationship because it has been—and remains—a particular concern for social psychologists interested in attitudes (e.g., Eagly & Chaiken, 1993). Moreover, the extent to which attitudes are predictive of behavior, resistant to persuasion, or influential with respect to information processing are not mutually exclusive. For example, attitudes that are more predictive of behavior are likely to be more resistant to persuasion and to exert greater influence on information processing. Thus, by focusing attention on the attitude–behavior relationship, it is possible to examine the effects of pliability and information processing in the context of attitude–behavior relations. The focus of this chapter is therefore on the attitude–behavior relationship and the way in which other properties of attitudes, such as pliability, might be influenced by (or indeed influence) the attitude–behavior relationship.

## Attitudinal ambivalence

Traditionally, attitudes have been conceptualized as unidimensional bipolar constructs, meaning that individuals may only be positively disposed, negatively disposed or neutral about a particular attitude object (such as a behavior). The assumption underpinning this conceptualization is that people approach positively evaluated objects and avoid negatively evaluated objects. However, because the evidence for this predicted relationship between attitudes and behavior has proven somewhat inconsistent (e.g., Kraus, 1995; Wicker, 1969), research attention has been directed at identifying the conditions under which attitudes *do* predict behavior. One approach to understanding this "gap" between attitudes and behavior has been to consider various properties of attitudes, notably the *strength* of attitudes. The idea is that strong attitudes will be more predictive of subsequent behavior. Several different dimensions of attitude strength have been identified, for example, the extremity of one's attitude, the certainty with which one holds a particular attitude, or whether one has a vested interest in the attitude object (e.g., Petty & Krosnick, 1995). Consistent across most attempts at understanding attitude strength, however, is the idea that attitudes are unidimensional, bipolar constructs. In contrast, the bidimensional view of attitudes provides both an index of attitude strength as well as a reconceptualization of the concept of attitude.

The bidimensional model of attitudes extends the unidimensional view of attitudes by arguing that individuals can simultaneously hold positive *and* negative attitudes that are not perfectly (negatively) correlated with one another. In other words, it is possible for individuals to simultaneously evaluate an attitude object as being positive *and* negative, or to be *attitudinally ambivalent*. Conner and Sparks (2002) identify two defining characteristics of attitudinal ambivalence, namely: (a) how *intense* the positive and negative evaluations are; (b) the extent to which the positive and negative evaluations are *similar*. This view is captured in Thompson, Zanna, and Griffin's (1995, p. 367) definition of ambivalence as being when an individual "is inclined to give it [an attitude object] equivalently strong positive and negative evaluations". Research into attitudinal ambivalence has expanded in recent years, primarily because less ambivalent attitudes are thought to share a number of the characteristics associated with "strong" attitudes, namely: predictive validity, stability over time, resistance to persuasion and influence on information processing (Krosnick & Petty, 1995; for recent reviews see Conner & Sparks, 2002; Jonas, Brömer, & Diehl, 2000). To further elucidate the concept of attitudinal ambivalence, we first consider the way in which ambivalence has been operationalized before reviewing the effects of attitudinal ambivalence on the attitude–behavior relationship.

### Measurement of attitudinal ambivalence

There is currently a lack of consensus about the best means to measure ambivalence (Breckler, 1994; Conner & Sparks, 2002; Priester & Petty, 1996; Thompson et al., 1995). Conner and Sparks (2002) identify three dimensions along which ambivalence measures differ.

First, measures of ambivalence differ in terms of the content of ambivalence judgments. Attitudes are commonly regarded as consisting of distinct evaluative, affective and cognitive components (e.g., Eagly & Chaiken, 1993). In other words, people respond to attitude objects by making evaluations, expressing feelings or by cognitively processing aspects of the object. Thus, individuals may experience intra-attitudinal conflicts within the evaluative, cognitive, and affective components, or inter-attitudinal conflicts between cognitive/affective, evaluative/affective and evaluative/cognitive components. We return to these distinctions later in the chapter.

Second, measures of ambivalence differ in terms of whether they are felt (direct) or potential (indirect). Measures of felt ambivalence tap the subjective impression of the extent to which the individual's attitude is experienced as "mixed" or consisting of both positive and negative evaluations, beliefs or feelings. For example, Priester and Petty (1996) asked participants to rate their subjective ("felt") ambivalence on 11-point scales anchored with *feel no conflict at all, feel no indecision at all* (= 0) and *feel maximum conflict, feel maximum indecision* (= 10), respectively. Such measures may be important in tapping the extent to which ambivalence is experienced as unpleasant (i.e., similar to the idea of cognitive dissonance, high levels of felt ambivalence may motivate individuals to attempt to resolve the ambivalence, see Festinger, 1957). However, in general, such measures appear to be more open to extraneous influences that can undermine their validity (Bassili, 1996). For example, Newby-Clark, McGregor, and Zanna (2002) have shown that the relationship between felt and potential ambivalence is dependent upon the extent to which the opposing poles are salient. Thus, people's felt ambivalence may be affected by extraneous influences, and—with the exception of studies that deliberately manipulate salience—it is not clear whether the information upon which to form judgments of felt ambivalence are ordinarily available to consciousness.

Measures of potential ambivalence employ separate measures of the positive and negative thoughts, feelings or beliefs that an attitude object produces. Such measures possess some similarity to Bassili's (1996) operative indices of attitude strength. Operative indices of attitude strength are derived from the attitude judgment process or its outcomes (e.g., response latency). Such measures are to be preferred to the extent that they do not require the respondent to combine the positive and negative evaluations in a biased manner. Nevertheless, the term potential ambivalence would appear appropriate because the individual with high levels of potential ambivalence may not experience high levels of experienced ambivalence unless both positive and negative evaluations upon which the potential ambivalence is based is similarly highly accessible (Conner & Sparks, 2002; Newby-Clark et al., 2002).

Third, ambivalence measures can differ in whether the measures tap beliefs or overall evaluations. Belief-based measures of ambivalence can either be closed ended or open ended. Closed-ended measures typically ask respondents to select the most important beliefs about an attitude object and then compute a measure of ambivalence from the number of positive and negative beliefs selected (e.g., van der Pligt, de Vries, Manstead, & van Harreveld, 2000). Open-ended belief-based measures require respondents to first generate and then evaluate positively and negatively valenced beliefs about the attitude object (e.g., Maio, Bell, & Esses, 1996; Povey, Wellens, & Conner, 2001). Such measures appear to have considerable face validity compared with other measures of ambivalence.

There are now several "overall evaluation" based measures of attitudinal ambivalence, with most being based upon the *split semantic differential* scale (Kaplan, 1972), the evolution of which is shown in Figure 6.1 (see also Jonas et al., 2000). Traditionally, participants are asked to rate their attitude toward an object on a 7-point bipolar ($-3$ to $+3$) semantic differential scale anchored with antonymous adjectives, such as *bad* ($-3$) and *good* ($+3$), as shown in Figure 6.1, panel A(i). By splitting the bipolar scale at the midpoint (Figure 6.1, panel Aii), it is possible to ask participants to rate the positive and negative poles independently (Figure 6.1, panel B). Typically, participants are asked to focus on the positive (negative) aspects of a particular attitude object while ignoring all the negative (positive) aspects of that object. These evaluations are then combined according to one of seven formulae (see Jonas et al., 2000), of which the "Griffin index" (Thompson et al., 1995) arguably

A (i): Semantic differential scale

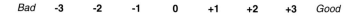

Bad  -3   -2   -1   0   +1   +2   +3   Good

A (ii): Semantic differential scale

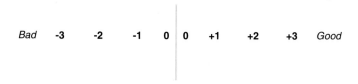

Bad  -3   -2   -1   0 | 0   +1   +2   +3   Good

B: Split semantic differential scale (e.g., Kaplan, 1972)

Not at all   4   3   2   1 | Extremely
bad                          | bad

                  Not at all | 1   2   3   4   Extremely
                       good  |                 good

*Figure 6.1* Evolution of the split semantic differential scale.

produces the measure of ambivalence with the most desirable characteristics. The Griffin index (Thompson et al., 1995) captures the intensity of the positive and negative evaluations as well as the level of similarity between the two evaluations, thus:

Ambivalence = (positive + negative)/2 – | positive – negative |

In other words, greater ambivalence is associated with positive and negative evaluations that are both intense and similar (e.g., Breckler, 1994). Interestingly, both Riketta (2000) and Priester and Petty (1996) have reported that the Griffin index is more closely correlated with experienced ambivalence than any other index ($rs$ = .62 and .44, respectively). This implies that the

Griffin measure of potential ambivalence is closer to felt ambivalence than any other measure.

### Consequences of attitudinal ambivalence

Attitudinal ambivalence has traditionally been treated as a measure of attitude strength with lower levels of ambivalence being associated with a strong attitude. Although there have been several empirical studies of the interrelationship of attitude strength measures (e.g., Bassili, 1996; Eagly & Chaiken, 1993; Jonas et al., 2000; Krosnick, Boninger, Chuang, Berent, & Carnot, 1993; Pomerantz, Chaiken, & Tordesillas, 1995), the relationship of ambivalence to the full range of attitude strength measures remains under-researched (Conner & Sparks, 2002). Ambivalence is found to be associated with lower accessibility of the attitude (Bargh, Chaiken, Govender, & Pratto, 1992; Brömer, 1998), lower attitude extremity (Maio et al., 1996), lower attitude certainty (Bassili, 1996; Jonas, Diehl, & Brömer, 1997), but is unrelated to evaluative-cognitive or evaluative-affective consistency (Maio et al., 1996). However, the relationship of ambivalence to other attitude strength dimensions such as attitude importance, knowledge, interest, involvement and intensity remains an issue for further research. In addition, prior research has examined each correlate of attitudinal ambivalence for only single attitude objects or a small set of attitude objects; the relations across a range of attitude objects should be examined.

If attitudinal ambivalence is regarded as a facet of attitude strength, one would expect that, compared with univalent attitudes, ambivalent attitudes should be less stable over time, more pliable, exert less influence on information processing and, perhaps most importantly, be less predictive of behavior (Conner & Sparks, 2002). Before focusing on research into the effects of ambivalence on the attitude–behavior relationship, we will briefly consider the rationale for expecting less ambivalent attitudes to be more predictive of behavior.

A key prediction for a measure of attitude strength is that strong attitudes should be more likely to predict behavior than weak attitudes (Converse, 1995, p. xi; Krosnick & Petty, 1995, p. 3). As Schwartz (1978) noted, an attitude assessed at one time is unlikely to predict behavior at a later time if the attitude does not persist over the intervening time interval. Thus, at least part of the greater impact of strong attitudes on behavior may be attributable to strong attitudes being more likely to persist over time. In spite of a number of null findings (see Conner & Sparks, 2002 for a review), there does seem to be evidence to support the idea that univalent attitudes are more stable than ambivalent attitudes. For example, Bargh et al. (1992) reported that attitudinal ambivalence was negatively correlated with attitude stability. More recently, Conner (2004a, Study 2) found that inducing attitudinal ambivalence actually produced significantly more stable attitudes in a low ambivalence group compared with a high ambivalence group.

## Attitudes-as-constructions model

Wilson and Hodges' (1992) *attitudes-as-constructions* model (see also Erber, Hodges, & Wilson, 1995; Zaller & Feldman, 1992) provides one account of why ambivalent attitudes might be less stable than univalent attitudes. The attitudes-as-constructions model argues that attitudes are temporary constructs, meaning that when they are required (e.g., for decision making), they are constructed on the spot (i.e., from accessible information). Thus, the degree of attitude stability is a function of the extent to which similarly valenced information is retrieved each time the attitude is constructed, which in turn is dependent upon the consistency of the underlying database. In other words, attitudes based on an evaluatively consistent database of information are more stable than attitudes based on an evaluatively inconsistent database (see Erber et al., 1995). Armitage (2003) has extended this approach to examine attitude–behavior relations per se, finding that attitudes based on homogeneous sets of beliefs (i.e., an evaluatively consistent database) were significantly more predictive of subsequent behavior than were attitudes based on heterogeneous belief sets (i.e., an evaluatively inconsistent database).

In terms of attitudinal ambivalence, one would therefore predict that attitudes based only on positive or negative information about the attitude object (i.e., univalent attitudes) will be temporally stable and more predictive of subsequent behavior. In contrast, assuming that the information search is not completely exhaustive, ambivalent individuals are more likely to retrieve information that varies in valence from occasion to occasion. In other words, the retrieved set of information will be positive on some occasions and negative on others. If this occurs, respondents will appear to have attitudes that switch in valence. This is likely to result in less stable attitudes and lower consistency between attitudes and behavior because the behavior may be based upon a different attitude to that generated in response to the initial measurement of attitude. One consequence of this analysis is that ambivalence is more likely to moderate attitude–behavior relationships when the interval between the measurement of the two is prolonged.

However, other mechanisms may also influence the ability of strong (univalent) attitudes to influence behavior compared to weaker (ambivalent) attitudes. For example, Fazio (1986, 1995) has argued that attitudes influence our behavior in part by shaping our perceptions of the world. That is, the capacity of an attitude to predict behavior is partly dependent on the ability of the attitude to bias perceptions of the attitude object and the context in which the behavior is performed. Strong attitudes are assumed to be more readily accessible and so more likely to produce these biasing effects. Demonstrating such an effect for ambivalence would support the view that ambivalence is a component of attitude strength. The following sections focus on the relationship between attitudes and behavior.

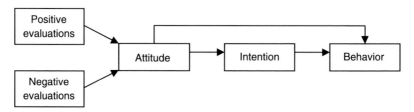

*Figure 6.2* Attitude–intention–behavior model.

## Behavioral intentions as mediators of the attitude–behavior relationship

Thus far, we have considered the impact that attitudinal ambivalence might have on the strength of one's attitude, focusing on the effects on attitude–behavior relations. In other words, we have considered the potential moderating effect of attitudinal ambivalence on the attitude–behavior relationship (Baron & Kenny, 1986). Before we give in depth consideration to the moderating effects of attitudinal ambivalence, it is worth discussing possible *mediators* of the effects of attitudes on behavior. In other words, it is important to consider variables through which attitudes affect behavior. Perhaps the most widely researched mediator is *behavioral intention* (e.g., Ajzen, 1991; Fishbein & Ajzen, 1975, see Figure 6.2). Behavioral intentions are defined as people's decisions to perform particular behaviors and represent a summary of people's motivation to act: the more an individual *intends* to do something, the more likely that behavior is to be performed (for a review see Sheeran, 2002).[1]

Behavioral intentions are most closely associated with research into the theories of reasoned action (Fishbein & Ajzen, 1975) and planned behavior (Ajzen, 1991). Of particular relevance to the present discussion is the fact that both theories argue that the lack of correspondence between attitudes and behavior can be attributed in part to the mediating role of behavioral intentions. Consistent with accumulated research (e.g., Armitage & Conner, 2001), the model in Figure 6.2 shows that attitudes do not (necessarily) determine behavior directly and that the effects of attitudes on behavior can be mediated through behavioral intentions. In fact, some researchers regard behavioral intentions as being so closely related to behavior that they use intentions as proxy measures of behavior (e.g., Jonas et al., 1997). Nonetheless, the implication is that researchers interested in the relationship between attitudes and

---

1 Note that behavioral intentions encapsulate the influences of a number of other motivational variables, most notably subjective norms and perceived behavioral control (see Ajzen, 1991). These variables are not considered here because they are regarded as being independent of attitudes and because they consistently explain less variance in behavioral intentions than do attitudes (see Armitage & Conner, 2001).

behavior might need to consider controlling for the potential effects of behavioral intentions. More importantly, the model presented in Figure 6.2 raises three key questions as to the role of attitudinal ambivalence and its influence on behavior. The first question concerns the attitude–intention relationship: does ambivalence moderate the attitude–intention relationship? If, as expected, less ambivalent attitudes are more predictive of intentions, the question then arises: what are the implications for the intention–behavior relationship (question 2)? Given that intentions are expected to mediate the attitude–behavior relationship, one possibility is that intentions formed on the basis of ambivalent attitudes will be undermined and therefore less predictive of subsequent behavior. The third question relates to the attitude–behavior relationship: if the effects of attitude on behavior are mediated by intention in all cases, one might expect that ambivalence would exert no direct effect on the attitude–behavior relationship. Alternatively, is it possible for sufficiently univalent attitudes to be so strong as to "by-pass" intentions and exert a direct effect on behavior? These issues are addressed in the following sections.

### *Summary*

Univalent attitudes are likely to be more predictive of behavior than ambivalent attitudes. However, given that behavioral intentions have been shown to consistently mediate the relationship between attitudes and behavior, the question then arises: What is the role of attitudinal ambivalence with respect to the relationships between attitudes, intentions *and* behavior? The following sections deal with research into the moderating effects of attitudinal ambivalence by examining each of the component relationships in turn, beginning with the attitude–intention relationship, followed by the attitude–behavior relationship and finally the intention–behavior relationship (see Figure 6.2).

In examining the moderating effects of attitudinal ambivalence two important difficulties need to be overcome. First, simple comparisons of correlations between variables (e.g., attitude and behavior) in high and low ambivalence groups can be inappropriate because the two groups usually vary in terms of variance in attitudes. This can be addressed by comparing variances in the two groups or through the use of moderated regression analysis examining the significance of the interaction between attitudes and ambivalence after taking account of the independent effects of these two variables (Baron & Kenny, 1986). Second, the confound between ambivalence and attitude extremity needs to be taken into account: univalent attitudes tend to be more extreme than ambivalent attitudes. For example, Krosnick et al. (1993) report a correlation of $-.90$ between ambivalence and attitude extremity (see also Thompson et al., 1995) and independent manipulations of attitude extremity have been shown to increase attitude–behavior correspondence from $r = .19$ to $r = .85$ (Kallgren & Wood, 1986). The extent of this problem can be identified by examining the correlation between ambivalence and attitude extremity (e.g., Conner, Sparks, Povey, James, Shepherd, & Armitage, 2002). Alternatively, a median split procedure can be employed to classify individuals into higher and lower ambivalence groups at each level of the attitude measure and so disconfound ambivalence from attitude extremity (e.g., Conner, Povey, Sparks, James, & Shepherd, 2002).

## Attitude–intention relationship

Research into the influence of ambivalence on the attitude–intention relationship has typically utilized cross-sectional survey designs. One study reported by Sparks, Conner, James, Shepherd, and Povey (2001) provides a useful example. Sparks et al.'s (2001) study was designed to examine the influence of attitudinal ambivalence on attitudes towards meat ($n = 156$) and chocolate consumption ($n = 154$). Participants completed standard measures of attitude and behavioral intention; attitudinal ambivalence was computed in accordance with the Griffin index (Thompson et al., 1995). Consistent with Baron and Kenny's (1986) recommendations, which take account of differences in variance between high and low ambivalence groups, behavioral intention was regressed on attitude, ambivalence and the attitude-by-ambivalence interaction term. These analyses revealed a significant negative $\beta$-weight for the attitude $x$ ambivalence interaction term for both meat and chocolate consumption. This indicates that greater levels of ambivalence were associated with weaker attitude–intention relations. In a related study of intentions to consume meat, vegetarian, or vegan diets, Povey et al. (2001) reported comparable findings using an open-ended belief-based measure of ambivalence: ambivalent attitudes were again less predictive of intentions than were univalent attitudes.

However, not all tests of the effects of ambivalence on the attitude–intention relationship have produced consistent findings. For example, using similar measures across 20 different eating behaviors and controlling for the effects of attitude extremity, Conner et al. (2003) did not find that attitudinal ambivalence moderated the attitude–intention relationship in multivariate analyses of between-participants data or univariate analyses of within-participants data. Conner, Sherlock, and Orbell (1998) similarly failed to find that attitudinal ambivalence attenuated the relationship between attitudes and intention with respect to taking ecstasy. There are a number of potential explanations for the inconsistencies between these studies, but we will focus on the two that seem most relevant. First, Conner et al.'s (1998, 2003) studies essentially reveal null effects, which are difficult to interpret because they might reflect sampling bias or measurement error. The second explanation relates to the cross-sectional designs that were employed in these studies: cross-sectional designs increase the likelihood that the data will be affected by a desire to respond consistently to questionnaires that are presented concurrently, thereby artificially inflating the strength of the attitude–intention relations, independently of ambivalence. Indeed, a growing body of research demonstrates that such concurrent measurement introduces a host of social judgment biases (e.g., Haddock & Carrick, 1999; Schwarz & Bless, 1992).

There have been very few attempts to experimentally manipulate attitudinal ambivalence. Jonas et al. (1997) present two experimental tests of the influence of attitudinal ambivalence on the attitude–intention relationship. Jonas et al. (1997) randomized participants to receive either an evaluatively consistent or evaluatively inconsistent message about novel shampoos, and asked them to rate their attitudes, intentions and ambivalence. The message manipulation successfully increased attitudinal ambivalence in the evaluatively inconsistent group. Interestingly, Jonas et al. (1997) hypothesized that attitudinal ambivalence would *augment* the relationship between attitude and intention. This was based on the rationale that evaluative inconsistency would reduce people's confidence in their attitudes, thereby increasing systematic message processing and increasing attitude–intention consistency. Jonas et al.'s (1997) findings corroborated their hypotheses: attitudinal ambivalence was associated with both increased systematic information processing and augmented attitude–intention relationships.

Although Jonas et al. (1997) replicated their findings in two experimental studies, there are a number of additional factors that might explain why the findings seem to be at odds with the theory underpinning attitudinal ambivalence. Indeed, as Jonas et al. (1997) argue: "under *certain* conditions attitudinal ambivalence may actually increase the consistency between attitudes and intentions" (p. 193, emphasis added), and it is these conditions we now consider. First, there are differences between the attitude objects used by Jonas et al. (1997) and those used by (for example) Sparks et al. (2001) and Povey et al. (2001). Whereas Jonas et al. (1997) asked people to rate fictional shampoos, Sparks et al. (2001) and Povey et al. (2001) asked people about their personal food choices. In terms of Wilson and Hodges' (1992) attitudes-as-constructions model, rating novel shampoo involves constructing a new attitude whereas food choices are likely to have been made before. Thus Jonas et al.'s (1997) task may have been more difficult (i.e., one demanding systematic processing) than rating food choices that are encountered in everyday life. Jonas et al.'s (1997) findings might therefore be explained as: ambivalence further increases systematic processing under demanding conditions. Second, Jonas et al. (1997) used an alternative measure of ambivalence (the Kaplan 1972 index), which has different properties to the Griffin index, notably that it fails to conform fully with Breckler's (1994) recommendations concerning the measurement of ambivalence (see Thompson et al., 1995 for further details). Although the Kaplan and Griffin indices are correlated, one might expect that manipulation of ambivalence would exacerbate any inconsistencies. In spite of these reservations, Jonas et al.'s (1997) findings are intriguing and warrant further investigation. In particular, it would be interesting to contrast the effects of novel and familiar stimuli on judgments made under conditions of ambivalence. Overall, then, the weak and inconsistent effects of ambivalence on the attitude–intention relationship support a need for more use of prospective designs and more experimental manipulations of ambivalence.

Armitage and Conner (2000, Study 1) used a prospective design to examine people's attitudes and intentions with respect to eating a low-fat diet. Attitude and ambivalence were measured contemporaneously while behavioral intention was measured five months later. Armitage and Conner (2000, Study 1) found that univalent attitudes were significantly more predictive of intentions five months later than were ambivalent attitudes. Similarly, Conner (2004b) attempted to address a number of these problems by manipulating ambivalence experimentally and then assessing the moderating effects of ambivalence on attitude–intention relationships both cross-sectionally and prospectively (over a period of two weeks). The target behavior was visiting a specific World Wide Web site. Ambivalence was manipulated through the presentation of a balanced set of arguments in favor and against visiting this website. Given the definition of ambivalence employed here, as perceiving equivalently strong positive and negative evaluations, it was expected that the presentation of strong arguments *both* in favor and against visiting the website would produce high levels of ambivalence and so attenuate the attitude–intention relationship compared to the presentation of weak arguments both in favor and against visiting the website. Attitudes and intentions were assessed after reading the arguments and two weeks later (along with an objective measure of behavior; see below). The manipulation was shown to have no impact on overall attitudes but produced two groups varying in attitudinal ambivalence. For both the cross-sectional comparison and prospective comparison, the relationship between attitudes and intentions were significantly weaker in the high ambivalence group compared to the low ambivalence group.

In sum, the weight of evidence would support the idea that attitudinal ambivalence moderates the attitude–intention relationship, such that univalent attitudes are more predictive of intentions than ambivalent attitudes (see Table 6.1 for a summary of these findings). Moreover, the effects can persist over periods of up to five months, suggesting that attitudinal ambivalence is an important facet of attitude strength. However, it seems that studies employing cross-sectional designs produce inconsistent findings, possibly because they are vulnerable to social judgment effects. Further studies employing prospective and experimental designs are required to determine the factors underlying the different moderating effects of ambivalence on attitude–intention relationships. Moreover, given that intentions do not always predict behavior (Sheeran, 2002), the question remains as to the nature of the relationships between attitudinal ambivalence, intention, and actual behavior.

## Attitude–behavior relationship

The second pathway of interest in Figure 6.2 concerns the direct relationship between attitudes and behavior. One early test of the moderating effect of

*Table 6.1* Summary of the effects of attitudinal ambivalence on attitude–intention–
behavior relations

| Authors | Design | A → I | A → B | I → B |
|---|---|---|---|---|
| Armitage and Conner (2000) Study 1, eating a low-fat diet | Prospective | √ | √ | × |
| Conner (2004b) visiting a World Wide Website | Experimental | √ | √ | √ |
| Conner et al. (1998) Study 2, using ecstasy | Cross-sectional for intention; prospective for behavior | 0 | 0 | √ |
| Conner et al. (2003) 20 healthy eating behaviors | Cross-sectional for intention; prospective for behavior | 0 | √ | × |
| Conner et al. (2002) Study 1, eating a low-fat diet | Cross-sectional for intention; prospective for behavior | 0 | √ | 0 |
| Conner et al. (2002) Study 1, eating five portions of fruit and vegetables per day | Cross-sectional for intention; prospective for behavior | 0 | √ | 0 |
| Conner et al. (2002) Study 2, eating a low-fat diet | Cross-sectional for intention; prospective for behavior | 0 | √ | 0 |
| Jonas et al. (1997) Study 1, choosing novel shampoos | Experimental | × | N/A | N/A |
| Jonas et al. (1997) Study 2, choosing novel shampoos | Experimental | × | N/A | N/A |
| Moore (1973)[a] voting for reinstatement of capital punishment | Cross-sectional | N/A | √ | N/A |
| Moore (1980)[a] recycling | Cross-sectional | N/A | √ | N/A |
| Moore (1980)[a] gambling | Cross-sectional | √ | N/A | N/A |
| Moore (1980)[a] pet owning[b] | Cross-sectional | √ | √ | N/A |
| Povey et al. (2001) eating a meat diet | Cross-sectional | √ | N/A | N/A |
| Povey et al. (2001) eating a vegetarian diet | Cross-sectional | √ | N/A | N/A |
| Povey et al. (2001) eating a vegan diet | Cross-sectional | √ | N/A | N/A |
| Sparks et al. (2001) chocolate consumption | Cross-sectional | √ | N/A | N/A |
| Sparks et al. (2001) meat consumption | Cross-sectional | √ | N/A | N/A |

*Note.* A → I = Attitude–Intention Relationship; A → B = Attitude–Behavior Relationship; I → B = Intention–Behavior Relationship. √ = greater ambivalence *attenuates* the specified relationship; 0 = no significant effect of ambivalence; × = greater ambivalence *augments* the specified relationship. [a]These papers do not report formal tests of the moderator hypothesis, but the magnitude of the zero-order correlations is in the predicted direction. [b]Participants were asked to report "their intended or actual pet ownership" (Moore, 1980, p. 206).

ambivalence on the attitude-behavior relationship was conducted by Moore (1973), who showed that ambivalent attitudes were less predictive of whether or not students voted to have capital punishment reinstated than were univalent attitudes. However, consistent with work on the attitude–intention relationship Moore's (1973) study was cross-sectional, reducing confidence in the generalizability of the findings. In fact, the attitude–behavior pathway has received less research attention than the attitude–intention relationship because of the logistics associated with conducting studies with prospective designs. For example, it is important to ensure a large retest sample as well as a satisfactory measure of behavior. Two recent studies by Conner et al. (2002) examined the effects of attitudinal ambivalence on food intake and used a validated nutrition measure to obtain details about dietary intake. In order to rule out competing explanations of the findings, Study 1 tested the attitude–behavior relationship across one month and Study 2 examined the attitude–behavior relationship across three months. Consistent with predictions, both studies showed that lower levels of attitudinal ambivalence (as measured by the Griffin index) were associated with attitudes that were more predictive of behavior. Importantly, these findings remained when the effects of past behavior were statistically controlled (Conner et al., 2002, Study 2).

Conner et al. (2003) extended this work by explicitly controlling for the potential confound between ambivalence and extremity of attitudes. Moreover, rather than focusing solely on between-participants analyses, Conner et al. (2003) also examined the moderating effects of ambivalence within-participants by examining attitudes toward 20 healthy eating behaviors (e.g., eating a healthy breakfast, eating food containing vitamins). The within-person analyses allowed Conner et al. (2003) to examine the behavioral decision-making process more closely than traditional between-persons analyses, which assume that what a person does is best described in relation to others. Both forms of analyses were consistent: ambivalence moderated the attitude–behavior relationship such that greater ambivalence was associated with attenuated attitude–behavior relations. These findings are important because within- and between-persons analyses are independent, nevertheless similar findings emerged even in the presence of alternative sources of variation (Conner et al., 2003).

Armitage and Conner (2000, Study 1) extended these findings by controlling for the effects of behavioral intentions. The target behavior was eating a low-fat diet. Univalent attitudes were found to be significantly more predictive of behavior than were ambivalent attitudes. Importantly, not only were the effects on behavior tested across an eight-month time period, but the analyses also controlled for the effects of behavioral intention. The latter finding is of particular interest because it suggests that sufficiently univalent attitudes can actually "by-pass" intentions (Figure 6.2). This finding would seem to contradict models such as the theory of planned behavior, which regard behavioral intentions as complete mediators of the attitude–behavior relationship (e.g., Ajzen, 1991). The implication is that attitudes can be directly predictive of behavior when they are univalent but that when attitudes are ambivalent, behavior is determined by other variables such as behavioral intentions. This is important because many studies employ a measure of behavioral intention to act as a proxy for actual behavior: Armitage and Conner's (2000, Study 1) work suggests that this assumption is likely to be unwarranted for a large proportion of people.

More recently, Conner (2004b) examined the effects of manipulating ambivalence on the relationship between attitudes and subsequent behavior. Consistent with Conner et al. (2002, Study 2) and Armitage and Conner (2000, Study 1), the ambivalence manipulation attenuated the prospective relationship between attitudes and an objective measure of behavior (visiting a specified World Wide Web site) such that ambivalent attitudes were significantly weaker predictors of behavior than univalent attitudes. Thus, consistent with predictions, univalent attitudes are more predictive of behavior than ambivalent attitudes (see Table 6.1 for a summary of these findings).

## Intention–behavior relationship

The third pathway displayed in Figure 6.2 is that between intention and behavior. Although not intuitively linked with research into attitudinal ambivalence, there are grounds for expecting attitudinal ambivalence to influence the intention–behavior relationship. First, we have already noted that intention and behavior are largely driven by univalent attitudes, and so the question arises as to what drives the behavior of individuals with ambivalent attitudes. Given that the majority of research suggests that intentions are based principally on attitudes (e.g., Armitage & Conner, 2001) and that intentions based upon attitudes are more predictive of subsequent behavior than attitudes based on subjective norms (see Sheeran, Norman, & Orbell, 1999), one possibility is that attitudinal ambivalence might attenuate the intention–behavior relationship. Thus, weaker (i.e., ambivalent) attitudes might weaken intentions and thereby weaken intention–behavior correspondence. One mechanism for such effects might be stability: given that intention stability exerts similar effects to attitude stability, namely that stable intentions/attitudes are more predictive of behavior (e.g., Conner, Sheeran, Norman, & Armitage, 2000), it is possible that unstable attitudes create unstable intentions that are less predictive of behavior. The alternative view is that attitudinal ambivalence might *augment* the intention–behavior relationship: if people *feel* ambivalent about an attitude object, they may not want to base their decisions (i.e., intentions) on their attitudes. Instead, they might look to others for guidance, or behave in ways that are consistent with their habits. In other words, it is possible that attitudinal ambivalence might enhance intention–behavior correspondence because the intentions of people with ambivalent attitudes may be based on norms, habits, or other determinants of behavioral intentions (e.g., Conner & Armitage, 1998).

The second line of reasoning that links attitudinal ambivalence with intention–behavior relations concerns the effects of attitudinal ambivalence on information processing. For example, Jonas et al. (1997) have shown that attitudinal ambivalence is closely associated with increased systematic information processing (see also Maio et al., 1996; Maio, Esses, & Bell, 2000; Maio, Greenland, Bernard, & Esses, 2001). These studies suggest that individuals with ambivalent attitudes try to reconcile the positive and negative poles of their attitudes through greater information processing. Independent lines of research suggest that enhanced systematic information processing leads to better-formed intentions (see Bagozzi & Yi, 1989). In sum, research to date suggests that attitudinal ambivalence is likely to influence the intention–behavior relationship, although it is not clear whether the relationship is likely to be augmented or attenuated with increased attitudinal ambivalence.

In fact, four studies have investigated the effects of attitudinal ambivalence on the intention–behavior relationship. Conner et al. (1998) examined the role of attitudinal ambivalence in relation to ecstasy use, "to see if those with lower levels of ambivalence (stronger attitudes) showed significantly stronger relationships between TPB [theory of planned behavior] components and subsequent behavior" (p. 298). Conner et al. (1998) found that, consistent with their predictions, greater attitudinal ambivalence was associated with an attenuated intention–behavior relationship. The implication is that weaker, more ambivalent attitudes undermine the intention–behavior relationship. However, Conner et al. (1998) found no moderating effect of ambivalence on either attitude–intention or attitude–behavior relations, suggesting that ambivalence did not exert its influence via attitude. This finding is of particular interest because it implies that ambivalence exerted direct effects on intention. Moreover, Conner (2004b) has shown that a manipulation of ambivalence attenuated the prospective relationship between intentions and an objective measure of behavior such that intentions formed in the high ambivalence condition were significantly weaker predictors of behavior than intentions formed in the low ambivalence condition. Thus, it seems that if it is possible for people to simultaneously possess both positive and negative evaluations, it must also be possible to have conflicting intentions.

Armitage and Conner (2000, Study 1) also investigated the effects of attitudinal ambivalence on the intention–behavior relationship. Controlling for the effects of attitude, Armitage and Conner (2000, Study 1) found that when attitudes were ambivalent, behavioral intentions with respect to eating a low-fat diet were significantly more predictive of behavior. These findings were interpreted as showing evidence of systematic information processing. Armitage and Conner (2000) reasoned that, consistent with Bagozzi and Yi's (1989) intention formation manipulation, participants with ambivalent attitudes were more likely to weigh up the pros and cons associated with engaging in a particular behavior (cf. Jonas et al., 1997; Maio et al., 2000; Maio et al., 2001). Controlling for the effects of attitude extremity, Conner et al. (2003) replicated this finding by showing that the behavioral intentions of individuals low in ambivalence were not significantly related to behavior ($\beta$ = .05, *ns*), unlike those of high ambivalence participants ($\beta$ = .60, $p < .001$).[2] Importantly, Conner et al. (2003) included variables from the theory of planned behavior in order to explore the hypothesis that individuals with ambivalent attitudes are more likely to base their intentions on variables other than attitudes. Contrary to expectations, there were no differences between the univalent and ambivalent attitude groups and further research is required to see whether variables such as habits better predict the behavior of individuals with ambivalent attitudes.

The discrepancy between the studies by Conner et al. (1998) and Conner (2004b) on the one hand and by Armitage and Conner (2000, Study 1) and Conner et al. (2003) on the other might be accounted for by the nature of the attitude object. Notably, both Armitage and Conner and Conner et al. (2003) examined food choice, whereas Conner et al. (1998) studied ecstasy use and Conner (2004b) looked at visiting a web site. Aside from the more obvious dissimilarities, Conner et al. (1998) found that, out of the 12 different behaviors they tested, ecstasy use produced the least amount of ambivalence ($M$ = 0.22). Moreover, ecstasy ambivalence differed significantly from ambivalence about reducing fat intake ($M$ = 0.34). One intriguing possibility is that up to a certain level (perhaps before the individual *feels* ambivalent), potential ambivalence undermines the intention–behavior relationship, but once a person starts to experience ambivalence, efforts are made to resolve the ambivalence, resulting in increased systematic information processing and an augmented intention–behavior relationship (cf. Armitage, Povey, & Arden, 2003; Jonas et al., 1997; Maio et al., 1996; Maio et al., 2000; Maio et al., 2001).

In sum, the studies reviewed above suggest that attitudinal ambivalence generally moderates the intention–behavior relationship (see Table 6.1 for a summary of these findings). However, whether greater ambivalence is associated with an augmented or attenuated intention–behavior relationship is clearly a matter for future research. Clearly, further work that more systematically examines the direction of the moderator effect is required. One possible avenue for this research might be to consider the roles of both potential (operative) and felt (meta-judgmental) ambivalence in moderating the intention–behavior relationship.

---

2 Note that although differences were found between $\beta$ coefficients, examination of the zero-order correlations reveals a slightly different pattern of findings. Although nonsignificant, differences in the between-persons zero-order correlations actually go in the opposite direction (i.e., greater ambivalence was associated with attenuated intention–behavior relations). Again, the zero-order within-person correlations did not differ significantly between the ambivalent and univalent groups, but here greater ambivalence was associated with an *augmented* intention–behavior relationship.

## Summary and directions for future research

This chapter shows that attitudinal ambivalence exerts effects on the relationships between attitudes, intentions and behavior. Univalent attitudes are clearly more predictive of subsequent behavior, whether felt or potential ambivalence is measured. Less clear, however, are the effects of ambivalence on attitude–intention and intention–behavior relationships. Although some studies show that ambivalence attenuates these relationships, others show that ambivalence augments them. Given that the effects of ambivalence on the attitude–behavior relationship seem so unambiguous, the implication is that further research into the effects of ambivalence on intentions per se is required. Moreover, in reviewing this research, it is clear that there are currently a number of gaps in knowledge.

First, the vast majority of studies (with the exceptions of Conner, 2002a, 2004b; Conner et al., 1998; Jonas et al., 1997) have investigated attitudinal ambivalence in the domain of food choice. In fact, several commentators have noted that various aspects of food choice are particularly likely to generate ambivalence (e.g., Conner & Armitage, 2002). For example, Sparks et al. (2001) point out that "people may have mixed feelings about consuming animal products because the sensory appeal of such products may be accompanied by moral concerns with animal welfare issues" (p. 56). By the same token, the positive evaluations concerning the palatability of a chocolate bar may be experienced simultaneously with negative evaluations associated with potential weight gain. It is possible that food choice may be a domain in which the concept of attitudinal ambivalence is a particularly helpful aid to our understanding of the relationship between attitudes and behavior. Although this is undoubtedly the case, there have been demonstrations of attitudinal ambivalence in relation to interpersonal relationships (Priester & Petty, 2001); social groups (Maio et al., 2000); and alcohol consumption (Morgan & Grube, 1994).

The next step is to examine these attitude–behavior relations in a broader range of contexts. A related issue concerns measuring behavior: more robust indices of behavior are required to increase confidence in conclusions drawn. For example, self-reports of the frequency with which behavior is performed are often used as a proxy measure of behavior when objective assessments are unavailable, yet the validity of these data are rarely assessed. Nonetheless, early findings are encouraging: studies that have employed more objective assessments of behavior are broadly consistent with previous studies (e.g., Conner, 2004b).

The second area that requires further research attention concerns experimental manipulation of ambivalence. As far as we are aware, only Conner (2004b) has manipulated ambivalence and then studied the attitude–intention–behavior relationship. Further experimental tests are required to establish a causal link between the induction of ambivalence and the attenuation of the attitude–behavior relationship.

## Intra- and inter-component ambivalence

This chapter has focused primarily on attitudinal ambivalence, defined as a state in which an attitude object is simultaneously evaluated positively *and* negatively (e.g., Thompson et al., 1995). However, attitudes are commonly regarded as consisting of distinct evaluative, affective and cognitive components (e.g., Eagly & Chaiken, 1993). In other words, people respond to attitude objects by making evaluations, expressing feelings or by cognitively processing aspects of the object. Thus, the present chapter focuses on one aspect of intra-component ambivalence: intra-evaluative ambivalence. Indeed, whereas much of the research presented here has measured ambivalence evaluatively by asking participants to rate separately the positive or negative *things* associated with an attitude object (Armitage & Conner, 2000, p. 1423),[3] other researchers have specifically asked participants to consider the positive/negative *feelings* (Bargh et al., 1992, p. 896) or the positive/negative *thoughts* (Jonas et al., 1997, pp. 196, 200) associated with an attitude object. Further research is required to examine the differential effects of intra-evaluative, intra-cognitive ("mixed thoughts") and intra-affective ("mixed feelings") ambivalence on attitude–intention–behavior relations. Theoretically, one would predict consistent effects across the different types of ambivalence, with intra-affective ambivalence attenuating the affective attitude–behavior relationship compared with intra-affective univalence (e.g., Conner & Sparks, 2002). However, it is almost certainly the case that certain attitude objects are likely to elicit more conflicting thoughts than feelings and vice versa (e.g., minority groups versus the death penalty).

In addition to the different aspects of intra-component ambivalence, there are also likely to be discrepancies between the components of attitude, or *inter-component ambivalence* (e.g., Maio et al., 2000). Inter-component ambivalence refers to conflict between these components, for example, when a large cream cake is simultaneously evaluated as "nice" (affective, positive) but "fattening" (cognitive, negative). For example, MacDonald and Zanna (1998) found that cross-dimensionally ambivalent men tended to rate their *admiration* for feminists as being positive, but their *affection* for them negatively; these men were also more likely to be influenced by unconscious priming. In other words discrepancies between components of attitudes also produce attitudes that are weaker. To date, however, the vast majority of research into ambivalence has treated inter- and intra-component ambivalence as being mutually exclusive: one goal for future research is to redress this balance. This suggestion is not trivial: studies that have examined intra-component ambivalence have not controlled for the potential effects of inter-component ambivalence. This is important because it seems likely that

---

3 By "measured ambivalence evaluatively" we are referring to studies that have not specified feelings or thoughts, and so allow participants to consider both affective and cognitive aspects of their positive/negative poles.

inter-component ambivalence will exert a powerful effect on intra-component ambivalence (cf. Maio et al., 2000). This might provide a further explanation for inconsistencies between the studies of intra-component ambivalence reviewed above.

## Summary and conclusions

The concept of attitudinal ambivalence represents a reconceptualization of the unidimensional bipolar attitude into a bidimensional model. More importantly, attitudinal ambivalence exerts a powerful effect on key determinants of behavior, namely attitudes and intentions. Attitudes that are univalent tend to be more predictive of subsequent behavioral intentions and subsequent behavior, whether measured using self-report or a more objective index. Thus attitudinal ambivalence seems to represent a key facet of attitude strength. Somewhat counterintuitively, attitudinal ambivalence also seems to affect intention formation, although determining when the intention–behavior relationship will be attenuated and when it will be augmented is a matter for future research. Further research into this important domain is required, most notably with respect to extending the findings to domains other than food choice and by investigating different forms of attitudinal ambivalence.

## References

Ajzen, I. (1991). The theory of planned behavior. *Organizational Behavior and Human Decision Processes, 50*, 179–211.

Armitage, C. J. (2003). Effects of belief homogeneity on attitude-intention-behaviour relations. Beyond attitudinal ambivalence: Effects. *European Journal of Social Psychology, 33*, 551–563.

Armitage, C. J., & Conner, M. (2000). Attitudinal ambivalence: A test of three key hypotheses. *Personality and Social Psychology Bulletin, 26*, 1421–1432.

Armitage, C. J., & Conner, M. (2001). Efficacy of the theory of planned behavior: A meta-analytic review. *British Journal of Social Psychology, 40*, 471–499.

Armitage, C. J., Povey, R., & Arden, M. A. (in press). Evidence for discontinuity patterns across the stages of change: A role for attitudinal ambivalence. *Psychology and Health.*

Bagozzi, R. P., & Yi, Y. (1989). The degree of intention formation as a moderator of the attitude-behavior relationship. *Social Psychology Quarterly, 52*, 266–279.

Bargh, J. A., Chaiken, S., Govender, R., & Pratto, F. (1992). The generality of the automatic attitude activation effect. *Journal of Personality and Social Psychology, 62*, 893–912.

Baron, R. M., & Kenny, D. A. (1986). The moderator-mediator variable distinction in social psychological research: Conceptual, strategic, and statistical considerations. *Journal of Personality and Social Psychology, 51*, 1173–1182.

Bassili, J. N. (1996). Meta-judgmental versus operative indexes of psychological attributes: The case of measures of attitude strength. *Journal of Personality and Social Psychology, 71*, 637–653.

Breckler, S. J. (1994). A comparison of numerical indexes for measuring attitudinal ambivalence. *Educational and Psychological Measurement, 54*, 350–365.

Brömer, P. (1998). Ambivalent attitudes and information processing. *Swiss Journal of Psychology, 57*, 225–234.

Conner, M. (2004a). *Attitudinal ambivalence and the stability of attitudes.* Manuscript submitted for publication.

Conner, M. (2004b). *Attitudinal ambivalence and the attitude-intention-behavior relationship.* Manuscript submitted for publication.

Conner, M., & Armitage, C. J. (1998). Extending the theory of planned behavior: A review and avenues for further research. *Journal of Applied Social Psychology, 28*, 1429–1464.

Conner, M., & Armitage, C. J. (2002). *The social psychology of food.* Buckingham, UK: Open University Press.

Conner, M., Povey, R., Sparks, P., James, R., & Shepherd, R. (1998). Understanding dietary choice and dietary change: Contributions from social psychology. In A. Murcott (Ed.), *The nation's diet: The social science of food choice* (pp. 43–56). London: Longman.

Conner, M., Povey, R., Sparks, P., James, R., & Shepherd, R. (2003). Moderating role of attitudinal ambivalence within the theory of planned behavior. *British Journal of Social Psychology, 42*, 75–94.

Conner, M., Sheeran, P., Norman, P., & Armitage, C. J. (2000). Temporal stability as a moderator of relationships in the theory of planned behavior. *British Journal of Social Psychology, 39*, 469–493.

Conner, M., Sherlock, K., & Orbell, S. (1998). Psychosocial determinants of ecstasy use in young people in the UK. *British Journal of Health Psychology, 3*, 295–317.

Conner, M., & Sparks, P. (2002). Ambivalence and attitudes. *European Review of Social Psychology, 12*, 37–70.

Conner, M., Sparks, P., Povey, R., James, R., Shepherd, R., & Armitage, C. J. (2002). Moderator effects of attitudinal ambivalence on attitude-behavior relationships. *European Journal of Social Psychology, 32*, 705–718.

Converse, P. E. (1995). Foreword. In R. E. Petty & J. A. Krosnick (Eds.), *Attitude strength: Antecedents and consequences* (pp. xi–xvii). Mahwah, NJ: Lawrence Erlbaum Associates, Inc.

Eagly, A. H. (1992). Uneven progress: Social psychology and the study of attitudes. *Journal of Personality and Social Psychology, 63*, 693–710.

Eagly, A. H., & Chaiken, S. (1993). *The psychology of attitudes.* Fort Worth, TX: Harcourt Brace Jovanovich.

Erber, M. W., Hodges, S. D., & Wilson, T. D. (1995). Attitude strength, attitude stability, and the effects of analyzing reasons. In R. E. Petty & J. A. Krosnick (Eds.), *Attitude strength: Antecedents and consequences* (pp. 433–454). Mahwah, NJ: Lawrence Erlbaum Associates, Inc.

Fazio, R. H. (1986). How do attitudes guide behavior? In R. M. Sorrentino & E. T. Higgins (Eds.), *Handbook of motivation and cognition: Foundations of social behavior* (Vol. 1, pp. 204–243). New York: Guilford Press.

Fazio, R. H. (1995). Attitudes as object-evaluation associations: Determinants, consequences, and correlates of attitude accessibility. In R. E. Petty & J. A. Krosnick (Eds.), *Attitude strength: Antecedents and consequences* (pp. 247–282). Mahwah, NJ: Lawrence Erlbaum Associates, Inc.

Festinger, L. (1957). *A theory of cognitive dissonance*. Stanford, CA: Stanford University Press.

Fishbein, M., & Ajzen, I. (1975). *Belief, attitude, intention and behavior: An introduction to theory and research*. Reading, MA: Addison-Wesley.

Haddock, G., & Carrick, R. (1999). How to make a politician more likeable and effective: Framing political judgments through the numeric values of a rating scale. *Social Cognition, 17*, 298–311.

Jonas, K., Brömer, P., & Diehl, M. (2000). Attitudinal ambivalence. *European Review of Social Psychology, 11*, 35–74.

Jonas, K., Diehl, M., & Brömer, P. (1997). Effects of attitudinal ambivalence on information processing and attitude-intention consistency. *Journal of Experimental Social Psychology, 33*, 190–210.

Kallgren, C. A., & Wood, W. (1986). Access to attitude-relevant information in memory as a determinant of attitude-behavior consistency. *Journal of Experimental Social Psychology, 22*, 328–338.

Kaplan, K. J. (1972). On the ambivalence-indifference problem in attitude theory and measurement: A suggested modification of the semantic differential technique. *Psychological Bulletin, 77*, 361–372.

Kraus, S. J. (1995). Attitudes and the prediction of behavior: A meta-analysis of the empirical literature. *Personality and Social Psychology Bulletin, 21*, 58–75.

Krosnick, J. A., Boninger, D. S., Chuang, Y. C., Berent, M. K., & Carnot, C. G. (1993). Attitude strength: One construct or many related constructs? *Journal of Personality and Social Psychology, 65*, 1132–1151.

Krosnick, J. A., & Petty, R. E. (1995). Attitude strength: An overview. In R. E. Petty & J. A. Krosnick (Eds.), *Attitude strength: Antecedents and consequences* (pp. 1–24). Mahwah, NJ: Lawrence Erlbaum Associates, Inc.

MacDonald, T. K., & Zanna, M. P. (1998). Cross-dimension ambivalence toward social groups: Can ambivalence affect intentions to hire feminists? *Personality and Social Psychology Bulletin, 24*, 427–441.

Maio, G. R., Bell, D. W., & Esses, V. M. (1996). Ambivalence and persuasion: The processing of messages about immigrant groups. *Journal of Experimental Social Psychology, 32*, 513–536.

Maio, G. R., Esses, V. M., & Bell, D. W. (2000). Examining conflict between components of attitudes: Ambivalence and inconsistency are distinct constructs. *Canadian Journal of Behavioral Science, 32*, 71–83.

Maio, G. R., Greenland, K., Bernard, M., & Esses, V. M. (2001). Effects of intergroup ambivalence on information processing: The role of physiological arousal. *Group Processes and Intergroup Relations, 4*, 355–372.

Moore, M. (1973). Ambivalence in attitude measurement. *Educational and Psychological Measurement, 33*, 481–483.

Moore, M. (1980). Validation of the attitude toward any practice scale through the use of ambivalence as a moderator variable. *Educational and Psychological Measurement, 40*, 205–208.

Morgan, M., & Grube, J. W. (1994). The Irish and alcohol: A classic case of ambivalence. *The Irish Journal of Psychology, 15*, 390–403.

Newby-Clark, I. R., McGregor, I., & Zanna, M. P. (2002). Thinking and caring about cognitive inconsistency: When and for whom does attitudinal ambivalence feel uncomfortable? *Journal of Personality and Social Psychology, 82*, 157–166.

Petty, R. E., & Krosnick, J. A. (1995). *Attitude strength: Antecedents and consequences*. Mahwah, NJ: Lawrence Erlbaum Associates, Inc.

Pomerantz, E. V., Chaiken, S., & Tordesillas, R. S. (1995). Attitude strength and resistance processes. *Journal of Personality and Social Psychology, 69*, 408–419.

Povey, R., Wellens, B., & Conner, M. (2001). Attitudes towards following meat, vegetarian and vegan diets: An examination of the role of ambivalence. *Appetite, 37*, 15–26.

Priester, J. R., & Petty, R. E. (1996). The gradual threshold model of ambivalence: Relating the positive and negative bases of attitudes to subjective ambivalence. *Journal of Personality and Social Psychology, 71*, 431–449.

Priester, J. R., & Petty, R. E. (2001). Extending the bases of subjective attitudinal ambivalence: Interpersonal and intrapersonal antecedents of evaluative tension. *Journal of Personality and Social Psychology, 80*, 19–34.

Riketta, M. (2000). Discriminative validation of numerical indices of attitude ambivalence. *Current Research in Social Psychology, 5*, 1–9.

Schwarz, N., & Bless, H. (1992). Scandals and the public's trust in politicians: Assimilation and contrast effects. *Personality and Social Psychology Bulletin, 18*, 574–579.

Schwartz, S. H. (1978). Temporal instability as a moderator of the attitude-behavior relationship. *Journal of Personality and Social Psychology, 36*, 715–724.

Sheeran, P. (2002). Intention-behavior relations: A conceptual and empirical review. *European Review of Social Psychology, 12*, 1–36.

Sheeran, P., Norman, P., & Orbell, S. (1999). Evidence that intentions based on attitudes better predict behavior than intentions based on subjective norms. *European Journal of Social Psychology, 29*, 403–406.

Sparks, P., Conner, M., James, R., Shepherd, R., & Povey, R. (2001). Ambivalence about health-related behaviors: An exploration in the domain of food choice. *British Journal of Health Psychology, 6*, 53–68.

Thompson, M. M., Zanna, M. P., & Griffin, D. W. (1995). Let's not be indifferent about (attitudinal) ambivalence. In R. E. Petty & J. A. Krosnick (Eds.), *Attitude strength: Antecedents and consequences* (pp. 361–386). Mahwah, NJ: Lawrence Erlbaum Associates, Inc.

van der Pligt, J., de Vries, N. K., Manstead, A. S. R., & van Harreveld, F. (2000). The importance of being selective: Weighing the role of attribute importance in attitudinal judgment. In M. P. Zanna (Ed.), *Advances in experimental social psychology* (Vol. 32, pp. 135–200). San Diego, CA: Academic Press.

Wicker, A. W. (1969). Attitudes versus actions: The relationship of verbal and overt behavioral responses to attitude objects. *Journal of Social Issues, 25*, 41–47.

Wilson, T. D., & Hodges, S. D. (1992). Attitudes as temporary constructions. In A. Tesser & L. Martin (Eds.), *The construction of social judgment* (pp. 37–65). Hillsdale, NJ: Lawrence Erlbaum Associates, Inc.

Zaller, J., & Feldman, S. (1992). A simple theory of the survey response: Answering questions versus revealing preferences. *American Journal of Political Science, 36*, 579–616.

# 7 Intention–behavior relations

## A self-regulation perspective

*Sheina Orbell*

### Attitudes, intentions and behavior

Several deliberative models of decision making and social behavior including the theory of reasoned action (Fishbein, 1980), the theory of planned behavior (Ajzen, 1985, 2001), the model of goal-directed behavior (Perugini & Bagozzi, 2001) and protection–motivation theory (Rogers, 1983) as well as theories of goal striving (e.g. Emmons, 1996; Sheldon & Elliott, 1999) propose that the proximal determinant of a person's behavior is his or her intention to act. Behavioral intention, according to each of these models, mediates the impact of prior variables on subsequent behavior. Indeed the genesis of the theory of reasoned action is attributable in large part to the assertion that the relationship of attitude (and subjective norm) to behavior is mediated by the formation of a behavioral intention. Similarly, protection–motivation theory proposes intention as the important motivational construct mediating the effects of threat and coping appraisal processes on subsequent behavior. The model of goal-directed behavior also asserts that intention is the proximal cause of behavior, mediating the effects of behavioral desire and its antecedents (goal desire, positive and negative anticipated emotions, attitude, subjective norms and perceived behavioral control). Both the model of goal-directed behavior and the theory of planned behavior posit that intentions are the proximal determinants of behavior but allow for the possibility that, in some circumstances, a person may not have complete control over behavior and therefore, be unable to act upon his or her intention. Thus, behavior in these models may be predicted from intention and perceived behavioral control. A fundamental issue for each of these theories must therefore be to consider how satisfactory is the theoretically causal relationship between intention and behavior.

How might an intention be defined? I once explained to a friend that I was conducting research on intentions. She queried what I meant by asking the following instructive question: "Is an intention something you haven't done yet?" Implicit in the notion of an intention is that it expresses a person's plans to act: "I intend to do Z," "I will do Z." An intention may be either positive ("I intend to do Z") or negative ("I do not intend to Z") and is assumed by most theoretical models to capture the motivational import of prior variables so as to determine the tenacity with which an individual intends to pursue a given behavior or goal. An intention that is strongly held is supposed to be pursued with more vigor and be more likely to lead to enactment.

In this chapter, I begin by reviewing evidence concerning the strength of the relationship between intentions and behavior. Next, an analysis of the nature of inconsistency between intention and behavior is presented. It is argued that there are good empirical and theoretical grounds for supposing that positive intentions do not always translate into intended actions. While intentions (and their deliberative determinants) are one very important prerequisite for achieving behavioral goals, attention needs also to be given to mechanisms mediating the effects of intentions on behavior. One important approach to this difficulty is to identify self-regulatory processes that overcome problems in initiating or maintaining goal-directed behavior.

## How strong is the relationship between intention and behavior?

Many studies concerned with a wide range of behaviors have considered the relationship of intentions to behavior. Importantly, many tests of the intention–behavior relation are available with respect to ecologically valid behaviors occurring in natural contexts and many studies have utilized non-student samples (cf. Sears, 1986). If we are to evaluate (and improve upon) the ability of intentions to determine behavior, it is important that we do so in social contexts where possible obstacles to translating an intention into behavior are permitted to occur naturally, as they do in everyday life. Such studies have examined a wide range of behaviors including illicit drug use (e.g. Conner, Sherlock, & Orbell, 1998; Orbell, Blair, Sherlock, & Conner, 2001), health service uptake (e.g. Orbell & Sheeran, 1998a; Sheeran, & Orbell, 2000b), physical activity (e.g. Hagger, Chatzisarantis, Biddle, & Orbell, 2001; Sheeran, & Orbell, 1999a), vehicle driver behavior (e.g. Parker, Manstead, & Stradling, 1995), blood donation (e.g. Warshaw, Calantone, & Joyce, 1986), studying (e.g. Orbell, 2003) and diet and weight loss (e.g. Bagozzi & Warshaw, 1990).

Fortunately, several meta-analytic reviews are available to assist in evaluating the size of the association between intention and behavior. Reviews provide evidence of the size of the relationship between intention and subsequent behavior derived from literatures relating to specific behaviors such as physical activity (Hagger, Chatzisarantis, & Biddle, 2002), condom use (Sheeran & Orbell, 1998) and health behaviors (Godin & Kok, 1996), or specific theories such as the theory of reasoned action (Sheppard, Hartwick, & Warshaw, 1988), the theory of planned behavior (Armitage & Conner, 2001) or protection–motivation theory (Milne, Sheeran, & Orbell, 2000). Recently, Sheeran (2002) attempted to provide an overview of meta-analytic evidence from studies relating to these different theories and behavior by performing a meta-analysis of 10 previously published meta-analyses, giving a total sample size of $N = 82,107$, and 422 hypothesis tests. His analysis shows that although correlations between intentions and behavior obtained in individual meta-analyses ranged from $r = 0.40$ to 0.82, the overall sample weighted average correlation was $r = 0.53$ with a 95% confidence interval from 0.52 to 0.53. In regression terms, this implies that intentions account for 28% of the variance in behavior, on average, in prospective studies. According to Cohen's (1992) criteria for interpreting the size of correlations, an $r = 0.10$ might be considered a "small" effect size, an $r = .30$ a "medium" effect and an $r = .50$ a "large" effect. The $r = 0.53$ result Sheeran obtained should therefore be considered a large effect and the ability of the intention construct to predict behavior classed as pretty good.

A strong statistical relationship between intention and behavior is particularly likely when careful attention is given to methodological issues that might attenuate the size of the association (see Ajzen, 1991, Ajzen, 2002; Sutton, 1998 for reviews). The reliability with which intentions and behavior are assessed will constrain the possible obtainable correlation between the variables. For example, two variables with internal reliabilities of .70 can achieve a maximum correlation of just .49 (.70 × .70) whereas measures with reliabilities of .80 could achieve a correlation of .64 (.80 × .80) *if they were in reality perfectly correlated.* It has long been established within the theory of reasoned action, that conceptualization of behavior in terms of the action, target, time and context must correspond to the conceptualization of intention (Ajzen & Fishbein, 1973, 1974). Global behavioral measures, or those that describe goals or end states are best predicted by global intention measures. Conversely, specific behaviors are best predicted by specific intentions. Compatibility of scales used to assess intentions and behavior has also been subject to empirical test. Courneya and McAuley (1994) showed that prediction of the number of times that respondents exercised in the past four weeks was greatest when a frequency measure of intention (number of times participants intended to exercise in the next four weeks) was utilized, compared with a measure of intention which assessed only the likelihood of exercising ("I intend to exercise in the next four weeks"; extremely likely–extremely unlikely). Similar limitations might occur if an intention item specified only intensity (as opposed to likelihood) of intention to perform a repeated behavior ("I intend to eat breakfast in the next week"; strongly agree–strongly disagree) and behavior were assessed in terms of the number of times breakfast was eaten during the past week. Thus, the strength of association that can be observed between intention and behavior is certainly indicative of a substantial statistical association.

## Origins of the "gap" between intentions and behavior

Notwithstanding the power of behavioral intentions to account for substantial variance in subsequent behavior, and the possible impact that correcting for measurement might have on the size of the correlations (see Kim &

Hunter, 1993), there are both theoretical and empirical grounds for supposing that not all people who intend to perform a given behavior will actually do so. In essence, the high positive correlations obtained between intention and behavior can tell us only that those who intend to act are more likely to act than those who do not intend to act. While this is clearly reassuring for all deliberative accounts of human action, in fact there are two possible sources of consistency and two possible sources of inconsistency between intention and behavior which cannot be readily discerned from correlational data (or from regression analyses) (McBroom & Reid, 1992; Orbell & Sheeran,1998a). If intention and behavior are cross-tabulated (Figure 7.1) it can be shown that *consistency* between intention and behavior will arise when those with positive intentions act or when those with negative intentions do not act. Conversely, *inconsistency* between intention and behavior will arise when those with positive intentions do not act or those with negative intentions do act. It is useful to recognize that this analysis applies to the *direction* of an intention, irrespective of whether the focal behavior is an *approach* behavior (e.g. "I intend to give blood" [positive] versus "I do not intend to give blood" [negative]) or an *avoidance* behavior (e.g. "I intend to try not to eat snacks" [positive] versus "I do not intend to try not to eat snacks" [negative]). In this latter instance, an individual who intends to avoid snacking and does so is correctly classified as an "inclined actor" and an individual who does not intend to avoid snacking and does not do so is correctly classified as a "disinclined abstainer."

Orbell and Sheeran (1998a) examined data from a one-year prospective study of screening uptake, an objectively verifiable behavior, in order to partition the four discrete patterns of intention–behavior relationship illustrated

|  | Positive intention | Negative intention |
|---|---|---|
| Acts | Inclined actor | Disinclined actor |
| Does not act | Inclined abstainer | Disinclined abstainer |

*Figure 7.1* Decomposition of sources of consistency between intentions and behavior.

in Figure 7.1: inclined actors, inclined abstainers, disinclined actors, disinclined abstainers. By examining the data in this manner, it was possible to reveal that the *main source of consistency in intention–behavior relations is derived from the perhaps unremarkable ability of non-intenders not to act.* We are, it would appear, very good at not doing what we do not intend to do. Some 88% of the disinclined acted consistently with their intention and were classified as disinclined abstainers, compared with only 12% classified as inconsistent disinclined actors. Intenders on the other hand were much less likely to carry out their intention to act. Just 43% of this group were screened during the year and classified as inclined actors, while some 57% behaved in a way that was inconsistent with their intention and were classified as inclined abstainers.

Orbell and Sheeran's (1998a) finding can be corroborated by evidence from other studies and data concerning different types of behavior. Young, DeSarbo, and Morwitz (1998) for example, examined correspondence between consumer intentions to purchase a diet drink and actual behavior and found that only 62% of intenders actually purchased the product. Table 7.1 illustrates the decomposition of inclined actors, disinclined abstainers, inclined abstainers and disinclined actors for studies concerned with three classes of health-related behavior. Approach behaviors that are discrete acts require that an intender perform a focal behavior once, such as in the case of a single attendance at cancer screening (Sheeran, & Orbell, 2000b; Sutton, Bickler, Sancho-Aldridge, & Saidi, 1994). Approach behaviors that involve repeated behaviors, such as regular physical activity (Orbell, 2000a; Sheeran, & Orbell, 2000a) or consistent condom use (Gallois, Kashima, Terry, McCamish, Timmins, & Chauvin, 1992; Orbell, 2001; Stanton et al., 1996) require that intenders consistently perform the focal behavior over a period of time. The third class is avoidance behaviors in which an intender must successfully resist performing a focal behavior consistently over a period of time (e.g. Orbell & Sheeran, 2002). For each class of intention–behavior relationship, intenders were more likely to fail to act on their intentions (median number of inclined abstainers = 46%) than were non-intenders (median number of disinclined actors = 9.5%).

While these observations do not represent a comprehensive review of all available evidence, findings to date provide reasonable evidence that the main source of inconsistency between intention and behavior and that which leaves most variance in behavior unaccounted for is derived from the tendency of people with positive intentions not to act on them. Moreover, this relationship obtains whether we consider intentions to approach or avoid a focal behavior, whether we consider single behaviors or repeated behaviors and whether we employ objectively verifiable or self-report measures of behavior.

*Table 7.1* Percentages of samples from different studies behaving consistently and inconsistently with their intentions by type of behavioral intention

|  | Consistent | | Inconsistent | |
|---|---|---|---|---|
| *Behavior type* | *Inclined actors* % | *Disinclined abstainers* % | *Inclined abstainers* % | *Disinclined actors* % |
| *Approach: Discrete* | | | | |
| Screening uptake (Orbell & Sheeran, 1998a) | 43 | 88 | 57 | 12 |
| Screening uptake[1] (Sheeran & Orbell, 2000b) | 70 | 97 | 30 | 3 |
| Screening uptake[1] (Sutton et al., 1994) | 74 | 65 | 26 | 35 |
| *Approach: Repeated* | | | | |
| Condom use (Orbell, 2001) | 33 | 98 | 67 | 2 |
| Condom use[1] (Gallois et al., 1992) | 43 | 90 | 57 | 10 |
| Condom use[1] (Stanton et.al, 1994) | 61 | 100 | 39 | 0 |
| Exercise[1] (Sheeran & Orbell, 2001) | 46 | 97 | 54 | 3 |
| Sports club attendance (Orbell, 2000) | 63 | 83 | 37 | 17 |
| *Avoidance: Repeated* | | | | |
| Not eating late night junk food (Orbell & Sheeran, 2002) | 38 | 91 | 62 | 9 |

[1] Figures based on secondary analysis of data presented in Sheeran (2002).

## Do variables in deliberative models discriminate intenders who act from intenders who do not act?

Given the emphasis in models of social behavior on intention and its various determinants as predictors of behavior, an important issue for our understanding of intention–behavior inconsistency is to consider whether the variables contained in those models might be able to discriminate between inclined actors and inclined abstainers. Orbell and Sheeran (1998a) conducted just such a discriminant analysis using variables from protection–motivation theory (perceived susceptibility, perceived severity, worry, response efficacy, response costs and self-efficacy). Although these variables were able to provide reasonable prediction of behavior for the sample as a whole, and to discriminate the inclined from the disinclined, it was not possible to derive a significant discriminant function capable of distinguishing between inclined actors and inclined abstainers. To my knowledge, just one other study has attempted such an analysis (Sheeran, 2002) using data from Sheeran and Orbell's (1999a) study of exercise. In that analysis theory of planned behavior variables were similarly able to discriminate the inclined from the disinclined but were unable to discriminate inclined actors from disinclined actors. Thus, it would appear that people with statistically equivalent motivation as assessed by at least two deliberative models might nonetheless differ in their likelihood of performing a behavior.

## Substantive explanations for poor correspondence between intention and behavior

The intention–behavior relationship has been the subject of previous conceptual analyses (e.g. Ajzen, 1991, 2001; Greve, 2001; Sheeran, 2002) pointing in particular to the need to address properties of intentions that might affect their stability or the tenacity with which they are held. According to this perspective, equivalent intentions, assessed in terms of direction and intensity, may differ in other properties, and it is these properties that affect their relationship to behavior. Alternatively, it might even be suggested that the failure of people to turn their intentions into action be taken as indicative of the need to turn to alternative, non-deliberative and non-conscious explanations of human action (e.g. Wegner & Wheatley, 1999). Each of these positions has empirical support and will be briefly considered here before turning to the issue of self-regulatory processes in action initiation and maintenance.

One obvious reason why people may not appear to enact their positive intentions is that they change those intentions over time. Since deliberative models are based on the assumption that people form intentions derived from their attitudes, subjective normative influences, perceptions of control, perceptions of personal susceptibility and severity of disease and so on, it is perfectly plausible that they might modify their intentions in the time interval between assessing intention and behavior (Ajzen, 1985, 1991; Ajzen & Fishbein, 1980; Fishbein, 1980; Fishbein & Ajzen, 1975). There is both indirect and direct evidence for the stability hypothesis. Indirect tests based upon comparisons of the strength of the intention–behavior correlation where there is a short time interval between the two measures versus a long time interval show evidence of moderation for within-behavior comparisons (Sheeran & Orbell, 1998) but not for across-behavior comparisons (Randall & Wolff, 1994). Sheeran, Orbell, and Trafimow (1999) conducted a direct test in which intention stability was measured by computing within-participants' correlations between intention scores at two time points, prior to assessing behavior. Their findings showed that stable intentions were indeed better predictors of subsequent behavior than unstable intentions. Moreover, when intentions were stable, past behavior was no longer a significant determinant of future behavior (cf. Ajzen, 2002; Conner & Norman, 2002; Conner, Sheeran, Norman, & Armitage, 2000). These findings, together with evidence for a moderating role of other variables which are themselves presumed to influence intention–behavior relations by their influence on temporal stability (e.g. degree of intention formation, Bagozzi & Yi, 1989; Sheeran, Norman,

& Orbell, 1999, anticipated regret, Parker et al., 1995; Sheeran & Orbell, 1999b; Sheeran & Abraham, 2002, self-schemas; Sheeran & Orbell, 2000a) are persuasive. One might consider, however, whether instability ought, in practice, to be equally likely to occur amongst people with initially positive or negative intentions. If this were the case, we might generally expect to observe equivalent inconsistency between intention and behavior amongst people holding either positive or negative intentions, which we do not (Table 7.1).

An alternative viewpoint, that intention does not have a *causal* relationship with behavior is supported by evidence that primes outside of conscious awareness can have substantive effects on overt behavior. Perugini and Bagozzi (Chapter 8, this volume) estimated the size of effect that might be attributed to automatic processes in classic experiments by Bargh, Chen, and Burrows (1996) and by Chen and Bargh (1999). Based on 11 manipulations, Perugini and Bagozzi estimate that automaticity might account for 13% of variance in behavior, clearly leaving substantial variance unaccounted for. Such automatic processes can certainly be demonstrated, even outside the laboratory and with general population samples. For example, Orbell and Guinote (2002) showed that older people attending two day centers could be induced to speed or slow their walking pace after being primed with a youthful or positive elderly prime, respectively. Notwithstanding this finding, it remains uncertain how enduring such priming effects might be or how frequently such primes might actually occur in everyday life. The role of automatic processes might be viewed as similar to the role of genes in determining variation in human behavior. That is, their role cannot be denied but the extent of their influence should be seen in the context of multiple determinants of complex behaviors in ecologically valid environments.

Notwithstanding evidence for automatic processes, within a self-regulatory perspective two lines of argument lead to the conclusion that further exploration of the intention–behavior relationship is worthwhile. As will be seen in the following sections of this chapter, there are reasons to believe that behaviors may originate as intentional acts and become automatic after satisfactory repetition (cf. Ajzen, 2002; Brandstatter, Lengfelder, & Gollwitzer, 2001). The ability of past behavior to predict behavior over and above behavioral intention has also been seen as indicative of a role for automatic, usually referred to as habitual processes in predicting future actions. While this issue remains open to further research, it might be argued that even if past behavior effects were attributed to habit, this raises the important self-regulatory question of how people might overcome past behavioral tendencies and act according to their intentions (cf. Orbell, Hodgkins, & Sheeran, 1997).

## Self-regulation: Turning intentions into action

Having formed a behavioral intention, the actor may encounter a host of problems in actually translating those intentions into action. People are notoriously optimistic about what they will accomplish and how long it will take them to accomplish it, a phenomenon referred to as the planning fallacy (Kahneman & Tversky, 1979, c.f. Koole & Spijker, 2000). For example, people may possess intentions that cannot be enacted immediately but have to await a suitable opportunity; they may procrastinate about getting started; they may possess other competing intentions which gain priority or they may have difficulty sticking to a behavior which requires repeated performance or sustained effort and avoiding getting distracted by other goals en route (Kuhl, 1985). The identification of self-regulatory solutions to these difficulties represents an important step forward in explaining the intention–behavior relation.

An important contribution to understanding the intention–behavior relation in recent years is Gollwitzer's concept of an implementation intention (Gollwitzer, 1993, 1999; Gollwitzer & Brandstatter, 1997). An implementation intention is a powerful self-regulatory strategy, which takes the form "If I encounter situation X, then I will perform behavior Y." Implementation intentions should be distinguished from intentions to achieve certain outcomes or perform certain behaviors, which have been the focus of the chapter up to now. Whereas a goal intention of this sort simply reflects an individual's positive orientation towards the behavior or outcome and the intensity of that intention, an implementation intention is proposed to commit the individual to action initiation. This is because when an implementation intention is formed, a mental link is created between a future specific situation and the intended response. As a consequence of this mental link, suitable opportunities for initiating action are not missed or forgotten or overlooked because attention is directed elsewhere.

There is now considerable evidence from a number of behavioral domains that supplementing a positive intention with an implementation intention specifying where and when to initiate behavior can increase the likelihood that the intention will be translated into action. Gollwitzer and Brandstatter (1997, Studies 1 and 2) provided both correlational and experimental evidence that students' intentions to complete a personal project over the Christmas vacation were more likely to be fulfilled when they were supplemented by an implementation intention. In Study 2, 70% of students who formed an implementation intention to write a report on Christmas Eve did so compared with just 30% of those who possessed an intention, but did not form an implementation intention committing them to a time and place to act upon it. That study clearly demonstrates the potential for this self-regulatory strategy to overcome the obstacles presented at a busy and distracting time. A number of other studies concerning a wide variety of behavioral domains have similarly shown that implementation intentions can ensure that opportunities for completing a goal intention are not missed (Table 7.2). Evidence shows not only that behaviors are *more likely* to be performed, but that they are likely to be performed *sooner* (e.g. Koole & Spijker, 2000), suggesting that behavior will be initiated at the first available

*Table 7.2* Behavioral outcome of forming an implementation intention

| Behavior type | Behavioral outcome amongst those forming implementation intentions | Behavioral outcome amongst those not forming implementation intentions |
| --- | --- | --- |
| *Discrete behaviors* | | |
| Write a report at Christmas (Gollwitzer & Brandstatter, 1997, Study 2) | 70% completion | 30% completion |
| Complete an assignment (Koole & Spijker, 2000) | Completed after 1.02 days | Completed after 2.90 days |
| Collect an assignment (Dholakia & Bagozzi, in press, Study 1) | 72% (low difficulty) 10% (high difficulty) | 9.5% 0 % |
| Check a website (Dholakia & Bagozzi, 2003, Study 2) | 70% completion | 33% completion |
| Collect a coupon (Aarts et al., 1999) | 80% completion | 50% completion |
| Perform BSE (Orbell et al., 1997) | 64% completion | 14% completion |
| Resume functional activity after surgery (older adults) (Orbell & Sheeran, 2000) | 18/32 activities resumed faster than those without imps | – |
| Uptake cervical screening test (Sheeran & Orbell, 2000b) | 92% uptake | 69% uptake |
| Exercise (Milne et al., 2002) | 91% completion | 29% completion |
| Attend worksite fire training (Sheeran & Silverman, 2003) | 39% attendance | 12% attendance |
| Write a CV (opiate withdrawal patients) (Brandstatter et al., 2002, Study 1) | 80% completion | 0% completion |
| Write a CV (post-withdrawal patients) (Brandstatter et al., 2002, Study 1) | 40% completion | 0% completion |
| Exercise (Orbell & Verplanken, 2002) | 79% completion | 54% completion |
| *Repeated behaviors* | | |
| Recycling drinking cartons (Rise et al., 2003) | imps $r = 0.58$ with behavior | – |
| Exercise (Rise et al., 2003) | imps $r = 0.67$ with behavior | – |
| Dental flossing daily (Orbell & Verplanken, 2004) | *Mean* = flossed 10/14 days | *Mean* = flossed 4/14 days |

*Table 7.2* contd.

| Behavior type | Behavioral outcome amongst those forming implementation intentions | Behavioral outcome amongst those not forming implementation intentions |
|---|---|---|
| Take a daily vitamin pill (Sheeran & Orbell, 1999, Study 1) | *Mean* = 1.57/21 days missed | *Mean* = 3.53/21 days missed |
| Take a daily vitamin pill (Sheeran & Orbell, 1999, Study 2) | *Mean* = .90/21 days missed, 26% missed a pill | *Mean* = 2.50/21 days missed, 61% missed a pill |
| Healthy eating index (Verplanken & Faes, 1999) | *Mean* = 6.63 | *Mean* = 5.45 |
| Writing date on six test material sheets of paper (older adults) (Chasteen et al., 2001) | *Mean* = .57/6.0 sheets dated | *Mean* = .22/6.0 sheets dated |
| Drinking fluids during exercise session (Hagger & Orbell, 2003) | *Mean* = 10.36 drinks/hour | *Mean* = 5.0 drinks/hour |

opportunity, or as soon as the contextual cue for action is encountered. Behaviors that may be perceived as costly or unpleasant to perform are also promoted by forming implementation intentions. For example, Orbell et al. (1997) showed that women were four times as likely to perform a breast self-examination if they supplemented their intention with an implementation intention. The powerful effects of implementation intentions are not restricted to discrete behavioral acts. Behaviors which have to be repeated, where frequent performance (e.g. dental hygiene, Orbell & Verplanken, 2004) or not forgetting (e.g. taking a daily vitamin pill, Sheeran & Orbell, 1999b) is crucial can also be established by forming an implementation intention. Implementation intentions have also been shown to facilitate action initiation amongst older adult samples, where prospective memory (e.g. Guynn, McDaniel, & Einstein, 2001) may be particularly poor (Chasteen, Park, & Schwarz, 2001) and amongst opiate withdrawal patients (Brandstatter et al., 2001). In sum, the effects of implementation intentions are dramatic, generalizable to a wide range of behaviors and populations and have been well established utilizing both self-report and objectively verifiable behaviors.

Given the remarkable success of implementation intentions, one might wonder if people actually possess the tendency to spontaneously form such plans in order to self-regulate their behavior. Several lines of evidence suggest that they may. Orbell and Sheeran (2000) gave participants booklets in which they had to form their own implementation intentions on a weekly basis over a 12-week period. Rise, Thompson, and Verplanken

(2003) have developed a multi-item method for measuring implementation intentions in correlational research and shown that the measure predicts significant variance in behavior independent of goal intention. Similarly, in a retrospective study, Webb and Sheeran (in press) showed that goal achievement was associated with self-reported formation of an implementation intention.

Implementation intentions are proposed to supplement the effects of goal intentions on behavioral performance. Important for the analysis of inclined abstainers, most studies have sought to demonstrate that participants possess positive intentions before being asked to form an implementation intention (e.g. Brandstatter et al., 2001). These studies show that amongst people *equally motivated to act*, in terms of their goal intention, forming an implementation intention regarding when and where to initiate action significantly increases goal completion (e.g. Orbell et.al., 1997; Sheeran & Orbell, 1999b). Two studies which investigated the combined effects of a motivational intervention based on protection motivation theory with an implementation intention intervention (Milne, Orbell, & Sheeran, 2002; Milne & Sheeran, 2001) each showed that motivation is necessary but not sufficient for action initiation. Dholakia and Bagozzi (2003) also investigated the dual effects of manipulating commitment to a goal intention and implementation intentions and obtained evidence that combined effects maximized behavioral enactment of short fuse behaviors (actions that must be enacted within a very limited window of opportunity). Orbell et al. (1997) and Sheeran and Orbell (1999b) additionally examined the possibility that implementation intentions might alter or specifically, increase commitment to goal intentions. In both studies, intention was unaltered by the formation of an implementation intention, indicating that the process by which implementation intentions lead to behavioral enactment can be attributed to post-deliberative processes affecting the translation of an intention into action.

Given that implementation intentions do not operate by modifying traditional motivational or deliberative variables (e.g. by modifying intentions) how do they exert their effects? Gollwitzer (1993, 1999) proposed that the critical feature of implementation intentions is the linking of action to a specified context in memory. When the context is encountered, action is proposed to follow (a) immediately, (b) efficiently, that is without requiring much cognitive processing capacity, and (c) without conscious intent. Put another way, implementation intentions delegate control of behavior to the environment. Various forms of evidence speak to these proposed mechanisms. Orbell et al. (1997), for example, showed that all but one person in their study reported enacting breast self-examination in the time and place specified in their implementation intentions one month previously. While these findings suggest that people are able to detect situations specified in their implementation intentions, they do not speak directly to speed in detecting those contexts, nor to speed of action initiation, once those contexts are detected. Gollwitzer and Brandstatter (1997, Study 3) demonstrated that participants who formed implementation intentions regarding suitable opportunities to present counterarguments in a debate were faster to seize opportunities to express themselves when those opportunities arose, than were participants who only identified suitable opportunities. Similarly, Aarts and Dijksterhuis (2000) showed that people who formed implementation intentions regarding travel mode choices were faster to respond with choices specified in their implementation intentions when presented with computer-generated cues regarding journeys they might make. Aarts, Dijksterhuis, and Midden (1999) further showed that the heightened accessibility of environmental cues specified in an implementation intention to collect a coupon on the way to the cafeteria mediated the likelihood of actually collecting that coupon. Thus, supplementing an intention with an implementation intention ensures that situations for enactment are rapidly detected, and acted upon, even in the chaos of everyday life, as in students heading for the cafeteria, or participants in Orbell et al.'s (1997) study going about their daily routines.

In fact, many of the experiments described above have been conducted in ecologically valid environments where goal intentions under investigation might be considered to be competing with other cognitive activities (e.g. Sheeran & Orbell, 1999b, 2000b, Milne et al., 2002). This does not, however, constitute hard evidence that implementation intentions operate efficiently, requiring limited processing capacity. Recently, Brandstatter et al. (2001) have provided just such evidence by examining the effects of forming implementation intentions under conditions of high cognitive load. Brandstatter et al. (Study 1) showed that opiate withdrawal patients who formed an implementation intention regarding where and when they would write a curriculum vitae were dramatically more likely to complete their goal by the end of the day (80%) than were those who formed an irrelevant implementation intention (0%). Their subsequent studies showed that schizophrenic patients (Study 2) and students under cognitive load generated by a dual task (Studies 3 & 4) were faster to respond in a Go–NoGo computerized task than those who had not formed implementation intentions. Thus, implementation intentions produce behavior in an efficient manner. In fact, it is intriguing to note from Brandstatter et al.'s recent findings that the effects appear to be enhanced by higher cognitive load, suggesting that the willful act of forming an implementation intention can ensure action initiation, especially where a person has a great many competing intentions.

It might be argued that evidence that implementation intentions produce responses to stimuli rapidly and efficiently does not provide conclusive evidence of automaticity because the stimulus cues in studies to date have not been presented outside of conscious awareness. Bayer, Moskowitz, and Gollwitzer (2002) have examined this proposition. They showed (Study 1) that people who had formed an implementation intention to retaliate to rude behavior showed faster reading times of words related to being rude when presented with subliminal rude faces, compared to participants who only formed a goal intention to complain. Their second study demonstrated that the behavior specified in an implementation intention (classifying geometrical figures) was enacted faster in response to a subliminal cue. This recent evidence suggests that having formed a goal intention and supplemented it by an implementation intention, the initiation of behavior does not require further conscious intent.

Evidence to date provides strong support for the notion that implementation intentions operate by delegating control to the environment (Gollwitzer, 1993, 1999). Evidence that the situational context specified in an implementation intention is capable of producing responses (a) immediately, (b) efficiently and (c) outside conscious awareness constitute three critical features of automatic responding (e.g. Bargh, 1994, 1996, 1997). This is an intriguing possibility, indicating that the deliberative processes, which might lead to development of a goal intention, can, by virtue of being supplemented by the willful act of forming an implementation intention, ultimately produce responses that may be characterized as automatic. In terms of understanding the establishment of novel behaviors, this implies that implementation intentions are a simple and willful means of creating habits. Habits also possess the characteristics of automaticity but, crucially, are developed as a result of repeated behavioral responses to a particular environmental cue, rather than as a result of a conscious mental act of forming an implementation intention (Verplanken & Aarts, 1999; Wood, Quinn, & Kashy, 2002).

In practical terms, this analysis implies that "good" habits might be created rather quickly if implementation intentions were employed in intervention studies. Recently, Verplanken and Orbell (2003) developed a self-report habit index (SRHI), which provides a measure of meta-subjective awareness of automaticity in behavioral responding. The measure is not intended to capture automaticity as it occurs, but captures people's awareness that they do something, or have done something, automatically, perhaps without realizing they were doing it, for example, "Behavior X is something I do without having to consciously remember." "Behavior X is something that would require effort not to do" (agree–disagree). The index is based on a theoretical analysis of features of habit, namely a history of repetition, automaticity and expressing one's identity (Verplanken & Aarts, 1999; Verplanken, Myrbakk, & Rudi, in press). A series of studies showed that the index possesses high internal and test–retest reliability and was capable of discriminating between behaviors that differed in frequency as measured three weeks earlier. Since the measure provides an assessment of *quality* of behavioral responses, it may have particular value in research where memory for *frequency* of behavior is unreliable, but people are able to characterize their behavior, using this measure, as occurring automatically. In preliminary studies, Orbell and Verplanken (2003, 2004) have shown that an implementation intention manipulation produces rapid increases in scores on the SRHI, in two behavioral domains. Moreover, Orbell and Verplanken (2003) also obtained evidence that forming an implementation intention is capable of attenuating the impact of pre-manipulation (previous) habit on subsequent exercise behavior. In regression analyses, previous habit contributed significant variance to the prediction of subsequent behavior over and above behavioral intention amongst controls. However, for the group who formed implementation intentions the addition of previous habit to the regression model did not contribute to the prediction of behavior over and above behavioral intention. These findings point to the validity of the measure in that it is sensitive to a manipulation (i.e., formation of an implementation intention), which has been independently demonstrated to create automatic responses.

## Self-regulation and pursuit of complex goals

Thus far we have been primarily concerned with the pursuit of relatively simple goal intentions referring to specific behavioral responses (e.g. "I intend to perform breast self-examination," "I intend to floss my teeth"). However, in considering the tasks of self-regulation it is useful to distinguish other forms of goal intention (cf. Bagozzi, 1992; Bagozzi & Dholakia, 1999). The general conceptualization ("I intend to do Z") may also apply to the achievement of more complex behavioral goals where a number of behavioral steps are required in order to reach the intended behavior (e.g. "I intend to catch my plane," "I intend to study hard for my exams," "I intend to stop snacking," "I intend to give up smoking") or to the outcomes of behaviors (e.g. "I intend to get fit," "I intend to lose weight," "I intend to get an 'A' in my course"). These more complex goal intentions require attention to (a) the identification of instrumental acts which might lead to goal achievement and (b) the self-regulatory skills which might contribute to those acts being successfully initiated and maintained. The formation of a goal intention to achieve a complex goal or to achieve an outcome may initiate a search for means (cf. implemental mindsets, Gollwitzer, 1999; Taylor & Gollwitzer, 1995) or the formation of plans as to what instrumental acts are needed in order to pursue a goal. The extent to which these activities lead to goal attainment will depend, however, upon the selection of appropriate (effective) instrumental acts and the successful execution of those acts.

In a preliminary investigation of the role of implementation intentions in pursuit of a complex behavioral goal, Sheeran and Orbell (2000b) theorized that the goal intention to go and get a cervical screening test would be achieved by performing the instrumental act of ringing up to make an appointment ("I intend to do Y in order to achieve behavioral goal Z"). Participants in that study were asked to form implementation intentions regarding when and where they would make an appointment to have a screening test ("If I encounter situation X, I will do Y, in order to achieve behavioral goal Z"). In that study, implementation intentions were highly successful in both ensuring that the instrumental act was performed, and consequently, that participants underwent a cervical screening test. While appropriate means to an end may be readily apparent in some instances, such as in forming an implementation intention to book a taxi to the airport in order to achieve the goal of catching the plane, in other instances the identification of instrumental acts and the execution of those acts may be less clear. The plethora of pamphlets and publications relating to how to give up smoking, how to lose weight, or how to be promoted attests to this fact. In a series of studies, Orbell and Sheeran (2002) (cf. Schaal & Gollwitzer, 1999) have recently examined the role of implementation intentions in achieving these more truly complex behavioral goals. A preliminary study investigated people's knowledge of possible instrumental acts that might contribute to avoiding eating snacks. While people were able to suggest three distinct strategies that they might use to achieve this goal, subsequent studies showed that only one type of strategy was actually effective in reducing snack consumption. When people formed an implementation intention to enact this strategy, they were not only more likely to use the strategy, and presumably did so in an automatic manner, but were more likely to achieve the goal of reducing snack consumption.

Some goal intentions may be difficult to achieve, not only because of the difficulty in initiating a behavioral intention or an intention to pursue an instrumental act, but because it may be difficult to stick with a behavior requiring concentration, deal with setbacks, or resume activity following an interruption. Consider, for example, the efforts required to finish painting the spare room in a single day, win the game of pool you are playing, finish the book chapter you are writing or do all of the weeding. These capacities are the focus of Kuhl's (1996, 2000; Kuhl & Kazen, 1994) personality systems interactions (PSI) theory. Kuhl suggests that an individual may possess positive intentions to enact a goal but lack the necessary volitional abilities to actually perform that behavior. PSI theory describes the complex interplay of conscious and non-conscious processes (e.g. emotions, attention, arousal, cognitive processing), which comprise two distinct types of volitional efficiency; *goal maintenance*, which is achieved by mechanisms of self-control, and *self-maintenance*, which is achieved by mechanisms of *self-regulation*.

Self-control was originally referred to as "action control" in the theory of action control (Kuhl, 1981, 1984, 1985, 1992) and functionally supports the maintenance and enactment of conscious goals and intentions in an explicit memory structure. Self-control is akin to common notions of "willpower" and essentially refers to conscious processes such as planning which inhibit other cognitive and emotional processes in order to protect an ongoing intention from competing alternatives. Because processes related to the self are suppressed when operating in this mode (self-control: "control of self"), self-control can permit an individual to pursue goals which may not be self-chosen or which have been assigned by others.

Unlike action control theory, personality systems interactions theory postulates a second mode of volition referred to as self-regulation. Self-regulation (self as agent) maintains actions in line with the needs, values and beliefs of the self. When operating in this volitional mode, self-generated actions and goals are protected and maintained by means of largely unconscious processes that integrate as many cognitive and emotional subsystems as possible for the support of a chosen action. Since the self-regulation mode relies upon access to the self-system, an individual operating in this mode will have access to self-motivational and cognitive resources for finding new solutions and will be able to identify and reject self-alien "unwanted thoughts" or social demands set by others which might otherwise interfere with goal directed activity. While self-control is facilitated by negative mood, self-regulation is facilitated by positive mood.

An exciting development in recent years has been the availability of scales to assess the various functional volitional components proposed by personality systems interactions theory (Kuhl & Fuhrmann, 1998). The Volitional Competence Inventory (VCI) assesses subjective concomitants of the various functions of self-control and self-regulation under conditions that require the person to overcome difficulties of enactment such as competing motivations, strong habitual tendencies, over- or under-arousal. Scales assessing *self-regulation* include attention control, implicit attention control, motivation control, emotion control, self-determination and decision control, while *self-control* competencies include intention control, planning, initiating, impulse control, failure control.

The availability of VCI scales facilitates exploration of the role of volitional competence in respect to a wide range of complex behavioral and outcome goals. One important issue for such research relates to their ability to provide improved prediction of behavior, over that provided by motivational models. If the scales are capable of capturing elements of volitional competence essential to the successful completion of complex or arduous goals, we would expect those individuals possessing such competence to be more likely to translate their intentions into action. Orbell (2003) examined the ability of volitional competence as assessed by the VCI to enhance prediction of a challenging behavior after taking account of intensity of intention and prior variables. When faced with a challenging task such as studying, a person who can activate the self-system by employing self-regulation is hypothesized to experience positive mood which in turn enhances access to memory and causes an increase in motivational energy for strengthening commitment to self-compatible goals, so that he/she can stay focused on the self-chosen activity and avoid unwanted self-alien thoughts (Kuhl, 2000). Consistent with PSI theory, Orbell (2003) found that participants with high scores on scales assessing these competencies, conscious attention control, implicit attention control and self-determination were more likely to translate their intentions into action. Moreover, participants with low subjective norms (which might be interpreted as low social support for studying or self-alien demands), were able to perform at least as well as those with high subjective norm if they employed self-regulation. These findings indicate an important role for self-regulatory processes in understanding the intention–behavior gap.

Further research might usefully examine other effects of volitional competence posed by this intriguing PSI theory. For example, the achievement of complex behavioral goals such as smoking cessation are hypothesized to require the operation of both self-regulatory competence and self-control competence. Self-regulation is necessary to maintain aspects of the self that support the goal ("what I want") while self-control is necessary to ensure that appropriate strategies are enacted to maintain that goal when confronted with competing motivations. The VCI also contains scales that purport to assess the extent to which an individual might behave spontaneously, or in accordance with established behavioral routines, raising the interesting possibility of individual differences in the extent to which given behaviors might be predictable from intentions versus behavioral habits.

## Concluding remarks

Intentions remain a very important determinant of human actions in contemporary social psychology, as does the study of the determinants of those intentions. However, there are good conceptual reasons for supposing that a host of self-regulatory difficulties haunt the proverbial intention–behavior gap. In particular, the inconsistency of intentions with behavior characterized by the analysis of "inclined abstainers" points to particular difficulties in intention maintenance and enactment amongst those with positive intentions, rather than to a more generalized tendency to simply change one's intentions, perhaps as a result of additional deliberation. The identification of self-regulatory mechanisms such as implementation intentions and the recent availability of scales for assessing a wide range of volitional competencies provides a basis for moving beyond deliberative processes to provide a fuller account of human goal achievement. Some progress has been made in establishing that where motivation can be shown to be equivalent, individuals will nonetheless differ in their likelihood of achieving simple behavioral goals. The delineation of competencies required for the completion of more complex goals will be an important issue for future research. Other important issues relate to the roles of behavioral control and habitual tendencies in determining behavior. It is not clear, for example, whether direct effects of perceived control on behavior might be considered markers for volitional competence in overcoming barriers to goal achievement, although Orbell's (2003) study suggests that this may be the case. Perhaps most challenging for theories of self-regulation is the possibility that volitional competencies might attenuate the pervasive effects of past behavior in tests of deliberative models. While there is good evidence that implementation intentions may successfully attenuate past behavioral tendencies, because the use of an implementation intention enables the translation of intention into action (Orbell et al., 1997; cf. Ajzen, 2002), only recently has it been possible to examine the interplay of self-regulation and habit. The recent availability of the SRHI (Verplanken & Orbell, 2003) to assess habitual tendencies may assist this research endeavor. Perhaps most challenging is the possibility of closing the intention–behavior gap for avoidance behaviors such as snacking. As shown in Figure 7.1, those with positive intentions to avoid acting are just as vulnerable to becoming inclined abstainers as are those with positive intentions to act. To overcome a past habit by enacting an intention not to do something represents a challenge indeed both for self-regulation theories and for the ongoing contest between intended and automatic behavior.

## References

Aarts, H., & Dijksterhuis, A. (2000). Habits as knowledge structures: Automaticity in goal-directed behaviors. *Journal of Personality and Social Psychology, 78,* 53–63.

Aarts, H., Dijksterhuis, A., & Midden, C. (1999). To plan or not to plan? Goal achievement or interrupting the performance of mundane behaviors. *European Journal of Social Psychology, 29,* 971–979.

Ajzen, I. (1985). From intentions to actions: A theory of planned behavior. In J. Kuhl & J. Beckmann (Eds.), *Action control: From cognition to behavior* (pp. 11–39). Berlin: Springer-Verlag.

Ajzen, I. (1991). The theory of planned behavior. *Organizational Behavior and Human Decision Processes, 50,* 179–211.

Ajzen, I. (2001). Nature and operation of attitudes. *Annual Review of Psychology, 52,* 27–58.

Ajzen, I. (2002). Residual effects of past on later behavior: Habituation and reasoned action explanations. *Personality and Social Psychology Review, 6,* 107–122.

Ajzen, I., & Fishbein, M. (1973). Attitudinal and normative variables as predictors of specific behaviors. *Journal of Personality and Social Psychology, 27,* 41–57.

Ajzen, I., & Fishbein, M. (1974). Factors influencing intentions and the intention-behavior relation. *Human Relations, 27,* 1–15.

Ajzen, I., & Fishbein, M. (1980). *Understanding attitudes and predicting social behavior.* Englewood Cliffs, NJ: Prentice Hall.

Armitage, C. J., & Conner, M. (2001). Efficacy of the theory of planned behavior: A meta-analytic review. *British Journal of Social Psychology, 40,* 471–499.

Bagozzi, R. P. (1992). The self-regulation of attitudes, intentions and behavior. *Social Psychology Quarterly, 55,* 178–204.

Bagozzi, R. P., & Dholakia, U. (1999). Goal setting and goal striving in consumer behavior. *Journal of Marketing, 63,* 19–32.

Bagozzi, R. P., & Warshaw, R. P. (1990). Trying to consume. *Journal of Consumer Research, 17,* 127–140.

Bagozzi, R. P., & Yi, Y. (1989). The degree of intention formation as a moderator of the attitude-behavior relationship. *Social Psychology Quarterly, 52,* 266–279.

Bargh, J. A. (1994). The four horsemen of automaticity: Awareness, intention, efficiency and control in social cognition. In R. S. Wyer, Jr. & T. K. Srull (Eds.), *Handbook of social cognition* (2nd ed., pp. 1–40). Hillsdale, NJ: Lawrence Erlbaum Associates, Inc.

Bargh, J. A. (1996). Principles of automaticity. In E. T. Higgins & A. Kruglanski

(Eds.), *Social psychology: Handbook of basic principles* (pp. 169–183). New York: Guilford Press.

Bargh, J. A. (1997). The automaticity of everyday life. In R. S. Wyer, Jr. (Ed.), *The automaticity of everyday life: Advances in social cognition* (Vol. 10, pp. 1–61). Mahwah, NJ: Lawrence Erlbaum Associates Inc.

Bargh, J. A., Chen, M., & Burrows, L. (1996). Automaticity of social behavior: Direct effects of trait construct and stereotype activation on action. *Journal of Personality and Social Psychology*, *71*, 230–244.

Bayer, U. C., Moskowitz, G. B., & Gollwitzer, P. M. (2002). *Implementation intentions and action initiation without conscious intent*. Manuscript under review.

Brandstatter, V., Lengfelder, A., & Gollwitzer, P. M. (2001). Implementation intentions and efficient action initiation. *Journal of Personality and Social Psychology 81*, 946–960.

Chasteen, A. L., Park, D. C., & Schwarz, N. (2001) Implementation intentions and facilitation of prospective memory. *Psychological Science*, *12*, 457–461.

Chen, M., & Bargh, J. A. (1999). Consequences of automatic evaluation: Immediate behavioral predispositions to approach or avoid the stimulus. *Personality and Social Psychology Bulletin*, *25*, 215–224.

Cohen, J. (1992). A power primer. *Psychological Bulletin*, *112*, 155–159.

Conner, M., & Norman, P. (2002). The theory of planned behavior and dietary change. *Health Psychology*, *21*, 194–201.

Conner, M., Sheeran, P., Norman, P., & Armitage, C. J. (2000). Temporal stability as a moderator of relationships in the theory of planned behavior. *British Journal of Social Psychology*, *39*, 469–494.

Conner, M., Sherlock, K., & Orbell, S. (1998). Psychosocial determinants of ecstasy use in young people in the UK. *British Journal of Health Psychology*, *3*, 295–317.

Courneya, K. S., & McAuley, E. (1994). Factors affecting the intention–physical activity relationship: Intention versus expectation and scale correspondence. *Research Quarterly for Exercise and Sport*, *65*, 280–285.

Dholakia, U. M., & Bagozzi, R. P. (2003). As time goes by: How implementation intentions influence enactment of short-fuse behaviors. *Journal of Applied Social Psychology*, *33*, 889–922.

Emmons, R. A. (1996). Striving and feeling: personal goals and subjective wellbeing. In P. M. Gollwitzer & J. A. Bargh (Eds.), *The psychology of action: Linking cognition and motivation to behavior* (pp. 313–337). New York: Guilford Press.

Fishbein, M. (1980). A theory of reasoned action: Some applications and implications. In H. Howe & M. Page (Eds.), *Nebraska symposium on motivation* (Vol. 27, pp. 65–116). Lincoln, NB: University of Nebraska Press.

Fishbein, M., & Ajzen, I. (1975). *Belief, attitude, intention and behavior: An introduction to theory and research*. Reading, MA: Addison-Wesley.

Gallois, C., Kashima, Y., Terry, D., McCamish, M., Timmins, P., & Chauvin, A. (1992). Safe and unsafe sexual intentions and behavior: The effects of norms and attitudes. *Journal of Applied Social Psychology*, *22*, 1521–1545.

Godin, G., & Kok, G. (1996). The theory of planned behavior: A review of its applications to health-related behaviors. *American Journal of Health Promotion*, *11*, 97–98.

Gollwitzer, P. M. (1993). Goal achievement: The role of intentions. *European Review of Social Psychology*, *4*, 141–185.

Gollwitzer, P. M. (1999). Implementation intentions: Strong effects of simple plans. *American Psychologist*, *54*, 493–503.

Gollwitzer, P. M., & Brandstatter, V. (1997). Implementation intentions and effective goal pursuit. *Journal of Personality and Social Psychology*, *73*, 186–199.

Gollwitzer, P. M., Heckhausen, H., & Stellar, B. (1990). Deliberative and implemental mindsets – cognitive tuning toward congruous thoughts and information. *Journal of Personality and Social Psychology*, *59*, 1119–1127.

Greve, W. (2001). Traps and gaps in action explanation: Theoretical problems of a psychology of human action. *Psychological Review*, *108*, 435–451.

Guynn, M. J., McDaniel, M., & Einstein, G. O. (2001). Remembering to perform actions: A different type of memory? In H. D. Zimmer, R. L. Cohen, M. J. Guynn, J. Engelkamp, R. Kormi-Nouri, & M. A. Foley (Eds.), *Memory for action: A distinct form of episodic memory?* (pp. 25–48). Oxford: Oxford University Press.

Hagger, M., Chatzisarantis, N., Biddle, S., & Orbell, S. (2001). Antecedents of children's physical activity intentions and behavior: Predictive validity and longitudinal effects. *Psychology and Health*, *16*, 391–407.

Hagger, M. S., Chatzisarantis, N. L. D., & Biddle, S. J. H. (2002). A meta-analytic review of the theories of reasoned action and planned behavior in physical activity: Predictive validity and the contribution of additional variables. *Journal of Sport and Exercise Psychology*, *24*, 3–32.

Hagger, M. S., & Orbell, S. (2003). *Implementation intentions, self-determination and establishment of healthy hydration habits during exercise.* Manuscript in preparation, University of Essex.

Hodgkins, S., & Orbell, S. (1998) Does protection–motivation theory predict behavior? A longitudinal test and exploration of the role of previous behavior. *Psychology and Health*, *13*, 237–250.

Kahneman, D., & Tversky, A. (1979). Intuitive prediction: Biases and corrective procedures. *TIMS Studies in Management Science*, *12*, 313–327.

Kim, M. S., & Hunter, J. E. (1993). Relationships among attitudes, behavioral intentions, and behavior: A meta-analysis of past research, Part 2. *Communication Research*, *20*, 331–364.

Koole, S., & Spijker, M. (2000). Overcoming the planning fallacy through willpower: Effects of implementation intentions on actual and predicted task-completion times. *European Journal of Social Psychology*, *30*, 873–888.

Kuhl, J. (1981). Motivational and functional helplessness: The moderating effect of state versus action orientation. *Journal of Personality and Social Psychology*, *40*, 155–170.

Kuhl, J. (1984). Volitional aspects of achievement motivation and learned helplessness: Toward a comprehensive theory of action control. In B. A. Maher (Ed.), *Progress in Experimental Personality Research* (Vol. 13, pp. 99–171). New York: Academic Press.

Kuhl, J. (1985). Volitional mediators of cognition-behavior consistency: Self-regulatory processes and action control. In J. Kuhl & J. Beckmann (Eds.), *Action control: From cognition to behavior* (pp.101–128). Berlin: Springer-Verlag.

Kuhl, J. (1992). A theory of self-regulation: Action versus state orientation, self-discrimination and some applications. *Applied Psychology: An International Review*, *41*, 97–129.

Kuhl, J. (1996). Who controls whom when "I control myself"? *Psychological Inquiry*, *7*, 61–68.

Kuhl, J. (2000). A functional-design approach to motivation and self-regulation: The dynamics of personality systems interactions. In M. Boekaerts, P. R. Pintrich, &

M. Zeidner (Eds.), *Self-regulation: Directions and challenges for future research* (pp. 111–169). New York: Academic Press.

Kuhl, J., & Fuhrmann, A. (1998). Decomposing self-regulation and self-control: The volitional components checklist. In J. Heckhausen & C. Dweck (Eds.), *Life span perspectives on motivation and control* (pp.15–49). Mahwah, NJ: Lawrence Erlbaum Associates, Inc.

Kuhl, J., & Kazen, M. (1994). Self-discrimination and memory: State orientation and false self-ascription of assigned activities. *Journal of Personality and Social Psychology, 66*, 1103–1115.

McBroom, W. H., & Reid, F. W. (1992). Towards a reconceptualization of attitude-behavior consistency. *Social Psychology Quarterly, 55*, 205–216.

Milne, S., Sheeran, P., & Orbell, S. (2000). Prediction and intervention in health related behavior: A meta-analytic review of protection–motivation theory. *Journal of Applied Social Psychology, 30*, 106–143.

Milne, S. E., Orbell, S., & Sheeran, P. (2002). Combining motivational and volitional interventions to promote exercise participation: Protection–motivation theory and implementation intentions. *British Journal of Health Psychology, 7*, 163–184.

Milne, S. E., & Sheeran, P. (2001). *Testing interaction effects in implementation intentions.* Paper presented at the annual conference of the Division of Health Psychology of the British Psychological Society, St Andrews, Scotland.

Orbell, S. (2000a). *Acquiring a novel behavior: Development of attitudes and intentions during the establishment of a regular behavior.* Unpublished raw data. University of Essex, UK.

Orbell, S. (2000b). *The theory of planned behavior and behavior change.* Unpublished raw data. University of Essex, U.K.

Orbell, S. (2001). *Attitudes, intentions and consideration of future consequences as determinants of consistent condom use.* Unpublished raw data. University of Essex, UK.

Orbell, S. (2003). Personality systems interactions theory and the theory of planned behavior: Evidence that self-regulatory volitional components enhance enactment of studying behavior. *British Journal of Social Psychology, 42*, 95–112.

Orbell, S., Blair, C., Sherlock, K., & Conner, M. (2001). The theory of planned behavior and ecstasy use: Roles for habit and perceived control over taking versus obtaining substances. *Journal of Applied Social Psychology, 31*, 31–47.

Orbell, S., Gollwitzer, P. M., & Sheeran, P. (2002). *Implementation intentions and complex goals.* Manuscript in preparation.

Orbell, S., & Guinote, A. (2002). *Priming activity in older people.* Unpublished raw data. University of Essex, UK.

Orbell, S., Hodgkins, S., & Sheeran, P. (1997). Implementation intentions and the theory of planned behavior *Personality and Social Psychology Bulletin, 23*, 953–962.

Orbell, S., & Sheeran, P. (1998a). "Inclined abstainers": A problem for predicting health behavior. *British Journal of Social Psychology, 37*, 151–166.

Orbell, S., & Sheeran, P. (1998b). Regulation of behavior in pursuit of health goals. *Psychology and Health, 13*, 753.

Orbell, S., & Sheeran, P. (2000). Motivational and volitional processes in action initiation: A field study of implementation intentions. *Journal of Applied Social Psychology, 30*, 780–797.

Orbell, S., & Sheeran, P. (2002). Changing health behaviours: The role of implementation intentions. In D. Rutter & L. Quine (Eds.), *Changing health behaviour:*

*Intervention and research with social cognition models* (pp. 123–137). Buckingham, UK: Open University Press.

Orbell, S., & Sheeran, P. (2002). *Implementation intentions and complex goals.* Manuscript in preparation.

Orbell, S., & Verplanken, B. (2003a) *Implementation intentions and the SRHI.* Manuscript in preparation.

Orbell, S., & Verplanken, B. (2004). *Measuring and modifying habituation in goal-directed behavior: Can implementation intentions enhance habit formation?* Manuscript submitted for publication.

Parker, D., Manstead, A. S. R., & Stradling, S. G. (1995). Extending the theory of planned behavior: The role of personal norm. *British Journal of Social Psychology, 34,* 127–137.

Perugini, M., & Bagozzi, R. P. (2001). The role of desires and anticipated emotions in goal-directed behaviors: Broadening and deepening the theory of planned behavior. *British Journal of Social Psychology, 40,* 79–98.

Perugini, M., & Bagozzi, R. P. (2004). An alternative view of pre-volitional processes in decision-making: Conceptual issues and empirical evidence. In G. R. Maio & G. Haddock (Eds.), *Contemporary perspectives on the psychology of attitudes.* Hove, UK: Psychology Press.

Randall, D. M., & Wolff, J. A. (1994). The time interval in the intention-behavior relationship: Meta-analysis. *British Journal of Social Psychology, 33,* 405–418.

Rise, J., Thompson, M., & Verplanken, B. (2003). Measuring implementation intentions in the context of the theory of planned behavior. *Scandinavian Journal of Psychology, 44,* 87–95.

Rogers, R. W. (1983). Cognitive and physiological processes in fear appeals and attitude change: A revised theory of protection motivation. In B. L. Cacioppo & L. L. Petty (Eds.), *Social psychophysiology: A source book* (pp. 153–176). New York: Guilford Press.

Schaal, B., & Gollwitzer, P. M. (1999). *Implementation intentions and resistance to temptation.* Cited in Gollwitzer (1999).

Sears, D. O. (1986). College sophomores in the laboratory: Influences of a narrow data base on social psychology's view of human nature. *Journal of Personality and Social Psychology, 51,* 515–530.

Sheeran, P. (2002). *Intention–behavior relations: A conceptual and empirical review.* In W. Stroebe and M. Hewstone (Eds.), *European Review of Social Psychology, 12,* 1–36.

Sheeran, P., & Abraham, C. (2002). Mediator of moderators: Temporal stability of intention and the intention–behavior relation. *Personality and Social Psychology Bulletin, 29,* 205–215.

Sheeran, P., Norman, P., & Orbell, S. (1999). Evidence that intentions based on attitudes better predict behavior than intentions based on subjective norms. *European Journal of Social Psychology, 29,* 403–406.

Sheeran, P., & Orbell, S. (1998) Does intention predict condom use? A meta-analysis and test of four moderators. *British Journal of Social Psychology, 37,* 231–250.

Sheeran, P., & Orbell, S. (1999a). Augmenting the theory of planned behavior: Roles for anticipated regret and descriptive norms. *Journal of Applied Social Psychology, 29,* 2107–2142.

Sheeran, P., & Orbell, S. (1999b). Implementation intentions and repeated behaviors: Enhancing the predictive validity of the theory of planned behavior. *European Journal of Social Psychology, 29,* 349–369.

Sheeran, P., & Orbell, S. (2000a). Self-schemas and the theory of planned behavior. *European Journal of Social Psychology, 30,* 533–550.

Sheeran, P., & Orbell, S. (2000b). Using implementation intentions to increase attendance for cervical cancer screening. *Health Psychology, 19,* 283–289.

Sheeran, P., Orbell, S., & Trafimow, D. (1999). Does the temporal stability of behavioral intentions moderate intention–behavior and past behavior–future behavior relations? *Personality and Social Psychology Bulletin, 25,* 721–730.

Sheeran, P., & Silverman, M. (2003). Evaluation of three interventions to promote workplace health and safety: Evidence for the utility of implementation intentions. *Social Science and Medicine, 56,* 2153–2163.

Sheldon, K. M., & Elliot, A. J. (1999). Goal striving, need satisfaction and longitudinal well-being: The self-concordance model. *Journal of Personality and Social Psychology, 76,* 482–497.

Sheppard, B. H., Hartwick, J., & Warshaw, P. R. (1988). The theory of reasoned action: A meta-analysis of past research with recommendations for modifications and future research. *Journal of Consumer Research, 15,* 325–342.

Stanton, B. F., Li, X., Black, M. M., Ricardo, I., Galbraith, J., Feigelman, S., & Kaljee, L. (1996). Longitudinal stability and predictability of sexual perceptions, intentions and behaviors among early adolescent African-Americans. *Journal of Adolescent Health, 18,* 10–19.

Sutton, S. (1998). Predicting and explaining intentions and behavior: How well are we doing? *Journal of Applied Social Psychology, 28,* 1317–1338.

Sutton, S., Bickler, G., Sancho-Aldridge, J., & Saidi, G. (1994). Prospective study of predictors of attendance for breast screening in inner London. *Journal of Epidemiology and Community Health, 48,* 65–73.

Taylor, S., & Gollwitzer, P. M. (1995). Effects of mindset on positive illusions. *Journal of Personality and Social Psychology, 69,* 213–226.

Verplanken, B., & Aarts, H. (1999) Habit, attitude and planned behavior: Is habit an empty construct or an interesting case of goal-directed automaticity? *European Review of Social Psychology, 10,* 101–134.

Verplanken, B., & Faes, S. (1999). Good intentions, bad habits and effects of forming implementation intentions on healthy eating. *European Journal of Social Psychology, 29,* 591–604.

Verplanken, B., Myrbakk, V., & Rudi, E. (in press). The measurement of habit. In T. Betsch & S. Haberstroh (Eds.), *The routines of decision making.* Mahwah, NJ: Lawrence Erlbaum Associates, Inc.

Verplanken, B., & Orbell, S. (2003). Reflections on past behavior: A self-report index of habit strength. *Journal of Applied Social Psychology, 33,* 1313–1330.

Warshaw, P. R., Calantone, R., & Joyce, M. (1986). A field application of the Fishbein and Ajzen intention model. *Journal of Social Psychology, 126,* 135–136.

Webb, T. L., & Sheeran, P. (in press). Integrating concepts from goal theories to understand the achievment of personal goals. *European Journal of Social Psychology.*

Wegner, D. M., & Wheatley, T. (1999). Apparent mental causation: Sources of the experience of will. *American Psychologist, 54,* 480–492.

Wood, W., Quinn, J. M., & Kashy, D. A. (2002). Habits in everyday life: Thought, emotion and action. *Journal of Personality and Social Psychology, 83,* 1281–1297.

Young, M., DeSarbo, W. S., & Morwitz, V. G. (1998). The stochastic modeling of purchase intentions and behavior. *Management Science, 44,* 188–202.

# 8 An alternative view of pre-volitional processes in decision making

## Conceptual issues and empirical evidence

*Marco Perugini and*
*Richard P. Bagozzi*

The last 20 years have seen a series of developments within attitude theory that are likely to shape the field in the next decades. Two main approaches to decision making within this field have emerged: automatic and deliberative (Eagly & Chaiken, 1998). These two approaches have been repeatedly sketched in the so-called dual theories, for instance in models of attitude change and persuasive messages (e.g., Chen & Chaiken, 1999; Petty & Wegener, 1999), whereby both routes are considered as possible, depending on variables such as motivation and ability, as well as in theories where the emphasis has been placed on one of the two approaches, such as the motivation and opportunity as determinants (MODE) model proposed by Fazio (1990) and the theory of planned behavior (TPB) developed by Ajzen (1991).

In this chapter we will briefly examine the two positions. We will argue that, although recent evidence emphasizes the importance of automatic processes and momentum appears to be with this approach, the automatic approach still falls short from offering a comprehensive view and a satisfactory prediction of behavior. In particular, we will argue that, whereas it is clear that automatic processes play an important role and should be taken into account in any attempt to explain and predict human behaviors, they alone cannot suffice to fully explain behavior. We will then review the mainstream approach within the deliberative camp and identify areas for improvement. The core of this chapter will be on proposing an alternative conceptualization of attitude theory that offers a deeper understanding and improved prediction of prevolitional processes. We also review empirical evidence supporting our conceptualization. Finally, we will discuss possible extensions of the models and future directions of research.

## Automatic approaches to attitudes

The automatic, effortless, and implicit aspects of human information processing are currently at the center of attention in attitude research. Several recent studies have shown that implicit attitudes can be activated automatically and guide behavior directly (e.g., Bargh, Chen, & Burrows, 1996; Chen & Bargh, 1999; Dovidio, Kawakami, Johnson, Johnson, & Howard, 1997; Fazio & Dunton, 1997). Other studies have found that attitude accessibility moderates the link between attitudes and behavior (e.g., Fazio, Sanbonmatsu, Powell, & Kardes, 1986; Fazio & Williams, 1986; Posovac, Sanbonmatsu, & Fazio, 1997). Fazio's MODE model encapsulates this empirical evidence by proposing that attitudes that are automatically accessed, via strength of the object-evaluation association, bias perceptions of the object and lead directly to behavior without any conscious reasoning processes occurring (Fazio, 1990). Still other studies have emphasized implicit attitudes that are thought to direct people's reactions to attitude objects outside of conscious awareness (Greenwald & Banaji, 1995). The Implicit Association Test (Greenwald, McGhee, & Schwartz, 1998) has been specifically developed to measure implicit attitudes and used in several studies (e.g., Cunningham, Preacher, & Banaji, 2001; Dasgupta, McGhee, Greenwald, & Banaji, 2000; Greenwald, Banaji, Rudman, Farnham, Nosek, & Mellott, 2002; Greenwald & Farnham, 2000). Altogether, there is growing and convincing evidence that automatic processes play an important role in human cognition and that they can direct behavior even when it is complex (e.g., Bargh, Gollwitzer, Lee-Chai, Barndollar, & Trötschel, 2001; see also Vargas, Chapter 12 this volume).

However, the extent to which these studies imply that reasoned processes are only marginally or not at all relevant for the prediction of human behavior is a more controversial issue. It is outside the scope of the present chapter to deal with this issue. Interested readers are referred to Ajzen (2001) and Eagly and Chaiken (1998), who review the theoretical and practical importance of considering reasoned or deliberative decision-making models. We will briefly focus here merely on one issue not dealt with previously: namely, the empirical evidence produced so far falls well short of showing that automatic processes explain much of the richness of human behaviors (cf. Bargh & Chartrand, 1999). If one analyzes the empirical evidence in more detail, the role of automaticity in predicting behavior appears to be more limited than claimed.

For purposes of illustration, we will consider three among the most famous studies in the field.[1] The study by Bargh et al. (1996) is a widely cited example of automaticity in action. The experiments show the influence of subliminally priming (1) the concept of rudeness on increasing the likelihood with which participants interrupt the experimenter (Experiment 1); (2) stereotypes of

---

1 It is outside the scope of this chapter to embark into a systematic analysis of all studies conducted on automaticity. The selectivity of our review is exclusively done for purposes of exemplification. However, we believe that by analyzing three among the most famous and widely cited examples of "automaticity in action" general considerations can still be reasonably made.

elderly people on the speed of walking (Exps. 2a, 2b); (3) stereotypes of African American on producing hostile behaviors (Exp. 3). Equally well known is the paper by Chartrand and Bargh (1999) studying the *chameleon effect*: that is, the nonconscious mimicry of the postures of the experimenter displayed by participants. This mimicry effect was investigated in three experiments with several dependent variables. Finally, the study by Djikstheruis and Van Knippenberg (1998) presents four experiments showing that priming a stereo-type or a trait (professors or soccer hooligans) leads to improved or decreased performance in a Trivial Pursuit game. All the above studies have been often cited as exemplary evidence for the automaticity of behavior.[2]

Using the method suggested by Rosenthal and Rubin (1982), we have calculated the variance explained in behavior from the effects found in the experiments (see Table 8.1). The amount of variance explained by the experimental manipulations that are due to the automaticity effect ranges from .06 to .37, with a simple average value of .13 across the 18 dependent variables. That is, the above studies finding automaticity in action predict only 13% of the variance in behavior on average.

In closing this section, we would like to emphasize that our goal is not to trivialize the results obtained within the automaticity paradigm. We truly believe that the paradigm and findings to date represent important contribu-tions to the field of attitude research. The studies clearly show that people need not necessarily form an intention in order to perform a behavior. Thus, the conscious deliberative link between attitude and behavior can be bypassed. Nevertheless, we argue that this does not imply that intentions do not play any role or that intentions are simply epiphenomenal attributions made by people to explain to themselves why they do what they do (Wegner & Wheatley, 1999). On logical grounds, the argument claiming that intentions are epiphenomena is self-contradictory (cf. Yanchar, 2000). On pragmatic grounds, we believe it would be wiser and scientifically more productive to acknowledge that reasoned and deliberative approaches cannot be dismissed out of hand, if one wants truly to explain and predict a realistic range of ecologically relevant behaviors. As we argue below, the empirical evidence clearly supports the importance of constructs such as intention and volition in predicting human behavior, over and above the contributions provided by automatic attitudinal effects.

## Deliberative approaches to attitudes

Expectancy-value approaches have been dominant within the deliberative tradition, and the leading contemporary model in this tradition is Ajzen's theory of planned behavior (TPB; Ajzen, 1991, 2001).

Under the TPB, the proximal cause of behavior is an intention to perform that given behavior. Moreover, attitude is only one of the determinants of

2 The three studies have been cited a total of 184 times by other published works (August 2002).

*Table 8.1* Variance explained in behavior in the experiments of Bargh, Chen, and Burrows (1996), Chartrand and Bargh (1999), Dijksterhuis and Van Knippenberg (1998)

| Study | DV | Value | df | R | R² |
|---|---|---|---|---|---|
| **Bargh, Chen, and Burrow (1996)** | | | | | |
| *Exp. 1 (Rudeness)* | | | | | |
| Counting of rude behavior[a] | % | 73.5 vs. 26.5 | 1 | .36 | .13 |
| *Exp. 2 (Elderly people)* | | | | | |
| (a) Walking speed | t | 2.86 | 28 | .48 | .23 |
| (b) Walking speed | t | 2.16 | 28 | .38 | .14 |
| *Exp. 3 (African American)* | | | | | |
| Hostility rating (by coders) | F | 6.95 | 39 | .39 | .15 |
| **Chartrand and Bargh (1999)** | | | | | |
| *Exp. 1 (Mimicry between strangers)* | | | | | |
| (1) Facial expression (by coders) | F | 20.31 | 34 | .61 | .37 |
| (2) Face rubbing | F | 5.71 | 34 | .38 | .14 |
| (3) Foot shaking | F | 3.76 | 34 | .32 | .10 |
| (4) Smiling | F | 4.16 | 34 | .33 | .11 |
| *Exp. 2 (Adaptive function)* | | | | | |
| (1) Liking | F | 5.55 | 70 | .27 | .07 |
| (2) Smoothness | F | 4.08 | 70 | .23 | .06 |
| *Exp. 3 (Individual differences)* | | | | | |
| For high perspective-takers | | | | | |
| (1) Combined face rubbing and foot shaking | F | 3.85 | 48 | .27 | .07 |
| **Dijksterhuis and Van Knippenberg (1998)** | | | | | |
| *Exp. 1 (Professors)* | | | | | |
| (1) Correct answers (Prof. vs. Secret.) | F | 10.45 | 57 | .39 | .15 |
| (2) (Prof. vs. No-prime) | F | 5.84 | 57 | .30 | .09 |
| *Exp. 2 (Length of priming)* | | | | | |
| (1) Correct answers (2 min vs. No-prime) | F | 4.83 | 55 | .28 | .08 |
| (2) (9 min vs. No-prime) | F | 16.36 | 55 | .48 | .23 |
| *Exp. 3 (Soccer hooligans)* | | | | | |
| (1) Correct answers (2 min vs. No-prime) | F | 1.35 | 92 | .12 | .01 |
| (2) (9 min vs. No-prime) | F | 10.58 | 92 | .32 | .10 |
| *Exp. 4 (Direction of prime)* | | | | | |
| Correct answers | F | 7.12 | 39 | .39 | .15 |
| **Average** | | | | **.35** | **.13** |

*Notes*
[a] = The primary dependent variable of this experiment (number of seconds the participants waited before interrupting the experimenter) could not be used to calculate the variance because the authors do not report the *t*-values for pairwise comparisons. We used the secondary dependent variable (percentage of participants in each priming condition who interrupted at all) that could be approximately inferred from Figure 8.1.

intention. Subjective norms (i.e., the perceived social pressure to perform a given behavior) and perceived behavioral control (i.e., the perceived ease or difficulty of performing the given behavior) are also hypothesized to influence one's intention. Both constructs are formed in parallel summative manners:

normative beliefs times motivations to comply for subjective norms and control beliefs times perceived power for perceived behavioral control. Perceived behavioral control is also posited to have a direct influence on behavior, to the extent that it corresponds to actual behavioral control (Ajzen & Madden, 1986).

From an empirical point of view, the performance of the TPB has been assessed in a number of recent meta-analytic studies. Godin and Kok (1996) reviewed 76 applications of the TPB in the domain of health-related behaviors, and found an average of 41% of variance explained in intentions and 34% in behavior. Similar findings were obtained by Armitage and Conner (2001) who examined 185 empirical tests of the TPB and found that the TPB accounted on average for 39% of the variance in intention and 27% of the variance in behavior. A recent meta-analysis of meta-analyses by Sheeran (2002) found that over a total sample of $N = 82,107$, whereby the TPB as well as other theoretical models that include intention as predictors of behavior were scrutinized, the average sample-weighted correlation between intention and behavior was .53, corresponding to 28% of variance in behavior explained by the intention to behave. This latter value should be compared with the average value of 13% across the experiments by Bargh and colleagues (Table 8.1). Despite the differences across studies which limit direct comparisons, it is obvious that explanations in terms of automaticity of behavior that exclude any role played by intentions do not offer pragmatically superior alternatives. These data support the notion that, at least on pragmatic grounds, the construct of intention cannot be dismissed as irrelevant. On the contrary, given that the empirical evidence supports the important role played by intentions and volitions in explaining and predicting behavior, the question of how people come to form intentions or volitions remains a key issue.

## An alternative view of pre-volitional processes in decision making

The TPB provides a robust explanation of the pre-volitional processes in decision making and predicts a remarkable amount of variance in intention, as testified by the average value of 39% in Armitage and Conner's meta-analysis (2001). Yet, the findings suggest that there is still room for improvement in both explanatory and predictive senses. Several proposals to improve the TPB have been offered, often with a mix of new theoretical and empirical contributions. The weak point of the TPB, it has been often argued, is its sufficiency. Researchers have proposed additions to the TPB addressing self-identity processes (Sparks & Shephard, 1992), moral norms (Beck & Ajzen, 1991; Parker, Manstead, & Stradling, 1995), the distinction between perceptions of control and self-efficacy (Armitage & Conner, 1999; Terry & O'Leary, 1995), anticipated emotions (Parker et al., 1995; Richard, van der Pligt, & de Vries, 1995), and habit or past behavior (Bagozzi, 1981;

Ouellette & Wood, 1998). The focus of these proposals is on the addition of independent variables as parallel predictors of behavioral intentions and behaviors, along with the established predictors. The rationale is that more variance can be accounted for by specifying processes formally contained in error terms in tests of the theory and that the resulting theoretical under-standing of the decision-making process can be broadened. Four main areas of improvement over the TPB can be identified: (a) automatic pro-cesses; (b) affective processes; (c) motivational processes; (d) means–end analyses. Below, we review these areas and present two recently developed models that offer alternative views of pre-volitional decision-making processes.

## Automatic processes

> Consuetudine quasi altera quandam naturam [Habit is practically our second nature].
>
> Cicero, 45 BC, *De finibus bonorum et malorum*, Lib. 5, Cap. 25, Par. 74

The role of automatic processes in decision making can hardly be exagger-ated. As we have argued above, there is impressive experimental evidence in this regard. Additional evidence can be found in previous studies whereby past behavior and habit was shown to explain additional variance in behavior, over and above that explained by intentions (e.g., Bagozzi, 1981; Bentler & Speckart, 1979, 1981). Ajzen (1991) criticized the use of past behavior on grounds that it offers no explanatory content, although he allowed that past behavior provides a methodological control in tests of any theory: "past behavior can be used to test the sufficiency of any model designed to predict future behavior" (Ajzen, 1991, p. 202). Further, Ajzen (1991) argued that the inclusion of perceived behavioral control (PBC) in the TPB should preclude the need for past behavior, in that PBC should mediate any residual effects of past behavior. This was one of the main reasons why the TPB superseded its predecessor Theory of Reasoned Action (Fishbein & Ajzen, 1975). However, recent empirical work finds that past behavior still predicts intentions and behavior in tests of the TPB (e.g., Bagozzi & Kimmel, 1995; Beck & Ajzen, 1991; Leone, Perugini, & Ercolani, 1999).

The question remains what the effects of past behavior might represent. A meta-analysis recently found robust evidence for the impact of frequency of past behavior on both intentions and behavior (Ouellette & Wood, 1998). Ouellette and Wood (1998) proposed two processes through which frequency of past behavior guides future behavior. When a behavior is well learned and practised in a non-changing environment, frequency of past behavior reflects habit strengths and therefore shows a direct effect on future behavior. When a behavior is novel or performed in non-stable contexts, frequency of past behavior influences intentions on the grounds that people like to do things that they have done in the past.

Another proposal has been to partition the effects of past behavior into frequency and recency effects (Bagozzi & Warshaw, 1990). Although seemingly related, frequency and recency effects are conceptually distinct and therefore might carry independent information. For instance, one may have a long history of performing a given behavior without having performed it recently or one may have recently taken up an activity with no prior experience with it. Recency of behavior performance should influence future behavior to the degree that availability and anchoring/adjustment biases occur in information processing (e.g., Tversky & Kahneman, 1974) and to the degree that an activity, whether established or not, has been recently initiated. The recent initiation of an activity may carry implicit information about intentions over and above the degree to which intentions are accessible to conscious awareness. Recency may therefore serve as an indirect indicator that an intention has been activated and therefore be positively associated with subsequent performance of the behavior.

The concept of habit as the key explanatory variable underlying the role of past behavior has also been proposed by other researchers (for a review, see Verplanken & Aarts, 1999). For instance, Aarts and Dijksterhuis (2000) define habit as a form of goal-directed automatic behavior, which is activated automatically by the presence of relevant environmental cues (cf. the automotive model, Bargh, 1990), provided that the relevant goal is activated. Measures relying on habit strength and on aspects of automaticity have been proposed by Verplanken and colleagues. A different view has been recently put forward by Ajzen (2002). Ajzen maintains that the empirical evidence produced so far does not offer sound theoretical explanations of the role of past behavior in terms of habitualized responses. He argues that other explanations, such as the instability of intentions or the presence of unrealistic optimism and inadequate planning should instead be considered before claiming that past behavior (habit) provides a theoretical basis for predictions.

To sum up, the evidence of the role played by past behavior in *predicting* future behavior is very strong. However, there is a range of opinions concerning its role in *explaining* future behavior. Either way, we believe that any comprehensive decision-making model in this field should include past behavior, if for no other reason than to improve the prediction of intentions and behavior and/or control for unmeasured determinants.

## Affective processes

> . . . I shall endeavour to prove *first*, that reason alone can never be a motive to any action of the will; and *secondly*, that it can never oppose passion in the direction of the will.
>
> Hume, 1739, *A Treatise of Human Nature*, Section III, p. 413

The TPB has traditionally emphasized the cognitive-evaluative component of attitude and neglected the affective component. Attitude is conceived as "a psychological tendency that is expressed by evaluating a particular entity with some degree of favor or disfavor" (Eagly & Chaiken, 1993, p. 1, emphasis in original removed). Under the TPB, attitude is usually formulated to refer to a target behavior and its overall measure consists of bipolar semantic differential items such as good–bad, harmful–beneficial, rewarding–punishing, and unpleasant–pleasant (Ajzen, 1991). Therefore, depending on the specific pair of adjectives used in a study, an overall measure of attitude in practice can be characterized mostly by cognitive aspects, by affective aspects or, more frequently, by a variable mix of the two. In this sense, the original conception of the TPB did focus mostly on the evaluative aspect without explicitly dealing with the specific contribution of the affective and cognitive components. Some authors have instead argued for an explicit distinction between the evaluative and affective components of attitude and collected empirical support for this distinction (e.g., Breckler & Wiggins, 1989; Trafimow & Sheeran, 1998; Verplanken, Hofstee, & Janssen, 1998). The affective component has been defined as an affective disposition to respond in a favorable or unfavorable manner. A person is expected to acquire over a period of time or through repeated contact accompanied by reinforcement an affective orientation toward an object or act that, once learned, can be triggered automatically when one is exposed to the object or act or thinks about it (Fazio, 1995).

An alternative approach has been proposed by Bagozzi, Baumgartner, and Pieters (1998), who introduced the concept of anticipated emotions as predictors of intentions to act. An attitude, either affective or cognitive, is typically constant over reasonable periods of time and it is not formulated as a response contingent on the occurrence of particular happenings to be appraised. By contrast, the processes behind the functioning of anticipated emotions are more dynamic and entail self-regulation in response to feedback (Bagozzi, 1992; Carver & Scheier, 1998). They are specifically contingent on one's appraisal of achievement or failure, which changes from time to time, depending on the context. An implicit comparison is made between one's goal as a standard or reference value and achieving and failing to achieve that goal, with anticipated emotions as consequences.

This functioning of anticipated emotions is related to counterfactual thinking. Counterfactuals are conditional statements that contain both an antecedent expressed as a hypothetical (e.g., "If X happens") and a consequent expressed as an implication ("then Y will occur"). Quite a bit of research has been conducted in recent years with respect to the cognitive processes underlying "backward-looking" counterfactuals, wherein people consider what might have been, if certain things had happened differently than they did (e.g., Roese & Olson, 1995). Less frequently studied has been the function of anticipated counterfactuals, where people consider future prospects and evaluate the consequences of alternative, contingent outcomes. Gleicher, Boninger, Strathman, Armor, Hetts, & Ahn (1995, p. 294) call such anticipated counterfactuals "prefactuals."

With regard to negative outcomes, two mechanisms were hypothesized by Gleicher et al. (1995, pp. 294–295) for serving as the basis by which counterfactuals operate to influence intentions and behavior:

> First, when a person generates a counterfactual that reverses a negative outcome, he or she is likely to make the attribution that there is an effective action that can be taken in the future ... [Second] when an individual thinks about a counterfactual in advance, the motivation to avoid this negative affect influences behavioural choices.

Parker et al. (1995) were among the first to find that anticipated regret (measured with "make me feel sorry" and "make me feel good" items) affected expectations that one would commit certain automotive driving violations. Likewise, Richard et al. (1995) found that negative anticipated emotions (called anticipated postbehavioral affective reactions and measured with "worried–not worried", "regret–no regret", and "tense–relaxed" items) increased expectations that people would refrain from sexual intercourse or would use condoms in casual encounters. In these, as well as in other works, the emphasis has been placed on a few negative anticipated emotions, especially on regret.

However, the range of negative anticipated emotions potentially affecting one's intention to perform a given behavior is much greater (e.g., shame, disappointment, anger, guilt, sadness). Moreover, parallel processes can be hypothesized for positive outcomes. People should be motivated to make choices promoting positive affects such as gladness, satisfaction, happiness, and pride. Whether positive or negative anticipated emotions play a more important role in decision-making processes may depend on the kind of behavior, for instance, whether it is a preventive or a detection behavior (Rothman & Salovey, 1997), or on the kind of person, for instance, whether one is promotion or prevention focused (Higgins, 1996). Within each cluster of positive and negative emotions, even more specific predictions concerning which emotion is more likely to play an important role can be made by relying on emotional appraisal theories such as the one proposed by Roseman, Antoniou, and Jose (1996).

A question that can be raised is whether anticipated emotions overlap with the affective component of attitude and its measures. Although both conceptualizations attempt to tap affective processes in decision making, they do so in fundamentally different ways.

Attitude focuses upon "the evaluation of an object, concept, or behavior, along a dimension of favor or disfavor, good or bad, like or dislike" (Ajzen & Fishbein, 2000, p. 3). It has also been argued that attitude should be sharply distinguished from affect, given that the operational definition of attitude assesses an evaluative dimension, which may include affective evaluations, rather than a properly affective or emotional component (Ajzen & Fishbein, 2000, p. 3). By contrast, anticipated emotions are dynamic, self-regulatory, and based on contingent appraisals of the consequences of alternative outcomes. They refer to anticipated affective consequences of failure or success rather than to static evaluations. Anticipated emotions are hypothesized also to affect the intention to perform a given behavior (through their effect on desires, as developed below). Finally, another difference occurs at the level of measurement. When people are asked to respond with their attitudes, they are forced to make a choice of favorability or unfavorability. This is a consequence of the recommended practice of using bipolar items to indicate respondents' attitudes. By contrast, anticipated emotions are better measured by using unipolar items (e.g., the experience of disappointment along a "not at all" to "very much" continuum). In a study of affect, Bagozzi, Wong, and Yi (1999) found that positive and negative affect can be positively related, negatively related, or unrelated to each other, depending on conditions such as the independence vs. interdependence of the culture where people had their upbringing and live. This finding is in line with related evidence for basic differences between positive and negative emotional reactions, in terms of static structural representations of affect (e.g., Russell & Barrett, 1999), basic functioning of physiological systems (e.g., Gray, 1990), behavioral strategies (e.g., Higgins, 1996), anticipation of future consumption (e.g., Loewenstein, 1987), decision making (e.g., van der Pligt, Zeelenberg, van Dijk, de Vries, & Richard, 1998) and effects on behavior (e.g., Cacioppo & Berntson, 1994). To use a bipolar scale to measure affective features (as it is routinely done in attitude theory) would make positive and negative affect mutually exclusive by definition and not permit respondents the opportunity to express their differential relevance.

To sum up, the TPB does not pay sufficient attention to the role played by affective processes in decision making. One possibility is to construe affect as another component of attitudes. An alternative possibility that we believe to be more fruitful is to examine affective processes as instances of pre-factual thinking where people are asked to anticipate what their emotional responses would be to the occurrence and non-occurrence of a future event. Analogous to the notion of prospect-based emotions (e.g., Ortony, Clore, & Collins 1988), anticipated emotions can be hypothesized to be integrated with attitudes, subjective norms, and perceived behavioral control as a basis for intention formation.

## Motivational processes

> I believe that I will die someday, and make a mistake today, but I intend to do neither. What is lacking is desire, the motivational element in intention.
>
> Davis (1984, p. 45)

Another weak area of the TPB concerns the motivational processes in decision making. It has been argued that the TPB fails to consider how intentions become energized (Bagozzi, 1992; Fazio, 1995, pp. 271–272). Attitudes, subjective norms, and perceived behavioral control provide reasons for acting, but do not incorporate explicit motivational content needed to induce an intention to act. Bagozzi (1992, pp. 184–186) early on proposed that desires provide the motivational impetus for intentions and suggested that attitudes work through desires to influence intentions. Expanding on Bagozzi's (1992) arguments, Perugini and Bagozzi (2001) proposed that desire is a stronger predictor of intentions than attitudes, subjective norms, and perceived behavioral control, and it plays a key mediational role in transforming reasons to perform a given behavior into a motivation to do so. From this perspective, the usual TPB predictors do not directly determine behavioral intentions, but rather indirectly through desires.

The concept of desires is rarely mentioned in contemporary attitude theory presentations. Mainstream attitude models (e.g., Ajzen, 1991; Eagly & Chaiken, 1993; Fazio, 1990) do not consider desires at all or else seemingly lump them together with intentions. On the other hand, philosophers make a clear distinction between desires and intentions (Audi, 1986; Bratman, 1987; Davidson, 1963; Davis, 1984; Mele & Moser, 1994; Schueler, 1995). Although theoretical disagreements exist concerning the specific way in which desires and intentions are related, the distinction is one of the central tenets of philosophical treatments of action, dating back at least to Aristotle. The dominant model in this stream of work within the so-called philosophy of action is some variant of a three-facet model of decision making, based on a distinction between beliefs and desires and their influence on corresponding intentions. For philosophers, desires are thought to have a fundamental role in decision making. Likewise people in everyday life distinguish between desiring to act or obtain something and intending to do or to achieve it, respectively, placing much emphasis on the concept of desire in one's thoughts, interpersonal relations, and actions. That desires and intentions are distinct can be witnessed in familiar or conventional problem solving: John feels a desire to take a vacation but for various reasons intends not to do so; Janet lacks a desire to attend a lecture yet plans to attend it nevertheless.

Recent empirical evidence supports this important distinction. Theoretically, the distinction between the two constructs has been developed by Malle and Knobe (2001) and by Perugini and Bagozzi (2004). Malle and Knobe (2001) approach this issue from a social perceiver perspective and argue that social perceivers are well aware of the distinction embedded in these two mental states. For instance, people are relying more on someone else's intentions than desires when trying to make accurate predictions, because they are aware that desires can be highly conflicting whereas intentions are less so. Moreover, they are aware that an intention is a further step in the decision-making process and does imply some form of even partial commitment to action, whereas a desire can be more fleeting and might not involve any decision to act upon it.

Perugini and Bagozzi (2004) approach the issue from a decision maker's perspective and proposed three criteria to distinguish between desires and intentions: *perceived performability* (desires being typically perceived as less performable than intentions); *action-connectedness* (desires are less connected to actions); and *temporal frame* (desires are relatively more future oriented than intentions). In two studies, they have found evidence that people perceive their own desires as less connected to specific actions, as more framed in longer temporal horizons, and as perceived as less obtainable than their own intentions. In other words, people do appreciate that, in their own decision-making flow, a desire comes before an intention, it does imply a more limited commitment to action, and it does not always lead to an intention to act. This appeared to be the case even when focusing on action rather than goal content, which is a special situation whereby the differences between desires and intentions should be minimized (cf. Malle & Knobe, 2001).

Empirically, there is recent correlational and experimental evidence supporting the distinction between desires and intentions. In their meta-analysis of TPB studies, Armitage and Conner (2001) showed that attitudes, subjective norms and perceived behavioral control predicted significantly more variance in desires than in intentions, and that intention was a better predictor of behavior than desires. We will review additional correlational evidence below. Malle and Knobe (2001) reported the results of a series of scenario-based experiments finding clear empirical evidence for the distinction. Finally, Perugini and Bagozzi (2004) provided empirical support for this distinction in two experiments.

Interestingly, whereas desire is rarely mentioned[3] in the literature, the concept of desirability is often used in social psychology to explain a wide range of phenomena. Particularly interesting is the temporal construal theory proposed by Liberman and Trope (1998) which focuses on the mental construction of events at different levels of abstraction and under different time frames. Liberman and Trope (1998) propose that feasibility and desirability are key elements in choosing between temporally near and distant alternative courses of action. Desirability, reflecting the superordinate "why" aspects of an action (cf. Vallacher & Wegner, 1987), was defined as the valence of an action's end state and hypothesized to be a main reason to act, especially for distant future scenarios; feasibility, defined as the ease or difficulty of

---

3 One exception is given by the model of action phases (Gollwizter, 1996; Heckhausen & Gollwitzer, 1987). The first stage of this model (pre-decisional stage) consists of the contemplation of different wishes and desires and the setting of preferences among them. The culmination of this stage is the formation of a goal intention, which is initiated and executed in the following two stages (pre-actional and actional). However, Gollwitzer does not consider extensively how these goal intentions come about (e.g., on the basis of which criteria a goal is chosen) but rather focuses on subsequent action phases.

reaching the end state, was argued to be more relevant for near-future actions (Liberman & Trope, 1998, p. 7).

The emphasis of research on desirability has been more on the value of a particular goal outcome (e.g., the valence of an action's end state) than on the role of the agent and the processes of valuation and their impact on action initiation, per se. However, whether an agent will act in relation to a "desirable" end state depends on the agent's desire to achieve that end state. A definition of desire resting on the valence attributed to an object or action would seem to be empty without reference to the motivational state of mind of the agent. In other words, a key causal element in action is the personal motivation (*desire*) to achieve an end state and not an inherent objective property of the end state itself (i.e., its *desirability*).[4] Otherwise, we might end up believing that it was the nice car that caused me to buy it, and not my desire to have it.

Furthermore, whether one desires to perform a certain action does not necessarily imply that he/she will intend to do it. We often have desires, fleeting or otherwise, that we never intend to act upon. However, an intention to perform an action generally follows a volitional desire (i.e., behavioral desire or desire to act) which represents the motivational state of mind wherein appraisals and reasons to act are transformed into a personal motivation to do so.

## Model of goal-directed behavior

An alternative account of the decision-making processes whereby these three areas (automatic, affective, motivational) are integrated is given by the model of goal-directed behavior (MGB; Perugini & Bagozzi, 2001). The main focus of the MGB is on the pre-volitional stages of decision making which involve a number of new components. The MGB begins with the basic constructs of the TPB but focuses additionally on the three relatively overlooked areas. The MGB is depicted in Figure 8.1. Note that for the sake of simplicity the figure does not include behavior as an outcome, given that the MGB focuses mostly on pre-volitional processes.

The MGB does not simply add other variables to the TPB but rather redefines the decision-making process. A key construct introduced in the MGB is desire. As argued above, desires are distinct from intentions and represent the motivational state of mind in which appraisals and reasons to

4 Obviously there are circumstances where it might be a reasonable approximation to assume that a certain end state is desirable. Yet, strictly speaking, even in extreme cases this would generally be a matter of interpretation. Most people would agree that it is more desirable to be alive than to die, or to be rich than to be poor, yet some individuals prefer to die instead of live (euthanasia, martyrdom) or to choose poverty rather than wealth (ascetics, religious people).

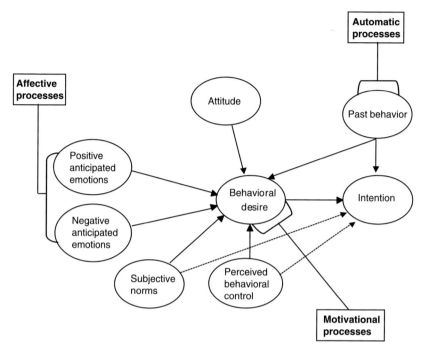

*Figure 8.1* Model of goal-directed behavior (MGB).

act are reconciled. Desires perform energizing and transformative functions for the antecedents of decision making and represent the most proximal determinants of intentions. Unlike Ajzen (1991, p. 181) who maintains that "intentions are assumed to capture the motivational factors that influence a behavior," we argue that intentions in and of themselves do not have specific motivational content. Rather, intentions perform planning (Bratman, 1987) and directive functions. The motivational content in decision making is constituted by the desire to perform a certain behavior. It is this desire which energizes intentions.

Among the determinants of desires are positive and negative anticipated emotions which refer to anticipated affective reactions to failure and success. Unlike recent proposals where some affect-related variables have been added to improve the prediction of intention and behavior (e.g., Conner & Abraham, 2001; Parker et al., 1995; Richard et al., 1995), the MGB stipulates that anticipated emotions represent a form of counterfactual (prefactual) thought processes where the emotional consequences of achievement and failure are appraised. Moreover, a more comprehensive set of both positive and negative emotions, assessed separately for perspectives of success and of failure, is introduced. Based on a previous study by Bagozzi et al. (1998), 17 emotions (7 positive and 10 negative) were originally proposed by Perugini and Bagozzi

(2001). However, the number and content of the anticipated emotions could be different depending on the specific goal and behavior under investigation.

Finally, past behavior is introduced as a proxy for habit and also given a substantive interpretation. As argued above, past behavior has been repeatedly found to have independent effects on intentions (for a review see Conner & Armitage, 1998). In contrast to Ajzen's conclusion that "although past behavior may well reflect the impact of factors that influence later behavior, it can usually not be considered as a causal factor in its own right" (1991, p. 203; see also Ajzen, 2002), recent thinking provides a theoretical rationale for the causal influence of past behavior or habit on current behavior (e.g., Aarts & Dijksterhuis, 2000; Albarracin & Wyer, 2000; Bargh, 1990; Oullette & Wood, 1998; Verplanken & Aarts, 1999). A similar rationale can be extended to explain the influence of past behavior on the motivational and volitional stages in decision making, as proposed under the MGB. Perugini and Bagozzi (2001) distinguished between frequency and recency as two related but separate mechanisms through which the influence of past behavior can be conceptualized. Other possible explanations are self-identity (Ouellette & Wood, 1998) and habit (Verplanken, Aarts, & van Knippenberg, 1997). Whatever the specific mechanisms behind past behavior, the general point is that automatic processes can have an unmediated impact on pre-volitional states, especially on desire and intention, and should be included in any comprehensive modeling of decision making.

The MGB proposes that volitive desires mediate the effects of deliberative processes on intentions. However, there are two ways that reasons for acting can have direct effects on intentions, one methodological, one substantive. Methodologically, to the extent that the measures of desires fail to capture its full nature or scope, empirical tests of the MGB may find direct paths from the reasons for acting to intentions. Substantively, to the extent that the reasons for acting reflect non-deliberative processes, we might expect direct effects from the reasons to intentions. The latter direct effects would reflect automatic activation of intentions. In sum, although we expect that desires generally mediate the effects of the reasons for acting on intentions, it is possible to find partial mediation or direct effects on intentions depending on the presence of random and systematic error in measures of desires and of automatic processes.

To sum up, the MGB redefines the theoretical mechanisms of the decision-making process and incorporates three important new theoretical areas (affective, motivational, and automatic processes) that are overlooked by the TPB. While the MGB was originally conceived as an integration of goal and behavioral criteria, as implied by the focus of anticipated affective reactions on goals instead of behavior (cf. Perugini & Bagozzi, 2001), we believe that it is more useful to conceive it as a model at a behavioral level. The focus of anticipated emotional reactions can be defined at the level of behavioral outcomes or goal outcomes, but to fully explain goal-directed behavior the MGB must be extended, as developed below.

## Means–end analysis

> The origin of action—its efficient, not its final cause—is choice, and that of
> choice is desire and reasoning with a view to an end.
>                    Aristotle, c. 340 BC, *Nicomachean Ethics*, 1139a 31–2

Goals play a central role in the explanation of many behaviors because these
behaviors are chosen as means to goal achievement (e.g., Gollwitzer &
Moskowitz, 1996). Yet, in attitude theory only rarely have behaviors been
studied in relation to the goals for which they are performed. The focus has
been restricted to specific behaviors in isolation from the broader context
which justify their performance (Eagly & Chaiken, 1998).

Vallacher and Wegner (1987) have suggested that actions may be represented at different hierarchical levels, in terms of superordinate or sub-
ordinate goals, and have found that people tend to define their actions
mostly in terms of higher levels of abstraction (the *why* aspects of an
action). Gollwitzer (1990) proposed a model of action phases, whereby the
first stage (pre-decisional stage) consists in the contemplation of different
goals and the setting of preferences among them (*goal setting*). The culmination of this stage is the formation of a goal intention, which is initiated
and executed in the following two stages (pre-actional and actional, *goal
striving*; see also Bagozzi & Edwards, 1998). Other research (e.g., Deci &
Ryan, 1991; Locke & Latham, 1990) also shows that goals play a central
role in understanding behavioral intentions. Despite these findings, work on
goals has had limited impact on mainstream attitude research. The implicit
assumption is that goals represent distal determinants of behavior whose
influence is fully mediated by more proximal determinants of behaviors (cf.
Eagly & Chaiken, 1993). Therefore, the analysis of goal-related constructs is
assumed not to be useful to improve the prediction of behavioral intentions,
once the proximal determinants are taken into account. However, no relevant empirical data support this mediational hypothesis. On the contrary, to
the extent that a goal can be realized in different ways through different
behaviors, it is not obvious that the cognitive determinants of a goal-
directed behavior would be sufficient to predict the volition to perform it.
The distinction between goals and behaviors, their simultaneous analysis,
and the specification of how goals translate into behavioral volitions may
add to the prediction of these volitions over and above their most proximal
determinants.

In choosing a goal, two variables have been identified as central: goal desirability and goal feasibility (cf. Gollwitzer & Moskowitz, 1996). Actually, goal
desirability and goal feasibility, interpreted as desire and belief, are classical
concepts in the philosophy of action (Mele, 1997), dating back at least to
Hume, and rediscovered periodically ever since. As we argued above, goal
desirability emphasizes the personal *value* which is attached to a certain goal
outcome, while at the same time neglecting the personal *motivation* to achieve
that goal outcome, which is central in philosophical analysis (e.g., Davis,

1984; Mele, 1995). Moreover, research within the goal tradition emphasizes the direct link between goal intentions and behavior. In other words, the standard assumption is that a goal is a direct organizer of actions.

To sum up, while research within the attitude tradition has usually focused on the behavioral level alone, research within the goal tradition has focused on the goal level alone. Rarely has an explicit interplay between goal and behavioral levels been articulated. Yet, this seems to be a common situation: when people behave, they often do so because they want to achieve a goal and they have preferences and evaluations both for the behavior and the goal. Expressions such as "I want to get a good degree [goal] but I do not fancy studying hard [behavior]" make perfect sense in everyday conversation and convey different evaluations and motivations at the goal and behavioral levels. Whether a student will study hard depends on the balance between how much he/she wants to achieve a good degree and how much he/she dislikes studying hard. By focusing on one level alone, we would miss important aspects of the decision making process.

## Extended model of goal-directed behavior

Building on the MGB, Perugini and Conner (2000) recently proposed the extended model of goal-directed behavior (EMGB), depicted in Figure 8.2.

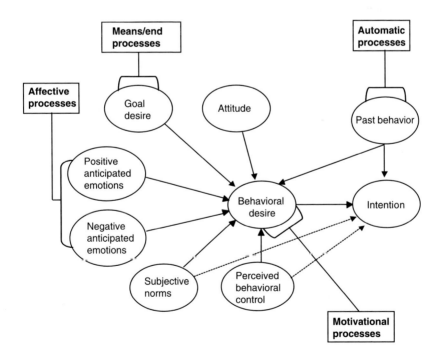

*Figure 8.2* Extended model of goal-directed behavior (EMGB).

As in the MGB, the focus of the EMGB is on the pre-volitional stages of decision making. Under the EMGB, however, the concept of desires is further developed, and a distinction is drawn between goal (or outcome) and behavioral (or action) desires. This distinction reflects a refinement in the conceptualization of desires and their differences from intentions. Building on distinctions between intrinsic and extrinsic desires made in philosophy (Mele, 1995), Perugini and Conner (2000) proposed that both goal desires and behavioral desires play a role in decision making concerning goal-directed actions. This follows from the assumption that most relevant behaviors can be better understood in the light of the interplay between the goal and behavioral levels. It is maintained that the influence of a desire to achieve a certain goal will influence the desire to perform a certain behavior that is subjectively felt to be instrumental for goal attainment. As a result, the behavioral desire will be the most proximal determinant of the intention to perform the behavior in question, and goal desire will have an indirect effect on intentions through behavioral desire (Bagozzi, Dholakia, & Basuroy, 2003).

This distinction between goal and behavioral desires is consistent with the previously described criteria differentiating desires from intentions. In particular, the distinction between goal and behavioral desires accommodates the notion that an intention has an action content, whereas a desire can have goal or action content. Furthermore, the notion that goal desires are different from behavioral desires and have different roles in decision making allows us to understand motivation and its manifestation at the goal and behavioral levels of analysis. In this way, goal desires represent the wishes of the decision maker as they guide further planning and elaboration concerning how to fulfill desires. The "how" (i.e., behavioral) level in turn requires behavioral desires for initiation, which resemble the concept of extrinsic desire, that is "a desire for something for its believed conduciveness to something else that one desires" (Mele, 1995, p. 391).

## Why two models?

The MGB and the EMGB are two models that can increase theoretical understanding and, as we will show, the empirical predictions of pre-volitional processes. A question might be posed on the need for both models. We believe that the best way to conceptualize them is to consider the EMGB as providing an additional ladder over the MGB, which is therefore the basic model. In other words, one way to compare and interpret the models is in terms of the level of analysis. To the extent that one wants to emphasize both the behavioral and goal aspects of decision making, the EMGB is the most comprehensive model because it provides an additional ladder. In this context, anticipated emotions are redefined and anchored in terms of goals, as proposed by Bagozzi et al. (1998) and initially incorporated in the MGB (Perugini & Bagozzi, 2001). Quite a bit of research has focused on the importance of goals in influencing action (for a review, see Gollwitzer &

Moskowitz, 1996). We believe that attitude-based models can and will be enriched by focusing on the more distal determinants of action, such as the desire to achieve a given goal by means of some more specific behaviors. However, this would imply a more detailed and richer analysis of both the goal and the behaviors that can be functional to achieve it.

We acknowledge that practical considerations might prevent a researcher from including both levels of analysis in a specific study. For instance, there are some applied contexts in which the key question is to predict and understand the behavior itself, rather than its distal determinants. Moreover, the links between goals and behaviors are multidetermined: a given goal can be achieved in multiple ways (i.e., with different behaviors) and a given behavior can be functional to achieve different goals, both within and between persons. Therefore, the simultaneous examination of both the goal and behavioral levels requires a simplification of both levels, which occasionally might not be the best strategy given the specific research question. Indeed, there are circumstances in which the theoretical interest of the researcher will focus solely on a specific behavior that happens to be functional to achieve a number of goals at the same time. In these circumstances, it might become too complicated to enlarge the analysis to both levels simultaneously. Finally, there also specific cases whereby the distinction between goal and behavior is difficult to draw, and therefore the analysis of their interplay would not add much. In all these cases, the MGB can be the best alternative.

In short, there are pros and cons for using either model. As a general rule, when the focus and interest are on both goals and behaviors, the EMGB is the best choice, whereas when the focus is or must be restricted to behavior only, the MGB is the best choice.

## Empirical evidence

### *Distinction between desires and intentions*

Besides the previously mentioned experimental evidence, correlational evidence also supports a distinction between desires and intentions for actions or goals. We located 13 studies where both desires and intentions were measured (Bagozzi & Edwards, 1998; Bagozzi & Kimmel, 1995; Capozza, Cesco, Dazzi, Voci, & Martines, 1999; Leone, Perugini, & Ercolani, 1999, 2002; Perugini, 2002; Perugini & Bagozzi, 2001; Perugini & Conner, 2000). The domains of application were varied, including bodyweight regulation, studying, helping charities, and dieting. Multiple measures were available for each construct (see Perugini & Conner, 2000, for typical examples of items). The relation between desires and intentions was investigated using confirmatory factor analysis (CFA). The models tested formally the discriminant validity of the constructs and provided unbiased (corrected for measurement error) estimates of their correlation. The average correlation between the constructs of desires and intentions over the 13 studies was 0.75 (raw correlation = 0.68),

188 *Pre-volitional processes*

with values ranging from 0.52 to 0.94. Formal tests of discriminant validity showed that the hypothesis that desires and intentions are different constructs cannot be rejected.[5] Furthermore, it should be emphasized that these correlations are likely to be inflated due to common method biases and that they are upward corrected for measurement error. In sum, the estimated correlations at the latent variable level suggest that discriminant validity between observed measures is achieved, even after correcting for measurement error and using a common method.

### Comparison between MGB, EMGB, and TPB

In addition to theoretical arguments supporting the MGB and EMGB, it is also possible to provide empirical evidence to support the predictive power of the models and to compare them with the TPB. This empirical evidence has started to accumulate in a series of studies (Perugini & Bagozzi, 2001; Perugini & Conner, 2000; Leone, Perugini, & Ercolani, 2002; Taylor, Bagozzi, & Gaither, 2001). In Table 8.2, we summarize a set of studies where all three models were tested. The set included such varied goals and behaviors as studying efforts, weight control, learning SPSS, helping charities, and keeping fit. Additional studies are ongoing and include socializing, dental flossing, drinking, eating with friends, and nutrition choices.

In the first set of seven studies, the TPB and the MGB were tested (five in Italy, two in the USA), whereas in the remaining four studies, performed in the UK, the EMGB was also tested. Considering first the five Italian and two US studies, the average prediction for the TPB was 32% of the variance for intentions and 20% for behavior. These values are comparable to results reported in previous meta-analytic reviews. The MGB produced a dramatic improvement in predictive power over the TPB, with averages of 58% of variance for desires, 58% for intentions, and 26% for behavior explained. Note that the improvement is especially strong for pre-volitional and volitional constructs, due to the main focus of the MGB on these aspects. On average, an additional 26% of the variance in intentions was gained by introducing the concept of desires. One might also wish to compare the prediction

---

5 At least three procedures can be used to test the discriminant validity of two constructs using CFA. One approach is to inspect the confidence interval of the estimated correlation between the latent constructs. If the confidence interval, built by considering ± 2 standard errors from the point-estimate, does not include 1, then the constructs are discriminated. A second procedure is to compare two models, the first with the observed variables loading on two correlated factors and the second with the variables loading on a single overall factor. A third procedure, which perhaps is superior to the first two, is to compare two models, the first with the correlation between latent constructs set free and the second with the correlation fixed to unity. If the latent variables are not significantly different, one cannot reject the hypothesis that the two constructs are the same. Hence, a significant difference is needed to provide evidence of discriminant validity.

Table 8.2 Summary of predictive power of TPB, MGB, and EMGB

| STUDY / N | Goal | Behavior | TPB | | MGB | | | EMGB | |
|---|---|---|---|---|---|---|---|---|---|
| | | | $R^2$ Int. | $R^2$ Beh. | $R^2$ Des. | $R^2$ Int. | $R^2$ Beh. | $R^2$ Des. | $R^2$ Int. |
| **Perugini and Bagozzi (2001)** | | | | | | | | | |
| 108 | Weight control | Dieting | .34 | .19 | .54 | .74 | .25 | na | na |
| 122 | Studying | Exercising | .58 | .38 | .72 | .78 | .46 | na | na |
| | | Free choice | .34 | .15 | .49 | .53 | .24 | na | na |
| **Leone, Perugini, and Ercolani (2002)** | | | | | | | | | |
| 102 | Learning SPSS | Handbook | .37 | .18 | .52 | .58 | .27 | na | na |
| | | Practice | .24 | .16 | .41 | .38 | .27 | na | na |
| **Bagozzi and Dholakia (2004)** | | | | | | | | | |
| 154 | Group participation | Riding, Shopping, Socializing | .12 | .21 | .80 | .64 | .22 | na | na |
| 255 | Group participation | Riding, Shopping, Socializing | .23 | .14 | .58 | .41 | .14 | na | na |
| | | Average | **.32** | **.20** | **.58** | **.58** | **.26** | – | – |
| **Perugini and Conner (2000)** | | | | | | | | | |
| 104 | Weight/Studying | Free choice | .30 | na | .46 | .74 | na | .62 | .76 |
| **Perugini (2002)** | | | | | | | | | |
| 107 | Keeping fit | Free choice | .37 | na | .69 | .79 | na | .79 | .80 |
| 101 | Look after health | Free choice | .31 | na | .66 | .81 | na | .70 | .82 |
| **Perugini and Bagozzi (2001)** | | | | | | | | | |
| 102 | Helping charity | Free choice | .28 | na | .72 | .79 | na | .74 | .79 |
| | | Average | **.32** | – | **.63** | **.78** | – | **.71** | **.79** |
| | | Total average | **.35** | **.21** | **.58** | **.68** | **.30** | **.71** | **.79** |

Notes: Int = Intention, Beh = Behavior, Des = Desire; na = not available.

of intentions under the TPB with that of desires under the MGB, given that they are functionally equivalent under the two theories: in both cases they are meant to represent the outcome of a decision-maker's weighting of various reasons for acting. In this case, the MGB explains 26% more variance in desires than the TPB does in intentions. The EMGB improves further the predictive power of the MGB.

Focusing on the average values of the second set of four studies, where all three models were tested, the TPB explains 32%, the MGB 78%, and the EMGB 79% of the variance in intentions. Furthermore, the MGB explains 63% and the EMGB 71% of the variance in behavioral desires. Again the differences in predictive power are substantial, and both the MGB and the EMGB clearly outperform the TPB. The EMGB shows a moderate improvement in the prediction of behavioral desires, with an increase of 8% in explained variance. As argued elsewhere (Perugini & Conner, 2001), it is fair to note that this is not the ideal arena to test the TPB, especially because items in the questionnaires are explicitly worded as functional to goals (e.g., "I intend to do X in order to achieve Y" vs. "I intend to do X"). Nevertheless, the differences in predictive power are so great as to suggest that the MGB and EMGB capture essential determinants of decisions neglected by the TPB. It is important to note too that these differences are equally great if we base our comparisons on the results of recent meta-analytic reviews which included "traditional" TPB studies.

A closer look at the estimates for structural paths specified by the MGB (Table 8.3) shows interesting results. The average values for estimates, which are based on a total sample of 1155 participants, suggest that all paths are likely to play a significant role. However, it can be seen that which specific path is significant varies considerably depending on the study. For instance, attitudes show a significant path on desires in seven of the nine studies, whereas subjective norms reveal it in five studies. Never is it the case that all predictors are significant in the same study. However, which specific construct plays a more important role varies among studies, and this therefore suggests the importance of considering them all. In other words, the antecedents function in a compensatory way and do so differentially, depending on the context.

Similar to expectations for the predictors of intentions in the TPB, there is no claim that all predictors of desires under the MGB should always be significant. But of course the implicit expectation is that a considerable portion of variance should be explained by the set of predictors, leaving it an empirical matter which predictor should be significant in any particular study. Note that in eight of the ten studies either positive or negative anticipated emotions have significant influences on desires, and in one study both are significant. Past behavior also plays an important role in predicting both desires and intentions. This result is in line with recent emphasis on automatic processes in decision making and behavior. The influence of desires on intentions is always strong, but never such that one could claim that they

Table 8.3 Summary of structural paths of MGB

| | PB1 | PB2 | LPE1 | LPE2 | PC | P1 | P2 | PB3 | BD1 | BD2 | Average |
|---|---|---|---|---|---|---|---|---|---|---|---|
| PAE → Desires | .28* | -.14 | .11 | .35* | .47* | -.01 | -.05 | -.05 | .23** | .28*** | **.15** |
| NAE → Desires | .12 | .32* | .12 | .04 | .08 | .14 | .35* | .39* | .10* | .01 | **.17** |
| Attitudes → Desires | .17 | .41* | .39* | .01 | .13 | .49* | .20* | .19* | .13* | .24*** | **.24** |
| Subjective norms → Desires | .24* | .16* | .15 | .17 | .14 | .07 | .26* | .03 | .24*** | .11* | **.16** |
| PBC → Desires | -.08[a], .61[b] | .37* | .19* | .21* | .34* | -.11 | .08 | .23* | .05 | .07 | **.18** |
| Past behavior → Desires | .24* | .24* | .12[c] | .29*[c] | .10 | .42* | .39* | .51* | na | na | **.31** |
| Desires → Intentions | .77* | .66* | .71* | .60* | .85* | .62* | .62* | .76* | .78*** | .78*** | **.72** |
| Past behavior → Intentions | .16* | .14 | .12[c] | .04[c] | .03 | .34* | .35* | .17 | na | na | **.17** |

*Notes*: PAE = Positive anticipated emotions; NAE = Negative anticipated emotions; PBC = Perceived behavioral control. PB1 = Perugini and Bagozzi, 2001, Weight control; PB2 = Perugini and Bagozzi, 2001, Studying; LPE1 = Leone, Perugini, and Ercolani, 2002, Learning SPSS, Handbook; LPE2 = Leone, Perugini, and Ercolani, 2002, Learning SPSS, Practice; PC = Perugini and Conner, 2000, Weight/Studying; P1 = Perugini, 2002, Keeping fit; P2 = Perugini, 2002, Look after health; PB3 = Perugini and Bagozzi, 2001, Helping charity; BD1 = Bagozzi and Dholakia, 2004, Study 1; BD2 = Bagozzi and Dholakia, Study 2.
[a] = Dieting; [b] = Exercising; [c] = Recency

are indistinguishable constructs, even after correcting for measurement error.

Likewise the values of the structural paths specified by the EMGB (Table 8.4) show that all variables play an important role. The introduction of goal desires proves important, as the construct always significantly predicts behavioral desires. Note, however, that the measures of goal and behavioral desires achieve discriminant validity, even after correcting for measurement error. These results support the view that the interplay between goal and behavioral levels of analysis represents an important element to understand the decision-making process. Note that, although anticipated emotions have a significant impact on behavioral desires in three out of four studies, their average impact is substantially lower than that found under the MGB. It is possible that the introduction of goal desires reduces the impact of antici-pated emotions on behavioral desires, as both sets of constructs have goals as their referents. As for the MGB, past behavior shows a substantial impact on both behavioral desires and intentions. Finally note that, considering both the MGB and the EMGB, the impact of perceived behavioral control on desires is moderate but often smaller in magnitude than the path from past behavior to desires.

## Conclusions

The MGB and EMGB provide a fuller understanding of decision making than the TPB. On the face of it, it seems that the advantages of the MGB and EMGB come at the cost of loss of parsimony. However, there is a sense in which the MGB and EMGB are more parsimonious than the TPB. If we focus on the proximal determinants of intentions, we see that the MGB and EMGB actually specify fewer direct antecedents to intentions than the TPB. More importantly, it should be pointed out that the theories are based on

*Table 8.4* Summary of structural paths of EMGB

|  | PC | P1 | P2 | PB3 | Average |
|---|---|---|---|---|---|
| Goal desires → Behavioral desires | .52* | .44* | .28* | .27* | **.38** |
| PAE → Behavioral desires | .38* | −.04 | −.13 | −.10 | **.03** |
| NAE → Behavioral desires | −.28 | −.03 | .24* | .25* | **.04** |
| Attitudes → Behavioral desires | .17* | .44* | .15 | .15 | **.23** |
| Subjective norms → Behavioral desires | .13 | .07 | .25* | .03 | **.12** |
| PBC → Behavioral desires | .28* | −.07 | .04 | .17* | **.11** |
| Past behavior → Behavioral desires | .12 | .26* | .34* | .41* | **.28** |
| Behavioral desires → Intentions | .85* | .64* | .63* | .76* | **.72** |
| Past behavior → Intentions | .03 | .32* | .34* | .18 | **.22** |

*Notes*: PAE = Positive anticipated emotions; NAE = Negative anticipated emotions; PBC = Perceived behavioral control; PC = Perugini and Conner, 2000, Weight/Studying; P1 = Perugini, 2002, Keeping fit; P2 = Perugini, 2002, Look after health; PB3 = Perugini and Connor, 2000, Helping charity.

fundamentally different theoretical processes. The TPB assumes that intentions summarize the effects of attitudes, subjective norms, and perceived behavioral control, and that these antecedents each provide motivational impetus for intending to act. The processes are deterministic, and it is left to empirical research to ascertain which of the antecedents are operative in any particular setting. By contrast, under the MGB and EMGB the antecedents are regarded as reasons for acting that do not, in and of themselves, contain motivations to act. Rather, a decision maker must personally decide and accept these as inner private concerns and experience their meaning as a desire to act. Desire, then, introduces an element of self-regulation into human behavior, an element missing from the TPB (see also Orbell on self-regulation, Chapter 7 in this book). Desire transforms the reasons for acting into intentions and is the proximal cause of intentions.

It remains an open question whether other reasons for acting influence intentions and action. Under the MGB and EMGB, as noted above, we acknowledge that automatic processes can have direct effects on action. It has been shown that implicit evaluations can trigger behavior automatically. However, it might be argued that the power for automatic activation of action resides also in learned motives or desires that become triggered or primed in the proper situation. That is, it can be hypothesized that alongside the automatic activation effect on behavior due to the triggering of an implicit evaluation, implicit desires can be automatically triggered as well. We have argued extensively and provided empirical evidence that desires are broader than evaluations (i.e., attitudes) and represent the integration of different reasons to act into a personal motivation to do so. Hence, they are more important than attitudes in determining behavior via intention. It might be argued that desires are more important than attitudes also at an implicit or automatic level. This would imply that people have not only associative networks organized in terms of valence (e.g., Greenwald et al., 2002), but also in terms of wishes. In other words, it looks reasonable that people create associations not only between objects and evaluations, but also between objects and desires or wishes. The activation by proper cues of these latter associations could directly lead to action bypassing intentions.

Another key related issue concerns the interplay between implicit and explicit determinants of action. The two traditions have developed largely in isolation and few attempts have been made to develop a comprehensive framework. Wilson, Lindsey, and Schooler (2000) have recently proposed a model of dual attitudes, defined as different evaluations, implicit and explicit, of the same attitude object. They suggest the coexistence in memory of implicit and explicit attitudes toward the same attitude object. In this framework, implicit attitudes are assumed to direct behavior that people do not monitor consciously or that they do not see as an expression of their attitude, whereas explicit attitudes tend to predict controlled behaviors or behaviors that they see as expressive of their attitudes. The empirical evidence supporting these claims comes mainly from research on prejudice and stereotyping (e.g., Fazio, Jackson, Dunton, & Williams, 1995; see also Vargas, Chapter 12 in this book). Despite the useful framework provided by Wilson and colleagues, there are still important questions that are unanswered. One of these questions concerns the interplay between implicit and explicit attitudes. The theoretical elaboration of Wilson and colleagues is focused only on cases of conflicts between implicit and explicit attitudes. But what happens when implicit and explicit attitudes are congruent? Do implicit attitudes interact with explicit attitudes in affecting behavior? Is the influence of implicit attitudes mediated, at least partly, by deliberative intentions or by desires? These and similar questions represent an important avenue for future investigations. Both the MGB and EMGB might represent a comprehensive theoretical framework that could be expanded by incorporating implicit determinants of action and might ultimately provide a common ground for both traditions.

The TPB, MGB, and EMGB are basically psychological explanations of action and accommodate social processes only through the impact of subjective norms. Bagozzi (2000) and Bagozzi and Lee (2002) recently reconceptualized intentions to apply in social or group situations. Heretofore, psychologists have studied what might be called personal intentions to perform an individual act (e.g., "I intend to read a novel this evening"). A personal intention is a "conscious plan to exert effort to carry out a behavior" (Eagly & Chaiken, 1993, p. 168) by oneself, where the behavior is the performance of an individual action. There are two types of social intentions found frequently in group situations. One is a personal intention to perform one's part of a group action (e.g., "I intend to play bridge with my friends on Thursday evening"). A second is a shared intention to engage in a group act (e.g., "We intend to have a vacation in the Canadian Rockies this summer"). Under a shared intention, a person plans to participate in a joint activity, but he/she conceives it not so much as an individual performing a personal act that contributes to a group performance, but rather as a group action where one is a member of the group. Under a personal intention to perform a group act, the person thinks of a group activity in an atomistic sense such that members of the group, and especially the self, are distinct entities who come together but act individually to contribute to the group activity. Under a shared intention, in contrast, the person thinks of a group activity holistically, such that one sees the self as part of a social representation (e.g., a family, club, team, work organization), and it is the group that acts.

Bagozzi and Lee (2002) differentiated between three social reasons for acting as explanations of social intentions: compliance (e.g., interpersonal pressure), internalization (e.g., group norms), and social identity (i.e., cognitive self-awareness of membership in a group, affective commitment to the group, and collective self-esteem). This has been tested in the context of the MGB as applied to friendship groups that were organized around ownership of Harley Davidson motorcycles (Bagozzi & Dholakia, 2004).

Thus, the MGB and EMGB can be expanded to explain social behavior by reconceptualizing individual intentions to accommodate social intentions and introducing compliance, internalization, and social identity processes as additional antecedents of desire. Other antecedents or reasons for acting might be relevant to consider, depending on the particular action, person and situation in which the action is performed. For example, Bagozzi and Lee (2002) found that culture moderates the effects of reasons for acting on intentions with social identity more important in group- or interdependent-based cultures and group norms more salient in individual- or independent-based cultures. It is important to stress, however, that desire is the proximal determinant of intentions, and additional reasons for acting will be translated typically through desire, if they have significance in decision making.

In conclusion, we believe that researchers should take into consideration both deliberative and automatic processes in decision making. An approach focused exclusively on the automatic links between attitudes and behavior, which seems very fashionable these days, does not provide a theoretically and pragmatically superior alternative. An approach focused only on the deliberative decision-making processes would exclude important theoretical aspects and neglect a key direct route to action whereby explicit intentions and volitions are bypassed. More research is needed into the conditions governing the operation of automatic and deliberative processes, including inquiry into when one or the other functions or when both are at work.

The MGB and EMGB provide an alternative conceptualization of decision-making processes developed within the deliberative camp but that also tries to accommodate automatic processes. The main focus of both models is on pre-volitional processes, yet they can be easily integrated with approaches that focus on post-volitional and pre-actional processes. By their very nature, both models are open to improvements and extensions. The data collected so far are sufficient to claim that the MGB and EMGB deserve closer scrutiny and investigation, and that they are real alternatives to the TPB. Future research should aim at testing the two models in an extensive range of domains and at refining some of the mechanisms that underlie them.

## Acknowledgments

We wish to thank Geoff Haddock and an anonymous reviewer for useful comments and suggestions.

## References

Aarts, H., & Dijksterhuis, A. (2000). Habits as knowledge structures: Automaticity in goal-directed behavior. *Journal of Personality and Social Psychology, 78*, 53–63.

Ajzen, I. (1991). The theory of planned behavior. *Organizational Behavior and Human Decision Processes, 50*, 179–211.

Ajzen, I. (2001). Nature and operation of attitudes. *Annual Review of Psychology, 52*.

Ajzen, I. (2002). Residual effects of past on later behavior: Habituation and reasoned perspectives. *Personality and Social Psychology Review, 6,* 107–122.

Ajzen, I., & Fishbein, M. (2000). Attitudes and the attitude–behavior relation: Reasoned and automatic processes. In W. Stroebe & M. Hewstone (Eds.), *European Review of Social Psychology, 11,* 1–33.

Ajzen, I., & Madden, T. J. (1986). Prediction of goal-directed behavior: Attitudes, intentions, and perceived behavioral control. *Journal of Experimental Social Psychology, 22,* 453–474.

Albarracin, D., & Wyer, R. S. (2000). The cognitive impact of past behavior: Influences on beliefs, attitudes, and future behavioral decisions. *Journal of Personality and Social Psychology, 79,* 5–22.

Armitage, C. J., & Conner, M. (1999). Distinguishing perceptions of control from self-efficacy: Predicting consumption of a low fat diet using the theory of planned behavior. *Journal of Applied Social Psychology, 29,* 72–90.

Armitage, C. J., & Conner, M. (2001). Efficacy of the theory of planned behavior: A meta-analytic review. *British Journal of Social Psychology, 40,* 471–799.

Aarts, H., & Dijksterhuis, A. (2000). Habit as knowledge structure: Automaticity in goal-directed behavior. *Journal of Personality and Social Psychology, 78,* 53–63.

Audi, R (1986). Acting for reasons. *Philosophical Review, 95,* 511–546.

Bagozzi, R. P. (1981). Attitudes, intentions and behavior: A test of some key hypothesis. *Journal of Personality and Social Psychology, 41,* 607–627.

Bagozzi, R. P. (1992). The self-regulation of attitudes, intentions, and behavior. *Social Psychology Quarterly, 55,* 178–204.

Bagozzi, R. P. (2000). On the concept of intentional social action in consumer behavior. *Journal of Consumer Research, 27,* 388–396.

Bagozzi, R. P., Baumgartner, H., & Pieters, R. (1998). Goal-directed emotions. *Cognition and Emotion, 12,* 1–26.

Bagozzi, R. P., & Dholakia, U. M. (2004). *Brand community behavior: Psychological and social antecedents plus purchase consequences.* Unpublished working paper.

Bagozzi, R. P., Dholakia, U. M., & Basuroy, S. (2003). How effortful decisions get enacted: The motivating role of decision processes, desires, and anticipated emotions. *Journal of Behavioral Decision Making, 16,* 273–295.

Bagozzi, R. P., & Edwards, E. A. (1998). Goal setting and goal pursuit in the regulation of body weight. *Psychology and Health, 13,* 593–621.

Bagozzi, R. P., & Kimmel, S. K. (1995). A comparison of leading theories for the prediction of goal-directed behaviors. *British Journal of Social Psychology, 34,* 437–461.

Bagozzi, R. P., & Lee, K.-H. (2002). Multiple routes for social influence: The role of compliance, internalization, and social identity. *Social Psychology Quarterly, 65,* 226–247.

Bagozzi, R. P., & Warshaw, P. R. (1990). Trying to consume. *Journal of Consumer Research, 17,* 127–140.

Bagozzi, R. P., Wong, N., & Yi, Y. (1999). The role of culture and gender in the relationship between positive and negative effect. *Cognition and Emotion, 13,* 641–672.

Bargh, J. A. (1990). Auto-motives: Preconscious determinants of social interaction. In R. M. Sorrentino & E. T. Higgins (Eds.), *Handbook of motivation and cognition* (pp.93–130). New York: Guilford Press.

Bargh, J. A., & Chartrand, T. L. (1999). The unbearable automaticity of being. *American Psychologist, 54,* 462–479.

Bargh, J. A., Chen, M., & Burrows, L. (1996). Automaticity of social behavior: Direct effects of trait construct and stereotype activation on action. *Journal of Personality and Social Psychology, 71*, 230–244.

Bargh, J. A., Gollwitzer, P. M., Lee-Chai, A., Barndollar, K., & Trötschel, R. (2001). The automated will: Nonconscious activation and pursuit of behavioral goals. *Journal of Personality and Social Psychology, 81*, 1014–1027.

Beck, L., & Ajzen, I. (1991). Predicting dishonest actions using the theory of planned behavior. *Journal of Research in Personality, 25*, 285–301.

Bentler, P. M., & Speckart, G. (1979). Models of attitude–behavior relations. *Psychological Review, 86*, 452–464.

Bentler, P. M., & Speckart, G. (1981). Attitudes "cause" behaviors: A structural equation analysis. *Journal of Personality and Social Psychology, 40*, 226–238.

Bratman, M. E. (1987). *Intentions, plans, and practical reason.* Cambridge, MA: Harvard University Press.

Breckler, S. J., & Wiggins, E. C. (1989). Affect versus evaluation in the structure of attitudes. *Journal of Experimental Social Psychology, 25*, 253–271.

Cacioppo, J. T., & Berntson, G. G. (1994). Relationship between attitudes and evaluative space: A critical review, with emphasis on the separability of positive and negative substrates. *Psychological Bulletin, 115*, 401–423.

Capozza, D., Cesco, V., Dazzi, C., Voci, A., & Martines, D. (1999). Verifica di teorie delle intenzioni tramite modelli di equazioni strutturali [Test of intention theories through structural equation models]. *TPM, 6*, 133–146.

Carver, C. S., & Scheier, M. F. (1998). *On the self-regulation of behavior.* Cambridge, UK: Cambridge University Press.

Chartrand, T. L., & Bargh, J. A. (1999). The chameleon effect: The perception–behavior link and social interaction. *Journal of Personality and Social Psychology, 76*, 893–910.

Chen, M., & Bargh, J. A. (1999). Consequences of automatic evaluation: Immediate behavioral predispositions to approach or avoid the stimulus. *Personality and Social Psychology Bulletin, 25*, 215–224.

Chen, S., & Chaiken, S. (1999). The heuristic-systematic model in its broader context. In S. Chaiken & Y. Trope (Eds.), *Dual-process theories in social psychology* (pp. 73–96). New York: Guilford Press.

Conner, M., & Abraham, C. (2001). Conscientiousness and the theory of planned behavior: Toward a more complete model of the antecedents of intentions and behavior. *Personality and Social Psychology Bulletin, 27*, 1547–1561.

Conner, M., & Armitage, C. J. (1998). Theory of planned behavior: A review and avenues for future research. *Journal of Applied Social Psychology, 28*, 1430–1464.

Cunningham, W. A., Preacher, K. J., & Banaji, M. R. (2001). Implicit attitude measures: Consistency, stability, and convergent validity. *Psychological Science, 12*, 163–170.

Dasgupta, N., McGhee, D. E., Greenwald, A. G., & Banaji, M. R. (2000). Automatic preference for White Americans: Eliminating the familiarity explanation. *Journal of Experimental Social Psychology, 36*, 316–328.

Davidson, D. (1963) Actions, reasons, and causes. *Journal of Philosophy, 60*, 685–700.

Davis, W. A. (1984). A causal theory of intending. *American Philosophical Quarterly, 21*, 43–54.

Deci, E. L., & Ryan, R. M. (1991). A motivational approach to self: Integration in personality. In R. Dienstbier (Ed.), *Nebraska Symposium on Motivation* (vol. 38, pp. 199–255). Lincoln: University of Nebraska Press.

Dijksterhuis, A., & van Knippenberg, A. (1998). The relation between perception and behavior or how to win a game of Trivial Pursuit. *Journal of Personality and Social Psychology, 74*, 865–877.

Dovidio, J. F., Kawakami, K., Johnson, C., Johnson, B., & Howard, A. (1997). On the nature of prejudice: Automatic and controlled processes. *Journal of Experimental Social Psychology, 33*, 510–554.

Eagly, A. H., & Chaiken, S. (1993). *The psychology of attitudes.* Fort Worth, TX: Harcourt Brace Jovanovich.

Eagly, A.H., & Chaiken, S. (1998). Attitude structure and function. In D. T. Gilbert, S. T. Fiske, & G. Lindzey (Eds.), *The handbook of social psychology* (4th ed., Vol. 1, pp. 269–322). New York: McGraw-Hill.

Fazio, R. H. (1990). Multiple processes by which attitudes guide behavior: The MODE model as an integrative framework. In M. P. Zanna (Ed.), *Advances in experimental social psychology* (Vol. 23, pp. 75–109). New York: Academic Press.

Fazio, R. H. (1995). Attitudes as object-evaluation associations: Determinants, consequences, and correlates of attitude accessibility. In R. E. Petty & J. A. Krosnick (Eds.), *Attitude strength: Antecedents and consequences* (Vol. 4, pp. 247–282). Hillsdale, NJ: Lawrence Erlbaum Associates, Inc.

Fazio, R. H., & Dunton, B. C. (1997). Categorization by race: The impact of automatic and controlled components of racial prejudice. *Journal of Experimental Social Psychology, 33*, 451–470.

Fazio, R. H., Jackson, J. R., Dunton, B. C., & Williams, C. J. (1995). Variability in automatic activation as an unobstrusive measure of racial attitudes: A bona fide pipeline? *Journal of Personality and Social Psychology, 69*, 1013–1027.

Fazio, R. H., Sanbonmatsu, D. M, Powell, M. C. & Kardes, F. R. (1986). On the automatic activation of attitudes. *Journal of Personality and Social Psychology, 50*, 229–238.

Fazio, R. H., & Williams, C. J. (1986). Attitude accessibility as a moderator of the attitude–perception and attitude–behavior relations: An investigation of the 1984 presidential election. *Journal of Personality and Social Psychology, 51*, 505–514.

Fishbein, M., & Ajzen, I. (1975). *Belief, attitude, intention and behavior: An introduction to theory and research.* Reading, MA: Addison-Wesley.

Gleicher, F., Boninger, D. S., Strathman, A., Armor, D., Hetts, J., & Ahn, M. (1995). With an eye toward the future: The impact of counterfactual thinking on affect, attitudes, and behavior. In N. J. Roese & M. M. Olson (Eds.), *What might have been: The social psychology of counterfactual thinking* (pp. 283–304). Mahwah, NJ: Lawrence Erlbaum Associates, Inc.

Godin, G., & Kok, G. (1996). The theory of planned behavior: A review of its applications to health-related behaviors. *American Journal of Health Promotion, 11*, 87–98.

Gollwitzer, P. M. (1990). Action phases and mind-sets. In E. T. Higgins & R. M. Sorrentino (Eds.), *Handbook of motivation and cognition* (Vol. 2, pp. 53–92). New York: Guilford Press.

Gollwitzer, P. M. (1996). The volitional benefits of planning. In P. Gollwitzer & J. A. Bargh (Eds.), *The psychology of action: Linking cognition and motivation to behavior* (pp. 287–312). New York: Guilford Press.

Gollwitzer, P. M., & Moskowitz, G. B. (1996). Goal effects on action and cognition. In E. T. Higgins & A. W. Kruglanski (Eds.), *Social psychology: Handbook of basic principles* (pp. 361–399). New York: Guilford Press.

Gray, J. A. (1990). Brain systems that mediate both emotion and cognition. *Cognition and Emotion, 4*, 269–288.

Greenwald, A. G., & Banaji, M. R. (1995). Implicit social cognition: Attitudes, self-esteem, and stereotypes. *Psychological Review, 102*, 4–27.

Greenwald, A. G., Banaji, M. R., Rudman, L. A., Farnham, S. D., Nosek, B. A., & Mellott, D. S. (2002). A unified theory of implicit attitudes, stereotypes, self-esteem, and self-concept. *Psychological Review, 109*, 3–25.

Greenwald, A. G., & Farnham, S. D. (2000). Using the Implicit Association Test to measure self-esteem and self-concept. *Journal of Personality and Social Psychology, 79*, 1022–1038.

Greenwald, A. G., McGhee, D. E., & Schwartz, J. K. L. (1998). Measuring individual differences in implicit cognition: The Implicit Association Test. *Journal of Personality and Social Psychology, 74*, 1464–1480.

Heckhausen, H., & Gollwitzer, P. M. (1987). Thought contents and cognitive functioning in motivational versus volitional states of mind. *Motivation and Emotion, 11*, 101–120.

Higgins, E. T. (1996). Ideals, oughts, and regulatory focus. In P. M. Gollwitzer & J. A. Bargh (Eds.), *The psychology of action* (pp. 119–145). New York: Guilford Press.

Karpinski, A., & Hilton, J. L. (2001). Attitudes and the Implicit Association Test. *Journal of Personality and Social Psychology, 81*, 774–778.

Leone, L., Perugini, M., & Ercolani, A. P. (1999). A comparison of three models of attitude–behavior relationships in studying behavior domain. *European Journal of Social Psychology, 29*, 161–189.

Leone, L., Perugini, M., & Ercolani, A. P. (2002). *A test of the Model of Goal-directed Behavior (MGB)*. Unpublished manuscript.

Liberman, N., & Trope, Y. (1998). The role of feasibility and desirability considerations in near and distant future decisions: A test of temporal construal theory. *Journal of Personality and Social Psychology, 75*, 5–18.

Locke, E. A., & Latham, G. P. (1990). Work motivation and satisfaction: Light at the end of the tunnel. *Psychological Science, 1*, 240–246.

Loewenstein, G. (1987). Anticipation and the valuation of delayed consumption. *Economic Journal, 97*, 666–684.

Malle, B. F., & Knobe, J. (2001). The distinction between desire and intention: A folk-conceptual analysis. In B. F. Malle, L. J. Moses, & D. A. Baldwin (Eds.), *Intentions and intentionality: Foundations of social cognition*. Cambridge, MA: MIT Press.

Mele, A. R. (1995). Motivation: Essentially motivation-constituting attitudes. *Philosophical Review, 104*, 387–423.

Mele, A. R. (Ed.) (1997). *The philosophy of action*. New York: Oxford University Press.

Mele, A. R., & Moser, P. K. (1994). Intentional action. *Nous, 28*, 39–68.

Ortony, A., Clore, G. L., & Collins, A. (1988). *The cognitive structure of emotions*. Cambridge, UK: Cambridge University Press.

Ouellette, J. A., & Wood, W. (1998). Habit and intention in everyday life: The multiple processes by which past behavior predicts future behavior. *Psychological Bulletin, 124*, 54–74.

Parker, D., Manstead, A. S. R., & Stradling, S. G. (1995). Extending the theory of planned behavior: The role of personal norm. *British Journal of Social Psychology, 34*, 127–137.

Perugini, M. (2002). *A test of the Extended Model of Goal-directed Behavior in three domains*. Unpublished raw data.

Perugini, M., & Bagozzi, R. P. (2001). The role of desires and anticipated emotions in goal-directed behaviors: Broadening and deepening the Theory of Planned Behavior. *British Journal of Social Psychology*, *40*, 79–98.

Perugini, M., & Bagozzi, R. P. (2004). The distinction between desires and intentions. *European Journal of Social Psychology*, *34*, 69–84.

Perugini, M., & Conner, M. T. (2000). Predicting and understanding behavioral volitions: The interplay between goals and behaviors. *European Journal of Social Psychology*, *30*, 705–731.

Petty, R. E., & Wegener, D. T. (1999). The elaboration likelihood model: Current status and controversies. In S. Chaiken & Y. Trope (Eds.), *Dual-process theories in social psychology* (pp. 37–72). New York: Guilford Press.

Posavac, S. S, Sanbonmatsu, D. M., & Fazio, R. H. (1997). Considering the best choice: Effects of the salience and accessibility of alternatives on attitude-decision consistency. *Journal of Personality and Social Psychology*, *72*, 253–261.

Richard, R., van der Pligt, J., & de Vries, N. (1995). Anticipated affective reactions and prevention of AIDS. *British Journal of Social Psychology*, *34*, 9–21.

Roese, N. J., & Olson, J. M. (Eds.) (1995). *What might have been: The social psychology of counterfactual thinking*. Mahwah, NJ: Lawrence Erlbaum Associates, Inc.

Roseman, I. J., Antoniou, A. A., & Jose, P. E. (1996). Appraisal determinants of emotions: Constructing a more accurate and comprehensive theory. *Cognition and Emotion*, *10*, 241–277.

Rosenthal, R., & Rubin, D.B. (1982). Comparing effect sizes of independent studies. *Psychological Bulletin*, *92*, 500–504.

Rothman, A. J. & Salovey, P. (1997). Shaping perceptions to motivate healthy behavior: The role of message framing. *Psychological Bulletin*, *121*, 3–19.

Russell, J. A., & Barrett, L. F. (1999). Core affect, prototypical emotional episodes, and other things called emotion: Dissecting the elephant. *Journal of Personality and Social Psychology*, *76*, 805–819.

Schueler, G. F. (1995). *Desire: Its role in practical reasons and the explanation of action*. Cambridge, MA: MIT Press.

Sheeran, P. (2002). Intention–behavior relations: A conceptual and empirical review. In M. Hewstone & W. Stroebe (Eds.), *European Review of Social Psychology* (Vol. 12, pp. 1–36). Chichester, UK: Wiley.

Sparks, P., & Shepherd, R. (1992). Self-identity and the theory of planned behavior: Assessing the role of identification with green consumerism. *Social Psychology Quarterly*, *55*, 388–399.

Taylor, S. D., Bagozzi, R. P., & Gaither, C. A. (2001). Gender differences in the self-regulation of hypertension. *Journal of Behavioral Medicine*, *24*, 469–487.

Terry, D. J., & O'Leary, J. E. (1995). The theory of planned behavior: The effects of perceived behavioural control and self-efficacy. *British Journal of Social Psychology*, *34*, 199–220.

Trafimow, D., & Sheeran, P. (1998). Some tests of the distinction between cognitive and affective beliefs. *Journal of Experimental Social Psychology*, *34*, 378–397.

Tversky, A., & Kahneman, D. (1974). Judgment under uncertainty: Heuristics and biases. *Science*, *185*, 1124–1131.

Vallacher, R. R., & Wegner, D. M. (1987). What do people think they're doing? Action identification and human behavior. *Psychological Review*, *94*, 3–15.

van der Pligt, J., Zeelenberg, M., van Dijk, W. W., de Vries, N. K., & Richard, R. (1998). Affect, attitudes and decisions: Let's be more specific. In W. Stroebe &

M. Hewstone (Eds.), *European Review of Social Psychology* (Vol. 8, pp. 33–66). Chichester, UK: Wiley.

Verplanken, B. & Aarts, H. (1999). Habit, attitude, and planned behavior: Is habit an empty construct or an interesting case of goal-directed automaticity? In W. Stroebe & M. Hewstone (Eds.), *European Review of Social Psychology* (Vol. 10, pp. 101–134). Chichester, UK: Wiley.

Verplanken, B., Aarts, H., & van Knippenberg, A. (1997). Habit, information acquisition, and the process of making travel mode choices. *European Journal of Social Psychology*, *27*, 539–560.

Verplanken, B., Aarts, H., van Knippenberg, A., & Moonen, A. (1998). Habit versus planned behavior: A field experiment. *British Journal of Social Psychology*, 37, 111–128.

Verplanken, B., Hofstee, G., & Janssen, H. J. W. (1998). Accessibility of affective versus cognitive components of attitudes. *European Journal of Social Psychology*, *28*, 23–35.

Wegner, D. M., & Wheatley, T. (1999). Apparent mental causation: Sources of the experience of will. *American Psychologist*, 54, 480–492.

Wilson, T. D., Lindsey, S., & Schooler, T. Y. (2000). A model of dual attitudes. *Psychological Review*, *107*, 101–126.

Yanchar, S.C. (2000). Some problems with Humean causality. *American Psychologist*, *55*, 767–768.

# Part II

# Attitude awareness, attitude representations, and change

# 9 Self-validation processes

## The role of thought confidence in persuasion

*Pablo Briñol and Richard E. Petty*

What determines whether or not people change their attitudes? Early empirical research focused on the idea that attitude change depended on the extent to which people were able to comprehend and retain the information contained in a persuasive message (e.g., Hovland, Janis, & Kelley, 1953; Hovland, Lumsdaine, & Sheffield, 1949). Later, it was shown that the ability to learn the information (e.g., message arguments) was not as important in attitude change processes as how individuals cognitively responded to or elaborated upon that information (e.g., Brock, 1967; Greenwald, 1968; McGuire, 1964; Petty, Ostrom, & Brock, 1981).

This *cognitive response* approach contends that persuasion depends on the extent to which individuals generate and rehearse their own idiosyncratic thoughts to the information presented. The cognitive response perspective maintains that individuals are active participants in the persuasion process who attempt to relate message elements to their existing repertoires of information. According to this framework, an appeal that elicits issue-relevant thoughts that are primarily favorable toward a particular recommendation would be expected to produce agreement, whereas an appeal that elicits issue-relevant thoughts that are predominantly unfavorable toward the recommendation would be expected to be ineffective in achieving attitude change. Experimental research is consistent with this view and has shown that the polarity of one's issue-relevant thoughts (e.g., positive minus negative thoughts) is a good predictor of post-message attitude change, especially when a person's motivation and ability to think are high (Eagly & Chaiken, 1993; Petty & Cacioppo, 1986).

In the present chapter we focus mostly on situations in which people are active processors of the information provided to them. However, the available research has demonstrated clearly that attitude change can occur even in situations where people are not thinking very carefully or effortfully about the information provided to them (e.g., see Chaiken, Liberman, & Eagly, 1989; Petty & Cacioppo, 1981, 1986; Petty & Wegener, 1999). In contemporary models of persuasion such as the elaboration likelihood model (ELM; Petty & Cacioppo, 1986) and the heuristic-systematic model (HSM; Chaiken et al., 1989), the extent of thinking is understood as a continuum ranging from low to high amounts of message-relevant thought (e.g., Chaiken, Duckworth, & Darke, 1999; Kruglanski & Thompson, 1999; Petty, Wheeler, & Bizer, 1999). When thinking is high, attitude change is related to the number and valence (i.e., favorable and unfavorable) of issue-relevant thoughts that people generate. When thinking is low, attitude change is determined less by one's issue-relevant thoughts and more by a variety of lower effort processes such as classical conditioning (Staats & Staats, 1957), self-perception (Bem, 1972), and the use of decision heuristics (Chaiken, 1980; see Eagly & Chaiken, 1993; Petty & Wegener, 1998). Changed attitudes based on a low amount of thinking tend to be less accessible, enduring, and resistant to subsequent attacking messages than attitudes based on careful processing (Petty, Haugtvedt, & Smith, 1995; see Petty & Krosnick, 1995, for more on the determinants and consequences of attitude strength).

We postulate that under high elaboration conditions, another aspect of thinking—meta-cognition—can play an important role in attitude change. Meta-cognition refers to people's awareness of and thoughts about their own or others' thoughts or thought processes (i.e., cognition about cognition; see Jost, Kruglanski, & Nelson, 1998). In this chapter, we argue for the conceptual importance of and utility of examining the impact of one meta-cognitive factor—thought confidence—in persuasion. More specifically, the goal of this chapter is to review recent research that has shown that in addition to generating mostly favorable thoughts, individuals also need to have confidence in the validity of their thoughts in order for thoughtful attitude change to occur. Furthermore, with respect to resistance, thoughtful individuals not only need to generate counterarguments, but they also need to have confidence in those counterarguments. After documenting the importance of meta-cognitive processes and thought confidence in particular, we discuss a number of variables that can influence people's confidence in their thoughts and thereby influence the extent of attitude change.

## Meta-cognitive responses

The topic of meta-cognition has received considerable theoretical and research attention recently, being considered one of the "top 100 topics" of psychological research (Nelson, 1992, p. ix). Meta-cognition is important because it enables individuals to better manage their thoughts and cognitive skills. In general terms, meta-cognitions have important consequences for people's judgments and behavior (see Koriat & Goldsmith, 1996; Nelson & Narens, 1994). For example, the stronger one's feeling of knowing about an elusive name, the more time one is likely to spend searching for it before giving up (e.g., Costermans, Lories, & Ansay, 1992; Nelson & Narens, 1990). The urge to bring the search to an end is all the more intense when one feels that the name is on the "tip of the tongue" and is about to emerge into consciousness (Yzerbyt, Lories, & Dardenne, 1999).

The meta-cognition of interest in this chapter concerns people's subjective confidence in their thoughts. The idea that people evaluate their thoughts is prevalent in a number of psychological domains. For instance, evaluating one's thoughts is critical to some forms of clinical practice. Indeed, the main goal of cognitive-behavior therapy is to get individuals to decrease the perceived validity of or confidence in negative or irrational thoughts by questioning them or assessing the evidence for them (e.g., Beck & Greenberg, 1994; Ellis, 1962). The role of thought confidence in judgment also plays a prominent role in social-cognitive theories. For example, Kruglanski's (1980, 1989) lay epistemic theory emphasizes a two-phase sequence of thinking in which hypotheses (beliefs) are first generated and then validated. Validating one's hypotheses would presumably enhance confidence in them, whereas invalidating them would reduce confidence.

## Confidence in thoughts and persuasion

In considering the role of meta-cognition in attitude change, it should matter whether or not people have confidence or doubt in the validity of the thoughts that they generate while thinking about an attitude issue or in response to a persuasive message.[1] Specifically, when one's attitude-relevant thoughts are perceived as valid, they should have a strong impact on attitudes, but when one's attitude-relevant thoughts are perceived as invalid, they should not. The proposed relationship between thought confidence and attitudes in many ways parallels the relationship between attitude confidence and corresponding behavior (for a review, see Gross, Holtz, & Miller, 1995). That is, the more confidence one has in one's attitude, the more one is willing to act on it (e.g., Fazio & Zanna, 1978). Attitude confidence is defined in this context as a subjective sense of conviction or validity regarding one's attitude (Festinger, 1950, 1954). Similarly, thought confidence refers to a sense of conviction or validity regarding one's thoughts. Just as confident attitudes are more likely to guide behavior, we suggest that confident thoughts will be more likely to guide attitudes.[2]

Applying this *self-validation hypothesis* to persuasion suggests that increasing confidence in one's own thoughts could conceivably increase or decrease

---

1 We note that the current work is focused on meta-cognitions about the *contents* of one's thoughts. It may prove equally fruitful to examine meta-cognitions about one's thought *processes* in persuasion settings. For example, to the extent that people become aware that they have followed the peripheral route to persuasion and that this has produced an unsatisfactory outcome, they might switch to the central route (Mazursky & Schul, 2000). Prior work on how one's desired level of confidence matches one's obtained level is consistent with a meta-cognitive perspective on persuasion processes (see Bohner, Rank, Reinhard, Einwiller, & Erb, 1998; Chaiken et al., 1989).

2 Overall confidence in a thought could be based on a number of factors. For example, confidence in the thought that "If we raise tuition, I'll find the books I need in the library" might

attitude change as could increasing doubt in one's thoughts. The effect obtained would depend on the nature of the thoughts elicited by the persuasive communication. When the thoughts in response to a message are primarily favorable, increasing confidence in their validity should increase persuasion, but increasing doubt about their validity should decrease persuasion. When thoughts are primarily unfavorable, however, increasing confidence in their validity should decrease persuasion, but increasing doubt about their validity should increase persuasion. Thus, the meta-cognitive factor of confidence should interact with the dominant thought valence in determining persuasion.

### *Initial self-validation experiments*

In an initial series of studies designed to test the self-validation hypothesis, Petty, Briñol, and Tormala (2002) found evidence supporting the notion that thought confidence can increase or decrease persuasion depending on the favorability of the cognitive responses to a message. In one of the studies (Petty et al., 2002, Study 1), participants were asked to read a persuasive message about a campus issue, to think carefully about the proposal, and to list what they thought might be some of its consequences. Following this task, participants reported the overall confidence they had in the consequences they listed as well as their attitudes toward the proposal. In accord with the self-validation hypothesis, the relationship between thoughts (i.e., direction of the consequences listed) and attitudes was significantly greater to the extent that confidence was relatively high rather than low. In other words, to the extent that people had confidence in their thoughts, persuasion depended on the valence of those thoughts. On the other hand, to the extent that people lacked confidence in their thoughts, persuasion was less dependent on thought valence.

In a second study, rather than asking participants to list all the thoughts they had while reading a message, they were asked to generate and to write down only pro-arguments in favor of the message or only counterarguments against it. Because measuring thought confidence before attitudes (as in the first study) could increase its accessibility, thought confidence was measured after the attitude reports in Study 2. In addition, thought confidence was assessed individually for each thought (rather than for all thoughts together). We replicated the self-validation pattern observed in the first study. Again, thoughts became more important in determining attitudes as confidence was increased. When individuals wrote favorable thoughts, increased confidence

---

be based on one's confidence in the likelihood that this will occur (Smith & Swinyard, 1988) or confidence in the desirability of the consequence. Confidence in likelihoods or desirabilities might reflect the range of likelihoods or desirabilities considered plausible (Petty et al., 2002). That is, the greater the range of likelihoods or desirabilities considered reasonable, the less confidence one has in any particular likelihood or desirability.

was associated with more persuasion, but when individuals wrote negative thoughts, increased confidence was associated with reduced persuasion. Thus, these two studies showed that the amount of confidence people have in their thoughts can moderate the ability of cognitive responses to predict attitudes. Nevertheless, because confidence in participants' thoughts was measured rather than manipulated in both studies, it was important to manipulate thought confidence to isolate the causal effects of this variable.

Thus, in a third experiment, both the valence of the thoughts and the confidence in those thoughts were manipulated. In order to ensure that participants generated mostly positive or negative thoughts, the cogency of the arguments in the persuasive message was varied (Petty, Wells, & Brock, 1976). Individuals who received strong arguments were expected to produce mostly favorable thoughts, whereas individuals who received weak arguments were expected to produce mostly unfavorable thoughts. In order to manipulate thought confidence, after listing their thoughts about the topic, participants were asked to recall personal experiences in which they had felt confidence or doubt in what they were thinking (ostensibly as part of an unrelated experiment). This manipulation was expected to influence the confidence with which people held their thoughts through a misattribution-like procedure. Both manipulations were successful. Individuals exposed to the strong message generated mostly favorable thoughts, whereas people exposed to the weak message generated mostly unfavorable thoughts. Furthermore, when confidence in those thoughts was assessed following the confidence manipulation, people who wrote about past experiences of confidence expressed greater confidence in the validity of their thoughts than did individuals who wrote about past experiences of doubt.

In this study we also measured the extent to which people reported thinking about the issue. Individuals who reported relatively high amounts of thinking (as determined by a tertiary split on this measure) showed the self-validation effect. That is, manipulated thought confidence interacted with argument quality to influence attitudes (see Figure 9.1). Participants exposed to the strong message reported more favorable attitudes when confidence was manipulated to be high rather than low. In contrast, participants exposed to the weak version of the message reported less favorable attitudes when confidence was manipulated to be high rather than low. These findings provide initial evidence that having confidence in one's thoughts *causes* people to be more reliant on them when expressing attitudes in response to a persuasive message—at least when the level of thinking is high.

### Role of elaboration likelihood

The fact that the self-validation effect was obtained in Study 3 only for individuals who reported relatively high amounts of thinking about the issue is consistent with the notion that self-validation effects are not typically automatic, but instead requires some attention and cognitive effort. When

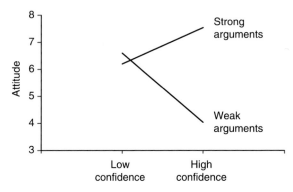

*Figure 9.1* The-two way interaction on post-message attitudes between argument quality and thought confidence for high elaboration participants (adapted from Petty, Briñol, & Tormala, 2002).

attempting to implement a meta-cognition (i.e., thoughts about one's own cognitive responses), controlled thinking is often required. Meta-cognitive beliefs such as "I'd rather not think like this" or "Something is wrong with this thought" appear to involve some conscious control (e.g., Wegner, 1989), at least until such thinking becomes routinized (Smith, Stewart, & Buttram, 1992) such as when an attitude issue becomes overly familiar.

In accord with this reasoning, self-validation effects are expected to be most apparent when the likelihood of thinking is high. There are at least two reasons for this. First, if people have few thoughts about a persuasive communication, there would be few thoughts to validate or invalidate, thereby attenuating any effects. Second, the same factors that would likely motivate high amounts of message scrutiny in general (e.g., high personal importance of the issue, accountability, and so on; see Petty & Cacioppo, 1986) would also likely motivate people to scrutinize and evaluate the validity of their thoughts.

In order to motivate participants to elaborate upon the information presented, in the first two studies described earlier (Petty, et al., 2002, Exps. 1 and 2), we used a topic with high personal relevance and participants explicitly were asked to pay attention to and think about the information. In Study 3, participants were divided into two different groups according to their own reports about the extent to which they paid attention to the message and thought about its content. The results of these studies were consistent with the idea that confidence in thoughts affects attitude change when the likelihood of elaboration is relatively high.

The effects of these studies are especially interesting to compare with prior work on high elaboration and persuasion. Past studies have been reasonably consistent in their finding that under high thinking conditions people are more responsive to the quality of the arguments in a persuasive message than under low thinking conditions (see Petty & Wegener, 1998, for a review). The research on self-validation (Petty et al., 2002) shows that the impact of argument quality on attitudes under high elaboration conditions can be attenuated and even eliminated when thoughtful people lack confidence in the thoughts that they have generated.

## Thought confidence and other thought dimensions

Thought confidence refers to an individual's subjective assessment of the validity of his or her own thought. Thus, thought confidence can be distinguished from other properties of thoughts that have already proven important in attitude change, such as the expectancy (i.e., likelihood) and the value (i.e., desirability) properties of beliefs (Fishbein & Ajzen, 1975; Petty & Wegener, 1991; Wegener, Petty, & Klein, 1994). We argue that having high (or low) confidence in a thought such as "If we raise taxes, the roads will be improved" does not necessarily imply that fixing the roads is better or worse, or more or less likely to occur if taxes are raised. To verify this, we conducted two studies to demonstrate that thought confidence accounted for variance in attitudes above and beyond the likelihood and desirability components of thoughts (Petty et al., 2002).

In one study (Petty et al., 2002, Exp. 1), we asked participants to read a persuasive message and to list what they thought might be some of its consequences. Following this task, participants reported the confidence they had in the consequences they listed, as well as how likely and desirable they thought each consequence was. As noted earlier, in this study we found that the relationship between thoughts (i.e., direction of consequences) and attitudes was greater to the extent that confidence was relatively high rather than low. Furthermore, although we found that thought confidence was reliably correlated with thought likelihood and desirability, these constructs did not account for the role that thought confidence had in moderating the relationship between thought valence and attitudes.

In a second study conducted in order to differentiate thought confidence from other properties, participants wrote down consequences that they thought would be relatively likely, and consequences that would be relatively unlikely to occur if marijuana were to be legalized. Then, confidence in those thoughts was manipulated by asking participants to recall previous experiences of confidence or doubt. Results showed that increasing confidence had opposite effects on the relatively likely and unlikely consequences. That is, increasing confidence in relatively likely consequences increased the perceived likelihood of occurrence, but increasing confidence in relatively unlikely consequences decreased perceived likelihood. Thus, across the full range of consequences, likelihood and confidence were uncorrelated. In sum, these studies demonstrated that thought confidence, likelihood, and desirability are not only conceptually distinct but are empirically separable.

Our research also suggested that thought confidence is relatively independent of the objective accuracy or inherent quality of the thoughts. For example, in one of our studies (Petty et al., 2002, Exp. 2), we had impartial judges rate the thoughts that the participants generated for quality, and there was no relationship between a person's confidence in a thought and its rated quality. Even more compelling evidence comes from the studies in which perceived confidence was manipulated (Petty et al., 2002, Exps. 3 and 4). Since participants were randomly assigned to the high and low confidence manipulation which followed the listing of thoughts, participants in the high and low confidence conditions must have generated thoughts of equal quality. Nevertheless, when confidence in thoughts was manipulated to be low, people relied on those thoughts less than when confidence was manipulated to be high.

In consonance with findings outside the persuasion domain, (see reviews by Deffenbacher, 1984; Wells & Murray, 1983), our studies clearly indicate that people's confidence in their thoughts can be independent of their actual quality. Future research should explore, however, the specific circumstances under which thought confidence might be associated with thought quality. For example, thought confidence can be based on a careful consideration of information that is diagnostic for the validity of the thought, or it can be based on the elaboration of irrelevant information. When the confidence with which people hold their thoughts is based on effortful analyses of diagnostic information, then such thought confidence would not only predict attitudes but may also be associated with qualities such as accessibility, durability, stability, and resistance. On the other hand, when thought confidence is based on less relevant information or less careful thought, the confidence might be relatively weaker in terms of accessibility, durability, stability, and resistance. Importantly, future research should also explore whether attitudes based on the former form of confidence would be more accurate and functional, whereas attitudes based on the later type of weak confidence may be associated with overconfidence effects.

### Summary

We presented evidence showing that the extent to which people have confidence in the validity of their cognitive responses can play a significant role in persuasion. In accord with the self-validation hypothesis, as thought confidence increased, valenced cognitive responses were more predictive of attitudes. Importantly, across our initial studies, the self-validation hypothesis was supported whether thought confidence was measured or manipulated. We also used two different kinds of measures of thought confidence— assessing confidence in each individual thought or in all of one's thoughts. We measured confidence both before and after attitude expression. We also used different ways to vary the valence of thinking. None of these differences changed the self-validation effects observed. That is, with respect to attitude change, the current research showed that when people's thoughts were largely favorable (either because they were instructed to be favorable or because favorable thoughts were naturally produced to strong arguments), increasing thought confidence (whether measured or manipulated) increased persuasion. On the other hand, when people's thoughts were largely unfavorable (either because they were instructed to counterargue or because unfavorable thoughts were naturally produced to weak arguments), increasing thought confidence reduced persuasion.

Another contribution of our initial research has been to specify under what circumstances the evaluations of our own thoughts are more likely to influence our judgments. We postulated and found that self-validation effects are fostered when motivation and ability to think are high rather than low. Finally, across the studies we were able to demonstrate that the effects of thought confidence on attitudes are not accounted for by related constructs, such as belief likelihood or desirability.

## Implications of self-validation

There are a number of important implications of the self-validation notion. On a practical level, for example, persuasion researchers might not only get respondents to rate their thoughts for valence, but also for subjective confidence because additional heretofore unexplained variance in attitudes can be captured by this dimension. Prior research has shown clearly that thoughts are more predictive of attitudes under high than low elaboration conditions (e.g., Chaiken, 1980; Petty & Cacioppo, 1979), but even under high elaboration conditions, attitude–thought correlations are often only modest (e.g., .5 to .6; for a review see Petty & Cacioppo, 1986). The self-validation hypothesis suggests, however, that the typical correlations reported under high elaboration conditions may conceal additional and previously unrecognized differences that exist between individuals who have relatively high versus low confidence in their thoughts. In fact, combining the data from the studies we reported in the earlier section (Petty et al., 2002), we found that attitude–thought correlations were higher for individuals with high confidence in their thoughts, and lower for individuals with low confidence in their thoughts. Thus, although previous work has clearly shown that persuasion depends on the thoughts that are generated in response to a message—at least when the elaboration likelihood is high (Petty et al., 1981), the self-validation research demonstrates that what people think about their cognitive responses is a potentially important additional factor to consider.

Another example of the potential utility of the self-validation framework comes from the extent to which thought confidence might affect overall confidence in one's attitude. Confidence in attitudes is important because attitudes held with great confidence are stronger than those held with low confidence (see Petty & Krosnick, 1995, for a review of attitude strength work). That is, confident attitudes guide judgments and behavior better than attitudes about which one has doubt, and are more resistant to change (e.g., Fazio & Zanna, 1978; see Gross et al., 1995 for a review). In one of the studies described earlier in this chapter (Petty et al., 2002, Exp. 2), we found that attitudes based on highly confident thoughts were not only more evaluatively congruent with those thoughts than attitudes based on thoughts held with low confidence, but the resulting attitudes were also held with greater confidence. Thus, we showed that thought confidence can have implications for attitude strength, at least when attitude strength is assessed by subjective confidence in the attitude. Of course, future research should examine whether attitudes based on highly confident thoughts are also more stable, accessible, resistant to further challenges, and better predictors of future behavior than attitudes based on thoughts held with low confidence. We suspect, as noted earlier, that the basis of the thought confidence may have important implications for the impact of thought confidence on attitude confidence.

In brief, the current research indicates that there is a third important dimension of thinking in addition to the *extent* of thinking (i.e., amount) and *direction* of thinking (i.e., valence) that have garnered the lion's share of prior research attention in the persuasion literature (see Petty & Cacioppo, 1986; Petty & Wegener, 1999). This meta-cognitive dimension—thought confidence—has been shown to be able to increase or decrease persuasion depending on the nature of the thoughts generated in response to a persuasive proposal. As a consequence, based on self-validation processes, there are implications for a new conceptual understanding of a diversity of attitude change phenomena. That is, variations in thought confidence might provide a plausible alternative explanation for a number of attitude change effects that had been attributed previously to other mechanisms. As an example of the potential utility of the self-validation framework to provide a novel explanation for diverse attitude change phenomena, we next describe two recent lines of research. In each case, we examine a well-known paradigm in the literature of persuasion that can be reinterpreted in terms of self-validation processes.

## Applying self-validation to various persuasion phenomena

### *Effects of overt head movements on persuasion*

One effect to which self-validation processes appear to apply is the effects of overt head movements on persuasion. In the original study on this topic, Wells and Petty (1980) asked participants to move their heads in an up-and-down (vertical or "yes") manner, in a side-to-side (horizontal or "no") manner, or gave no instructions about head movements, as they listened to music and an editorial over headphones. The primary result was that attitudes were more in accord with the position advocated in the message when participants nodded rather than shook their heads. In a conceptual replication of this finding, Tom, Pettersen, Lau, Burton, and Cook (1991) found that nodding head movements resulted in the establishment of increased preference for a previously neutral object, whereas shaking head movements led to a decline in preference for the neutral object (see Förster & Strack, 1996, for another application of this paradigm).

There are a number of possible explanations for the impact of head movements on attitudes. First, Wells and Petty argued that head movements could have biased the content of people's thoughts about the message or attitude object and these biased thoughts made attitudes more favorable in the vertical than in the horizontal head movement conditions. Although thought content was not assessed, Wells and Petty speculated that when nodding, favorable thoughts would be facilitated and unfavorable thoughts inhibited, but when shaking, unfavorable thoughts would be facilitated and favorable thoughts inhibited. A second possibility is that head movements might induce a simple inference that leads one to agree with or reject the proposal (e.g., if I shook my head I must not like it; cf., Chaiken, 1987). Finally, head movements might induce positive or negative affective states that become associated with the advocacy through a classical conditioning process (see Tom et al., 1991; for this point of view).

The self-validation hypothesis holds out yet another possible explanation for the persuasive effects of head movements. This analysis also assumes that head movements prime the agreement and disagreement concepts, but that agreement/disagreement is associated with one's thoughts about the message rather than the message position per se. That is, just as vertical movements from others would enhance the perceived validity of what you are saying because others agree with you (i.e., social validation, see Festinger, 1954), one's own vertical head movements might instill greater confidence in what one is thinking through a process of self-validation (i.e., "I agree with my thoughts").

One key implication of the self-validation hypothesis that differs from all the others is that in the self-validation framework either vertical or horizontal head movements can increase or decrease persuasion depending on the nature of the thoughts elicited by the message. If thoughts are predominantly favorable, then, relative to shaking, nodding should enhance persuasion because such movements would inspire confidence in (or signal approval of) these favorable thoughts. This is the direction of the effects found in all prior studies on head movements. More interestingly, the self-validation hypothesis makes a unique prediction when individuals' thoughts are predominately negative. Here, nodding should reduce persuasion relative to shaking because it would inspire confidence in one's unfavorable thoughts about the communication. Shaking would enhance persuasion relative to nodding by undermining confidence in one's negative thoughts. This reverses the typical effect of head movements found in all prior studies.

To examine the self-validation hypothesis that one's own head movements can serve as a cue to the validity of what one is thinking, we conducted several experiments (Briñol & Petty, 2003). In the first study, we instructed participants to nod or shake their heads in conjunction with a message containing either strong or weak arguments on a topic of interest to the college student participants. The primary finding was a message quality × head movement interaction (see Figure 9.2). When participants generated mostly

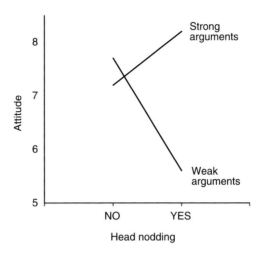

*Figure 9.2* The two-way interaction on post-message attitudes between argument quality and direction of head nodding (from Briñol & Petty, 2003).

favorable thoughts (i.e., to the strong arguments), nodding produced more agreement with the proposal than shaking, replicating the original Wells and Petty (1980) findings. In stark contrast, however, shaking actually led to more persuasion than nodding when the message contained weak arguments and people's thoughts were largely unfavorable rather than favorable.

Following a similar paradigm, in a second study we examined whether this self-validation effect would occur mostly when the likelihood of thinking about the message was low or high. As described earlier, our hypothesis was that the self-validation effect should be more likely to occur when the likelihood of thinking is high since people need motivation and ability to evaluate the thoughts they have generated. Elaboration was manipulated with a combination of motivational and ability factors. In the low elaboration condition, the message was made to seem less important and it was also presented a bit faster over the headphones. As expected, a three-way interaction (head movement × argument quality × elaboration) emerged on the measure of attitude toward the focal issue. Under the high elaboration conditions, we replicated the two-way interaction of head movements and argument quality found in Exp. 1. Under low elaboration conditions, no significant effects were obtained.

In another study in this series, we replicated the attitude findings from the previous studies, and also showed that head movements have an effect on confidence in thoughts, but not in the nature (valence) of the thoughts themselves. Furthermore, confidence in one's thoughts mediated the effects of head movements on attitudes. In summary, our studies demonstrated that head nodding enhances confidence in one's own thoughts relative to shaking, and can thereby either enhance or reduce persuasion depending on the valence of the dominant thought.

## Effects of ease of retrieval on persuasion

In persuasion paradigms, the ease of retrieval idea suggests that people who try to generate many favorable thoughts about a position can be less persuaded than people who try to generate few favorable thoughts (see Wänke, Bless, & Biller, 1996). The dominant explanation for this surprising effect is based on the availability heuristic (Tversky & Kahneman, 1973). The explanation begins with the assumption that generating few arguments is easy, but that generating many arguments is difficult. When people have a hard time generating arguments, they might infer that there are few such arguments available, but when they have an easy time generating arguments, they might infer that there are many such favorable arguments. These inferences of argument availability translate into inferences about how good the position is (Rothman & Schwarz, 1998). That is, one's subjective experience of ease or difficulty of argument generation leads to a simple inference about argument availability. This simple availability heuristic inference, like other simple inferences (e.g., Chaiken, 1980), is postulated to be more impactful on judgments when the extent of cognitive processing is relatively low (e.g., Chen & Chaiken, 1999; Rothhman & Schwarz, 1998; Schwarz, Bless, Strack, Klumpp, Rittenauer-Schatka, & Simons, 1991; see also Wänke & Bless, 2000).

In accord with the self-validation hypothesis, the ease of retrieval effect might be explained by an alternative psychological mechanism. That is, when it is easy to generate arguments, people might have more confidence in the arguments they generate than when it is more difficult to generate them. According to the self-validation hypothesis, we predicted the ease of retrieval effects would be mediated by the confidence individuals have in their thoughts with greater ease of retrieval producing more thought confidence, and ultimately more thought-congruent attitudes. Furthermore, since considering thought confidence requires sufficient motivation and ability to think and assess one's thoughts, we expected the ease of retrieval effects to be more likely to occur under high elaboration conditions than under low elaboration conditions (see, Benjamin & Bjork, 1996; Gill, Swann, & Silvera, 1998 for other links between fluency and confidence).

Tormala, Petty, and Briñol (2002) conducted a number of studies in which participants were asked to read a persuasive message and were induced to generate either a low or high number of positive (or negative) thoughts in response to it. According to the self-validation notion, we predicted that under high elaboration conditions, generating a high number of thoughts would be difficult, and thus people would rely on these thoughts less than when generating a smaller and easier number of thoughts. That is, the effect of generation difficulty on attitudes would be mediated by the confidence participants had in the thoughts they listed. Under low elaboration conditions, we expected that thought confidence would not matter, since under these conditions participants are less motivated (or able) to attend to their own thinking. In accord with prior research on the number heuristic (Pelham, Sumarta, & Myaskovsky, 1994; Petty & Cacioppo, 1984), low elaboration participants were expected to be more influenced by the actual number of thoughts they generated (e.g., favoring the issue more after listing ten than two favorable thoughts).

As expected, Tormala et al. (2002, Exp. 1) found in one study that high elaboration participants opposed a new policy more after generating few rather than many arguments *against* a message supporting the policy. This study demonstrated that experienced ease of generating arguments can decrease persuasion under high elaboration conditions when the thoughts generated are unfavorable toward the proposal. In two additional studies, Tormala et al. (2002, Exps. 2 and 3) found that high elaboration participants favored a new policy more after generating few rather than many *positive* thoughts in response to a message supporting the policy. Importantly, we argued and found in these studies that the effects were mediated by the confidence participants had in the thoughts they listed in response to the persuasive message. That is, the easier it felt to generate positive thoughts (because only few were requested), the more confidence one had in those thoughts, and the more favorable attitudes that resulted. Confidence in the thoughts that underlie one's attitudes might be responsible for the enhanced attitude confidence that has been observed when people find it easy rather than difficult to generate thoughts on an issue (Haddock, Rothman, Reber, & Schwarz, 1999).[3]

Finally, individuals engaging in a high level of elaboration seem to be the most motivated to assess their own thought confidence and then rely on this meta-cognition to include or discount their thoughts when forming an attitude on the issue. Low elaboration participants, on the other hand, tended to show the opposite results, reporting more thought-congruent attitudes after generating a high number of such thoughts.

In conclusion, our work on the self-validation hypothesis suggests that individuals who are highly motivated to think pay close attention to their subjective feelings of confidence while generating thoughts. Although in the prior work on self-validation described earlier in this chapter (Petty et al.,

---

3 To ensure that attitude confidence did not account for our thought confidence effects, in one study we measured both and showed that controlling for attitude confidence did not eliminate the thought confidence effects. Although attitude and thought confidence bear some relation, they are independent constructs (Petty et al., 2002). Notably, whereas attitude confidence effects in the ease paradigm are readily derived from the availability heuristic (i.e., greater perceived information available on an issue could translate into greater global attitude confidence), thought confidence effects are not as readily derived from the availability heuristic. That is, greater perceived information available in general should not affect confidence in any individual component of that knowledge. Rather, the feeling of ease of generating the thoughts per se is what presumably produces the confidence (i.e., unmediated by the perceived availability of arguments).

2002) confidence was manipulated fairly directly, we argued that other components of subjective experience (e.g., experienced ease of retrieval; head movements) might also affect confidence for individuals attuned to that experience (i.e., those motivated and able to think about the issue). Our studies on ease of retrieval are consistent with this argument, and inconsistent with the previous notion that ease of retrieval affects attitudes solely by an availability heuristic process that operates when motivation or ability to think are low. In fact, our findings suggest that ease of retrieval effects do not necessarily reflect the availability heuristic as assumed in previous research (e.g., Schwarz, 1998), but may stem from a consideration of the confidence people have in their thoughts.

## Conclusions: A new role for variables in persuasion

Our work on self-validation shows that in addition to the *extent* (i.e., amount) of thinking and *direction* (i.e., valence) of thinking, a new dimension of thinking—thought confidence—can play a significant role in persuasion. In accord with the self-validation hypothesis, the effects of the valence of a person's cognitive responses were shown to be greater for people with high thought confidence than those with relatively low thought confidence. In operational terms, as thought confidence increased, favorable and unfavorable cognitive responses were more predictive of attitudes.

Self-validation processes have clear implications for current persuasion theory. Within the framework of the elaboration likelihood model (ELM) of persuasion (Petty & Cacioppo, 1986), for example, the current research appears to suggest a new role that variables can take on in persuasion settings. Prior research on the ELM has focused on four roles that persuasion variables can assume in different situations. That is, any one variable (e.g., source credibility, mood) can, depending on the elaboration likelihood, affect persuasion by invoking different mechanisms. The ELM holds that when the elaboration likelihood is high, a variable can serve as an argument (i.e., a piece of evidence regarding the merits of the issue) if it is relevant to the merits of the issue, or the variable can determine the nature of the ongoing information-processing activity (e.g., it might bias the ongoing thinking). On the other hand, when the elaboration likelihood is low, evaluations are likely to be the result of relatively simple associations or inferences based on salient cues and thus variables are likely to influence attitudes in this way when thinking is low. Finally, when the elaboration likelihood is moderate, people may examine the persuasion context for indications (e.g., is the source credible?) of whether or not they are interested in or should process the message.

Research on self-validation suggests another role for variables in persuasion. That is, under high elaboration conditions a variable might influence attitudes by affecting people's confidence in their thoughts (see Petty &

Briñol, 2002, for a review of multiple roles in persuasion).[4] For example, in this chapter we described how people's overt behavior (i.e., head nodding; Briñol & Petty, 2003) can influence persuasion by increasing (e.g., nodding) or decreasing (e.g., shaking) the confidence with which people hold their own thoughts in response to a message. We also presented evidence demonstrating that the ease with which thoughts come to mind can have an impact on persuasion by influencing thought confidence (Tormala et al., 2002). When it is easy to generate arguments, thought confidence increases, enhancing thought-congruent attitudes. However, when it is more difficult to generate thoughts, thought confidence decreases, reducing thought-congruent attitudes. Of course, there may be a wide variety of other variables that instill or reduce confidence in people's thoughts. The factors affecting confidence likely range from individual variables such as a person's current mood state (Briñol, Petty, & Barden, 2004; Wyer, Clore, & Isbell, 1999) to situational factors like the credibility of the source associated with the message (Briñol, Petty, & Tormala, 2004). The research we reviewed in this chapter suggests that some persuasion variables are capable of influencing people's confidence in their thoughts. Many other such variables may also be amenable to a self-validation analysis, and if so the self-validation hypothesis may ultimately prove useful in providing a novel explanation for diverse attitude change phenomena.

As one final example, consider classic work on the sleeper effect whereby a message that is initially ineffective gains in impact over time (e.g., Kelman & Hovland, 1953). Contemporary research strongly indicates that the sleeper effect is most likely to occur when people first receive a compelling message that is then discredited by declaring it false, or associating it with a low credibility source (Pratkanis, Greenwald, Leippe, & Baumgardner, 1988). The most prominently mentioned account for the increased impact of this discredited message is that over time people disassociate the discrediting cue from the message position (e.g., Cook, Gruder, Hennigan, & Flay, 1979). However, it is possible that self-validation processes are also at work. That is, a person might have many favorable thoughts to a strong message, but lose

---

4 When confidence is induced prior to message exposure, and elaboration is not constrained to be high or low, confidence might affect the extent of information processing, with confident people engaging in less thought than people lacking in confidence (Tiedens & Linton, 2001). If confidence is induced after extensive message processing, as in the current research, however, it appears to affect confidence in the thoughts that have been generated—enhancing persuasion if the thoughts were favorable, but reducing persuasion if the thoughts were unfavorable. If confidence is induced prior to a message and elaboration is constrained to be low (e.g., by presence of distraction; Petty et al., 1976), then a feeling of confidence might enhance using one's own attitude as a peripheral cue. If confidence is induced prior to a message and elaboration is high, then confidence might enhance attitudinally biased information processing (Lord, Ross, & Lepper, 1979). The multiple possible roles for feelings of confidence should be explored in future research.

confidence in these thoughts when the message is discredited (e.g., "everything I was thinking must be wrong"). Over time, however, confidence in one's own thoughts might increase again, thus restoring the impact of the message. Our point is not that the self-validation hypothesis necessarily explains the sleeper effect finding, but rather that there may be numerous source, message, context, and recipient variables that influence attitudes by affecting people's confidence in their thoughts, and thereby have an impact on persuasion. These issues should be investigated in future studies.

In closing, we note that the self-validation framework might also be extended from understanding attitudes about issues (as in the examples provided in the present chapter) to other attitude domains, such as attitudes about oneself (i.e., self-esteem). For instance, we conducted an experiment to provide additional evidence of the potential of the self-validation hypothesis to explain the impact of overt behavior on thought confidence and its implications for self-esteem (Briñol & Petty, 2003, Exp. 4). As part of a presumed graphology study, participants in this experiment were required to think about and write down their best or worse qualities (thought-direction manipulation) using their dominant or non-dominant hand (overt behavior manipulation). Then, participants rated the confidence in those thoughts and reported their self-esteem. Since writing with the non-dominant hand is very infrequent and difficult, and whatever is written with the non-dominant may appear "shaky," we expected and found that using the non-dominant hand decreased the confidence with which people held the thoughts they listed. As found in the head nodding studies, this impact of behavior on thought confidence occurred despite the fact that the actual quality of the thoughts did not vary across the hand conditions. As a consequence of the differential thought confidence, the effect of the direction of thoughts (positive/negative) on current self-esteem was significantly greater when participants wrote those thoughts with their dominant rather than their non-dominant hand. That is, writing positive thoughts about oneself with the dominant hand increased self-esteem relative to writing positive thoughts with the non-dominant hand, but writing negative thoughts with the dominant hand resulted in the reversed effect. Thus, as head nodding did, using the dominant hand affected participants' attitudes (toward themselves) by influencing the confidence in the validity of their own thoughts.

The studies described in this chapter have shown that what people do (e.g., head movements and use of dominant hand) while they process relevant information (e.g., listening to a persuasive message or self-generating arguments and thoughts) can influence the confidence people have in their thoughts, and this confidence mediates the effects of behavior on attitudes. Thus, it might be worthwhile for future research to examine other behavioral treatments that could be linked to self-validation processes. Future research might explore whether facial expression of emotions during thinking could signal that one is happy or displeased with one's cognitions. Future research might explore the self-validation role of different body postures and actions (e.g., arm flexion and extension) during information processing. The research we reported in this chapter suggests that the self-validation framework has the potential to generate novel explanations for existing findings as well as generate new effects.

## References

Beck, A. T., & Greenberg, R. L. (1994). Brief cognitive therapies. In A. E. Bergin & S. L. Garfield (Eds.), *Handbook of psychotherapy and behavior change* (pp. 230–249). New York: Wiley.

Bem, D. J. (1972). Self-perception theory. In L. Berkowitz (Ed.), *Advances in experimental social psychology* (pp. 1–62). New York: Academic Press.

Benjamin, A. S., & Bjork, R. A. (1996). Retrieval fluency as a metacognitive index. In L. M. Reder (Ed.), *Implicit memory and metacognition* (pp. 309–338). Mahwah, NJ Lawrence: Erlbaum Associates, Inc.

Bohner, G., Rank, S., Reinhard, M., Einwiller, S., & Erb H. (1998). Motivational determinants of systematic processing: Expectancy moderates effects of desired confidence on processing effort. *European Journal of Social Psychology, 28*, 185–206.

Briñol, P., & Petty, R. E. (2003). Overt head movements and persuasion: A self-validation analysis. *Journal of Personality and Social Psychology, 84*, 1123–1139.

Briñol, P., Petty, R. E., & Barden, J. (2004). *Mood and persuasion: A self-validation analysis.* Working paper. Ohio State University, Columbus, OH.

Briñol, P., Petty, R. E., & Tormala, Z. L. (2004). The self-validation of cognitive responses to advertisements. *Journal of Consumer Research, 31*, 559–573.

Brock, T. C. (1967). Communication discrepancy and intent to persuade as determinants of counterargument production. *Journal of Experimental Social Psychology, 3*, 269–309.

Chaiken, S. (1980). Heuristic versus systematic information processing in the use of source versus message cues in persuasion. *Journal of Personality and Social Psychology, 39*, 752–766.

Chaiken, S. (1987). The heuristic model of persuasion. In M. P. Zanna, J. M. Olson, & C. P. Herman (Eds.), *Social influence: The Ontario symposium* (Vol. 5, pp. 3–39). Hillsdale, NJ: Lawrence Erlbaum Associates, Inc.

Chaiken, S., Duckworth, K. L., & Darke, P. (1999). When parsimony fails . . . *Psychological Inquiry, 10*, 118–123.

Chaiken, S., Liberman, A., & Eagly, A. H. (1989). Heuristic and systematic processing within and beyond the persuasion context. In J. S. Uleman & J. A. Bargh (Eds.), *Unintended thought* (pp. 212–252). New York: Guilford Press.

Chen, S. & Chaiken, S. (1999). The heuristic-systematic model in its broader context. In S. Chaiken and Y. Trope (Eds.), *Dual-process theories in social psychology* (pp. 73–96). New York: Guilford Press.

Cook, T. D., Gruder, C. L., Hennigan, K. M., & Flay, B. R. (1979). History of the sleeper effect: Some logical pitfalls in accepting the null hypothesis. *Psychological Bulletin, 86*, 662–679.

Costermans, J., Lories, G., & Ansay, C. (1992). Confidence level and feeling of knowing in question answering: The weight of inferential processes. *Journal of Experimental Psychology: Learning, Memory, & Cognition, 18*, 142–150.

Deffenbacher, K. A. (1984). Experimental psychology actually can assist triers of fact. *American Psychologist, 39,* 1066–1068.

Eagly A. H., & Chaiken, S. (1993). *The psychology of attitudes.* Fort Worth, TX: Harcourt, Brace, Jovanivich.

Ellis, A. (1962). *Reason and emotion in psychotherapy.* New York: Lyle Stuart.

Fazio, R. H., & Zanna, M. P. (1978). Attitudinal qualities relating to the strength of the attitude–behavior relationship. *Journal of Experimental Social Psychology, 14,* 398–408.

Festinger, L. (1950). Informal social communication. *Psychological Review, 57,* 271–282.

Festinger, L. (1954). A theory of social comparison processes. *Human Relations, 7,* 117–140.

Fishbein, M., & Ajzen, I. (1975). *Belief, attitude, intention, and behavior: An introduction to theory and research.* Menlo Park, CA: Addison-Wesley.

Förster, J., & Strack, F. (1996). Influence of overt head movements on memory for valence words: A case of conceptual-motor compatibility. *Journal of Personality and Social Psychology, 71,* 421–430.

Gill, M. J., Swann, W. S. Jr., & Silvera, D. H. (1998). On the genesis of confidence. *Journal of Personality and Social Psychology, 75,* 1101–1114.

Greenwald, A. G. (1968). Cognitive learning, cognitive response persuasion, and attitude change. In A. G. Greenwald, T. C. Brock, & T. M. Ostrom (Eds.), *Psychological foundations of attitudes.* New York: Academic Press.

Gross, S., Holtz, R., & Miller, N. (1995). Attitude certainty. In R. E. Petty & J. A. Krosnick (Eds.), *Attitude strength: Antecedents and consequences* (pp. 215–245). Mahwah, NJ: Lawrence Erlbaum Associates, Inc.

Haddock, G., Rothman, A. J., Reber, R., & Schwarz, N. (1999). Forming judgments of attitude certainty, intensity, and importance: The role of subjective experiences. *Personality and Social Psychology Bulletin, 25,* 771–782.

Hovland, C. I., Janis, I. L., & Kelley, H. H. (1953). *Communication and persuasion.* New Haven: Yale University Press.

Hovland, C. I., Lumsdaine, A. A., & Sheffield, F. D. (1949). *Experiments on mass communication.* Princeton: Princeton University Press.

Jost, J. T., Kruglanski, A. W., & Nelson, T. O. (1998). Social metacognition: An expansionist review. *Personality and Social Psychology Review, 2,* 137–154.

Kelman, H. C., & Hovland, C. I. (1953). Reinstatement of the communicator in delayed measurement of opinion change. *Journal of Abnormal and Social Psychology, 48,* 327–335.

Koriat, A., & Goldsmith, M. (1996). Monitoring and control processes in the strategic regulation of memory accuracy. *Psychological Review, 103,* 490–517.

Kruglanski, A. W. (1980). Lay epistemo-logic-process and contents: Another look at attribution theory. *Psychological Review, 87,* 70–87.

Kruglanski, A. W. (1989). *Lay epistemics and human knowledge: Cognitive and motivational bases.* New York: Plenum Press.

Kruglanski, A. W., & Thompson, E. P. (1999). Persuasion by a single route: A view from the unimodel. *Psychological Inquiry, 10,* 83–109.

Lord, C. G., Ross, L., & Lepper, M. R. (1979). Biased assimilation and attitude polarization: The effects of prior theories on subsequently considered evidence. *Journal of Personality and Social Psychology, 37,* 2098–2109.

Mazursky, D., & Schul, Y. (2000). In the aftermath of invalidation: Shaping judgment rules on learning that previous information was invalid. *Journal of Consumer Psychology*, *9*, 213–222.

McGuire, W. J. (1964). Inducing resistance to persuasion: Some contemporary approaches. In L. Berkowitz (Ed.), *Advances in experimental social psychology*. New York: Academic Press.

Nelson, T. O. (1992). *Metacognition: Core readings*. Boston: Allyn & Bacon.

Nelson, T. O., & Narens, L. (1990). Metamemory: A theoretical framework and new findings. In G. Bower (Ed.), *The psychology of learning and motivation* (pp. 125–173). New York: Academic Press.

Nelson, T. O., & Narens, L. (1994). Why investigate metacognition? In J. Metcalfe & A. Shimamura (Eds.), *Metacognition: Knowing about knowing* (pp. 1–25). Cambridge, MA: MIT Press.

Pelham, B. W., Sumarta, T. T., & Myaskovsky, L. (1994). The easy path from many to much: The numerosity heuristic. *Cognitive Psychology*, *26*, 103–133.

Petty, R.E., & Briñol, P. (2002). Attitude change: The elaboration likelihood model. In G. Bartels & W. Nielissen (Eds.), *Marketing for sustainability: Towards transactional policy making* (pp. 176–190). Amsterdam: IOS Press.

Petty, R.E., Briñol, P, & Tormala, Z. L. (2002). Thought confidence as a determinant of persuasion: The self-validation hypothesis. *Journal of Personality and Social Psychology*, *82*, 722–741.

Petty, R. E., & Cacioppo, J. T. (1979). Issue involvement can increase or decrease persuasion by enhancing message-relevant cognitive responses. *Journal of Personality and Social Psychology*, *37*, 1915–1926.

Petty, R. E., & Cacioppo, J. T. (1981). *Attitudes and persuasion: Classic and contemporary approaches*. Dubuque, IA: Wm. C. Brown.

Petty, R. E., & Cacioppo, J. T. (1984). Source factors and the elaboration likelihood model of persuasion. *Advances in Consumer Research*, *11*, 668–672.

Petty, R. E., & Cacioppo, J. T. (1986). *Communication and persuasion: Central and peripheral routes to attitude change*. New York: Springer-Verlag.

Petty, R. E., Haugtvedt, C., & Smith, S. M. (1995). Elaboration as a determinant of attitude strength: Creating attitudes that are persistent, resistant, and predictive of behavior. In R. E. Petty & J. A. Krosnick (Eds.), *Attitude strength: Antecedents and consequences* (pp. 93–130). Mahwah, NJ: Lawrence Erlbaum Associates, Inc.

Petty, R. E., & Krosnick, J. A. (Eds.) (1995). *Attitude strength: Antecedents and consequences*. Mahway, NJ: Lawrence Erlbaum Associates, Inc.

Petty, R. E., Ostrom, T. M., & Brock, T. C. (1981). Historical foundations of the cognitive response approach to attitudes and persuasion. In R. Petty, T. Ostrom, & T. Brock (Eds.), *Cognitive responses in persuasion* (pp. 5–29). Hillsdale, NJ: Lawrence Erlbaum Associates, Inc.

Petty, R. E., & Wegener, D. T. (1991). Thought systems, argument quality, and persuasion. In R. S. Wyer & T. K. Srull (Eds.), *Advances in social cognition* (Vol. 4, pp. 147–161). Hillsdale, NJ: Lawrence Erlbaum Associates, Inc.

Petty, R. E., & Wegener, D. T. (1998). Attitude change: Multiple roles for persuasion variables. In D. Gilbert, S. Fiske, & G. Lindzey (Eds.), *The handbook of social psychology* (4th ed.). New York: McGraw-Hill.

Petty, R. E., & Wegener, D. T. (1999). The elaboration likelihood model: Current status and controversies. In S. Chaiken & Y. Trope (Eds.), *Dual-process theories in social psychology* (pp. 37–72). New York: Guilford Press.

Petty, R. E., Wells, G. L., & Brock, T. C. (1976). Distraction can enhance or reduce yielding to propaganda: Thought disruption versus effort justification. *Journal of Personality and Social Psychology, 34*, 874–884.

Petty, R. E., Wheeler, S. C., & Bizer, G. Y. (1999). Is there one persuasion process or more? Lumping versus splitting in attitude change theories. *Psychological Inquiry, 10*, 156–163.

Pratkanis, A. R., Greenwald, A. G., Leippe, M. R., & Baumgardner, M. H. (1988). In search of reliable persuasion effects: III. The sleeper effect is dead. Long live the sleeper effect. *Journal of Personality and Social Psychology, 54*, 203–218.

Rothman, A.J., & Schwarz, N. (1998). Constructing perceptions of vulnerability: Personal relevance and the use of experiential information in health judgments. *Personality and Social Psychology Bulletin, 24*, 1053–1064.

Schwarz, N. (1998). Accessible content and accessibility experiences: The interplay of declarative and experiential information in judgment. *Personality and Social Psychology Review, 2*, 87–99.

Schwarz, N., Bless, H., Strack, F., Klumpp, G., Rittenauer-Schatka, H., & Simons, A. (1991). Ease of retrieval as information: Another look at the availability heuristic. *Journal of Personality and Social Psychology, 61*, 195–202.

Smith, E. R., Stewart, T. L., & Buttram, R. T. (1992). Inferring a trait from a behavior has long-term, highly specific effects. *Journal of Personality and Social Psychology, 62*, 753–759.

Smith, R. E., & Swinyard, W. R. (1988). Cognitive response to advertising and trial. Belief strength, belief confidence and product curiosity. *Journal of Advertising, 17*, 3–14.

Staats, A. W., & Staats, C. (1958). Attitudes established by classical conditioning. *Journal of Abnormal and Social Psychology, 67*, 159–167.

Tiedens, L. Z., & Linton, S. (2001). Judgment under emotional certainty and uncertainty: The effects of specific emotions on information processing. *Journal of Personality and Social Psychology, 81*, 973–988.

Tom, G., Pettersen, P., Lau, T., Burton, T., & Cook, J. (1991). The role of overt head movement in the formation of affect. *Basic and Applied Social Psychology, 12*, 281–289.

Tormala, Z., Petty, R. E., & Briñol, P. (2002). Ease of retrieval effects in persuasion: The roles of elaboration and thought confidence. *Personality and Social Psychology Bulletin, 28*, 1700–1712.

Tversky, A., & Kahneman, D. (1973). Availability: A heuristic for judging frequency and probability. *Cognitive Psychology, 5*, 207–232.

Wänke, M., & Bless, H. (2000). The effects of subjective ease of retrieval on attitudinal judgments: The moderating role of processing motivation. In H. Bless & J. P. Forgas (Eds.), *The message within: The role of subjective experience in social cognition and behavior* (pp. 143–161). Philadelphia, PA: Taylor & Francis.

Wänke, M., Bless, H., & Biller, B. (1996). Subjective experience versus content of information in the construction of attitude judgments. *Personality and Social Psychology Bulletin, 22*, 1105–1113.

Wegener, D. T., Petty, R. E., & Klein, D. J. (1994). Effects of mood on high elaboration attitude change: The mediating role of likelihood judgments. *European Journal of Social Psychology, 23*, 25–44.

Wegner, D. M. (1989). *White bears and other unwanted thoughts*. New York: Viking Press.

Wells, G. L., & Murray, D. M. (1983). What can psychology say about the Neil v.

Biggers criteria for judging eyewitness accuracy? *Journal of Applied Psychology, 68,* 347–362.

Wells, G. L., & Petty, R. E. (1980). The effects of overt head movements on persuasion: Compatibility and incompatibility of responses. *Basic and Applied Social Psychology, 1,* 219–230.

Wyer, R. S., Clore, G. L., & Isbell, L. M. (1999). Affect and information processing. In M. P. Zanna (Ed.), *Advances in experimental social psychology* (Vol. 31, pp. 1–77). San Diego, CA: Academic Press.

Yzerbyt, V. Y., Lories, G., & Dardenne, B. (1998). *Metacognition: Cognitive and social dimensions.* Thousand Oaks, CA: Sage.

# 10 Coping with invalid messages by increasing or decreasing processing complexity

*Yaacov Schul*

Lying is a fact of everyday life. DePaulo, Kashy, Kirkendol, Wyer, and Epstein (1996) report that participants from a diverse community sample disclosed that they lie in one out of five social interactions, and college students reported lying in one out of three interactions (see also DePaulo & Kashy, 1998; Feldman, Forrest, & Happ, 2002). Consumers are often exposed to invalid claims when they are given information about products. Such claims may result from deliberate attempts to mislead (e.g., Dyer & Kuehl, 1978; Mazis & Adkinson, 1976; Schul & Mazursky, 1990) or from more mundane errors that are not the consequence of an intention to deceive (e.g., when a reduced price tag is unintentionally misplaced).

This chapter reviews evidence concerning the ways in which individuals cope with persuasion attempts when they suspect that some of the information is invalid. The problem recipients have in this case grows from the realization that if an invalid message is identified correctly, it can often be handled more or less successfully. However, if an invalid message is not identified as such, or a valid message is misidentified as invalid, receivers incur a cost. Thus, to understand how individuals cope when they suspect false messages, we must understand the knowledge they bring to the situation about their success in identifying deception as well as their ability to counter the deception once it is identified (for a similar approach see Friestad & Wright, 1994).

This chapter therefore begins with a brief discussion of the difficulties people have in their attempts to uncover deception. Then it proceeds to examine what happens when falsehoods are detected. Are people able to ignore invalid claims? Can consumers discount a dishonest source? This is followed by a discussion of how people's experience with invalid messages influences their future coping with invalidity. For example, how is readers' encoding of newspaper reports modified after they find out that a particular reporter is not trustworthy? How do jurors react to new witnesses after they have been informed that another witness lied to them? We present evidence showing that individuals prepare for invalid messages in one of two opposite ways. Sometimes they increase the degree of elaborateness of message processing. On other times, however, people prepare for invalid messages by using simplified processing, relying to a greater extent on heuristic cues. The chapter ends by viewing these conflicting strategies within a more general set of models of social psychological phenomena.

## Uncovering deception in interpersonal interactions

After thousands of years of interpersonal perception human beings should have evolved into highly accurate receivers. Yet many dozens of studies of interpersonal perception suggest that accuracy is modest at best, attesting to the complexity of the task people face when trying to perceive others (Funder, 1995). This is especially true when the others try to mask their thoughts and feelings. As people's interpersonal perception skills have evolved, so too have their skills in masking their inner states, leading to a perpetual struggle between the former and the latter. In this battle, accuracy succumbs more often than not. There is ample evidence to show that people's competency in unmasking deception is poor (DePaulo & Friedman, 1998).

Ekman and O'Sullivan (1991) examine the success of individuals whose profession involves detection of lies. They show that members of the secret service can uncover deception on a level which is significantly better than chance, although even these professionals are far from perfect. Notwithstanding, Ekman and Sullivan report that the performance of members of the other groups of professionals (federal poligraphers, robbery investigators, judges, and psychiatrists) was not significantly different from chance. In other words, on average even people whose task involves the need to identify deception could not reliably separate truthtellers from liars. Moreover, it seems that people are not aware of their poor performance, as indicated by the null relationship between confidence in detection accuracy and actual accuracy (DePaulo, Charlton, Cooper, Lindsay & Muhlenbruck, 1997).

In this context, it is particularly interesting to explore the moderating role of the amount of information the perceiver has about the speaker. Consider the influence of perceiver–speaker acquaintance on the success of detecting deception. At first glance, the prediction seems straightforward. Since close friends are familiar with each other (Funder, Kolar, & Blackman, 1995) and tend to self-disclose, they should be more accurate than strangers in unmasking deception. Moreover, as Miller, Mongeau, and Sleight (1986) note, in order to detect deception, perceivers must be sensitive to slight departures of verbal and nonverbal expressions from the ordinary, that is, deviations from the baseline level present during communication of truth (Feeley & deTurch, 1995). Fiedler and Walka (1993) refer to this phenomenon as nonverbal conspicuousness. Because of their familiarity with the sender of the communication, friends have a target-specific baseline with which the potentially deceptive behavior might be compared. In contrast, by definition, strangers lack baseline levels for the specific communicator. As a result, they must compare verbal or nonverbal expressions to a global baseline. Accordingly, friends should have an advantage over strangers—that is, they should be more skillful in uncovering configurations of cues associated with deceit (cf., Mann, Vrij, & Bull, 2002). Nevertheless, research exploring the effect of acquaintance on the success of detection of deception has failed to show that friends are more successful than strangers in unmasking deception (Anderson, DePaulo, Ansfield, Tickle, & Green, 1999; McCornack & Parks, 1986).

The null effect associated with acquaintance is consistent with the suggestion that face-to-face contact with the potentially deceptive target may actually interfere with the success of uncovering deception. Ruback and Hopper (1986) examined the recommendations of parole officers. Each officer made two predictions about the likelihood that an inmate would complete his or her parole successfully, the first after reading the inmate's file, and the second after interviewing him or her. The study explored whether these predictions were accurate by comparing them to the actual success of the parole. It was found that the pre-interview predictions distinguished between inmates whose parole was revoked and those whose parole was completed successfully. In contrast, the post-interview predictions failed to distinguish between the two groups, suggesting that the parole officers became less accurate after the interview. It is interesting to note that the post-interview prediction was highly related to the parole officer's perception of the inmate's honesty during the interview. I speculate that the face-to-face interview induced a clinical or experiential mode of thinking (Einhorn, 1986; Epstein & Pacini, 1999), which may have limited the officers' ability to focus on those diagnostic cues that were useful for uncovering deception. This speculation is discussed further at the end of the chapter.

It should be noted that the impairment associated with the face-to-face interview occurred even though perceivers could have used the interview effectively to extract cues that would allow some separation of truthtellers from falsifiers. For example, Fiedler and Walka (1993) and Vrij, Edward, and Bull (2001) suggest that deceptive communication tends to be factual whereas communication of truth is associated with more perception-like qualities. Other valid cues come from the work of Mann et al. (2002) who examined police interviews. They suggest that when interviewees attempt to deceive they blink less frequently and make longer pauses than when they make truthful statements. However, it appears that interviewers rarely use such stylistic or behavioral cues without special coaching. Consequently, a face-to-face interview might draw the interviewer's attention from potentially diagnostic cues to non-diagnostic cues, thereby impairing detection of deception.

The inconspicuousness of cues for deception has two important consequences. First, perceivers often fail in their attempts to uncover deception. Second, because people are often aware of the difficulty involved in unmasking deception, whenever they have to cope with potentially invalid information they tend to search for configurations of cues that might help them separate truth from falsehood and distinguish cheaters from honest persons. As we shall see in the next section, when there are many messages, some valid and some not, attempts to prepare for handling invalid messages can lead to an increase in the density of the associative network that links the valid and invalid messages. This can in turn have a profound effect on people's success in coping with invalid messages, *even* when such messages have been identified.

## Discounting invalid messages

Because using false information from others is costly, pervasive, and inherent to social life, receivers should have developed skills that allow them to discount invalid information successfully. However, as past research suggests, the success of discounting such information is limited (see more detailed reviews in Golding & MacLeod, 1998). In order to understand this outcome it is useful to consider such discounting from two vantage points: making the judgment (after one knows which messages are valid and which are not) and time of encoding (before one learns which messages are invalid). Broadly speaking, two main findings have been reported. From the perspective of judgment, discounting seems to be a correction process, with those factors that increase the magnitude of correction tending to increase the magnitude of discounting. We shall focus on one important factor, the motivation to discount. Taking the vantage point of encoding, research suggests that success in discounting varies as a function of the density of the associative links between the invalid (to-be-ignored) and valid (to-be-used) messages. However, as we shall see below, the impact of density is not as free from ambiguity as was initially assumed.

### *Discounting as a correction process*

By definition, in order to succeed in discounting, receivers must base their judgments on the valid information only. However, because the valid information may contain meanings and associations that were added to it by the invalid information, it is not sufficient to attempt to consider the valid information "by itself" while making the judgment. Ideally, receivers could have removed the contamination by thinking only about the valid messages and encoding them again as if the invalid messages had not been presented. However, evidence suggests that re-encoding is unlikely (Schul & Burnstein, 1985; Wyer, Srull, Gordon, & Hartwick, 1982). To combat the contaminating influence produced by the to-be-ignored information, receivers could correct their initial judgment so as to remove its impact (Wilson & Brekke, 1994).

This analysis likens discounting to correction, thus predicting that, other things being equal (e.g., awareness of the bias, cognitive resources, see Martin, Seta, & Crelia, 1990; Schwarz & Bless, 1992; Strack & Hannover, 1996), as the motivation for discounting increases, discounting ought to be more successful. Generally, this seems to be the case. Evidence from two very different paradigms on this issue is discussed below.

Consider the reasons given to people for ignoring testimony in a study simulating jury decision making. A testimony could be ruled inadmissible because the witness could not have seen the events he or she describes (e.g., Elliott, Farrington, & Manheimer, 1988; Hatvany & Strack, 1980; Loftus, 1974; Schul & Manzury, 1990; Weinberg & Baron, 1982), or because the testimony reflects a vested interest of the witness (e.g., Kassin & Wrightsman, 1981). In these cases there seems to be a sound reason to believe that the evidence is completely invalid. Similar types of reasons can be found in the marketing domain. An advertisement could be found misleading because it makes false claims (see Wilkie, McNeill, & Mazis, 1984, for several real examples). Requests to ignore a message that provides substantive reasons to cast doubt on the validity of the message are termed *substantive requests*.

A testimony could also be ruled inadmissible because it violates the justice procedure. For example, after hearing a testimony about a recorded conversation, jurors may find that the conversation was recorded illegally, and therefore, is inadmissible and must be ignored (Carretta & Moreland, 1983; Kassin & Sommers, 1997; Lenehan & O'Neill, 1981). Under certain conditions, the jury might also be instructed to ignore prior convictions as evidence that the defendant has a bad character, or to disregard hearsay information (Pickel, 1995). In such cases the to-be-ignored testimony may or may not be true. However, regardless of its truth value, receivers are asked to ignore the testimony because its use violates the rules of the game—the rules of evidence. Such requests are termed *procedural requests*. Clearly, substantive requests are stronger than procedural requests because they are based on both the motivation to be accurate and the motivation to comply with the rules of the game.

Studies that compare the two types of requests show that respondents discount invalid information more successfully when the request is substantive than when it is procedural (Golding et al., 1990; Golding & Hauselt, 1994; Kassin & Sommers, 1997; Schul & Goren, 1997; Schul & Mayo, 1999). When the requests stress the unreliability of the testimony, discounting often succeeds (Elliott et al., 1988; Hatvany & Strack, 1980; Schul & Manzury, 1990; Weinberg & Baron, 1982). Failure in discounting is more prevalent when the request to ignore a testimony is procedural (Tanford & Penrod, 1984; Pickel, 1995). Nevertheless, it should be noted that even procedural requests do lead to some sort of adjustment, so that the to-be-discounted evidence does not make its full impact.

Interestingly, the motivation to discount invalid information properly might also be influenced by manipulations that affect the respondent's perception that the invalid message has unduly contaminated his or her judgment. Based on the research on correction, it is predicted that an invalid message should be discounted more strongly when it is perceived as having a high impact on one's judgments than when it is viewed as having only little such impact. Analogous predictions have been made with respect to the correction of various other biases, such as the effect of context (Martin, 1986; Petty & Wegener, 1993), the impact of situational pressures (Gilbert & Osborne, 1989), the effect of attractiveness of the source (Petty, Wegener, & Fabrigar, 1997), and the effect of priming (Lombardi, Higgins, & Bargh,

1987; Martin et al., 1990; Strack, Schwarz, Bless, Kubler, & Wänke, 1993; see review in Strack & Hannover, 1996). In the context of discounting, this prediction is particularly interesting because it suggests that, other things being equal, it should be easier to discount a highly persuasive claim (i.e., one that has a strong impact on judgments) than a mildly persuasive one, when each is found to be invalid at a later point in time. That is to say, even though the more persuasive claim is more likely to sway receivers and affect their judgment, receivers are more likely to be aware of its influence and therefore more likely to correct for its contamination. As a result, following a discounting request, a weak claim may have more residual impact on judgments than a strong claim.

To examine this prediction, Schul and Goren (1997) manipulated the persuasive impact of invalid messages. The cover story involved a trial about a car accident. Participants were given several testimonies about the case, one of which was provided by a young witness. After being exposed to that testimony, respondents in the discounting conditions were informed that they should ignore it when making their judgment. The persuasive potential of the critical testimony was manipulated in three different ways: the confidence of the witness (assuming that high confidence makes a more persuasive testimony, see Schul & Goren, 1997 for detailed discussion of the rationale of the manipulatons), the style of the language used by the witness (assuming that a matter-of-fact description of the accident is more persuasive than a testimony including linguistic phrases that could remind receivers of the witness's age), and the normality of the events described in the critical testimony (assuming that a testimony about a routine action would be less persuasive, and would have less impact than a testimony about an abnormal action).

The general prediction of Schul and Goren (1997) was that participants who *used* the critical testimony would find the defendant guiltier when the testimony was strong than when it was weak. Yet, because the perception of strength provides a cue for the extent of contamination the testimony can have, correction should be more pronounced in the case of a strong testimony. As a result, even though the strong testimony should be more persuasive, it should also lead to a more successful discounting performance. This was indeed the case.

This phenomenon might explain the difference in people's success in discounting positive and negative testimonies that were found to be invalid. Hatvany and Strack (1980), Thompson, Fong, and Rosenhan (1981), and Wyer and Budesheim (1987) observed that judges ignore negative messages successfully but fail to ignore positive messages. Because receivers may presume negative messages have a greater potential to influence them, they make greater correction efforts when discounting a negative message than when discounting a positive one. Conceptually similar explanations may account for the relative success with which individuals ignore forced confessions when they are elicited by punishment, but the reluctance to ignore such confessions when they are elicited by a promise of reward (Kassin & Wrightsman, 1981).

Promises of reward may thus be considered a weaker incentive to confess than threats of punishment. It follows that confessions obtained by promises are more likely to be true, and therefore they evoke less motivation to correct for their impact on judgment than do confessions obtained by threats.

### The moderating role of integrative encoding

At first glance, the role of integrative encoding is straightforward. Discounting appears to be more successful if, at the time of encoding, receivers are prevented from elaborating on and integrating the valid and invalid messages than when they are not prevented from doing so (Fleming & Arrowood, 1979; Schul & Burnstein, 1985). Conversely, discounting is less successful when receivers are induced to encode the two kinds of messages integratively (e.g., Anderson, Lepper, & Ross, 1980; Schul & Manzury, 1990; Schul & Mazursky, 1990). Additional support for the notion that integrative encoding tends to hinder successful discounting has been obtained by Wyer and Budesheim (1987). These authors show that discounting is facilitated when the to-be-used and to-be-ignored messages refer to unrelated issues, and it is impaired when they refer to the same issue. In the latter case it is likely that receivers integrate the information even without being instructed to do so explicitly.

However, we have shown that the role of integrative encoding is more complex than past research has suggested (Schul & Mayo, 1999). In this study we explored what happens when a single source provides two messages, only one of which is valid. It is suggested that in such a case integrative encoding is not necessarily associated with greater failure in discounting. Rather, integrative encoding can either facilitate or impair discounting, depending on the relationship between the valid and the invalid messages. This research is described here in some detail because it sheds light on the cognitive operations involved in coping with invalidity.

Schul and Mayo (1999) analyzed discounting from two opposite perspectives: using the valid (unchallenged) messages, and disregarding the invalid (challenged) messages. These perspectives are important because, as noted above, discounting requires receivers to engage in two simultaneous operations: to suppress or block the influence of the invalid messages, and, at the same time, to utilize the full persuasive potential of the valid messages. We suggested that correction techniques could be used to offset the contamination by the invalid information. However, as the discussion below suggests, when the different messages are associatively linked, that is, when they are integrated, attempts to perform one operation may interfere with the other. In particular, attempts at correction might lead to appropriate discounting, too much discounting (over-correction), or too little discounting (under-correction), even if the impact of the contamination, that is, that of the invalid message by itself, is accurately gauged.

Consider first how using a valid message could impair the suppression of the impact of the invalid message. By definition, in order to ignore an invalid message, one needs to block all its implications. When a valid message is associatively linked with the invalid message, thinking about the former may interfere with one's ability to block the latter. This occurs because the contemplation of the valid message leads to activation and utilization of inferences that are associated with the invalid message since the two have been integrated. As an illustration, imagine that Jim is applying for the position of copywriter at an advertising agency. The members of the selection committee are considering two reference letters about Jim. One indicates that he is lazy, while the other states that he is overly competitive. Assume that the letters are integrated, that is, that they are interpreted jointly so that their meanings become interdependent. In this example "lazy" and "overly competitive" may be associated with an image of a person who will do anything to climb the professional ladder, yet, because he is lazy, will resort to unethical means. Imagine that at a later time the committee members find out that the message about the applicant's competitiveness is unreliable and should therefore be ignored. At this point they have to use the valid message about his laziness uncontaminated by the implications of the invalid message about his competitiveness. However, since the two messages have been integrated, the unfavorable implications of competitiveness (the invalid information) are added to the implications of laziness (the valid information). This should lead to a *more unfavorable* evaluation of the candidate compared with a condition in which only the message about laziness was provided.

Consider now the other perspective, namely the attempt to suppress the impact of the invalid information. Our analysis suggests that such suppression may lead receivers to *underuse* the valid recommendation. Specifically, since the valid and invalid recommendations are highly associated, when one suppresses the invalid information one tends to suppress the valid information as well. In the example given above, blocking the impact of "overly competitive" (the invalid message) can result in blocking some of the implications of "lazy" (the valid message). When the valid message is unfavorable, blocking its implications leads to a *more favorable* evaluation of the candidate. This might be interpreted as over-correction.

This analysis suggests that manipulations that increase the density of integrative encoding, that is, facilitate the formation of associative links between the different messages, can either facilitate discounting (to a point of over-correction) or interfere with it. In Schul and Mayo (1999) the density of associative network between the valid and invalid messages was manipulated by attributing them either to a single source or to two different sources. When the messages come from the same source they are more likely to be cognitively integrated (McConnell, Sherman, & Hamilton,1997; Wyer, Bodenhausen, & Srull, 1984). Comparing judgments from the single source condition with those from the different-sources condition can tell whether the impact of using the valid message on blocking the invalid message is greater than, equal to, or less than the impact of suppressing the invalid message on using the valid information.

Schul and Mayo (1999, Exp. 2) examined a case in which the valid and the invalid messages indicated different negative qualities. When these messages were attributed to different sources, respondents discounted the invalid message appropriately. However, when messages were attributed to a single source, respondents under-used the valid message. In other words, their judgments were overly positive, as compared to judgments of individuals who received only valid information.

What are the implications of these lines of research? Consider, for example, a situation in which two individuals, Tom and Tina, are engaged in a conversation. Tom wants to present himself in a favorable way, as he wants to impress Tina. So he exaggerates a little and lies a little (see Feldman et al., 2002). Yet, not everything that Tom says is false. In fact, the majority of his statements are accurate. Imagine that at a later point in time Tina finds out that a particular statement made by Tom was false. Can she discount this particular statement properly? The findings presented above offer a theoretically challenging yet empirically complex view about her success. In contrast to the early research that appeared to show that Tina would be unable to discount the false statement, recent research points to conditions that might help or impede successful discounting. That is, there is a shift in the theoretical emphasis from questions about existence ("Is there an interesting phenomenon?") to questions about incidence ("When does the phenomenon occur?") and, perhaps more interestingly, about understanding ("What are the mechanisms that give rise to it?"). Greater insight into these mechanisms may allow us to devise ways that facilitate coping with invalid messages. The next section is a first step in this direction, as it discusses how past experience of coping with invalidity influences the success of future coping with invalidity.

## Preparing to cope with invalid messages

The early research on belief perseverance appears to show that people fail to ignore invalid information even when they know it is invalid. As a result, beliefs persist even after their original evidential bases have been completely falsified. Ross, Lepper, and Hubbard (1975), for example, gave students false feedback indicating that they had failed (or succeeded) on an experimental task. Later, these respondents were thoroughly debriefed about the fictitious nature of the feedback. Still, even though they had learned that the feedback was invalid, the respondents persisted in their erroneous beliefs about themselves (see also Fleming & Arrowood, 1979; Ross, Lepper, Strack, & Steinmetz, 1977). This finding has been generalized to situations that do not involve judgments about the self or, for that matter, about any specific individual (Anderson et al., 1980; Anderson, New, & Speer, 1985; Schul & Burnstein, 1985; Wyer & Budesheim, 1987).

A different picture emerges, however, from the research exploring discounting in situations known to involve deception, and in particular, from research about judgments of mock jurors. It is often found that judgments of guilt or verdicts of respondents who are instructed to disregard invalid target testimony are not significantly different from judgments of control respondents who have not received the target testimony at all (Elliott et al., 1988; Hatvany & Strack, 1980; Weinberg & Baron, 1982; but see Loftus, 1974, for failures to discount), suggesting that people can ignore invalid evidence in making judgments.

As hinted above, one potential difference between belief perseverance and the court paradigms has to do with the a priori expectations that individuals have regarding the validity of the information. In the typical belief perseverance study respondents receive information that pertains to a rather unfamiliar domain (e.g., their ability to detect suicide notes) from a highly credible source (i.e., the experimenter). Consequently, they have very little reason to suspect that the information might be inaccurate or invalid. Jurors, in contrast, are well aware that some witnesses may be lying and that testimonies are sometimes invalid. This is highlighted by the procedure of witness cross-examination. Thus, the court setting generally embodies an implicit warning as well as reminders about the potential for deception, while the belief perseverance situation generally does not. The relative success of discounting in a court situation may reflect this difference.

Several lines of research have tested this suggestion. Schul and Manzury (1990) examined the success of discounting in simulated court settings. In line with the findings of other research about discounting in a court setting, Schul and Manzury found that respondents discounted the to-be-ignored testimony successfully when making judgments about the defendant's guilt. Importantly, however, respondents made two additional types of judgments, one about the defendant's aggressiveness and another about the defendant's likability. Unlike its impact on the judgments of guilt, the to-be-ignored testimony did influence the judgments of aggressiveness and likability. We believe that this phenomenon occurred because court settings activate a schema that leads people to deliberately correct for potential biases regarding the relevant guilt judgments. Since other judgments are less central within the court schema, they are not actively monitored and consequently they are more susceptible to the effects of a to-be-ignored testimony (cf., Strack et al., 1993).

Schul and Manzury's (1990) experiment highlights one general mechanism that allows receivers to fare better when coping with invalid messages. When individuals are put on a non-specific alert to the potential bias of invalid information, they are more successful in discounting such information once they discover the specific falsehood. The warning, or the increase in alertness, may be triggered by the properties of one of the messages (e.g., Schul, 1993; Schul & Goren, 1997) and/or by the individuals' experience in similar situations (Schul & Manzury, 1990).

A second general mechanism for coping with invalidity operates at the encoding stage. I have already discussed the hindrance for successful discounting that integrative encoding creates, especially in cases in which the invalid and valid messages have different implications. Let us return to the interaction between Tom and Tina. Assume that Tina has read Schul and Mayo's (1999) paper before revising her impression of Tom and is thus aware of the difficulties that integrative encoding can induce. In order to prepare for undoing the impact of the invalid information, she can employ one of the following two strategies. On the one hand, Tina may reduce processing complexity so that the invalid messages (but also the valid ones) receive only minimal attention and elaboration, and hence are represented in a rather unintegrated fashion. Accordingly, she may try to encode the information about Tom in a discrete fashion, attempting to remember what Tom said without forming an overall impression (Bless, Hamilton & Mackie, 1992; Hartwick, 1979; Schul & Burnstein, 1985). According to this line of reasoning, a reduction in elaborative processing would allow receivers to minimize or even undo the impact of bad information completely once they find out that the information is indeed bad. However, this strategy is very difficult to implement, as it is virtually impossible to inhibit the tendency to categorize the interacting partner evaluatively.

Alternatively, Tina can prepare to cope with invalid information by increasing rather than decreasing the complexity of processing. Kruglanski's lay epistemic theory suggests that when people suspect that a belief is invalid, they delay the "freezing" of this belief and continue to look for other alternatives (Kruglanski, 1989; Kruglanski & Freund, 1983). As the cost of a mistake increases, people seek more relevant information and examine it more carefully (Kruglanski & Mayseless, 1987; Kruglanski, Peri & Zakai, 1991). Our own research (Schul, 1993; Schul, Burnstein, & Bardi, 1996) supports the hypothesis that preparatory activity leads to additional processing of the message information. Specifically, when respondents had to read several messages about the same person, those who were made suspicious about the validity of one of the messages needed more time to read the messages and integrate them than those who were not made suspicious. This phenomenon occurred even though the importance of accurate judgment was equally stressed to suspicious as well as unsuspicious respondents, so that they did not differ with respect to the cost of mistakes.

At first glance, increasing the complexity of encoding may seem counterproductive for coping with invalidity and for inducing successful discounting. However, note that the increase in the complexity of encoding is not done around a single focus. Rather than thinking about Tom along a single dimension, Tina may attempt to think about Tom in multiple ways, as if his statements are true and, simultaneously, as if what he says is false. Schul et al., (1996), as well as Fein and coworkers (Fein, Hilton, & Miller, 1990; Fein, McCloskey, & Tomlinson, 1997; Hilton, Fein, & Miller, 1993) suggest that when individuals interpret information in several different ways, thus creating multiple counter-scenarios, they are better able to discount invalid information. Fein's research shows, for example, that people who discover a possible hidden motivation that may account for the protagonist's behavior engage in more complex encoding than those who do not suspect a hidden motive. Specifically, suspicious respondents behave as if they are examining the protagonist's behavior in two scenarios: one consistent with the explicit motive given in the story and the other consistent with the hidden motive.

In the Tom and Tina example it seems that Tina may find it difficult to prepare to process invalid information by decreasing the complexity with which she processes the information about Tom. Naturally, this raises a question about the conditions in which such strategy can be useful. Below we consider some of the factors that can influence the amount and nature of the processing of message information.

The typical paradigm for studying the processing of invalid messages attempts to make receivers focus on the message information. Receivers usually get information about a single protagonist, and they are either forewarned that some of the information relevant to the protagonist may be invalid, or they are led to discover the potential for invalidity while processing the information. In either case, they do not have any clear diagnostic information that allows them to separate the true messages from the false ones. The discussion of deception detection presented above points out several characteristics of this situation that may lead to an increase in processing complexity.

First, few processing demands are posed on one's capacity by other tasks. Thus, individuals can devote all their mental resources to attempting to find out those cues that may allow them to detect deception. It is speculated that as demands from concurrent tasks increase, individuals shift their processing away from tasks that involve uncertainty. This strategy is particularly likely when the other tasks are not seen as primary and when mistakes are not costly.

Second, the cues for invalidity in the typical suspicion paradigm are either nonexistent or only probabilistic (e.g., the protagonist may have ulterior motives for performing an action, but he or she may also perform it because of intrinsic motivation). Consequently, receivers tend to encode the message information in counter-scenarios. However, as cues become more diagnostic of invalidity, receivers' tendency to elaborate on the invalid information may decrease.

Third, it is functional to elaborate on information if one anticipates using it later. Such a strategy, however, becomes less useful as the amount of potentially invalid information increases. For example, participants in Schul et al.'s (1996) experiments were informed that just one of the eight messages about each protagonist might be invalid, hence most of the messages were valid. Imagine, however, that the number of potentially invalid messages increases to the point that the majority of messages are invalid. My conjecture is that extensive elaboration and reinterpretation within multiple counter-scenarios are counterproductive when the number of potentially invalid messages is high.

It is interesting to note that Wegner's (1994) model of mental control makes similar predictions about the impact of cognitive load on discounting when one knows which message is false. According to Wegner, it is easy to monitor and suppress the impact of an invalid message since upon detecting the invalid message the perceiver can minimize its influence by counter-arguing. Importantly, however, the actual consequences of counterargumentation depend on the cognitive load: under high load condition, the more perceivers attempt to avoid being misled by the invalid message, the less likely it is that they will be able to discount it. Note, however, that this cannot happen when perceivers do not know whether a message is valid or invalid. In such a case, perceivers cannot monitor whether they are being misled upon encoding a message. The monitoring process, therefore, cannot moderate the effect of cognitive load on discounting. Nevertheless, cognitive load is likely to reduce the extent of elaborative encoding and consequently decrease the likelihood that the person will be capable of generating counter-scenarios. If so, this should result in a weakening of the resistance to invalid information that is usually afforded by processing under suspicion.

Finally, the increase or decrease in the complexity of processing may reflect the receiver's response to the realization that his or her habitual mode of processing leads him/her astray. That is, receivers' recent experience with relevant episodes involving coping with invalidity may influence how they process new messages. To study this influence, Mazursky and Schul (2000) exposed respondents to information about six attributes of cars (Exp. 1) or computers (Exp. 2). Shortly afterwards, the respondents found out that the message about one of the attributes was invalid and should be ignored. They then made a series of judgments about the quality of the products. At a later point in the experiment, respondents were given information about different cars (or computers). This information was attributed either to the same source of information as in the first phase or to a new, highly credible source. During this phase no attribute was discounted and respondents were supposed to use all attributes in evaluating the new products. Thus, following the first phase of the study, half of the respondents experienced coping with false information and half of the respondents experienced using valid information. The question of interest is whether people's experience in the first part of the experiment influences how they process information in the second part of the experiment. In particular, we explored whether respondents increased or decreased the complexity of their processing in the second phase.

The study used three different markers to indicate complexity of processing. First, complex processors should be more sensitive than simplified processors to the attribute information. Because the cars were constructed to have different attributes and consequently different overall degree of desirability, it was expected that respondents using a complex processing strategy would distinguish between the cars more clearly than those using a simplified processing strategy. A second indicator of complexity of processing is judgment latency. Complex processing is more laborious than simplified processing, and should therefore take more time. Third, participants may simplify processing by using a heuristic cue for evaluating the cars (Chen & Chaiken,

1999; Petty & Wegener, 1999). Specifically, participants were exposed to product information attributed to one of two sources, either the same source that was used in the first phase, or a source considered by the respondent population to be a highly credible person. Therefore, when participants engage in *simplified* processing and rely on a given source in evaluating products, the difference between the two sources should be pronounced. Under these conditions, evaluations based on information conveyed by a superior (highly credible) source ought to be more favorable than evaluations based on information conveyed by the source from the first phase. Conversely, when processing is *complex*, difference as a function of the two sources in evaluations of the cars should be attenuated, because under complex processing the evaluations are based mainly on the qualities of the cars.

Mazursky and Schul (2000) explored which of the following three tendencies characterizes our respondents' judgments after they encountered an untrustworthy source of information: (1) increased complexity of processing for everyone; (2) decreased complexity of processing for everyone; (3) decreased complexity for those who are complex processors in the product domain and increased complexity for those who use habitually simplified processing in the product domain. The latter tendency necessitate a priori classification of the respondents as complex or simplified processors. In Experiment 1 individuals were classified as habitually simplified versus complex processors, according to their status of car ownership. We predicted (and found) that car owners will have more complex processing strategies regarding cars than non-owners. In Experiment 2 whether a person used habitually simplified versus complex processing strategies was determined according to participants' involvement with the product. It was predicted that those who were highly involved with computers would show more complex processing regarding computers than those who were not involved.

Figures 10.1, 10.2 and 10.3 present the results of Experiment 1. It is important to compare phase2 judgments of those who have not undergone an experience of invalidation in the first phase (the no invalidation baseline condition) with those who experienced invalidation in the first phase. As the figures show, the experience of invalidation had different consequences for car owners and non-owners. Relative to the baseline condition, owners who had experienced invalidation in the first phase of the experiment shifted to more simplified processing, as indicated by a marked decrease in their differentiation among the cars, a decrease in the time they took to produce the judgments, and an increase in their reliance on the trustworthiness of the source of information. Non-owners, on the other hand, shifted in the opposite direction. Relative to the baseline respondents (who did not experience invalidation during the first phase of the experiment), non-owners who experienced invalidation in the first phase employed more a complex processing strategy in the second phase. This is indicated by an increase in their differentiation among cars, an increase in the time needed to make the judgments, and a decrease in their reliance on the source of information. A second

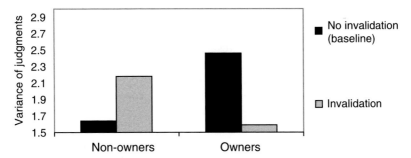

*Figure 10.1* Differentiation among phase2 cars as indicated by variance of quality-of-car judgments (based on Mazursky and Schul, 2000, Exp. 1).

*Note*: Simplified processing is indicated by small differentiation among cars with different attributes whereas complex processing is indicated by large differentiation.

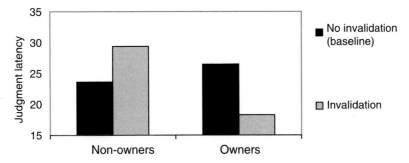

*Figure 10.2* Latency of judgments concerning phase2 cars (based on Mazursky & Schul, 2000, Exp. 1).

*Note*: Simplified processing is indicated by fast judgments whereas complex processing is indicated by slow judgments.

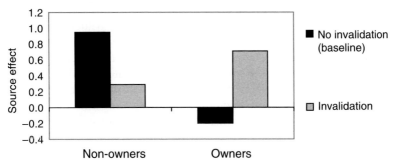

*Figure 10.3* Source effects (high credibility vs. low credibility) in judgments concerning phase2 cars (based on Mazursky & Schul, 2000, Exp. 1).

*Note*: Simplified processing is indicated by judgments which are heavily influenced by credibility of phase2 source whereas complex processing is indicated by judgments that are not influenced by credibility.

experiment replicated this complex pattern of results, using a different product class (computers) and a different construct to define habitually complex and habitually simplified processors.

Mazursky and Schul's (2000) results suggest that individuals learn from their invalidation experience and systematically change their habitual mode of processing. Those who tend to be complex processors in the particular domain of judgment shift to a more simplified processing, while those who tend to process information in a simplified way, shift to more complex processing. I believe that these shifts occur through the following mechanisms.

To begin with, having encountered an untrustworthy source of information highlights weaknesses in the process of attitude formation or in the judgment procedure. For people who tend to focus on message information in making judgments about the product (complex processors), the experience highlights the importance of the source's trustworthiness, thus increasing the impact of information about the source. On the other hand, for those who habitually use the source as a primary cue for evaluating products (simplified processors), the experience highlights the problems associated with relying on a simple heuristic cue. Therefore, these individuals shift to a greater reliance on message itself.

The choice of processing strategy may also reflect the correspondence between the amount of cognitive resources required by the task and the processing strategy that receivers employ for the task. Receivers who use complex processing (and therefore have little processing capacity to spare) tend to resort to simpler processing strategies following message invalidation. In contrast, receivers who use simple processing when not exposed to message invalidation (and therefore have a great deal of processing capacity to spare) can use a more complex strategy following message invalidation that may increase their chances of detecting false messages.

Finally, the change in people's processing strategy may reflect their motivations. Habitually complex processors (in the particular domain of judgments) may start out with high motivation, coupled with high confidence in their ability to form judgments successfully. Finding out that a message was invalid can therefore produce frustration, resulting in a shift to a more simplified processing strategy. In contrast, those who are less invested in the domain of judgments (non-owners, or people less interested in the products used in the study) have lower motivation to perform accurately. They are more likely to use the least number of cues allowing them to satisfy the requirements of the task. Finding out that a message was invalid may make the task more challenging. This may result in an increase in processing complexity. Clearly, these alternative mechanisms are not mutually exclusive.

It should be noted that each of the two processing strategies by itself might be costly. Consider, for example, what might happen to consumers who are exposed to deceptive marketing practices, such as being shown false information about products or services, being given misleading or incomplete information, or having been subjected to deceptive pricing policies (see examples in Tellis, 1998). Simplifiers may decide to reduce processing effort, to limit and control the potential bias of the message information. Such a strategy, however, is likely to lead them to ignore useful product information, impairing the optimality of their purchasing decisions. Others may attempt to cope with practices of deceptive marketing by increasing their processing complexity. This, however, may spill over to other social exchanges, which may not involve deception. At the extreme, such individuals might mistrust any transaction or information exchange, thus limiting their ability to enjoy many (or most) social interactions which are based on trust. I believe, therefore, that only a well-balanced mixture of the two coping strategies allows one proper functioning in reality that contains many truthful communications and a few deceptive ones.

## Summary and speculation

We have discussed evidence consistent with the following claims about individuals' success in detecting and handling invalid messages:

1 People are relatively poor detectors of deception.
2 Increased familiarity with the source of information does not improve success in detecting deception and may actually diminish it.
3 Once a message is found invalid, and receivers are asked to ignore it, the nature of the request matters, with requests based on substantive grounds resulting in more successful discounting than requests based on procedural considerations.
4 Messages that elicit a perception of high contamination are discounted to a greater extent than those evoking a perception of low contamination.
5 Integrative encoding can lead to judgments that appear as either under-correction, appropriate, or over-correction, depending on the relationship between the to-be-ignored and the to-be-used messages.
6 Individuals can prepare for coping with invalid messages by increasing the degree of elaborateness of message processing, thus encoding the messages with the use of different counter-scenarios.
7 People also prepare for invalid messages by using simplified processing, relying to a greater extent on heuristic cues.

The central thread in the story we have told is the oscillation between the two poles of processing complexity. People can cope with invalid messages by increasing or decreasing processing complexity. The distinction between complex and simplified processing is not new. It appears in several different models of social psychological phenomena, describing person perception (Brewer & Harasty Feinstein, 1999; Fiske, Lin, & Neuberg, 1999), stereotyping (Bodenhausen, Macrae, & Sherman, 1999), as well as attitude formation and change (Chen & Chaiken, 1999; Petty & Wegener, 1999). At an even more general level, the two poles could be linked to the recent suggestion that there are two distinct modes of information processing: experiential and rational (Epstein, 1994; Lieberman, 2000; Nisbett, Peng, Choi, & Norenzayan, 2001; Sloman, 1996; Smith & DeCoster, 2000).

There are many interesting differences between the experiential and the rational systems (Epstein & Pacini, 1999; Smith & DeCoster, 2000). I would like to stress one characteristic that is particularly important in the context of social judgments. The experiential system tends to operate according to well-rehearsed patterns. The rational system, in contrast, allows individuals to deal with abstractions and to make a cogitated response rather than an automatic one.

Schul and Mayo (2003) speculate that in dealing with uncertainty one tends to use the experiential mode of thinking (Epstein & Pacini, 1999). This is particularly likely when individuals attribute uncertainty to deception (rather than to chance). I believe that, paradoxically, the greater likelihood of using the experiential mode of thinking in detecting deception stems from the receivers' attempts to understand how the sender of information operates, as well as from their attempts to use the suspect message in the specific context. Put differently, in such cases people try not only to deal with immediate uncertainty, but also to gain deeper insight into the deception strategies of the sender. However, although such attempts allow people to be responsive to minute details and sensitive to the configuration of informational cues, they prevent them from thinking about events in an abstract way. Decision makers are often not cognizant of the possibility that minute details can reflect error variance and that using them might lead them astray (Einhorn, 1986).

Only when one's trust in the experiential system is shaken will one be willing to give up this habitual mode of processing for a less involving, and perhaps less committing, option. It seems that such a choice is possible when the cost of error is low. Thus, it is speculated that, perhaps paradoxically, when people attribute uncertainty to deception by others and when mistakes are very costly, they are likely to persist in using the experiential system, resisting the pressure to switch to rational processing. When there are no diagnostic cues for detecting invalid messages, such a strategy may not be very harmful. However, when there are diagnostic cues that allow the detection of invalid messages with probabilities above chance, using the experiential system is likely to diminish successful coping with invalid messages.

## Acknowledgments

Preparation of this chapter was supported by grants from the United States–Israel Binational Science Foundation (BSF) and by the Israel Foundation Trustees. I would like to thank Ruth Mayo and David Mazursky for commenting on an earlier version of this chapter.

# References

Anderson, C. A., Lepper, M. R., & Ross, L. (1980). Perseverance of social theories: The role of explanation in the persistence of discredited information. *Journal of Personality and Social Psychology*, *39*, 1037–1049.

Anderson, C. A., New, B. L., & Speer, J. P. (1985). Argument availability as a mediator of social theory perseverance. *Social Cognition*, *3*, 235–249.

Anderson, D. E., DePaulo, B. M., Ansfield, M. E., Tickle, J. J., & Green, E. (1999). Beliefs about cues to deception: Mindless stereotypes or untapped wisdom. *Journal of Nonverbal Behavior*, *23*, 66–89.

Bless, H., Hamilton, D. L., & Mackie, D. M. (1992). Mood effects on the organization of person information. *European Journal of Social Psychology*, *22*, 497–509.

Bodenhausen, G. V., Macrae, C. N., & Sherman, J. W. (1999). On the dialectics of discrimination: Dual processes in social stereotyping. In S. Chaiken & Y. Trope (Eds.), *Dual process theories in social psychology* (pp. 271–290). New York: Guilford Press.

Brewer, M. B., & Harasty Feinstein, A. S. (1999). Dual processes in the cognitive representation of persons and social categories. In S. Chaiken & Y. Trope (Eds.), *Dual process theories in social psychology* (pp. 255–270). New York: Guilford Press.

Carretta, T. S., & Moreland, R. L. (1983). The direct and indirect effects of inadmissible evidence. *Journal of Applied Social Psychology*, *13*, 291–309.

Chen, S., & Chaiken, S. (1999). The heuristic-systematic model in its broader context. In S. Chaiken & Y. Trope (Eds.), *Dual process theories in social psychology* (pp. 73–96). New York: Guilford Press.

Dawes, R. M. (1994). *House of cards*. New York: Free Press.

DePaulo, B. M., Charlton, K., Cooper, H., Lindsay, J. J., & Muhlenbruck, L. (1997). The accuracy–confidence correlation in the detection of deception. *Personality and Social Psychology Review*, *1*, 346–357.

DePaulo, B. M., & Friedman, H. S. (1998). Nonverbal communication. In D. T. Gilbert, S. T. Fiske, & G. Lindsey (Eds.), *The handbook of social psychology* (Vol. 2, pp. 3–40). Boston, MA: McGraw-Hill.

DePaulo, B. M., & Kashy, D. H. (1998). Everyday lies in close and casual relationships. *Journal of Personality and Social Psychology*, *74*, 63–79.

DePaulo, B. M., Kashy, D. A., Kirkendol, E. E., Wyer, M. M., & Epstein, J. A. (1996). Lying in everyday life. *Journal of Personality and Social Psychology*, *70*, 979–995.

Dyer, R. F., & Kuehl, P. G. (1978). A longitudinal study of corrective advertising. *Journal of Marketing Research*, *15*, 39–48.

Einhorn, H. J. (1986). Accepting error to make less error. *Journal of Personality Assessment*, *50*, 387–395.

Ekman, P., & O'Sullivan, M. (1991). Who can catch a liar? *American Psychologist*, *46*, 913–920.

Elliott, R., Farrington, B., & Manheimer, H. (1988). Eyewitnesses credible and discredible. *Journal of Applied Social Psychology*, *18*, 1411–1422.

Epstein, S. (1994) Integration of the cognitive and the psychodynamic unconscious. *American Psychologist*, *49*, 709–724.

Epstein, S., & Pacini, R. (1999). Some basic issues regarding dual-process theories from the perspective of cognitive-experiential-self theory. In S. Chaiken & Y. Trope (Eds.), *Dual process theories in social psychology* (pp. 462–482). New York: Guilford Press.

Feeley, T. H., & deTurch, M. A. (1995). Global cue usage in behavioral lie detection. *Communication Quarterly*, *43*, 420–430.

Feeley, T. H., & deTurch, M. A. (1998). The behavioral correlates of sanctioned and unsanctioned deceptive communication. *Journal of Nonverbal Behavior*, *22*, 189–204.

Fein, S., Hilton, J. L., & Miller, D. T. (1990). Suspicion of ulterior motivation and correspondence bias. *Journal of Personality and Social Psychology*, *58*, 753–764.

Fein, S., McCloskey, A. L., & Tomlinson, T. M. (1997). Can the jury disregard that information? The use of suspicion to reduce the prejudicial effects of pretrial and inadmissible testimony. *Personality and Social Psychology Bulletin*, *23*, 1215–1226.

Feldman, R. S., Forrest, J. A., & Happ, B. R. (2002). Self-presentation and verbal deception: Do self-presenters lie more? *Basic and Applied Social Psychology*, *24*, 163–170.

Fiedler, K., & Walka, I. (1993). Training lie detectors to use nonverbal cues instead of global heuristics. *Human Communication Research*, *20*, 199–223.

Fiske, S. T., Lin, M., & Neuberg, S. L. (1999). The continuum model: Ten years later. In S. Chaiken & Y. Trope (Eds.), *Dual process theories in social psychology* (pp. 231–254). New York: Guilford Press.

Fleming, I., & Arrowood, J. (1979). Information processing and the perseverance of discredited self-perceptions. *Personality and Social Psychology Bulletin*, *5*, 201–205.

Friestad, M., & Wright, P (1994). The persuasion knowledge model: How people cope with persuasion attempts. *Journal of Consumer Research*, *21*, 1–31.

Funder, D. C. (1995). On the accuracy of personality judgment: A realistic approach. *Psychological Review*, *102*, 652–671.

Funder, D. C., Kolar, D. C., & Blackman, M. C. (1995). Agreement among judges of personality: Interpersonal relations, similarity, and acquaintanceship. *Journal of Personality and Social Psychology*, *69*, 656–672.

Gilbert, D. T., & Osborne, R. E. (1989). Thinking backwards: Some curable and incurable consequences of cognitive busyness. *Journal of Personality and Social Psychology*, *57*, 940–949.

Golding, J. M., Fowler, S. B., Long, D. L., & Latta, H. (1990). Instructions to disregard potentially useful information: The effects of pragmatics on evaluative judgments and recall, *Journal of Memory and Language*, *29*, 212–227.

Golding, J. M., & Hauselt, J. (1994). When instructions to forget become instructions to remember. *Personality and Social Psychology Bulletin*, *20*, 178–183.

Golding, J. M., & MacLeod, C. (1998). *Intentional forgetting: Interdisciplinary approaches*. Mahwah, NJ: Lawrence Erlbaum Associates, Inc.

Hartwick, J. (1979). Memory for trait information: A signal detection analysis. *JESP*, *15*, 533–552.

Hatvany, N., & Strack, F. (1980). The impact of a discredited key witness. *Journal of Applied Social Psychology*, *10*, 490–509.

Hilton J. L., Fein, S., & Miller, D. T. (1993). Suspicion and dispositional inference. *Personality and Social Psychology Bulletin*, *19*, 501–512.

Kassin, S. M., & Sommers, S. R. (1997). Inadmissible testimony, instructions to disregard, and the jury: Substantive versus procedural considerations. *Personality and Social Psychology Bulletin*, *23*, 1046–1055.

Kassin, S. M., & Wrightsman, L. S. (1981). Coerced confessions, judicial instruction, and mock juror verdicts. *Journal of Applied Social Psychology*, *11*, 489–506.

Kruglanski, A., & Freund, T. (1983). The freezing of lay inferences effects of impressional primacy, ethnic stereotyping and numerical anchoring. *Journal of Experimental Social Psychology, 19*, 448–468.

Kruglanski, A. W. (1989). *Lay epistemics and human knowledge.* New York: Plenum Press.

Kruglanski, A. W., & Mayseless, O. (1987). Motivational effects in the social-comparison of opinions. *Journal of Personality and Social Psychology, 53*, 834–842.

Kruglanski, A. W., Peri, N., & Zakai, D. (1991). Interactive effects of need for closure and initial confidence on social information seeking. *Social Cognition, 9*, 127–148.

Lenehan, G. E., & O'Neill, P. (1981). Reactance and conflict as determinants of judgments in a mock jury trial. *Journal of Applied Social Psychology, 11*, 231–239.

Lieberman, M. D. (2000). Intuition: A social cognitive neuroscience approach. *Psychological Bulletin, 126*, 109–137.

Loftus, E. (1974). The incredible eyewitness. *Psychology Today, 8*, 116–119.

Lombardi, W. J., Higgins, E. T., & Bargh, J. A. (1987). The role of consciousness in priming effects on categorization. *Personality and Social Psychology Bulletin, 13*, 411–429.

Mann, S., Vrij, A., & Bull, R. (2002). Suspects, lies, and videotape: An analysis of authentic high-stake liars. *Law and Human Behavior, 26*, 365–376.

Martin, L. L. (1986). Set/reset: Use and disuse of concepts in impression formation. *Journal of Personality and Social Psychology, 51*, 493–504.

Martin, L. L., Seta, J. J., & Crelia, R. A. (1990). Assimilation and contrast as a function of people's willingness and ability to expend effort in forming an impression. *Journal of Personality and Social Psychology, 59*, 27–37.

Mazis M. B., & Adkinson J. E. (1976). An experimental evaluation of a proposed corrective advertising remedy. *Journal of Marketing Research, 13*, 178–183.

Mazursky, D., & Schul, Y. (2000). In the aftermath of invalidation: Shaping judgment rules on learning that previous information was invalid. *Journal of Consumer Psychology, 9*, 213–222

McConnell, A. R., Sherman, S. J., & Hamilton, D. L. (1997). Target entitivity: Implications for information processing about individual and group targets. *Journal of Personality and Social Psychology, 72*, 750–762.

McCornack, S. A., & Parks, M. R. (1986). Deception detection and relationship development: The other side of trust. *Communication Yearbook, 9*, 377–389.

Miller, G. R., Mongeau, P. A., Sleight, C. (1986). Fudging with friends and lying to lovers: Deceptive communication in personal relationship. *Journal of Social and Personal Relationship, 3*, 495–512.

Nisbett, R. E., Peng, K., Choi, I., & Norenzayan, A. (2001). Culture and systems of thought: Holistic versus analytic cognition. *Psychological Review, 108*, 291–310.

Petty, R. E., & Wegener, D. T. (1993). Flexible correction processes in social judgment: Correcting for context-induced contrast. *Journal of Experimental Social Psychology, 29*, 137–175.

Petty, R. E., & Wegener, D. T. (1999). The Elaboration Likelihood model: Current status and controversies. In S. Chaiken & Y. Trope (Eds.), *Dual process theories in social psychology* (pp. 41–72). New York: Guilford Press.

Petty, R. E., Wegener, D. T., & Fabrigar, L. R. (1997). Attitude and attitude change. *Annural Review, 48*, 609–647.

Petty, R. E., Wegener, D. T., & White, P. H. (1998). Flexible correction process in social judgment: Implications for persuasion. *Social Cognition, 16*, 93–113.

Pickel, K. L. (1995). Inducing jurors to disregard inadmissible evidence: A legal explanation does not help. *Law and Human Behavior 19*, 407–424.

Ross, L., & Nisbett, R.E. (1991). *The person and the situation.* New York: McGraw-Hill.

Ross, L., Lepper, M. R., & Hubbard, M. (1975). Perseverance in self-perception and social perception: Biased attributional processes in the debriefing paradigm, *Journal of Personality and Social Psychology, 32*, 880–892.

Ross, L., Lepper, M. R., Strack, F., & Steinmetz, J. (1977). Social explanations and social expectations: Effects of real and hypothetical explanations on subjective likelihood. *Journal of Personality and Social Psychology, 35*, 817–829.

Ruback, B. R., & Hopper, C. H. (1986). Decision making by parole interviewers: The effect of case and interview factors. *Law and Human behavior, 10*, 203–214.

Schul, Y. (1993). When warning succeeds: The effect of warning on success of ignoring invalid information. *Journal of Experimental Social Psychology, 29*, 42–62.

Schul, Y., & Burnstein, E. (1985). When discounting fails: Conditions under which individuals use discredited information in making a judgment. *Journal of Personality and Social Psychology, 49*, 894–903.

Schul, Y., & Burnstein, E. (1998). Suspicion and discounting: Ignoring invalid information in an uncertain environment. In J. M. Golding & C. MacLeod (Eds.), *Intentional forgetting: Interdisciplinary approaches* (pp. 321–348). Mahwah, NJ: Lawrence Erlbaum Associates, Inc.

Schul, Y., Burnstein, E., & Bardi, A. (1996). Dealing with deceptions that are difficult to detect: Encoding and judgment as a function of preparing to receive invalid information. *Journal of Experimental Social Psychology, 32*, 228–253.

Schul, Y., & Goren, H. (1997). When strong evidence has less impact than weak evidence: Bias, adjustment, and instructions to ignore. *Social Cognition 15*, 133–155.

Schul, Y., & Manzury, F. (1990). The effect of type of encoding and strength of discounting appeal on the success of ignoring an invalid testimony. *European Journal of Social Psychology, 20*, 337–349.

Schul, Y., & Mayo, R. (1999). Two sources are better than one: The effects of ignoring one message on using a different message from the same source. *Journal of Experimental Social Psychology, 35*, 327–345.

Schul, Y., & Mayo, R. (2003). Searching for certainty in an uncertain world: The difficulty of giving up the experiential for the rational mode of thinking. *Journal of Behavioral Decision Making, 16*, 93–106.

Schul, Y., & Mazursky, D. (1990). Conditions facilitating successful discounting in consumer decision making: Type of discounting cue, message encoding, and kind of judgment. *Journal of Consumer Research, 16*, 442–451.

Schwarz, N., & Bless, H. (1992). Scandals and the public trust in politicians: Assimilation and contrast effects. *Personality and Social Psychology Bulletin, 18*, 574–579.

Sloman, S. A. (1996). The empirical case for two systems of reasoning. *Psychological Bulletin, 119*, 3–22.

Smith, E. R., & DeCoster, J. (2000). Dual-process models in social and cognitive psychology: Conceptual integration and links to underlying memory system. *Personality and Social Psychology Review, 4*, 108–131.

Strack, F., & Hannover, B. (1996). Awareness of influence as a precondition for implementing correctional goals. In P. M. Gollwitzer & J. A. Bargh (Eds.), *The psychology of action: Linking motivation and cognition to behavior* (pp. 579–596). New York: Guilford Press.

Strack, F., Schwarz, N., Bless, H., Kubler, A., & Wänke, M. (1993). Awareness of the influence as a determinant of assimilation versus contrast. *European Journal of Social Psychology*, *23*, 53–62.

Tanford, S., & Penrod, S. (1984). Social inference processes in juror judgments of multiple-offense trials. *Journal of Personality and Social Psychology*, *47*, 749–765.

Tellis, G. J. (1998) *Advertising and sales promotion strategy*. New York: Addison-Wesley.

Thompson, W. C., Fong, G. T., & Rosenhan, D. L. (1981). Inadmissible evidence and juror verdicts. *Journal of Personality and Social Psychology*, *40*, 453–463.

Vrij, A., Edward, K., & Bull, R. (2001). Stereotypical verbal and nonverbal responses while deceiving others. *Personality and Social Psychology Bulletin*, *27*, 899–909.

Wegner, D. M. (1994). Ironic processes of mental control. *Psychological Review*, *101*, 34–52.

Weinberg, H. I., & Baron, R. S. (1982). The discredible eyewitness. *Personality and Social Psychology Bulletin*, *8*, 60–67.

Wilkie, W. L., McNeill, D. L., & Mazis, M. B. (1983). Marketing's "scarlet letter": The theory and practice of corrective advertising. *Journal of Marketing*, *48*, 11–31.

Wilson, T. D., & Brekke, N. (1994). Mental contamination and mental correction: Unwanted influences on judgments and evaluations. *Psychological Bulletin*, *116*, 117–142.

Wood, W. (2000). Attitude change: Persuasion and social influence. *Annual Review*, *51*, 539–570.

Wyer, R. S., Bodenhausen, G. V., & Srull, T. K. (1984). The cognitive representation of persons and groups and its effect on recall and recognition memory. *Journal of Experimental Social Psychology*, *20*, 445–469.

Wyer, R. S., & Budesheim, T. L. (1987). Person memory and judgments: The impact of information that one is told to disregard. *Journal of Personality and Social Psychology*, *53*, 14–29.

Wyer, R. S., Srull, T. K., Gordon, S. E., & Hartwick, J. (1982). Effects of processing objectives on the recall of material. *Journal of Personality and Social Psychology*, *43*, 674–668.

Wyer, R. S., & Unverzagt, W. H. (1985). Effects of instructions to disregard information on its subsequent recall and use in making judgments. *Journal of Personality and Social Psychology*, *48*, 533–549.

# 11 The value-account model of attitude formation

*Tilmann Betsch, Henning Plessner and Elke Schallies*

## Introduction

How do people form attitudes? This question has concerned social psychologists ever since the construct of attitudes was introduced by Thomas and Znaniecki (1918) and elaborated on by Gordon Allport (1935). The second half of the twentieth century witnessed the emergence of numerous models of attitude formation and change. After the Second World War, attitude formation was largely conceived to follow general learning processes such as classical and operant conditioning (Berkowitz & Knurek, 1969; Hovland & Rosenberg, 1960; Insko, 1965; Staats & Staats, 1958; Verplanck, 1955). Findings obtained from this domain of research suggest that attitudes are largely shaped by the context. According to this view, the actor plays a rather passive role. Attitudes unwittingly emerge as a by-product of learning and socialization.

Beginning with the "new look" movement (e.g., Bruner, 1957), attitude researchers became more concerned with cognitive processes. Consequently, attitude formation and change was viewed as an active, cognitive process involving understanding and elaboration of persuasive information (McGuire, 1968). At the same time, formal models from other disciplines, mainly statistics and probabilistic decision theory, were imported into psychology and employed to describe mental operations (e.g., Edwards, 1954). The zeitgeist of the early 1960s advocated rational concepts of the human mind. Judgements and decisions were assumed to primarily reflect thinking and reasoning rather than automatic operations. Not surprisingly, the emphasis of deliberative cognitive processes also precipitated attitude theory. The theory of reasoned action (Fishbein & Ajzen, 1975) represents the most prominent example of this line of theorizing. The core assumptions of this model are borrowed from subjectively expected utility theory (Edwards, 1954) which itself is based on economic theory (von Neumann & Morgenstern, 1944). According to the theory of reasoned action, attitudes are the product of explicit deliberation (cf., Ajzen & Fishbein, 1980, p. 5) involving the anticipation and weighted integration of valued consequences associated with an attitude object. Models rooted in the rationality approach still have a strong impact in social psychology (Eagly & Chaiken, 1993).

The emergence of the heuristics and biases program in the 1970s, however, cast the view of human rationality into doubt (see Kahneman, Slovic, & Tversky, 1982, for an overview). Henceforth, empirical evidence accumulated showing that individuals employ simple judgmental heuristics instead of systematic and deliberative modes of information processing (e.g., Nisbett & Ross, 1980). In attitude research, this insight fostered the development of dual process models (e.g., Chaiken, 1980, Petty & Cacioppo, 1986). These models postulate that both systematic/central and heuristic/peripheral processing strategies contribute to attitude formation and change. For example, when motivation and ability is low, people may construe an attitude on the basis of peripheral cues such as the attractiveness of a communicator (Petty & Cacioppo, 1986) or simply by adopting the opinion shared by a salient majority (Bohner, Moskowitz, & Chaiken, 1995).

The focus in mainstream social psychology on heuristic processing paved the way for studying the role of automaticity in attitudes and social cognition (e.g., Bargh, 1996; Fazio, 1990). At present, the automatic or *implicit* facets of attitudes (Greenwald & Banaji, 1995) receive increasing attention as evidenced, for instance, by recent journal special issue publications on attitude measurement (De Hower & Hermans, 2001; Plessner & Banse, 2001).

How do people form attitudes? The brief overview of research might give rise to the interpretation that we are back to where we started in the 1950s. Surely, this would be a misinterpretation. Research has identified a number of mechanisms of both implicit and explicit attitude formation. We know that attitudes can be implicitly acquired via classical, operant or evaluative conditioning. Several heuristics have been described in the literature helping people to explicitly form attitudes on the spot with little cognitive effort (e.g., Schwarz, 2000). Under certain conditions (high accuracy motivation, high ability) explicit attitude formation may even involve a thorough and rational analysis of values and expectations (e.g., Fazio, 1990).

Nevertheless, implicit and explicit processes are often described in separate, local models rather than in integrative theoretical frameworks. The few general frameworks which consider both implicit and explicit strategies of attitude formation are capable of predicting intensities of information elaboration rather than application of particular mechanisms of attitude formation. Consider for example the elaboration likelihood model (ELM) of persuasion (Petty & Cacioppo, 1986). Although the ELM spells out conditions that foster central or peripheral routes to attitude formation and change, it cannot predict strategy choice on a molecular level. A key assumption of the model is that when motivation is low and processing capacities are constrained, people should be likely to elaborate on the incoming information in a shallow or peripheral fashion which involves the application of simple judgmental heuristics (e.g., conform with the majority's opinion) and even unconscious mechanisms such as conditioning. However, the ELM cannot predict application of a particular strategy, i.e., under which conditions, for example, people rely on a judgmental shortcut or on automatic mechanisms which are described in the conditioning literature. Consequently, the model is silent about information integration processes in implicit and explicit attitude formation. Similar problems arise with other dual process models (e.g., the heuristic-systematic model, Bohner et al., 1995, Chaiken 1980). Fazio's MODE model (1990) can be considered an exception. It is specific with regard to strategy selection. Depending on motivation and opportunity, people are assumed either to rely on an automatic activated attitude or engage in scrutinizing beliefs and evaluation. In accordance with Fishbein and Ajzen's expectancy-value model, the MODE model describes information integration in *explicit* attitude formation to obey a signed summation model. Albeit, the MODE model is silent about the mechanisms of *implicit* attitude formation.

In the next section, we provide an attempt to integrate implicit and explicit processes of attitude formation in one theory. The major concern of our approach is to spell out the mechanisms of information integration. One of the chief assumptions of the model states that implicit attitude formation is guided by a summation principle, whereas explicit attitude formation is guided by an averaging principle. After an overview of the model, we will introduce a research paradigm designed for testing the model's predictions. Later, we will substantiate our theory by evidence obtained from our own research.

## Value-account model of attitude formation

### *Scope of theory, definitions, and basic assumptions*

The value-account model attempts to explain and predict implicit and explicit attitude formation for situations in which value-charged information about an entity (self, person, group, object, behavior, abstract concepts) is encoded. By the term "value charged" we refer to the potential of a stimulus to evoke any sort of internal reaction in the perceiver which can be placed on the evaluative dimension. In other words, application of our theory requires the association of an entity's representation in working memory and any sort of internal positive or negative reaction as an antecedent condition. For example, Tom listens to a speech of a politician during an election campaign. The politician supports military strikes against all countries hosting international terrorists. Assume that these statements evoke negative reactions such as indignance or fear in Tom. Consider another example. Tina has been encouraged by her finance advisor to buy shares of a big car company. Subsequently, she watches reports of the stock market on the news channel. During the first week, the price of her shares keeps falling constantly, which causes her considerable distress. During the next week, the price begins to rise again, evoking more positive thoughts and feelings in Tina. The two examples refer to experiences evoking affective reactions in the judges. The value-account model predicts how such pieces of value-charged information can contribute to both implicit and explicit attitude formation.

We use the term "implicit" in accordance with the definition of implicit cognition provided by Greenwald and Banaji (1995). Accordingly, implicit attitude formation is conceived as a mental process which is unintentionally or automatically started and performed. The process of information integration cannot be accessed via introspection and cannot be verbally reported. Moreover, implicit processes consume a minimum of cognitive resources only. In contrast, explicit attitude formation consumes cognitive resources and is bounded by capacity constraints. Explicit processes are controlled by the individual. They start with the intention to arrive at an attitude judgment. Individuals are aware that they are evaluating the target entity. At least partly, individuals are able to give verbal reports about these processes. For example, they may remember pieces of information they have considered (e.g., arguments, pros and cons) and are able to write them down during a thought listing procedure (e.g., Petty & Cacioppo, 1986). Depending on the situation they may have more or less control about strategy choice, weighting of information (e.g., consideration of probability or importance) and other procedural aspects. Some of these operations are also subject to meta-cognitive representation and report.

It is a basic assumption of our model that individuals can utilize different types of representations of value-charged information when they form an attitude. In a similar vein as in dual-representation models (e.g., Srull & Wyer, 1989) we distinguish between a concrete and a global level of memory representation. On the concrete level, the memory system can store specific value-charged episodes or events. For instance, Tom may later remember that the politician supported military strikes against other countries in his speech. Tina may remember an outstanding increase of her shares' value, e.g., when the shares doubled in value at a particular trading date. Such events can be stored in close association to their valence and a representation of the attitude entity to whom they pertain (e.g., the politician). Representations on the concrete level conserve the input of an encounter episode. In turn, aggregate or global representations conserve the output of an attitude formation process. The output provides a summary evaluation (attitude) towards an entity. Assume that Tom has arrived at the judgment that he extremely dislikes the politician. Subsequently, this summary evaluation (EV) can be stored in long-term memory.

In addition, we assume that implicitly formed attitudes are simultaneously conserved in long-term memory independent from explicitly formed evaluations. We term these hypothetical memory structures value accounts (VA). A VA is proposed to result from an implicit accumulation of value-charged experiences with an attitude entity. VAs are thought to be closely associated with the representation of the entity in memory. Therefore, they are immediately accessible whenever the attitude entity is activated from memory. Moreover, we assume that the extremity and polarity of a VA are conveyed by the affective system. Accordingly, a VA which stems from many and/or intensive positive experiences made with an entity (person, object, behavior) will evoke stronger positive feelings in the individual than a VA which stems from few and/or weak positive experiences.

### Implicit formation of attitudes

We propose that whenever value-charged information about an entity is encoded it will be implicitly aggregated into a memory structure which we term value account (VA). The VA is associated with the entity in memory. The subjectively experienced intensities of the positive and negative reactions provide the input values to the process of implicit information integration. As a key assumption, we posit that implicit integration of value-charged information obeys the principles of a *weighted summation model*. If a VA has been already established, the new information is incremented or decremented to the existing VA.

The weight of an input value depends on personal factors (e.g., motivational state) and the context (e.g., salience of the stimulus). Moreover we assume that weighting depends on the prior magnitude of a VA. The greater the magnitude of the VA, the lower is the weight of a new entry. Formally speaking we assume that the magnitude of a value account follows a negatively accelerated growth function when it is constantly incremented or decremented over time. The integration model for implicit online formation or change of a VA is summarized by the following equation:

$$\text{new } VA_{ES} = \text{old } VA_{ES} + \sum_i w_i v_i \qquad [1]$$

whereas $w$ and $v$ denote the *w*eighted *v*alue of a reaction $i$ towards the entity. The subscript ES refers to the entity in a particular type of situation. Assume that one of your friends is a politician. You might have different attitudes towards this person. Perhaps you like him as a friend but you dislike him as a politician. Different situations may cue different preformed attitudes—implicit and explicit ones. Let us briefly consider how implicit attitudes towards your friend will change according to equation 1. A particular type of situation will activate a pre-established VA. For example, listening to your friend addressing the parliament may automatically evoke a negative feeling according to the extremity or magnitude of your implicit attitude (old $VA_{Friend-S1}$). Assume further that in his speech your friend supports military strikes against countries hosting terrorists. The weighted value $v$ of the internal reaction evoked by this new statement will be automatically added to the old VA. Other implicit attitudes, for instance, the positive affection you hold towards them in private settings ($VA_{Friend-S2}$) will remain unchanged.

So far, we have been concerned with the mechanisms of implicit *online* formation of attitudes. It is also possible, however, that individuals implicitly change their attitudes from *retrospection*. Assume, you have attended the presentation of a guest professor at the research colloquium of your institute. The next day you brief a colleague about the talk. Suddenly your colleague asks you whether you like the guest professor. Assume you would give a spontaneous answer without further deliberating on the recalled aspects of the previous day's episode. How do you form an attitude judgment? Our assumption is that such retrospective, spontaneous attitude judgments are guided by the same implicit processes that are outlined above. Accordingly, a spontaneously formed attitude is a joint function of a previously formed VA and the weighted values of the positive and negative reactions evoked by the events and features which are *currently* activated from memory.

### Explicit formation of attitudes

Individuals can also construe attitudes in an explicit or controlled fashion. Explicit attitude formation often starts with the intention to evaluate an entity. Explicit information processing can involve more or less deliberative activities which consume cognitive resources. Therefore, application of explicit modes is constrained by time, ability, and cognitive capacity. A substantial part of those operations can be accessed by self-report or introspection. We do not propose, however, that individuals have complete insight into the dynamics of information integration which underlies their subsequent judgments.

We posit that information integration in explicit attitude formation is guided by a *weighted averaging principle*. Averaging models are widespread in the literature on evaluative judgments. Probably the most influential formulation of a general averaging model stems from Norman Anderson (1971, 1981). His information integration theory had a pronounced impact on various field of psychology, and especially on attitude research (cf. Eagly & Chaiken, 1993). Recently, a shortcut version of the weighted averaging model has been put forward by Kahneman and collaborators (Fredrickson & Kahneman, 1993; Kahneman, Fredrickson, Schreiber, & Redelmeier, 1993; Redelmeier & Kahneman, 1996). They suggested that individuals can employ the so-called "peak-and-end heuristic" in retrospective (memory-based) evaluation. Accordingly, the resulting summary evaluation is a function of some outstanding events of a prior encounter episode which can be recalled at the time of judgment. Outstanding events, such as experiences with extreme values (peaks) or those which occurred recently (end), can be subsequently easily retrieved from memory. Formally speaking, the resulting summary evaluation is the *average* of a subset of values which receive the weight of 1, whereas the values of other aspects of the encounter episode are attached with a weight of zero.

In contrast to a summation model, an averaging model predicts that summary evaluations are normalized, for example, by the size of the sampled (or considered) values. A general averaging model can take the following form:

$$EV_{ES} = \frac{\sum_i w_i e_i}{\sum_i w_i} \qquad [2]$$

whereas EV denotes the summary evaluation resulting from an explicit consideration of the attitude object. Parameter *e* denotes the value of the evaluation of a particular aspect, feature or outcome *i* associated with the entity E in a situation S. Given a pre-established explicit summary evaluation of the entity is accessed in memory (e.g., a prior attitude judgment), the equation reads:

$$\text{new } EV_{ES} = \frac{w_o EV_o + \sum_i w_i e_i}{w_o + \sum_i w_i} \qquad [3]$$

whereas $EV_o$ is the "old" evaluation and $w_o$ the weight it receives in the current situation. This equation applies to situations in which both a prior summary evaluation and other pieces of value charged information are available. If only the prior summary evaluation can be retrieved from memory, then the new evaluation equals the prior one (new $EV_{ES} = EV_o$). Formula 3 converges with the averaging rule for attitude formation as suggested by Norman Anderson (1981). In contrast to his approach, we suggest, however, that the averaging principle applies to *explicit* attitude formation only.

Note that summary evaluations (EVs) and value accounts (VAs) are two distinct hypothetical constructs. We propose that they constitute different *memory structures* which are developed and stored independently from each other. Explicit processing cannot directly handle VAs. Conversely, EVs are only subject to controlled processes. An EV can be mentally represented in different ways, for instance, as a verbal statement or even as a number one has circled on a response scale in a survey questionnaire. In contrast, a VA itself cannot be directly accessed by introspection. The person can only witness its effects, namely the feelings of liking and disliking which arise when an entity is encountered. We propose that these feelings, especially if they are subtle, cannot be handled by deliberative operations. They might fade or vanish when the person attempts to elaborate on them. In rare cases, if these feelings are strong, they might be utilized indirectly in an explicit manner. For instance, if a decision maker realizes that the presence of a particular entity influences her affective state, than she can use these feelings as information in the explicit evaluation process (cf., Schwarz & Clore, 1988). Thus, affective reactions can indirectly influence explicit attitude formation but only via an active appraisal process.

### Forming attitude judgments

The value-account model assumes that people can form and store multiple attitudes towards an entity, which in turn can be produced by different modes of information processing. Implicit modes produce holistic, implicit attitudes (VA) which conserve the entire stream of positive and negative reactions (for a certain significant type of situation). Explicit modes produce EVs which can be accessed on a meta-cognitive level. Moreover, we proposed two distinct mechanisms underlying implicit and explicit attitude formation (summation vs. averaging). When will attitude judgments be based on VAs and the summation principle, and when will people use EVs and an averaging rule to arrive at their judgments?

We first assume that reliance on VA is the default strategy when judgments are made without much deliberation and/or concrete information about the entity is difficult to be accessed. Second, if concrete information can be accessed at the time of judgment, then we propose that application of explicit strategies becomes more likely. However, with increasing time and capacity constraints, attitude judgments again will be likely to reflect VAs.

As already noted, we assume that the content of VAs are conveyed by the affective system. Those feelings immediately arise whenever the attitude object is encountered again. If time and capacity constraints are severe, attitude judgments will reflect these feelings. If, simultaneously, other aspects of the encounter situation evoke additional positive or negative reactions they will be altogether integrated according to the summation principle stated in equation 1. The resulting attitude judgment will reflect the updated implicit attitude (new $VA_{ES}$). The more time and cognitive resources available, the more likely it is that attitude judgments will reflect EV and, consequently, concrete pieces of information which are available at the time of judgment. Information integration in this case will follow the averaging principle as stated in equations 2 and 3. It is noteworthy to mention that the amount of time and capacity resources available at the time of judgment may also result from a resource allocation decision (Zakay, 1993). In such, time and capacity are not only a function of situational and physiological variables but also of motivational processes.

## Empirical evidence

The empirical substantiation of our theory requires, as a prerequisite, rigorous experimental control over implicit and explicit modes of attitude formation. Recall the distinction between implicit and explicit cognition which we adopted from Greenwald and Banaji (1995). The key aspect of their definition pertains to meta-cognitive insight. First, the content of explicit cognition can be accessed by self-report and introspection, whereas implicit cognition cannot. Accordingly, individuals should be able to report causes and reasons underlying their *explicitly* formed attitudes. Conversely, in *implicit* attitude formation, judges should not systematically be able to subsequently access traces of information in memory which contributed to their attitudes. Second, the process of explicit attitude formation is to a considerable extent under volitional control. Implicit processes, in contrast, are activated and performed automatically. As a consequence, explicit processes consume more time and cognitive resources than implicit processes do.

## *Experimental paradigm*

The implications for the experimental procedure are straightforward. To study implicit attitude formation, processing capacities must be severely constrained. Moreover, volitional influences should be reduced. Accordingly, participants should not have the intention to evaluate a target while they are encoding value-charged information about it. As a manipulation check, one has to demonstrate that participants neither have access to event memory which is diagnostic to attitude formation nor that they are aware that they have formed an attitude. Statistically, this should manifest in zero-correlations between memory and attitude measures. On the other hand, to foster explicit processes, participants must have sufficient cognitive resources available at the time they form an attitude. They should be more likely to engage in scrutinizing pieces of information about the target. In turn, they should be able to memorize attitude-relevant information. Therefore, memory and attitude measures in these participants should correlate.

In the laboratory, explicit attitude formation can be easily studied. One simply has to present participants with some pieces of information about a target and to ask them to form an attitude judgment. It is somehow more difficult to prevent people from explicitly forming an attitude, especially in the presence of value-charged information. To inhibit operation of the explicit mode of attitude formation, we often employed a dual-task procedure. Participants were asked to work on two tasks at the same time. The secondary task was framed as a "distracter" task. Its ostensible purpose was to render the work on the primary task more difficult. The distracter task, however, required the participants to encode value-charged information about attitude objects. To further constrain explicit elaboration of the stimuli, we increased the amount of information and the pace in which it has to be processed to the extreme. As a manipulation check, we subsequently probed event memory of our participants. Specifically, we asked them to recall pieces of information from the primary and the secondary task. In numerous studies, information overload proved to be a technique highly effective in constraining memory. In general, we obtained valid recall for the primary task, but not for the "distracter" task which contained the information about the attitude objects.

Figure 11.1 depicts an example of such a dual-task procedure. Participants were presented with videotaped ads on a TV or a PC monitor. They believed they were participating in a study on consumer research. Their primary task

Supan +14    Elskar +6    Navig +32    Patel +50    Söd

*Figure 11.1* Screen shot of stimulus presentation in the dual-task paradigm. Video-taped ads appear in the background. Return values of shares (gains achieved at a particular trading date at the stock market in DEM) appear on a running caption at the bottom of the screen.

was to remember as accurately as possible the content of the ads. Simultaneously they were to read aloud information about the performance of shares at the stock market which appeared on running caption at the bottom of the screen ("distracter" task). Each of the fictitious shares (ELSKAR, NAVIG, PATEL, etc.) appeared several times. Participants were initially instructed that a value indicates the absolute *increase* or gain of a share's value on a particular trading date at the stock market (in Deutsche Mark). For instance, ELSKAR +6 means that the value of this share has increased by 6 DEM at that trading date. The performance of each share in the presentation was shown for a period of up to 20 trading dates. The whole presentation lasted between 7 and 15 minutes involving up to 130 pieces of information about shares and 30 commercial clips. After the presentation, we assessed participants' attitudes towards the shares.

We employed the dual-task paradigm in a series of experiments which will be reviewed below. From post-experimental interviews and recall data it became evident in these studies that the method effectively prevents participants from explicit online formation of attitudes towards the shares.

Subsequent experiments revealed, however, that it is not generally necessary to employ a dual task procedure. Often, it suffices to have participants focus on certain aspects of the presentation which are unrelated to the evaluative aspect of the task. In a series of studies, we asked participants to check numerous utterances of fictitious politicians for syntactical correctness under slight time pressure. Subsequently, participants were not able to recall the politicians' utterances. As will be shown later, however, their implicit attitudes were remarkable sensitive to the entire set of statements a politician had made in the presentation. In another experiment, we presented participants with forecasts of the weather in different cities. The ostensible task was to evaluate the voices of the speakers (style, grammar, slang etc.). Participants subsequently lacked any concrete memories about the weather in the various cities. Their spontaneous attitudes towards the cities, however, reflected the entire set of weather forecasts given for each cities over a couple of days. We now present empirical evidence for our theory. In all of the studies we employed one of the experimental paradigms we have described so far. The empirical evidence is summarized in Table 11.1.

### Implicit attitude formation

The first assumption of our theory holds that implicit attitudes are formed or changed *automatically* and stored in memory whenever value-charged information about an entity is encoded. Accordingly, individuals should be able to differentiate between entities (shares, politicians, cities) in terms of their valence. Most importantly, this should be the case even if they had previously not intended to evaluate these objects and even if they lack concrete memories about the encounter episode at the time of judgment.

The first assumption was consistently supported in all of our studies. As an example, Figure 11.2 depicts the results of our first experiment (Betsch et al., 2001a, Exp. 1). It shows spontaneous attitude judgments towards shares which differed with regard to their objective sum of return values. In all of our studies, we performed repeated measure analyses of variance on spontaneous attitudes judgments towards the objects. These analyses generally produced significant effects, indicating that participants hold different attitudes towards the objects. Inspection of Table 11.1 reveals that effect sizes are moderate on average. Note that these results were obtained in an experimental paradigm which prevents participants from explicit online evaluation of the attitude objects. Post-experimental interviews revealed that participants had no insight into the fact that they were capable of systematically differentiating between the objects. Memory measures further substantiate the validity of these observations. After the presentations, participants were unable to systematically recall evaluative information about the objects.

A central assumption of the value-account model holds that implicit attitude formation is guided by a summation principle. Consequently, individuals' intuitions should reflect the frequency and intensity of the *entire*

*Table 11.1* Empirical evidence for the value-account model

| Study | Attitude objects | IAF reflects sum of prior experiences* | Further findings |
|---|---|---|---|
| Betsch et al. (2001a) | | | |
| Experiment 1 | shares | $\eta^2 = .42$ | |
| Experiment 2 | shares | $.30 < \eta^2 < .94$ | IAF reflects summation and averaging. |
| Experiment 3 | shares | $\eta^2 = .20$ | Attitude judgments reflect IA under time pressure. Access to event memory fosters EAF. |
| Betsch et al. (2001b) | | | |
| Experiment 1 | shares | *not studied* | EAF reflects averaging. |
| Experiment 2 | shares | $\eta^2 = .10$ | EAF reflects averaging. Access to event memory fosters EAF. |
| Experiment 3 | shares | $\eta^2 = .10$ | EAF reflects averaging. Access to event memory fosters EAF. |
| Betsch et al. (2003) | shares | $\eta^2 = .21$ | Intuitive attitude judgments are not influenced by ease of recognition. |
| Plessner et al. (2001) | | | |
| Experiment 1 | shares | $.33 < \eta^2 < .90$ | Thinking reduces the impact of IA on attitude judgments. |
| Experiment 2 | shares | $\eta^2 = .35$ | Thinking reduces the impact of IA on attitude judgments. Access to event memory fosters EAF. |
| Plessner et al. (2003) | | | |
| Experiment 1 | politicians | $\eta^2 = .41$ | |
| Experiment 2 | politicians | $\eta^2 = .35$ | Convergence between scroll-bar measure of IA and the Implicit Association Test (Greenwald et al., 1998). |
| Plessner et al. (2002) | | | |
| Experiment 1 | shares | $\eta^2 = .80$ | Immediate attitude judgments reflect EAF, delayed judgments reflect IAF. |
| | politicians | $\eta^2 = .33$ | Stability of IA over time. |
| Pavel (2001) | politicians | $\eta^2 = .30$ | IAF is robust against valence of context information. |
| Höhle et al. (2001) | cities | $\eta^2 = .22$ | Applicable anchors reduce impact of IA on attitude judgments. |

*Notes*: * Effect sizes are obtained from repeated measure analyses of the evaluations of target objects. IA: Implicit attitude(s). IAF: Implicit attitude formation. EAF: Explicit attitude formation.

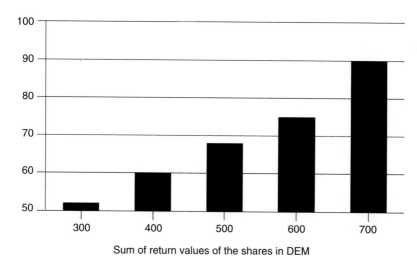

*Figure 11.2* Attitude judgments of five shares from a study on implicit attitude formation (Betsch et al., 2001a, Exp. 1). Stimulus shares which differ with
regard to their sum of return values in Deutsche Mark (DEM) obtained
on the stock market over several trading days. Higher values (standardized scores) indicate more favorable attitude judgments.

stream of value-charged experiences they have made with an entity. Empirical results strongly corroborate this prediction. In the monetary domain,
we systematically varied the return values of shares at the stock market.
The shares differed with regard to their sum of gains achieved over a period
of trading days. In our studies, we repeatedly found a perfect rank order
correlation between intuitive attitude judgments and the actual yield of the
shares. Most notably, when we asked our participants to rank the shares
according to their monetary yield they were unable to do so (Betsch et al.,
2001a). This lack of meta-cognitive insight provides further evidence for the
notion that attitude formation in our participants indeed happened in an
uncontrolled, automatic fashion. These findings could be successfully replicated in other domains. We systematically varied, for instance, the valence
of statements of fictitious politicians. Although participants subsequently
were not able to remember the content of the speeches (because they were
occupied with judging syntactical features of the utterances) their intuitive
judgments reflected the sum of the pre-tested scale values of all the statements a politician had made (e.g., Plessner, Betsch, Schallies, & Schwieren,
2003).

The consistent finding of high rank order correlations between actual sum
of values and liking of the attitude objects confirms the predictions of the
summation principle. However, these findings alone do not allow us to
cogently outrule alternative interpretations in terms of an averaging principle, since sum and average of value distributions are always confounded if

presentation frequency of the stimuli is kept constant. In order to show that information aggregation in implicit attitude formation really obeys a summation and not an averaging principle we slightly changed the stimulus material of the share paradigm. Before the presentation, participants were informed that the data files of the shares were incomplete. In the case of missing data, the share's name on the running caption was accompanied by a sign, indicating that a return value for this particular trading date was not available (see Betsch et al., 2001a, Exp. 2, for details). Including missing data, allows us to orthogonally vary sum and average of return distributions while keeping presentation frequency of the stimuli constant. Specifically, one share, the SUM winner, yielded a higher sum but lower average of return values than its competitor, the AVERAGE winner. The results of this study (Betsch et al., 2001a, Exp. 2) and its subsequent replications (Betsch et al., 2001b) corroborated the core assumption of our theory. Implicitly formed attitudes were sensitive to the entire sum and not the average of value-charged experiences with an attitude object. In concrete, participants liked the SUM winner better than the AVERAGE winner, given that they lacked concrete event memories about the encounter episode. We emphasize the latter point, because access to event memories would allow the participant to form attitudes in an explicit fashion. As we will see below, we find a reversal of this pattern of results when the situation fosters explicit attitude formation.

### Explicit attitude formation

Numerous studies have provided evidence for the notion that attitude formation is guided by an averaging principle (e.g., Anderson, 1981; Fredrickson & Kahneman, 1993; Kahneman et al., 1993; Redelmeier & Kahneman, 1996). We propose, however, that averaging is not a general principle of information integration but is limited to explicit attitude formation. Hence, we had to demonstrate that different mechanisms of information integration apply to different modes of judgment.

For this purpose, we again employed the share paradigm because it allows perfect control over the crucial parameters of the distribution such as sum and average. In the former experiments we ensured that information overload was extremely high so that participants were not able to form attitudes explicitly. High information overload was achieved by having participants encode up to 130 pieces of information about the shares. The effectiveness of this manipulation was evident by the fact that participants were subsequently unable to recall instances of returns produced by a particular share, nor were they able to estimate crucial aspects of the return distributions such as the sum or the average value of the return distributions (although their intuitive attitude judgments perfectly reflected the sum of return values).

In another study (Betsch et al., 2001b, Exp. 1) we reduced the number of shares and share exposures. Specifically, participants were presented with only two shares, a SUM winner (high sum of returns, low average return) and an AVERAGE winner (low sum of returns, high average return). Moreover, each share appeared only eight times in random order. In other words, the number of share exposures during the presentation was reduced from over 130 in the study on implicit attitude formation (Betsch et al., 2001a, Exp. 2) to 16. Not surprisingly, under these conditions the participants were able to reliably recall instances of the return distribution. They were also able to correctly estimate sum and average of the return distributions of the two shares. The results on the memory measures show that reducing the amount of information successfully reduced information overload compared to the former study. Consequently, participants should now have been able to form their attitudes towards the shares *explicitly* on the basis of recalled information. Under such conditions, the value-account model predicts that attitude formation is guided by an averaging principle. Accordingly, participants should no longer prefer the SUM winner above the AVERAGE winner as they did in the former study with high information overload. Results clearly corroborated this prediction. Participants liked the AVERAGE more than the SUM winner. The results of this study on *explicit* attitude formation (Betsch et al., 2001b, Exp. 1) and those from the former study on *implicit* attitude formation (Betsch et al., 2001a, Exp. 2) are depicted in Figure 11.3.

The pattern of results shown in Figure 11.3 was replicated in two follow-up studies (Betsch et al., 2001b, Exp. 2, Exp. 3) which employed different techniques to manipulate cognitive load. We obtained additional evidence from another study (Betsch et al., 2001a, Exp. 3). In this experiment, participants

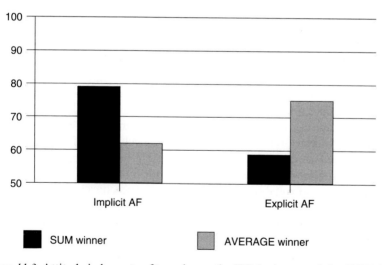

*Figure 11.3* Attitude judgments of two shares, the SUM winner and the AVERAGE winner, from a study on implicit attitude formation (high information overload at the time of encoding, Betsch et al., 2001a, Exp. 2) and a study on explicit attitude formation (no information overload at the time of encoding, Betsch et al., 2001b, Exp. 1). Higher values (standardized scores) indicate more favourable attitude judgments.

were able to recall a subset of the information from the presentation. When they had enough time to explicitly form their attitude judgment, they no longer preferred the SUM winner. They did prefer the SUM winner, however, under time pressure which impaired their ability to explicitly form attitudes on the basis of recalled information. Altogether, these results provide converging evidence supporting the assumption that explicit information integration is guided by an averaging principle.

### Conditions that moderate utilization of implicit attitudes

The value-account model proposes that in the absence of concrete memories attitude judgments will reflect implicit attitudes, i.e., the magnitude of value accounts reflecting the sum of prior experiences. In the preceding sections it should have become evident that this assumption has been consistently confirmed. However, our initial assumption was more specific. We additionally claimed that reliance on implicit attitudes is the default strategy in spontaneous judgment. Additionally we assumed that thinking can block utilization of implicit attitudes in judgment. We conducted two experiments which address these assumptions (Plessner, Haberstroh, & Betsch, 2001). The results are in line with our model. Half of the subjects were requested to consider their intuitive feelings about the objects (shares) and to use them in making their judgments. In this condition, implicit attitudes had no impact on the ratings of the targets as evident from a null correlation of the actual sum of the shares' values and judgments. In the counter-condition, participants were instructed to *ignore* their intuition. Those individuals could not avoid the influence of implicit attitudes as evident from a significant rank–order correlation between the actual sum of the shares' values and judgments. Altogether these results indicate that utilization of implicit attitudes might not be under deliberative control.

What happens if judges have access to concrete information about the targets in memory? As predicted by our theory, people are likely to use this information unless cognitive capacities are constrained. This has been demonstrated by the above reported studies on the mechanism of explicit attitude formation (Betsch et al., 2001b). These results also suggest that high motivation is not necessary as an antecedent condition for using concrete information in judgment. Probably, concrete information is conceived as being more appropriate an informational base in judgment compared to vague feelings of liking or disliking. However, under capacity constraints individuals again relied on their implicit attitudes even if concrete information could be accessed (Betsch et al., 2001a, Exp. 3)—as predicted by the value-account model.

### Further findings

In most of our studies we assessed attitude judgments by means of a vertical scroll bar ("good"–"bad") participants could adjust by moving the computer mouse to express their intuitive feelings of liking or disliking. Under time pressure, in the absence of concrete event memory, or merely when people were instructed to make their judgments in a spontaneous fashion, attitudes assessed with this measure reflected the sum of previous experiences. These findings suggest that the scroll bar device can indeed detect implicit attitudes. Nevertheless, it is a direct measure, since participants are explicitly requested to judge the targets. To assess the validity of the scroll bar device as a measure of implicit attitudes, we employed indirect measures as well. In one experiment (Plessner, Betsch, Schallies, & Schwieren, 2003, Exp. 2) we employed the Implicit Association Test (IAT, Greenwald et al., 1998). There is a good deal of evidence, both empirical and theoretical, indicating that the IAT can actually diagnose implicit evaluative orientations (see Greenwald & Nosek, 2001, for an overview). Results obtained with the IAT converge with our previous results. In the absence of concrete memories, attitudes towards politicians reflected the sum of prior experiences regardless whether they were assessed with the IAT or with the scroll bar device.

In the share paradigm we often—though not generally—confounded the sum of return values and exposure frequency of a share's distribution. Therefore the results might offer an alternative interpretation. Judgments of liking might reflect the ease by a which a target is recognized at the time of judgment rather than implicitly formed attitudes. Recognition has been found to be an important variable in heuristic judgment and decision making (e.g., Gigerenzer, Todd, & ABC Research group, 1999; Goldstein & Gigerenzer, 2002; Klein, 1999). This caveat has already been ruled out in our first experiments (Betsch et al., 2001a) in which either presentation frequency has been reduced for the SUM winner (Exp. 1) or has been kept constant across all shares (Exp. 2). However, in these experiments we did not measure ease of recognition and thus could not directly assess its mediating effects on attitude judgment. In a recent demonstration (Betsch et al., 2003) we disentangled the influence of exposure frequency and sum of return values of the shares within our dual-task paradigm. The SUM winner appeared only 5 times whereas another share with a lower sum of values appeared 17 times in the presentation (EXPOSURE winner). Again it was ensured that participants subsequently lacked any concrete memories about the return values of the shares. As dependent measures we assessed recognition latency and attitudes towards the shares. We found a negative correlation between the ease of recognition (recognition latency) and attitudes (judgments of liking). Specifically, the SUM winner was judged more positively but was slower recognized as the EXPOSURE winner. These results clearly rule out an alternative interpretation of our results in terms of heuristics that rely on the ease of recognition. Moreover the results dovetail with the primacy-of-affect view which has been put forward early in psychology (Wundt, 1907; Zajonc 1968).

Stability of attitudes has always been a controversial issue in the literature (e.g., Eagly & Chaiken, 1993; Schwarz, 2000). The value-account model takes over a differentiated view on this issue. Implicit attitudes are assumed to be relatively stable over time in such that they are stored in memory and attached to the entity. They are relatively unstable in such that they are changed by each positive or negative experience with the entity. In the absence of such experiences, however, the implicit attitude is assumed to be kept unchanged in memory. Under conditions which foster the reliance on implicit attitudes (e.g., absence of concrete memories, spontaneous judgment), attitude judgments should reveal a stable evaluative orientation towards the entity over time. We obtained first empirical evidence in support of this prediction. We assessed participants' spontaneous evaluations of politicians directly after the presentation or one week later. In both conditions, judgments reflected the sum of value-charged experiences with the politicians (Plessner, Betsch, & Schallies, 2002).

Finally, two other results are worth mentioning. The first underlines the robustness of the processes by which implicit attitudes are formed. Pavel (2001) systematically varied the valence of background information presented at the time when participants encoded value-charged information about targets (politicians). Specifically, participants were requested to memorize the position of pictures on the screen while they were listening to speeches of politicians. The pictures aroused positive and negative affect as ensured by pre-tests. As a result, implicit attitudes were uninfluenced by the affective load of the pictures but again reflected the sum of value-charged information about the targets. These findings suggest that implicit attitude formation is tuned to only those pieces of value-charged information which are directly associated with the attitude object.

The last finding to be mentioned in this review again illustrates that the impact of implicit attitudes on judgment is likely to decrease if concrete relevant information is accessible. Höhle, Molter, and Betsch (2001) varied the applicability of judgmental anchors. Specifically, attitude judgments about targets (cities) were preceded by an evaluation task which either addressed a similar or a dissimilar judgmental domain. If the preceding task provided an applicable anchor (similar domain) judgments did not reflect prior experiences with the cities. Conversely, if no applicable anchor was provided, judgments reflected the sum of prior experiences.

## Discussion

In the present chapter, we outlined the value-account model of attitude formation and change. Moreover, we reviewed recent research which substantiates the core assumptions of our theory. The value-account model is a dual process theory. It distinguishes between implicit and explicit strategies of attitude formation. Its major assumption states that these modes involve different mechanisms of information integration. Specifically it posits that implicit attitude formation is guided by a summation principle, whereas explicit attitude formation follows an averaging principle. Implicit processes are not constrained by processing capacities. The resulting implicit attitudes (value accounts, VA) are therefore assumed to reflect the entire sum of prior value-charged experiences with an attitude object. In such, implicit attitudes are holistic but they are blind to sample size, since values are simply accumulated. In contrast, explicit attitudes (summary evaluations, EV) can reflect sample size due to the underlying averaging mechanism. However, with a growing amount of information they are likely to be based on a subset of information since explicit processes are bounded by capacity constraints. The formation of VAs was assumed to be instantiated automatically whenever value-charged information about entities is encoded. The resulting implicit attitudes should be readily accessible whenever the entity is encountered again. Therefore, reliance on implicit attitudes was assumed to serve as a default strategy in attitude judgment. Specifically, judges should be prone to rely on implicitly formed attitudes if either concrete information about the entity to be judged cannot be accessed or if processing capacities are constrained at the time of judgment. The experiments reported above provide converging evidence for these core assumptions of the value-account model.

The value-account model provides an integrative theoretical account to attitude formation and change. On the conceptual level it postulates two distinct modes of information processing involving different principles of information integration and makes specific assumptions about mode application. It posits that individuals can develop multiple attitudes towards an entity and rely on multiple sources of knowledge when forming an attitude judgment. Moreover, the model spells out the conditions under which particular attitudes guide attitude judgment. On the phenomenological level, the value-account model covers automatic and deliberative processes, as well as affect-based and knowledge-based strategies in attitude formation.

Due to its broad scope, the value-account model is capable of addressing a variety of phenomena which have been described so far in quite unrelated areas of attitude research. Specifically, it covers implicit or automatic processes of attitude formation as they have been described in the literature on classical (e.g., Staats & Staats, 1958), evaluative (e.g., Walther, 2002) and operant conditioning of attitudes (e.g., Verplanck, 1955). On the other hand, the value-account model also addresses explicit processes involving the consideration of concrete evaluative information. Such processes have been seized by completely different approaches rooted in the tradition of expectancy-value models (e.g., Ajzen, 1991; Anderson, 1981, Fishbein & Ajzen, 1975) and the heuristics-and-biases program (Kahneman et al., 1993). Although these approaches share some background assumptions, they differ with regard to the postulated principles of information integration. The theory of planned behavior and its predecessor the model of reasoned action assume that attitude formation is guided by a signed summation principle (Ajzen, 1991; Fishbein & Ajzen, 1975). Information integration theory, in contrast, puts forward a weighted averaging rule as a universal principle of attitude formation and change (Anderson, 1981). Anderson devoted a great deal of effort to substantiate his claim empirically. He developed a scaling procedure termed "functional measurement" which allows for a critical test of the predictions of summation and averaging models. The averaging model has been repeatedly supported by studies involving participants to *explicitly* form their attitudes either online (Anderson, 1981) or from retrospection (Kahneman et al., 1993). The value-account model integrates both views. It claims that the summation principle applies to implicit and the averaging principle to explicit attitude formation. The research reviewed above strongly supports this notion.

It is worthwhile to point out the differences between VAs and other concepts of learned attitudes. Let us consider the MODE model (Fazio, 1990) and the model of dual attitudes (Wilson, Lindsey, & Schooler, 2000) as two prominent examples. These models jointly assume that an attitude, after it has been formed, can be stored in memory in association with an attitude object. In accordance with basic learning principles, the association between the attitude and the object is assumed to increase as a function of the frequency of joint activation (and other factors which need not to be considered here). In the case in which an attitude–object association has become strong, the mere encounter or recognition of an attitude object will automatically activate the pre-established attitude from memory. Both the MODE model and the dual attitude model view the learned attitude as a relatively stable evaluative orientation. Wilson and colleagues (2000) even claim that the prior attitude is resistant against change. They postulate that new attitudes do not overwrite old ones, but that both will coexist in memory. According to these models, learning processes change the *association* between the object and the attitude, but not the *value* (extremity, polarity) of the attitude. The notion of VA differs sharply from this view. We assume that VAs are constantly changed with each incoming peace of value-charged information about the attitude object. In such, a value account reflects the strength of association between an object and the positive and negative affective system rather than the strength of association between the object and a stable evaluation (see Betsch, 2002, for an elaboration of this position).

Taken together, the value-account model is capable of integrating a wide range of phenomena. It allows us to derive clear-cut and unique predictions about how attitudes are formed, stored in memory and used in attitude judgment. There are a number of predictions and implications to be derived from the theory which have not yet been studied, for example, the affect–cognition distinction and some other facets of the multiple attitude view, especially the idea that value accounts are learned and stored in relation to distinct types of situations. The empirical work reviewed in this chapter provides first empirical support for the validity of the value-account model. We thus find it worthwhile to pursue this line of research in the future.

## Acknowledgements

Our research was financially supported by the Deutsche Forschungsgemein-schaft (Grant BE 2012/1–2 to the first author). We thank Bronwyn Bosse for commenting on a draft version of this chapter.

## References

Ajzen, I. (1991). The theory of planned behavior. *Organizational Behavior and Human Decision Processes, 50*, 179–211.

Ajzen, I., & Fishbein, M. (1980). *Understanding attitudes and predicting social behavior*. Englewood Cliffs, NJ: Prentice-Hall.

Allport, G. W. (1935). Attitudes. In C. Murchison (Ed.), *Handbook of social psychology* (pp. 798–844). Worcester, MA: Clark University Press.

Anderson, N. H. (1971). Integration theory and attitude change. *Psychological Review, 78*, 171–206.

Anderson, N. H. (1981). Integration theory applied to cognitive responses and attitudes. In R. E. Petty, T. M. Ostrom & T. C. Brock (Eds.), *Cognitive responses in persuasion* (pp. 361–397). Hillsdale, NJ: Lawrence Erlbaum Associates, Inc.

Bargh, J. A. (1996). Principles of automaticity. In E. T. Higgins & A. Kruglanski (Eds.), *Social psychology: Handbook of basic principles* (pp. 169–183). New York: Guilford Press.

Berkowitz, L., & Knurek, D. A. (1969). Label-mediated hostility generalization. *Journal of Personality and Social Psychology, 13*, 200–206.

Betsch, T. (in press). Preference theory—an affect-based approach to recurrent decision making. In T. Betsch & S. Haberstroh (Eds.), *The routines of decision making*. Mahwah, NJ: Lawrence Erlbaum Associates, Inc.

Betsch, T., Hoffmann, K., Hoffrage, U., & Plessner, H. (2003). Intuition beyond recognition: When less familiar events are liked more. *Experimental Psychology, 50*, 49–54.

Betsch, T., Plessner, H., Hoffmann, K., Gütig, R., & Schwieren, C. (2001b). *Different mechanisms of information integration in implicit and explicit attitude formation*. Research paper, University of Heidelberg.

Betsch, T., Plessner, H., Schwieren, C., & Gütig, R. (2001a). I like it but I don't know why: a value-account approach to implicit attitude formation. *Personality and Social Psychology Bulletin, 27*, 242–253.

Bohner, G., Moskowitz, G. B., & Chaiken, S. (1995). The interplay of heuristic and systematic processing of social information. In W. Stroebe & M. Hewstone (Eds.), *European Review of Social Psychology, 6*, 33–68.

Bruner, J. S. (1957). Going beyond the information given. In H. Gulber et al. (Eds.), *Contemporary approaches to cognition* (pp. 41–69). Cambridge: Cambridge University Press.

Chaiken, S. (1980). Heuristic versus systematic information processing and the use of source versus message cues in persuasion. *Journal of Personality and Social Psychology, 39*, 752–766.

De Hower, J., & Hermans, D. (Eds.) (2001). Automatic affective processing [special issue]. *Cognition and Emotion, 15*.

Eagly, A. H., & Chaiken, S. (1993). *The psychology of attitudes.* Fort Worth, TX: Harcourt Brace Jovanovich.

Edwards, W. (1954). The theory of decision making. *Psychological Bulletin, 51,* 380–417.

Fazio, R. H. (1990). Multiple processes by which attitudes guide behavior: The MODE model as an integrative framework. *Advances in Experimental Social Psychology, 23,* 75–109.

Fishbein, M., & Ajzen, I. (1975). *Belief, attitude, intention and behavior: An introduction to theory and research.* Reading, MA: Addison-Wesley.

Fredrickson, B. L., & Kahnemann, D. (1993). Duration neglect in retrospective evaluations of affective episodes. *Journal of Personality and Social Psychology, 65,* 45–55.

Gigerenzer, G., Todd, P. M., & ABC Research Group (1999). *Simple heuristics that make us smart.* Oxford: Oxford University Press.

Goldstein, D. G., & Gigerenzer, G. (2002). Models of ecological rationality: The recognition heuristic. *Psychological Review, 109,* 75–90.

Greenwald, A. G., & Banaji, M. R. (1995). Implicit social cognition: Attitudes, self-esteem, and stereotypes. *Psychological Review, 102,* 4–27.

Greenwald, A. G., McGhee, D., & Schwartz, J. (1998). Measuring individual differences in implicit cognition: The implicit association test. *Journal of Personality and Social Psychology, 74,* 1464–1480.

Greenwald, A. G., & Nosek, B. A. (2001). Health of the Implicit Association Test at age 3. *Zeitschrift für Experimentelle Psychologie/Journal of Experimental Psychology, 48,* 85–93.

Höhle, C., Molter, B., & Betsch, T. (2001). *Retrospective evaluation under time pressure: Intuitive judgments reflect the entire sum of prior experiences.* Paper presented at the 18th SPUDM Conference in Amsterdam, Netherlands, 12–15 August.

Hovland, C. I., & Rosenberg, M. J. (1960). Summary and further theoretical issues. In C. I. Hovland & M. J. Rosenberg (Eds.), *Attitude organization and change: An analysis of consistency among attitude components* (pp. 198–232). New Haven, CT: Yale University Press.

Insko, C. A. (1965). Verbal reinforcement of attitude. *Journal of Personality and Social Psychology, 2,* 621–623.

Kahnemann, D., Fredrickson, B. L., Schreiber, C. A., & Redelmeier, D. A. (1993). When more pain is preferred to less: Adding a better end. *Psychological Science, 4,* 401–405.

Kahneman, D., Slovic, P., & Tversky, A. (Eds.) (1982). *Judgment under uncertainty: Heuristics and biases.* Cambridge: Cambridge University Press.

Klein, G. (1999). *Sources of power. How people make decisions.* Cambridge, MA: MIT Press.

McGuire, W. J. (1968). Personality and attitude change: An information-processing theory. In A. G. Greenwald, T. C. Brock, & T. M. Ostrom (Eds.), *Psychological foundations of attitudes* (pp. 171–196). New York: Academic Press.

Nisbett, R. E., & Ross, L. (1980). *Human inference and shortcoming of social judgment.* Englewood-Cliffs, NJ: Prentice-Hall.

Pavel, K. (2001). *Kontexteinfluesse auf die implizite Einstellungsbildung* [Context influences on implicit attitude formation]. Diploma thesis, University of Heidelberg.

Petty, R. E., & Cacioppo, J. T. (1986). The elaboration likelihood model of persuasion. In L. Berkowitz (Ed.), *Advances in experimental social psychology* (Vol. 19, pp. 123–205). San Diego, CA: Academic Press.

Plessner, H., & Banse, R. (Eds.) (2001). Attitude measurement using the Implicit Association Test (IAT) [special issue]. *Zeitschrift für Experimentelle Psychologie, 48* (2).

Plessner, H., Betsch, T., & Schallies, E. (2002). *Die Stabilität impliziter Nutzenkonten als Basis von Einstellungsurteilen über die Zeit* [The stability of value accounts as a basis of attitude judgements over time]. Unpublished raw data.

Plessner, H., Betsch, T., Schallies, E., & Schwieren, C. (2003). *Automatic on-line formation of implicit attitudes towards politicians.* Manuscript submitted for publication.

Plessner, H., Haberstroh, S., & Betsch, T. (2001). *Paradoxical effects in judgments and decisions as a consequence of implicit attitude formation.* Research paper, University of Heidelberg.

Redelmeier, D. A. & Kahnemann, D. (1996). Patient's memories of painful medical treatments: real-time and retrospective evaluations of two minimally invasive procedures. *Pain, 66,* 3–8.

Schwarz, N. (2000). AGENDA 2000—social judgment and attitudes: Warmer, more social, and less conscious. *European Journal of Social Psychology, 30,* 149–176.

Schwarz, N. & Clore, G. L. (1988). How do I feel about it? Informative functions of affective states. In K. Fiedler & J. Forgas (Eds.), *Affect, cognition and social behavior* (pp. 44–62). Toronto: Hogrefe.

Srull, T. K., & Wyer, R. S. Jr. (1989). Person memory and judgment. *Psychological Review, 96,* 58–83.

Staats, A. W., & Staats, C. K. (1958). Attitudes established by classical conditioning. *Journal of Abnormal Social Psychology, 57,* 37–40.

Thomas, W. I., & Znaniecki, F. (1918). *The Polish peasant in Europe and America.* Boston: Badger.

Verplanck, W. S. (1955). The control of the content of conversation: Reinforcement of statements of opinion. *Journal of Abnormal and Social Psychology, 51,* 668–676.

Von Neumann, J., & Morgenstern, O. (1944). *Theory of games and economic behavior.* Princeton: Princeton University Press.

Walther, E. (2002). Guilty by mere association: Evaluative conditioning and the spreading attitude effect. *Journal of Personality and Social Psychology, 82,* 919–934.

Wilson, T. D., Lindsey, S., & Schooler, J. W. (2000). A model of dual attitudes. *Psychological Review, 107,* 101–126.

Wundt, W. (1907). *Outlines of psychology.* Leipzig: Wilhelm Engelmann.

Zajonc, R. B. (1968). Attitudinal effects of mere exposure. *Journal of Personality and Social Psychology, 9* (Part 2, no. 2).

Zakay, D. (1993). The impact of time perception processes on decision making under time stress. In O. Svenson & A. J. Maule (Eds.), *Time pressure and stress in human judgment and decision making* (pp. 59–72). New York: Plenum Press.

# 12 The relationship between implicit attitudes and behavior

## Some lessons from the past, and directions for the future

*Patrick T. Vargas*

Under what conditions do our attitudes predict behavior? This question has received a great deal of attention during the past 75 years. However, the attention devoted to the question has focused almost exclusively on explicit (i.e., direct, self-report) measures of attitudes. Although implicit (i.e., indirect) measures have been in existence almost as long as explicit measures, relatively little research has examined the relationship between implicit attitudes and behavior. There are a number of reasons for the discrepancy in amount of research available on explicit attitude–behavior relations and implicit attitude–behavior relations, including the nearly complete disappearance of implicit attitude measures during the 1970s and 1980s. In the past ten years implicit attitude measures have made a remarkable comeback—indeed, in November 2001 an entire section of social psychology's flagship journal was devoted to implicit attitude measures.

This chapter attempts to re-examine a variety of issues relevant to explicit attitude–behavior relations in the light of current work on implicit attitude–behavior relations. Lessons learned in social psychology 25 and even 40 years ago can shed light on the current efforts to make sense of the relationship between implicit attitudes and behavior. This chapter has two main goals. First, it shows how the correspondence principle (Ajzen & Fishbein, 1977), and the theory of transfer appropriate processing (Blaxton, 1989; Morris, Bransford, & Franks, 1977; Roediger, 1990) might be applied to increase understanding of the relationship between implicit attitudes and behavior. Original research addressing the relationship between implicit attitudes and behavior will be presented to support this position. Second, the chapter presents a reintroduction of another classic piece of social psychological literature, Cook and Selltiz's (1964) call for multiple indicators of attitudes. It is proposed that Cook and Selltiz's taxonomy of attitude measures is still valid, and that it might be used to address weaknesses in the current position, and guide future research on the relationship between attitudes (both implicit and explicit) and behavior.

## Measuring explicit attitudes, and explicit attitude–behavior relations

Definitions of attitudes have become more constrained over the years, as attitude theory and measurement have influenced one another (Ostrom, 1989). Allport's (1935) definition of attitude was exceptionally broad: "An attitude is a mental and neural state of readiness, organized through experience, exerting a directive or dynamic influence upon the individual's response to all objects and situations with which it is related" (p. 810). As noted by Ostrom (1989), this definition includes a wide variety of states of readiness— awaiting the start of a footrace, judging the value of a painting, willingness to donate money at church, and so forth. Allport believed the evaluative dimension of attitudes to be a rather primitive aspect of the attitude concept. Krech and Crutchfield (1948) defined attitude as "an enduring organization of motivational, emotional, perceptual, and cognitive processes with respect to some aspect of the individual's world" (p. 152). Campbell's (1963) definition of attitudes, published nearly 30 years after Allport's, is similarly broad. He believed that attitudes were acquired behavioral dispositions that contained "residues of experience of such a nature as to guide, bias, or otherwise influence later behavior" (p. 97). But largely due to difficulties in measuring such a complex and far-reaching construct, researchers have tended to conceptualize attitudes in more narrow terms. Eagly and Chaiken's (1993) current definition of attitude is more specific, focusing on the evaluative nature of attitudes: "Attitude is a psychological tendency that is expressed by evaluating a particular entity with some degree of favor or disfavor" (p. 1). Attitude measurement techniques have developed alongside these different conceptual definitions, but have focused primarily on the evaluative component of attitudes.

Attitude measurement also has a long and conceptually varied history. However, this history is covered extensively elsewhere (see Himmelfarb, 1993; Ostrom, 1989). At present let us consider only explicit, or self-report, measures (e.g., Likert, Thustone, semantic differential scales). All of these measures assume that attitudes can be conceptualized as evaluative tendencies lying on a continuum ranging from extremely favorable toward the object to extremely unfavorable toward the object. Further, these measures assume that respondents can draw upon stored, evaluative, declarative knowledge to report their attitudes. Despite these similarities in explicit measures, the relationship between attitudes and behavior has been tumultuous.

The attitude concept held great promise for the prediction of behavior. Allport (1935) referred to attitudes as the cornerstone of social psychological research. Cohen (1964) noted that most researchers assumed that attitudes have a direct influence on behavior. However, others were less enthusiastic about the attitude construct (Corey, 1937; La Piere, 1934). Wicker's (1969) famous article attacking the utility of the attitude construct reviewed 33 published articles and found "correlation coefficients relating [attitudes and behavior] are rarely above .30, and often are near zero" (p. 65). Wicker concluded with the idea that perhaps abandoning the attitude construct would lead to more fruitful lines of research. Fortunately, rather than abandoning the attitude construct, researchers began to explore conditions under which attitudes did reliably predict behaviors.

One line of research addressing conditions under which explicit attitude measures predict behavior focused on the way in which behaviors were assessed. Fishbein and Ajzen (1974) distinguished between multiple-act and single-act criteria. The former refers to the single observation of a single act, or repeated observations of the same act; the latter refers to single or repeated observations of different behaviors. Fishbein and Ajzen noted that general attitude measures should not be expected to predict single-act criteria because attitudes toward objects may cause a variety of different responses to identical attitude objects. Thus, any single behavior is not necessarily a good indicator of attitude. Conversely, general attitude measures should be predictive of a variety of different acts over a period of time. An examination of environmental attitudes (Weigel & Newman, 1976) offered strong support for this notion: attitude correlations with 14 different single-act criteria ranged from .12 to .57. When these 14 individual behaviors were grouped into categories of behavior (smaller multiple-act criteria, ranging from two to eight behaviors), attitude correlations ranged from .36 to .50. When all 14 behaviors were grouped to form a behavioral index the correlation with attitudes was .62. Behavioral prediction was vastly improved when multiple-act criteria are used instead of single-act criteria (see also Davidson & Jaccard, 1979). Fishbein and Ajzen (1974) also noted that the behavioral criteria could be scaled according to Guttman, Thurstone, and Likert operating characteristics. Matching the operating characteristics of attitude scales and behavioral criteria also increased attitude–behavior correlations, although not as much as using multiple-act criteria instead of single-act criteria. Refining behavioral criteria accounts for only half of the attitude–behavior relationship.

A second line of research addressing conditions under which explicit attitude measures are correlated with behavior focused on the way in which attitudes were measured. Ajzen and Fishbein (1977) proposed that attitude–behavior correlations would be maximized to the extent that they are matched, or correspond to one another with regard to their target, action, context, and time elements. Behaviors are actions performed toward a particular target, in particular contexts, and times, and attitudes can be assessed with reference to these four criteria, as well. Ajzen and Fishbein (1977) identified studies that varied in the extent to which the attitude measure and the behavioral criteria corresponded. Among studies with low correspondence, 26 showed non-significant attitude–behavior correlations, 1 showed low or inconsistent correlation (defined as $r < .40$), and none showed high correlation ($r >$ or $= .40$). Among studies with partial correspondence, 20 showed low correlations, 47 showed low or inconsistent correlations, and 4 showed high correlations. Among studies with high correspondence, none showed non-significant correlation, 9 showed low or inconsistent correlations, and 37 showed high correlations. More recently, Kraus's (1995) meta-analysis of attitude–behavior relations demonstrated a large effect of correspondence on attitude–behavior relations. There are, of course, other variables that moderate the strength of the attitude–behavior relationship: affective-cognitive consistency (Norman, 1975), direct experience (Fazio, Zanna, & Cooper, 1978), the time interval between attitude and behavior measurement (Davidson & Jaccard, 1979), attitude strength (Kraus, 1995; Petty & Krosnick, 1995), and social desirability concerns.

When respondents are unwilling and/or unable to report their true attitudes, one would expect attitude–behavior relations to suffer. People may be unwilling to report their true attitudes due to social desirability concerns, or unable to report attitudes for unfamiliar objects. Consider social desirability concerns, for example. Corey (1937) measured students' attitudes toward cheating and tried to predict actual cheating behavior throughout the course of a school semester. He found that the correlation between attitudes toward cheating and actual cheating behavior was .024. Of course, it may be argued here that Corey could not expect high attitude–behavior correlations because he used a single-act criterion and had only moderate correspondence between the attitude measure and the behavior. Nevertheless, despite researchers' best abilities to measure both attitudes and behaviors, if respondents are unwilling to report their true attitudes it is unlikely that explicit attitude measures will be good predictors of behavior. When social desirability concerns are expected to limit the efficacy of explicit measures, researchers have turned to more indirect, or implicit attitude measures.

Implicit attitude measures can also assess evaluative tendencies, but they do not require respondents to consciously recall stored evaluative information. Throughout this chapter "implicit" is used in the same sense that cognitive psychologists refer to implicit memory measures: "Implicit tests of retention measure transfer (or priming) from past experience on tasks that do not require conscious recollection of recent experiences for their performance" (Roediger, 1990, p. 1043). This is consistent with Greenwald and Banaji's (1995) definition of implicit attitudes as "*introspectively unidentified (or inaccurately identified) traces of past experience* that mediate favorable or unfavorable feeling, thought, or action toward social objects" (p. 8; emphasis added).

Implicit attitude measures were developed shortly after Thurstone's (1928) initial work on attitude measurement (e.g., Proshansky, 1943). These measures come in a variety of different forms, including disguised self-reports (e.g., Hammond, 1948; Selltiz & Cook, 1966; Thistlethwaite, 1950), behavioral indicators (e.g., Byrne, Ervin, & Lamberth, 1970; Milgram, Mann, & Harter, 1965; Webb, Campbell, Schwartz, Sechrest, & Grove, 1981), physiological procedures (e.g., Cacioppo, Petty, Losch, & Kim, 1986), and most recently response-time and priming-based measures (e.g., Dovidio & Gaertner, 1991; Dovidio, Kawakami, Johnson, Johnson, & Howard 1997; Fazio, Jackson, Dunton, & Williams, 1995; Greenwald, McGhee, & Schwartz, 1998). The use of implicit attitude measures in social psychological research has wavered over the years. Disguised self-reports fell out of favor due to perceived concerns about their reliability and validity (e.g., Lemon, 1973). If one is studying attitude–behavior relations, the use of behavioral indicators may be considered redundant (i.e., using behavior to predict behavior; but see Albarracin & Wyer, 2000; Ouellette & Wood, 1998). Physiological procedures are not widely used because they tend to require careful training and sophisticated (and expensive) equipment. However, there has been a recent flurry of research using priming and response time based measures. Let us now consider some of this research in light of attitude–behavior relations.

## The relationship between explicit and implicit attitude measures

There are at least two curious findings regarding explicit and implicit attitude measures, their relationship with one another, and with behavior. First, explicit and implicit attitude measures, although ostensibly tapping a single construct, are not consistently correlated with each other (e.g., Bosson, Swann, & Pennebaker, 2000). This inconsistency does not appear to be attributable to social desirability alone as even within one attitude domain (e.g., racial prejudice) some studies report reliable correlations between explicit and implicit measures (e.g., Cunningham, Preacher, & Banaji, 2001; Hense, Penner, & Nelson, 1995; Kawakami, Dion, & Dovidio, 1998; Wittenbrink, Judd, & Park, 1997), whereas others do not (e.g., Fazio et al., 1995; Greenwald et al., 1998). Even within methods, the relationship between explicit and implicit measures varies: Dovidio et al. (1997) report a significant correlation in one study, and no correlation in another using identical methods. Wavering correlations are not the only dissociation between the measures; they also can be differentially related to relevant behavior.

Implicit and explicit attitude measures, when uncorrelated, tend to predict qualitatively different types of behaviors (see Wilson, Lindsey, & Schooler, 2000, for a review). Implicit attitude measures tend to predict behaviors that are spontaneous, uncontrollable, and/or not consciously monitored, but do not seem to be related to more deliberative, consciously controlled behaviors. Conversely, explicit attitude measures tend to predict deliberative, controlled behaviors, but do not seem to be related to unmonitored or uncontrollable behaviors. For example, in work by Fazio and colleagues (1995), a priming-based implicit measure tapping participants' implicit attitudes toward African-Americans correlated with an African-American experimenter's judgments of participants' friendliness and involvement, but not with participants' ratings of the justness of the Rodney King verdict. An explicit attitude measure showed the opposite set of relationships (see also Dovidio et al., 1997; and see Spalding & Hardin, 1999, for an example unrelated to prejudice). When explicit and implicit measures are uncorrelated, why should explicit measures predict only deliberative behavior, and implicit measures predict only spontaneous behavior?

Wilson et al. (2000) proposed a model of dual attitudes to explain the differential predictive ability of implicit and explicit attitude measures. According to this perspective, explicit and implicit attitudes toward a single object can coexist in memory (see also Dovidio et al., 1997; Greenwald & Banaji, 1995). Upon encountering an attitude object for which an individual has dual attitudes, implicit attitudes are activated automatically, whereas explicit attitudes must be called to mind with effort. Wilson and colleagues propose four distinct types of dual attitudes, and explicate conditions under which implicit and explicit attitudes are endorsed. They suggest that implicit attitudes influence behaviors that people cannot or do not consciously control (e.g., nonverbal behaviors such as blinking and stuttering), regardless of whether the explicit attitude has been retrieved. Explicit attitudes, on the other hand, influence consciously controlled behaviors. This perspective on the differential predictive ability of implicit and explicit attitude measures is related to classic work on attitude–behavior correspondence.

Again, the general principle of correspondence (Ajzen & Fishbein, 1977) states that attitude–behavior correlations will be maximized to the extent that attitude measures and behaviors are matched in their level of specificity, especially with regard to action, target, context, and time. We can draw on compatibility theory to extend the logic of Wilson et al. and better understand the aforementioned relationships among explicit and implicit measures and deliberative and spontaneous behaviors. The level of correspondence between explicit measures and deliberative behaviors should be relatively high, because explicit measures require individuals to consciously and deliberatively access stored attitudinal information, just as deliberative behaviors require individuals to consciously choose a course of action. Thus the cognitive activities required to retrieve stored attitudes match the activities required to make juridic judgments and the like. Similarly, the level of correspondence between implicit measures and spontaneous behaviors should be relatively high, because implicit measures rely on automatic, non-conscious information processing, just as spontaneous behaviors rely on automatic, non-conscious information processing. Thus, the cognitive activities required to respond to implicit attitude measures match the activities required to perform spontaneous behaviors (see Fazio, 1990, for a related argument).

Conversely, the degree of correspondence between explicit measures and spontaneous behaviors, and between implicit measures and deliberative behaviors, should be relatively low because of the discordance in cognitive processes. Thus the differential correlations among explicit and implicit measures and deliberative and spontaneous behaviors reported by Fazio et al. (1995), Dovidio et al. (1997) and Spalding and Hardin (1999) may be attributed to differential compatibility of the cognitive processing underlying attitude measures and behaviors. Extending this logic, we can propose that the previous failure of implicit measures to predict deliberative behavior, as well as that of explicit measures to predict spontaneous behavior, may be attributable to a confounding of type of attitude measure and level of information processing required to respond to it.

## Unconfounding measures and underlying processes

Although not previously recognized, it seems that type of information processing (spontaneous versus deliberative) can be orthogonal to type of attitude measure (implicit versus explicit). As can be seen in Table 12.1, the measures used in the contemporary studies described above fall into two of the possible four quadrants. In the top, right cell we have questionnaire measures that are explicit and require deliberative processing. In the bottom, left cell are priming and response time based measures that are implicit and rely on spontaneous, non-conscious processing. But what of the other cells in the 2 × 2? In the top, left cell are explicit measures (i.e., require intentional recall of stored attitudes) that rely on spontaneous processing; and, in the bottom, right cell are measures that are implicit (i.e., do not require conscious recall of stored attitudes) but rely on deliberative information processing. What are these measures and what relationships would such measures have with spontaneous and deliberative behaviors?

Wilson et al. (2000) have proposed an explicit, spontaneous measure, wherein respondents must report their attitudes within a short (3 sec.) time frame. Wilson et al. suggest that this method causes participants to rely on habitual, stored responses, rather than on newly formed attitudes. A spontaneous, explicit measure (e.g., speeded responses, or responses given under a cognitive load manipulation, as in Gilbert & Hixon, 1991) may thus be used to tap individuals' habitual responses to attitude objects. Although Wilson et al. (2000) do not hypothesize how such a measure might relate to behavior, such a spontaneous explicit measure may reliably predict variance in spontaneous behavior, to the extent that the measure and the behavior both rely on spontaneous information processing.

A deliberative implicit attitude measure would require effortful information processing, and yet would not require respondents to intentionally access their stored attitudes. Regarding deliberative implicit attitude measures, there

*Table 12.1* Type of attitude measure by level of information processing factorial

| Type of attitude measure | Level of information processing | |
| --- | --- | --- |
| | *Spontaneous* | *Deliberative* |
| *Explicit* | Speeded response, cognitive load | Semantic differential, Likert scales |
| *Implicit* | Implicit Association Test, priming measures | Projective tests |

are two issues that must be addressed. The first is whether they can predict deliberative behaviors. If so, the second is whether they can predict behavior above and beyond deliberative explicit attitude measures. The first issue is addressed below, and the second will be addressed later. According to the current perspective, deliberative implicit measures should predict deliberative behaviors because the measure and the behavior have a high degree of correspondence with respect to the level of information processing required. The logic behind this prediction is derived from the notion of *transfer appropriate processing* (Blaxton, 1989; Morris et al., 1977; Roediger, 1990).

Transfer appropriate processing theory has been used to explain dissociations between explicit and implicit memory tests. One illustrative study may be useful in describing these dissociations. Smith and Branscombe (1988) conducted an experiment in which participants first studied words either by reading them or generating them from relevant phrases (e.g., "attended church three times a week") and the first letter of each word (e.g., "r———"). Three types of memory tests—one explicit and two implicit—showed two divergent results. Free recall (an explicit memory test) performance was best when participants had generated words; word fragment completion (an implicit memory test) was best when participants had read words; and category accessibility (an implicit memory test) performance was best when participants had generated words. How to explain divergent results from two implicit memory tests?

Roediger and colleagues have explained such results by suggesting that memory performance is best when the type of cognitive processing at study matches the type of cognitive processing at testing. In the Smith and Branscombe (1988) study, generating words, free recall, and category accessibility tests all rely on conceptual processing, whereas reading words and word fragment completion rely on perceptual (i.e., data-driven) processing. Thus the divergent memory results among the three tests can be explained in terms of transfer appropriate processing. The present research relies on a similar application of transfer appropriate processing: it is expected that implicit measures for which respondents must engage in deliberative cognitive processing will reliably predict deliberative behaviors. Importantly, as will be explained shortly, these implicit deliberative measures should sometimes predict behavior *over and above* explicit deliberative measures. Interestingly, although not widely recognized, deliberative implicit measures have been developed and used in prior attitude research. These procedures have typically been referred to as providing "indirect" measures of attitudes (e.g., Petty & Cacioppo, 1986).

## Classic work on deliberative, implicit (indirect) attitude measures

A number of studies have shown that implicit attitude measures that do not rely on spontaneous information processing can be related to both explicit attitudes and deliberative behaviors. In one study (Proshansky, 1943), students known to have pro- and anti-labor union attitudes were shown a series of images (previously judged to be neither pro- nor anti-labor) and asked to write for two and a half minutes about each picture. Three judges coded the responses as either favorable or unfavorable toward union labor. This "projective technique" was found to be highly correlated with a traditional measure of attitudes toward labor unions.

Other researchers have also used measures that may be considered both implicit and deliberative. Hammond's (1948) error-choice technique, for example, required respondents to take a test ostensibly assessing their knowledge about current events. In fact, the "test" featured two types of questions: the first featured response options that were equidistant and in opposite directions from the true answers, e.g., "Man-days lost because of strikes from January to June, 1946, were (1) 34.5 (2) 98.6 million" (Hammond, 1948), p. 48). The second featured questions that were indeterminate, e.g., "Molotov is known in diplomatic circles for his (1) excellent (2) poor manners" (Hammond, 1948, p. 48). The respondent's attitude was inferred from the direction of the response. If a respondent tended to select as true those items that were more favorable toward union labor (e.g., choice 1 in the first example), one can infer a positive attitude toward unions, and vice versa. Importantly, Hammond noted: "The particular effect with which we shall be concerned here will be the systematic *error in perception and recall*" due to the influence of attitudes (p. 38, emphasis in original). Thistlethwaite (1950) examined distortions in logical reasoning as a function of attitudes, finding attitude-congruent distortions (e.g., students at Northern colleges and universities were more likely to accept logically flawed, but emotionally charged arguments in favor of integration, students at Southern colleges were more likely to accept the opposite arguments). Waly and Cook (1965) and Selltiz and Cook (1966) used similar techniques.

## Deliberative implicit measures should predict behavior

As explained above, contemporary research on the relationship between explicit and implicit attitude measures and different types of behavior suggests that when implicit measures diverge from explicit ones, the implicit measures should not be predictive of deliberative, controlled behaviors. On the other hand, the logic inherent to transfer appropriate processing and classic research on implicit (indirect) attitude measures indicates that deliberative implicit attitude measures might be used to predict deliberative behavior. Importantly, it is also possible that deliberative implicit attitude measures could predict unique variance in deliberative behavior, above and beyond the level of prediction gained by traditional, direct, explicit attitude measures.

In order to understand why deliberative implicit attitude measures might predict unique variance in deliberative behavior (i.e., over and above deliberative explicit attitude measures), it is helpful to consider an example:

> Mary didn't go to church once the whole time she was in college, but she claimed that she was still a very religious person. She said that she prayed occasionally, and that she believed in Christian ideals. Sometimes she watched religious programs on TV like the 700 Club, or the Billy Graham Crusade.

Based on the above information, how religious would you judge Mary to be? As explained further shortly, if you thought she was quite religious, you show evidence of a non-religious attitude. If you thought she was not very religious, however, you show evidence of a religious attitude. The above description of Mary is actually one item in a series of vignettes that describe characters behaving in somewhat discrepant ways. Following each vignette, respondents are asked to rate the targets with respect to the attitude object under consideration. For example, following the brief description of Mary, respondents would rate the extent to which they believe that Mary is religious. This measure is deliberative, in that it requires effortful consideration of the religiosity displayed by a protagonist in a scenario, and implicit, in that it does not require intentional retrieval of respondents' own attitudes toward religion in order to respond.

According to the logic behind this measure, different people should *encode* these scenarios in different ways (Hastorf & Cantril, 1954). Specifically, judgments about Mary's religiosity should be unintentionally influenced by the perceiver's own attitudes toward religion. Respondents likely do not pause to consider their own attitudes toward religion before making social judgments—Mary just *seems* to be one way or another. Because Mary behaves in both religious (occasional prayer, watching religious TV programming) and non-religious (skipping church for years) ways, her behavior should be discrepant for both religious and atheistic people, alike. Thus, the behaviors should lie in both religious and atheistic people's latitudes of rejection, and should be contrasted away by both (Sherif & Hovland, 1961). Very religious people should see Mary's behaviors as rather non-religious. Very atheistic people should see Mary's behaviors as rather religious. So, to the extent that individuals interpret the behaviors as relatively religious, one can infer that the perceivers, themselves, are not religious.

This differential interpretation of events has the potential to be an important independent determinant of how an individual responds to an object, person, or situation. The way in which one interprets an event, favorably or unfavorably, should cause differential positive or negative behavior. Consider, for example, two people reading an article about capital punishment. One sees a series of well-argued, valid points; the other sees a series of poorly argued, trivial points. Both are privy to the same series of arguments, but their differential interpretations of the arguments encourage voting for or against capital punishment, respectively (Lord, Ross, & Lepper, 1979;

Vallone, Ross, & Lepper, 1985). Indeed, it is often these biases in information processing that justify or enable the individual's preferential response to an attitude object (see Fazio, 1990; Karpinski & von Hippel, 1996; Kunda, 1990). Presumably, not all individuals use their attitudes to the same extent to interpret the surrounding environment. To the extent that a deliberative implicit measure taps into the tendency for a person's attitudes to bias interpretation of situations, this measure could contribute to behavioral prediction above and beyond a deliberative explicit measure that does not tap into this bias.

## Research using deliberative implicit attitude measures

A series of three studies based on these ideas attempted to demonstrate that deliberative implicit attitude measures tapping biased information processing are distinct from traditional attitude measures, and can be used to predict unique variance in behavior for a wide variety of attitude objects (Vargas, von Hippel, & Petty, 2004). A first study examined an attitude object for which social desirability concerns were expected to limit the efficacy of traditional, explicit attitude measures, viz., dishonesty. There were two critical dependent measures in the study. First, participants were given the opportunity to cheat on an anagram test (single-act criterion). Second, participants completed a self-report checklist of dishonest behaviors they may have performed (multiple-act criteria). Participants first completed the anagram test, scored their own answers, and then completed a counterbalanced packet containing a deliberative explicit measure (a semantic differential assessing attitudes toward being dishonest), a deliberative implicit measure (described below), and a variety of other measures (including the Balanced Inventory of Desirable Responding, BIDR; Paulhus, 1991).

The deliberative implicit measure consisted of a series of vignettes describing different people engaged in ambiguously dishonest behaviors. For example, one vignette was about a woman who had checked out a rare book from her school library. The woman had received a notice that the book was overdue, and she decided to keep it by reporting it as lost and paying a relatively small fine. Following each vignette, participants were asked to indicate how honest they thought the characters in the vignettes were. According to the logic behind this measure, different participants should encode the scenarios in different ways. Because the targets of the scenarios behave in moderately dishonest ways, their behavior should be discrepant for honest and dishonest people alike; that is, their behavior should lie in both honest and dishonest people's latitudes of rejection, and should be contrasted away (Sherif & Hovland, 1961). Thus, the processing bias tapped by this measure is a contrast effect. Honest people (or those favorable toward honesty) should see the ambiguous behaviors as rather dishonest. Dishonest people (or those favorable toward dishonesty), on the other hand, should see the ambiguous behaviors as "opportunities" or as "clever behaviors" rather than dishonest.

A variety of predictions regarding the explicit attitude measure might be made here. According to processing-based correspondence principles, a deliberative explicit measure might predict both actual cheating behavior and a self-reported index of dishonest behavior because both require deliberative information processing. According to traditional correspondence principles (action, target, time, context), a deliberative explicit measure assessing attitudes toward "being dishonest" should be a moderate predictor of multiple behaviors, because the broad (i.e., non-specific) attitude measure should correspond with a wide variety of behaviors. According to single/multiple-act criteria, a deliberative explicit measure should only predict the comprehensive behavioral index of dishonest behaviors. But perhaps most importantly for the present study, considering social desirability concerns associated with attitudes toward dishonesty, a deliberative explicit attitude measure should predict neither behavior. Thus, expectations for the deliberative explicit measure were low. But what about the deliberative implicit measure?

According to processing-based correspondence theory, a deliberative implicit measure should predict both actual cheating and a self-reported index of dishonest behavior because both require deliberative information processing. According to traditional correspondence principles (action, target, time, context), a deliberative implicit measure relying on judgments about individuals engaged in ambiguously dishonest behaviors should predict only behaviors that correspond to the behaviors presented in the vignettes. According to single/multiple act criteria, a deliberative implicit measure should only predict the comprehensive behavioral index of dishonest behaviors. Considering social desirability concerns associated with attitudes toward dishonesty, a deliberative implicit attitude measure should predict both actual behavior and overall self-reported dishonesty, because social desirability concerns should not influence responses to implicit measures. Finally, to the extent that the deliberative implicit measure taps biased processing it should predict variance in behavior beyond that predicted by an explicit measure.

The deliberative explicit and implicit attitude measures[1] were not reliably correlated with one another, $r = .11$. Simultaneous multiple regression analyses[2] revealed that both the deliberative explicit and deliberative implicit measures reliably predicted self-reported dishonest behavior (betas = .15 and .21, respectively), even after controlling for impression management, self-deception, and students' high school GPA (interestingly, all of these measures reliably predicted self-reported dishonesty—betas −.46, .15, and −.21, respectively). A second regression analysis examining an actual instance

1 Reliability scores (Cronbach's alpha) were adequate: .89 for the semantic differential, .70 for the deliberative implicit measure.
2 Simultaneous multiple regression analyses are reported throughout for the sake of simplicity. Hierarchical regression analyses were also performed on all data sets, and the obtained results were identical to those reported.

of cheating revealed that only the deliberative implicit attitude measure was a reliable predictor (beta = .20; all other betas < .15). Thus, there is some evidence suggesting that level of information processing might be important in understanding when implicit attitude measures predict behavior. When the level of information processing is matched, implicit measures can predict unique variance in both self-reported and actual behavior, beyond that predicted by traditional, deliberative explicit measures. But it is possible that the predictive advantage conferred by the deliberative implicit measure is due to social desirability concerns limiting the efficacy of explicit measures. A second study sought to test the efficacy of deliberative implicit measures when social desirability concerns are nonexistent. Pretesting helped determine that attitudes toward political conservatism were almost completely independent of social desirability concerns.

In a second study participants again completed a counterbalanced packet of materials, including two deliberative explicit measures assessing attitudes toward being conservative (one semantic differential, and a revised version of the Wilson Conservatism Scale, Wilson, 1985), and one deliberative implicit attitude measure that was conceptually identical to the ones described above. In this measure, target characters behaved in ways that were ambiguously or conflictingly politically conservative. There were again two dependent measures in this study: the first was a self-report index of liberal and conservative behaviors; the second was a page appended to the back of the experimental packets indicating that students could sign one of two lines to request information from campus political groups.

According to processing-based correspondence principles, deliberative explicit measures should predict both actual political behavior, and a self-reported index of liberal/conservative behavior because both require deliberative information processing. According to traditional correspondence principles (action, target, time, context), deliberative explicit measures assessing attitudes toward "political conservatism" should be moderate predictors of multiple behaviors. According to single/multiple-act criteria, deliberative explicit measures should only predict the comprehensive behavioral index of dishonest behaviors. And the deliberative implicit measure?

According to processing-based correspondence theory, a deliberative implicit measure should predict both actual political behavior and a self-reported index of liberal/conservative behavior because both require deliberative information processing. According to traditional correspondence principles (action, target, time, context), a deliberative implicit measure relying on judgments about individuals engaged in ambiguously conservative behaviors should predict only behaviors that correspond to the behaviors presented in the vignettes. According to single/multiple-act criteria, a deliberative implicit measure should only predict the behavioral index of liberal/conservative behaviors. Finally, the biased processing tapped by the deliberative implicit measure should allow it to predict unique variance in behavior, beyond that predicted by explicit measures.

As would be expected, the two deliberative explicit measures were reliably correlated with one another, $r = .60$. However, neither was reliably correlated with the deliberative implicit measure, $rs < .06$.[3] Simultaneous multiple regression analyses examining the behavioral index revealed that both deliberative explicit measures reliably predicted unique variance (betas = .38 and .50). However, the deliberative implicit measure was only a marginal predictor (beta = .11). Identical analysis of the actual political behavior revealed that one of the deliberative explicit measures reliably predicted unique variance (the semantic differential, beta = .32), whereas the other was marginally significant (beta = .21). Importantly, the deliberative implicit measure reliably predicted unique variance in an actual behavior (beta = .25), beyond what was predicted by traditional deliberative explicit measures. This suggests that the information-processing correspondence is relevant and meaningful, and that the biased processing tapped by this measure has the potential to add to explained variance in behavior. However, it is somewhat surprising that two deliberative explicit measures would predict unique variance beyond one another. This suggests the possibility that there is nothing unique about the deliberative implicit measure, and that simply adding more deliberative explicit measures might function equally well. In order to test whether a deliberative implicit measure can predict unique variance in behavior beyond that predicted by a number of deliberative explicit measures, a third study was conducted.

As in study two, a domain in which social desirability concerns were minimized was sought, and religious attitudes and behavior seemed to fulfill this characteristic.[4] In this study, all measures were presented to participants in a split-half, split-method technique. At time one, participants in the study completed counterbalanced packets containing half of each of the measures (three deliberative explicit measures, one deliberative implicit measure, a comprehensive behavioral checklist of religious and non-religious behaviors). At time two they completed the second half of the measures presented in a random order via MediaLab experimental software (Jarvis, 2002). The split-half, split-method technique allowed the separation of five separate deliberative explicit attitude measures (for those keeping score, it should have been six, but one of the measures was omitted from the regression analysis due to collinearity concerns).[5] Also, this study included an Implicit Association Test, administered at time two. The dependent measure used in this study was

---

3 Reliability scores (Cronbach's alpha) were adequate: .95 for the semantic differential, .79 for the conservatism scale, and .63 for the deliberative implicit measure.

4 Correlations among religious attitudes (as indexed by three deliberative explicit measures) and the impression management subscale of the BIDR were less than .12.

5 The one-item measure and the semantic differential were correlated at .82 at Time 1. The one item measure was collapsed across both times to obviate collinearity concerns.

a modified version of the comprehensive behavioral index of religious behaviors used in Fishbein and Ajzen (1974).

Again, according to processing-based correspondence principles, deliberative explicit measures should be correlated with the comprehensive index of religious behavior because both the measure and the behavior require deliberative information processing. According to traditional correspondence principles (action, target, time, context) deliberative explicit measures should be moderate predictors of multiple behaviors. According to single/multiple-act criteria, deliberative explicit measures should predict the comprehensive behavioral index of dishonest behaviors. Thus, expectations for the deliberative explicit measures were high. And regarding the deliberative implicit measure?

According to processing-based correspondence theory, the deliberative implicit measure should predict the self-reported index of liberal/conservative behavior. According to traditional correspondence principles (action, target, time, context), a deliberative implicit measure should predict only behaviors that correspond to the behaviors presented in the vignettes. According to single/multiple-act criteria, a deliberative implicit measure should predict the behavioral index of liberal/conservative behaviors. Further, if the deliberative implicit attitude measure predicts unique variance in self-reported religious behavior beyond that predicted by five deliberative explicit measures, it seems reasonable to suggest that the deliberative implicit measure is indeed tapping something unique. But what about the spontaneous implicit measure, the IAT? According to processing-based correspondence, the IAT should not predict deliberative behaviors because the measure and the behaviors do not rely on the same level of information processing. According to traditional correspondence principles, the IAT should be moderately related to the comprehensive behavioral index. According to the single/multiple-act criteria, the IAT should be related to the multiple-act criteria.

The three deliberative explicit measures were reliably correlated with one another $.41 < rs < .77$. However, none of these measures were reliably correlated with the deliberative implicit measure, $rs < .04$. Two of the three deliberative explicit measures (the semantic differential and the one-item measure) were reliably correlated with the IAT, $rs = .23$ and $.25$, respectively; the RAS was marginally correlated with the IAT, $r = .12$.[6] When all of the measures were entered into a simultaneous multiple regression equation, three of the five deliberative explicit measures were reliable predictors, and the deliberative implicit measure continued to reliably predict unique variance in self-reported behavior. The IAT did not predict unique variance in the behavioral index. Study three provides further support for the utility of implicit attitude measures, in that one was able to reliably predict unique variance in self-reported

6 Split-half/split-method correlations were roughly comparable with one another: .30 for the RAS, .68 for the semantic differential, .51 for the one-item measure, and .45 for the deliberative implicit measure.

behavior beyond that predicted by a number of explicit measures. Also, study three provides additional evidence of the importance of the processing-based correspondence principle, in that a deliberative implicit measure reliably predicted unique variance in deliberative behaviors, but a spontaneous implicit measure did not. Finally, study three also suggests that the deliberative implicit measure is indeed tapping something other than what can be assessed with explicit measures.

## Some new developments

More recent research has offered some mixed evidence regarding the principle of processing-based correspondence. Supporting the notion of processing-based correspondence, a conceptual replication of the Fazio et al. (1995) paper by McConnell and Leibold (2001) used deliberative explicit measures and the IAT to predict prejudiced behavior toward an African-American experimenter. Consistent with processing-based correspondence, the IAT, a spontaneous implicit measure, predicted spontaneous behaviors (speaking time, smiling, speech errors, speech hesitation); whereas explicit measures were unrelated to spontaneous behaviors.

There are also some studies providing potentially disconfirming evidence for the processing-based correspondence idea. Work on the prediction of condom use by Marsh et al. (2001) has demonstrated that deliberative explicit measures reliably predicted the tendency to use condoms with stable partners, but that the IAT predicted the tendency to use condoms among casual partners. The extent to which condom use with casual partners is a spontaneous or deliberative behavior is debatable, at least. People may be very deliberative about engaging in sex with casual partners. Thus, it is unclear whether the Marsh et al. research contradicts the current position. Further work examining the extent to which condom use under different conditions is spontaneous or deliberative is needed.

Other work provides more compelling evidence that spontaneous implicit measures can predict deliberative behavior. In one study by Swanson, Rudman, and Greenwald (2001), IATs assessing attitudes toward smoking and vegetarianism reliably predicted those deliberative behaviors. Of course, it is possible that smoking and vegetarianism are sufficiently habitualized or proceduralized, behaviors that they require no deliberative thought (Anderson, 1982; Smith, 1994). Another study by Wänke et al. (2002) demonstrated that the IAT can predict consumer choices that are at least somewhat deliberative. Participants completed a deliberative explicit measure of their attitudes toward different brands of coffee, and a spontaneous implicit measure (IAT) assessing coffee preferences. In simultaneous multiple regression analyses both deliberative explicit and spontaneous implicit measures reliably predicted unique variance in the type and number of free coffee samples selected.

Thus, it seems that even spontaneous implicit measures might be more useful than previously thought—that is, both spontaneous and deliberative implicit measures may have utility in predicting deliberative behavior beyond that provided by explicit measures. Rather than focusing on implicit *versus* explicit attitude measures, it may be more fruitful, from a behavioral prediction standpoint, to focus on the simultaneous use of both implicit *and* explicit measures. But are attitude researchers limited to only two classes of attitude measures?

## Classes of measures and multiple indicators

In 1964 Stuart Cook and Claire Selltiz published a prescient paper identifying five classes of attitude measures, and calling for the use of multiple indicators in attitude measurement. Remarkably, after nearly four decades of attitude research, the five classes of measures identified by Cook and Selltiz clearly encompass all contemporary attitude measures. The first group "measures in which the material from which inferences are drawn consists of self-reports of beliefs, feelings, behavior, etc., toward an object or class of objects" (p. 39) is now commonly referred to as explicit attitude measures. The second group, behavioral measures, is now commonly viewed as attitudinal outcomes, rather than measures. For the purposes of the present research, there seems little to be gained by attempting to predict behavior, on the basis of behavior. A third group of attitude measures is physiological.

A fourth group, which has frequently been employed in the service of behavioral prediction, encompasses contemporary implicit attitude measures. In this group, inferences about attitudes are made on the basis of performance on "objective" tasks. As defined by Cook and Selltiz: "Approaches in this category present the respondent with specific tasks to be performed; they are presented as tests of information or ability, or simply as jobs that need to be done. The assumption common to all of them is that performance may be influenced by attitude, and that a systematic bias in performance reflects the influence of the attitude" (1964, p. 50). It is clear that this group of attitude measures would encompass priming-based implicit attitude measures, and the IAT. Both rely on the automatic activation of attitudes, and the influence of attitude activation on simple, objective tasks such as lexical decisions and categorization. Attitude researchers have largely overlooked the final group of measures.

Measures relying on the interpretation of partially structured stimuli, as defined by Cook and Selltiz, are similar to objective measures in "that, while there may be no attempt to disguise the reference to the attitudinal object, the subject is not asked to state his own reactions directly; he is ostensibly describing a scene, a character, or the behavior of a third person" (p. 47). Classic attitude measures belonging to this group include projective tests (e.g., Proshansky, 1943). More recent use of such a measure is, of course, described above: the vignettes employed as deliberative implicit measures may best be thought of as partially structured attitude measures. Another example of a more contemporary attitude measure from this category is respondents' style of completing sentence stubs (von Hippel, Sekaquaptewa, & Vargas, 1995, 1997; Sekaquaptewa, Espinoza, Thompson, Vargas, & von Hippel, in press). For example, Sekaquaptewa et al. (2003, Study 2) presented participants with a series of sentence beginnings that were stereotype congruent and incongruent for African-Americans. Participants were asked to complete the sentences however they saw fit. The tendency to make external attributions for stereotype-incongruent behavior by African-Americans, and internal attributions for stereotype-congruent behavior by African-Americans reliably predicted the positivity of social interactions with an African-American confederate.

Perhaps most importantly, Cook and Selltiz acknowledged that any single attitude index provides a relatively crude measure of the latent attitude construct: "This orientation leads to emphasis on the need for a number of different measurement approaches to provide a basis for estimating the common underlying disposition, and to the expectation that data from these approaches will not be perfectly correlated" (p. 37). Different types of attitude measures, even when assessing attitudes toward the same construct, might thus be expected to be only moderately correlated with one another. Further, to the extent that different types of measures tap different aspects of attitudes, multiple indicators might work together to enhance behavioral prediction.

## Conclusions

In the 75 years since Thurstone declared that attitudes can be measured, a number of methods for doing so have been developed. Most of these methods have relied on explicit self-reports and have assessed individuals' evaluative feelings, beliefs, and thoughts about attitude objects. Implicit, or indirect, attitude measures traditionally have been seen as secondary measures, to be used only when explicit measures might be suspect (such as when social desirability concerns are apparent) and when people might attempt to conceal their true attitudes on explicit measures. Based on most contemporary literature, then, one might recommend that researchers include implicit attitude measures in two situations: first, when trying to predict a socially undesirable behavior (e.g., cheating, racial prejudice); second, to predict behavior that is automatic, spontaneous, or not consciously controlled. Based on the existing literature, one would *not* recommend that researchers include implicit measures in order to aid prediction of more mundane behaviors (e.g., simply requesting information from one of the major political parties, engaging in a variety of religious behaviors). The present research suggests that these widely accepted assumptions are likely to be incorrect.

The current research demonstrates that implicit attitude measures might be of much wider utility in predicting behavior and can yield information beyond that provided by explicit attitude measures for a variety of behaviors, even when social desirability is a not a concern. It is believed that deliberative implicit attitude measures (partially structured measures, in Cook & Selltiz's terms), such as the ones used in this study, are effective beyond explicit measures, and beyond spontaneous implicit measures (objective measures, in Cook & Selltiz's terms), because the deliberative implicit/partially structured measures rely on attitude use, or the tendency for attitudes to bias information processing. As noted by Cook and Selltiz, partially structured attitude measures assess individuals' biased perception of attitude-relevant stimuli as a proxy for direct evaluations. Projective techniques, for example, rely on respondents' interpretations of ambiguous images. Proshansky (1943) suggested that his projective method was sensitive to two potential biases that could be useful for inferring attitudes: first, attitudes might have distorted perception, such that respondents would tend to perceive the slides as attitude congruent; second, attitudes might have influenced memory such that respondents would tend to recall more attitude-congruent information about the pictures.

The notion that psychological factors such as mood, expectancies, and attitudes influence information processing is one of the oldest and most pervasive ideas in social psychology (e.g., Bruner, 1957; James, 1890; Lewin, 1935). Consider the classic definitions of the attitude construct by Allport, Kretch and Crutchfield, and Campbell presented at the beginning of this chapter. The deliberative implicit/partially structured measures described above tap something other than the stored evaluative tendencies tapped by explicit attitude measures; they tap biased information processing. Because the attitude construct gains utility as a function of the strength of the relationship between attitudes and behavior, the inclusion of processing biases as an active area of attitudinal research seems to have considerable potential to increase the utility and scope of the attitude construct.

Most fundamentally, the notion that attitudes contain an important processing component shifts the conceptualization of attitudes away from a static collection of feelings and beliefs toward a set of active processing strategies or styles that can and should be assessed. The point of this approach to the psychology of attitudes is that, rather than measuring attitudes solely in terms of evaluative content, it might be profitable to measure them in terms of a complex interrelationship between processes, proclivities, and content. In so doing, the processing approach to attitudes emphasizes that *how* we think can be just as important as *what* we think.

## Acknowledgments

This research was supported in part by a National Science Foundation Grant #0111646, and a grant from the University of Illinois Research Board. I thank William von Hippel and Richard E. Petty for their helpful comments and insights regarding this work.
Correspondence should be addressed to Patrick T. Vargas, Department of

Advertising, University of Illinois, 810 S. Wright St., MC-462, Urbana, IL 61801; email: pvargas@uiuc.edu.

## References

Albarracin, D., & Wyer, R. S., Jr. (2000). The cognitive impact of past behavior: Influences of beliefs, attitudes, and future behavioral decisions. *Journal of Personality and Social Psychology, 79*, 5–22.

Ajzen, I., & Fishbein, M. (1977). Attitude–behavior relations: A theoretical analysis and review of empirical research. *Psychological Bulletin, 84*, 888–918.

Allport, G. W. (1935). Attitudes. In C. Murchison (Ed.), *Handbook of social psychology* (pp. 133–175). Worcester, MA: Clark University Press.

Anderson, J. R. (1982). Acquisition of cognitive skill. *Psychological Review, 89*, 369–406.

Blaxton, T. A. (1989). Investigating dissociations among memory measures: Support for a transfer appropriate processing framework. *Journal of Experimental Psychology: Learning, Memory, and Cognition, 15*, 657–668.

Bosson, J. K., Swann, W. B., & Pennebaker, J. W. (2000). Stalking the perfect measure of implicit self-esteem: The blind men and the elephant revisited? *Journal of Personality and Social Psychology, 79*, 631–643.

Bruner, J. W. (1957). On perceptual readiness. *Psychological Review, 64*, 123–152.

Byrne, D., Ervin, C. R., & Lamberth, J. (1970). Continuity between the experimental study of attraction and "real life" computer dating. *Journal of Personality and Social Psychology, 16*, 157–165.

Cacioppo, J. T., Petty, R. E., Losch, M. E., & Kim, H. S. (1986). Electromyographic activity over facial muscle regions can differentiate the valence and intensity of affective reactions. *Journal of Personality and Social Psychology, 50*, 260–268.

Campbell, D. T. (1963). Social attitudes and other acquired behavioral dispositions. In S. Koch (Ed.), *Psychology: A study of a science* (Vol. 6, pp. 94–172). New York: McGraw-Hill.

Cohen, A. R. (1964). *Attitude change and social influence*. New York: Basic Books.

Cook, S. W., & Selltiz, C. (1964). A multiple-indicator approach to attitude measurement. *Psychological Bulletin, 62*, 36–55.

Corey, S. M. (1937). Professed attitudes and actual behavior. *Journal of Educational Psychology, 28*, 217–280.

Cunningham, W. A., Preacher, K. J., & Banaji, M. R. (2001). Implicit attitude measures: Consistency, stability, convergent validity. *Psychological Science, 121*, 163–170.

Davidson, A. R., & Jaccard, J. (1979). Variables that moderate the attitude–behavior relation: Results of a longitudinal survey. *Journal of Personality and Social Psychology, 37*, 1364–1376.

Dovidio, J. F. & Gaertner, S. L. (1991). Changes in the nature of assessment of racial prejudice. In H. Knopke, J. Norrill, & R. Rogers (Eds.), *Opening doors: An appraisal of race relations in contemporary America* (pp. 201–241). Tuscaloosa, AL: University of Alabama Press.

Dovidio, J. F., Kawakami, K., Johnson, C., Johnson, B., & Howard, A. (1997). On the nature of prejudice: Automatic and controlled processes. *Journal of Experimental Social Psychology, 33*, 510–540.

Eagly, A. H., & Chaiken, S. (1993). *The psychology of attitudes.* Fort Worth, TX: Harcourt Brace Jovanovich.

Fazio, R. H. (1990). Multiple processes by which attitudes guide behavior: The MODE model as an integrative framework. In M. P. Zanna (Ed.), *Advances in experimental social psychology* (Vol. 23, pp. 75–109). San Francisco: Academic Press.

Fazio, R. H., Jackson, J. R., Dunton, B. C., & Williams, C. J. (1995). Variability in automatic activation as an unobtrusive measure of racial attitudes: A bona fide pipeline? *Journal of Personality and Social Psychology, 69,* 1013–1027.

Fazio, R. H., Zanna, M. P., & Cooper, J. (1978). Direct experience and attitude–behavior consistency. *Personality and Social Psychology Bulletin, 4,* 48–51.

Fishbein, M., & Ajzen, I. (1974). Attitudes toward objects as predictors of single and multiple behavioral criteria. *Psychological Review, 81,* 59–74.

Gilbert, D. T., & Hixon, J. G. (1991). The trouble of thinking: Activation and application of stereotypic beliefs. *Journal of Personality and Social Psychology, 60,* 509–517.

Greenwald, A. G., & Banaji, M. R. (1995). Implicit social cognition: Attitudes, self-esteem, and stereotypes. *Psychological Review, 102,* 4–27.

Greenwald, A. G., McGhee, D. E., & Schwartz, J. L. K. (1998). Measuring individual differences in implicit social cognition: The implicit association test. *Journal of Personality and Social Psychology, 74,* 1464–1480.

Hammond, K. R. (1948). Measuring attitudes by error choice: An indirect method. *Journal of Abnormal and Social Psychology, 43,* 38–48.

Hastorf, A. H., & Cantril, H. (1954). They saw a game: A case study. *Journal of Abnormal and Social Psychology, 49,* 129–134.

Hense, R. L., Penner, L. A., & Nelson, D. L. (1995). Implicit memory for age stereotypes. *Social Cognition, 13,* 399–415.

Himmelfarb, S. (1993). The measurement of attitudes. In A. Eagly & S. Chaiken (Eds.), *The psychology of attitudes* (pp. 23–43). Fort Worth, TX: Harcourt Brace Jovanovich.

Houston, D. A., & Fazio, R. H. (1989). Biased processing as a function of attitude accessibility: Making objective judgments subjectively. *Social Cognition, 7,* 51–66.

James, W. (1890). *The principles of psychology.* New York: Dover.

Jarvis, W. B. G. (2002). MediaLab by Empirisoft Research Software.

Karpinski, A. T., & von Hippel, W. (1996). The role of the linguistic intergroup bias in expectancy maintenance. *Social Cognition, 14,* 141–163.

Kawakami, K., Dion, K. L., & Dovidio, J. F. (1998). Racial prejudice and stereotype activation. *Personality and Social Psychology Bulletin, 24,* 407–416.

Kraus, S. J. (1995). Attitudes and the prediction of behavior: A meta-analysis of the empirical literature. *Personality and Social Psychology Bulletin, 21,* 58–75.

Krech, D., & Crutchfield, R. (1948). *Theory & problems of social psychology.* New York: McGraw-Hill.

Kunda, Z. (1990). The case for motivated reasoning. *Psychological Bulletin, 108,* 480–498.

LaPiere, R. T. (1934). Attitudes versus actions. *Social Forces, 13,* 230–237.

Lemon, N. (1973). *Attitudes and their measurement.* New York: Wiley.

Lewin, K. (1935). *A dynamic theory of personality.* New York: McGraw-Hill.

Lord, C. G., Ross, L., & Lepper, M. (1979). Biased assimilation and attitude polarization: The effects of prior theories on subsequently considered evidence. *Journal of Personality and Social Psychology, 37,* 2098–2109.

Marsh, K. L., Johnson, B. T., Scott-Sheldon, L. A. (2001). Heart versus reason in condom use: Implicit versus explicit attitudinal predictors of sexual behavior. *Zeitschrift fuer Experimentelle Psychologie, 48,* 161–175.

McConnell, A. R., & Leibold, J. M. (2001). Relations among the Implicit Association Test, discriminatory behavior, and explicit measures of racial attitudes. *Journal of Experimental Social Psychology, 37,* 435–442.

Milgram, S. L., Mann, L., & Harter, S. (1965). The lost-letter technique: A tool of social science research. *Public Opinion Quarterly, 29,* 437–438.

Morris, C. D., Bransford, J. D., & Franks, J. J. (1977). Levels of processing versus transfer appropriate processing. *Journal of Verbal Learning and Verbal Behavior, 16,* 519–533.

Norman, R. (1975). Affective-cognitive consistency, attitudes, conformity, and behavior. *Journal of Personality and Social Psychology, 32,* 83–91.

Ostrom, T. M. (1969). The relationship between the affective, behavioral, and cognitive components of attitude. *Journal of Experimental Social Psychology, 5,* 12–30.

Ostrom, T. M. (1989). The interdependence of attitude theory and measurement. In A. R. Pratkanis, S. J. Breckler, & A. G. Greenwald (Eds.), *Attitude structure and function* (pp. 11–36). Hillsdale, NJ: Lawrence Erlbaum Associates, Inc.

Ouellette, J. A., & Wood, W. (1998). Habit and intention in everyday life: The processes by which past behavior predicts future behavior. *Psychological Bulletin, 124,* 54–74.

Paulhus, D. L. (1991). Measurement and control of response bias. In J. P. Robinson, P. R. Shaver, & L. S. Wrightsman (Eds.), *Measures of personality and social psychological attitudes,* San Diego: Academic Press.

Petty, R. E., & Cacioppo, J. T. (1986). *Communication and persuasion: Central and peripheral routes to attitude change.* New York: Springer-Verlag.

Petty, R. E., & Krosnick, J. A. (Eds.) (1995). *Attitude strength: Causes and consequences.* Hillsdale, NJ: Lawrence Erlbaum Associates, Inc.

Proshansky, H. M. (1943). A projective method for the study of attitudes. *Journal of Abnormal and Social Psychology, 38,* 393–395.

Roediger, H. L. (1990). Implicit memory: Retention without remembering. *American Psychologist, 45,* 1043–1056.

Sekaquaptewa, D., Espinoza, P., Thompson, M., Vargas, P., & von Hippel, W. (2003). Stereotypic explanatory bias: Implicit stereotyping as a predictor of behavior. *Journal of Experimental Social Psychology, 39,* 75–82.

Selltiz, C., & Cook, S. W. (1966). Racial attitude as a determinant of judgments of plausibility. *Journal of Social Psychology, 70,* 139–147.

Sherif, M., & Hovland, C. T. (1961). *Social judgment: Assimilation and contrast effects in communication and attitude change.* New Haven, CT: Yale University Press.

Smith, E. R. (1994). Procedural knowledge and processing strategies in social cognition. In R. S. Wyer & T. K. Srull (Eds.), *Handbook of social cognition* (Vol. 1). Hillsdale, NJ: Lawrence Erlbaum Associates, Inc.

Smith, E. R., & Branscombe, N. R. (1988). Category accessibility as implicit memory. *Journal of Experimental Social Psychology, 24,* 490–504.

Spalding, L. R., & Hardin, C. D. (1999). Unconscious unease and self-handicapping: Behavioral consequences of individual differences in implicit and explicit self-esteem. *Psychological Science, 10,* 535–539.

Swanson, J. E., Rudman, L. A., & Greenwald, A. G. (2001). Using the Implicit

Association Test to investigate attitude–behavior consistency for stigmatized behavior. *Cognition and Emotion, 15*, 207–230.

Thistlethwaite, D. L. (1950). Attitude and structure as factors in the distortion in reasoning. *Journal of Abnormal and Social Psychology, 45*, 442–458.

Thurstone, L. L. (1928). Attitudes can be measured. *American Journal of Sociology, 33*, 529–554.

Vallone, R. P., Ross, L., & Lepper, M. R. (1985). The hostile media phenomenon: Biased perception and perceptions of media bias in coverage of the Beirut massacre. *Journal of Personality and Social Psychology, 49*, 577–585.

Vargas, P., von Hippel, W., & Petty, R. E. (2004). Using partially structured attitude measures to enhance the attitude–behavior relationship. *Personality and Social Psychology Bulletin, 30*, 197–211.

von Hippel, W., Sekaquaptewa, D., & Vargas, P. (1995). On the role of encoding processes in stereotype maintenance. *Advances in Experimental Social Psychology, 27*, 177–254.

von Hippel, W., Sekaquaptewa, D., & Vargas, P. (1997). The linguistic intergroup bias as an implicit indicator of prejudice. *Journal of Experimental Social Psychology, 33*, 490–509.

Waly, P., & Cook, S. W. (1965). Effect of attitude on judgments of plausibility. *Journal of Personality and Social Psychology, 2*, 745–749.

Wänke, M., Plessner, H., & Friese, M. (2002). *When implicit attitude measures predict brand choice—and when they don't.* Paper presented at the symposium, "Predicting Consumer Behavior by Implicit Attitudes," at the Association for Consumer Research, Asia-Pacific Conference, Beijing, China.

Webb, E. J., Campbell, D. T., Schwartz, R. D., Sechrest, L., & Grove, J. B. (1981). *Nonreactive measures in the social sciences* (2nd ed.). Boston, MA: Houghton Mifflin.

Weigel, R. H., & Newman, L. S. (1976). Increasing attitude–behavior correspondence by broadening the scope of the behavioral measure. *Journal of Personality and Social Psychology, 33*, 793–802.

Wicker, A. W. (1969). Attitudes versus actions: The relationship of verbal and overt behavioral responses to attitude objects. *Journal of Social Issues, 25*, 41–78.

Wilson, G. D. (1985). The "catchphrase" approach to attitude measurement. *Personality and Individual Differences, 6*, 31–37.

Wilson, T. D., Lindsey, S., & Schooler, T. Y. (2000). A model of dual attitudes. *Psychological Review, 107*, 101–126.

Wittenbrink, B., Judd, C. M., & Park, B. (1997). Evidence for racial prejudice at the implicit level and its relationship with questionnaire measures. *Journal of Personality and Social Psychology, 72*, 262–274.

# 13 The role of exemplar stability in attitude consistency and attitude change

*Charles G. Lord*

In the early years of social psychology, theorists were full of optimism about research on attitudes. Gordon Allport, writing in the *Handbook of Social Psychology*, for instance, held that: "The concept of attitude is probably the most distinctive and indispensable concept in contemporary American social psychology" (1935, p. 798). He also commented that the attitude concept had "established itself as the keystone in the edifice of American social psychology" (1935, p. 798). Not only Allport but other theorists as well believed that attitudes could be used to predict what people will see, hear, feel, think, and do. They also believed that unwanted attitudes could be changed by well-designed persuasive techniques, if only we understood enough about how they work. Subsequent research, however, revealed two major problems with the attitude construct.

## The attitude–behavior problem

The first problem with the attitude construct might be termed the "attitude–behavior problem." Once sufficient research had accumulated, it became possible to estimate the extent to which attitudes predicted what people would do in empirical studies, both inside and outside the psychology laboratory. Extensive reviews estimated the correlation between attitudes and behavior in the .30 to .40 range, which is considered only a moderate relationship (Schuman & Johnson, 1976; Wicker, 1969). Modern meta-analyses have since established a more exact figure, which appears to be .40 (Kraus, 1995; Wallace, Paulson, Stokes-Zoota, Lord, & Bond, 2002). Although a .40 relationship is on the high side of empirical relationships within the discipline of social psychology (Richard, Bond, & Stokes-Zoota, 2002), it is relatively disappointing when compared to the importance that Allport and other early theorists had attached to attitudes. It is hard to reconcile a .40 relationship with a construct that was supposed to predict with confidence what people would see, hear, feel, think, and do.

The second problem with the attitude construct might be termed the "attitude–object problem." Although early theorists had expressed confidence that well-designed persuasive techniques might ameliorate socially unwanted attitudes, for instance, toward unfairly stigmatized minority groups, the research results proved disappointing. What were at first believed to be simple relationships between a manipulation and attitude change proved to be complex (Eagly & Chaiken, 1993; Hovland, Janis, & Kelley, 1953; McGuire, 1985). Attitude change techniques worked well for some people, but either did not work or backfired in others.

It proved impossible to change "all of the people all of the time" because some individuals seemed to have developed very effective ways to resist and to counteract even evidence that might on the surface seem overwhelming (Lord, Ross, & Lepper, 1979; Mazursky & Schul, 2000; Ross, 1977). Targets of persuasive attempts proved very adept at altering their interpretation of the attitude object in such a way as to retain their initial attitudes. They resisted attitude change after positive contact with an admittedly likable member of a disliked group, for instance, by deciding that the specific person was "the exception that proves the rule" (Hewstone & Brown, 1986; Hewstone & Lord, 1998). Thus they cognitively redefined the attitude object (a disliked social group or category) to exclude the person with whom they had positive contact, and retained negative attitudes by changing the attitude object's meaning (Zanna & Hamilton, 1977; Zanna & Rempel, 1988).

The attitude–behavior problem has often been illustrated by reference to LaPiere's 1934 study. Although that study had many flaws that by modern standards clouded its interpretation, it stands as a very salient example of an instance in which attitudes not only did not predict, but also were at odds with observed behavior. Richard LaPiere was a Stanford professor who toured California and adjacent states with close personal friends—a Chinese couple. Because of prejudices that had been reported in the media, LaPiere and his friends were very worried about being able to find places to stay or to eat. When they started touring, however, LaPiere and his friends were pleasantly surprised. They were served courteously at all but one of 128 establishments.

LaPiere's surprise at his Chinese friends' reception was so pronounced that he decided to send an attitude questionnaire to the places they had visited and to other similar restaurants and hotels in the same area to check on whether they had just happened to stumble upon the only 127 establishments in that part of the country that would accept Chinese customers. The most important question on the form that he sent these establishments was "Will you accept members of the Chinese race in your establishment?" The respondent could choose from "yes," "no," and "depend upon the circumstances."

LaPiere received a good sample of responses, both from hotels and restaurants that he and his Chinese friends had visited and from other similar establishments in the same part of the country. Imagine his surprise when more than 90% of respondents, both from the places they had visited and from the other similar places, chose "no." Respondents had the option, remember, of choosing "depend upon the circumstances," yet they chose "no," thus reporting very negative attitudes toward serving Chinese customers.

To what might we attribute these seemingly incongruous results? LaPiere blamed the questionnaire technique. He wrote: "The questionnaire may be constructed with elaborate skill and hidden with consummate cunning in a maze of supplementary or even irrelevant questions yet all that has been obtained is a symbolic response to a symbolic situation" (1934, p. 230). He went on to speculate: "A questionnaire will reveal what Mr. A writes or says when confronted with a certain combination of words. But not what he will do or say when he meets Mr. B. Mr. B is more than a series of words. He is a man and he acts. His action is not necessarily what Mr. A 'imagines' it will be when he reacts verbally to the symbol 'Mr. B' "(1934, p. 236). People might have one thing in mind when they fill out a questionnaire, but confront a different person in a different situation than they had imagined.

LaPiere (1934) admitted that his Chinese friends were polite, smiling, and educated—a far cry from what the questionnaire respondents probably had in mind at a time when local media were presenting stereotypes of uncouth, ill-mannered coolie laborers "stealing" Americans' jobs. Had LaPiere (1934) inquired further, many of his respondents, when questioned about their apparent lack of attitude–behavior consistency, might have replied "When I said I would refuse to serve Chinese people, I didn't mean Chinese professors!" As we shall see, LaPiere's explanation of his results in terms of "symbolic responses to symbolic situations" fits well with modern explanations of the attitude–behavior problem.

## The attitude–object problem

Before describing those modern explanations, however, it is also instructive to consider the attitude–object problem, which is that people maintain their attitudes by changing the meaning of the attitude object. A prime example of the attitude–object problem came when Solomon Asch (1940) studied the effects of normative information on attitudes. Asch asked students in a control condition to rank ten professions (accountancy, business, dentistry, engineering, journalism, law, medicine, music, politics, and teaching) on four dimensions (conscientiousness, character, idealism, and social usefulness). On average, these students expressed a relatively low opinion of politics by ranking it next to last on all four dimensions.

In the experimental group, Asch asked other students to make the same ranking, but first told them that 500 of their peers had ranked politics first on all four dimensions. Students who were given this (factually inaccurate) normative information, on average, ranked politics in the top half of these respected professions. The normative information, then, had a large impact on the attitudes that students expressed toward politics.

To explain the results, Asch (1940) emphasized changes in how students interpreted the word "politics." When questioned, students in the control condition thought they were ranking people like Boss Tweed, leader of the notorious Tammany Hall political machine, and other party hacks known to be involved in corruption and scandal. With exemplars such as these in mind, it is small wonder that they expressed a very low opinion of the profession.

Students in the experimental condition, in contrast, said that when they ranked politics they were thinking of statesmen like Franklin Roosevelt and Winston Churchill. With such respected exemplars in mind, their relatively high rankings also made sense. The important difference between the two groups appears to have been the exemplars that they called to mind to represent the profession identified on paper as "politics." In Asch's elegant phrase "the characteristic of the process under investigation entails *a change in the object of judgment, rather than in the judgment of the object*" (1940, p. 458, italics in original).

## One explanation for both problems

LaPiere's (1934) explanation of his attitude–behavior results and Asch's (1940) explanation of his attitude change results suggest that the attitude–behavior problem and the attitude–object problem might involve similar mechanisms. These mechanisms can be understood by reference to the attitude construct. "Attitude" is a hypothetical construct that psychologists use to describe an individual's bias toward favorable or unfavorable evaluative responses. Eagly and Chaiken, in what is perhaps the most widely used modern definition, describe an attitude as "*a psychological tendency that is expressed by evaluating a particular entity with some degree of favor or disfavor*" (1993, p. 1, italics in original). They also define attitude-relevant evaluative responses as overt or covert, cognitive, affective, or behavioral.

One interpretation of Eagly and Chaiken's (1993) definition is that attitudes are sets of evaluative responses, including thoughts, feelings, and actions toward an attitude object (Breckler, 1984), that have a tendency to be either favorable or unfavorable. Tendencies are probabilistic rather than a sure thing. An individual might have an overall positive attitude toward an attitude object, therefore, and still have a mixture of thoughts, feelings, and actions, some of which are positive, some neutral, and possibly a few that are slightly negative. We might imagine, then, situations in which one of an individual's evaluative responses does not match another.

By LaPiere's (1934) explanation, that is exactly what happened in his study. As shown in the top row of Table 13.1, people who operated or worked at various restaurants and hotels made two evaluative responses that did not match. In one evaluative response, they served a well-dressed, cultured Chinese couple. In the other, they checked "No" on a question about their willingness to serve "Chinese." In all likelihood they had in mind an entirely different type of Chinese people when they checked "No" than when they granted service.

By Asch's (1940) explanation, as shown in the second row of Table 13.1, a similar mechanism was involved in his study. Participants in two separate groups made different evaluative responses to what on the surface seems the

*Table 13.1* Explanations of mismatching evaluative responses

| Reference | Evaluative response 1 | Evaluative response 2 | Explanation |
|---|---|---|---|
| LaPiere (1934) | Served Chinese couple courteously | Reported negative attitude toward serving Chinese | Thinking of different Chinese for Evaluative Response 1 than for Evaluative Response 2 |
| Asch (1940) | Control group ranked politicians next to last | Experimental group ranked politicians in top half | Thinking of different politicians for Evaluative Response 1 than for Evaluative Response 2 |
| Lord and Lepper (1999) | Assume/perceive attitude object's identity | Assume/perceive attitude object's identity | Activate different assumptions and/or perceptions for Evaluative Response 1 than for Evaluative Response 2 |

same stimulus—a set of professions. Some participants ranked politics next to last among ten professions, whereas other participants ranked politics in the top half. By their own admission, participants in the control group had in mind an entirely different subset of politicians than did participants in the experimental group, possibly because the fictitious subjective norms suggested a different culturally shared representation (Eiser, Claessen, & Loose, 1998).

Based on these converging explanations of attitude–behavior consistency and attitude change, Lord and Lepper (1999) proposed attitude representation theory (ART), which includes a model of how people make attitude-relevant evaluative responses. According to ART, in attitude-relevant situations people activate assumptions about exemplars and characteristics of the attitude object, actions and emotions associated with the attitude object, and contextual or situational constraints. When the only stimulus is words on an attitude questionnaire, as in one part of LaPiere's (1934) study, these assumptions are likely to determine the evaluative response. When the stimulus involves an actual other person, as in the behavioral part of LaPiere's (1934) study, the assumptions must be combined with perceptions of the immediate situation to determine the evaluative response. Thus ART predicts, as shown in the bottom row of Table 13.1, that evaluative responses will not match when assumptions about the attitude object do not match perceptions of the actual behavioral situation. Similarly, even when both evaluative responses are made to the same words on paper, as in both conditions of Asch's (1940) study, respondents might activate different assumptions at two different times.

It is important to note that Lord and Lepper's (1999) ART model conceptualizes an attitude as a set of evaluative responses. According to ART, the term "attitude–behavior consistency" so widely used in the literature is more a shorthand convenience than a precise description. LaPiere's (1934) study, for instance, did not literally address "attitude–behavior consistency." It actually addressed consistency between two evaluative responses—one on the questionnaire and one in person. Neither of these evaluative responses constitutes an attitude, because an attitude is a set of evaluative responses.

Figure 13.1 shows a hypothetical individual's attitude toward an attitude object. The X axis represents the valence of various evaluative responses to the attitude object, ordered from the most negative to the most positive. The Y axis represents the number of times that the individual responded at each level of valence. These responses can include thoughts, feelings, and actions (Breckler, 1984). During the time period in question, the individual had 12 evaluative responses. One was very negative, three were moderately negative, four were slightly negative, two were neutral, one was slightly positive, and one was moderately positive. Overall, the individual's attitude might be described by its mean, which is slightly negative. None of these 12 evaluative responses constitutes the individual's attitude, however, even if the evaluative response in question is a self-reported point on an attitude questionnaire in answer to the question "What is your attitude?"

Using Figure 13.1, it is entirely possible that one of LaPiere's (1934) respondents might have provided an attitude report (on the questionnaire) that was very negative and yet enacted a behavior (when the Chinese couple requested service) that was moderately positive. The precise description of such a pattern is that the two evaluative responses were inconsistent with each other, but not that the respondent's "attitude" was inconsistent with his or her "behavior." A behavior is only one evaluative response within an attitude,

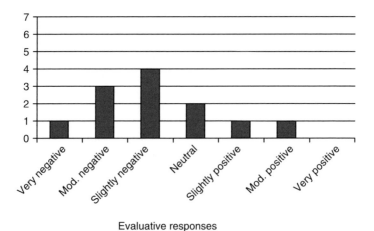

Evaluative responses

*Figure 13.1* An attitude with a slightly negative mean and relatively high variance.

so almost all investigations that have been included in literature reviews of "attitude–behavior consistency" have actually measured consistency between one evaluative response (typically an attitude report) and another (typically a specific behavior or behavioral intention). It is important to bear in mind when reading such reviews that the term "attitude–behavior consistency" is merely a shorthand phrase that is used for convenience.

Similarly, consider Asch's (1940) study of "attitude change." Even if the same students had first rated politics next to last and then, following the manipulation, rated politics in the top half of professions, how much would they have changed their attitudes? The individual whose attitude is depicted in Figure 13.1 might have provided an extremely negative opinion at one time and a slightly positive opinion at another, but without changing very radically the overall distribution of his or her evaluative responses. This is not to deny that attitude change is impossible, however, because new evaluative responses might accumulate to move the central tendency of the distribution toward either the positive or the negative side.

If Figure 13.1 represents an individual's attitude, then attitudes have several properties that have received little attention in reviews of either attitude–behavior consistency or attitude change. Attitudes have a mean, a median, and a mode. Attitudes have skew, range, and variance. It is possible, for instance, to characterize the attitude shown in Figure 13.1 as having a slightly negative mean, positive skew, and a relatively high variance of evaluative responses.

## Attitude variance

Figure 13.2 presents an attitude that also consists of 12 evaluative responses, but has relatively low variance. It is obvious from comparing Figures 13.1 and 13.2 that high variance attitudes differ from low variance attitudes in the likelihood that two randomly selected evaluative responses within the attitude will correspond in valence. Thus individuals who have relatively high variance attitudes will, all else being equal, display less of what is usually referred to as "attitude–behavior consistency" than will individuals who have relatively low variance attitudes. Similarly, individuals who have relatively high variance attitudes will, all else being equal, display more of what is usually referred to as "attitude change" than will individuals who have relatively low variance attitudes.

Attitude variance is similar to but conceptually distinct from other attitude constructs. It is similar to but distinct from, for example, attitude ambivalence. Attitude ambivalence occurs when an individual's evaluative responses differ from each other (Armitage & Conner, 2000; Breckler, 1994; Katz, 1981; Lavine, Thomsen, Zanna, & Borgida, 1998; Priester & Petty, 2001). One way to picture attitude ambivalence is to imagine a bimodal distribution in either Figure 13.1 or Figure 13.2, with some of the individual's evaluative responses clustered on the positive side and others clustered on the negative side. Although it is more likely that ambivalent attitudes will have high than low

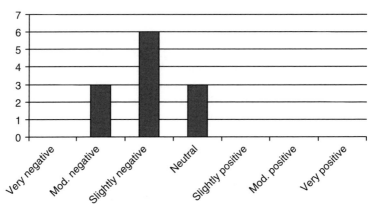

*Figure 13.2* An attitude with a slightly negative mean and relatively low variance.

variance, the relationship is not mathematically necessary. An individual whose attitude consisted of 12 evaluative responses, 6 of them moderately positive and 6 moderately negative, might have an ambivalent attitude without an unusually high degree of attitude variance. The causes and consequences of attitude ambivalence, which have been examined in several theories and programs of research, are not necessarily the same as the causes and consequences of attitude variance.

Attitude variance is also similar to but conceptually distinct from attitude range, which has been investigated in research on "latitudes of acceptance" (Sherif & Hovland, 1961). Evaluative responses differ in the range of valences that an individual finds acceptable. In a typical questionnaire to measure latitudes of acceptance, the individual indicates his or her attitude (actually an attitude report) on a scale with points from very negative to very positive. The individual then indicates the most positive and least positive positions on that scale that the individual would be willing to accept. The area between the most and least positive points is termed the individual's "latitude of acceptance." The remaining areas of the scale are termed the individual's "latitude of rejection." All else being equal, people with wide latitudes of acceptance are likely to have relatively large attitude variance, but the relationship is not mathematically necessary. Thus the causes and consequences of wide versus narrow latitudes of acceptance, which have been examined in several theories and programs of research, are not necessarily the same as the causes and consequences of attitude variance.

## Exemplars and attitude variance

Attitude variance has at least two causes. The first and more obvious cause is that an individual's evaluative responses might occur in situations that differ in their situational constraints. We might term this type of variance "induced attitude variance," because it is variance that is prompted by something about the specific situation. To take just one example, imagine an individual who behaves toward an attitude object first in the company of three valued associates who very much want and expect positive behaviors, a week later in the company of three other valued associates who very much want and expect negative behaviors, and a week after that in the company of three additional valued associates who very much want and expect neutral behaviors.

From everything that we know about social psychology, including research on conformity (Asch, 1956), context effects (Schwarz, 1994), and the theories of reasoned action (Ajzen & Fishbein, 1980) and planned behavior (Ajzen, 1985), we would not be surprised to observe three dramatically different evaluative responses from the same individual, who would have exhibited, at least across these three behavioral opportunities, high attitude variance. Changes in the immediate subjective norms can cause attitude variance, as can changes in the information provided to the individual, for instance, in studies that examine the impact of persuasive communications (Petty & Cacioppo, 1986).

The other type of attitude variance might be termed "spontaneous attitude variance," to indicate that it occurs spontaneously, without any alterations in the external circumstances that surround and can influence evaluative responses. An individual might, for instance, report an extremely negative attitude toward an attitude object today and yet report a neutral attitude toward the same attitude object on the same scale, completed in exactly the same physical setting, next week.

One reaction to spontaneous attitude variance is to dismiss it as "error variance," attributable to imperfections in the measurement process. Error variance no doubt explains some of it, but the thesis of this chapter is that much of what appears to be spontaneous attitude variance is not attributable to error variance, but instead to systematic aspects of the process by which people arrive at their evaluative responses (Tourangeau & Rasinski, 1988). To reiterate, Lord and Lepper (1999) described that process as one in which assumptions about the attitude object are activated and, barring external constraints, inform the evaluative response. One of the assumptions is that the attitude object can be represented by specific exemplars, which can vary from one time to the next. The average person has less than .70 probability of activating the same exemplar for a category from one month to the next (Bellezza, 1984).

If people spontaneously activate different exemplars to represent an attitude object from one time to the next, then differences in the valence of evaluative responses might occur because of differences in evaluative implications of the activated exemplars. If an individual in Asch's (1940) study were to interpret "politicians" on one occasion as meaning "thieves like Boss Tweed" and interpret "politicians" on another occasion as meaning "statesmen like Franklin Roosevelt," then the individual might have a very negative evaluative response one time, and a very positive evaluative response the next. The individual's attitude variance across those two evaluative responses would be high, not because anything about the situation or the information changed, but because different exemplars happened to be activated. The information did not change, because the individual knew about both Boss Tweed and Franklin Roosevelt, but one of them came to mind on one occasion and the other came to mind on a different occasion. The same exemplars were available for both evaluative responses, but their accessibility changed (Schwarz, 1998).

Lord and Lepper (1999) are not the only theorists to describe a process in which the evaluative response of the moment depends on whatever assumptions about the attitude object happen to be activated at that specific time. Schwarz and Bless, for instance, wrote: "Evaluation of a target is based on information that is included in the temporary representation that individuals construct of it" (1992, p. 219). Similarly, Wilson and Hodges wrote: "People often have a large, conflicting 'data base' relevant to their attitudes on any given topic, and the attitude they have at any time depends on the subset of these data to which they attend" (1992, p. 38). Of all the pieces of information that an individual knows about an attitude object, some presumably have a higher probability than others of being activated and informing a specific evaluative response, but at some other time the same individual's evaluative response might be informed by a different piece of information, possibly with different evaluative implications.

Thus the two individuals whose attitudes are shown in Figures 13.1 and 13.2 might differ in the variance of their evaluative responses even without differences in the external situations that surround those evaluative responses, merely because the individual in Figure 13.1 tends to activate evaluatively dissimilar pieces of information each time an evaluative response occurs, whereas the individual in Figure 13.2 tends to activate evaluatively similar pieces of information for each evaluative response. Table 13.2 provides a more concrete example of such differences in attitude variance toward politicians as a function of two individuals having the same versus different politician exemplars come to mind on four separate occasions. The two individuals of Table 13.2 might have the same mean attitude, but Individual 2, who activates different exemplars from one time to the next, has greater attitude variance.

**Consequences for attitude–behavior consistency**

If individuals can differ in exemplar stability, then it seems reasonable to ask what consequences such individual differences might have for attitude–behavior consistency. From inspecting Figures 13.1 and 13.2, plus Table 13.2, the consequences seem obvious. If all of an individual's evaluative responses (including thoughts, actions, and feelings) have matched in the past, then the likelihood is that the next two evaluative responses, one an attitude

*Table 13.2* Temporal stability of activated exemplars can influence attitude variance

| Time | Activated exemplar | Evaluative response | Favorability |
|------|--------------------|--------------------|--------------|
| **Individual 1** | | | |
| 1 | Roosevelt | Positive attitude report | +2 |
| 2 | Roosevelt | Positive behavior (donation) | +2 |
| 3 | Roosevelt | Positive behavior (voting) | +2 |
| 4 | Roosevelt | Positive attitude report | +2 |
| | | Mean evaluative response | +2 |
| **Individual 2** | | | |
| 1 | Roosevelt | Positive attitude report | +5 |
| 2 | Boss Tweed | Negative behavior (no donation) | −1 |
| 3 | Churchill | Positive behavior (voting) | +5 |
| 4 | Party Hack | Negative attitude report | −1 |
| | | Mean evaluative response | +2 |

report and the other a behavior or behavioral intention, will match. If an individual's previous evaluative responses have varied widely, in contrast, then it would be relatively difficult to predict from one of the next two evaluative responses to the other. Thus individuals who have in the past had high attitude variance will display less of what is usually termed attitude–behavior consistency than will individuals who have in the past had low attitude variance.

Table 13.2, however, implies a novel prediction that goes beyond the fact of spontaneous attitude variance to address one of its causes—the activation of exemplars. The table suggests that individuals who activate different exemplars to represent an attitude object from one time to the next will display less attitude–behavior consistency than will individuals who always activate the same exemplar to represent the attitude object. An individual who activates Franklin Roosevelt on one occasion and Boss Tweed on the next, for instance, is likely to display less attitude–behavior consistency than an individual who activates Roosevelt or Tweed both times. The prediction assumes, of course, that different exemplars of a social category have a higher likelihood of being differently liked than would the same exemplar over time, but with that assumption, the prediction follows logically from work by LaPiere (1934), Asch (1940), and Lord and Lepper (1999).

The prediction also suggests a corollary, which is that it might be possible to predict not just attitude–behavior inconsistency, but also the *direction* of attitude behavior consistency. An individual who activates a less liked exemplar at the time of behavior than for the attitude report, that is, would be predicted not only to display low attitude–behavior consistency, but also to behave more negatively than the initial attitude report would have indicated. Conversely, an individual who activates a more liked exemplar at the time of behavior than for the attitude report would be predicted to behave more positively than the initial attitude report would have indicated

Sia, Lord, Blessum, Ratcliff, and Lepper (1997, Exp. 2) tested just such a prediction in a three-session experiment. In the first session, adapting a free response listing procedure that had been developed by Esses, Haddock, and Zanna (1994) and Eagly, Mladinic, and Otto (1994), the researchers asked undergraduates to name exemplars that came to mind spontaneously for each of seven social categories, two of which were politicians and gay men. They also asked each student to report his or her attitude toward each of the categories.

In the second session, two weeks later, a different experimenter asked the same students how much they liked each of 150 well-known people and objects (e.g., sports cars, Rice Krispies, Bill Clinton). Although the students had no reason to suspect any connection between the two sessions, the list of 150 had been tailored to include specific politicians and gay men that the individual student had named as exemplars in the first session.

The third session, two weeks after the second and one month after the first, had two parts that were disguised as unrelated. In the first part, the experimenter from session one had the students answer the same questions that they had answered one month earlier. That experimenter collected the questionnaires and left the room. In the second part of session three a third experimenter, supposedly working for the student council, entered the room and distributed petitions that asked the university administration to bring more of various types of speakers, including environmentalists, politicians, and gays, to campus.

For each type of speaker, the student had to decide whether to sign or not sign the petition. The student also had to indicate his or her willingness to engage in 24 volunteer activities that would aid in making that type of speaker's visits a success. The activities included writing letters, making phone calls, and getting others to attend the talks. Signing or not signing the petition, then, served as a dichotomous measure of behavior. The student's mean willingness to engage in the 24 supportive activities served as a continuous measure of behavioral intentions. Subsequent questions established that all students believed they would be asked at a later date to fulfill what they considered a commitment to their behavioral intentions.

To analyze attitude–behavior consistency toward politicians, the researchers first identified one group of students who had named the same first politician exemplar in session three as they had in session one, and a second group of students who had named a different politician first exemplar in session three than they had in session one. They made the same distinction for gay men exemplars. Approximately equal numbers of participants fell in each group for each category. Then, to test the central hypothesis, the researchers correlated session one's initial attitudes with session three's behavioral intentions (mean willingness to perform the 24 supportive activities for that category) and behaviors (signing the petition versus refusing to sign it).

Table 13.3 summarizes the attitude–behavior consistency results. For both categories, students who named a different first exemplar in session three than they had in session one displayed less attitude–behavior consistency

*Table 13.3* Temporal stability of activated exemplars affects consistency between an attitude report and two types of behavior (abstracted from Sia, Lord, Blessum, Ratcliff, & Lepper, 1997, Exp. 2)

Correlation between reported attitude and willingness to perform supportive behaviors

|                   | Named same exemplar | Named different exemplars |
|-------------------|---------------------|---------------------------|
| Politician speaker | .45                 | −.08                      |
| Gay man speaker    | .59                 | −.03                      |

Correlation between reported attitude and signing the petition

|                   | Named same exemplar | Named different exemplars |
|-------------------|---------------------|---------------------------|
| Politician speaker | .50                 | −.25                      |
| Gay man speaker    | .56                 | −.06                      |

than did students who named the same first exemplar both times. Inconsistency in activating exemplars of a category from one month to the next predicted inconsistency between two evaluative responses from one month to the next.

Furthermore, the researchers were able to predict, for the first time in the study of spontaneous attitude–behavior inconsistency, the *direction* in which behavior or behavioral intentions would deviate from attitude reports. Among students who had named different exemplars (of either category) in session three than in session one, those who named an exemplar that they liked more (from their session two ratings) behaved more positively than their session one attitude reports would have suggested. They were, for example, more likely than one would have predicted from their earlier attitude reports to sign the petition and more willing to volunteer for activities that would help make that type of speakers' visits successful. Students who had named a less likable exemplar in session three than in session one, in contrast, were less likely than one would have predicted from their earlier attitude reports to sign the petition and less willing to volunteer for activities that would help make that type of speakers' visits successful.

Sia and her associates (1997) thus extended previous findings of moderators to attitude–behavior consistency by predicting not just when inconsistency would occur, but also the *direction* in which behavioral measures would differ from each student's initial attitude report. The results fit well with theoretically derived ideas about the role of fluctuating mental representations in spontaneous attitude variance. Not all of attitude variance is random error. Some of it is systematic error caused by a tendency to activate different rather than the same pieces of information about an attitude object from one time to the next. The results thus offered additional insights into the processes that underlie evaluative responses to an attitude object, and suggested principled reasons for expecting less consistency within attitude-relevant responses from some individuals than from others.

### Consequences for attitude change

A more recent experiment applied similar reasoning about spontaneous attitude variance to the study of attitude change. Attitude change, like attitude consistency, depends in part on people trying to maintain a valid understanding of reality (Wood, 2000). Is it possible that the "reality" of a social category's exemplars might remain more stable for some individuals than for others? Consider again the two attitudes shown in Figures 13.1 and 13.2. The attitude in Figure 13.1 has relatively high variance, whereas the attitude in Figure 13.2 has relatively low variance. Suppose that we were to try changing both attitudes by inducing a new evaluative response that would be either more positive or more negative than the mean. In which case might we expect greater success? Intuitively, it seems more likely that we could induce the wanted evaluative response in the Figure 13.1 attitude than in the Figure 13.2 attitude.

An attitude like the one in Figure 13.1, in which evaluative responses fluctuate spontaneously in their valence from one time to the next, seems intuitively more susceptible to the introduction of a new evaluative response different from the mean than does the attitude in Figure 13.2, in which evaluative responses tend to remain relatively stable. An attitude like the one in Figure 13.1 is composed of evaluative responses that shift so readily that getting the individual to have a new evaluative response more positive or more negative than its central tendency seems relatively easy. An attitude like the one in Figure 13.2 is composed of evaluative responses that stay so stable that getting the individual to have a new evaluative response more positive or more negative than its central tendency seems relatively difficult.

As in Sia et al.'s (1997) experiment, however, the emphasis in the current reasoning is not so much on attitude variance, but on inconsistent exemplar activation as a possible cause of attitude variance. If evaluative responses are informed by whichever pieces of information are spontaneously activated about the attitude object, then individuals who spontaneously activate different exemplars of a social category from one time to the next should display greater attitude change than those who spontaneously activate the same exemplar from one time to the next, even when they are both confronted with the same new information that contradicts their reported attitudes. Thus instability of exemplar activation imparts susceptibility to change in attitude reports.

Lord, Paulson, Sia, Thomas, and Lepper (2002, Exp. 1) tested just such a prediction about the relationship between exemplar stability and attitude change in an experiment that had six sessions, each one week after the other. In session one, they asked undergraduate students to report their attitudes toward several social categories, one of which was politicians. In sessions two through five, which were identical, a different experimenter asked the same students to name an exemplar of each social category by answering a question about that category, for instance "If someone said they saw a photograph of a politician, which politician would you picture?" In each of these four sessions, the students also completed the same attitude questionnaire that they had completed in session one.

Session six had two parts. In the first part, to disguise any intent to change attitudes, a third experimenter asked the students to critique an essay that had supposedly been developed as part of the stimulus materials for an experiment that might be conducted in a later semester. In reality, the essay that each student read was an attempt to change that student's attitude report, because it took a position directly opposite to the student's attitude report in session one.

Students who had reported an initial negative attitude toward politicians read an essay that praised the profession, the central themes of which were that politics serves a more valuable function than ever in an increasingly complex world and that politics is a more demanding, challenging profession today than it has ever been in the past. Students who had reported an initial positive attitude, in contrast, read an essay that disparaged the profession, the central themes of which were that the political process today is rife with corruption because of the undue influence exerted by "big money" and that campaign finance reform and other restraints against influence peddling are more needed today than they have ever been in the past. It is important to note, however, that neither the pro-politics message nor the anti-politics message mentioned any specific politician exemplar, either directly or indirectly, because the experimenters wanted to avoid making new or different exemplars more accessible.

To insure that students read the disguised persuasive message, they were required to summarize the author's position, list the author's main arguments, and list examples that the author had used to buttress the central arguments. Students' answers indicated that they had read and understood the materials. All students at least comprehended the message that was intended to sway their attitude reports. The dependent measure of interest, though, was change in those evaluative responses.

To analyze the data, the researchers first identified individuals who had named the same politician exemplar all five of the first five weeks. They also identified individuals who had named at least two different politician exemplars during those same five weeks. Approximately equal numbers of participants fell in each group. Further, approximately half of the students in each group had reported positive initial attitudes toward politicians, and half had reported negative initial attitudes toward politicians, so half received the negative message and half received the positive message.

These differences in which message they received, however, proved insignificant. Figure 13.3 displays mean change in the direction of the sixth week's persuasive message by students who started with either positive or negative attitudes and named either the same or different exemplars across the first five weeks. Regardless of which message they received, students who had named different politician exemplars across time were more influenced by the persuasive message to alter their attitude reports in the direction of

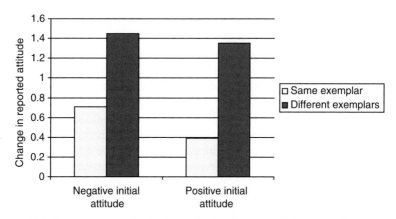

*Figure 13.3* Spontaneous attitude change in the direction of the persuasive message.

that message. Exemplar instability seemed to render participants susceptible to changes in their attitude reports.

The researchers also addressed a salient alternative explanation of the results—namely, that people who tend to have different exemplars come to mind from one time to the next are the same people who harbor relatively weak attitudes. These individuals' evaluative responses might be more varied than those who name the same exemplar every time, but their evaluative responses might also be less extreme, and thus more susceptible to attitude change. This alternative explanation was addressed by statistically controlling for the extremity of reported initial attitudes. Even controlling for initial extremity, the relationship between exemplar instability and attitude change remained significant, so individuals with relatively unstable exemplars might report less extreme attitudes, but that difference cannot explain the exemplar stability effect.

Lord and his associates were unable, however, to address several other plausible alternative explanations with data from what was essentially a cor-relational rather than experimental design. The relationship between spon-taneous exemplar instability and susceptibility to changing attitude reports might have occurred because people who name different exemplars over time are also low in need for cognition (Cacioppo & Petty, 1982), low in need for cognitive closure (Kruglanski, 1990), high in attitude ambivalence (Maio, Esses, & Bell, 2000), low in attitude certainty (Haddock, Rothman, Reber, & Schwarz, 1999), or any of countless other possibly correlated individual dif-ferences. Because it would be impossible to measure all the plausible indi-vidual differences that might have accounted for the result, the researchers realized that an experimental manipulation of exemplar stability might add weight to their arguments. They might have greater confidence in the relation-ship between exemplar instability and susceptibility to attitude change if exemplar instability were manipulated in randomly selected participants.

When we contemplate manipulating exemplar stability and instability, however, the logic behind these experiments at first seems to be violated. The reasoning that led to the experiments involved individual differences in *spontaneous* attitude variance, not *induced* attitude variance. Even if we could somehow get participants to name different exemplars of a category from one time to the next, and even if naming different exemplars caused them to report varying attitudes, why would such an artificial procedure have any effect on susceptibility to attitude change? Wouldn't an initial attitude like that in Figure 13.1 remain as susceptible to attitude change as it had been before the manipulation? Wouldn't an initial attitude like that in Figure 13.2 remain as resistant to attitude change as it had been before the manipulation?

The answer to this question is that attitude reports might be transformed by such a manipulation, because one of the pieces of information that goes into an attitude report is the individual's previous evaluative responses, either as specific memories or as summary evaluations (Betsch, Plessner, Schwieren, & Guetig, 2001). Many theories of attitude change, such as cognitive dissonance theory (Festinger, 1957) and self-perception theory (Bem, 1972) state this principle either implicitly or explicitly. According to these theories, individuals base their attitude reports in part on memories of previous evaluative responses, such as favorable or unfavorable actions toward the attitude object. In Lord and Lepper's (1999) ART model as well, each new evaluative response is informed in part by "associated responses," which include previous thoughts, feelings, and actions toward the attitude object.

It should be possible, then, to transform an attitude of average variance into one of either above-average or below-average variance simply by adding a set of new evaluative responses that are either very inconsistent or very consistent with each other. Lessons derived from experiments on cognitive dissonance and self-perception, of course, suggest that the initial attitude might not be transformed if the new evaluative responses were so coerced that they were not perceived by the individual as self-diagnostic (Gilbert, 1998; Jones & Davis, 1965), but with a subtle enough manipulation, new evaluative responses might simply be added to the mental representation that the individual activates in choosing the next evaluative response (Smith & DeCoster, 1998). Through a suitably subtle manipulation, then, it might be possible to manipulate exemplar stability and influence susceptibility to attitude change in randomly selected participants.

Lord and his associates (2002, Exp. 2) borrowed just such a subtle manipulation from Bodenhausen, Schwarz, Bless, and Wänke, (1995). These previous researchers had asked participants to estimate the height of several famous people, the last one of whom was either a well-liked African-American (Michael Jordan or Oprah Winfrey) or a white person. Immediately after estimating these heights, the participants reported their opinions on whether "discrimination against Blacks is no longer a significant problem in the U.S." (Bodenhausen, et al., 1995, p. 53). As predicted, students who had just rated Michael or Oprah were more likely to regard discrimination against blacks as a continuing problem than were students who had just rated a white person. Sia and her associates (1997, Exp. 3) had also used this manipulation to prime either positive or negative politician exemplars, with significant effects on their participants' reported attitudes toward politicians.

To manipulate exemplar stability, therefore, Lord and his associates (2002) had undergraduate students participate in five weekly sessions. In session one, the students reported their attitudes toward and listed exemplars of several social categories, one of which was politicians. They also indicated how much they liked each of the exemplars that they had listed. Of the participants 75% reported non-neutral attitudes and listed three or more politician exemplars that they liked differently, thus qualifying as individuals who could be randomly assigned to one of three conditions for sessions two through four.

Students in all three conditions estimated the height of famous people in week two, the weight of famous people in week three, and the age of famous people in week four. For students who had been randomly assigned to the "same exemplar" condition, the last name on the list of people to be rated was the same each week—namely, the first politician exemplar that they had listed in session one. For students who had been randomly assigned to the "different exemplars" condition, the last name on the list of people to be rated each week was a different (and differently liked) one of the politicians that they had listed in session one. For the remaining students, in the "no exemplar" control condition, the last name on the list, like all the other names, was that of a non-politician. After making their ratings each week, students in all three conditions also repeated the attitude questionnaire from week one, but listed only one exemplar for each category.

Session five had two parts that were similar to those used in the study of spontaneous exemplar stability and attitude change. Briefly, all students critiqued an essay opposed to their initial reported attitude toward politicians and then completed a final attitude questionnaire that served as the measure of attitude change. The pro-politics and anti-politics essays were the same as described earlier.

Lord and his associates (2002) used several manipulation checks. First, they established that students who had been primed with different exemplars each week had listed a larger number of different exemplars across those three weeks of the manipulation than had students who had been primed with the same exemplar every week. Second, they showed that students in the different exemplars condition were more likely to name the primed exemplar each week than would have been expected by chance. Third, they showed that students in the different exemplars condition gave attitude reports that varied more in valence across the three weeks of the manipulation than did students in the same exemplar condition. On these manipulation checks, interestingly, the different exemplars condition differed significantly from both the same exemplar condition and the control condition, but those two conditions did not differ. The manipulation checks thus suggested that it is easier to induce high than low variance in randomly selected attitudes.

The central hypothesis, however, was tested by attitude change in the direction of the essay. As Figure 13.4 shows, attitude reports changed more in the direction of the persuasive message for students who had been primed with different exemplars than for students who had been primed with either the same exemplar or no exemplars. The result held for both students who received the pro-politics message and students who received the anti-politics message. It also held when extremity of initial attitude reports was statistically controlled. It proved possible, then, to decrease randomly selected participants' resistance to persuasion by reminding them of a differently liked exemplar of the category each week, in the process prompting several new evaluative responses that increased the attitude's variance.

An alternative explanation of these results might be that the manipulation made students publicly commit themselves to an attitude each week, which induced self-presentational processes extraneous to exemplar stability. This alternative explanation, however, seems better suited to explaining why students in the same exemplar condition might have changed their attitudes less than students in the no exemplar condition (which did not happen) than explaining why students in the different exemplar condition changed their attitudes more than students in the no exemplar condition (which did happen). Reporting an attitude every week might introduce concerns about looking consistent to the experimenters, but such concerns about looking consistent should have worked against the hypothesis that priming different exemplars would increase susceptibility to attitude change.

## Concluding remarks

Taken together, these results suggest that exemplar stability plays a role in the phenomena conventionally designated as attitude–behavior consistency and attitude change. Its precise role in such phenomena, however, remains unexplored and raises several interesting questions. First, from the experi-

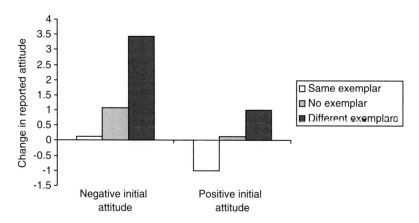

*Figure 13.4* Induced attitude change in the direction of the persuasive message.

ments that have been conducted, we do not know the precise mechanisms by which people who have stable exemplars resist and people who have unstable exemplars succumb to attacks on their attitudes. One intriguing possibility is that those who have stable exemplars maintain an active defense against persuasion (Eagly, Kulesa, Brannon, Shaw, & Hutson-Comeaux, 2000) by citing their favorite exemplars as counter-examples, as in "This essay claims that modern politics requires high morality, but what about Bill Clinton?" Conversely, those who have unstable exemplars might be all too prone to "recognize" within persuasive arguments exemplars that imply an attitude different from what they had previously reported. To explore such possibilities, it would be necessary to examine in greater detail the cognitive processes that occur while participants are reading counterattitudinal information (Priester & Fleming, 1997).

Second, we also do not know, at this point, how closely exemplar stability and attitude variance are related to other factors that have proved important in past research, such as attitude strength (Krosnick, Boninger, Chuang, Berent, & Carnot, 1993), attitude accessibility (Fazio, 1990), direct experience with the attitude object (Fazio & Zanna, 1981), and attitude ambivalence (Armitage & Conner, 2000). People who have unstable exemplars for a category might have relatively high attitude variance, but is that in part because other pieces of information also vary for them in their temporal stability (Conner, Sheeran, Norman, & Armitage, 2000; Sheeran, Orbell, & Trafimow, 1999)? Do manipulations of exemplar stability affect the stability of other pieces of information that inform evaluative responses, such as the characteristics that the individual attributes to typical members of the social category (Lord, Lepper, & Mackie, 1984), the emotions and desires that the individual associates with the category (Perugini & Bagozzi, 2001), or the past actions that the individual remembers having taken toward members of the category?

Third, we do not know whether exemplar stability influences attitude–behavior consistency and attitude change for attitude objects other than social groups and categories (i.e., gay men and politicians). One could claim, however, that all attitude objects have exemplars and that all reported attitudes might vary with the exemplar that is activated. Attitudes toward inanimate objects such as trucks might depend on whether we are thinking of pickups or eighteen-wheelers. Attitudes toward activities such as dieting might depend on whether we are thinking of a low carbohydrate diet or a diet of scotch whisky. Attitudes toward issues such as abortion might depend on whether we are thinking of abortions in the first or third trimester. Even attitudes toward one person, such as Bill Clinton, might depend on whether we are thinking of him as a president or as a husband. Although the empirical evidence is currently lacking, it seems likely that spontaneous exemplar stability, without any alteration in the information available to the individual, would affect attitude–behavior consistency and attitude change for any and all attitude objects.

Fourth, we might wonder whether other aspects of evaluative responses, not just exemplars, might differ from one individual to the next in the temporal stability of their activation. Might some individuals make the same emotional associations to an attitude object on every occasion, whereas others make different emotional associations from one time to the next? Might some individuals recall the same ones of their previous actions toward an attitude object every time, and others recall different ones of their previous actions on different occasions? Might some individuals heed the same subjective norms for every evaluative response toward an attitude object, whereas others activate different subjective norms, with different evaluative implications, next week than they did today? If so, then might one expect individuals who activate different emotions, actions, and subjective norms across time to display less attitude–behavior consistency and greater susceptibility to attitude change than would their counterparts whose activated assumptions about the attitude object tend to be more stable?

These are but a few of the interesting research questions that arise when one follows the suggestions of LaPiere (1934) and Asch (1940) that attitude reports are no more than symbolic responses to symbolic situations. "Attitudes are never directly observed" (Allport, 1935, p. 839), because attitude is a hypothetical construct (Eagly & Chaiken, 1993) used to describe a set of evaluative responses to an attitude object (Lord & Lepper, 1999). The research described in this chapter suggests that when evaluative responses are informed by a stable exemplar, that attitude is like a house built on rock. It can withstand attack. If the evaluative responses are informed by constantly changing exemplars, in contrast, that attitude seems more like a house built on sand. When the rains of contradiction, the floods of new information, and the winds of competing perspectives beat upon such a house, it tends to collapse.

# References

Ajzen, I. (1985). From intentions to actions: A theory of planned behavior. In J. Kuhl & J. Beckman (Eds.), *Action-control: From cognition to behavior*. Heidelberg: Springer.

Ajzen, I., & Fishbein, M. (1980). *Understanding attitudes and predicting social behavior*. Englewood Cliffs, NJ: Prentice-Hall.

Allport, G. W. (1935). Attitudes. In C. Murchison (Ed.), *A handbook of social psychology* (pp. 798–844). Worcester, MA: Clark University Press.

Armitage, C. J., & Conner, M. (2000). Attitudinal ambivalence: A test of three key hypotheses, *Personality and Social Psychology Bulletin, 26*, 1421–1432.

Asch, S. E. (1940). Studies in the principles of judgments and attitudes: II. Determination of judgments by group and by ego standards. *The Journal of Social Psychology, S.P.S.S.I. Bulletin, 12*, 433–465.

Asch, S. E. (1956). Studies of independence and conformity: I. A minority of one against a unanimous majority. *Psychological Monographs, 70* (Whole no. 416).

Bellezza, F. S. (1984). Reliability of retrieval from semantic memory: Common categories. *Bulletin of the Psychonomic Society, 22*, 324–326.

Bem, D. J. (1972). Self-perception theory. In L. Berkowitz (Ed.), *Advances in experimental social psychology* (Vol. 6, pp. 1–62). New York: Academic Press.

Betsch, T., Plessner, H., Schwieren, C., & Guetig, R. (2001). I like it but I don't know why: A value-account approach to implicit attitude formation. *Personality and Social Psychology Bulletin, 27,* 242–253.

Bodenhausen, G. V., Schwarz, N., Bless, H., & Wänke, M. (1995). Effects of atypical exemplars on racial beliefs: Enlightened racism or generalized appraisals? *Journal of Experimental Social Psychology, 31,* 48–63.

Breckler, S. J. (1984). Empirical validation of affect, behavior, and cognition as distinct components of attitude. *Journal of Personality and Social Psychology, 47,* 1191–1205.

Breckler, S. J. (1994). A comparison of numerical indexes for measuring attitude ambivalence. *Educational and Psychological Measurement, 54,* 350–365.

Cacioppo, J. T., & Petty, R. E. (1982). The need for cognition. *Journal of Personality and Social Psychology, 42,* 116–131.

Conner, M., Sheeran, P., Norman, P., & Armitage, C. J. (2000). Temporal stability as a moderator of relationships in the Theory of Planned behavior. *British Journal of Social Psychology, 39,* 469–493.

Eagly, A. H., & Chaiken, S. (1993). *The psychology of attitudes.* New York: Harcourt, Brace, Jovanovich.

Eagly, A. H., Kulesa, P., Brannon, L. A., Shaw, K., & Hutson-Comeaux, S. (2000). Why counterattitudinal messages are as memorable as proattitudinal messages: The importance of active defense against attack. *Personality and Social Psychology Bulletin, 26,* 1392–1408.

Eagly, A. H., Mladinic, A., & Otto, S. (1994). Cognitive and affective bases of attitudes toward social groups and social policies. *Journal of Experimental Social Psychology, 30,* 113–137.

Eiser, J. R., Claessen, M. J. A., & Loose, J. L. (1998). Attitudes, beliefs, and other minds: Shared representations in self-organizing systems. In S. J. Read & L. C. Miller (Eds.), *Connectionist models of social reasoning and social behavior* (pp. 313–354). Mahwah, NJ: Lawrence Erlbaum Associates, Inc.

Esses, V. M., Haddock, G., & Zanna, M. P. (1994). The role of mood in the expression of intergroup stereotypes. In M. P. Zanna & J. M. Olson (Eds.), *The psychology of prejudice: The Ontario symposium* (Vol. 7, pp. 77–101). Hillsdale, NJ: Lawrence Erlbaum Associates, Inc.

Fazio, R. H. (1990). Multiple processes by which attitudes guide behavior: The MODE model as an integrative framework. In M. P. Zanna (Ed.), *Advances in experimental social psychology* (Vol. 23, pp. 75–109). New York: Academic Press.

Fazio, R. H., & Zanna, M. P. (1981). Direct experience and attitude–behavior consistency. In L. Berkowitz (Ed.), *Advances in experimental social psychology* (Vol. 14, pp. 161–202). New York: Academic Press.

Festinger, L. (1957). *A theory of cognitive dissonance.* Stanford, CA: Stanford University Press.

Gilbert, D. T. (1998). Ordinary personology. In D. T. Gilbert, S. T. Fiske, & G. Lindzey (Eds.), *The Handbook of Social Psychology* (Vol. 2, pp. 89–150). Boston, MA: McGraw-Hill.

Haddock, G., Rothman, A. J., Reber, R., & Schwarz, N. (1999). Forming judgments of attitude certainty, intensity, and importance: The role of subjective experiences. *Personality and Social Psychology Bulletin, 25,* 771–782.

Hewstone, M., & Brown, R. (1986). Contact is not enough: An intergroup perspective on the "contact hypothesis." In M. Hewstone & R. Brown (Eds.), *Contact and conflict in intergroup encounters*. New York: Blackwell.

Hewstone, M., & Lord, C. G. (1998). Changing intergroup cognitions and intergroup behavior: The role of typicality. In C. Sedikides, J. Schopler, & C. A. Insko (Eds.), *Intergroup cognition and intergroup behavior*. Mahwah, NJ: Lawrence Erlbaum Associates, Inc.

Hovland, C. I., Janis, I. L., & Kelley, H. H. (1953). *Communication and persuasion: Psychological studies of opinion change*. New Haven, CT: Yale University Press.

Jones, E. E., & Davis, K. E. (1965). From acts to dispositions. The attribution process in person perception. In L. Berkowitz (Ed.), *Advances in experimental social psychology* (Vol. 2). New York: Academic Press.

Katz, I. (1981). *Stigma: A social psychological analysis*. Hillsdale, NJ: Lawrence Erlbaum Associates, Inc.

Kraus, S. J. (1995). Attitudes and the prediction of behavior: A meta-analysis of the empirical literature. *Personality and Social Psychology Bulletin, 21*, 58–75.

Krosnick, J. A., Boninger, D. S., Chuang, Y. C., Berent, M. K., & Carnot, C. G. (1993). Attitude strength: One construct or many related constructs? *Journal of Personality and Social Psychology, 65*, 1132–1151.

Kruglanski, A. W. (1990). Motivations for judging and knowing: Implications for causal attribution. In E. T. Higgins & R. M. Sorrentino (Eds.), *Handbook of motivation and cognition: Foundations of social behavior* (Vol. 2, pp. 333–368). New York: Guilford Press.

LaPiere, R. T. (1934). Attitudes versus actions. *Social Forces, 13*, 230–237.

Lavine, H., Thomsen, C. J., Zanna, M. P., & Borgida, E. (1998). On the primacy of affect in the determination of attitudes and behavior: The moderating role of affective-cognitive ambivalence. *Journal of Experimental Social Psychology, 34*, 398–421.

Lord, C. G., & Lepper, M. R. (1999). Attitude representation theory. In M. P. Zanna (Ed.), *Advances in experimental social psychology* (Vol. 31, pp. 265–343). San Diego, CA: Academic Press.

Lord, C. G., Lepper, M. R., & Mackie, D. (1984). Attitude prototypes as determinants of attitude–behavior consistency. *Journal of Personality and Social Psychology, 46*, 1254–1266.

Lord, C. G., Paulson, R. M., Sia, T. L., Thomas, J. C., & Lepper, M. R. (2002). *Houses built on sand: Effects of exemplar variability on susceptibility to attitude change*. Unpublished manuscript.

Lord, C. G., Ross, L., & Lepper, M. R. (1979). Biased assimilation and attitude polarization: The effects of prior theories on subsequently considered evidence. *Journal of Personality and Social Psychology, 37*, 2098–2109.

Maio, G. R., Esses, V. M., & Bell, D. W. (1994). The formation of attitudes toward new immigrant groups. *Journal of Applied Social Psychology, 24*, 1762–1776.

Maio, G. R., Esses, V. M., & Bell, D. W. (2000). Examining conflict between components of attitudes: Ambivalence and inconsistency are distinct constructs. *Canadian Journal of Behavioural Science, 32*, 58–70.

Mazursky, D., & Schul, Y. (2000). In the aftermath of invalidation: Shaping judgment rules on learning that previous information was invalid. *Journal of Consumer Psychology, 9*, 213–222.

McGuire, W. J. (1985). Attitudes and attitude change. In G. Lindzey & E. Aronson (Eds.), *Handbook of social psychology* (Vol. 2). New York: Random House.

Perugini, M., & Bagozzi, R. P. (2001). The role of desires and anticipated emotions in goal-directed behaviors: Broadening and deepening the theory of planned behavior. *British Journal of Social Psychology, 40*, 79–98.

Petty, R. E., & Cacioppo, J. T. (1986). *Communication and persuasion: Central and peripheral routes to attitude change.* New York: Springer-Verlag.

Priester, J. R., & Fleming, M. A. (1997). Artifact or meaningful theoretical constructs? Examining evidence for non-belief and belief-based attitude change processes. *Journal of Consumer Psychology, 6*, 67–76.

Priester, J. R., & Petty, R. E. (2001). Extending the bases of subjective attitudinal ambivalence: Interpersonal and intrapersonal antecedents of evaluative tension. *Journal of Personality and Social Psychology, 80*, 19–34.

Richard, D., Bond, C. F., Jr., & Stokes-Zoota, J. (2002). *One hundred years of social psychology quantitatively described.* Unpublished manuscript.

Ross, L. (1977). The intuitive psychologist and his shortcomings: Distortions in the attribution process. In L. Berkowitz (Ed.), *Advances in experimental social psychology* (Vol. 10, pp. 174–221). New York: Academic Press.

Schuman, H., & Johnson, M. P. (1976). Attitudes and behavior. *Annual Review of Sociology, 2*, 161–207.

Schwarz, N. (1994). Judgments in a social context: Biases, shortcomings, and the logic of conversation. In M. P. Zanna (Ed.), *Advances in experimental social psychology* (Vol. 26, pp. 123–162). San Diego, CA: Academic Press.

Schwarz, N. (1998). Accessible content and accessibility experiences: The interplay of declarative and experiential information in judgment. *Personality and Social Psychology Rreview, 2*, 87–99.

Schwarz, N., & Bless, H. (1992). Constructing reality and its alternatives: An inclusion/exclusion model of assimilation and contrast effects in social judgment. In L. L. Martin & A. Tesser (Eds.), *The construction of social judgments* (pp. 217–245). Hillsdale, NJ: Lawrence Erlbaum Associates, Inc.

Sheeran, S., Orbell, S., & Trafimow, D. (1999). Does the temporal stability of behavioral intentions moderate intention–behavior and past behavior–future behavior relations? *Personality and Social Psychology Bulletin, 25*, 721–730.

Sherif, M., & Hovland, C. I. (1961). *Social judgment: Assimilation and contrast effects in communication and attitude change.* New Haven: Yale University Press.

Sia, T. L., Lord, C. G., Blessum, K., Ratcliff, C.D., & Lepper, M. R. (1997). Is a rose always a rose? The role of social category exemplar-change in attitude stability and attitude-behavior consistency. *Journal of Personality and Social Psychology, 72*, 501–514.

Smith, E. R., & DeCoster, J. (1998). Knowledge acquisition, accessibility, and use in person perception and stereotyping: Simulation with a recurrent connectionist network. *Journal of Personality and Social Psychology, 74*, 21–35.

Tourangeau, R., & Rasinski, K. A. (1988). Cognitive processes underlying context effects in attitude measurement. *Psychological Bulletin, 103*, 299–314.

Wallace, D. S., Paulson, R. M., Stokes-Zoota, J. J., Lord, C. G., & Bond, C. F., Jr. (2002). *Which behaviors do attitudes predict? Meta-analyzing the effects of social desirability and difficulty.* Unpublished manuscript.

Wicker, A. W. (1969). Attitude versus actions: The relationship of verbal and overt behavioral responses to attitude objects. *Journal of Social Issues, 25*, 41–78.

Wilson, T. D., & Hodges, S. D. (1992). Attitudes as temporary constructions. In L. L. Martin & A. Tesser (Eds.), *The construction of social judgments*. Hillsdale, NJ: Lawrence Erlbaum Associates, Inc.

Wood, W. (2000). Attitude change: Persuasion and social influence. *Annual Review of Psychology, 51*, 539–570.

Zanna, M. P., & Hamilton, D. L. (1977). Further evidence for meaning change in impression formation. *Journal of Experimental Social Psychology, 13*, 224–238.

Zanna, M. P., & Rempel, J. K. (1988). Attitudes: A new look at an old concept. In D. Bar-Tal & A. W. Kruglanski (Eds.), *The social psychology of knowledge*. Cambridge: Cambridge University Press.

# 14 Putting Humpty together again

## Attitude organization from a connectionist perspective

*J. Richard Eiser*

Humpty Dumpty sat on a wall.
Humpty Dumpty had a great fall.
All the king's horses and all the king's men
Couldn't put Humpty together again.

Mind you, it didn't help that Humpty was an egg. But even if Humpty had not had the handicap of a fragile external shell, his disintegration would have been difficult to reverse. All living and physical systems sustain coherence only so long as the forces that hold them together are stronger than those that would pull them apart. But when we consider how well we understand such processes of coherence and disintegration, there is a remarkable asymmetry. A friend once used to sign off his emails with the proverb: "Life is what stops when you stomp on it." Put differently, we know how to break an egg, but not how to make one. An unbroken egg is—well—just an egg. It is as though we take it for granted that the world consists of ready-made and complete objects and creatures, and regard any change from this state of affairs as a form of deviation. It's not just that we can't *see* molecules, electromagnetic fields, DNA, or the formation of chemical compounds; it's rather that it seems unnatural even to *think* of objects that way, unless we have been specially educated to do so.

So it has been with attitudes, which are, in a less immediate but still important sense, physical systems too. Attitude theorists have tended to start from the view that attitudes are coherent structures, and to treat incoherence as a problem to be explained. In order to explain incoherence, where it occurs, researchers have tended to break up the concept of attitude into its presumed constituents, which then in turn need explaining in terms of ever smaller constituents. Our methods and our theories have not simply become more refined, but finer grained. We have achieved greater precision in our predictions, but at the price, often, of restricting the range of contexts in which such predictions apply.

Take, for example, one of the most enduring issues in attitude research, that of discrepancies between attitudes, intentions, and behavior (e.g., Ajzen

& Fishbein, 1977; this volume, Armitage & Connor, Chapter 6; Orbell, Chapter 7). The "problem" here is defined in terms of why attitudes *don't* perfectly predict intentions, or intentions perfectly predict behavior. But why should they? Likewise, our beliefs about objects or people don't always match our emotional feelings towards them. But again, why should they? These questions go to the heart of what we think attitudes are and, more specifically, how attitudes are *organized*.

Previous theoretical views on attitude organization can be characterized broadly as before-the-fall and after-the-fall. This distinction is only approximately chronological. After all, there is no agreed or perhaps even single date for Humpty's fall. It refers more to the starting assumptions of different perspectives on how attitudinal thoughts, feelings and behaviors hang together (if and when they do). Without straining spatial metaphors very much at all, before-the fall theories can be thought of as top-down (i.e., they start with general organizing principles), whereas after-the-fall theories are bottom-up (i.e., they start with a focus on relationships at a simpler and more context-specific level).

## Attitude organization before the fall

The before-the-fall theoretical principle par excellence is that of cognitive consistency. For present purposes, this can be defined broadly to cover not only the theory of cognitive balance as originally formulated by Heider (1946), but also its various adaptations including especially cognitive dissonance theory (Festinger, 1957) and the large experimental literature to which this gave rise. All these theories claim that individuals may change specific beliefs and feelings, including expressed attitudes, personal feelings and evaluations of own and others' behavior, to bring them into line with a pre-existing structure, or conception of reality. This all reflects a homeostatic process whereby established attitudes resist change, and keep their balance even when exposed to contrary influences. Alongside this is the assumption that, when presented with inconclusive or incomplete information, individuals will engage in a search for structure. But this will not be just *any* structure. It will be one that conforms to Gestalt principles of greatest simplicity, symmetry, and completeness. To sustain this search for structure, it is proposed that we are motivated to perceive, construct and protect psychologically "consistent" structures while we experience "inconsistency" as disturbing and unpleasant—in dissonance theory's terms, as a state of noxious arousal.

This perspective was hugely influential throughout the second half of the last century. However, it is hampered by (at least) two general difficulties. The first is the question of the level, or levels, of analysis at which this motivation for consistency is supposed to occur. When we talk of an attitude, are we talking about just one evaluative belief about an object, a momentary affective reaction, or some accumulation of these? In fact, research on "affective-cognitive consistency" asserts that individuals' beliefs and affective reactions will tend to influence one another (Chaiken & Yates, 1985; Rosenberg, 1960). How long do such beliefs or reactions need to last for to count as an attitude? Is consistency purely an intrapersonal matter, or does it apply to interpersonal relations too, and if so to how many people at one time? In fairness to Heider (1946), he offered an answer, at least by implication. Consistency—as a Gestalt principle that is independent of content—should apply at *all* levels. More explicitly, he proposed that individuals would want to see *both* evaluative consistency in the different attributes or aspects of a single object or issue *and* interpersonal consistency, in terms of a match between attitudinal agreement and social relationships of liking or belonging. What is less clear is how any given individual is to decide the appropriate level of analysis for detecting inconsistency and/or achieving consistency. Alternatively, if consistency motives are assumed to operate simultaneously at all levels of generality or specificity, there seems no guarantee that they will pull in the same direction when it comes to the need for change in particular cognitions. Put differently, the possibility of different levels of analysis opens up the possibility of independent pulls towards potentially *inconsistent* forms of consistency.

The second difficulty, related to the first, is the question of relevance, or selectivity. Before we can ask if elements of a structure are organized consistently or inconsistently, we need some basis for deciding which objects and events are to be included as elements of that structure and which are not. Applying the cognitive consistency notion to the special issue of reactions to persuasive messages, Osgood and Tannenbaum (1955, p. 43) proposed that "changes in evaluation are always in the direction of increased congruity with the existing frame of reference." This statement unmasks the problem but does not solve it. What constitutes "the existing frame of reference?" This is essentially the same problem identified by Lewin (1943) as that of defining the "field at a given time." We have to take the perspective of the individual. The structure, or frame of reference, is *subjective*.

If we already know what specific judgments of approval or disapproval, relationships of liking or disliking, evaluative beliefs, subjective norms, and so on and so forth, are salient or personally relevant to the individual, we have most of what we need to *predict* his or her attitudes and behavior. But unless we can account for *why* these specific judgments, etc., are salient, and others aren't, we really haven't *explained* very much at all. If we focus only on the attitudes of single individuals, but fail to consider why and how different individuals and groups *disagree* on many issues—sometimes violently—we are ducking the big questions against which the intellectual and practical value of our theories must be measured. So, before we can start talking about consistency, we must define the "field," "life space," or "frame of reference" within which any motive or "strain" towards symmetry and consistency can come into play. More precisely, we must define how individuals construct and organize this frame of reference for themselves. But if we can't define organization purely in terms of Gestalt principles of good form, where else should we turn? Appealing to the subjective content of an individual's frame of reference is all very well, but is it going to help, rather than hinder, the development of objective methods and usable theories?

### Did Humpty jump, or was he pushed?

Sadly, although many attitude researchers have respected the importance of individual frames of reference, others have argued in a different direction. Historically, probably the most influential of these was Thurstone. In proposing that attitudes could be objectively measured, he did not care to be reminded of their intrinsic complexity:

> It will be conceded at the outset that an attitude is a complex affair which cannot be wholly described by any single numerical index. For the problem of measurement this statement is analogous to the observation that an ordinary table is a complex affair which cannot be wholly described by any single numerical index. Nevertheless, we do not hesitate to say that we measure the table. The context usually implies what it is about the table that we propose to measure. We say without hesitation that we measure a man when we take some anthropometric measurements of him. The context may well imply without explicit declaration what aspect of the man we are measuring, his cephalic index, his height or weight or what not. Just in the same sense we shall say here that we are measuring attitudes. We shall state or imply by the context the aspect of people's attitudes that we are measuring. The point is that it is just as legitimate to say that we are measuring attitudes as it is to say that we are measuring tables or men.
>
> (Thurstone, 1928, p. 530)

Thanks to Thurstone and the methods of scale construction he developed, attitude research became an indispensable and undisputed part of quantitative social science. Now that attitudes could be defined in numerical terms, researchers could conduct experiments with attitudes as a dependent variable and measure the statistical significance of attitude change. Likewise, they could look at what predicted, and followed from, individual differences in opinions on any given issue. For reasons of pragmatic convenience, as well as conceptual preference on the part of many researchers, the emphasis moved away from issues of organization and complexity towards more straightforward questions of predicting simple evaluations of single objects. Reservations about this new technology, expressed, for instance, by Allport, seem to have been swiftly pushed aside:

> Measurement can only deal with attitudes that are *common*, and there are relatively few attitudes that are common enough to be profitably scaled.

In forcing attitudes into a scale form, violence is necessarily done to the unique structure of a man's mind. Attitude scales should be regarded only as the roughest approximations of the way in which attitudes actually exist in the mental life of individuals.

(Allport, 1935, p. 842)

## Attitude organization after the fall

Better remembered than his lack of appetite for scaling techniques is the definition that Allport offered to future attitude researchers:

An attitude is a mental and neural state of readiness, organized through experience, exerting a directive and dynamic influence upon the individual's response to all objects with which it is related.

(Allport, 1935, p. 810)

The perspective expressed in this definition is a remarkably contemporary one. The notion of attitudes being "related" to objects implies that they are not just free-floating "feelings" but have a quality of "aboutness" (Eiser, 1994), or reference. In other words, attitudes make *public* claims about what is and what is not the case. They do not just express *private* feelings. They are forms of representation, evaluative as well as descriptive, that can be, and frequently are, disputed. These exert a dynamic influence in the sense that attitudinal and other responses change over time and can affect each other. The mention of a neural basis for attitudes could point to new theoretical and methodological links with cognitive neuroscience. Above all, though, it is the phrase "organized through experience" which needs to be taken to heart. Attitudes do not just happen, they are acquired through learning and interaction with the environment. We build up individual experiences into more organized representational and motivational structures. To the extent that such structures display consistency, such consistency is itself something that is learnt and acquired. Put differently, consistency, where it exists, is not given, but achieved.

But how is consistency or any other such principle of organization achieved? How does experience organize mental events and reactions into what we call attitudes? The answer is in two parts, neither of which is complete without the other. The first part is that we, that is to say, in this context, our brains, have evolved to form associations between events. This assumption runs right through from philosophical associationism (Hume, 1740/1911) through theories of classical and instrumental conditioning (Dickinson, 1980; Rescorla & Solomon, 1967) through to contemporary research on connectionism. Along the way, we have the speculation from Hebb (1949) that the way learning is instantiated in the brain is through the strengthening of the synaptic connections between any (assemblies of) neurons that are simultaneously activated. Subsequently, we have several applications of the "spreading activation" model of memory (e.g., Bower, 1981) according to which activation of any given memory will lead to the easier retrieval of other memories with which it is associated. The notion of associative memory is now very much part of contemporary attitude theory (Fazio, 1995, 2001).

The second part of the answer is that we inhabit a physical and social environment that itself exhibits considerable structure. This part sometimes tends to be forgotten in talk about the relativity of different individuals' constructions of events. Of course we do not all interpret events in exactly the same way (there would be no work for attitude researchers if we did). Likewise, at a more basic level, our sensory capacities are physically limited, selective and species specific. But still, in a profoundly important sense, the truth is "out there." There has to be *something* for our sensory, interpretative and representational processes to get to work on. This is essentially the same problem as confronted associationist accounts of causality. If cause–effect relations, as proposed by Hume, boil down simply to the experience of if–then succession, then anything could be said to be the cause of anything else that it happened to precede. And so it could be, if the world itself were random, and exhibited no inherent structure. If, however, the world has structure, an information-processing system capable of pattern discrimination can detect that structure and build an organized representation of the world through the associations between separate events and aspects of experience.

In the remainder of this chapter, I shall describe two illustrations of how attitude organization can be built up through learnt associations. Both illustrations rely on computer simulations involving connectionist neural networks. First, though, let me outline the aims, advantages and acknowledged limitations of simulation as an investigatory technique, and provide a short primer in relevant connectionist principles and methods.

## Why simulate?

Simulation is not a substitute for empirical investigation. Simulations can imitate reality, they can elucidate underlying processes, but they cannot establish what is or is not the case. Having said this, empirical investigations also attempt to do more than merely describe what happens to be the case. Typically, they attempt to test predictions and hypotheses in specific contexts. But, of course, not all hypotheses are confirmed. There can be many reasons for this. The underlying general assumption of one's theory may be incorrect. The specific context in which the hypothesis is being tested may involve unforeseen additional causal influences and sources of error. Or the reasoning by which a specific prediction is derived from the underlying general assumption may be flawed. Hence empirical investigations, while they offer us "facts," may not always provide us with a firm basis for extrapolating to other contexts nor for definitely accepting or rejecting a particular theoretical account.

Simulations, on the other hand, do not offer "facts," but they do tell us what *might* be the case in specific situations, if particular theoretical assumptions are actually correct. This means that simulations can help us formulate predictions that can then be submitted to empirical test. But this is the very least that they can do. In cases where simulations successfully imitate or reproduce existing empirical effects, we can have added faith in the theoretical assumptions underlying the predictions. This is because, for any simulation program to work at all, the processes have to be specified in terms of a far tighter and more precise logic than is typical of more discursive approaches to theory building. In other words, the activity of designing a simulation demands that we specify precisely how we expect particular processes to operate under particular conditions. Another advantage is that simulations are not restricted by the same practical constraints of time and resources that apply to laboratory experiments or real-life observations. Far more complex situations can be simulated than reproduced in a controlled experiment. Multiple high-order interactions are relatively easy to study through simulation and repeated measures (to look at the evolution of effects over time) are no problem at all. In other words, simulations can provide *plausible inferences* about what would happen to a standard effect if new factors were introduced, or the context changed or extended in some way.

## Why connectionism?

Whereas most forms of computer simulation and mathematical modeling offer added theoretical precision for the reasons detailed above, the approach known as *connectionism* (e.g., Ellis & Humphreys, 1999; Gurney, 1997; McLeod, Plunkett & Rolls, 1998) goes even further. Here the relationship between method and theory is both intimate and reciprocal. As a technique, connectionism differs radically from previous methods such as expert systems and traditional artificial intelligence (AI). Broadly, these previous approaches rely on sets of predefined rules for translating a particular set of inputs into a particular set of output. These translation rules remain constant, until revised by the programmer. Another way of expressing this is that such systems *apply* knowledge, but do not *acquire* it. Connectionist systems, by contrast, are designed not simply to give answers but to *ask* questions of the information with which they are presented. In other words, such systems are designed to identify relationships within the information presented to them and respond adaptively. In short, they are programmed to *learn*.

Before describing how this is achieved, it is important to appreciate that what is on offer here is not simply a set of techniques, but a rather particular conceptual perspective on the nature of cognition (Seidenberg, 1993). For sure, the techniques *can* be used without strong commitment to the theory, and the theory *can* be discussed without reliance on any particular set of techniques, but neither exercise progresses quite as far or as satisfactorily in such isolation. At base, the unifying assumption is that thought (in all its forms) is a *physical* process achieved by the systematic activity of the brain. Brains, of course, are immensely complex systems, but their basic constituents—neurons—are, relatively speaking, far more simple. Any given neuron can be thought of as a kind of switching device that receives information, in the form of impulses, from other neurons, accumulates it, and then activates other neurons in its turn. Among the factors that influence this transmission of information (activation) is the strength of the connections at the synapses between neurons. Hence, brain processes may be described essentially in terms of two sets of dimensions or parameters: (a) the activation of different (assemblies of) neurons, or centers in the brain, at any given time; (b) the interconnectedness of different neurons through "circuits" that control how activation is passed between and within centers. At a broad level, the latter is constrained by the evolved neuroanatomy of the brain, but at a finer grain level the strength of connections at any given moment is assumed to reflect various factors, including previous learning. In short, learning is reflected in modified brain activity by influencing how activation is transmitted from one neural assembly to another. Of course, this description is extremely crude, but the meta-theoretical point still applies. Complexity in a system does not at all require that the constituents or components of the system are themselves complex. What is needed rather is that the separate components can combine and recombine with each other in many different (and often adaptive) ways. Extremely crudely again, what makes brains so complex is not the neurons in themselves, but the billions of ways in which they interconnect.

Connectionist simulation incorporates this metatheory—albeit with plenty of disclaimers about any close resemblance to actual brains—by exploring the potential of systems termed neural networks. In simple terms, a neural network is a mathematical structure consisting of a number of separate *units* (analogous to neurons) that are (partially or completely) interconnected with each other. The *architecture* of the network specifies the number and arrangement of the separate units, in particular which units receive input from which others. Each unit has an *activation* that varies according to input information it receives from other units (or external "stimulus" input). Each link from one unit to another is associated with a *connection weight*. At any point in time, the activation level of any given (receiving) unit is a function of the activations sent to it, multiplied by the connection weights attached to the relevant links (more or less as, in multiple regression, the value of a dependent variable is derived from the values of the predictor variables, multiplied by the respective coefficients).

Crucially, these connection weights are not fixed in advance, but modified during the course of the simulation until the network reaches a solution to whatever problem is presented to it. Thus, the connection weights both determine how information is processed by the network and define the "memory" of the network. In short, the network "learns" by modifying its connection weights. This can be achieved in a number of different ways, and considerable work has been done evaluating how effectively different kinds of learning algorithms allow networks with particular architectures to solve particular kinds of problems. This is a rapidly evolving field, but for present purposes it is sufficient to distinguish between two broad types of learning algorithm (which can sometimes be used in combination). *Unsupervised* learning is roughly analogous to classical (Pavlovian) conditioning, and works by the strengthening of connections between units as a function of their respective activations. For instance, the Hebbian rule (cf. Hebb, 1949) works by strengthening the link between units that are simultaneously active. *Supervised* learning is roughly analogous to instrumental conditioning, and works by having the network generate an output in response to an input. This output is then compared with a previously defined "target" value and an error is computed. The connection weights are then adjusted to reduce this error. The use of supervised learning has implications for the network architecture. As a minimum, there needs to be a distinction between "input units" that receive stimulus information and "output units" that receive activation from the input units and generate an output. It is also very common (and for many problems, essential) to add a layer of "hidden units" between the input and output layers. These units process and condense the information from the input layer before passing it on to the output layer. The most common way of training such "multi-layer, feed-forward" networks is through the "back-propagation of error" learning algorithm (Rumelhart, Hinton & Williams, 1986). Examples of both types of simulations will now be described.

## Simulating Heiderian balance in multiperson groups

The simulations described in this section have been reported in more detail by Eiser, Claessen, and Loose (1998). Their focus is the archetypical (before-the-fall) theory of attitude organization, Heider's (1946) theory of cognitive balance. As will be familiar, Heider proposed that our attitudes towards other people and towards objects or issues mutually influence each other. We tend to agree more with people whom we like, and tend to like people more if they agree with us. This implies that certain kinds of structures, termed "balanced" by Heider, will be more stable and self-sustaining. Specifically, they are those where we agree with our friends or disagree with our enemies. Our concern was not directly with whether this theory is supported empirically (we already know that other factors affect interpersonal liking and agreement). Rather, we were interested first in whether this principle could be translated into connectionist terms, and second whether, if so, we could extrapolate the theory to contexts that were previously difficult to investigate by standard experimental methods.

The first part of the task, then, was to translate the standard Heiderian structure, the triad involving a person or perceiver ($P$), another person ($O$) and an object or issue ($X$). This is commonly represented as a triangle with the three "elements" ($P$, $O$, $X$) at the different points, connected by lines representing either liking/approval or disliking/disapproval. We represented this by a simple bond of two units (corresponding to $P$ and $O$) interconnected

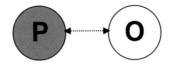

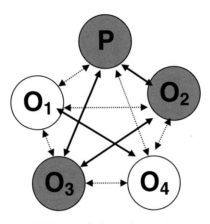

*Figure 14.1* Illustration of Heiderian balance in two-person and five-person structures. Unfilled circles indicate that the person's attitude towards an object
X is positive, filled circles indicate a negative attitude. Solid arrows
indicate mutual liking, dashed arrows, mutual disliking.

by two-way links (see Figure 14.1). As in the triangular representation, these
links reflect interpersonal liking. However, they also fulfil an additional function. We assume that *P* and *O* communicate with each other, and that these
links will control the effect of this communication, as will soon be explained.
The object *X* no longer appears as a separate element in the structure, but the
relevant information is represented in the activations of the units P and O.
Simply, the activation of unit P is more positive, the more *P* approves of *X*,
and more negative, the more *P* disapproves of *X*. *O*'s approval or disapproval
of *X* is likewise represented by the activation of unit O. Note that this allows
for a more continuous representation of both liking (connection weights) and
approval or attitude (activations) than was typical in early balance theory
research. However, there is an even more important advantage of this
approach. As noted by Cartwright and Harary (1956), the balance principle
should be applicable to groups much larger than a dyad. Figure 14.1 also
shows a structure composed of five interconnected units, each representing
a separate individual with relationships of liking or disliking to all other
individuals in the group.

In fact, our simulations used an even more complex structure than that
presented in Figure 14.1. We examined what would be predicted to happen, *if*

balance theory were correct, in a group consisting of ten individuals, each with an attitude towards the same single issue, and each communicating with everyone else in the group to equal extents. What remains to be done is to define a learning algorithm that appropriately translates the central assumption of balance theory, that liking increases attitudinal agreement and agreement increases liking. To achieve this, the algorithm first determined the change (on each trial) in activation of each single unit (P) as a function of the activations of all the other units ($O_1$ to $O_9$), multiplied by the connection weights associated with the links from each of these other units to P. (This was done for all units, i.e., all units took it in turn to be P.) Next, the algorithm adjusted the connection weights between each pair of units as a function of their respective activations. If the two activations shared the same sign or valence (i.e., both represented approval, or both disapproval), the connection weights were strengthened (positively) in inverse proportion to the difference between them. If the activations had different signs, the algorithm adjusted the weights so that they became more negative.

A series of simulations were performed using this algorithm, starting from an initial random setting of weights and activation levels and continuing until a clear structure emerged. Under standard conditions, perfect balance (and reciprocity of liking relationships) was achieved very rapidly. However, recall that Heider is silent on whether balance should be achieved by changes in relationships (e.g., deciding to like others you agree with) or changes in attitude (e.g., deciding to agree with others you like). In fact, the findings of the simulations point strongly to the answer that, in such larger groups, relationships change more than attitudes. The activations drift towards greater extremity, but in the direction of their initial valance. In other words, approval stays as approval and disapproval as disapproval. The connection weights also become more polarized, with some highly positive and some highly negative, but in this case this involves many instances where an initial liking relationship turn into one of strong dislike, and vice versa. Moreover, when the parameter settings are changed so as to slow down the learning rate at which that connection weights can be modified (relative to activations), the ability of the network to settle into an overall balanced solution is drastically impaired.

This makes sense in terms of the fact that there are more degrees of freedom associated with the relationships rather than the attitude. Put differently, there is more chance of organizing your relationships so that you are friends with those who share your opinion than the other way round; changing your attitude to make a friend of one person could mean that you make an enemy of someone else. In more concrete terms, suppose that P likes $O_1$ and $O_2$ and dislikes $O_3$ and $O_4$. At the same time, P agrees with $O_1$ and $O_3$ but disagrees with $O_2$ and $O_4$. In other words, the substructures (Heiderian triads) involving P with $O_1$ and $O_4$ are balanced, and those involving P with $O_2$ and $O_3$ are imbalanced. The latter two substructures *could* be rendered balanced by changing P's attitude, but then the other two substructures will immediately become imbalanced. On the other hand, if the relationships are changed, so that $o_2$ becomes disliked as well as still disagreed with, and $o_3$ becomes liked as well as still agreed with, then restoration of balance within one substructure can be achieved without disrupting it elsewhere.

What are the implications for real relationships? Probably a fairer question is: what are the implications for *theories* of real relationships? A highly influential notion is that we choose as friends others who are similar in various ways to ourselves (Byrne, 1961). The dynamic feature of Heiderian balance, reflected in our simulation, stresses that similarity should not simply be treated as a cause and attraction as an effect. We may also *perceive* others as more similar to ourselves (in attitude or other characteristics) if we are more attracted to them. We may also *change* our own attitudes to achieve greater (perceived) similarity with our friends. However, in contexts of many individuals but a single issue, balance may more easily be achieved through relationship change than attitude change. This implies that balance processes can be closely involved in phenomena of group polarization (e.g., Mackie, 1986; Mackie & Cooper, 1984). Members of larger groups may split into mutually opposed subgroups, and these subgroups themselves become more cohesive (in terms of relationships) and well as homogeneous (in terms of attitudes) as a consequence of processes that hitherto have been considered almost always in the context of dyads. These simulations therefore suggest that there may be unrecognized common ground between balance theory and a number of theories of group processes, such as social identity theory (Tajfel, 1982), with respect to their basic underlying assumptions. Both approaches, after all, assume that people are motivated to make sense of their social world in terms of simple evaluative categorizations, and will frame their social relationships and behavior accordingly.

At the same time, the limitations of these simulations must be stressed. One is that we represented separate individuals by single units, so that the only way balance could be resolved was interpersonally. Related to this is the fact that we dealt with only a single attitude issue, and agreement or disagreement on this one issue was the only factor influencing relationship change. If we allowed the "individuals" to hold several "attitudes" simultaneously, then agreement with a friend on one issue might compensate for disagreement on another. Of course this would be more like real life, but there is still quite a lot of real life where situational constraints and/or personal motives mean that a single issue *can* dominate, or have a disproportionate effect on, social relationships. Taken as they stand, our findings suggest that single-issue political activity or controversy is particularly likely to lead to individuals being polarized into opposing camps. This is another advantage of simulation. We have to define not just the process we want to simulate, but the context within which we believe this process applies.

## Simulating attitude learning

The second set of simulations addresses the question of how we acquire attitudes through interaction with our environment. (For a more detailed account, see Eiser, Fazio, Stafford, & Prescott, 2003.) Our main purpose was to explore potential asymmetries in the learning of favorable and unfavorable attitudes. Specifically, we sought to clarify the implications of the following assumptions: (a) attitudes are based on acquired object-evaluation associations and expectancies (Fazio, 1995); (b) acquired associations and expectancies guide behavior so that individuals will approach attitude objects that they evaluate positively and avoid objects they evaluate negatively; (c) hence, other things being equal, individuals will have more experience of interaction with positively than negatively evaluated objects; (d) avoidance of objects believed to be negative can lead to false negative beliefs remaining uncorrected for longer than false positive beliefs.

The simulations reported were conducted alongside human experiments (Fazio & Eiser, 2000; Fazio, Eiser, & Shook, in press) that involved participants playing a computer game in which they inhabited a virtual world in which, to survive, they had to discriminate between edible and inedible objects, or "beans." Eating good beans provided energy, whereas eating bad beans (or not eating at all) resulted in a loss of energy, with too much energy loss resulting in "death." These beans varied in terms of two dimensions: shape (from round to oblong) and number of speckles (1 to 10). There were 36 beans involved, half of them good and half of them bad, located in six different "regions" of the two dimensional space, as shown in Figure 14.2. The critical aspect of the game is that participants can only discover if a bean is good or bad by first trying (i.e., eating) it. If they don't eat, they don't learn. This implies an asymmetry in the extent to which positive and negative attitudes are open to disconfirmation. If you think a bean is good, you'll eat it, and so find out if it really was good or bad. If you think it's bad, you'll avoid it, and so won't find out if you are right or wrong. The main finding from the human data is that participants find this task quite difficult, and in particular fail to identify all the good beans with which they are presented. In other words, while participants correctly avoid most bad beans, they incorrectly avoid some of the good beans too.

To simulate this, a variant of a standard feedforward network was designed. This involved: (a) a layer of 22 input units, 11 of which provided a distributed coding of the shape dimension and 11 a coding of the number of speckles;[1] (b) a layer of 3 hidden units; (c) a single output unit, with activation

---

1 Each level of an attribute (shape or speckles) was represented by activation (>0) on up to 6 of the 11 units. For example, one speckle would be encoded by the vector [1,1,0.5,0.25,0,0,0,0,0,0,0], four speckles as [0,0.25,0.5,1,1,0.5,0.25,0,0,0,0], through to ten speckles as [0,0,0,0,0,0,0,0.25,0.5,1,1]. The effect of this is that any two adjacent levels of an attribute will share one input unit in common where the activation level is at its maximum (1). Because each attribute level is encoded by more that one input unit, and the individual input

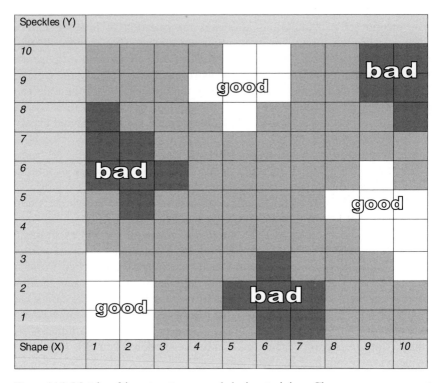

*Figure 14.2* Matrix of input patterns used during training. Clear squares represent
good beans and dark grey squares represent bad beans. The remaining 64
squares represent attribute combinations not used during training, but
presented afterwards to test for generalization.

bounded within the range 0 to 1, so that activations below 0.5 represented
avoidance and activations of 0.5 or above represented approach (eating the
bean); (d) alongside the hidden layer and connected to it, a single unit representing the aspect of the human experiment whereby "energy level" varied as
a consequence of eating good or bad beans, and declined with time if no bean
were eaten at all.

   This network was trained on the 36 beans for a total of 5000 epochs (each
epoch involving a single presentation of each of the 36 beans in a random
order). (The learning rate parameter was set at 0.02, and the momentum
parameter at 0.06.) The activations provided to these 36 input patterns were

units contribute to the encoding of more than one attribute level, the network achieves a
*distributed* (rather than localist) representation of the different stimuli. This enables the network to encode location in the space in such a way as to also take account of proximity. (Note,
that this is only one of many possible methods of achieving a distributed representation of the
input space.)

then inspected. Additionally, in order to see how well the network could generalize, the activations to new input patterns, not presented during training, were inspected. This procedure was replicated ten times (in each condition) with different random initial settings of the connection weights (within the range −0.3 to 0.3).

The network was trained by comparing its outputs with target values, set at 0.9 for good beans and 0.1 for bad beans. The difference or error score ($\Delta$) between the output and target was then used as a basis for modifying the connection weights throughout the network. Three different learning algorithms were employed. A "full feedback" condition used the standard backpropagation of error (backprop) algorithm. This meant that the network received feedback as to whether it was generating correct or incorrect responses, regardless of whether it had categorized a bean as good or bad. This essentially provides a benchmark about how well the different types of beans could be discriminated with no extra constraints. Next, a "contingent feedback" condition was introduced. This was intended to simulate the constraint that no information was gained unless a bean was "eaten." The algorithm employed was equivalent to full feedback whenever the network produced an output of 0.5 or above. However, if the network produced an output below 0.5, equivalent to not eating, no feedback modification of the weights took place on that trial. Finally, a "confirmation bias" condition adapted the contingent feedback algorithm to reflect the notion that avoidance may partly be self-reinforcing, even without confirmation that an avoided bean was bad. For example, classic studies of avoidance learning in animals (Solomon & Wynne, 1954) suggest that avoidance of an anticipated negative event (e.g., shock) is not simply processed as a non-event, but may reduce fear and hence be reinforcing. To simulate this, on all trials where the network "avoided" (i.e., produced an output < 0.5), *regardless of the true target value for the input*, a $\Delta$ was calculated as though the target value was 0.1 (i.e., as though it was a bad bean). This $\Delta$ was then arbitrarily divided by 10 and the connection weights were updated by the backprop algorithm in the normal way. Thus, all avoidance, whether correct or incorrect, was reinforced, the strength of the reinforcement being equivalent to one-tenth of that received for *correct* avoidance under full feedback training for an output activation at the same level.

The simulations indicated that, under full feedback, the network distinguished the good and bad beans with essentially perfect reliability. In all 10 replications, all 18 good beans were categorized as good and all 18 bad beans as bad. The mean $\Delta$ was also close to zero for both sets of beans. By comparison, in the contingent feedback and confirmation bias conditions, the network showed a clear asymmetry in its learning. Categorization of bad beans was again perfect, or nearly so (only one replication under contingent feedback misclassified any of the 18 inputs), although the mean $\Delta$s for each set of beans were higher than in the full feedback condition. However, the mean discrimination of the good beans was far less reliable, with, on average, 5.4 of the 18 good beans misclassified as bad under contingent feedback, and 4.9 under confirmation bias. The most noticeable effect of the confirmation bias algorithm was to reduce the $\Delta$ for outputs to the bad beans.

This asymmetry in learning carried over to the outputs produced by the network to the 64 novel beans not presented during training. On average, these were significantly below the 0.5 threshold value following contingent feedback (0.42) and confirmation bias (0.41) but not full feedback (0.53). In other words, the network tended to predict that more of the novel beans were bad than good. Additional analyses indicated that this reflected a generalization based on proximity. That is, patterns close to original inputs that had been classified as good were also predicted to be good, whereas those close to inputs that had (rightly or wrongly) been classified as bad were also predicted to be bad.

## Attitudes as dynamic systems

The two sets of simulations described here both attempt to look at contextual constraints on how systems come to differentiated objects as "good" or "bad." Immediately, it must be stressed that—from the point of view of the network—there is nothing intrinsically evaluative about the differentiations achieved. The network—any network—is merely an abstract system that performs mathematical operations. Establishing what these operations and their outputs could stand for in the real world demands intuitions and arguments that come from elsewhere. It is therefore important to state the intuitions underlying the claim that these simulations might have anything to do with "real" attitudes.

The intuition underlying the first set of simulations, as originally proposed by Heider (1946), is that our attitudes towards objects and other people influence one another. We are more likely to agree with our friends and be friends with those who share our opinions. In these simulations, approval or disapproval of *objects* was represented by higher or lower activations of individual units. Defining higher activations as standing for approval rather than disapproval was completely arbitrary, since we assumed no asymmetry between the processes underlying favorable and unfavorable opinions. However, the sign of the connection weights linking the different units was crucial. In balance theory terms, positive liking leads to greater sharing of opinions. In connectionist terms, a positive connection weight means that a sending unit will directly influence a receiving unit, leading to greater correspondence between their respective activation levels. Hence, it makes theoretical sense to say that positive connection weights can stand for liking, and negative weights for disliking, since the difference in the effect of such weights on the performance of the network is analogous to the difference between positive and negative interpersonal relationships (according to balance theory).

The second set of simulations was based on the intuition that we acquire attitudes by exploring our social environment or life space, but that our exploration is selectively focused in directions we anticipate to be rewarding. In other words, we approach things we expect to be good and give pleasure, and avoid things we expect to be bad and give pain. This can lead us to identify sufficiently safe and/or rewarding experiences, albeit at the price of leaving some other potentially rewarding regions of our life space unexplored. As a result of this response bias towards false negatives, for many of us positive experiences will tend to predominate over negative ones. According to Parducci (1984), this will lead to feelings of happiness. In fact, it may be for this reason that, on average, people tend to describe themselves as above average in happiness (Klar & Giladi, 1999) and positive traits (Hoorens, 1995) and less vulnerable to ill health or other risks (Weinstein, 1989). Less encouragingly, though, people may persist in negative and preju- dicial beliefs through a lack of any learning experience to contradict such beliefs. This intuition, however, rests on a limiting condition, namely that choices are free and that we can avoid things we dislike or fear. Where, as is too often the case, this does not apply, the same processes of learning can have very different effects. Where choices are not free, and where abuse, oppression and exclusion are frequent and inescapable, this assumption of a predominance of positive over negative experiences will no longer be valid. Instead the preconditions will exist for feelings of learned helplessness (Abramson, Seligman, & Teasdale, 1978; Alloy, Abramson, & Francis, 1999).

Within each set of simulations and the theoretical assumptions they explore, there is a yet more general principle. An attitude is not just an output or reaction, even an evaluative one. As Allport (1935) put it, an attitude exerts "a directive and dynamic influence upon the individual's response to all objects with which it is related." Attitudes have consequences, and these consequences in their turn change the environment around which these same attitudes are organized. Our attitudes may influence our choice of friends, who in turn influence our attitudes. Our attitudes may influence our approach and avoidance behaviors, and these in turn influence those experiences that in their turn reinforce what we approach in the expectation of pleasure or gain, and what we avoid through fear of pain or loss. We are, in short, looking at *dynamic systems* that evolve over time (Eiser, 1994), and achieve a coherent structure, not because they are searching for some pre-ordained template of "good form," but because changes in the direction of greater organization are continually self-reinforced through a cycle of positive feedback. Attitude is not simply organized through experience, it organizes experience. Con- nectionism offers not merely a set of techniques to complement traditional experimentation. Conceptually it treats attitude as a system, continually being organized and reorganized through the dynamic interactions of affect, cognition and behavior. There may be hope for Humpty yet!

# References

Abramson, L. Y., Seligman, M. E. P., & Teasdale, J. D. (1978). Learned helplessness in humans: Critique and reformulation. *Journal of Abnormal Psychology*, *87*, 49–74.

Ajzen, I., & Fishbein, M. (1977). Attitude–behavior relations: A theoretical analysis and review of empirical research. *Psychological Bulletin*, *84*, 888–918.

Alloy, L. B., Abramson, L. Y., & Francis, E. L. (1999). Do negative cognitive styles confer vulnerability to depression? *Current Directions in Psychological Science*, *8*, 128–132.

Allport, G. W. (1935). Attitudes. In C. Murchison (Ed.), *Handbook of social psychology* (pp. 798–844). Worcester, MA: Clark University Press.

Bower, G. H. (1981). Mood and memory. *American Psychologist*, *36*, 129–148.

Byrne, D. (1961). Interpersonal attraction and attitude similarity. *Journal of Abnormal and Social Psychology*, *62*, 713–715.

Cartwright, D., & Harary, F. (1956). Structural balance: A generalization of Heider's theory. *Psychological Review*, *63*, 277–293.

Chaiken, S., & Yates, S. M. (1985). Affective-cognitive consistency and thought-induced attitude polarization. *Journal of Personality and Social Psychology*, *49*, 1470–1481.

Dickinson, A. (1980). *Contemporary animal learning theory*. Cambridge: Cambridge University Press.

Eiser, J. R. (1994). *Attitudes, chaos and the connectionist mind*. Oxford, Blackwell.

Eiser, J. R., Claessen, M. J. A., & Loose, J. J. (1998). Attitudes, beliefs and other minds: Shared representations in self-organizing systems. In S. J. Read & L. C. Miller (Eds.), *Connectionist models of social reasoning and social behavior* (pp. 313–354). Mahwah, NJ: Lawrence Erlbaum Associates, Inc.

Eiser, J. R., Fazio, R. H., Stafford, T., & Prescott, T. J. Connectionist simulation of attitude learning: Asymmetries in the acquisition of positive and negative evaluations. *Personality and Social Psychology Bulletin*, *29*, 1221–1235.

Ellis, R., & Humphreys, G. (Eds.) (1999). *Connectionist psychology: A text with readings*. Hove, UK: Psychology Press.

Fazio, R. H. (1995). Attitudes as object-evaluation associations: Determinants, consequences, and correlates of attitude accessibility. In R. E. Petty & J. A. Krosnick, (Eds.), *Attitude strength: Antecedents and consequences* (pp. 247–282). Mahwah, NJ: Lawrence Erlbaum Associates, Inc.

Fazio, R. H. (2001). On the automatic evaluation of associated evaluations: An overview. *Cognition and Emotion*, *15*, 115–141.

Fazio, R. H., & Eiser, J. R. (2000). *Attitude formation through associative learning: Valence asymmetries*. Paper presented to the annual meeting of the Society for Experimental Social Psychology, Atlanta, GA, October.

Fazio, R. H., Eiser, J. R., & Shook, N. J. (in press). Attitude formation through exploration: Valence asymmetries. *Journal of Personality and Social Psychology*.

Festinger, L. (1957). *A theory of cognitive dissonance*. Evanston, IL: Row, Peterson.

Gurney, K. (1997). *An introduction to neural networks*. London: UCL Press.

Hebb, D. O. (1949). *The organization of behavior*. New York: Wiley.

Heider, F. (1946). Attitudes and cognitive organization. *Journal of Psychology*, *21*, 107–112.

Hoorens, V. (1995). Self-favoring biases, self-presentation, and the self-other asymmetry in social comparison. *Journal of Personality*, *63*, 793–817.

Hume, D. (1740/1911). *A treatise of human nature.* London: Dent.

Klar, Y., & Giladi, E. E. (1999). Are most people happier than their peers, or are they just happy? *Personality and Social Psychology Bulletin, 25,* 585–594.

Lewin, K. (1943). Defining the "field at a given time." *Psychological Review, 50,* 292–310.

Mackie, D. M. (1986). Social identification effects in group polarization. *Journal of Personality and Social Psychology, 50,* 720–728.

Mackie, D. M., & Cooper, J. (1984). Attitude polarization: Effects of groups membership. *Journal of Personality and Social Psychology, 46,* 575–585.

McLeod, P., Plunkett, K., & Rolls, E.T. (1998). *Introduction to connectionist modelling of cognitive processes.* Oxford: Oxford University Press.

Osgood, C. E., & Tannenbaum, P. H. (1955). The principle of congruity in the prediction of attitude change. *Psychological Review, 62,* 42–55.

Parducci, A. (1984). Value judgments: Toward a relational theory of happiness. In J. R. Eiser (Ed.), *Attitudinal judgment* (pp. 3–21). New York: Springer-Verlag.

Rescorla, R. A., & Solomon, R. L. (1967). Two-process learning theory: Relationships between Pavlovian conditioning and instrumental learning. *Psychological Review, 74,* 151–182.

Rosenberg, M. J. (1960). An analysis of affective-cognitive consistency. In C. I. Hovland & M. J. Rosenberg (Eds.), *Attitude organization and change: An analysis of consistency among attitude components* (pp. 15–64). New Haven, CT: Yale University Press.

Rumelhart, D. E., Hinton, G. E., & Williams, R. J. (1986). Learning internal representations by error propagation. In D. E. Rumelhart, J. L. McClelland, & PDP Research Group (Eds.), *Parallel distributed processing: Explorations in the microstructure of cognition* (Vol. 1, pp. 318–362). Cambridge, MA: MIT Press.

Seidenberg, M. S. (1993). Connectionist models and cognitive theory. *Psychological Science, 4,* 228–235.

Solomon, R. L., & Wynne, L. C. (1954). Traumatic avoidance learning: The principles of anxiety conservation and partial irreversibility. *Psychological Review, 61,* 353–385.

Tajfel, H. (Ed.) (1982). *Social identity and intergroup relations.* Cambridge: Cambridge University Press.

Thurstone. L. L. (1928). Attitudes can be measured. *American Journal of Sociology, 33,* 529–554.

Weinstein, N. D. (1989). Effects of personal experience on self-protective behavior. *Psychological Bulletin, 105,* 31–50.

# 15 Connectionist modeling of attitudes and cognitive dissonance

*Karen Jordens and*
*Frank Van Overwalle*

How are attitudes represented in human memory, and how are they changed after direct experiences or messages that contradict earlier opinions? In this chapter, the question of attitude representation and change is analyzed from a connectionist approach. This novel framework has been introduced in social psychology during the last decade, inspired by the increasing success of connectionism in cognitive psychology. Connectionist models offer a new perspective on diverse social psychological phenomena, including person impression formation (Smith & DeCoster, 1998; Van Overwalle & Labiouse, 2004), causal attribution (Read & Montoya, 1999; Van Overwalle, 1998), group biases (Kashima, Woolcock, & Kashima, 2000; Van Rooy, Van Overwalle, Vanhoomissen, Labiouse, & French, 2003) and cognitive dissonance (Van Overwalle & Jordens, 2002; for an overview, see Read & Miller, 1998). A key difference from earlier models is that the connectionist architecture and processing mechanisms are founded on the neurological properties of the brain. This allows a view of the mind as an adaptive learning mechanism that develops an accurate mental representation of the world. Learning is modeled as a process of online adaptation of existing knowledge to novel information provided by the environment.

We propose a connectionist perspective on attitude formation and cognitive dissonance that integrates various prior perspectives. The model adopts not only the three-component view on attitudes as consisting of beliefs, evaluations, and behavioral tendencies (Katz & Stotland, 1959; Rosenberg & Hovland, 1960), but also incorporates earlier algebraic models of attitude formation (Fishbein & Ajzen, 1975) and an attributional perspective on cognitive dissonance and attitude formation (cf. Cooper & Fazio, 1984). In our perspective, beliefs are representations of outcomes or attributes of the attitude object; evaluations are negative or positive preferences and emotional experiences associated with the attitude object, and behavioral tendencies are simply the verbal responses or approach or avoidance reactions with respect to the attitude object. Although most researchers agree that evaluative reactions are the major constituent of an attitude, we conceive both evaluations and behavioral responses as determinants of someone's attitude. As we will see later, this is most evident and relevant when behaviors do not express someone's preferences, but are rather discrepant with it.

In the model, the attitude object and other contextual factors reflect the causes that drive the evaluative reactions (like or dislike) or behavioral responses (approach or avoidance). Each of the causal input factors and outcome responses is represented by (a set of) nodes connected by adjustable connections. Indeed, one of the key advantages of connectionist models is that connections are not fixed or determined a priori, but are adjusted on the basis of incoming information. This adjustment process is governed by a learning algorithm that processes information on a lower local level that involves changes in only a limited set of nodes, which obliterates the need for a central executive or supervisory module. Moreover, these changes are executed in parallel so that they allow for efficient and fast processing.

Thus, according to a connectionist approach, attitudes can be learned and changed with little awareness, intention or mental effort. This view is in line with the recent emphasis in social psychology on implicit processing in social perception and judgment (Bargh & Chartrand, 1999; Schwarz, 2000). Rather than governed by one's conscious control, many inferences and judgments—including attitudes—seem to be characterized as effortless, without intention or awareness (Bargh, 1984; Fazio, 1986). From a connectionist perspective, we assume that most often only the outcome of this adjustment process is open to conscious awareness, although it is possible that people may become aware of some aspects of the adjustment process, or that deliberative processes may interfere with or override this automatic process.

This chapter is organized as follows. We will first provide a short description on earlier work on attitude formation and change, and then discuss the features of the proposed connectionist model of attitude. Next, we present some simulations with the connectionist model, and we end with empirical data that support some unique predictions of the model.

## A short history of attitude models

### *Early learning theories*

Early attitude theories in the 1950s assumed that attitudes are developed through conditional learning and that affective experiences determine the attitude or evaluative response. According to classical conditioning theory, an attitude is an evaluative response (conditioned response) established by the temporal association of a stimulus (unconditioned stimulus) eliciting an affective reaction (unconditioned response), with the judgmental target or attitude object (conditioned stimulus). For instance, in one of their first experiments, Staats and Staats (1958) presented names (Swedish or Dutch) paired with words having a positive or negative value (e.g., pretty, failure). Consistent with their prediction, participants reported a positive attitude towards names associated with positive words, while they developed a negative attitude towards names associated with negative words (see also Zanna, Kiesler, & Pilkonis, 1970). Recently, there is a renewed interest of social psychologists in the conditioning of evaluations (Dijksterhuis, 2002; Riketta & Dauenheimer, 2002; for an overview, see De Houwer, Thomas, & Baeyens, 2001). Moreover, as we will see shortly, associative models of conditioning (cf. Rescorla & Wagner, 1972) have many key elements in common with current connectionist models.

### *Algebraic models*

By the late 1960s, when the cognitive paradigm emerged in social psychology, attitude research focused more on the cognitive processes in attitude formation. Influential attitude theories suggested that people infer their attitudes in a deliberate and rational way from beliefs or information about the attitude object according to simple, algebraic rules. According to these algebraic models, different pieces of information and beliefs are combined and integrated into an overall attitude. One type of algebraic model is the weighted average model of Anderson (1971, 1981a, 1981b). Anderson's information integration theory assumes that attitudinal judgments are computed as the weighted average of attributes. Attitudinal judgments are modified when new information comes in and is integrated with the initial attitude of the person.

Expectancy-value models constitute another subset of algebraic models. A prototypical and well-known example is Fishbein's (1963) model of attitude formation, later reformulated as the theory of reasoned action (Fishbein & Ajzen, 1975). According to this model, attitudes are determined on the one hand by salient behavioral beliefs about the attitude object (defined as the subjective probability that one's behavior towards the attitude object has certain consequences) and on the other hand by the evaluation of the behavioral consequences. The attitude $A$ toward the object $o$ is expressed in the following equation (Fishbein & Ajzen, 1975):

$$A = \sum_{i=1}^{n} b_i e_i \qquad [1]$$

where $b_i$ is the belief about behavioral consequences i; $e_i$ is the evaluation of the behavioral consequences i; and $n$ is the number of salient behavioral consequences. Take, for example, different modes of transportation such as a car, a bicycle and a public bus to go to work. Each of these vehicles ($os$) has a number of consequences ($b_i$) such as speed (fast or slow), protection against rain (dry or wet) and causing (or not) air pollution, and each of these consequences is evaluated ($e_i$) as good, bad or neutral.

In addition to cognitive information, some algebraic models are capable of incorporating affective and behavioral information to determine attitudes. For instance, Kaplan (1991) empirically demonstrated that cognition and affect could be integrated into an overall evaluative judgment according to a weighted average rule.

### Associative network models

Still another class of models are the associative or spreading-activation network models of memory developed in the 1970s in cognitive psychology (e.g., Anderson & Bower, 1973). These models postulate that concepts are stored as nodes in memory, which are connected through associative links. Activation is spread automatically along those links, in such a way that association strength determines the rate of activation spread.

Associative network models have also been used in social cognition to account for memory processes (e.g., Bower, 1981; Hastie & Kumar, 1979). Fazio (1986) integrated the associative network model into the attitude domain by postulating that attitudes are associations in memory between a given object and its evaluation, developed through repeated pairings (i.e., repeated attitudinal expressions). Furthermore, the strength of the association determines the accessibility of the attitude from memory and, consequently, the likelihood that the attitude will be automatically activated upon the mere presence of the attitude object. However, Fazio claimed that only strong attitudes are activated automatically upon the presence of the attitude object, whereas a weak attitude would be constructed in a more deliberative way from current accessible thoughts. Fazio's view on the automatic activation of attitudes is reminiscent of Zajonc's (1980) concept of affective primacy. In his influential paper, Zajonc argued that attitudes (preferences) are affective responses that occur automatically and independently of cognition. In line with Fazio's theory, Zajonc suggested that the association of a positive or negative value with an object occurs automatically.

Recently, there is a renewed interest in the role of implicit processes in attitude formation (see Bargh & Chartrand, 1999; Schwarz, 2000; Wilson, Lindsey, & Schooler, 2000). For instance, dual-process models of attitudes (e.g., Chaiken, 1987; Petty & Cacioppo, 1986) emphasize the contribution of explicit and implicit processes. The explicit or central processes involve the deliberative processing of arguments from persuasive messages concerning the attitude object. Implicit or peripheral processes involve the use of mental heuristics or shortcuts that allow forming an opinion on the basis of contextual cues, rather than the arguments of the message. Other authors focused on other implicit and automatic processes in attitude formation, such as incidental or subliminal learning of attitude objects and valences (e.g., Betsch, Plessner, Schwieren, & Gütig 2001; Dijksterhuis, 2002; Krosnick, Betz, Jussim, & Lynn, 1992; Riketta & Dauenheimer, 2002).

Although spreading-activation network models share many features of connectionist models, one major limitation is that the strength of the associations cannot be determined or adjusted by the model itself. Hence, a spreading-activation network is fixed and cannot learn from novel information provided.

Instead, authors must set these associative strengths themselves and assume an unspecified process by which these associations develop and change.

## An adaptive connectionist model of attitudes and cognitive dissonance

The architecture and processing mechanism of connectionist models are inspired by biological properties of the brain (O'Reilly & Munakata, 2000). Connectionist models are built of different units or nodes connected via links, like neural networks in the brain. In contrast to associative network models that use localist encoding where each node represents a single "symbolic" concept, many connectionist models use a distributed representation where multiple nodes represent "subsymbolic" micro-features of a concept, which is a more realistic simulation of brain functioning (Thorpe, 1994; for an example, see Smith & DeCoster, 1998).

The connectionist framework also proposes a novel view on encoding, storage and retrieval of information in the brain. Long-term memory is represented in the model by encoding the stored knowledge in the connection weights, while short-term memory is represented by patterns of activation of nodes in the network. As noted earlier, a distinct advantage of connectionist models is that they are dynamic, that is, they not only allow activation to spread in the network, but they also adjust the weight of the connections after novel information (represented as external activation) is processed in the network.

In contrast to this general class of dynamic connectionist models, there are some models which are static, that is, they compute only how activation is spread but do not adjust the weight of the connections. An example of such network is the constraint satisfaction model of cognitive dissonance proposed by Shultz and Lepper (1996). Given the important limitation that the connection weights in such models are fixed a priori, we will not further consider this class of connectionist models, and focus only on adaptive models where weights are dynamically developed and adjusted on the basis of novel incoming information.

### Basic features of the model

#### Architecture

The connectionist model of attitudes that we propose is an adaptive feedforward network, in which a layer of input nodes is connected to a layer of output nodes via adjustable connections (McLeod, Plunkett, & Rolls, 1998). The input nodes represent the attitude object and other environmental factors and the output nodes represent the cognitive, evaluative and behavioral outcomes or responses. A person's attitude is reflected in the connections linking the attitude objects with the evaluative reactions (like or dislike) or behavioral responses (approach or avoidance). Figure 15.1 illustrates this

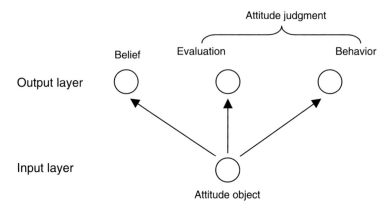

*Figure 15.1* A generic feedforward connectionist architecture reflecting the major components of an attitude; in the model, only evaluations and behaviors determine the attitude judgment.

feedforward architecture. The activation in a feedforward model typically spreads forward from input to output (hence the name feedforward). Although other, more complex architectures exist, they will not be considered because the purpose of this chapter is to demonstrate that even a very simple connectionist model is capable of explaining many attitude processes.

*Activation spreading*

When the attitude object and additional causal factors are present, their input nodes are activated and the level of activation is allowed to vary between −1 and +1. This external activation is automatically spread to the output nodes in proportion to the weight of the connections. The activations received from the input are linearly summed to determine the output activation, expressed as follows:

$$a_i^{out} = \Sigma \, (a_j^{in} \times w_{ij})$$ [2]

where $a_i^{out}$ is the output activation, $a_j^{in}$ the input activation and $w_{ij}$ the connection weight. The weights indicate the strength of the connections, analogous to synaptic strengths that reflect the efficiency with which a neuron receives its input from a synapse (O'Reilly & Munakata, 2000). Connection weights can be positive or negative, analogous to excitatory or inhibitory synapses, and typically range between −1 and +1.

*Learning mechanism*

As noted earlier, connectionist models focus on the dynamic properties of cognition and learning in addition to structural representations, unlike associative network models. The weights of the connections are adaptive, shaped by learning experiences. In our model, these weights are updated on the basis of an error-driven learning algorithm, the delta learning algorithm. The delta learning algorithm has been applied in most applications of connectionist models in social cognition (e.g., Read & Montoya, 1999; Smith & DeCoster, 1998; Van Overwalle, 1998; Van Overwalle & Jordens, 2002; Van Rooy et al., 2003). Interestingly, this learning algorithm is formally identical to the Rescorla-Wagner (1972) model of classical conditioning, which renders the present approach consistent with earlier (e.g., Staats & Staats, 1958) and current social conditioning research (e.g., De Houwer et al., 2001).

The learning algorithm operates after a pattern of external activation is presented to the input layer (i.e., the attitude object and other causal factors) and has spread out to the output layer. This output activation is also referred to as internal activation because it is generated by the network itself, and reflects the response predicted by the network. The goal of the delta learning algorithm is to generate internal output activation that corresponds as closely as possible with the external activation on the output layer (e.g., the individual's actual responses). How far off the network is from this external activation is measured by the discrepancy or error between the internal and external activation on the output layer. This error is used in the delta algorithm to adjust the connection weights and to decrease the error, and these adjustments are made proportional to a global learning rate parameter. The delta algorithm is mathematically expressed as follows:

$$\Delta w_{ij} = \varepsilon \times (a_i^{ex} - a_i^{out}) \times a_j^{in} \qquad [3]$$

where $\Delta w_{ij}$ reflects the weight adjustment, $\varepsilon$ is the learning rate, $a_i^{ex}$ the external activation of output node i, $a_i^{out}$ the internal activation of output node i and $a_j^{in}$ the external activation of input node j. As can be seen in the equation, the adjustments aim at minimizing the error or discrepancy between the internally generated output activation and the external activation of the output. If the network overestimated or underestimated the external activation, weights will be decreased or increased respectively. It can also be seen that each weight adjustment involves only one input node $a_j$ and one output node $a_i$, demonstrating that learning in a connectionist network occurs entirely at a lower level of processing without the need of a higher level supervisory system.

The learning rate $\varepsilon$ typically varies between 0 and +1. A high learning rate indicates that new information has strong priority over old information and leads to radical adjustments in the connection weights, whereas a low learning rate suggests conservative adjustments that preserve much of the knowledge in the weights acquired by old information. In the simulations presented, we set the learning rate to .05. This implies that only 5% of the error will be used to adjust the connection weights.

### Emergent connectionist properties

For the purpose of understanding attitude formation and change from a connectionist perspective, it is important to have a good understanding of some emergent properties of the delta learning algorithm: the properties of acquisition and competition.

*Acquisition property*

The acquisition property determines sample size effects that have been documented in several areas of social cognition. For example, when receiving more supportive information, people tend to hold more extreme impressions (Anderson, 1967, 1981a) and agree more with persuasive messages (Eagly & Chaiken, 1993).

How is this sample size effect explained in connectionist networks? As noted earlier, a key feature of adaptive connectionist networks using the delta algorithm is that connection weights are gradually adjusted when new information is processed. In general, the delta algorithm predicts that the more two nodes are positively activated together, the stronger their connection weight will become (i.e., acquisition property). This results in a pattern of increasing weights as more pieces of information are processed, reflecting the sample size effect. As illustrated in Figure 15.2(a), our model predicts that the more an attitude object A co-occurs with positive evaluative responses, the stronger the connection becomes, which results in stronger favorable attitudes.

*Competition property*

Another important emergent property of the delta algorithm is the competition property. Competition effects between connections arise when multiple causes compete in predicting the outcome. This produces effects similar to discounting and augmentation in causal attribution (Kelley, 1972). For instance, discounting of a cause occurs when alternative causes have already acquired strong causal weight. The attribution of an attitude to an actor is discounted given the presence of external pressures that may explain his or her behavior.

How does the delta algorithm produce discounting? The mechanism behind competition is that the internal output activation is determined by the sum of all activations received from the input (of the attitude object and all other causes present). As illustrated in the left panel of Figure 15.2(b), discounting of attitude A occurs when the connections of external factors F are already strong so that any additional activation by an attitude object A leads to overactivation of the output node and increased error. Therefore, any growth of connection weight of the attitude object A is blocked, resulting in discounting or a reduction of the weight from A to the output E. Thus, for instance, when strong external pressures forced a person to commit a

(a) Acquisition

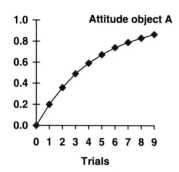

| ($a_i^{ex}$ | - | $a_i^{out}$) | × $a_j^{in}$ | × ε | = $\Delta W_{ij}$ | ⇒ $W_{ij}$ |
|---|---|---|---|---|---|---|
| (1 | - | .00) | × 1 | × .2 | = .20 | ⇒ .20 |
| (1 | - | .20) | × 1 | × .2 | = .16 | ⇒ .36 |
| (1 | - | .36) | × 1 | × .2 | = .13 | ⇒ .49 |
| (1 | - | .49) | × 1 | × .2 | = .10 | ⇒ .59 |
| (1 | - | .59) | × 1 | × .2 | = .08 | ⇒ .67 |
| (1 | - | .67) | × 1 | × .2 | = .07 | ⇒ .74 |
| (1 | - | .74) | × 1 | × .2 | = .05 | ⇒ .79 |
| (1 | - | .79) | × 1 | × .2 | = .04 | ⇒ .83 |
| (1 | - | .83) | × 1 | × .2 | = .03 | ⇒ .86 |

(b) Competition

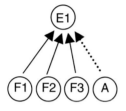 

*Figure 15.2* (a) Property of acquisition: an attitude object A is repeatedly paired with a positive evaluation. The graph on the left depicts the increase in connection weight between the attitude object and the evaluation. The table on the right shows the calculation of weight increase according to Equation 3, where the learning rate $ε = 0.20$, the attitude object has activation $a_j^{in} = 1$, the positive evaluation has activation $a_i^{ex} = 1$, and $a_i^{out}$ is the internal output activation computed by the network on the basis of the summed activation spread through the weights obtained at the previous trial (see Equation 2). Since there is only a single weight involved in this example, the internal activation is equal to the weight of the previous trial.
(b) Property of competition. A = attitude object, E = Evaluation, F = environmental factors. All nodes are activated together at a trial. Full lines denote strong connection weights while dotted lines denote weak weights.

particular act, additional explanations in terms of the person's attitude or traits will be discounted. In contrast, as illustrated in the right panel of Figure 15.2(b), when external forces are absent, the behavior will be attributed solely to the person's attitude.

## Model simulations

After clarifying the processing mechanisms of the feedforward network and, in particular, the emergent properties of acquisition and competition, we are now ready to illustrate attitude formation and cognitive dissonance with two simulations. Attitude formation is simulated through a replication of the theoretical prediction of Fishbein and Ajzen's (1975) model of reasoned action. Cognitive dissonance is simulated through a replication of an induced compliance experiment by Linder, Cooper, and Jones (1967).

### Simulation 1: Attitude formation

As described earlier in the chapter, one of the most influential theories in attitude research is the model of reasoned action by Fishbein and Ajzen (1975; later extended by Ajzen, 1991). According to this theory, attitudes are the product of two components. The first component consists of the belief or expectation, defined as the subjective probability that behavior will lead to a certain consequence or outcome. The second component is the evaluation of this outcome. To illustrate how our connectionist network can implement these two components, the earlier example of different modes of transportation will be used here. Thus, different attitude objects such as a car, a bicycle and a public bus have a number of consequences such as speed, weather protection and air pollution, which are each evaluated as good, bad or neutral.

### Architecture

The architecture of the feedforward model implementing our example is presented in Figure 15.3. The connections between the attitude objects and the cognitive outcomes represent the beliefs that the object is followed by a given consequence. For example, the different modes of transportation are linked

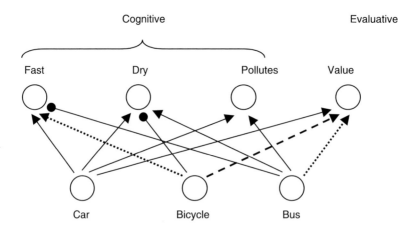

*Figure 15.3* Feedforward connectionist network of attitude formation according to the theory of reasoned action (localist representation). Positive connections are indicated with an arrow, negative connections with a circled endpoint, stronger connections with a full line, weaker connections with a dotted line.

with attributes like speed, weather comfort, and amount of pollution. The weights of these connections reflect the subjective probability or likelihood of these consequences. In addition, we also represent the evaluative responses to the attitude objects. As noted earlier, these evaluations express not only preferences, but also positive or negative emotional experiences, consistent with the view that affective responses play a central role in determining evaluative judgments or attitudes (e.g., Fazio, 1986; Staats & Staats, 1958; Zajonc, 1980). The connection between an attitude object and the evaluative output node represents the attitude towards the object. Behavioral outcomes are not included in the network, as they are assumed to consist of verbal responses that simply express the evaluative reaction.

*Learning history*

We assume that the subjective beliefs and evaluations have been developed during earlier experiences with the attitude objects, either directly through observation or indirectly through communication and messages by others. A schematic learning history that may reflect someone's experiences with various modes of transportation is depicted in Table 15.1. In correspondence with the acquisition principle, the frequency by which the attitude object co-occurs with a specific outcome determines the weight of the connection. That is, the more an attitude object is followed by a certain outcome, the stronger the weight becomes. More importantly, each time a behavioral outcome is experienced, this is also accompanied by a positive, neutral or negative evaluative response. These evaluative responses are accumulated by the acquisition property in the same manner as the cognitive consequences, except that this is done for all cognitive responses of an attitude object together. Specifically, each time a cognitive outcome node is activated, the value node is also activated, which means that the positive or negative evaluation of an object increases. Thus, the evaluative node represents the overall liking or disliking of the attitude object.

The acquisition mechanism in the evaluative node performs similar accumulation operations as the algebraic model of Fishbein and Ajzen (1975). In mathematical terms, according to Equation 3, the accumulated evaluation is the connection weight between the attitude object and the value node (expectation component) that is increased or decreased for each behavioral consequence by the positive, negative or neutral activation of the value node (evaluation component). However, these calculations are performed by simple delta learning adjustments that do not require sequential and conscious calculations as in the algebraic model. The assumption that attitudes are formed implicitly online through learning experiences is supported by recent research by Betsch, Plessner, and Schallies (2001; see also Chapter 11 this volume) on implicit online formation and storage of evaluations in memory via summative processes that are roughly equivalent with the acquisition mechanism of the delta learning algorithm.

*Table 15.1* Schematic learning history of attitude formation on the basis of beliefs on outcome consequences and their values

| | Causal factors | | | Outcomes | | | |
| --- | --- | --- | --- | --- | --- | --- | --- |
| | Car | Bicycle | Bus | Fast | Dry | Pollutes | Value |
| **Car** | | | | | | | |
| #10  Fast | 1 | 0 | 0 | 1 | 0 | 0 | 1 |
| #10  Dry | 1 | 0 | 0 | 0 | 1 | 0 | 1 |
| #10  Pollutes | 1 | 0 | 0 | 0 | 0 | 1 | −1 |
| **Bicycle** | | | | | | | |
| #5   Fast | 0 | 1 | 0 | 1 | 0 | 0 | 1 |
| #10  Wet | 0 | 1 | 0 | 0 | −1 | 0 | −1 |
| #10  Does not pollute | 0 | 1 | 0 | 0 | 0 | 0 | 0 |
| **Bus** | | | | | | | |
| #10  Slow | 0 | 0 | 1 | −1 | 0 | 0 | −1 |
| #5   Dry | 0 | 0 | 1 | 0 | 1 | 0 | 1 |
| #10  Pollutes | 0 | 0 | 1 | 0 | 0 | 1 | −1 |
| **Test** | | | | | | | |
| Attitude toward car | 1 | 0 | 0 | 0 | 0 | 0 | ? |
| Attitude toward bicycle | 0 | 1 | 0 | 0 | 0 | 0 | ? |
| Attitude toward bus | 0 | 0 | 1 | 0 | 0 | 0 | ? |

*Notes*: Each concept (column) was represented by 5 nodes with an activation randomly drawn from a Normal distribution ($M$ = cell entry, $SD$ = .20). This pattern was redrawn for each block of 10 trials to demonstrate that the simulation is not dependent on the particular activation pattern chosen. All trials were presented in a randomized order; # = number of trials.

An attitude is retrieved from memory as the activation of the value node after priming the attitude object node. Intuitively, this is similar to thinking about or being presented with the object, and sensing the subsequent like or dislike for the object. In a feedforward network, this retrieval procedure is equivalent to testing the connection between the attitude object and the evaluative outcome.

*Simulation*

Table 15.1 depicts our simulation of attitude formation based on experiences with different modes of transportation and their consequences. For the purpose of exposition, this simulation greatly simplifies the richness and abundance of real-life experiences. In contrast to the localist encoding of Figure 15.3 where each concept (i.e., attitude objects, beliefs and evaluations) was represented by a single node, in the simulation, we used a distributed encoding where each concept is represented by a set of five nodes which reflect a number of "subsymbolic" micro-features of the concept (Thorpe,

1994). The presence of a concept is represented by a noisy pattern of activation across this array of five nodes. Specifically, the activation pattern was drawn from a Normal distribution with the cell entries in Table 15.1 as mean and a standard deviation of .20 (for a similar encoding specification, see Smith & DeCoster, 1998). Although a distributed representation might appear somewhat more complex, it is a more realistic reflection of memory representation in the brain (see also McLeod et al., 1998; Smith, 1996) and its interpretation and workings are for the present simulations identical to a localist representation.

As can be seen in Table 15.1, the presence of an attitude-object is coded with a mean activation of 1, and its absence with a mean activation level of 0. Cognitive outcomes are coded with mean activations of +1, 0 or −1 to indicate the presence of an outcome, its absence or the opposite outcome respectively. Similarly, evaluative outcomes are coded with mean activation of +1, 0, or −1 to indicate a positive, neutral or negative evaluation. Connection weights, which reflect the likelihood of the outcomes, are developed on the basis of this co-occurrence of the attitude-objects and the outcomes.

We ran the feedforward network 50 times (i.e., with 50 "participants"). Each "participant" went through all trials in a randomized order to reflect the different orders of the learning experiences. Weight adjustments were performed after each trial, with a global learning rate of .05. At the end of the learning history, test trials were run in which the attitude object was turned on and the resulting output activation in the evaluative nodes was recorded to measure the attitude. This resulted in three attitude activations for each "participant." Next, we compared these activations with the theoretical predictions of Fishbein and Ajzen (1975; see also Equation 1). These predictions were calculated by taking the number of trials as estimate of the belief $b_i$ that certain consequences will occur, and the mean activation of the value node as estimate of the evaluation $e_i$ of these outcomes. Assuming that higher frequencies lead to stronger beliefs, we took the raw trial frequencies rather than proportions or probabilities. Hence, the predictions reflect the relative attitude towards each object; they are similar if taken proportional to the total number of trials.

*Simulation results*

Figure 15.4 shows the simulated values (broken line) and the values that would be predicted by the theory of reasoned action (bars). In the figure, the simulated data (averaged across all simulation runs) were rescaled by linear regression so that they matched most closely to the predictions of Fishbein and Ajzen (1975) and the model fit can be inspected visually. The reason is that only the pattern of activation produced by the simulation is of interest, not the exact activation values. As can be seen, the simulated data closely replicated the theoretical prediction. A between-subjects analysis of variance

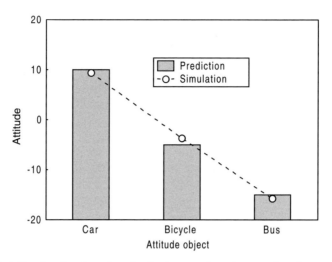

*Figure 15.4* Simulated and predicted attitude towards various modes of transportation.

(ANOVA) on the simulated data revealed that the differences between modes of transportation was highly significant, $F(2,147) = 799.69, p < .001$. To further evaluate the performance of the network (model fit), a correlation between the mean simulated data and the predicted values was calculated. Although the correlation was quite high, $r = 0.99, p < .05$, it merely serves as an indication because it involves only three data means.

### Simulation 2: Cognitive dissonance

According to Festinger (1957), cognitive dissonance arises when there are inconsistencies between cognitions that people have about oneself, one's behavior, or the external world. This cognitive discrepancy generates psychological discomfort or dissonance, an aversive state that motivates people to reduce it by changing their beliefs, attitudes or behavior. Numerous studies inspired by Festinger's (1957) cognitive dissonance theory have been conducted (for an overview, see Harmon-Jones & Mills, 1999). In particular, the influence of discrepant behavior contradicting one's initial attitude has been examined in a popular research paradigm, called the induced-compliance paradigm (Festinger & Carlsmith, 1959). On the basis of this paradigm, we will first discuss the major theoretical perspectives on cognitive dissonance and then turn to a simulation.

#### Prior theoretical accounts

In the induced-compliance paradigm, participants are induced to act in a way that is contrary to their initial attitude and are given sufficient or insufficient justification for doing so, for instance, by being given a high or low monetary reward. For example, in an experiment by Festinger and Carlsmith (1959), participants were given $20 or $1 to convince another student (actually a confederate) that the boring tasks in the experiment were enjoyable. According to cognitive dissonance theory, people would experience more dissonance in the $1 conditition than in the $20 condition since the low reward insufficiently justifies the discrepant behavior. Consequently, they would attempt to reduce this dissonance by changing their attitude in the direction of the lie. As predicted, participants in the $1 conditition showed more attitude change towards the boring tasks compared to participants in the $20 condition. Thus, a negative relationship between the amount of reward and the amount of attitude change was observed.

A radical different perspective was taken by reinforcement theory, which assumed that the higher the reward people receive for their discrepant behavior, the more they change their attitudes in line with that behavior. This theory thus predicts a positive relationship between the level of reward and the amount of attitude change. For example, Janis and Gilmore (1965) found more attitude change after engaging in a role-playing task in the high-reward condition than in the low-reward condition.

In several dissonance studies (e.g., Calder, Ross, & Insko, 1973; Holmes & Strickland, 1970), experimenters obtained reinforcement as well as dissonance effects. For instance, Linder et al. (1967) showed that a reinforcement effect occurs when people are forced to perform the counterattitudinal behavior, but when they have the freedom to engage in the discrepant behavior or not, the dissonance effect is obtained.

After Festinger's (1957) original formulation, several alternative accounts of cognitive dissonance theory have been advanced that stress the person's attributions. According to self-perception theory (Bem, 1967), people infer their attitudes from observing their behavior and the situation in which the behavior occurred. Although this theory makes the same predictions as cognitive dissonance theory, it differs from it by postulating that motivational mediating processes (i.e., aversive state of dissonance) are unnecessary in dissonance induction. Solely non-motivational, cognitive inferences on external cues determine one's attitude. If situational factors elicit the discrepant behavior, no inference can be made that the behavior reflects the person's true attitude. But if the discrepant behavior cannot be attributed to situational factors, one must conclude that the behavior reflects his or her true attitude. Thus, when one engages in discrepant behavior for a small reward that is not a sufficient justification for the behavior, one must infer that the person really enjoyed it.

Cooper and Fazio (1984) offered an attributional reformulation on the cognitive dissonance process. According to these authors, dissonance is not produced by inconsistent cognitions, but depends on the causal inference people made for their discrepant behavior and the arousal that results from the experienced discrepancies. In this perspective, dissonance only arises when an attribution is made to the person for unwanted, aversive consequences produced by the person's discrepant behavior. However, if the behavior is attributed to situational factors, no dissonance is experienced and as a consequence, no attitude change would be observed.

Although these later theoretical accounts present different underlying processes for explaining dissonance reduction, in general, their predictions largely agree on the point that insufficient justification or explanation by external factors increases dissonance and attitude change. However, none of these models is capable to explain the reinforcement effect when participants are forced to defend a given attitude position.

### A connectionist account

Although our connectionist approach implements an attributional view, as we will see, it is able to account for typical dissonance as well as reinforcement effects. The model extends and reframes Cooper and Fazio's (1984) perspective by focusing on attributions to the attitude object instead of responsibility attributions of the person. In addition, unexpected outcomes are assumed to predominantly cause dissonance instead of unwanted, aversive outcomes like in Cooper and Fazio's (1984) theory.

Unlike the connectionist simulation of attitude presented earlier, we included here not only evaluative responses, but also one's own behaviors towards an object as determinant of an attitude. The reason is that, especially when discrepant with earlier behaviors or preferences, approach or avoidance behavior towards an object also reveals the actor's attitude. Cognitive dissonance in the connectionist model is represented as the error or discrepancy of the delta algorithm; that is, the error between the predicted outcome based on the internal output activation and the external output activation from actual responses. This conceptualization of cognitive dissonance is in line with Festinger's (1957) view that cognitions map reality and that dissonance can arise when people receive information that disconfirms their cognitions or expectations (Festinger, Riecken, & Schachter, 1956). As Festinger (1957) stated: *"The reality which impinges on a person will exert pressures in the direction of bringing the appropriate cognitive elements into correspondence with that reality"* (p. 11, original italics).

As an illustration of our feedforward model of cognitive dissonance, we replicate here a simulation by Van Overwalle and Jordens (2002) of the induced-compliance experiment by Linder et al. (1967). Participants were asked to write a forceful counterattitudinal essay under choice or no-choice conditions and were paid either $0.5 or $2.5 for it. In the choice conditions, the classical dissonance effect was obtained, that is, participants changed their attitudes more in the low-reward condition compared to the high-reward condition. The reinforcement effect was observed in the no-choice conditions. Participants favored the advocated position more in the high-reward condition than in the low-reward condition (see also Figure 15.6).

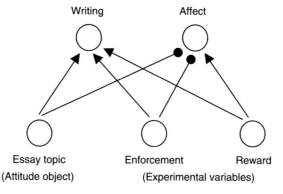

*Figure 15.5* A feedforward connectionist implementation (localist representation) of an induced-compliance experiment (Linder, Cooper, & Jones, 1967). Positive connections are indicated with an arrow and negative connections with a circled endpoint.

*Architecture*

Figure 15.5 shows the architecture of the feedforward model of induced compliance. The input nodes reflect the attitude object and external causal pressures that are linked to the output nodes representing behavioral and affective responses. This architecture is similar to the one used for attitude formation (Simulation 1), except that we did not include cognitive beliefs (as they do not directly affect the attitude). As noted earlier, we also included behavioral outcomes because in cognitive dissonance the behavior is not merely a reflection of an evaluative response, but rather opposed to it. Attitudinal judgments are assumed to be equally determined by evaluative and behavioral responses.

*Learning history*

The simulation of the Linder et al. (1967) experiment was run in two phases. In the first phase, the *pre-experimental phase*, connection weights were developed to simulate the assumption that participants begin the experiment with certain beliefs and evaluations. In the second phase, the *experimental phase*, the experimental manipulations of Linder et al. (1967) were closely replicated, that is, choice and no-choice conditions with either low or high reward were represented. Table 15.2 gives an overview of the learning experiences used in the simulations.

As can be seen, the learning history makes a number of assumptions on trial frequencies, levels of external factors (i.e., payment), and the nature and direction of behavioral and affective outcomes. First, we generally assumed in the pre-experimental learning history that single external factors would occur more frequently than the joint occurrences of these factors, although

*Table 15.2* Simulated learning experiences in the induced-compliance paradigm (Linder, Cooper, & Jones, 1967)

| | | *Factors* | | | *Outcomes* | |
|---|---|---|---|---|---|---|
| | | *Topic* | *Reward* | *Force* | *Writing* | *Affect* |
| **Pre-experimental learning history** | | | | | | |
| #20 | Counterattitudinal topic (T) | 1 | 0 | 0 | 0 | 0 |
| #10 | T + low reward (20% $) | 1 | .20 | 0 | 1 | 0 |
| #10 | T + high reward ($) | 1 | 1 | 0 | 1 | 0 |
| #10 | T + forced (F) | 1 | 0 | 1 | 1 | −1 |
| #5 | T + 20% $ + F | 1 | .20 | 1 | 1 | −1 |
| #5 | T + $ + F | 1 | 1 | 1 | 1 | 0 |
| **Experimental conditions** | | | | | | |
| **Choice** | | | | | | |
| #1 | Low reward: T + 20% $ | 1 | .20 | 0 | 1 | 0 |
| #1 | High reward: T + $ | 1 | 1 | 0 | 1 | 0 |
| **No choice** | | | | | | |
| #1 | Low reward: T + 20% $ + F | 1 | .20 | 1 | 1 | −1 |
| #1 | High reward: T + $ + F | 1 | 1 | 1 | 1 | 0 |
| **Test** | | | | | | |
| Attitude toward topic | | 1 | 0 | 0 | ? | ? |

*Notes*: Writing = writing a counterattitudinal essay; mean affect activation is coded as −1 (unpleasant) or 0 (neutral). All simulation specifications were similar as in Table 15.1, except that in the pre-experimental phase, at each trial, noise randomly drawn from a Normal distribution ($M = 0$, $SD = .50$) was added to the activation.

Van Overwalle and Jordens (2002) report that the chosen trial frequencies are not very crucial. In the experimental phase, we assumed one trial frequency to simulate the fact that after the experimental manipulation, participants would think at least once about the causes of their behavior and affect.

Second, the relative amount of low reward was simulated by activating the payment node for only 20% of the default level of +1 to reflect the same ratio of low ($0.5) to high ($2.5) payment in the experiment. However, other low levels of activation worked equally well (Van Overwalle & Jordens, 2002).

Third, in the pre-experimental phase, it was assumed that a person would not engage in writing a counterattitudinal essay without reward or enforcement. In the experimental phase, only compliant participants are considered, like in the original Linder et al. (1967) experiment.

Fourth, affective responses (negative, neutral or positive) in the pre- and experimental phase were based on the assumption that participants would experience pro-attitudinal behavior as pleasant, and their willingness to engage in counterattitudinal behavior as affectively neutral or at most mildly negative. These latter emotional experiences were coded as affectively neutral. Most crucial, we assumed that only the combination of two external constraints would lead to strong negative affect. Empirical evidence for these assumptions was provided by a survey in which major dissonance paradigms were described, including the specific procedures (Van Overwalle & Jordens, 2002). Participants reported that engaging in counterattitudinal behavior without external constraints was not experienced as overwhelmingly negative, but rather as mildly uncomfortable. More importantly, the highest levels of negative affect were reported when two unpleasant constraints were combined. This is contrary to the classic assumption that the lack of dissonance typically observed in this condition should produce the least discomfort.

*Simulation results*

Like in the previous simulation, we ran 50 "participants" for each experimental condition (or 200 "participants" overall). Each participant first went through all pre-experimental trials in a random order, and then went through a single experimental trial. In contrast to the previous simulation, to reproduce the notion that the attitude object in the pre-experimental phase was not identical to the advocacy in Linder et al.'s experiment, but rather reflects an accumulated history of experiences varying in similarity to the advocated speech, a dramatic amount of noise was added to each pre-experimental trial. Specifically, at each trial, noise was randomly drawn from a Normal distribution with a mean of 0 and a standard deviation of .50. There was no noise during the experimental trial. All other aspects of the simulation were identical to Simulation 1.

Figure 15.6 depicts the simulated and observed data. As can be seen, the simulation closely replicated the results by Linder et al. (1967). The observed interaction between reward and choice found in their study was also highly significant for the simulation data, $F(1,196) = 28.84$, $p < .001$. In addition, the correlation between observed and simulation means was .94, $p = .06$.

The interaction in the simulation demonstrates two effects. First, the feedforward network reproduced the dissonance effect in the choice conditions. This was accomplished by the discounting principle resulting from the competition property of the delta algorithm. When there is sufficient reward, the reward node sends sufficient positive activation to the behavioral and evaluative nodes to predict the presence of the discrepant behavior and neutral affect. Consequently, by the competition property, other potential explanations such as the person's attitude are discounted. However, when the activation of the reward node is lowered to .20 of its default value, it sends insufficient activation to predict the behavioral and evaluative responses. As a consequence, instead of discounting the person's attitude, the weight of this connection must be increased to compensate for the model's underestimation of the outcomes. This upward adjustment results in an increased attitude change in the direction of the discrepant behavior.

Second, the reinforcement effect in the no-choice conditions was also simulated. To obtain the reinforcement effect, the affective coding was crucial. In the high payment condition, the affective node was neutral so that the

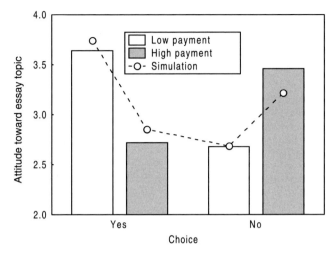

*Figure 15.6* Observed and simulation data of the induced-compliance study by
Linder, Cooper, and Jones (1967). The human data are adapted from
Table 3 in "Decision freedom as a determinant of the role of incentive
magnitude in attitude change," by D. E. Linder, J. Cooper, and E. E.
Jones, 1967, *Journal of Personality and Social Psychology, 6*, 245–254.
Copyright 1967 by the American Psychological Association.

attitude was relatively positive. In contrast, in the low payment condition
affect was assumed to be very negative because of the two unpleasant
external constraints (enforcement and low reward). This negative affective
outcome drives the connections downwards, resulting in negligible attitude
changes.

## Empirical validation of the cognitive dissonance model

One of the most critical assumptions in the simulation of the reinforcement
effect of Linder et al. (1967) is the role of negative affect in the low-choice,
low-payment condition. This assumption was tested by replicating the Linder
et al. (1967) experiment and extending the low-choice conditions with additional mood induction. The goal was to eliminate or reverse the reinforcement effect in the no-choice conditions by inducing the affect opposite to the
one assumed by the connectionist simulation. Specifically, we (Jordens & Van
Overwalle, 2004) induced positive affect in the low-reward condition (which
presumably would be experienced as very unpleasant) and negative affect
in the high-reward condition (which presumably would be experienced as
neutral). We hypothesized that by inducing the opposite affects, we would
counteract the affective feelings normally experienced during cognitive
dissonance, and so eliminate the reinforcement effect.

### Mood induction experiment

The experiment ran as follows. A few weeks before the beginning of the experiment, the initial attitude toward the issue of abolishing the university credit system was measured in an opinion questionnaire. Only students who were strongly opposed to the issue were selected for participation in the study. In a variation of the Linder et al. (1967) study, the expectation of reward was manipulated by announcing one week before the experiment that participation in the study would be rewarded 100 Belgian francs (about $2.22). The actual reward, however, was lower or higher than expected. This manipulation of expectation was necessitated because pilot studies indicated that without it, any level of reward was typically received with pleasure in our student population, eroding dissonance in all conditions.

The experimenter informed the participants that they would participate in two unrelated studies in which they would have to complete different tasks. In the first study, participants completed the "Standard Progressive Matrices" test of intelligence (Raven, 1958). This test would allow us to give false performance feedback as part of the mood induction at the end of the second study.

In the second experiment, dissonance was induced by giving participants low or high choice for writing the counterattitudinal essay on abolishing the credit system. In addition, they received a low (10 Belgian francs or $0.25) or high (400 Belgian francs or $2.25) reward for performing the counterattitudinal task. Participants were informed that the psychology department was collaborating with a commercial research bureau to examine students' opinions on different issues, including the abolition of the university credit system. Participants were told that enough arguments against abolishment of the credit system had already been sampled and that arguments in favor of abolishing the system were now needed. In the low-choice condition, participants were informed that they were randomly assigned to write the counterattitudinal essay. In the high-choice condition, on the other hand, the experimenter told them that the decision to write the counterattitudinal essay was entirely their own. Moreover, all participants were told that the reason for the discrepancy between the expected and actual reward was that the research bureau had decided to decrease (low-reward condition) or increase (high-reward condition) the monetary reward for participation. Participants in all conditions were paid before they started to write the essay.

After finishing the essay, in two additional low-choice conditions, mood was induced by giving positive or negative bogus performance feedback on the test completed in the first study. Finally, in all conditions, participants' attitudes toward abolishing the credit system were assessed.

### Results and discussion

The results indicated that the Linder et al. (1967) experiment had been successfully replicated. Consistent with the prediction of dissonance theory, participants in the high-choice conditions favored the counterattitudinal position in the essay more after a low reward than after a high reward. The reverse pattern was observed in the low-choice conditions. Consistent with the prediction of reinforcement theory, participants in the low-reward condition showed less attitude change than participants in the high-reward condition.

We then tested the critical role of affect in producing reinforcement under low-choice conditions by comparing the conditions with and without mood induction. Our prediction was that the reinforcement effect would be eliminated after inducing opposite mood, that is positive affect in the low-reward condition (which presumably elicits negative affect) and negative affect in the high-reward condition (which presumably elicits neutral affect). Figure 15.7 shows that, in line with our prediction, the reinforcement effect was eliminated by the induction of opposite mood. Compared to the no-mood conditions of the Linder et al. (1967) replication, participants changed their attitude more after positive mood induction in the low-reward condition and less after negative mood induction in the high-reward condition. A direct comparison between the positive-mood condition and the negative-mood condition revealed a marginal trend of a reversed reinforcement effect.

Taken together, the present results provide evidence for our hypothesis that the mechanism responsible for the reinforcement effect in a dissonant situation is affective in nature, a view that is shared by other authors (e.g., Carlsmith, Collins, & Helmreich, 1966; Shultz & Lepper, 1996). Compared to the no-mood conditions, participants in a positive mood changed their attitude more given a low reward, while participants in a negative mood changed

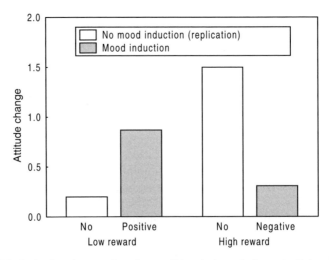

*Figure 15.7* Attitude change in the replicated low-choice conditions without mood induction and in the additional low-choice conditions with mood induction.

their attitude less given a high reward. This eliminated completely the typical reinforcement effect and even resulted in a slight reversal.

## General discussion

We presented a novel connectionist approach to attitude formation and cognitive dissonance. Unlike traditional attitude theories, the proposed model emphasizes associative memory processes in attitude formation and change that are adaptive in nature. Attitudes are represented as associations between attitude objects and one's evaluative or behavioral responses. Changes in these associations are incorporated through an error-correcting learning algorithm that adjusts the association weights (encoding long-term knowledge) whenever new information is processed.

This model is able to account for empirical data predicted by existing attitude theories. As an illustration, the model of reasoned action by Fishbein and Ajzen (1975) was simulated and shown to be driven basically by the acquisition property of the delta learning algorithm operating on the value component. As another example, cognitive dissonance in induced compliance (Linder et al., 1967) was simulated and shown to be driven by the competition property of the delta algorithm. This learning algorithm has also been applied to a wide range of other social cognitive phenomena like impression formation, categorization, causal attributions, and group biases (e.g., Smith & DeCoster, 1998; Read & Montoya, 1999; Van Overwalle, 1998; Van Overwalle & Labiouse, 2004; Van Rooy et al., 2003).

Perhaps more importantly, the empirical validity of the proposed connectionist model was explored by examining one of its critical predictions generated on the basis of computer simulations. This prediction was that not only the person's discrepant behavior, but also his or her current affective state plays a role in the dissonance reduction process. The unique contribution of the present connectionist approach is that it specifies the precise conditions where affect attenuates attitude change, namely, under the constraint of combined unpleasant conditions such as low choice and low reward. Given this hypothesis, the model reproduced the so-called reinforcement effect observed in the induced-compliance paradigm (for the same effect in other paradigms, see Van Overwalle & Jordens, 2002). This reinforcement effect could not been explained by cognitive dissonance theory (Festinger, 1957) or the attributional reformulation (Bem, 1967; Cooper & Fazio, 1984). This critical affective prediction of the model was then tested in a replication and extension of the induced-compliance experiment by Linder et al. (1967). In line with the connectionist prediction, the reinforcement effect was eliminated after the induction of opposite positive and negative affect.

This result underscores the utility of computer simulations. Although not very popular in social psychology, computer simulations provide a novel medium for theorizing, hypothesis generation and hypothesis testing. As Hastie and Stasser (2000) noted, they facilitate the construction and modification of theories through the formulation of explicit assumptions and derivation of precise hypotheses. However, as we have demonstrated, gathering human data remains necessary in order to test the predictions derived from connectionist models.

### Role of affect in attitude change

The impact of affect in our model is in line with affect priming and affect-as-information theories (e.g., Bower, 1981; Schwarz & Clore, 1983) that provide an account for mood-congruent judgments observed in numerous studies (for an overview, see Forgas, 2001). Affect priming theory (Bower, 1981; Isen, 1984) states that mood biases occur through mood-congruent attention, encoding and retrieval of information involved in judgmental processes. These biases were explained by the mechanism of activation spreading in an associative memory network. This is consistent with the present model, because affect is assumed to influence the evaluative component associated with an attitude object.

The affect-as-information approach (Schwarz, 1990; Schwarz & Clore, 1983), however, proposes an alternative mechanism of mood influence. According to this approach, affect has an informational value since people ask themselves "How do I feel about it?" when they evaluate persons or objects. Mood biases occur when people attribute (erroneously) the source of their affect to the attitude object, that is, when they are not made aware of the true source of their affective state. This is also consistent with our model, because strong associations of external factors with the evaluative/affective node will result in a discounting of the impact of these affective sources on the attitude, whereas if such associations do not exist or if people are not minimally aware of them, no such discounting will occur and affective sources will have more impact on the attitude.

Taken from this perspective, our results on mood induction in the extended induced-compliance experiment are entirely consistent with these earlier mood theories. These theories would predict that negative affect would result in more negative evaluative judgments, while positive affect would produce more positive evaluative judgments. This is indeed what we found in our empirical study (Jordens & Van Overwalle, 2002). However, it is evident that affect-priming and affect-as-information models do not take into account the effect of discrepant behavior on attitudes, whereas the connectionist assumption is that (discrepant) behavior and affect are aggregated to produce an attitude. Thus, the present network approach can accommodate a larger range of findings and phenomena.

### Unresolved questions

It is clear that a single study is insufficient to provide convincing empirical support for our connectionist approach. There are many assumptions of the model that remain untested and that should be verified in future research. A first empirical question is if and under which conditions the prediction of mood theories (Bower, 1981; Schwarz & Clore, 1983) and the connectionist approach diverge. As an illustration, imagine a dissonant situation where participants are induced to write arguments against a position that they initially favor (rather than disfavor as in most induced-compliance research). Mood theories would presumably predict that a positive mood would lead to a favorable attitude change and that a negative mood would result in an unfavorable attitude change. In contrast, our connectionist approach would predict that a positive mood would become associated with the discrepant behavior, that is, the writing of arguments against a favorable attitude. This would produce more attitude change in the direction of the unfavorable essay, while negative mood would produce little attitude change.

A second question is whether attitude formation will obey the acquisition principle under implicit and explicit processing of information. In Chapter 11 of this volume, Betsch, Plessner, and Schallies argue that implicit attitude formation is guided by a *summation* of valences, whereas explicit attitude formation is driven by an *averaging* of valences. Can this distinction be reconciled with the acquisition principle? Yes it can, and to understand this, it is important to realize that the delta algorithm reflects a negatively accelerating learning curve, that is, acquisition is fast and steep at the beginning, but then gradually slows down towards an asymptote. As can be seen in Figure 15.2(a), at the beginning of learning, at each trial, weight strength increases so that the delta algorithm reflects something like a summation of favorable valences. However, towards asymptote, weight strength converges to 1 so that it actually reflects the average of all positive valences. Other examples with a combination of strong and weak positive valences, or positive and negative valences, would also show an initial summation and then a convergence towards the average. Given the widely accepted idea that explicit learning is quite fast while implicit learning is much slower, our connectionist approach predicts that implicit learning often remains below asymptote while explicit learning reaches asymptote very early. This would predominantly result in summation during implicit learning and averaging during explicit learning, in line with the findings of Betch and colleagues.

A third question is whether different levels of weaker treatment (e.g., low reward) lead to different levels of dissonance reduction. Van Overwalle and Jordens (2002) predicted on the basis of their simulations that induced compliance is quite robust against different levels of reward for engaging in a counterattitudinal behavior. However, they also predicted that this might be less the case for other dissonant paradigms (e.g., prohibition, initiation) involving different levels of threat and punishment. These questions can be tested empirically by varying the different levels of external constraints on the dissonant behavior.

A final theoretical question is how the present connectionist account of attitude formation and change fits with recent dual-process models of attitude change (Chaiken, 1987; Petty & Cacioppo, 1986). According to dual-process models, people do not always form or update their attitudes by actively attending to and cognitively reflecting upon persuasive argumentation as assumed in algebraic models of attitude formation (e.g., Fishbein & Ajzen, 1975). In many cases, attitudes are created or changed in a more shallow or heuristic manner, by relying on heuristic shortcuts that utilize stored decision rules such as "experts can be trusted," "majority opinion is correct," and "long messages are valid messages." In the present simulations, we illustrated only how the connectionist model can account for the active processing of positive and negative experiences related to an attitude object (Simulation 1). It seems plausible that a similar process can explain how persuasive messages result in attitude formation based on the frequency and favorability of their arguments. However, it is less evident how heuristic processing might be accounted for by our connectionist perspective, although the recent unimodel developed by Kruglanski and Thompson (1999) seems to suggest that the distinction between central and peripheral processing is superfluous and that persuasion is governed by a single processing mechanism. Because a connectionist approach seems particularly suited to account for implicit processing, we are currently developing a single connectionist model to explain both heuristic and deliberative processes in persuasive communication.

## References

Ajzen, I. (1991). The theory of planned behavior. *Organizational Behavior and Human Decision Processes, 50,* 179–211.

Anderson, J. R., & Bower, G. H. (1973). *Human associative memory.* Washington, DC: Winston.

Anderson, N. H. (1967). Averaging model analysis of set size effect in impression formation. *Journal of Experimental Psychology, 75,* 158–165.

Anderson, N. H. (1971). Integration theory and attitude change. *Psychological Review, 78,* 171–206.

Anderson, N. H. (1981a). *Foundations of information integration theory.* New York: Academic Press.

Anderson, N. H. (1981b). Integration theory applied to cognitive responses and attitudes. In R. E. Petty, T. M. Ostrom, & T. C. Brock (Eds.), *Cognitive responses in persuasion* (pp. 361–397). Hillsdale, NJ: Lawrence Erlbaum Associates, Inc.

Bargh, J. A. (1984). Automatic and conscious processing of social information. In R. S. Wyer Jr. & T. K. Srull (Eds.), *Handbook of social cognition* (Vol. 3, pp. 1–43). Hillsdale, NJ: Lawrence Erlbaum Associates Inc.

Bargh, J. A., & Chartrand, T. L. (1999). The unbearable automaticity of being. *American Psychologist, 54,* 462–479.

Bem, D. J. (1967). Self-perception: An alternative interpretation of cognitive dissonance phenomena. *Psychological Review, 74,* 183–200.

Betsch, T., Plessner, H., Schwieren, C., & Gütig, R. (2001). I like it but I don't know why: A value-account approach to implicit attitude formation. *Personality and Social Psychology Bulletin, 27,* 242–253.

Betsch, T., Plessner, H., & Schallies, E. (2003). The value-account model of attitude formation. In G. Haddock & G. Maio (Eds.), *Theoretical perspectives on attitudes for the 21st century: The Gregynog symposium*. Hove, UK: Psychology Press.

Bower, G. H. (1981). Mood and memory. *American Psychologist, 36,* 129–148.

Calder, B. J., Ross, M., & Insko, C. A. (1973). Attitude change and attitude attribution: effects of incentive, choice, and consequences. *Journal of Personality and Social Psychology, 25,* 84–99.

Carlsmith, J. M., Collins, B. E., & Helmreich, R. L. (1966). Studies in forced compliance: I. The effect of pressure for compliance on attitude change produced by face-to-face role playing and anonymous essay writing. *Journal of Personality and Social Psychology, 4,* 1–13.

Chaiken, S. (1987). The heuristic model of persuasion. In M. P. Zanna, J. M. Olson, & C. P. Herman (Eds.), *Social influence: The Ontario symposium* (Vol. 5, pp. 3–39). Hillsdale, NJ: Lawrence Erlbaum Associates, Inc.

Cooper, J., & Fazio, R. H. (1984). A new look at dissonance theory. In L. Berkowitz (Ed.), *Advances in experimental social psychology* (Vol. 17, pp. 229–266). New York: Academic Press.

Cooper, J., Zanna, M. P., & Goethals, G. R. (1974). Mistreatment of an esteemed other as a consequence affecting dissonance reduction. *Journal of Experimental Social Psychology, 10,* 224–233.

De Houwer, K., Thomas, S., & Baeyens, F. (2001). Associative learning of likes and dislikes: A review of 25 years of research on human evaluative conditioning. *Psychological Bulletin, 127,* 853–869.

Dijksterhuis, A. (2002). *A subliminal road to happiness: Enhancing implicit self-esteem by subliminal evaluative conditioning.* Paper presented at the 4th European Social Cognition Network Meeting, Paris, France, September.

Eagly, A. H., & Chaiken, S. (1993). *The psychology of attitudes.* San Diego, CA: Harcourt Brace.

Fazio, R. H. (1986). How do attitudes guide behavior? In R. M. Sorrentino & E. T. Higgins (Eds.), *The handbook of motivation and cognition: Foundations of social behavior* (pp. 204–243). New York: Guilford Press.

Festinger, L. (1957). *A theory of cognitive dissonance.* Evanston, IL: Row, Peterson.

Festinger, L., & Carlsmith, J. M. (1959). Cognitive consequences of forced compliance. *Journal of Abnormal and Social Psychology, 58,* 203–210.

Festinger, L., Riecken, H. W., & Schachter, S. (1956). *When prophecy fails.* Minneapolis: University of Minnesota Press.

Fishbein, M. (1963). An investigation of the relationships between beliefs about an object and the attitude toward that object. *Human Relations, 16,* 233–240.

Fishbein, M., & Ajzen, I. (1975). *Belief attitude, intention and behavior an introduction to theory and research.* London: Addison-Wesley.

Forgas, J. P. (2001). *Handbook of affect and social cognition.* Hillsdale, NJ: Lawrence Erlbaum Associates, Inc.

Harmon-Jones, E., & Mills, J. (1999). *Cognitive dissonance: Progress on a pivotal theory in social psychology.* Washington, DC: American Psychological Association.

Hastie, R., & Kumar, P. A. (1979) Person memory: Personality traits as organizing principles in memory for behaviors. *Journal of Personality and Social Psychology, 37,* 25–38.

Hastie, R., & Stasser, G. (2000). Computer simulation methods for social psychology.

In H. T. Reis & C. M. Judd (Eds.), *Handbook of research methods in social and personality psychology* (pp. 85–114). New York: Cambridge University Press.

Holmes, J. G., & Strickland, L. H. (1970). Choice freedom and confirmation of incentive expectancy as determinants of attitude change. *Journal of Personality and Social Psychology*, *14*, 39–45.

Isen, A. M. (1984). Towards understanding the role of affect in cognition. In R. S. Wyer, Jr. & T. K. Srull (Eds.), *Handbook of social cognition* (Vol. 3, pp. 179–236). Hillsdale, NJ: Lawrence Erlbaum Associates Inc.

Janis, I. L., & Gilmore, J. B. (1965). The influence of incentive conditions on the success of role playing in modifying attitudes. *Journal of Personality and Social Psychology*, *1*, 17–27.

Jordens, K., & Van Overwalle, F. (2004). *Cognitive dissonance and affect: An empirical test of a connectionist account.* Manuscript submitted for publication.

Kaplan, M. F. (1991). The joint effects of cognition and affect on social judgment. In J. P. Forgas (Ed.), *Emotion and social judgments* (pp. 73–82). Oxford: Pergamon Press.

Kashima, Y., Woolcock, J., & Kashima, E. S. (2000). Group impression as dynamic configurations: The tensor product model of group impression formation and change. *Psychological Review*, *107*, 914–942.

Katz, D., & Stotland, E. (1959). A preliminary statement to a theory of attitude structure and change. In S. Koch (Ed.), *Psychology: A study of a science* (Vol. 3, pp. 423–475). New York: McGraw-Hill.

Kelley, H. H. (1972). Attribution in social interaction. In E. E. Jones, D. E. Kanouse, H. H. Kelley, R. E. Nisbett, S. Valins, & B. Weiner (Eds.), *Attribution: Perceiving the causes of behavior.* Morristown, NJ: General Learning Press.

Krosnick, J. A., Betz, A. L., Jussim, L. J., & Lynn, A. R. (1992). Subliminal conditioning of attitudes. *Personality and Social Psychology Bulletin*, *18*, 152–162.

Kruglanski, A. W., & Thompson, E. P. (1999). Persuasion by a single route: A view from the unimodel. *Psychological Inquiry*, *10*, 10, 83–109.

Linder, D. E., Cooper, J., & Jones, E. E. (1967). Decision freedom as a determinant of the role of incentive magnitude in attitude change. *Journal of Personality and Social Psychology*, *6*, 245–254.

McLeod, P., Plunkett, K., & Rolls, E. T. (1998). *Introduction to connectionist modeling of cognitive processes.* Oxford: Oxford University Press.

O'Reilly, R. C., & Munakata, Y. (2000). *Computational explorations in cognitive neuroscience.* Cambridge, MA: MIT Press.

Petty, R. E., & Cacioppo, J. T. (1986). The elaboration likelihood model of persuasion. In L. Berkowitz (Ed.), *Advances in experimental social psychology* (Vol. 19, pp. 123–205). San Diego, CA: Academic Press.

Raven, J. C. (1958). *Standard Progressive Matrices. Sets A, B, C, D and E.* London: Lewis.

Read, S. J., & Miller, L. C. (Eds.) (1998). *Connectionist models of social reasoning and social behavior.* Hillsdale, NJ: Lawrence Erlbaum Associates, Inc.

Read, S. J., & Montoya, J. A. (1999). An autoassociative model of causal reasoning and causal learning: Reply to Van Overwalle's critique of Read and Marcus-Newhall (1993). *Journal of Personality and Social Psychology*, *76*, 728–742.

Rescorla, R. A., & Wagner, A. R. (1972). A theory of Pavlovian conditioning: Variations in the effectiveness of reinforcement and nonreinforcement. In A. H. Black & W. F. Prokasy (Eds.), *Classical conditioning II: Current research and theory* (pp. 64–98). New York: Appleton-Century-Crofts.

Riketta, M., & Dauenheimer, D. (2002). *Manipulating self-esteem through subliminally presented words*. Manuscript submitted for publication.

Rosenberg, M. J., & Hovland, C. I. (1960). Cognitive, affective and behavioral components of attitudes. In C. I. Hovland & M. J. Rosenberg (Eds.), *Attitude organization and change: An analysis of consistency among attitude components* (pp. 1–14). New Haven, CT: Yale University Press.

Schwarz, N. (1990). Feelings as information: Informational and motivational functions of affective states. In E. T. Higgins & R. Sorrentino (Eds.), *Handbook of motivation and cognition: Foundations of social behavior* (Vol. 2). New York: Guilford Press.

Schwarz, N. (2000). Social judgment and attitudes: warmer, more social, and less conscious. *European Journal of Social Psychology*, *30*, 149–176.

Schwarz, N., & Clore G. L. (1983). Mood, misattribution, and judgments of well-being: Informative and directive functions of affective states. *Journal of Personality and Social Psychology*, *45*, 513–523.

Shultz, T., & Lepper, M. (1996). Cognitive dissonance reduction as constraint satisfaction. *Psychological Review*, *2*, 219–240.

Smith, E. R. (1996). What to connectionism and social psychology offer each other? *Journal of Personality and Social Psychology*, *70*, 893–912.

Smith, E. R., & DeCoster, J. (1998). Knowledge acquisition, accessibility, and use in person perception and stereotyping: Simulation with a recurrent connectionist network. *Journal of Personality and Social Psychology*, *74*, 21–35.

Staats, A. W., & Staats, C. K. (1958). Attitudes established by classic conditioning. *Journal of Abnormal Psychology*, *57*, 37–40.

Thorpe, S. (1994). Localized versus distributed representations. In M. A. Arbib (Ed.), *Handbook of brain theory and neural networks* (pp. 949–952). Cambridge, MA: MIT Press.

Van Overwalle, F. (1998). Causal explanation as constraint satisfaction: A critique and a feedforward connectionist alternative. *Journal of Personality and Social Psychology*, *74*, 312–328.

Van Overwalle, F., & Jordens, K. (2002) An adaptive connectionist model of cognitive dissonance. *Personality and Social Psychology Review*, *6*, 204–231.

Van Overwalle, F., & Labiouse, C. (2004). A recurrent connectionist model of person impression formation. *Personality and Social Review*, *8*, 28–61.

Van Rooy, D., Van Overwalle, F., Vanhoomissen, T., Labiouse, C., & French, R. (2003). A recurrent connectionist model of group biases. *Psychological Review*, *110*, 536–563.

Wilson, T. D., Lindsey, S., & Schooler, T. Y. (2000). A model of dual attitudes. *Psychological Review*, *107*, 101–126.

Zajonc, R. B. (1980). Feeling and thinking: Preferences need no inferences. *American Psychologist*, *35*, 151–175.

Zanna, M. P., Kiesler, C. A., & Pilkonis, P. A. (1970). Positive and negative attitudinal affect established by classical conditioning. *Journal of Personality and Social Psychology*, *14*, 321–328.

# 16 Investigating attitudes cross-culturally

## A case of cognitive dissonance among East Asians and North Americans

*Etsuko Hoshino-Browne,*
*Adam S. Zanna, Steven J. Spencer*
*and Mark P. Zanna*

### Introduction

During the last several decades, while the volume of cross-cultural research has steadily increased, experimental social psychologists' approach toward cross-cultural research on attitudes and attitude-relevant constructs seems to have gone through three stages or generations. In retrospect, we find that the first generation of cross-cultural research focused on identifying cross-cultural similarities, which tended to demonstrate universality in attitudes or attitude-relevant constructs. Over time, however, a second stage or generation of cross-cultural research emerged, that focused on identifying culture-specific psychological phenomena and generated findings that demonstrated cross-cultural differences in attitudes and their related constructs. The third generation, for which we provide empirical evidence below, can be characterized as a synthesis of the first and second generations. In particular, it is an approach to understand the role played by culture in shaping basic psychological functioning. It seeks to demonstrate not only that underlying psychological processes may be similar across cultures, but also that the situations in which the phenomenon is manifested and the manner according to which it operates may be culture specific. Of course, these distinctions between three generations of research are not as clear-cut as described above and some overlaps among them are seen in the literature. Nonetheless, we think that the above distinctions among three stages or generations capture the Zeitgeist, or the most important research questions for most people, of cross-cultural research at the time.

We prefer to use the term "generation" instead of terms such as "category" or "type" in order to underscore a trajectory of cross-cultural research on attitudes and attitude-relevant constructs that we review below. This does not mean, however, that we argue that universalist or cross-culturally specific findings obtained in the past were the product of either scholastic or methodological biases dominant at the time. Nor do we argue that past cross-cultural studies, portrayed as using a "universalist" or "culture-specific" approach, would produce different results were they to adopt the synthesized approach characteristic of the proposed third generation. They may or may not. Rather, we observe that in the first generation of cross-cultural research, researchers tended to study attitudes and their relevant constructs that were regarded as relatively universal. Similarly, in the second generation of cross-cultural research, we notice that researchers had a propensity to investigate attitudes and attitude-relevant constructs that were regarded as relatively culture specific. Finally, although we present evidence below demonstrating that a universal psychological phenomenon or underlying process may both manifest itself and operate according to a culturally distinct logic, we do not argue that all phenomena or processes can be explained in this manner. We believe that, whereas some psychological phenomena or processes are truly universal, others are culture specific.

### First generation of cross-cultural research on attitudes and attitude-relevant constructs

The first generation of cross-cultural research on attitudes or attitude-relevant constructs seemed to demonstrate universality across cultures or cross-cultural similarities. One attitude-relevant construct studied cross-culturally early on was semantic differentiation (Kumata & Schramm, 1956, as cited in Osgood, Suci, & Tannenbaum, 1957). Given that an attitude is a categorization of a target object along an evaluative dimension based on cognitive, affective, and behavioral information (Zanna & Rempel, 1988), one needs to make a clear semantic differentiation between two concepts or objects in order to make such an evaluative judgment. The semantic differentiation is, therefore, an integral part of an attitude.

Osgood et al. (1957) proposed a way to measure the meaning of a concept by arguing that each concept has a semantic space or a region of multiple dimensions that represents the meaning of the concept (e.g., stability, aggressiveness). The three most important dimensions in the semantic space are evaluation, potency, and activity. Each dimension consists of a set of semantic scales that are pairs of adjectives occupying polar ends of a continuum (e.g., *sharp–dull*). The evaluation dimension includes semantic scales such as *good–bad* and *positive–negative*, the potency dimension includes semantic scales such as *strong–weak* and *large–small*, and the activity dimension includes semantic scales such as *fast–slow* and *active–passive*. The meaning of each concept, such as "mother" or "ocean," is measured in multidimensional semantic space by allocating a point on a set of semantic scales like *good–bad* and *large–small*. Semantic differentiation or the difference in the meaning between two concepts is measured by the multidimensional distance between the two points allocated for the two concepts in the semantic space.

Based on this theory of the measurement of meaning proposed by Osgood and his colleagues, Kumata and Schramm (1956, as cited in Osgood et al., 1957) conducted a cross-cultural study to examine the comparability of semantic differentiation across languages and cultures using Japanese, Korean, and American college students. The participants were given 30 concepts (e.g., communism, police, labor union, father, waterfall, etc.) and asked to judge the concepts against 20 semantic scales (e.g., *good–bad, happy–sad, relaxed–tense, strong–weak, active–passive, sharp–dull*, etc.) selected primarily from the three most important dimensions (i.e., evaluation, potency, and activity). Each group of participants was tested twice. The Japanese and Korean participants were tested once in English and once in their native languages. Kumata and Schramm found cross-cultural similarities in semantic differentiation. That is, in judging the meaning of the concepts, participants used the dimensions in a highly similarly manner across the three languages. In addition, each of the three dimensions consisted of similar semantic scales across the three cultures. Thus, regardless of culture or language, people tend to judge the meaning of a concept using similar dimensions.

Values, another attitude-relevant construct, have also been studied cross-culturally. People's attitudes are likely to be guided by their values, and their attitudes are likely to reinforce their values. Schwartz and Bilsky (1987) summarized the definitions of values in the literature and proposed several features of values. Some features of values, such as their capacity to guide people's information processing (i.e., selection and evaluation) of both behavior and events, seem to be particularly relevant to attitudes. They further argued that values represent three universal human goals that are required for human existence: biological needs of humans as organisms, social or interactional needs for concerted interpersonal relationships, and societal or institutional needs for group survival and welfare. Based on these definitions of values, they proposed a universal typology of values that includes categories such as achievement, security, self-direction and conformity.

Schwartz (1992) further refined this typology of values and tested it cross-culturally. He examined 20 countries encompassing 13 different languages around the world. Most of the countries examined included participants representing two to three occupational groups comprised of teachers, university students, and the general public. Schwartz asked participants to rate each of 56 values representing 11 value types (e.g., achievement: ambitious, successful; hedonism: pleasure, enjoying life; self-direction: self-respect, freedom; benevolence: honest, helpful). The participants rated each value as a guiding principle in their lives on a 9-point scale ranging from "supreme importance" to "opposed to my values." The major finding was that most of the proposed value types (10 out of 11) appeared to be present across cultures. In addition, Schwartz found not only that people from different cultures regarded value types such as achievement and self-direction as the guiding principles in their lives, but also that the values constituting each value type tended to be similar across cultures. Moreover, people seemed to locate the 56 values in the postulated value types (e.g., successful in achievement, self-respect in self-direction), regardless of their cultural background. Finally, the structure of values, that is, the conflicts and compatibilities among values, appeared to be stable across cultures. Independent of the culture from which they derive, people tend to see consistent relationships among values: for example, conflict between achievement and benevolence and compatibility between conformity and tradition. Taken together, Schwartz found that, across different cultures, people hold relatively universal value types, value contents, and value structure.

To summarize, semantic differentiation is used to assess the meaning of a concept and has been shown to be cross-culturally invariable (Kumata & Schramm, 1956, as cited in Osgood et al., 1957). Relatedly, values that are used as the guiding principles in people's lives were found to be stable and consistent across cultures (Schwartz, 1992). Taken as representatives of the first generation of cross-cultural research on attitudes, these two sets of studies demonstrate cross-cultural similarities for attitude-relevant constructs.

### *Second generation of cross-cultural research on attitudes and attitude-relevant constructs*

Social psychology has been traditionally led by research conducted in Western cultures, and therefore, it has been significantly informed by Eurocentric cultural assumptions. Perhaps unsurprisingly, then, many social psychological phenomena or processes were initially assumed to be similar across cultures. However, fuelled by the recognition that such universalist assumptions risked obscuring distinct or culture-specific psychological phenomena, the second generation of cross-cultural research on attitudes and attitude-relevant constructs focused on phenomena or processes that did not seem to generalize across cultures. It recognized and demonstrated some important cross-cultural differences, especially between cultures that can be characterized as individualistic (e.g., North American culture) and those that can be characterized as collectivistic (e.g., East Asian culture).

Individualism tends to emphasize individual uniqueness and independence, whereas collectivism tends to emphasize group harmony and interdependence (Triandis, 1996). This individualism–collectivism dimension has been frequently used as the basis for studying cultural variability, because the dimension has been considered to foster strikingly different sets of self-concept, emotion, cognition, motivation, social behavior, social perception, interpersonal relationships, and intergroup relations (see Markus & Kitayama, 1991, for review). One aspect of the individualism–collectivism dimension that is particularly relevant to the literature we review here pertains to how an individual conceives of the self in each of the two opposed cultures. In individualistic cultures, the individual tends to be seen as an autonomous entity, separate from other people and the social context. The self is viewed as independent. In collectivistic cultures, by contrast, the individual tends to be regarded as being connected to others and embedded in the social context. The self is viewed as interdependent.

Similar cultural patterns can be seen in cross-cultural research on attribution. Although this research is not directly related to attitudes per se, we believe that reviewing these findings helps us understand the influence of culture more generally and aids in our understanding of the specific influence of culture on attitudes. With this in mind, we review a few studies that highlight the impact of culture on attribution.

Miller (1984) investigated cross-cultural differences between Americans and Hindus in attributions of another person's behavior. She also examined age differences in attributions and explanations of others' behaviors based on her belief that culture influences the development of such psychological processes. She argued that the individualistic cultural view of a person would lead to dispositional explanations of a behavior, reflecting the individualistic cultural assumption that an autonomous individual who is free from social constraints should be responsible for her own action. In contrast, the collectivistic cultural view of a person would lead to situational explanations of a behavior, because people in a collectivistic culture assume that a person's action reflects his duties and obligations for other people in the social network to which he belongs and that his action is strongly influenced by the social context. In addition, she argued that people in different cultures learn and acquire their respective culture's attributional logic as they grow older and that there should be age differences in behavioral attributions such that cross-cultural differences would be most apparent among adults.

In her study, Miller (1984) asked four age groups (8-, 11-, 15-year-olds and adults) of Americans in the United States and Hindus in India to describe two deviant and two prosocial behaviors of people that they knew well and to provide explanations for their behaviors. She found evidence in support of her arguments for cross-cultural and age differences. American adults used more general dispositions and personality characteristics (e.g., kind, insecure) than contextual factors (e.g., social norms, interpersonal relationships) to explain others' behaviors. In contrast, Hindu adults used more contextual or situational factors (e.g., he is her advisor, it was early in the morning) than general dispositions to explain others' behaviors. Furthermore, the striking cross-cultural differences obtained among adults were not observed among 8- and 11-year-old children. Miller found a significant linear age increase in the use of general dispositions among the American participants, but not among the Hindu counterparts. She also found a significant linear age increase in the use of contextual factors among the Hindus, but not among the Americans. Miller's (1984) findings are particularly important in understanding cultural influences on psychological phenomena and processes, given that they demonstrate developmental changes in social attributions in two different cultures.

More recently, Choi and Nisbett (1998) extended research on cross-cultural differences in social attributions in attempting to understand cross-cultural differences in the propensity to commit the fundamental attribution error, or the tendency to overestimate dispositional influences and underestimate situational influences on other people's behavior. Choi and Nisbett (1998) hypothesized that if Asians, in contrast to their North American counterparts, prefer situational explanations to dispositional ones in explaining others' behaviors, they ought to show less of a tendency to commit the fundamental attribution error in inferring others' attitudes. They examined European-American and Korean university students using the attitude attribution paradigm developed by Jones and Harris (1967). They found that when people merely learned that the target person was forced to write an essay, regardless of her true attitude toward capital punishment, European-Americans and Koreans evidenced an equal tendency to commit the fundamental attribution error in inferring the target's true attitude toward capital punishment.

The researchers thought that cross-cultural differences in making the fundamental attribution error would emerge if situational constraints that the target person had faced became more salient. Rather than merely learning that the target person was forced to write an essay, participants in the second study experienced the same situational constraints that the target person had faced, either by actually writing an essay regardless of their true attitudes toward capital punishment or by using the same arguments in writing their own essays that the target person used in her essay. As predicted, when situational constraints were made salient in these manners, Koreans demonstrated a clear tendency to become situationists, whereas European-Americans persisted in their preference for dispositionist explanations. Specifically, Koreans were significantly less likely to commit the fundamental attribution error when they experienced the same situational constraints that the target person had faced.

In contrast, European-Americans continued to commit the fundamental attribution error in inferring the target person's true attitude toward capital punishment, even after experiencing the same situational constraints as the target person. Furthermore, these researchers found cross-cultural differences in the actor–observer bias, the tendency to explain one's own behavior in terms of situational factors and others' behavior as due to dispositional factors. Regardless of the salience of situational constraints that the target person had experienced, European-Americans continued to be influenced by the actor–observer bias. They indicated that whereas the target person's essay reflected her true attitude, their own essays reflected the situational constraints. Among Koreans, in contrast, the actor–observer bias was eliminated once the situational constraints that the target person had faced were recognized. Taken together, these two studies clearly demonstrated cross-cultural differences in social attributions and propensity to commit the fundamental attribution error. Asians appear to be more adept at noticing and taking into account the impact of the social situation on people's behavior.

Another important area of attitude research that has demonstrated significant cross-cultural differences is in the domain of persuasion. Persuasive communications influence attitude formation and change. Considering the wide-ranging influence of culture on people's feelings, thoughts, and behaviors (Markus & Kitayama, 1991), different types of persuasive messages may very well influence people differently in cultures as distinct as North America and East Asia. Han and Shavitt (1994) postulated that cross-cultural differences on the dimension of individualism–collectivism would be reflected in magazine advertisements, and examined American and Korean magazine advertisements for persuasiveness. They found that American ads used individualistic appeals, which portray individuality, personal success, and self-reliance, more frequently than collectivistic appeals, which emphasize family integrity, group welfare, and interdependent relationships with others. Korean ads, on the other hand, used collectivistic appeals more frequently than individualistic appeals.

They also found that these two types of persuasive appeals differ in effectiveness in the two cultures. Both Americans and Koreans perceived that culturally consistent appeals (i.e., individualistic appeals for Americans and collectivistic appeals for Koreans) were more persuasive than culturally inconsistent appeals, particularly when they made purchase decisions for shared products such as detergent and electric irons. These findings indicate that cross-cultural differences exist in the content and effectiveness of persuasive messages.

It seems evident that there are cross-cultural differences in how people explain others' behavior, infer others' attitudes, and react to messages targeted at their own attitudes. What about attitudes toward the self, such as feelings of self-worth or self-regard? Recent research seems to indicate that there are indeed cross-cultural differences in people's attitudes toward themselves.

Heine, Lehman, Markus, and Kitayama (1999) argued that although North Americans tend to construe a positive self-regard as a universal human need and consider a positive self-view a prerequisite for mental health, the cross-cultural generalizability of this perspective is questionable. In particular, Heine and his colleagues argued that, unlike North Americans, Japanese, who live in a collectivistic culture, are not motivated to maintain such a positive self-regard. These researchers postulated a series of reasons, derived from collectivistic cultural ideals and values, capable of accounting for the apparent absence of a need to maintain a positive self-regard among Japanese. For instance, they argued that Japanese view themselves as relational entities and maintain their sense of self from their interdependent relationships with others or connectedness with others, and thus they do not need to sustain a positive self-view. They further argued that Japanese culture encourages strict self-discipline such as making efforts to improve oneself, persevering at a difficult task, and enduring hardships. Japanese also tend to hold self-critical attitudes and maintain feelings of both imperfection and dissatisfaction with current levels of performance. Self-discipline and self-critical attitudes among Japanese are thought to be important in both ensuring people's commitment to their ingroup and promoting group goals, but such cultural tendencies do not seem to be compatible with positive self-regard.

To support these arguments, Heine and his colleagues presented evidence for cross-cultural differences in self-esteem measured by Rosenberg's (1965) Self-esteem Scale. Among European-Canadians, for whom having a positive self-view is an individualistic cultural ideal, the self-esteem scores were distributed heavily toward the higher end of the scale. Their actual mean was much higher than the theoretical midpoint of the scale. On the other hand, among Japanese, the self-esteem scores were distributed along a normal bell curve. Their actual mean closely corresponded to the theoretical midpoint of the scale.

These researchers also examined the relation between self-esteem and the degree of independence and interdependence measured by Singelis's (1994) Independence/Interdependence Scale. Independence was highly positively correlated with self-esteem among both Japanese and European-Canadians, whereas interdependence was not related to self-esteem among Japanese and was negatively correlated with self-esteem among European-Canadians. This evidence corroborated Heine and his colleagues' argument that there are cross-cultural differences in self-view or attitudes toward the self. Given the importance placed on self-reliance and independence in individualistic cultures, people socialized in such cultures experience a greater need and desire to maintain a positive attitude toward themselves. Such a need for positive self-regard, at least insofar as it is conceptualized in individualistic North American culture, does not appear to be a universal need, as Japanese failed to show similar tendencies.

In summary, in the second generation of cross-cultural research on attitudes and attitude-relevant constructs, cross-cultural variability was demonstrated, especially between individualistic North American cultures and collectivistic East Asian cultures. The research found cross-cultural differences in many areas, including social attribution (Miller, 1984), the fundamental attribution error (Choi & Nisbett, 1998), persuasion (Han & Shavitt, 1994), self-concept (Markus & Kitayama, 1991), and positive self-regard (Heine et al., 1999).

### *Third generation of cross-cultural research on attitudes and attitude-relevant constructs*

Thus far, we have reviewed research demonstrating either cross-cultural similarities or cross-cultural differences. The third generation of cross-cultural research that we propose, for which we provide empirical evidence below, is best characterized as a new way of conceptualizing how culture influences psychological phenomena and processes. Specifically, we believe that many (but not all) psychological phenomena or fundamental processes operate consistently across cultures, but perhaps more importantly that culture configures the ways in which and the people among whom the phenomena or processes emerge. This new way of thinking about cultural influences is very different from both the first and second generations of cross-cultural research in that it does not treat a phenomenon or process as inherently universal or culture- specific. Rather, it assumes the existence of a cross-culturally consistent fundamental phenomenon or underlying process and seeks to ascertain how the phenomenon or process is manifested as a function of culture.

For example, consider the self-image maintenance process (Spencer, Josephs, & Steele, 1993), based on Steele's (1988) self-affirmation theory. According to the self-image maintenance process, people are motivated to maintain an image of self-integrity by affirming some positive, valuable aspects of the self when they feel an important aspect of the self is threatened by some negative event. We believe that such a basic psychological mechanism can operate across cultures. People in both Western and East Asian cultures engage in self-image maintenance processes. However, culture influences the ways in which people maintain their culturally valued sense of self because of the divergent self-concepts to which they subscribe and the differences in culturally ideal attributes and acts prevalent in the two cultures (see Figure 16.1). For instance, although both Westerners and East Asians are capable of experiencing threats to culturally valued dimensions of their respective self-concepts, Westerners are more likely to be sensitive to a threat to their independent self (e.g., failure), whereas East Asians might react more strongly to a threat to their interdependent self (e.g., not being a good group member). When culturally important self-concepts are threatened, the primary goal for members of both cultures would be to restore the integrity of a culturally valued sense of self by affirming themselves through culturally valued attributes and acts. Westerners might affirm themselves and restore their sense of self by enhancing their positive attributes or focusing on their unique personal qualities. East Asians might achieve the same end by addressing shortcomings or reminding themselves of important interpersonal relationships. By meeting their respective cultural ideals, individuals from both Western and East Asian cultures can affirm themselves and feel they are doing well.

In what circumstances do both Westerners and East Asians feel threats to their culturally important self-concepts and in turn engage in culturally ideal self-image maintenance processes? We argue that cognitive dissonance can be considered as part of a culturally ideal self-image maintenance process. Festinger (1957) proposed that cognitive dissonance, or psychological discomfort, arises when people have two incompatible cognitions and that they are motivated to reduce the dissonance or discomfort through various manners. Past research has demonstrated that people try to reduce dissonance by making one of the cognitions consistent with the other (e.g., Brehm, 1956; Festinger & Carlsmith, 1959) or by affirming an important aspect of the self (e.g., Heine & Lehman, 1997; Steele, 1988; Steele, Spencer, & Lynch, 1993).

Our basic premise is that cognitive dissonance and dissonance reduction are not phenomena specific to North American culture. According to this perspective, members of different cultures experience dissonance when culturally valued conceptions of the self are threatened by the possibility of making decisions that are not acceptable in their cultures or by behaving in ways that are not in line with culturally prevalent attitudes. However, the situations that are likely to give rise to the experience of dissonance would be a function of culture, because there would be cross-cultural differences conditioning when a culturally ideal self-concept is threatened and how the threat can be resolved. Below, we first review relevant cross-cultural research on cognitive dissonance. Then we provide empirical evidence that is in line with our argument for the third generation of cross-cultural research on attitudes.

## Empirical evidence for the third generation of cross-cultural research on attitudes

We were aware of only one published article demonstrating cross-cultural differences in cognitive dissonance before we started our investigation. Heine and Lehman (1997) investigated the relationship between cognitive dissonance and self-affirmation using a free-choice paradigm in which participants made a choice between two music CDs and found cross-cultural differences between Canadian and Japanese participants. In particular, Canadians demonstrated the usual rationalization of their choices of CDs. However, when provided with an opportunity to affirm themselves through positive feedback on a personality test, Canadian participants did not rationalize their decisions. Japanese participants, by contrast, were unaffected by self-affirmation opportunities. They did not show a tendency to rationalize their choices of CDs in any of the feedback conditions. Based on these findings, Heine and Lehman argued that Japanese participants do not rationalize their decisions because Asians do not experience dissonance. Appealing to core differences between the North American independent self-view and the East Asian interdependent self-view, they suggested that cognitive dissonance was a culturally constructed phenomenon specific to North America culture.

However, another line of research has demonstrated an opposed set of results with Asian samples. In particular, Sakai (1981; Sakai & Andow, 1980) found some evidence that Japanese experience cognitive dissonance and engage in dissonance reduction. In one study, Sakai and Andow (1980) examined the relation between personal responsibility and dissonance reduction among people who received an electric shock. The magnitude of the electric shock was determined by casting a die by the experimenter (the experimenter-caused condition) or by the participants themselves (the participant-caused condition). Although there were no differences in feelings of personal responsibility across condition, individuals in the participant-caused condition perceived the shock as less painful, estimated their own heart rate as slower, and perceived the experimenter as more favorable than those in the experimenter-caused condition. Sakai and Andow argued that less negative perceptions of the electric shock and the more favorable evaluations of the experimenter were due to dissonance reduction among those who determined the magnitude of the shock that they received.

In another study, Sakai (1981) investigated dissonance reduction in a forced compliance situation among Japanese high school students. He asked the students to make a counterattitudinal speech by agreeing with abolition of coeducation either publicly (i.e., included their names, affiliated classes, and grades in an audiotaped speech) or anonymously. He found that those who made the speech publicly showed significantly higher endorsement of the abolition of coeducation than those who made the speech anonymously. Sakai explained his findings in terms of cognitive dissonance. That is, individuals who made a public speech anticipated a counterargument from the audience, which in turn made the inconsistency between their private opinion and public speech salient to them. Subsequently, they engaged in dissonance reduction by agreeing more strongly with the abolition of coeducation than those who made an anonymous speech.

Such evidence suggests that cognitive dissonance is not specific to North American culture. How can we reconcile the inconsistent evidence on cognitive dissonance across cultures? We propose that this inconsistency can be reconciled by conceptualizing cognitive dissonance as part of the self-image maintenance processes operant among people in any culture. People experience cognitive dissonance when their culturally important self-concepts (e.g., an independent self for North Americans or an interdependent self for East Asians) are threatened by the possibility of making a culturally inappropriate decision or behaving in a manner that is incompatible with a culturally prevalent attitude. In such cases, individuals would try to maintain their culturally ideal self-image by rationalizing or justifying their decision or behavior. Alternatively, in the face of a threat to their culturally important self-concepts, people could maintain a culturally adaptive self-image through a self-affirmation process serving to reinforce the perception that they are living up to their cultural ideals (see Figure 16.1).

Cross-cultural differences in self-concepts have been highlighted by several social psychologists in recent years (e.g., Markus & Kitayama, 1991; Triandis, 1996). Some of these self-concept differences are particularly relevant to an understanding of cognitive dissonance as a means of maintaining a culturally ideal self-image. The North American conceptions of the independent self emphasize the importance of having the freedom to make one's own choices, expressing one's own desires and preferences, and maintaining consistency between one's attitudes (e.g., desires and preferences) and behaviors (e.g., making choices). For North Americans, therefore, making a rational decision means making a decision that is consistent with their desires and preferences. Recognizing that one's behavior (decision) is inconsistent with one's attitudes (desires and preferences) presents a serious threat to the independent "rational" self. This threat in turn leads people to justify their decisions so

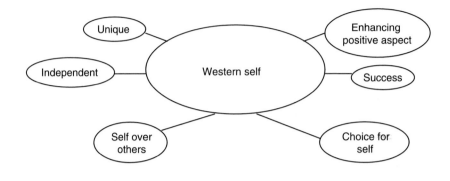

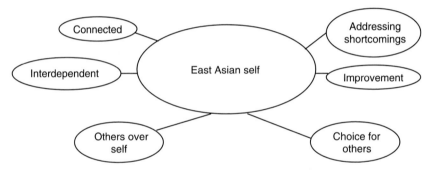

*Figure 16.1* A model of Western and East Asian self-systems.

that they can restore their rational self or threatened self-integrity. Providing individuals with opportunities for self-affirmation can also serve to counter such a threat, as demonstrated in past research (e.g., Heine & Lehman, 1997; Steele et al., 1993).

In contrast, East Asians, who hold an interdependent self-view, tend to attach greater importance to social roles and status in society, to interpersonal relationships, and to appropriate conduct in particular situations. Consequently, East Asians' behavior reflects their duties and obligations, deriving from their roles and status in a particular situation or relationship. Often, such duties and obligations include maintenance of group harmony and knowledge of others' desires and preferences. Specifically, in order to maintain harmonious relationships with ingroup members, people make decisions that reflect their group members' desires and preferences rather than their own. Given these characteristics of the interdependent self, the prospect of making a poor decision for their close other, such as a friend or a family member, may constitute a threatening situation capable of evoking cognitive dissonance for East Asian individuals. Recognizing that their decision indicates that they are not a good friend or family member, because they are not familiar with or did not anticipate correctly their close other's desires and preferences, can threaten to damage a culturally ideal image of an interdependent person. This threat can in turn lead people to rationalize their decision for their close other in order to maintain their sense of being a good group member. Can such a threat to the interdependent self be alleviated by a conventional self-affirmation procedure designed to affirm the independent self? We argue that for East Asian individuals to reduce threats to their interdependent self, they need to affirm their interdependent self, rather than their independent self.

In support of these arguments, there is some evidence that shows a relation between cognitive dissonance and interpersonal concerns. Consider Sakai's (1981) findings that Japanese high school students demonstrated dissonance reduction after public commitment by making a counterattitudinal, public speech. Making a counterattitudinal speech publicly can evoke interpersonal concerns, because people may anticipate defending themselves against their audience.

More recently, Kitayama and his colleagues (Kitayama, Conner Snibbe, Markus, & Suzuki, in press) also found evidence that East Asians experience cognitive dissonance when they have interpersonal concerns. They examined cognitive dissonance cross-culturally using a free choice paradigm and found that Japanese people engaged in dissonance reduction when they made a choice in reference to what other people might do or think (the reference-other). In one study, some participants rated and ranked ten CDs for an average college student, in addition to rating and ranking of ten CDs based their own CD preferences, before they made a choice between two music CDs taken from the participants' own preferences. Whereas those who were additionally asked to estimate an average college student's preferences (i.e., highlighted interpersonal concerns) showed dissonance reduction, those who were simply asked their own preferences of CDs (i.e., highlighted personal concerns) did not. In another study, dissonance reduction was demonstrated when the reference-other was a pleasant average college student, but not when the reference-other was an unpleasant or dislikable person. These researchers also found that their Japanese participants engaged in dissonance reduction when the reference-other was presented graphically as a schematic face, but not when the schematic face was not presented.

In contrast, the American counterparts in these studies did not show the effect of reference-other. They engaged in dissonance reduction regardless of condition. Kitayama and his colleagues (in press) argued that reference to relevant others evoked interpersonal concerns or worries among their Japanese participants, which in turn led them to justify their choices and reduce dissonance. These studies demonstrate that East Asians experience cognitive dissonance and engage in dissonance reduction, especially when they have interpersonal concerns.

In summary, we argue that the psychological phenomenon of cognitive dissonance can be observed across cultures as a way to maintain a culturally ideal self-image, but that the situations in which people experience dissonance depends on culture. Based on the arguments outlined above, we propose that cross-cultural differences in self-concept interact with cognitive dissonance. In particular, we expect that North Americans are likely to rationalize their decisions when the decisions pertain to themselves, because making a poor decision for oneself is threatening to the independent self. We predict that East Asians are likely to rationalize their decisions when the decisions pertain to their ingroup members, because making a bad decision for members of the ingroup is threatening to the interdependent self. We also contend that whereas affirming the independent self reduces dissonance for North Americans, affirming the interdependent self "takes the sting out of dissonance" for East Asians. In order to test these ideas, we conducted three studies.

### Study 1: Post-decision rationalization among European-Canadians and Asian-Canadians

In the first study, we examined the idea that cross-cultural differences in self-concept (independent self vs. interdependent self) influence when people are likely to rationalize their decisions. Adopting the free choice paradigm, we manipulated the target person for whom people make their decision: themselves or a close friend.

Participants were either Canadian-born European-Canadians or Asian-born Asian-Canadians. They were told that they were helping a soon-to-be-opened Chinese restaurant to create a special lunch menu. From a list of 25 Chinese entrées, participants selected the 10 most preferred items based on either their own preference or their perception of their close friend's preference. They ranked the 10 items in order of their own or their friend's preference. Upon completing this ranking task, the participants rated each of the 10 items in terms of how much they or their friend would like to order it. They were then presented with two gift certificates that were for the fifth and sixth ranked entrées on their initial ranking and were asked to choose one certificate for themselves or as a gift for their friend. After a 10-minute interval, during which the participants were left alone in the experimental room, they were presented with a sample menu that included detailed descriptions of each of the 25 entrées and asked to re-rate the 10 items they originally selected. The main dependent variable was the spread of alternatives, that is, the degree that the post-choice rating of the chosen alternative increased and the post-choice rating of the non-chosen alternative decreased.

We hypothesized that European-Canadians would show a greater spread of alternatives when they made decisions for themselves, rather than for their close friend. As for Asian-Canadians, we considered that the strength of their identification with their Asian culture might influence which self-concept, that is, an independent self or interdependent self, would interact with cognitive dissonance. We expected those Asian-Canadians, who only weakly identified with their Asian culture, would behave just like European-Canadians, presumably because they espouse an independent self-concept. Such weakly identified Asian-Canadians were expected to show a greater spread of alternatives when they made decisions for themselves, rather than for their close friend. On the other hand, we expected that Asian-Canadians who strongly identified with their Asian cultural background would espouse a more interdependent self-concept, which would in turn lead to a greater spread of alternatives when they made decisions for their close friend, rather than for themselves.

Figure 16.2 shows the results of the first study in a 3 (Cultural group: European-Canadians vs. Weakly-identified Asian-Canadians vs. Strongly identified Asian-Canadians) × 2 (Decision target: Self vs. Friend) design. As predicted, European-Canadians rationalized their choice of coupon for the Chinese entrée significantly more when they chose the coupon for themselves than when they chose it as a gift for their close friend. When they chose an entrée for themselves, they increased their own evaluation of the chosen entrée and decreased their own evaluation of the rejected entrée. This result, that European-Canadians justify their decisions when the decisions pertain to themselves, replicates past findings among North Americans (e.g., Brehm, 1956; Heine & Lehman, 1997; Steele et al., 1993). We also found predicted results among Asian-Canadians. Weakly identified Asian-Canadians, like their European-Canadian counterparts, rationalized their choice of coupon significantly more when they chose it for themselves than when they chose it as a gift for their close friend. In contrast, strongly identified Asian-Canadians justified their choice of coupon significantly more when they chose it for their close friend than when they chose it for themselves. When they chose an entrée as a gift for their close friend, they increased their perception of their close friend's evaluation of the chosen entrée and decreased their perception of their close friend's evaluation of the rejected

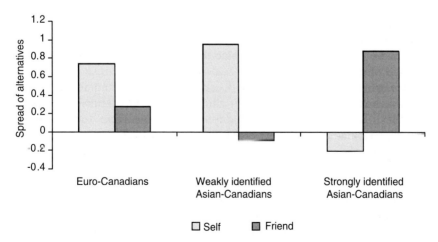

*Figure 16.2* Study 1: Post-decision rationalization (DV: mean spread of alternatives).

entrée. Thus, just like their European-Canadian counterparts, Asian-Canadians, too, showed significant post-decision rationalization. However, the situation in which they rationalized their decisions varied as a function of their strength of identification with Asian culture.

### Study 2: Interdependent self-affirmation

Past research has shown that self-affirmation reduces defensiveness and increases feelings of self-integrity, which in turn lead to less post-decision rationalization among European-Americans (Steele et al., 1993) and among European-Canadians (Heine & Lehman, 1997). Considering the result that strongly identified Asian-Canadians showed significant post-decision rationalization in the friend condition but not in the self condition in the first study, we predicted that for a self-affirmation manipulation to be successful for Asian-Canadians who strongly hold interdependent self-concepts, it must restore integrity to threatened aspects of the interdependent, and not the independent, self. Thus, in the second study, we devised an interdependent self-affirmation manipulation to affirm an interdependent self and tested the effects of both the independent and the newly devised interdependent self-affirmation manipulations on Asian-Canadians' state self-esteem.

The conventional self-affirmation manipulation, designed to affirm an independent self, uses a value survey. People are asked to choose one value from a list of six that is most important to them (e.g., business/economics, social life/relationships, religion/spirituality, etc.) and then to write about why the value is so important to them. Based on this procedure, we devised a new self-affirmation manipulation that could affirm an interdependent self, using the same list of six values. The interdependent self-affirmation procedure asks people to choose one value from the list of six that is most important to them and their family and then to write about why they and their family share this particular value. In order to make our independent self-affirmation more in parallel to this new interdependent self-affirmation, we revised the conventional self-affirmation slightly such that the value survey asks people to explain why the most important value they have chosen uniquely describes who they are.

To validate these manipulations, Asian-born Asian-Canadians were given either the revised independent self-affirmation manipulation or the new, interdependent self-affirmation manipulation. They were then asked to complete a state self-esteem scale (McFarland & Ross, 1982), which consists of 20 pairs of bipolar adjectives such as *good–bad, superior–inferior*, and *proud–ashamed*, rated on 7-point scales. We hypothesized that Asian-born Asian-Canadians, who were presumed to hold an interdependent view of the self, would evidence a higher level of state self-esteem when provided with an opportunity to affirm their interdependent self as compared to their independent self. As predicted, those Asian-Canadians who could affirm their interdependent self showed a significantly higher level of state self-esteem than those who affirmed their independent self. This result indicated that the newly devised interdependent self-affirmation procedure was successful in affirming the interdependent self.

Interestingly, the most popular value that was chosen was "social life/relationships" in both conditions. Regardless of whether the participants were asked to choose one value that was most important to them or to choose one value that was most important to them and their family, the majority chose "social life/relationships" as an important value. Moreover, they provided similar reasons in both conditions in explaining why the value is shared by them and their family or why the value uniquely describes them. For example, a participant who chose the value of social life/relationships in the interdependent self-affirmation condition wrote that "me [sic] and my family share this value because we feel it's extremely important to have close relationships so that we feel part of something, like we belong to a group (our family). We are very attentive to one another's feelings and so by being close, it brings us happiness and fulfillment in our lives." Another participant who chose the same value in the independent self-affirmation condition wrote that "having a good, harmonious relationship is important to my happiness and well-being. I tend to do well in school or work if I have a good social life with caring friends and family. If something goes wrong with school or at work, it helps me to get through it with supportive people around me. . . . It's easier to succeed and feel good about myself if I have a good social life."

A similar pattern was found with respect to the second most popular value, "science/pursuit of knowledge," which was chosen much less frequently than "social life/relationships." One participant in the interdependent self-affirmation condition wrote that "my family always watches TV shows which show the latest technologies developed. My parents always tell me to learn more stuff, as the more you know, the more successful you will be in life. We always try to buy the latest technologies like in computers, we try to upgrade to the fastest one that is out on the market." Another participant in the independent self-affirmation condition wrote that "I'm in the science faculty, so science is important to me. Knowledge is what I think is really important as it helps you to get ahead in life, in work, in school, etc. Since I am in school to learn and thinking about going to graduate school to learn more, I think that 'Pursuit of Knowledge' describes the type of person I am—doing well in school is very important to me."

It is important to note that regardless of the self-affirmation conditions, most of the Asian-Canadian participants chose the same values and listed similar reasons for their importance. Yet, the interdependent self-affirmation, which clearly induced participants to write (and presumably think) about why the value was important to them and their family (rather than simply to themselves), had a more positive effect on the participants' state self-esteem.

### Study 3: Post-decision rationalization and self-affirmation among strongly identified Asian-Canadians

In the third study, we examined the idea that a self-affirmation manipulation that affirms an interdependent self can reduce post-decision rationalization among Asian-Canadians who strongly identify with their Asian culture. We used both the revised independent self-affirmation and the newly devised interdependent self-affirmation procedures.

Participants were all Asian-born Asian-Canadians who strongly identified with their Asian culture. We used exactly the same materials as the first study and asked the strongly identified Asian-Canadians to choose a coupon of a Chinese entrée as a gift for their close friend. They made their choices in one of three self-affirmation conditions: no self-affirmation, independent self-affirmation, or interdependent self-affirmation.

We hypothesized that participants in the no self-affirmation and independent self-affirmation conditions would rationalize their choices, replicating the results obtained in the first study. We expected that those in the interdependent self-affirmation condition would not rationalize their choices, as the self-affirmation would reduce threatened feelings and lessen the need to justify their decisions.

Figure 16.3 shows the results of the third study in the three different self-affirmation conditions. As predicted, when Asian-Canadians who strongly identified with their Asian culture made their choices for their close friends, they rationalized their choices if they did not have an opportunity to affirm their interdependent self. In contrast, as hypothesized, those who had a chance to affirm their interdependent self did not rationalize their choices. They showed significantly less post-decision rationalization than those in the other two self-affirmation conditions. The third study replicated the result of the first study in the friend condition among strongly identified Asian-Canadians. It also demonstrated that affirming the interdependent self could

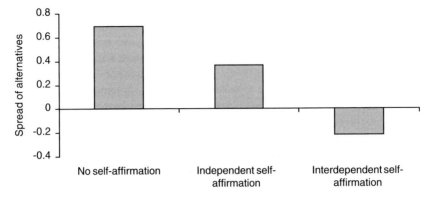

*Figure 16.3* Study 3: Post-decision rationalization by self-affirmation condition (DV: mean spread of alternatives).

reduce the threat of making poor decisions for close others among strongly identified Asian-Canadians.

Notice that the amount of post-decision rationalization in the independent self-affirmation condition is in between the amounts obtained in the no self-affirmation and interdependent self-affirmation conditions. Although all participants in the third study were Asian-born Asian-Canadians who strongly identified with their Asian background, it is conceivable that some of them identified with both Asian and Canadian cultures (i.e., they were biculturally identified) whereas others identified only with Asian culture. To the extent that Asian-Canadians identified with both individualistic Canadian culture and collectivistic Asian culture, it is conceivable that they could also be affirmed by an independent self-affirmation, which would in turn reduce the degree to which they engage in post-decision rationalization. Given that participants were all Asian-Canadians who strongly identified with their Asian culture and who all experienced a threat to their interdependent self, it is worth noting that identification with Canadian culture only seems to matter in independent self-affirmation condition. Theoretically, individuals in the no self-affirmation condition should show post-decision rationalization whether or not they identify with Canadian culture. Those in the interdependent self-affirmation condition should show attenuated post-decision rationalization regardless of the strength of identification with Canadian culture. To test this notion, we conducted a median split on the strength of identification with Canadian culture to examine the effect of independent self-affirmation on those who biculturally identified with Asian and Canadian cultures.

Figure 16.4 shows the results of the third study in a 2 (Identification with Canadian culture: Weak vs. Strong) × 2 (Self-affirmation: Independent self-affirmation vs. Interdependent self-affirmation) design. As we speculated, Asian-Canadians who strongly identified with Canadian culture (and, thus, were possessed of a strong bicultural identification with both Asian and Canadian cultures) showed less post-decision rationalization after having an opportunity to affirm their independent self. Those who weakly identified with Canadian culture (and, thus, strongly identified only with the Asian culture) were not affected by the independent self-affirmation, and therefore showed post-decision rationalization. The biculturally identified Asian-Canadians did not differ from the Asian-Canadians who identified only with the Asian culture in the interdependent self-affirmation condition, neither of whom had a tendency to rationalize their choices.[1] Incidentally, the result of the biculturally identified Asian-Canadians also provides strong evidence for the fluidity of self-affirmation (Steele, 1988). Although the Asian-Canadians experienced a threat to their interdependent self, the biculturally identified people could use their independent self to reduce the need to rationalize their

---

1 In the no self-affirmation (i.e., replication) condition, both groups had a tendency to rationalize their choices.

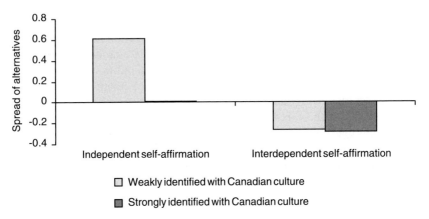

*Figure 16.4* Study 3: Post-decision rationalization by cultural identification (DV: mean spread of alternatives).

choices. It demonstrates that in order to affirm themselves and maintain an overall sense of integrity, individuals can use unrelated self-concepts to the ones that are being threatened.

### Summary of the three studies

Our cross-cultural research demonstrates that both North Americans and East Asians experience cognitive dissonance and consequently try to rationalize their decisions to alleviate their dissonance. European-Canadians rationalized their decisions when their independent self was threatened. This result replicates past findings in cognitive dissonance research conducted in North America. Asian-Canadians also rationalized their decisions when their culturally important self-concepts were threatened. Those who weakly identified with Asian culture justified their decisions when their independent self was at stake, just as their European-Canadian counterparts did. Those who strongly identified with Asian culture, on the other hand, justified their decisions when their interdependent self was threatened. However, when Asian-Canadians who strongly identified with their Asian culture could affirm their interdependent self, they no longer rationalized their decisions. Furthermore, when Asian-Canadians who biculturally identified with Asian and Canadian cultures could affirm either their interdependent or independent self, they did not rationalize their decisions in either case.

### Conclusion

In this chapter, we have presented our view of a historical trajectory of cross-cultural research on attitudes and attitude-relevant constructs. Whereas the first generation of cross-cultural research demonstrated similarities across cultures, the second generation demonstrated cross-cultural differences. We then proposed a third generation of cross-cultural research as a new way to conceptualize cross-cultural similarities and differences. In particular, we have argued that apparent cross-cultural differences might not be mere differences in psychological processes or lack of phenomenon. According to this perspective, although some underlying psychological processes are thought to be similar and consistent across cultures, the operation of such processes or the situations in which phenomena are manifested is a function of culture. In other words, culture influences how and when fundamental processes or phenomena emerge. We have suggested that self-image maintenance might be such a universal psychological process, especially in view of the fact that people strive to follow cultural norms and meet culturally ideal images of how they should be and act. Moreover, we have suggested that cognitive dissonance might be experienced when people's culturally important self-concepts are threatened by making decisions or engaging in behaviors that are incompatible with cultural ideals. We presented empirical evidence from our cross-cultural research on cognitive dissonance in support of these arguments.

By proposing and providing evidence for the third generation of cross-cultural research on attitudes and attitude-relevant constructs, we hope to draw attention to a new way of thinking about cross-cultural research on attitudes. Certain basic psychological phenomena or processes might be universal across cultures. However, differences in cultural norms, ideals, values, and the meaning of behavior might influence such basic psychological processes and these differences might emerge in the guise of differences in basic psychological processes or contribute to the appearance that such processes are culture specific. In such cases, we need to go beyond superficial differences and vigorously examine the cultural factors that produce the differences. To the extent that this third-generation approach is more widely adopted, we might find that basic processes manifest themselves and operate according to a distinct cultural logic, rather than prematurely conclude that they are altogether absent in either of the two cultures. Our own cross-cultural research indicates that taking such an approach is essential to further promoting our understanding of the basic psychological processes shaping attitudes.

Although in this chapter we focused on and argued for the superficial cross-cultural differences arising from a similar underlying psychological process, the converse could be true. That is, although a manifested psychological phenomenon may be similar across cultures, the actual mechanisms or underlying processes that create the superficial similarity may be quite different due to specific cultural factors such as norms and values. For instance, both East Asians and North Americans may experience cognitive dissonance in a similar situation, but the emotional experiences generating the discomfort may be different between these two cultural groups. We believe that extending the third-generation approach to investigate such cross-cultural similarities and variations is a promising way to go about understanding the psychology of attitudes.

## Acknowledgments

The research in this chapter was supported by a postgraduate scholarship from the National Science and Engineering Research Council of Canada (NSERC) to the first author, an Ontario Graduate Scholarship to the second author (who is now in Law School at McGill University), and a research grant from the Social Science and Humanities Research Council of Canada to the third and fourth authors.

Earlier versions of the research were reported at the 2001 (San Antonio, Texas) and 2002 (Savannah, Georgia) Annual Meeting of the Society of Personality and Social Psychology, the New Perspectives on Dissonance and Culture Symposium in Kyoto, Japan, in May 2001, and the 2001 (Toronto, Ontario) Annual Convention of the American Psychological Society.

We thank Dov Cohen for his helpful comments and suggestions on an earlier version of this chapter.

Correspondence concerning this chapter should be addressed to Etsuko Hoshino-Browne, Department of Psychology, University of Waterloo, Waterloo, Ontario, Canada N2L 3G1; email: ehoshino@watarts.uwaterloo.ca

## References

Brehm, J. W. (1956). Postdecision changes in the desirability of alternatives. *Journal of Abnormal and Social Psychology, 36*, 384–389.

Choi, I., & Nisbett, R. E. (1998). Situational salience and cultural differences in the correspondence bias and actor-observer bias. *Personality and Social Psychology Bulletin, 24*, 949–960.

Festinger, L. (1957). *A theory of cognitive dissonance.* Stanford, CA: Stanford University Press.

Festinger, L., & Carlsmith, J. M. (1959). Cognitive consequences of forced compliance. *Journal of Abnormal and Social Psychology, 58*, 203–210.

Han, S., & Shavitt, S. (1994). Persuasion and culture: Advertising appeals in individualistic and collectivistic societies. *Journal of Experimental Social Psychology, 30*, 326–350.

Heine, S. J., & Lehman, D. R. (1997). Culture, dissonance, and self-affirmation. *Personality and Social Psychology Bulletin, 23*, 389–400.

Heine, S. J., Lehman, D. R., Markus, H. R., & Kitayama, S. (1999). Is there a universal need for positive self-regard? *Psychological Review, 106*, 766–794.

Jones, E. E., & Harris, V. A. (1967). The attribution of attitudes. *Journal of Experimental Social Psychology, 3*, 1–24.

Kitayama, S., Conner Snibbe, A., Markus, H. R., & Suzuki, T. (in press). Is there any free choice? Self and dissonance in two cultures. *Psychological Science.*

Markus, H. R., & Kitayama, S. (1991). Culture and the self: Implications for cognition, emotion, and motivation. *Psychological Review, 98*, 224–253.

McFarland, C., & Ross, M. (1982). Impact of causal attributions on affective reactions to success and failure. *Journal of Personality and Social Psychology, 43*, 937–946.

Miller, J. G. (1984). Culture and the development everyday social explanation. *Journal of Personality and Social Psychology, 46*, 961–978.

Osgood, C. E., Suci, G. J., & Tannenbaum, P. H. (1957). *The measurement of meaning.* Urbana, IL: University of Illinois Press.

Rosenberg, M. (1965). *Society and the adolescent self-image.* Princeton, NJ: Princeton University Press.

Sakai, H. (1981). Induced compliance and opinion change. *Japanese Psychological Research, 23,* 1–8.

Sakai, H., & Andow, K. (1980). Attribution of personal responsibility and dissonance reduction. *Japanese Psychological Research, 22,* 32–41.

Schwartz, S. H. (1992). Universals in the content and structure of values: Theoretical advances and empirical tests in 20 countries. In M. P. Zanna (Ed.), *Advances in experimental social psychology* (Vol. 25, pp. 1–65). New York: Academic Press.

Schwartz, S. H., & Bilsky, W. (1987). Toward a universal psychological structure of human values. *Journal of Personality and Social Psychology, 53,* 550–562.

Singelis, T. M. (1994). The measurement of independent and interdependent self-construals. *Personality and Social Psychology Bulletin, 20,* 580–591.

Spencer, S. J., Josephs, R. A., & Steele, C. M. (1993). Low self-esteem: The uphill struggle for self-integrity. In R. F. Baumeister (Ed.), *Self-esteem: The puzzle of low self-regard* (pp. 21–36). New York: Plenum Press.

Steele, C. M. (1988). The psychology of self-affirmation: Sustaining the integrity of the self. In L. Berkowitz (Ed.), *Advances in experimental social psychology* (Vol. 21, pp. 261–302). San Diego, CA: Academic Press.

Steele, C. M., Spencer, S. J., & Lynch, M. (1993). Self-image resilience and dissonance: The role of affirmational resources. *Journal of Personality and Social Psychology, 64,* 885–896.

Triandis, H. C. (1996). The psychological measurement of cultural syndromes. *American Psychologist, 51,* 407–415.

Zanna, M. P., & Rempel, J. K. (1988). Attitudes: A new look at an old concept. In D. Bar-Tal & A. W. Kruglanski (Eds.), *The social psychology of knowledge* (pp. 315–334). New York: Cambridge University Press.

# 17 The parametric unimodel as a theory of persuasion

*Arie W. Kruglanski, Ayelet Fishbach,*
*Hans-Peter Erb, Antonio Pierro, and*
*Lucia Mannetti*

In a persuasion context, *recipients* (1) typically confront a *message* (2) originating from some *source* (3) and the essential question researchers have been posing is whether recipients' attitudes or opinions will change under these circumstances. To address this issue, early persuasion studies focused on the foregoing three, "phenotypically" salient, features of the persuasion context—the recipients, the source, and the message (c.f. Hovland, Janis, & Kelley, 1953; Lasswell, 1948), and treated them as relatively sequestered classes of factors relevant to persuasion. This has led to the compilation of variable lists in each of the "source," the "message" or the "recipient" categories and to an empirical investigation of their persuasive effects (for a review see e.g., McGuire, 1968).

Though of considerable historical importance, this pioneering research has run afoul of two major difficulties: (1) its fragmented nature failed to engender a comprehensive theory of the persuasion process; (2) its considerable crop of empirical findings yielded disappointingly inconsistent results. As Petty and Cacioppo (1986, p. 124) remarked: "Existing literature supported the view that nearly every independent variable studied increased persuasion in some situations, had no effect in others, and decreased persuasion in still other contexts."

An important theoretical and empirical breakthrough in understanding persuasion was accomplished by two seminal publications (Chaiken, 1980; Petty & Cacioppo, 1983). These launched two major models that have been guiding a preponderance of persuasion research ever since, specifically: (1) Petty and Cacioppo's (e.g., 1986) elaboration likelihood model (ELM); (2) Chaiken and Eagly's (Chaiken, Liberman, & Eagly, 1989) heuristic systematic model (HSM). Though distinct from each other in several respects (for discussions see Eagly & Chaiken, 1993; Petty, 1994), these models' fundamental view of persuasion shared some significant commonalities. Both approached it from a cognitive perspective (cf. Greenwald, 1968; Petty, Ostrom, & Brock, 1981) and located persuasive "action" within the recipient's ongoing mental processes. Relatedly, both assigned important role to recipients' processing motivation and cognitive capacity. Finally, and of special present relevance, both drew a distinction between *two* qualitatively different informational inputs impinging upon the recipient. One of these consisted of information contained in the *message arguments* or otherwise related to the issue or the topic under consideration. The second consisted of information *unrelated* to the topic or the issue yet capable of inducing persuasion under some circumstances.

In the HSM, such information was labeled as "heuristic cues," assumed to call to mind simple decision rules or "heuristics" to which a recipient may subscribe (Eagly & Chaiken, 1993, p. 327). In the ELM, it was referred to as "peripheral cues" that, while not formally defined, referred to a host of issue-extraneous factors such as source expertise, consensus information, number of arguments provided, speed of the communicator's speech, the recipients mood, etc. (for discussion see Petty & Cacioppo, 1986, p. 130).

In both the ELM and HSM, the processing of *cues* (whether "peripheral" or "heuristic") has been pervasively juxtaposed to the processing of *message* arguments or other issue-related information. Furthermore, as the various *source* factors (like expertise, consensus, likability, or speed of delivery) were typically classed as "cues," their apposition to message arguments echoes to some extent the "source" *versus* "message" partition of early persuasion work (cf. Hovland, Janis, & Kelley, 1953; Lasswell, 1948). Admittedly, however, both the "peripheral" and "heuristic" categories are much broader in conception than the category of source characteristics, and they include a host of additional issue-extraneous factors noted earlier.

A major common feature of the ELM and HSM is their integration of the motivation/capacity factors with the informational distinction between message arguments and (peripheral/heuristic) cues. It was that integration, specifically, which defined the two qualitatively distinct *modes of persuasion*, of pivotal importance to the ELM and HSM formulations: According to their analyses, when motivation and capacity are plentiful persuasion is accomplished via the "central" (in the ELM) or the "systematic" mode (in the HSM), consisting of the extensive elaboration and processing of *message or issue information*. By contrast, when motivation or capacity are scarce, persuasion is accomplished via the "peripheral" (ELM) or the "heuristic" (HSM) mode consisting of a relatively brief and shallow processing of various ("peripheral" or "heuristic") *cues*.

Numerous experimental studies yielded data consistent with the fundamental notion of the dual mode frameworks that the processing of cue information is carried out in a qualitatively different mode than the processing of message information (for reviews see Eagly & Chaiken, 1993; Petty & Cacioppo, 1986). This abundance of seemingly confirmatory findings notwithstanding, we presently describe an alternative theory of persuasion that dispenses with the concept of qualitatively distinct modes. Our theory, referred to as the *unimodel*, accounts for prior findings of persuasion research and affords novel predictions that set it apart from the dual mode paradigm.

## Persuasion according to the unimodel

Our point of departure is that persuasion represents a special case of judgment formation. To understand persuasion it is, therefore, useful to first conceptualize the process whereby judgments are arrived at. According to the lay epistemic theory (Kruglanski, 1989, 1990), to form a judgment an individual first comes up with some kind of information to serve as *evidence* for his or her conclusion. Nearly anything can serve as evidence under the appropriate circumstances: *What* was said (read or observed), the way (facial expression, posture) in which it was said, who was it said by, whether *others* agreed with it, *how* it made one *feel*, the *phenomenal experience* (Schwarz & Clore, 1996) it fostered, etc.

In order that a given bit of information serve as evidence, it should form part of a subjective syllogism. It should serve as a *minor premise* that combines with a previously held *major premise*, or an inference rule, to jointly afford a conclusion. In the process of making a judgment, a minor premise is given contextually whereas a major premise is retrieved from memory. Thus, for instance, one might encounter the information "Cucumbers are low in fat" (minor premise). This might serve as evidence for a conclusion "Cucumbers are healthy" if it instantiated an antecedent of a major premise in which the individual happened to believe, e.g., "All low fat foods are healthy" or "If low fat, then healthy." In general then, information would form a basis for judgment only wherever background knowledge allowed one to draw conclusions from it. Such background knowledge may come in a variety of representations and concern a wide variety of contents. It may contain attitudinally relevant knowledge about consumer products such as "low fat foods are healthy," stereotypic beliefs such as "MIT grads are intelligent," self-relevant meta-cognitive notions such as "If I feel good, I must be a generally happy person" (e.g., Schwarz & Clore, 1983), and so forth.

In describing the judgmental process as syllogistic we do not mean to imply that individuals necessarily engage in *explicit* syllogistic reasoning (e.g., Newell & Simon, 1972; Wason & Johnson-Laird, 1972). Nor do we mean to imply that knowledge is always represented as an abstract rule of the "All X are Y" or "If X then Y" variety, that it is consciously accessed in that form from working memory, or that individuals who use it (everyone, by present surmise) are familiar with the intricacies of formal logic, a proposition belied by over 30 years of research on the Wason (1966) card problem, among others. For instance, people might incorrectly treat an implicational "if a, then b" relation as an equivalence relation (*only if* a, then b) implying also that "if b, then a". We also accept that often people may be able to better recognize the "correct" implicational properties of concrete statements in familiar domains rather than of abstract, unfamiliar statements (Evans, 1989). None of this contradicts the notion that persons generally reason from subjectively relevant rules of the "if–then" format (see also Mischel & Shoda,

1995) that may or may not coincide with what some third party (e.g., the experimenter) had intended, or pronounced as correct.

### Fundamental parameters of judgment formation

According to the unimodel, the basic judgmental process of drawing conclusions from evidence is influenced by several major parameters described below.

#### Subjective relevance

The first parameter, stemming directly from the above notion of syllogistic reasoning, is that of subjective *relevance*, by which is meant the degree to which the individual believes in a linkage between the antecedent and the consequent terms in the major premise. For example, one may believe strongly or only weakly in the proposition "All low fat foods are healthy," with all the different shades of belief or disbelief in between. A strong belief renders the antecedent category and the information that instantiates it (in our prior example, the knowledge that "cucumbers are low in fat") highly relevant to the conclusion. In contrast, complete disbelief renders the information (instantiating the antecedent term) irrelevant as evidence. Consider the statement "All persons weighing above 150 lbs. are medical doctors." We all disbelieve this particular statement (we sincerely hope), and hence consider the information that a target weighs 162 lbs completely irrelevant to the judgment of whether she is a doctor. Degrees of belief in a linkage between the antecedent and the consequent terms in a given inference rule (a major premise) constitute a continuum defining the parameter of perceived relevance a given bit of information possesses regarding a given conclusion. We assume, quite unsurprisingly, that the greater the perceived relevance of the evidence to the conclusion, the greater its impact on judgments.

The subjective relevance parameter is of pivotal importance to the judgment process. It is the "jewel in the parametric crown" in reference to which the remaining judgmental parameters (described shortly) are auxiliary. As we shall see, the latter parameters refer to various *enabling conditions* affording the full realization of the relevance potential of the "information given" to, or actively wrested by, the individual. We turn to these enabling parameters next.

#### Processing difficulty

An important parameter in this category is experienced difficulty of the judgmental task. Its value may depend upon such factors as the *length and complexity* of the information confronted by the individual, the information's ordinal position in the informational sequence, its salience, and accessibility from memory of the pertinent inference rules, and our evolutionarily evolved capacity to deal with various information types (such as frequencies versus ratios, c.f., Cosmides & Tooby, 1996; Gigerenzer & Hoffrage, 1995; but see Evans, Handley, Perham, Over, & Thompson, 2000).

Within the *unimodel*, perceived difficulty is treated as a parameter ranging from great ease (e.g., when the information appears early, is simple, brief, salient, and fitting a highly accessible inference rule), to considerable hardship (e.g., when the information is late appearing, lengthy, complex, non-salient and/or fitting only a relatively inaccessible rule). Generally, the ease of information processing enables a quick and relatively effortless realization of its degree of judgmental relevance, whereas the difficulty of processing hinders such a realization.

*Magnitude of processing motivation*

The magnitude of motivation to engage in extensive information processing en route to a judgment is determined variously by the individual's information processing goals such as the goals of accuracy (Chaiken et al., 1989; Petty & Cacioppo, 1986), accountability (Tetlock, 1985), need for cognition (Cacioppo & Petty, 1982), need to evaluate (Jarvis & Petty, 1996), or need for cognitive closure (Kruglanski & Webster, 1996; Webster & Kruglanski, 1998). For instance, the higher the magnitude of the accuracy motivation or the need for cognition, the greater the degree of the processing motivation. By contrast, the higher the magnitude of the need for closure, the lesser the degree of such motivation.

Magnitude of processing motivation may be additionally determined by the desirability of initially formed beliefs. If such beliefs were desirable, the individual would be disinclined to engage in further information processing, lest the current conclusions be undermined by further data. On the other hand, if one's current beliefs were undesirable, the individual would be inclined to process further information that hopefully would serve to alter the initial, undesirable notions (Ditto & Lopez, 1992).

We assume, then, that the higher the degree of processing motivation, the greater the individual's readiness to invest efforts in information processing, and hence the greater her or his readiness to cope with difficult to process information. Thus, if some particularly relevant information was presented in a format that rendered it difficult to decipher, a considerable amount of processing motivation would be needed to *enable* the realization of its relevance.

*Cognitive capacity*

Another factor assumed to affect individuals' processing efforts is their momentary cognitive capacity determined by such factors as cognitive busyness (i.e., the alternative tasks they are attempting to execute in parallel), as well as by their degree of alertness and sense of energy versus feelings of exhaustion or mental fatigue (i.e., the result of prior information processing;

e.g., Bodenhausen, 1990; Webster, Richter, & Kruglanski, 1998). We assume that a recipient whose cognitive capacity is depleted would be less successful in decoding complex or lengthy information, and hence would be less impacted by such information as compared to an individual with a full cognitive capacity at his or her disposal. Capacity drainage will also favor the use of highly accessible as well as simple decision rules (and related evidence) over less accessible and/or more complex rules that are more difficult to retrieve from background knowledge (e.g., Chaiken et al., 1989). In short, the less one's cognitive capacity at a given moment, the less is her or his ability to process information, particularly if so doing appeared difficult, complicated and laborious.

*Motivational bias*

Occasionally, individuals do not particularly care about the judgmental outcome, i.e., the conclusion they may reach, or about the judgmental process whereby it was reached. Where they do care, we speak of *motivational bias* (see also Dunning, 1999; Kruglanski, 1989, 1990, 1999; Kunda, 1990; Kunda & Sinclair, 1999). In principle, all possible goals may induce such bias under the appropriate circumstances, rendering conclusions (judgments) congruent with the goal desirable and ones incongruent with the goal undesirable. Thus, the *ego-defensive, ego-enhancing,* and *impression management* goals discussed by Chaiken et al. (1989) may induce motivational biases, but many other goals (e.g., promotion and prevention goals; competency, autonomy, and relatedness goals; Higgins, 1997; Ryan, Sheldon, Kasser, & Deci, 1996) would also render the use of specific information (e.g., conversationally appropriate inference rules; Grice, 1975) or specific conclusions particularly desirable to the individual. Motivational biases may enhance the realization (or use) of subjectively relevant information yielding such conclusions, and hinder the realization of subjectively relevant information yielding the opposite conclusions (cf. Dunning, 1999; Kunda, 1999). Again, we view the degree of motivational bias as lying on a continuum ranging from an absence of bias to a considerable bias with regard to a given judgmental topic.

*Processing sequence*

Our final parameter concerns the sequence in which the individual considers the information. Specifically, conclusions derived from prior processing can serve as evidential input in which terms subsequent inferences are made. Thus, for example, several prior conclusions can combine to form a subsequent aggregate judgment (Anderson, 1971; Fishbein & Ajzen, 1975). In addition, prior conclusions can affect the construction of specific inference rules whereby subsequent ambiguous information is interpreted. Given that a source has been classified as "intelligent," for example, her or his subsequent, ambiguous pronouncements may be interpreted as "clever." Given that an actor has been classified as a "middle-class housewife," the epithet "hostile" may be interpreted as referring to "verbal aggressiveness." In contrast, if she has been classified as a "ghetto resident," "hostile" may be interpreted to mean "physical aggression" (cf. Duncan, 1976).

*Orthogonality of the parameters*

The foregoing judgmental parameters are assumed to be quasi-orthogonal to each other, hence, to form a multidimensional space containing a vast number of points, each representing a parametric intersection at different values. By contrast, the dual-process models typically isolate two such intersections (e.g., high processing difficulty, and high motivation and capacity versus low processing difficulty and low motivation or capacity), conjoin them to two separate types of content (e.g., message-related versus message-unrelated contents) and treat them as qualitatively distinct *modes* of judgment.

The orthogonality of the parameters derives from their generally independent determinants. Thus, subjective relevance of information may derive from a prior forging of conditional "if–then" links between informational categories, the magnitude of processing motivation may derive from the goal of accuracy, and the difficulty of processing may depend on accessibility of inference rules or the saliency of pertinent information, all representing clearly separate concerns. Nonetheless, the parameters may share some determinants and occasionally may affect one another and, in that sense, are only roughly (or quasi-) rather than "pristinely" orthogonal. For example, highly relevant information may be used more frequently than less relevant information, resulting in its greater accessibility, which in turn should lower the value of the processing difficulty parameter. Conversely, high accessibility of information may increase its perceived relevance in some contexts (e.g., Jacoby, Kelley, Brown, & Jasechko, 1989; Schwarz & Clore, 1996).

A similar case can be made for the influence of motivation on subjective relevance in that a given bit of information may be perceived as more relevant, the more desirable the conclusion it points to (e.g., Lord, Ross, & Lepper, 1979), or the more congruent its implications are with the individual's motivation. For instance, in order to justify their "freezing" on early information, persons under high need for closure may perceive it as more relevant to the judgment at hand than persons under low need for closure (Webster & Kruglanski, 1998). By contrast, individuals with a high need for cognition (Cacioppo & Petty, 1982) may perceive the early information as less relevant, hence they may carry on with their information-processing activity. Finally, limited cognitive capacity may reduce processing motivation or induce a need for cognitive closure (cf. Kruglanski & Webster, 1996), etc. Despite these interrelations, however, the judgmental parameters are relatively independent ("quasi-orthogonal") because many of their determinants are in fact unique or non-overlapping.

## The parametric unimodel as a theory of persuasion

If, as we presently assume, persuasion is a special case of judgment formation, the various judgmental parameters and their interactions afford a basis upon which a general theory of persuasion may be constructed. In what follows, we examine in the light of pertinent empirical evidence several hypotheses derived from that theory.

*Hypothesis 1: Relatively difficult to process information will exert*
*greater persuasive impact under high (vs. low) processing motivation*
*whereas relatively easy to process information will exert greater*
*persuasive impact under low (vs. high) processing motivation*

In our research we demonstrated the interactive effects of the processing difficulty and motivation parameters (Kruglanski & Thompson, 1999, Study 4) by presenting participants with a message containing arguments supporting the implementation of new comprehensive exams. The length and ordinal position of the message-argument information was manipulated. Participants read two initial, one-sentence arguments ostensibly submitted by an educator in response to a newsletter ad. These were followed by six arguments (of several sentences each) comprising a (fictitious) formal letter to the "National Board of Education" expressing the educator's support for the mandatory exam policy. Argument quality (weak vs. strong) was manipulated independently both for the initial brief arguments and for the subsequent lengthy arguments. Orthogonally, we manipulated issue involvement. Half the participants, assigned to the high involvement condition, were led to believe that the comprehensive exams would be introduced the next year so that they themselves would be impacted. The remaining half believed that the exams would be introduced ten years hence, so they would not be personally affected by the new policy. We predicted that under low involvement the strong (vs. the weak) initial brief, and hence easy to process, arguments would elicit a greater agreement with the message. However the strong (vs. the weak) subsequent lengthy, and hence difficult to process, arguments would not significantly differ in their persuasive impact. Under high involvement, however, we predicted that the strong (vs. weak) subsequent lengthy arguments would be more persuasive, but not the strong (vs. weak) initial brief arguments. The results supported these predictions (see Figure 17.1). It is noteworthy that the brief initial arguments *mimic* here the typical effects of *cue* information under low elaboration-likelihood conditions (cf. Petty, Cacioppo, & Goldman, 1981), whereas the subsequent lengthy arguments *replicate* here the typical message arguments' effects obtained in prior persuasion research (cf. Petty et al., 1981). These results are compatible with the unimodel's implication that what matters is the processing difficulty parameter rather than the type of information processed (e.g., whether classified as a "cue" or as a message argument).

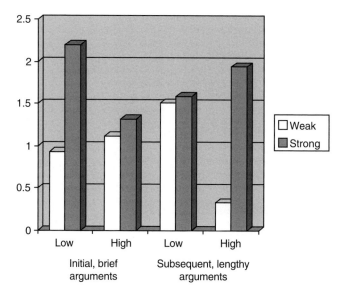

*Figure 17.1* Attitudes toward exams as a function of issue involvement and strength of initial, brief arguments, and as of subsequent, lengthy arguments.

*Hypothesis 2: Relatively difficult to process information will exert greater persuasive impact under high (vs. low) cognitive capacity whereas relatively easy to process information will exert greater persuasive impact under conditions of low (vs. high) cognitive capacity*

Whereas previous research (Petty, Wells, & Brock, 1976) demonstrated a decreased elaboration of *message arguments* under limited cognitive capacity, we sought to explore whether cognitive load should also impair the elaboration of equally lengthy and complex *expertise information*. To examine this possibility, Kruglanski and Thompson (1999, Study 2) presented a long description of expertise information (conveying via a one-page curriculum vitae that the communicator was expert or inexpert) followed by an equally lengthy set of message arguments, the same to all participants. Orthogonally, we manipulated cognitive load. Participants under load were shown a nine-digit number prior to reading the expertise information, and were asked to silently rehearse it so as to be able to reproduce it from memory later on. The remaining half of the participants, under the no-load condition, were given no such task. As shown in Figure 17.2, participants in the no-load condition were persuaded more by the expert than the inexpert source, whereas those under load were not persuaded differentially as a function of communicator expertise. It would seem then that to be adequately processed, relatively lengthy and complex heuristic information (about the source) requires sufficient cognitive capacity. When such capacity is depleted, participants are less able to realize the implications of information about the source.

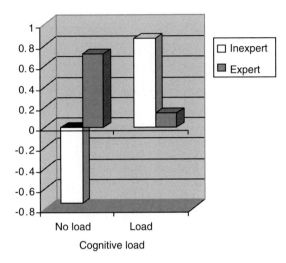

*Figure 17.2* Attitudes toward exams as function of source expertise and cognitive load.

As predicted by the unimodel, the heuristic information appears to behave identically to message argument information of comparable length-complexity that also is processed less effectively when recipients' mental capacity is taxed (Petty et al., 1976).

In a follow-up experiment, Kruglanski and Thompson (1999, Study 3) varied the length of the expertise information in addition to the degree of expertise and cognitive load. The expertise × load interaction obtained in the previous study was replicated when the source information was relatively lengthy. Specifically, the lengthy source information had the appropriate effect (high vs. low expertise leading to greater persuasion) in the absence as compared to the presence of cognitive load. The opposite pattern manifested itself when the source information was brief, and hence less difficult to process. Here expertise information had the greater effect under load versus no load (see Figure 17.3). Thus it appears that whereas lengthy (cue or message) information is interfered with by load, brief and simple information may actually benefit from load, or other "low elaboration likelihood" conditions because these prevent more complex and lengthy information from being properly processed, allowing the brief information to dominate persuasion.

*Hypothesis 3: The persuasive impact of message information will be enhanced by the activation of the appropriate inference rules that facilitate the processing of such information by lending it subjective relevance*

Thus far in the persuasion literature, the notion of rule activation was reserved for the processing of heuristic information assumed to proceed in a

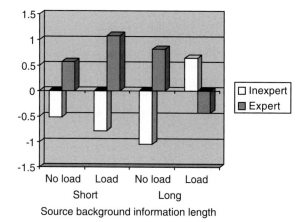

*Figure 17.3* Attitudes toward exams as function of source background information length, cognitive load, and source expertise.

"top-down" fashion (Chen, Duckworth, & Chaiken, 1999; Eagly & Chaiken, 1993) and was implied to be irrelevant to the processing of message information assumed to proceed in a "bottom-up" fashion (Norman & Bobrow, 1975). For instance, in a study by Chaiken, Axsom, Liberman, and Wilson (1992, cited in Eagly & Chaiken, 1993; Chen, Duckworth, & Chaiken, 1999) chronic users of a "length implies strength" heuristic (i.e., individuals for whom this rule enjoyed a high degree of chronic activation) were identified and additionally temporal accessibility of this heuristic was manipulated via a priming procedure in an ostensibly unrelated task prior to message exposure. Both chronic and momentary accessibility affected participants' use of the "length–strength" rule as demonstrated by higher (lower) agreement with the message when the message (that actually contained six arguments) was said to contain ten versus two arguments.

According to the unimodel, rule activation should play the same role in the processing of message contents as it does in the processing of heuristic cues external to the message. In the case of heuristics, the heuristic cue that the message is long represents a minor premise for which the rule "length equals strength" constitutes the major premise, jointly affording the conclusion that the lengthy message is compelling and should command agreement. The same process was expected to take place when dealing with message information. In a study designed to explore this possibility, we presented participants with a message extolling the virtues of a college that among its other attributes was described by the adjective "small" (Erb, Fishbach, & Kruglanski, 2002, Study 1). The relevance of the information was manipulated by either asserting that the size of classes in that college was generally small (of high relevance to evaluating the school as a whole) or that the college had a small program of industrial engineering (of low relevance to the school as a whole).

Orthogonally we activated the rule "less is better" in the context of a prior task, by having participants choose, for example, between cellular phones of different weights, or "more is better" by having participants choose, for example, between diamonds of different sizes. This priming manipulation resulted in a preference for a small school in the "less is better" versus "more is better" condition, only to the extent that the arguments were highly relevant to the judgment (see Figure 17.4). The fact that the mere mention of the word "small" in the low relevance condition did not induce a positive attitude toward the attitude object where the "small is better" rule was activated argues against a purely associationistic interpretation of our findings, whereby a connection established between "small" and "better" led to activation of the latter term upon a presentation of the former, thus affecting the attitude judgment mechanistically. As noted earlier, this did not happen. Instead, the effect occurred only in the high relevance condition where the term small could be taken in reference to the attitude object (i.e., the college) as a whole.

In a subsequent experiment we activated the "small is likable" and the "big is likable" rules in a different manner (Erb et al., Study 2). Participants were asked to answer various questions (e.g., "What is your opinion of George Bush?" "What is the size of a swordfish?") by recording their responses on one of two scales: one ranging between the "like" and "dislike" ends (appropriate for the question about Bush), the other ranging between the "small" and "large" ends (appropriate for the question about the swordfish). In one condition, "small" and "like" anchors were placed at the same end of the scale and "big" and "dislike" on the other; thus creating an association between the terms and presumably activating the "small is likable" and "big is dislikable" rules. In another condition, these terms' concordance was reversed, hence presumably activating the "big is likable" and "small is dislikable" rules. As hypothesized, compared with participants in a no prime condition, participants exposed to the "small–likable" rule reported a greater

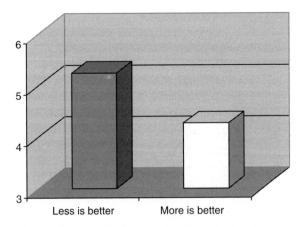

*Figure 17.4* Preference for a small school as function of rule prime.

preference for a small school in a message describing its virtues, whereas those exposed to the "big–likable" rule reported lesser preference for a small school (see Figure 17.5). These findings support the notion that the persuasiveness of message arguments (like the persuasiveness of heuristic cues) is positively affected by the activation of rules that lend relevance to the message contents, reducing the difficulty of coming up with such rules, and thus enhancing persuasion.

*Hypothesis 4: Early information can bias the processing of subsequent information provided the individual has sufficient motivation to process it*

Both the ELM and the HSM hold that central route or systematic processing can occasionally be biased by heuristic or peripheral cues (Bohner, Chaiken, & Hunyadi, 1994; Bohner, Ruder, & Erb, in press; Chaiken & Maheswaran, 1994; Darke, Chaiken, Bohner, Einwiller, Erb, & Hazelwood, 1998; Mackie, 1987; Petty, Schumann, Richman, & Strathman, 1993). Significantly, within the dual-process models, the biasing hypothesis is *asymmetrical*. It is the heuristic or peripheral cues that are presumed to bias subsequent processing of message information but not vice versa. The reason for the asymmetry is obvious. Because in prior persuasion studies "cues" typically appeared before the message arguments, it does not make much sense to ask whether their processing might be biased by the ("central" or "systematic") processing of message arguments. But the unimodel removes the constraint on processing sequence, hence it affords the question of whether *any* information type might be biased by preceding information, providing that one had a sufficient motivation to process the later appearing information. How might such a process unfold?

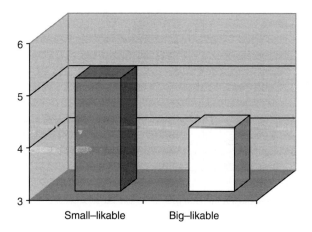

*Figure 17.5* Preference for a small school as function of rule prime.

Simply, the early information could make accessible certain conclusions serving as evidence for further inference rules in whose light the subsequent information might be interpreted (Higgins, Rholes, & Jones, 1977). We conducted two experiments to test this idea (Erb et al., 2002, Studies 4 and 5). In the first, we looked at the biasing effects of early *message arguments* on processing subsequent *message arguments*, and in the second, at biasing effects of early *message arguments* on processing subsequent *source information*.

Thus, in the first study participants were given information consisting entirely of message arguments about building a tunnel underneath the harbor of Rotterdam (the Netherlands). The initial argument was either of high or low quality as determined by a pretest. Specifically, it read: "The tunnel will bring [great] advantages for residents, because the traffic volume in adjacent neighborhoods will be reduced by about 80% [4%]. This means significantly [somewhat] less noise and exhaust fumes to be endured by residents." The subsequent five arguments, were *constant* for all the participants and were all of moderate quality or strength. They pertained to several additional aspects of the construction project, such as the benefits it may bring the local construction industry, the reduction of delays on a highly frequented highway between the cities of Delft and Rotterdam, and the proposed construction of additional green areas as well as leisure sites along with the tunnel. Orthogonally to the quality of initial arguments, we manipulated processing motivation (high vs. low) via accountability instructions. We found that attitude toward the aspects highlighted in the subsequent arguments (those constant for all the participants) was biased by the initial message argument, but this occurred only under high processing motivation. Specifically, in the high motivation condition attitude toward those aspects of the issue mentioned in the subsequent arguments was significantly more positive when the initial argument was of high versus low quality. In the low motivation condition this difference disappeared (see Figure 17.6).

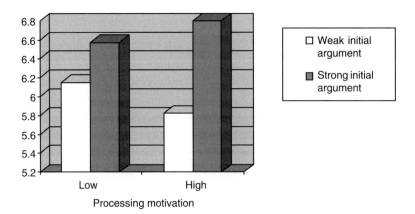

*Figure 17.6* Attitudes toward subsequent message aspects as function of initial argument quality and magnitude of processing motivation.

We also found that the *thoughts listed* in response to the subsequent five (constant) arguments were affected by initial argument quality, but only under high processing motivation. In that condition, thoughts generated in response to those arguments were more positive when the initial argument quality was high versus low (see Figure 17.7).

Path analyses additionally demonstrated that under high (but not under low) processing motivation persuasion was mediated by the biased processing of the subsequent arguments in light of the earlier arguments. In the high motivation condition, the effect of the initial argument on attitude judgments was fully mediated by biased processing of the subsequent arguments. Under low motivation the valence of the initial argument determined the thoughts about this particular argument, which in turn determined attitude judgments. There was no mediation here by thoughts about the subsequent arguments; hence no evidence for biased processing (see Figure 17.8).

Our second study reversed the typical order of presentation by placing in one condition the same initial message argument (of high or low quality) used in the preceding study *before* (rather than after) the source information. In another condition, the message-argument manipulation occurred after presentation of the source information. The latter information, constant for all participants, portrayed the source as of moderate expertise. Specifically, this individual was described as having some experience with planning traffic facilities (but not specifically with tunnels), living with his family in the Rotterdam area where the tunnel's impact would be greatest, running a construction company and being nominated for an award by the "Construction Industry Association of the Netherlands" for his proposal of a "Maas Rhine Channel." This description was pretested to be ambiguous in terms of eliciting thoughts that were neither strongly positive nor strongly negative with respect to the source.

All participants were placed under high processing motivation. The results

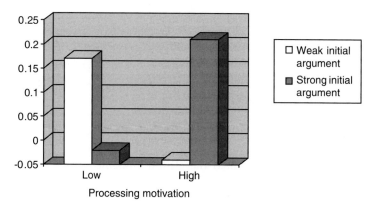

*Figure 17.7* Valence of cognitive responses to subsequent arguments as function of initial argument quality and magnitude of processing motivation.

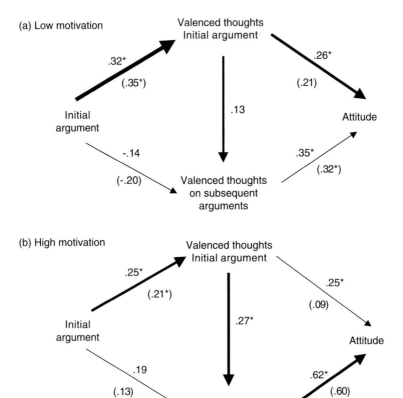

*Figure 17.8* Mediation of initial arguments' effect on attitudes by biased thought about subsequent arguments under high (b) but not low (a) processing motivation.

*Note*: Coefficients appearing above lines are beta weights for uncorrected paths. Coefficients in parentheses appearing below lines are beta weights for corrected paths (thoughts toward initial argument corrected for thought valence toward message arguments and vice versa). Predicted paths in bold lines. *p<.05.

revealed that the perceived expertise of the communicator was appropriately biased by the initial argument's quality but only when the argument preceded, and not when it succeeded the source information. Specifically, where the argument quality was high, the source's expertise was judged to be higher than where the argument quality was low. In turn, biased processing of the source information mediated the attitude judgments (see Figures 17.9 and 17.10).

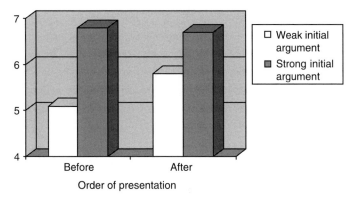

*Figure 17.9* Perceived expertise of the communicator as function of processing sequence and initial argument quality.

*Hypothesis 5: When the motivation to stop information processing early is high, the early appearing information will have more persuasive impact than the late appearing information*

In a typical persuasion study, the heuristic or peripheral information comes before the message information. Thus, a confounding exists between order of presentation (hence the processing sequence parameter) and information type (message-argument or heuristic/peripheral information). It is possible that part of the reason why the peripheral/heuristic source information exerted its effect primarily under low processing motivation is that the processing sequence matters and under low magnitude of processing motivation participants were inclined *to stop* information processing *sooner*, and hence to base their judgments on the early information. Consistent with this analysis, we (Erb et al. 2002, Studies 3 and 4) found that the need for closure, a variable known to affect the "seizing" and "freezing" on early information (Kruglanski & Webster, 1996; Webster & Kruglanski, 1998) enhanced the impact of the source *or* the message information where it appeared early in the informational sequence, prior to the alternative information type (i.e., message and source information respectively). These data are summarized in Figure 17.11.

## Conclusion

To summarize, the experiments we have described support the basic contention of the unimodel that the intersecting values of the judgmental parameters such as difficulty of processing (operationalized, e.g., by length/complexity of the information given, or rule accessibility), perceived relevance to the topic (operationalized by argument quality, and/or expertise information), magnitude of processing motivation (operationalized by issue

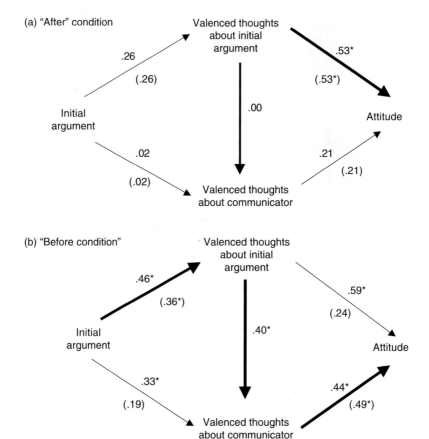

*Figure 17.10* Mediation of initial arguments' effect on attitudes by biased thought about the communicator in the "before" (b) but not in the "after" condition.

*Note*: Coefficients appearing above lines are beta weights for uncorrected paths. Coefficients in parentheses appearing below lines are beta weights for corrected paths (thoughts toward initial argument corrected for thought valence toward message arguments and vice versa). Predicted paths in bold lines. *p<.05.

involvement or need for closure), or processing sequence (i.e., early or late appearing information) determine persuasion. Controlling for parameter values, the contents or types of information, e.g., those inherent to the *message arguments* versus the *source information* external to the message, do not appear to have unique effects.

The research we described represents merely the first phase of the kind of work the present unimodel enables. It opens the way to a systematic exploration of the judgmental parameters and their interrelations as these may impact the formation and change of attitudes and opinions. In addition to the variables we have already investigated, one could investigate the

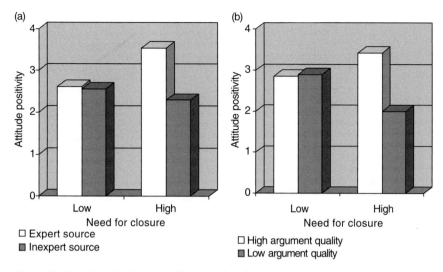

*Figure 17.11* (a) Attitudes toward comprehensive exams as function of early appearing source information and need for closure; (b) Attitudes toward comprehensive exams as function of early-appearing message argument information and need for closure.

persuasive effects of directional motivations, the relation between difficulty, motivation, and the quality of deduction performed by the recipients of persuasive message (represented by the logical consistency between these persons' premises and their conclusions), the effects of conclusion drawing on activation of relevant premises from memory, and other matters.

For example, the unimodel suggests that the effects of directional motivation on judgments would be less if the persuasive information was difficult versus easy to process because difficult-to-process information would consume individuals' resources such that fewer are left to carry out the distortion.

Furthermore, if the information was difficult to process individuals with low processing motivation (of the nondirectional variety) might be less able to carry out the appropriate deductions, and hence manifest lesser degree of coherence, or consistency between their premises and their conclusion than individuals with a high processing motivation. Such motivational differences might be less manifest if the information was an easy one to process.

It would also be important to relate our parameters to further persuasion phenomena, beyond attitude change, such as persistence of the change, resistance to counterpersuasion and the attitude–behavior relation. Specifically, according to the unimodel, resistance to change might relate to confidence with which one's opinions are held. Confidence, in turn, may depend on a degree to which the information was thoroughly examined and based on (subjectively) solid evidence as well as being determined by a variety of motivational factors of directional and nondirectional variety. For example, a strong directional motivation may effect a "freezing" (Kruglanski & Webster, 1996) and hence persistence and resistance to counterpersuasion to the extent that the opinions held were desirable, while at the same time promoting ready "unfreezing" (hence reducing persistence and resistance to counterpersuasion) with regard to undesirable opinions. Amassing considerable evidence for an opinion, as well as a nondirectional need for closure, should also affect persistence and resistance to counterpersuasion. According to the unimodel, all such effects should be independent of informational contents; thus, for instance, independent of whether the information in question constituted "peripheral" or "heuristic" cues or "message arguments."

On the practical level, the unimodel offers a flexible view of persuasion that removes the constraints of informational contents (inherent in the dual mode persuasion models) and extends the possibility of a thorough persuasion (whose effects may endure, and be resistant to counterpersuasion) independent of the recipients' familiarity with a given content domain of argumentation, e.g., through strongly believed premises related to the argumentation's *source*. Specifically, even if a recipient were unfamiliar with the intricacies of a medical, legal, or theological argument, he/she might be thoroughly and profoundly persuaded by such argument if he/she had amassed substantial evidence about the credibility of the source, or had a strong motivation to accept the source's conclusion.

Finally, on a theoretical level, the unimodel integrates contemporary persuasion work (Chaiken et al., 1989; Petty & Cacioppo, 1986) that stresses the role of cognitive and motivational resources with the work conducted in the 1970s on the logical structure of reasoning (McGuire, 1960; Wyer, 1970), and more generally on the function of evidence in opinion change. Perhaps of equal importance, it integrates current persuasion work with alternative social judgment phenomena in domains of impression formation (Brewer, 1988; Fiske & Neuberg, 1990), causal reasoning (cf. Trope & Alfieri, 1997; Chun, Spiegel, & Kruglanski, 2002), or indeed statistical reasoning that, according to the unimodel, are affected identically by the very same judgmental parameters that determine persuasion (for discussion see Erb, Kruglanski, Chun, Pierro, Mannetti & Spiegel, 2003).

## References

Anderson, N. H. (1971). Integration theory and attitude change. *Psychological Review, 78*, 171–206.
Bodenhausen, G. V. (1990). Stereotypes as judgmental heuristics: Evidence of circadian variations in discrimination. *Psychological Science, 1*, 319–322.
Bohner, G., Chaiken, S., & Hunyadi, P. (1994). The role of mood and message

ambiguity in the interplay of heuristic and systematic processing. *European Journal of Social Psychology*, *24*, 207–221.

Bohner, G., Ruder, M., & Erb, H.-P. (in press). When expertise backfires: Contrast and assimilation in persuasion. *British Journal of Social Psychology*.

Brewer, M. B. (1988). A dual process model of impression formation. In T. K. Srull & R. S. Wyer Jr. (Eds.), *Advances in social cognition* (Vol. 1, pp. 1–36), Hillsdale, NJ: Lawrence Erlbaum Associates, Inc.

Cacioppo, J. T., & Petty, R. E. (1982). The need for cognition. *Journal of Personality and Social Psychology*, *42*, 116–131.

Chaiken, S. (1980). Heuristic versus systematic information and the use of source versus message cues in persuasion. *Journal of Personality and Social Psychology*, *39*, 752–756.

Chaiken, S., Liberman, A., & Eagly, A. H. (1989). Heuristic and systematic processing within and beyond the persuasion context. In J. S. Uleman & J. A. Bargh (Eds.), *Unintended thought* (pp. 212–252). New York: Guilford Press.

Chaiken, S., & Maheswaran, D. (1994). Heuristic processing can bias systematic processing: Effects of source credibility, argument ambiguity, and task importance on attitude judgments. *Journal of Personality and Social Psychology*, *66*, 460–473.

Chen, S., Duckworth, K., & Chaiken, S. (1999). Motivated heuristic and systematic processing. *Psychological Inquiry*, *10*, 44–49.

Chun, W. Y., Spiegel, S., & Kruglanski, A. W. (2002). Assimilative behavior identification can also be resource-dependent: A unimodal perspective on personal-attribution phases. *Journal of Personality and Social Psychology*, *83*, 542–555.

Cosmides, L., & Tooby, J. (1996). Are humans good intuitive statisticians after all? Rethinking some conclusions from the literature on judgment under uncertainty. *Cognition*, *58*, 1–73.

Darke, P. R., Chaiken, S., Bohner, G., Einwiller, S., Erb, H.-P., & Hazelwood, D. (1998). Accuracy motivation, consensus information, and the law of large numbers: Effects on attitude judgments in the absence of argumentation. *Personality and Social Psychology Bulletin*, *24*, 1205–1215.

Ditto, P. H., & Lopez, D. F. (1992). Motivated skepticism: Use of differential decision criteria for preferred and nonpreferred conclusions. *Journal of Personality and Social Psychology*, *63*, 568–584.

Duncan, B. L. (1976). Differential social perception and attribution of intergroup violence: Testing the lower limits of stereotyping of blacks. *Journal of Personality and Social Psychology*, *34*, 590–598.

Dunning, D. (1999). A newer look: Motivated social cognition and the schematic representation of social concepts. *Psychological Inquiry*, *10*, 1–11.

Eagly, A. H., & Chaiken, S. (1993). *The psychology of attitudes*. Fort Worth, TX: Harcourt Brace Jovanovich.

Erb, H. P., Fishbach, A., & Kruglanski, A. W. (2002). *The effects of rule priming on social judgment*. Unpublished draft.

Erb, H.-P., Kruglanski, A. W., Chun, W. Y., Pierro, A., Mannetti, L., & Spiegel, S. (2003). Searching for commonalities in human judgment: The parametric unimodel and its dual mode alternatives. *European Review of Social Psychology*, *14*, 1–48.

Evans, J. St. B. T. (1989). *Bias in human reasoning: Causes and consequences*. Hove, UK: Lawrence Erlbaum Associates, Inc.

Evans, J. St. B. T., Handley, S. J., Perham, N., Over, D. E., & Thompson, V. A. (2000).

Frequency versus probability formats in statistical word problems. *Cognition, 77*, 197–213.

Fishbein, M., & Ajzen, I. (1975). *Belief, attitude, intention, and behavior: An introduction to theory and research*. Reading, MA: Addison-Wesley.

Fiske, S. T., & Neuberg, S. L. (1990). A continuum model of impression formation, from category-based to individuating processes: Influences of information and motivation on attention and interpretation. In M. P. Zanna (Ed.), *Advances in experimental social psychology* (Vol. 23, pp. 1–74). New York: Academic Press.

Gigerenzer, G., & Hoffrage, U. (1995). How to improve Bayesian reasoning without instruction: Frequency formats. *Psychological Review, 102*, 684–704.

Greenwald, A. G. (1968). Cognitive learning, cognitive response to persuasion, and attitude change. In A. G. Greenwald, T. C. Brock, & T. M. Ostrom (Eds.), *Psychological foundations of attitudes* (pp. 147–170). San Diego, CA: Academic Press.

Grice, H. P. (1975). Logic and conversation. In P. Cole & J. L. Morgan (Eds.), *Syntax and semantics 3: Speech acts* (pp. 41–58). San Diego, CA: Academic Press.

Higgins, E. T. (1997). Beyond pleasure and pain. *American Psychologist, 52*, 1280–1300.

Higgins, E. T., Rholes, W. S., & Jones, C. R. (1977). Category accessibility and impression formation. *Journal of Experimental Social Psychology, 13*, 141–154.

Hovland, C. I., Janis, I. L., & Kelley, H. H. (1953). *Communication and persuasion: Psychological studies of opinion change*. New Haven: Yale University Press.

Jacoby, L. L., Kelley, C. M., Brown, J., & Jasechko, J. (1989). Becoming famous overnight: Limits on the ability to avoid unconscious influences of the past. *Journal of Personality and Social Psychology, 56*, 326–338.

Jarvis, W. B. G., & Petty, E. E. (1996). The need to evaluate. *Journal of Personality and Social Psychology, 70*, 172–194.

Kruglanski, A. W. (1989). *Lay epistemics and human knowledge: Cognitive and motivational bases*. New York: Plenum Press.

Kruglanski, A. W. (1990). Lay epistemic theory in social cognitive psychology. (Target article for peer commentary). *Psychological Inquiry, 1*, 181–197.

Kruglanski, A. W. (1999). Motivation, cognition, and reality: Three memos for the next generation of research. *Psychological Inquiry, 10*, 54–58.

Kruglanski, A. W., & Thompson, E. P. (1999). Persuasion by a single route: A view from the unimodel. (Target article for peer commentary). *Psychological Inquiry, 10*, 83–109.

Kruglanski, A. W., & Webster, D. M. (1996). Motivated closing of the mind: "Seizing" and "freezing". *Psychological Review, 103*, 263–283.

Kunda, Z. (1990). The case of motivated reasoning. *Psychological Bulletin, 108*, 480–498.

Kunda, Z. (1999). *Social cognition: Making sense of people*. Cambridge: MIT Press.

Kunda, Z., & Sinclair, L. (1999). Motivated reasoning with stereotypes: Activation, application, and inhibition. *Psychological Inquiry, 10*, 12–22.

Lasswell, H. D. (1948). The structure and function of comunication in society. In L. Bryson (Ed.), *The communication of ideas: Religion and civilization series* (pp. 37–51). New York: Harper & Row.

Lord, C. G., Ross, L., & Lepper, M. R. (1979). Biased assimilation and attitude polarization: The effects of prior theories on subsequently considered evidence. *Journal of Personality and Social Psychology, 37*, 2098–2109.

Mackie, D. M. (1987). Systematic and nonsystematic processing of majority and minority persuasive communications. *Journal of Personality and Social Psychology*, *53*, 41–52.

McGuire, W. J. (1960). A syllogistic analysis of cognitive relationships. In C. I. Hovland, & M. J. Rosenberg (Eds.), *Attitude organization and change: An analysis of consistency among attitude components* (pp. 65–111). New Haven, CT: Yale University Press.

McGuire, W. J. (1968). Personality and attitude change: An information processing theory. In A. G. Greenwald, T. C. Brock, & T. M. Ostrom (Eds.), *Psychological foundations of attitudes* (pp. 171–196). San Diego, CA: Academic Press.

Mischel, W., & Shoda, Y. (1995). A cognitive-affective system theory of personality: Reconceptualizing situations, dispositions, dynamics and invariance in personality structure. *Psychological Review*, *102*, 246–268.

Newell, A., & Simon, H. A. (1972). *Human problem solving.* Englewood Cliffs, NJ: Prentice-Hall.

Norman, D. A., & Bobrow, D. G. (1975). On data-limited and resource-limited processes. *Cognitive Psychology*, *7*, 44–64.

Petty, R. E. (1994). Two routes to persuasion: State of the art. In G. d'Ydewalle, P. Eelen, & P. Berteleson (Eds.), *International perspectives on psychological science* (Vol. 2, pp. 229–247). Hillsdale, NJ: Lawrence Erlbaum Associates, Inc.

Petty, R. E., & Cacioppo, J. T. (1983). Central and peripheral routes to persuasion: Applications to advertising. In L. Percy & A. Woodside (Eds.), *Advertising and consumer psychology* (pp. 3–23). Lexington, MA: Heath.

Petty, R. E., & Cacioppo, J. T. (1986). The elaboration likelihood model of persuasion. In L. Berkowitz (Ed.), *Advances of experimental social psychology* (Vol. 19, pp. 123–205). San Diego, CA: Academic Press.

Petty, R. E., Cacioppo, J. T., & Goldman, R., (1981). Personal involvement as a determinant of argument-based persuasion. *Journal of Personality & Social Psychology*, *41*, 847–855.

Petty, R. E., Ostrom, T. M., & Brock, T. C. (Eds.) (1981). *Cognitive responses in persuasion.* Hillsdale, NJ: Lawrence Erlbaum Associates, Inc.

Petty, R. E., Schumann, D. W., Richman, S. A., & Strathman, A. J. (1993). Positive mood and persuasion: Different roles for affect under high- and low-elaboration conditions. *Journal of Personality and Social Psychology*, *64*, 5–20.

Petty, R. E., Wells, G. L., & Brock, T. C. (1976). Distraction can enhance or reduce yielding to propaganda: Thought disruption versus effort justification. *Journal of Personality and Social Psychology*, *34*, 874–884.

Ryan, R. M., Sheldon, K. M., Kasser, T., & Deci, E. L. (1996). All goals are not created equal: An organismic perspective on the nature of goals and their regulation. In P. M. Gollwitzer & J. A. Bargh (Eds.), *The psychology of action.* New York: Guilford Press.

Schwarz, N., & Clore, G. I. (1983). Mood, misattribution, and judgments of well-being: Informative and directive functions of affective states. *Journal of Personality and Social Psychology*, *45*, 513–523.

Schwarz, N., & Clore, G. L. (1996). Feelings and phenomenal experiences. In E. T. Higgins & A. W. Kruglanski (Eds.), *Social psychology: A handbook of basic principles* (pp. 433–465). New York: Guilford Press.

Tetlock, P. E. (1985). Accountability: A social check on the fundamental attribution error. *Social Psychology Quarterly*, *48*, 227–236.

Trope, Y., & Alfieri, T. (1997). Effortfulness and flexibility of dispositional judgment processes. *Journal of Personality and Social Psychology, 73,* 662–674.

Wason, P. C. (1966). *Reasoning.* In B. M. Foss (Ed.), *New horizons in psychology* (pp. 113–135). Harmondsworth, UK: Penguin.

Wason, P. C., & Johnson-Laird, P. N., (1972) *Psychology of reasoning: Structure and content.* Cambridge, MA: Harvard University Press.

Webster, D. M., & Kruglanski, A. W. (1998). Cognitive and social consequences of the need for cognitive closure. In W. Stroebe & M. Hewstone (Eds.), *European review of social psychology* (Vol. 8, pp. 133–141). Chichester, UK: Wiley.

Webster, D. M., Richter, L., & Kruglanski, A. W. (1998). On leaping to conclusions when feeling tired: Mental fatigue effects on impression formation. *Journal of Experimental Social Psychology, 32,* 181–195.

Wyer, R. S., Jr. (1970). Quantitative prediction of belief and opinion change: A further test of a subjective probability model. *Journal Personality and Social Psychology, 16,* 559–570.

# Part III
# Some final thoughts

# 18 Theories of attitude

## Creating a witches' brew

*Gregory R. Maio and*
*Geoffrey Haddock*

Jeff Keller (1999) penned the self-help book entitled *Attitude is Everything*. We agree. Countless individuals and groups state that attitudes are important, and in many walks of life (e.g., motivational experts, organizations, salespeople; Russell-McCloud, 1999; Ryan, 1999; Wal-Mart Canada, 1997). In social psychological research, Gordon Allport (1935) was among the first to speculate that attitude is a fundamental variable. This assertion spawned decades of attempts to capture properties of the attitude concept, using theory and empirical studies. Nonetheless, it is equivocal whether all these attempts to study attitudes actually examined precisely the same concept. In this chapter, we describe the ways in which the past research has used diverse conceptualizations of attitudes, and we describe an agenda for integrating and extending these theories.

### Lay versus social psychological conceptualizations of attitude

Before delving into theoretical conceptualizations of attitude, it is useful to consider the lay usage of this concept. Keller's (1999) book treats attitude as a broad approach to life and work, which is the focus of many other motivational experts in the self-help literature (e.g., Russell-McCloud, 1999; Ryan, 1999). In contrast, artists use the term to capture posture, styles of expression, and forms of artistic statement in everything from acting to dance. Standard dictionary definitions embrace the diversity of lay views. According to the *Pocket Oxford Dictionary* (Thompson, 1996) an attitude is: "1 an opinion or way of thinking; behavior reflecting this (don't like his attitude). 2 bodily posture; pose. 3 position of an aircraft etc. relative to given points."

Social psychological definitions of attitude correspond with some aspects of the lay descriptions. The most common feature of the social psychological definitions is that attitudes are tendencies to like or dislike specific attitude objects (Bem, 1970; Eagly & Chaiken, 1993; Fazio, 1990; Olson & Zanna, 1993; Petty, Wegener, & Fabrigar, 1997). The attitude objects can be anything that has the potential to be evaluated favorably or unfavorably, including individuals (e.g., the prime minister of Britain), groups of people (e.g., racial groups), social issues (e.g., censorship), abstract ideas (e.g., modern art), behaviors (e.g., eating meat), and specific objects (e.g., hamburgers). More important, the attitudinal orientations toward these attitude objects are subjective, because they reflect how a person sees an object and not necessarily how the object exists in reality.

Although the commonplace view of attitudes and the social psychological perspectives share an emphasis on attitudes as inclinations, they differ in the extent to which these inclinations are attached to things in general rather than to specific attitude objects. Lay perspectives often treat attitudes as trait-like orientations, such that a person with a positive attitude likes most things, and a person with a negative attitude dislikes most things. In contrast, the social psychological perspective emphasizes orientations toward specific objects, because social psychology has traditionally emphasized the ability of situational factors to alter attitudes. This emphasis explains how a person may have a positive attitude toward one thing (e.g., the media) and a negative attitude toward other things (e.g., the government). As a result, the social psychological concept allows flexibly for the possibility that a person may have similar attitudes toward different objects, but also have different attitudes toward different objects, and even have different attitudes toward the same object.

## The three witches in theories of attitude

Despite the shared emphasis on subjective, object-bound evaluations, past research on attitudes has included a variety of different assumptions about the way in which attitudes exist in the human mind. The theories cover three basic aspects of attitudes: content, structure, and function. To us, the operation of these three aspects is analogous to the way that three witches often work in folklore. Although a witch alone is capable of making a magical brew, three witches make the most potent brew together. This section reviews the independent "brews" in attitude theory, after which we describe the outcomes that might emerge from a common brew.

### Attitude content

Attempts to describe the content of attitudes have taken one of two perspectives. These perspectives make assumptions about the manner in which attitudes express more elemental psychological constructs, such as beliefs about the attitude object.

### The belief-based model

The traditional view of attitudes is that they express the totality of a person's relevant beliefs about the attitude object. For example, a person might believe that violent films are exciting, while also believing that the films cause society to become more tolerant of violence in the public and elicit an atmosphere of paranoia and distrust. As a result, the individual may hold a somewhat unfavorable attitude toward violent films, because the single positive belief about violent films is outnumbered by the two negative beliefs. Nonetheless, this example only partly describes the emergence of attitudes from beliefs. According to the well-known expectancy value perspective on attitudes, for example, Fishbein and Ajzen's (1975) *theory of reasoned action*, however, the situation is rarely this simple, because beliefs are associated with varying degrees of certainty and differing evaluative implications. A person may be 100% certain that violent films are exciting, but only 20% certain that they elicit violence and greater distrust in society. Moreover, the person might regard the impact on his or her own excitement as "very good," but regard the negative impacts on tolerance of violence and distrust as only "mildly bad." According to the expectancy-value model, beliefs have less impact on attitudes when they are less certain and less evaluatively extreme. This reasoning is summarized in a well-known equation:

$$A = \Sigma \, b_i e_i$$

where A is the total attitude toward the attitude object, $b_i$ is the subjective belief that the object possesses attribute *i* (e.g., the probability that violent films increase tolerance of violence), and $e_i$ is the evaluation of attribute *i* (e.g., the positive or negative value attached to the tolerance of violence).

Based on this view, some measures of attitudes ask people to rate (1) the probability that the object possesses each of many attributes and (2) the desirability of each attribute. The overall attitude is computed as the product of the probability and evaluative ratings for each attribute, and the products are summed across all of the attributes (e.g., Fishbein & Ajzen, 1975). Research has found that there are at least moderate relations between people's reports of their own attitudes and the summed products of the attitude-relevant expectancies and values (e.g., Budd, 1986; van der Pligt & de Vries, 1998). In addition, studies of persuasion have provided support for the notion that beliefs influence attitudes, because the persuasive messages used in these studies elicit specific positive or negative beliefs about an attitude object, and these positive beliefs, in turn, predict the emergence of more positive attitudes than do the negative beliefs (Chaiken, Liberman, & Eagly, 1989; Petty & Cacioppo, 1986; Thompson, Kruglanski, & Spiegel, 2000). It is also interesting that the relation between beliefs and attitudes is stronger when people possess high confidence about their beliefs than when people lack confidence about their beliefs (Briñol & Petty, Chapter 9 this volume). Thus, confidence about beliefs may be an important novel factor to consider in the belief-based models of attitude.

Nevertheless, an important implication of the belief-based model is that knowledge of the beliefs underlying attitudes should help to anticipate when the attitudes themselves predict behavior and are resistant to change (i.e., attitude strength; Petty & Krosnick, 1995). Specifically, attitudes should be stronger when the total number of accessible (i.e., easy to retrieve) attitude-relevant beliefs is high than when it is low. This effect should occur because the presence of abundant accessible beliefs provides people with many bits of information to counteract the potential influence of new information and may help people to retrieve the attitude from memory (see Wood, Rhodes, & Biek, 1995). A variety of evidence supports this reasoning. People who report a greater number of attitude-relevant beliefs are more likely to resist changing their attitude (e.g., Wood et al., 1995), possess biased perceptions of relevant messages (e.g., Vallone, Ross, & Lepper, 1985), and perform attitude-consistent behaviors (e.g., Kallgren & Wood, 1986).

*Three-component model*

The three-component model assumes that beliefs are not the sole antecedents of attitudes—attitudes can also express feelings and past behaviors regarding the attitude object (Eagly & Chaiken, 1998; Zanna & Rempel, 1988). That is, people usually have positive attitudes toward an object when their beliefs, feelings, and past behaviors express favorability toward the object, whereas people tend to have negative attitudes toward an object when their beliefs, feelings, and past behaviors express unfavorability toward the object. In this view, beliefs are associations between an object and its attributes in memory (e.g., "eating meat is unhealthy"); feelings are the pleasant or unpleasant sensations elicited by particular objects (e.g., "eating meat is disgusting"); and behaviors are overt acts that involve approaching or avoiding the object in some way (e.g., "I buy meat infrequently"). The attitude is a summary evaluation based on the beliefs, feelings, and past behaviors, and people may experience primarily this summary evaluation when they encounter the attitude object. That is, people can store their attitude as a statement in memory (e.g., "eating meat is bad"), in addition to storing the component beliefs, feelings, and behaviors. Moreover, the attitude can be highly consistent with the evaluative implications of the beliefs, feelings, and behaviors, or it can be at least partly inconsistent with them (Chaiken, Pomerantz, & Giner-Sorolla, 1995). The amount of consistency may depend on a variety of factors, including individual difference variables (Haddock & Huskinson, Chapter 2 this volume; Maio, Esses, Arnold & Olson, Chapter 1 this volume).

Measures of attitude that are based on this model attempt to assess all of the attitude-relevant beliefs, feelings, and behaviors. For example, open-ended measures ask participants to list their beliefs, feelings, and behaviors regarding the attitude object (Esses & Maio, 2002; Haddock & Zanna, 1998). Participants then rate the extent to which each response reflects something that is negative or positive about the attitude object. It is also possible to ask people to rate the extent to which a list of many beliefs, feelings, and behaviors describe them (cf. Crites et al., 1994). Such verbal measures can be supplemented by nonverbal data. For example, Breckler (1984) measured attitudes toward snakes by asking participants to rate their beliefs, feelings, and past behaviors toward snakes, using self-report scales. In addition, he recorded participants' heart rate (a nonverbal indicator of affect) and behavior in the presence of a live snake.

Researchers have found that these approaches yield beliefs, feelings, and behaviors that are correlated, but distinct (Breckler, 1984; Breckler & Wiggins, 1989; Crites et al., 1994; Haddock & Zanna, 1998). In addition, attitude-relevant feelings and beliefs may be clustered separately in memory (Trafimow & Sheeran, 1998, Chapter 3 this volume). Consistent with this separation of cognition and affect, cognitive responses are strong predictors of attitudes toward controversial issues (e.g., abortion, death penalty, nuclear arms; Breckler & Wiggins, 1989; Crites et al., 1994; Eagly, Mladinic, & Otto, 1994), whereas affective responses are strong predictors of attitudes toward blood donation (Breckler & Wiggins, 1989), intellectual pursuits (Crites et al., 1994), politicians (Glaser & Salovey, 1998), and smoking (Trafimow & Sheeran, 1998). In addition, affective associates of attitudes appear to be processed more easily (Reeder & Pryor, 2000) and more accessible (Verplanken, Hofstee, & Janssen, 1998; cf. Giner-Sorolla, 2001).

Drawing on the three-component model, attitudes should be stronger when they are evaluatively consistent with their components than when the attitudes and the components are somewhat discrepant (Chaiken et al., 1995). This effect of evaluative-cognitive consistency should occur because evaluatively consistent attitudes provide people with similarly valenced information about an attitude object when it is encountered in different situations. In contrast, evaluatively inconsistent attitudes may yield dissimilar information about the attitude object in different situations, depending on which aspects of the attitude object are salient. Past research has supported this reasoning by testing whether attitudes that are consistent with attitude-relevant beliefs (i.e., evaluative-cognitive consistency) are stronger than attitudes that are inconsistent with attitude-relevant beliefs (i.e., low evaluative-cognitive consistency). As expected, attitudes that are high in evaluative consistency are more stable, resistant to change, and predictive of behavior than attitudes that are low in evaluative consistency (see Chaiken et al., 1995).

### Attitude structure

Perspectives on attitude content are often treated as though they simply feature aspects of attitude *structure* (e.g., Eagly & Chaiken, 1993; Olson & Maio, in press). Extant evidence now forces a more explicit distinction between attitude content and structure, because the three-component model and the belief-based model are potentially compatible with different views on the manner in which attitudes summarize the positivity and negativity implied by beliefs, feelings, and behaviors. These models of attitude content traditionally assume that the components are combined to form an attitude that is positive or negative, but the possibility of emergent positive and negative evaluations exists.

*Unidimensional model*

The traditional perspective assumes that people may feel either positively or negatively about an attitude object, but not both at the same time. This perspective provides the basis for most for measures of attitude. Some measures ask people to rate their attitudes using semantic-differential scales that are anchored by a negative adjective at one end (e.g., bad) and a positive adjective at the other end (e.g., good). Other measures ask people to rate their agreement or disagreement with items that express favorability *or* unfavorability toward an attitude object (e.g., anti-terrorism laws). Such measures yield a total attitude score that represents favorability or unfavorability as polar opposites.

These unidimensional measures exhibit substantial criterion validity, because they yield attitude scores that reliably predict behavior (Ajzen & Fishbein, 1977; Kraus, 1995). Moreover, the extremity of these unidimensional evaluations from the neutral midpoint (i.e., the extent to which the individual's attitude is very favorable or very unfavorable) is important for understanding attitude strength (Abelson, 1995). Compared to less extreme attitudes, extreme attitudes are more predictive of behavior (e.g., Fazio & Zanna, 1978a), more resistant to influence (e.g., Osgood & Tannenbaum, 1955), and more strongly projected onto others (e.g., Allison & Messick, 1988).

Attitude strength is also influenced by the accessibility (i.e., ease of retrieval) of these unidimensional evaluations. When people can quickly report whether they like or dislike an attiude object, their attitude is likely to influence perceptions of attitude-relevant events (e.g., Houston & Fazio, 1989), predict behavior (Fazio, 1990; Kraus, 1995), and resist change (e.g., Bassili, 1996). In theory, the attitude object spontaneously activates highly accessible attitudes. As a result, these attitudes are more likely to exert an impact on judgments and behavior when the object is encountered.

*Bidimensional model*

The unidimensional model may be limited, despite its predictive power. A more powerful approach would allow for occasions when attitudes are both favorable and unfavorable toward the attitude object (i.e., ambivalent), in addition to encompassing the unidimensional prediction that attitudes can be (1) favorable, (2) unfavorable, and (3) neither favorable nor unfavorable. The bidimensional model encompasses this greater range of possibilities by proposing that attitudes subsume two dimensions of evaluation: one dimension varies in positivity and the other dimension varies in negativity.

Kaplan (1972) suggested that these separate dimensions may be assessed by "splitting" semantic differential scales into separate positive and negative dimensions (see Breckler, Chapter 4 this volume). For example, a measure of attitudes could include a semantic-differential scale from −3 (very bad) to

0 (neutral) and a semantic-differential scale from 0 (neutral) to 3 (very good), rather than use a single semantic-differential scale from −3 (very bad) to 3 (very good). It is also possible to use open-ended measures of attitude-relevant beliefs, feelings, and behaviors to assess separately the positivity and negativity in a person's attitude (see Esses & Maio, 2002; Haddock & Zanna, 1998). This approach involves examining the beliefs, feelings, and behaviors that respondents view as being positive separately from the beliefs, feelings, and behaviors that respondents view as being negative. Regardless of how the positivity and negativity scores are derived, the separate negative and positive dimension scores can be (1) analyzed separately; (2) summed to determine whether the attitude is primarily favorable, unfavorable, or neutral; (3) entered into formulae that enable the calculation of ambivalence (e.g., Bell, Esses, & Maio, 1996; Priester & Petty, 1996; Thompson, Zanna, & Griffin, 1995).

The success of the bidimensional model hinges on the relations between the separate positive and negative dimension scores, differences in their development and consequences, and the predictive power of ambivalence. First, if the bidimensional view is valid, favorability toward attitude objects should be at least somewhat unrelated to unfavorability toward the objects; otherwise, the two dimensions would supply redundant information. Consistent with the bidimensional view, researchers have found only moderate negative correlations between positivity and negativity, across a variety of attitude objects (e.g., different ethnic groups; Bell et al., 1996; Kaplan, 1972; Katz & Hass, 1988; Thompson et al., 1995; cf. Jonas, Diehl, & Brömer, 1997). Nonetheless, it is not yet known whether these correlations remain the same while simultaneously controlling random *and* systematic measurement error in the assessment of positivity and negativity. This issue is important because failure to control for both sources of error can artifactually make the positive and negative dimensions appear less strongly related than they are in reality (Green, Goldman, & Salovey, 1993).

Second, the positive and negative dimensions should have different developmental paths and outcomes. Consistent with this prediction, Cacioppo, Gardner, and Berntson (1997) describe a tendency for positivity to increase more slowly than negativity. Third, ambivalence should have unique psychological consequences that are not predicted by attitude valence alone. This prediction has been supported by evidence that ambivalence uniquely predicts the processing of persuasive messages (Hodson, Maio, & Esses, 2001; Jonas et al., 1997; Maio, Bell, & Esses, 1996) and attachment style in relationships (Maio, Fincham, & Lycett, 2001).

It has also been suggested that ambivalent attitudes have implications for understanding attitude strength, because ambivalent attitudes are easier to change (e.g., Armitage & Conner, Chapter 6 this volume) and less predictive of behavior (e.g., Lavine, Chapter 5 this volume) than nonambivalent attitudes. In addition, ambivalence polarizes relevant judgments of an attitude object when one of the positive or negative dimensions is made more salient than another (e.g., MacDonald & Zanna, 1998). For example, Bell and Esses

(2002) showed that individuals who possessed ambivalent attitudes toward Native Canadians made either more favorable or more unfavorable judgments about Native Canadian land claims depending on whether the participants were previously shown arguments supporting or opposing the land claims. In contrast, participants with nonambivalent attitudes were not affected by the different arguments.

Although one can use this evidence to conclude that ambivalent attitudes are weaker than nonambivalent attitudes (e.g., Armitage & Conner, Chapter 6 this volume), it is interesting to consider that the bidimensional model implies a slightly different conclusion. Specifically, the positive and negative evaluations themselves are stronger in ambivalent than in nonambivalent attitudes. This conclusion more closely fits the bidimensional model because this model treats the positive and negative dimensions as the real "attitude" dimensions, whereas the net "attitude" that is the average of these dimensions is a computational product that should have unique effects of its own.

### *Attitude function*

The above models of attitude content and structure are silent about the psychological motivations that attitudes fulfill. What needs and motives influence the valence and structure of attitudes? Why do people bother to form attitudes in the first place?

Two early models of attitude function (Katz, 1960; Smith, Bruner, & White, 1956) suggested overlapping answers to these questions. Smith et al. (1956) suggested that attitudes serve psychological needs to summarize the positive and negative attributes of objects in our environment (object-appraisal function), identify with people whom we like and dissociate from people whom we dislike (social-adjustment function), and defend the self against internal conflict (externalization function). Similarly, Katz (1960) proposed that attitudes serve needs to summarize information about attitude objects (knowledge function), maximize rewards and minimize punishments obtained from attitude objects (utilitarian function), express the self-concept and central values (value-expressive function), and protect self-esteem (ego-defense function).

More than 20 years after these models were proposed, several new models of attitude function emerged. Herek's (1986, 2000) theory of attitude function suggested a distinction between evaluative functions, which pertain to the ability of attitudes to summarize information about the attitude object itself, and expressive functions, which are fulfilled upon the expression of an attitude. He proposed three categories of evaluative functions. Experiential-specific attitudes help summarize favorable and unfavorable aspects of a specific attitude object (e.g., experiences with a particular member of a new immigrant group). Experiential-schematic attitudes summarize favorable and unfavorable information about a larger category of attitude objects (e.g., information about a new immigrant group from the media). Anticipatoryevaluative attitudes are based on the anticipated future utility of the attitude object (e.g., expectations that the minority group will contribute positively to the economy). He also proposed three expressive functions, which were the value-expressive, social-adjustive, and ego-defensive functions described above. In his model, all three expressive functions are fulfilled primarily when people use their attitudes as tools or symbols in their interactions with others. For example, people might protect their ties with other people (social-adjustive function) by communicating opinions that are shared by the others—the expression of these attitudes is a tool to achieve stronger bonds with the group.

Shavitt (1990) suggested three general categories of attitude function: utilitarian, social identity, and self-esteem maintenance. A unique feature of her model is the notion that some attitude objects should be tied to specific attitude functions (see also Han & Shavitt, 1994). For instance, air conditioners serve to make people comfortable and, therefore, attitudes toward them should primarily fulfill a utilitarian function. Similarly, flags, perfume, and clothing can serve a social identity purpose by expressing values and bonds to social groups. Attitudes toward controversial issues can serve a self-esteem maintenance function by making people feel good about their moral stance on topics.

Although it is equivocal whether any of the theories of attitude function adequately capture the full range of functions (see Maio et al. Chapter 1, this volume), there is evidence to support the importance of most of the proposed attitude functions (Maio & Olson, 2000). The object-appraisal function (which combines aspects of the utilitarian and knowledge functions) has received the most attention, because it can be argued that most attitudes simplify interaction with the environment in some way, regardless of whether the attitudes imply positivity or negativity toward the attitude object. Nonetheless, two sets of findings add caveats to this conclusion. First, researchers have found that highly accessible (i.e., easy-to-retrieve) attitudes increase the ease with which people make attitude-relevant judgments and decrease physiological arousal during these judgments (see Fazio, 1995, 2000). These findings support the conclusion that the object-appraisal function is more strongly served by attitudes that are spontaneously activated from memory when the object is encountered than by attitudes that are not spontaneously activated. Second, this object-appraisal function is more strongly served in the attitudes of individuals who are high in the need for closure, which is a "desire for a definite answer on some topic, *any* answer as opposed to confusion and ambiguity" (Kruglanski, 1989, p. 14). Through the object-appraisal function, attitudes can provide such "answers" by helping people to make decisions about attitude objects. Consequently, Kruglanski (1996) has predicted and found that a high need for closure increases the tendency to form and maintain attitudes, using an individual difference measure of need for closure and situational manipulations of the need for closure (which involve imposing or withdrawing situational pressures to resolve uncertainty).

Additional research has focused on the most well-known and important prediction of the theories of attitude function: Persuasive messages may yield more positive attitudes toward an attitude object when the messages successfully argue that the object fulfills a goal that message recipients aim to fulfill with their attitude than when the message addresses a goal that is irrelevant to message recipients' attitudes. A large amount of evidence supports this prediction (see Maio & Olson, 2000). For example, Shavitt (1990) found that advertisements for instrumental products (e.g., an air conditioner) were more persuasive when they emphasized instrumental features of the product than when they emphasized symbolic features (see also Han & Shavitt, 1994). In addition, DeBono (2000) predicted and found that low self-monitors (who typically possess utilitarian attitudes) are more persuaded by messages that emphasize utilitarian aspects of various products (e.g., whiskey, cigarettes) than are high self-monitors (whose attitudes typically fulfill social-adjustive functions). Petty and Wegener (1998) suggested that such effects occur because people process arguments that are relevant to the function of their attitude more carefully than they process arguments that are not relevant to the function of their attitude. As a result, these effects are more likely to occur when the persuasive arguments are strong than when the persuasive arguments are weak (Petty & Wegener, 1998).

## An agenda for theories of attitude

The three "witches" each describe important aspects of attitudes, but leave several issues unresolved. The purpose of this section is to describe the challenges to these descriptions of attitudes and some avenues that may be fruitful.

### Integration

It is possible to integrate the theories of attitude content, structure, and function, because they are compatible in many ways. For instance, the three-component model expands the expectancy-value formulation to consider different types of beliefs. This expansion is achieved by extending the belief-based model of attitude content to include distinctions between emotions and past behavior. The attitudes that are derived from these components may be formed along the positive and negative dimensions of the bidimensional model and on the positive versus negative dimension of the unidimensional model. The bidimensional model, however, allows for the same attitude positions as the unidimensional model (positive, negative, neutral), while also allowing for the existence of ambivalence. The bidimensional model may also apply more strongly to processes during attitude formation, where people perceive the attitude object on both positive and negative dimensions. These dimensions might then be integrated to form a single, unidimensional evaluation (see Cacioppo et al., 1997). Thus, it is possible that information from the three components feeds into positive and negative dimensions, which provide input for a single bipolar dimension.

At both the bidimensional and unidimensional level, the same attitude functions may operate, albeit to varying degrees. For instance, the object-appraisal function should be served more strongly by unidimensional attitudes than by bidimensional attitudes, because the bidimensional attitudes should evoke more decision conflict (except when only one dimension is salient). In addition, it is possible that social norms make it occasionally desirable to have high ambivalence in an attitude. Ambivalence may be desirable when an issue is controversial. In this situation, people who appear ambivalent may give the impression of being fair and knowledgeable. These individuals may also be inoffensive to others because they "agree" with everyone to some extent.

Despite the potential for integration, there have been few attempts so far, and none of the attempts have yet to address simultaneously attitude content, structure, and function. For instance, Maio and Olson's (2000; Maio et al., Chapter 1 this volume) function–structure model attempts to integrate ideas about attitude content with ideas about attitude function, but their model does not yet examine the role of attitude content at different levels of attitude dimensionality. Perhaps the strength of the interrelations between affect, cognition, and behavioral components are weaker at the bidimensional level of measurement than at the unidimensional level of measurement, because of the greater degree of integration between positivity and negativity required at the unidimensional level. This and other effects of attitude dimensionality have not yet been addressed in the function–structure model.

Similarly, Lord and Lepper's (1999; Lord, Chapter 13 this volume) attitude representation theory provides a new vantage point on the dominant models of attitude content and structure. This model proposes that people can be made aware of many exemplars of an attitude object, in addition to different attributes of each exemplar. For example, when thinking of their attitude toward politicians, people can recall the most recent politicians that they have seen in the news. The reported attitude will depend on which politicians are considered, because different politicians may be associated with different attributes and evaluations. It is likely that attitudes in general subsume many different exemplars of the attitude object, in addition to the varied attributes of the exemplars. Thus, this model provides an important and interesting caveat to the way that attitudes are conceived. Notably, however, this model does not yet explicitly consider the role of different attitude functions in attitude representations.

The same issue is relevant to the growing use of connectionist modeling to understand attitude structure. Both Eiser (Chapter 14 this volume) and Jordens and Van Overwalle (Chapter 15 this volume) propose that attitudes evolve from the association of feelings, beliefs, and past behaviors to an attitude object in a feedforward connectionist learning mechanism, which is a complex learning architecture (McClelland, Rumelhart, & Hinton, 1986).

Nonetheless, the links between this approach and the dimensionality and functioning of attitudes are not yet clear.

### Attitude formation and change

There are notable variations in the way that attitudes are formed. Classical conditioning of attitudes occurs when an attitude object comes to evoke an affective or behavioural response that it did not previously evoke, simply by being paired with another stimulus that already evokes that affective or behavioural response (e.g., Cacioppo, Marshall-Goodell, Tassinary, & Petty, 1992; Krosnick, Betz, Jussim, Lynn, & Stephens, 1992; Olson & Fazio, 2001; Staats & Staats, 1958). In this manner, for instance, consumer products that are paired with attractive models in advertisements might come to elicit positive feelings for people who view the advertisements. Mere exposure to an attitude object can also elicit positive affective responses to it (Zajonc, 1968). For example, an abstract painting might come to be liked over time as the painting becomes more familiar. An interesting feature of this effect is that it occurs even more strongly when people cannot consciously perceive or recognize the stimuli (e.g., Bornstein & D'Agostino, 1992; Moreland & Beach, 1992).

A challenge for researchers is to integrate knowledge about such mechanisms with conceptualizations of attitude content, structure, and function. As noted above, this integration is partly achieved by the evidence that persuasive messages are more successful when their content strongly addresses the function of the audience's attitude. It has also been suggested that persuasive messages are more successful when their content strongly addresses the affective versus cognitive bases of the audience's attitude (e.g., Edwards, 1990; Edwards & von Hippel, 1995; Fabrigar & Petty, 1999; Haddock & Huskinson, Chapter 2 this volume; cf. Millar & Millar, 1990). For instance, a message that uses conditioning to emphasize the positive feelings evoked by an object (e.g., a beverage) may cause positive attitudes toward the object among people who already possess many positive or negative feelings about it, but possess no beliefs about its other non-affective attributes (e.g., health value). In contrast, a message that emphasizes the nonaffective attributes of an object may cause positive attitudes toward the object among people who already possess many positive or negative beliefs about it, but possess few or no feelings about it. These potential effects of messages that match attitude function and content raise the possibility that strong persuasion is also elicited by messages that match a person's attitude structure. Specifically, one-sided persuasive messages (which highlight arguments for *or* against the attitude object) may be more persuasive when people hold unidimensional attitudes than when people hold bidimensional attitudes, whereas two-sided messages (which highlight arguments for *and* against the attitude object) may be more persuasive when people hold bidimensional attitudes than when they hold unidimensional attitudes. To our knowledge, this possibility has not yet been examined. Nonetheless, if this result occurs, it would suggest that the degree of match between persuasive messages and the psychological nature of targeted attitudes is important for understanding attitude formation and change, regardless of whether the message is tailored to attitude content, structure, or function.

This hypothesis is consistent with an important contemporary theory of attitude change—the *elaboration likelihood model* (Petty & Cacioppo, 1986). According to this model, a critical determinant of the effects of a persuasive message is the extent that the message is subjected to detailed processing. According to Petty, Wheeler, and Bizer (2000), messages that match the functions of message recipients' attitudes elicit more message elaboration than do messages that mismatch these functions of message recipients' attitudes. As a result, "matching" messages are more convincing only when their arguments are cogent and can withstand scrutiny. "Matching" messages that contain weak arguments appear flawed after close scrutiny, and therefore yield less persuasion than mismatching messages (Petty & Wegener, 1998). More important, Petty et al. (2000) presented evidence that similar enhancements of message scrutiny should occur whenever messages match any attribute of the message recipients, such as the content of their pre-message attitudes. Thus, a general principle may be that messages elicit more elaborate processing when they address the content, structure, and function of message recipients' attitudes.

Another important contemporary model attempts to integrate knowledge about attitude change with theories of the psychological nature of attitude, while focusing on the role of attitude function. Specifically, the *heuristic-systematic model* of persuasion (Chaiken et al., 1989) proposes that people process persuasive messages in a manner that enables them to attain attitudes that fulfil one of three goals: accuracy, social impression management, and ego defense. The accuracy motive causes people to pick out the strengths and weaknesses of persuasive messages, whereas the impression management and ego-defense motives cause people to process messages in ways that help them to maintain good social relations with others or to defend their self-esteem. There is some evidence to support these distinctions (Johnson & Eagly, 1989; Leippe & Elkin, 1987; Maio & Olson, 1995; cf. Petty & Cacioppo, 1990) and other predictions that are relevant to the match effects described above (Chen & Chaiken, 1999).

An interesting feature of both the elaboration-likelihood model of persuasion and the heuristic-systematic model of persuasion is their proposal that persuasive messages are processed through two routes. On the one hand, people may process the messages quickly and use simple decision cues to reach a post-message attitude. On the other hand, people may process the messages deliberately and use a careful consideration of the message arguments to reach a post-message attitude. Kruglanski, Fishbach, Erb, Pierro, and Mannetti's (Chapter 17 this volume) unimodel of persuasion challenges the distinction between these two routes, however, and strongly links message processing to the desire for accurate attitudes that fulfil the object-appraisal function. Also of interest, this desire for accurate attitudes is threatened when people encounter messages that may be deceptive or invalid, and Schul's (Chapter 10 this volume) research highlights how we cope with this situation. Overall, then, the recent research on attitude change uses diverse approaches to address the manner in which motivations and messages interact to influence attitude change, with an emphasis on the object-appraisal function of attitudes.

### Attention to attitude-relevant information

As discussed earlier, attitudes facilitate decisions about attitude objects, by enabling people to recognize the objects more quickly and more easily (Blascovich, Ernst, Tomaka, Kelsey, Salomon, & Fazio, 1993; Roskos-Ewoldsen & Fazio, 1992). This evidence is consistent with the notion that attitudes fulfill a need to have readily available guides to decisions about attitude objects (i.e., the object-appraisal function). Nonetheless, attitudes are useful guides only insofar as people believe that their attitudes are correct. If people have doubts about the veracity or utility of their attitudes, then they would need to reconsider the attitude object more fully. According to Festinger (1957), people experience an unpleasant tension from this type of self-scrutiny, and this tension motivates them to seek attitude-consistent information and avoid attitude-inconsistent information. A variety of evidence has supported this conclusion (e.g., Frey & Rosch, 1984; Olson & Zanna, 1979; Sweeney & Gruber, 1984; see also Hoshino-Browne, Zanna, Spencer, & Zanna, Chapter 16 this volume), although the evidence is strongest when the utility, novelty, and salience of consistent versus inconsistent information is controlled (Frey, 1986).

An interesting issue is whether such biased information searches are moderated by the content, structure, and function of attitudes. For instance, two people who positively evaluate the implementation of tougher laws to protect the environment may differ in their selective attention to information that supports their attitude, if their attitudes subsume different levels of ambivalence. A person who supports the tougher laws but possesses some ambivalence may seek out attitude congruent information more strongly than a person who supports tougher actions but possesses little ambivalence, because the attitude-congruent information would resolve the ambivalence and provide more closure for the ambivalent individual (see Maio et al., 1996). In addition, it is possible that attitudes bias information seeking more strongly when the attitudes are based on only one component (e.g., affect) than on many components. This effect may occur because a person whose attitude is based on only one component needs information from the other components to provide stronger support for the attitude, whereas attitudes that are already based on all three components do not require such consolidation of information across the components. Also, if the pursuit of attitude-consistent information is partly motivated by the need to believe in the veracity of attitudes, this tendency should be strongest when attitudes serve an object-appraisal function than some other function (e.g., ego defense, social adjustment). Regardless of whether these hypotheses are correct, theories of attitude should consider the implications of attitude content, structure, and function for understanding the pursuit of attitude-relevant information.

### *Interpretation and elaboration of attitude-relevant information*

An interesting feature of attitudes is that they motivate people to interpret information as more supportive of their attitudes than is actually the case. For example, Lord, Ross, and Lepper (1979) found that people's attitudes toward capital punishment predicted their ratings of the quality of an alleged scientific study that supported the deterrence value of the death penalty and another alleged scientific study that refuted the deterrence value of the death penalty. Participants more favorably evaluated the study that supported their own attitude than the study that refuted their attitude (cf. Houston & Fazio, 1989). This interpretational bias has other important implications. For instance, attitudes may interfere with people's ability to perceive change in an attitude object (Fazio, Ledbetter, & Towles-Schwen, 2000). Attitudes may also cause people to more easily recall attitudinally consistent information, although the evidence for this possibility is weak and inconsistent (see Eagly, Chen, Chaiken, & Shaw-Barnes, 1999). Finally, attitudes may influence spontaneous thinking about the attitude object, such that attitudes become polarized even in the absence of any new information (Tesser, 1978).

Perhaps these effects depend on attitude-relevant content. Indeed, polarization effects are stronger when people possess abundant information about the attitude object (Tesser, 1978). For instance, in the USA, polarization occurs more strongly when men think about scrimmage plays in American football and women think about fashions than when men think about fashions and women think about American football tactics (Tesser & Leone, 1977). Tesser and his colleagues assumed that this pattern occurred because men possess more elaborate schemas about American football tactics and women possess elaborate schemas about fashions. Presumably, however, these elaborate schemas included beliefs, feelings, and past behaviors regarding the topic, whereas the less elaborate schemas may have included only a few speculative beliefs. An interesting issue is whether more elaborate schemas lead to polarization more strongly when the knowledge is spread across attitude components than when it is restricted to a single component. In general, the strength of the effects of attitudes on interpretation, memory, and polarization may depend on the extent to which attitude-relevant knowledge is spread across the components.

These effects may also be less likely to occur when the attitude-relevant content is stored on separate negative and positive dimensions. Indirect support for this possibility again arises from the literature on attitude polarization, because polarization effects are stronger when beliefs and feelings about an object are similar in valence (see Chaiken & Yates, 1985). This similarity in valence may reflect a stronger tendency to store the beliefs and feelings on a single negative–positive dimension, rather than locate the beliefs and feelings on distinct negative and positive dimensions. Presumably, storage on a single dimension makes it more likely that focused thought leads to movement to a more extreme position on the dimension, whereas focused thoughts about two separate dimensions may lead to opposing movements and depolarization. Thus, attitude dimensionality may influence polarization effects, and, using similar logic, it could be argued that attitude dimensionality should influence attitude interpretation effects in general.

### Behavior toward the attitude object

Marketers, advertisers, and employers seek to influence attitudes because attitudes should predict behavior. From the point of view of an advertiser, for example, post-advertisement attitudes toward a commercial product should influence decisions to purchase the product. Similarly, from the perspective of an employer, attitudes toward one's job (i.e., job satisfaction) should predict the intensity of effort put into the job.

Attitudes are imperfect predictors of behavior (Wicker, 1969; cf. Kraus, 1995), however, because many factors influence this relationship. While noting the importance of intention as a proximal determinant of behavior (see Orbell, Chapter 7 this volume; Perugini & Bagozzi, Chapter 8 this volume), Ajzen and Fishbein (1977) observed that attitude–intention–behavior relations are stronger when the measure of attitude specifies the exact behavior of interest or when a measure of many relevant behaviors is used. There are also many attitude properties that moderate the magnitude of attitude–behavior relations. These relations become stronger when attitudes are based on direct experience (Fazio & Zanna, 1978b), held confidently (Fazio & Zanna, 1978a), easy to retrieve from memory (i.e., accessible; Fazio, 1990), extreme (Petersen & Dutton, 1975), based on high amounts of knowledge (Wood et al., 1995), evaluatively consistent with their constituent components (e.g., beliefs; Chaiken et al., 1995), and nonambivalent (Armitage & Conner, 2000).

Again, these results have implications for theories of attitude content, structure, and function. The effects of direct experience and high amounts of knowledge on attitude–behavior relations may be consistent with the general possibility that attitude–behavior relations are stronger when attitudes are based on information that is held across many components. In addition, the effects of evaluative consistency and ambivalence may be consistent with the notion that attitude–behavior relations are stronger when attitudes are stored on a single evaluative dimension, rather than separate negative and positive dimensions (which may separately direct behavior in different contexts).

Such possibilities might be addressed easily in expansions of existing models of attitude–behavior relations. The MODE model of attitude–behavior relations (Fazio, 1990) is a good example of a theory that might achieve this progress with a small amount of expansion. This model stipulates that attitudes influence judgment and behavior more strongly when the attitudes are spontaneously activated by the attitude object than when they are not spontaneously activated by the attitude object. As it stands, this model provides an elegant and comprehensive explanation of attitude–behavior relations. Thus far, however, the model focuses on attitudes that exist on a single evaluative dimension. This model could be potentially expanded to focus on the accessibility of both positive and negative evaluations (see Newby-Clark, McGregor, & Zanna, 2002). Alternatively, the emphasis on a single evaluative dimension may be usefully coupled with an explicit consideration of how the accessibility of this unidimensional attitude is influenced by attitude content, structure, and function. Perhaps, in general, attitudes are more accessible when they are based on diverse, evaluatively similar content, which is stored on a single dimension and serves many important psychological functions. If this is true, effects of attitude content, structure, and function on attitude accessibility may often mediate their effects on attitude–behavior relations.

### Attitudes and other constructs

The conceptual relations between attitudes and other social psychological constructs, such as values and ideologies, have not yet been fully explored and articulated. Several factors create high overlap between attitudes and these other constructs: the breadth of potential attitude objects, the focus on global evaluations in the attitude construct, and the assumption that attitudes subsume affective, cognitive, and behavioral content. Many of these features are possessed by social values, which are abstract ideals that people consider to be important guiding principles in their lives (e.g., freedom; Rokeach, 1973; Schwartz, 1992). Values can subsume a variety of abstract ideals, subsume global evaluations of these ideals, and include affective, cognitive, and behavioral components (Maio & Olson, 1998; Rohan, 2000). Moreover, theories of attitude function and theories of values indicate that the expression of values is a basic psychological function of attitudes (e.g., Herek, 1986; Katz, 1960; Rokeach, 1973), and many researchers have obtained evidence supporting the interconnection between these constructs (e.g., Gold & Robbins, 1979; Maio et al., 1996; Thomsen, Lavine, & Kounios, 1996).

Nevertheless, the extant research has also provided support for one of the principle characteristics that is said to differentiate values from attitudes. Specifically, according to Rokeach (1973) values exist at a higher level than attitudes in an hierarchical network of attitudes, beliefs, and values (see also Feather, 1995), such that a relatively small set of social values underlies most attitudes. This potential centrality of values is also reflected in Rosenberg's (1960, 1968) evaluative-cognitive consistency theory, which asserts that people strive for consistency between their attitudes and social values. This reasoning has been supported by research that has used priming paradigms to map the relations between values and attitudes in memory (Gold & Robbins, 1979; Thomsen et al., 1996).

The "importance" component of values also makes them distinct from attitudes (Feather, 1995: Maio & Olson, 1998), but there are reasons to further explore the role of importance in values and attitudes. The reason for examining this issue further is that value concepts and general attitude objects can be judged on dimensions of importance and valence. For instance, we could ask people to indicate the extent to which they *like* value concepts such as freedom, helpfulness, and equality. These responses would normally be labeled "attitudes" toward freedom, helpfulness, and equality. Do these attitudes convey the same information as ratings of value importance and, therefore, predict the same moral judgments and behaviors? We suspect that these attitudes do not convey the same information as ratings of value importance, because research on attitudes has indicated that importance judgments are distinct from judgments on other dimensions of attitude (e.g., certainty, intensity; Krosnick, Boninger, Chuang, Berent, & Carnot, 1993). Nevertheless, the answer to this empirical question would help to further elucidate the precise basis for distinguishing between values and attitudes.

### Inter-attitude structure

As researchers have learned about the manner in which attitudes form and change, researchers have also learned more about how attitudes influence each other. Heider (1958) predicted that people seek to hold attitudes that are logically consistent from the point of view of the person holding the attitudes. For instance, if Jim likes Lucy and Lucy likes Bill, Jim should be inclined to like Bill as well. A negative attitude toward Bill would create an unpleasant tension within Jim, which he would seek to reduce. Research that asks people to report how comfortable they would be in such scenarios has supported this reasoning (e.g., Jordan, 1953). Additional research has shown that people may experience a similar tension when their behaviors contradict their attitudes (see Harmon-Jones & Mills, 1999). Thus, we may have a general desire for evaluative consistency in the mental systems that contain our attitudes (Festinger, 1957; see also Eiser, Chapter 14 this volume).

In essence, attitudes can become antecedents of other attitudes, just as specific beliefs, feelings, and behaviors are components of attitudes. For instance, a person may dislike a right-wing political party because this party is unfavorable toward a reduction in greenhouse gas emissions. This situation can be characterized in one of two ways: (1) the person seeks consistency between his or her attitudes toward the party and his or her attitude toward the reduction of greenhouse gases; or (2) the person's attitude is based on the *belief* that the party will not reduce greenhouse gases, which is a consequence that the person evaluates very negatively. Thus, the attitude toward greenhouse gas emissions can be considered to be a *component* of the person's attitude toward the political party.

This possibility raises an important question: Do antecedent attitudes influence other (target) attitudes directly or do the components of the antecedent attitudes influence target attitudes? As shown in the top half of Figure 18.1 (Path A), the individual who would like a reduction in greenhouse gas emissions may hold this attitude because his or her asthma is debilitating during periods of increased smog. The attitude toward greenhouse gas reduction might, in turn, affect evaluations of the right-wing party that opposes these reductions. Alternatively, as shown in the bottom panel of Figure 18.1 (Path B), the person might believe that the right-wing party threatens his or her health because of the party's unwillingness to reduce smog. That is, the belief about the impact of greenhouse gases on the individual's health might directly shape the person's belief about the party's consequences for his or her health, and this belief about health might affect attitudes toward the party. It is interesting to consider the factors that determine when a component of an antecedent attitude (e.g., belief that smog worsens asthma) affects target attitudes directly (e.g., through belief that the right-wing party threatens health) rather than simply through the summary attitude that is based on the components (e.g., negative evaluation of greenhouse emissions). This issue is important because, if the matching principle is correct, the focus of persuasive messages on the topic should be more effective when they address the proximal determinants of the attitude. If the impact of the party on greenhouse gases is shaping attitudes toward the party, then messages should discuss this issue; if the impact of the party on people's health is

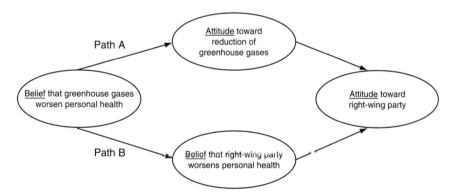

*Figure 18.1* The top panel (Path A) illustrates how a belief (greenhouse gases worsen personal health) might influence a target attitude (attitude toward the right-wing party) through an antecedent attitude (attitude toward reduction of greenhouse gases), whereas the bottom panel (Path B) indicates how a belief might influence a target attitude directly.

shaping attitudes toward the party, then messages should focus on alternative ways in which the party addresses health.

One possibility is that direct effects of components of the antecedent attitudes on target attitudes occur when the motivation to think about the rationale for the target attitude is low and the antecedent attitudes are highly consolidated and strong. In this situation, people might quickly base their target attitude on the attitudes that are linked to it, rather than deliberate on how the components of the antecedent attitudes are relevant to their target attitude. Some extant data support this reasoning. Specifically, Sanbonmatsu and Fazio (1990) gave participants information about two department stores that included camera departments and then, after a delay, asked participants where they would shop for a camera. One store was described favorably, but its camera department was described negatively. The other store was described unfavorably, but its camera department was described positively. Results indicated that participants were likely to base their decisions on the description of the camera department when they had received prior instructions asking them to form opinions of the stores *and* their camera departments. Participants were less likely to base their decisions on the description of the camera departments when the instructions encouraged them to form merely an opinion about the stores. More important, when the evaluations were not requested, the information about the camera departments was utilized only when participants were given instructions that motivated them to form an accurate decision and abundant time to reach their decision. These results show that more effort and ability may be required to search for and utilize weak evaluative beliefs that are components of attitudes than to search for strong attitudes that are based on the same information. Future theory and research should fully address this possibility by considering other attitude components (e.g., feelings).

### Attitude measurement

Theories of attitudes are inextricably bound to methods for assessing attitudes. As described above, the three-component model proposes different measures of attitude than the belief-based model, and the unidimensional model proposes different measures than the bidimensional model. The importance of these differences becomes even clearer when researchers attempt to assess the degree of correspondence between scores on a measure of attitude and scores on a measure of behavior. The measure of attitude can involve overt behaviors, such as simply circling a number on a scale or completing a series of more complex written descriptions of attitude. Conversely, the measure of behavior could primarily assess latent attitudes, as is the case when the "behavior" is simply a private expression of support for an attitude position. (For instance, a measure of voting behavior essentially asks for people's attitudes toward different candidates.) Thus, the question of "attitude–behavior" relations could be rephrased as a question of "behavior–

behavior" relations. The only reason that researchers often use the term "attitude–behavior" relations is that *theories* indicate how specific behaviors (e.g., scale ratings, response latencies) measure the latent construct that we call "attitude" (e.g., Lord, Chapter 13 this volume; Vargas, Chapter 12 this volume). Without these theories, we would be left with "behavior–behavior" relations and no reason to understand them in terms of attitudes rather than in terms of other constructs, such as habits and situational cues.

Recent innovations in attitude measurement are forcing more innovations in attitude theory. For instance, Bassili (1996) distinguished between "operative" and "meta-attitudinal" measures of attitude properties. Operative measures reflect attitude properties directly, whereas meta-attitudinal measures reflect the individual's conscious judgments about properties of their attitude. For example, the accessibility of an attitude can be assessed by directly timing how long it takes people to report their attitude when asked and by asking people to rate how easily they can remember their attitude. Bassili predicted and found that operative measures predict attitude resistance and stability more strongly than meta-attitudinal measures.

One of the problems with meta-attitudinal measures is that they may be affected by tendencies to respond in a manner that is socially desirable and consistent with personal motives (Paulhus, 1991). For example, people might be unwilling to report prejudice against ethnic groups because of the social stigma attached to prejudicial attitudes and because of conflict between any existing prejudice and egalitarian personal values. As a result, many techniques have been devised to overcome this problem. Some of these techniques use elaborate deceptive experimental procedures (e.g., bogus pipeline; Jones & Sigall, 1971) and psychophysiological techniques (e.g., brain-event potentials; facial electromyography, skin conductance; Cacioppo, Crites, & Gardner, 1996; Cacioppo, Petty, Losch, & Kim, 1986; Gardner, Cacioppo, Crites, & Berntson, 1994; Ohira, Winton, & Oyama, 1998; Petty & Cacioppo, 1983). Other techniques use priming procedures or response competition tasks to tap implicit, unconscious attitudes (e.g., Dovidio, Kawakami, Johnson, Johnson, & Howard, 1997; Fazio, Jackson, Dunton, & Williams, 1995; Greenwald, McGhee, & Schwartz, 1998). For example, people can be shown the name of different groups (e.g., blacks, whites) at subliminal levels and then asked to indicate whether a subsequent letter string is a word or nonword (Wittenbrink, Judd, & Park, 1997). Response times in this task can be used to calculate the extent to which the group names facilitated responding for positive versus negative trait words that appear as some of the letter strings.

Although virtually all of these operative measurement techniques have at least some evidence for their validity, an important issue is whether they actually tap the same construct. Indeed, the research cited above notes low correlations between measures. It is possible that some of these techniques yield "attitude" scores that are more closely linked to one attitude component than do others. Close ties to affect may be particularly true for some of the psychophysiological measures, such as eye blink latency and facial electromyography. An additional issue is whether some measures, such as measures of implicit attitudes, tap unidimensional attitudes more or less effectively than bidimensional attitudes (see Newby-Clark, McGregor, & Zanna, 2002). Also, as pointed out by Betsch, Plessner, and Schallies (Chapter 11 this volume), measures of implicit attitude may be influenced by different psychological processes for integrating prior information about attitude objects than are measures of explicit attitude. Resolving these issues is important for determining exactly how each measure fits with extant attitude theory.

## Conclusion

Despite the unresolved issues, attitude theories have made significant progress toward understanding attitude content, structure, and function. Now, an important agenda is to integrate the theories in these three domains into more powerful, comprehensive views of attitudes. The advances would include better understanding of attitude change, attention to attitude-relevant information, interpretation of attitude-relevant information, inter-attitude structure, and attitude measurement. As stated in a famous phrase, "Form ever follows function" (Louis Henry Sullivan). Thus, issues of attitude content, structure, and function are inextricably linked, and explicit delineation of these links would help address the substantial interest in the psychological nature of attitudes.

We are optimistic that such integration is emerging, and this integration will be an important issue for attitude researchers in the twenty-first century. The first century of research on attitudes yielded many of the basic principles for understanding attitudes and inspired considerable interest in this topic. The next hundred years of research on attitudes will consolidate this information and, we hope, inspire even greater interest.

## References

Abelson, R. P. (1995). Attitude extremity. In R. E. Petty & J. A. Krosnick (Eds.), *Attitude strength: Antecedents and consequences* (pp. 25–41). Mahwah, NJ: Lawrence Erlbaum Associates, Inc.

Ajzen, I., & Fishbein, M. (1977). Attitude–behavior relations: A theoretical analysis and review of empirical research. *Psychological Bulletin, 84*, 888–918.

Allison, S. T., & Messick, D. M. (1988). The feature-positive effect, attitude strength, and degree of perceived consensus. *Personality and Social Psychology Bulletin, 14*, 231–241.

Allport, G. W. (1935). Attitudes. In C. Murchison (Ed.), *Handbook of social psychology* (pp. 798–844). Worcester, MA: Clark University Press.

Armitage, C. J., & Conner, M. (2000). Attitude ambivalence: A test of three key hypotheses. *Personality and Social Psychology Bulletin, 26*, 1421–1432.

Bassili, J. N. (1996). Meta-judgmental versus operative indexes of psychological attributes: The case of measures of attitude strength. *Journal of Personality and Social Psychology, 71*, 637–653.

Bell, D. W., & Esses, V. M. (2002). Ambivalence and response amplification: A motivational perspective. *Personality and Social Psychology Bulletin, 28,* 1143–1152.

Bell, D. W., Esses, V. M., & Maio, G. R. (1996). The utility of open-ended measures to assess intergroup ambivalence. *Canadian Journal of Behavioural Science, 28,* 12–18.

Bem, D. J. (1970). *Beliefs, attitudes, and human affairs.* Belmont, CA: Brooks/Cole.

Blascovich, J., Ernst, J. M., Tomaka, J., Kelsey, R. M., Salomon, K. L., & Fazio, R. H. (1993). Attitude accessibility as a moderator of autonomic reactivity during decision making. *Journal of Personality and Social Psychology, 64,* 165–176.

Bornstein, R. F., & D'Agostino, P. R. (1992). Stimulus recognition and the mere exposure effect. *Journal of Personality and Social Psychology, 63,* 545–552.

Breckler, S. J. (1984). Empirical validation of affect, behavior, and cognition as distinct components of attitude. *Journal of Personality and Social Psychology, 47,* 1191–1205.

Breckler, S. J., & Wiggins, E. C. (1989). Affect versus evaluation in the structure of attitudes. *Journal of Experimental Social Psychology, 25,* 253–271.

Budd, R. J. (1986). Predicting cigarette use: The need to incorporate measures of salience in the theory of reasoned action. *Journal of Applied Social Psychology, 16,* 663–685.

Cacioppo, J. T., Crites, S. L., Jr., & Gardner, W. L. (1996). Attitudes to the right: Evaluative processing is associated with lateralized late positive event-related brain potentials. *Personality and Social Psychology Bulletin, 22,* 1205–1219.

Cacioppo, J. T., Gardner, W. L., & Berntson, G. G. (1997). Beyond bipolar conceptualizations and measures: The case of attitudes and evaluative space. *Personality and Social Psychology Review, 1,* 3–25.

Cacioppo, J. T., Marshall-Goodell, B. S., Tassinary, L. G., & Petty, R. E. (1992). Rudimentary determinants of attitudes: Classical conditioning is more effective when prior knowledge about the attitude stimulus is low than high. *Journal of Experimental Social Psychology, 28,* 207–233.

Cacioppo, J. T., Petty, R. E., Losch, M. E., & Kim, H. S. (1986). Electromyographic activity over facial muscle regions can differentiate the valence and intensity of affective reactions. *Journal of Personality and Social Psychology, 50,* 260–268.

Chaiken, S., Liberman, A., & Eagly, A. H. (1989). Heuristic and systematic processing within and beyond the persuasion context. In J. S. Uleman & J. A. Bargh (Eds.), *Unintended thought* (pp. 212–252). New York: Guilford Press.

Chaiken, S., Pomerantz, E. M., & Giner-Sorolla, R. (1995). Structural consistency and attitude strength. In R. E. Petty & J. A. Krosnick (Eds.), *Attitude strength: Antecedents and consequences* (pp. 387–412). Hillsdale, NJ: Lawrence Erlbaum Associates, Inc.

Chaiken, S., & Yates, S. (1985). Affective-cognitive consistency and thought-induced attitude polarization. *Journal of Personality and Social Psychology, 49,* 1470–1481.

Chen, S., & Chaiken, S. (1999). The heuristic-systematic model in its broader context. In S. Chaiken & Y. Trope (Eds.), *Dual-process theories in social psychology* (pp. 73–96). New York: Guilford Press.

Crites, S. L., Fabrigar, L. R., & Petty, R. E. (1994). Measuring the affective and cognitive properties of attitudes: Conceptual and methodological issues. *Personality and Social Psychology Bulletin, 20,* 619–634.

DeBono, K. G. (2000). Attitude functions and consumer psychology: Understanding perceptions of product quality. In G. R. Maio & J. M. Olson (Eds.), *Why we evaluate: Functions of attitudes* (pp. 1–36). Mahwah, NJ: Lawrence Erlbaum Associates, Inc.

Dovidio, J. F., Kawakami, K., Johnson, C., Johnson, B., & Howard, A. (1997). On the nature of prejudice: Automatic and controlled processes. *Journal of Experimental Social Psychology, 33*, 510–540.

Eagly, A. H., & Chaiken, S. (1993). *The psychology of attitudes.* Fort Worth, TX: Harcourt Brace Jovanovich.

Eagly, A. H., & Chaiken, S. (1998). Attitude structure and function. In D. T. Gilbert, S. T. Fiske, & G. Lindzey (Eds.), *The handbook of social psychology* (4th ed., Vol. 1, pp. 269–322). New York: McGraw-Hill.

Eagly, A. H., Chen, S., Chaiken, S., & Shaw-Barnes, K. (1999). The impact of attitudes on memory: An affair to remember. *Psychological Bulletin, 125*, 64–89.

Eagly, A. H., Mladinic, A., & Otto, S. (1994). Cognitive and affective bases of attitudes toward social groups and social policies. *Journal of Experimental Social Psychology, 30*, 113–137.

Edwards, K. (1990). The interplay of affect and cognition in attitude formation and change. *Journal of Personality and Social Psychology, 59*, 202–216.

Edwards, K., & von Hippel, W. (1995). Hearts and minds: The priority of affective and cognitive factors in person perception. *Personality and Social Psychology Bulletin, 21*, 996–1011.

Esses, V. M., & Maio, G. R. (2002). Expanding the assessment of attitude components and structure: The benefits of open-ended measures. In W. Stroebe & M. Hewstone (Eds.), *European review of social psychology* (Vol. 12, pp. 71–101) London: Wylie Press.

Fabrigar, L. R., & Petty, R. E. (1999). The role of affective and cognitive bases of attitudes in susceptibility to affectively and cognitively based persuasion. *Personality and Social Psychology Bulletin, 25*, 363–381.

Fazio, R. H. (1990). Multiple processes by which attitudes guide behavior: The MODE model as an integrative framework. In M. P. Zanna (Ed.), *Advances in experimental social psychology* (Vol. 23, pp. 75–109). San Diego, CA: Academic Press.

Fazio, R. H. (1995). Attitudes as object-evaluation associations: Determinants, consequences, and correlates of attitude accessibility. In R. E. Petty & J. A. Krosnick (Eds.), *Attitude strength: Antecedents and consequences* (pp. 247–282). Hillsdale, NJ: Lawrence Erlbaum Associates, Inc.

Fazio, R. H. (2000). Accessible attitudes as tools for object appraisal: Their costs and benefits. In G. R. Maio & J. M. Olson (Eds.), *Why we evaluate: Functions of attitudes* (pp. 1–36). Mahwah, NJ: Lawrence Erlbaum Associates, Inc.

Fazio, R. H., Jackson, J. R., Dunton, B. C., & Williams, C. J. (1995). Variability in automatic activation as an unobtrusive measure of racial attitudes: A bona fide pipeline? *Journal of Personality and Social Psychology, 69*, 1013–1027.

Fazio, R. H., Ledbetter, J. E., & Towles-Schwen, T. (2000). On the costs of accessible attitudes: Detecting that the attitude object has changed. *Journal of Personality and Social Psychology, 78*, 197–210.

Fazio, R. H., & Zanna, M. P. (1978a). Attitudinal qualities relating to the strength of the attitude–behavior relationship. *Journal of Experimental Social Psychology, 14*, 398–408.

Fazio, R. H., & Zanna, M. P. (1978b). On the predictive validity of attitudes: The role of direct experience and confidence. *Journal of Personality, 46*, 228–243.

Feather, N. (1995). Values, valences, and choice: The influence of values on the perceived attractiveness and choice of alternatives. *Journal of Personality and Social Psychology, 68*, 1135–1151.

Festinger, L. (1957). *A theory of cognitive dissonance*. Evanston, IL: Row, Peterson.

Fishbein, M., & Ajzen, I. (1975). *Belief, attitude, intention, and behavior: An introduction to theory and research*. Reading, MA: Addison-Wesley.

Frey, D. (1986). Recent research on selective exposure to information. In L. Berkowitz (Ed.), *Advances in experimental social psychology* (Vol. 19, pp. 41–80). San Diego, CA: Academic Press.

Frey, D., & Rosch, M. (1984). Information seeking after decisions: The roles of novelty of information and decision reversibility. *Personality and Social Psychology Bulletin, 10*, 91–98.

Gardner, W., Cacioppo, J. T., Crites, S., & Berntson, G. (1994). A late positive brain potential indexes between participant differences in evaluative categorizations. *Psychophysiology, 31*, S49.

Giner-Sorolla, R. (2001). Affective attitudes are not always faster: The moderating role of extremity. *Personality and Social Psychology Bulletin, 27*, 666–677.

Glaser, J., & Salovey, P. (1998). Affect in electoral politics. *Personality and Social Psychology Review, 2*, 156–172.

Gold, J. A., & Robbins, M. A. (1979). Attitudes and values: A further test of the semantic memory model. *Journal of Social Psychology, 108*, 75–81.

Green, D. P., Goldman, S. L., & Salovey, P. (1993). Measurement error masks bipolarity in affect ratings. *Journal of Personality and Social Psychology, 64*, 1029–1041.

Greenwald, A. G., McGhee, D. E., & Schwartz, J. L. K. (1998). Measuring individual differences in implicit cognition: The implicit association test. *Journal of Personality and Social Psychology, 74*, 1464–1480.

Haddock, G., & Zanna, M. P. (1998). On the use of open-ended measures to assess attitudinal components. *British Journal of Social Psychology, 37*, 129–149.

Han, S., & Shavitt, S. (1994). Persuasion and culture: Advertising appeals in individualistic and collectivistic societies. *Journal of Experimental Social Psychology, 30*, 326–350.

Harmon-Jones, E., & Mills, J. (Eds.) (1999). *Cognitive dissonance: progress on a pivotal theory in social psychology*. Washington, DC: American Psychological Association.

Heider, F. (1958). *The psychology of interpersonal relations*. New York: Wiley.

Herek, G. M. (1986). The instrumentality of attitudes: Toward a neofunctional theory. *Journal of Social Issues, 42*, 99–114.

Herek, G. M. (2000). The social construction of attitudes: Functional consensus and divergence in the U. S. public's reactions to AIDS. In G. R. Maio & J. M. Olson (Eds.), *Why we evaluate: Functions of attitudes* (pp. 325–364). Mahwah, NJ: Lawrence Erlbaum Associates, Inc.

Hodson, G., Maio, G. R., & Esses, V. M. (2001). The role of attitudinal ambivalence in susceptibility to consensus information. *Basic and Applied Social Psychology, 23*, 197–205.

Houston, D. A., & Fazio, R. H. (1989). Biased processing as a function of attitude accessibility: Making objective judgments subjectively. *Social Cognition, 7*, 51–66.

Johnson, B. T., & Eagly, A. H. (1989). Effects of involvement on persuasion: A meta-analysis. *Psychological Bulletin, 106*, 290–314.

Jonas, K., Diehl, M., & Brömer, P. (1997). Effects of attitude ambivalence on information processing and attitude-intention consistency. *Journal of Experimental Social Psychology, 33,* 190–210.

Jones, E. E., & Sigall, H. (1971). The bogus pipeline: A new paradigm for measuring affect and attitude. *Psychological Bulletin, 76,* 349–364.

Jordan, N. (1953). Behavioral forces that are a function of attitudes and of cognitive organization. *Human Relations, 6,* 273–287.

Kallgren, C. A., & Wood, W. (1986). Access to attitude-relevant information in memory as a determinant of attitude–behavior consistency. *Journal of Experimental Social Psychology, 22,* 328–338.

Kaplan, K. J. (1972). On the ambivalence–indifference problem in attitude theory and measurement: A suggested modification of the semantic differential technique. *Psychological Bulletin, 77,* 361–372.

Katz, D. (1960). The functional approach to the study of attitudes. *Public Opinion Quarterly, 24,* 163–204.

Katz, I., & Hass, R. G. (1988). Racial ambivalence and American value conflict: Correlational and priming studies of dual cognitive structures. *Journal of Personality and Social Psychology, 55,* 893–905.

Keller, J. (1999). *Attitude is everything: Change your attitude and you change your life.* Tampa, FL: INTI.

Kraus, S. J. (1995). Attitudes and the prediction of behavior: A meta-analysis of the empirical literature. *Personality and Social Psychology Bulletin, 21,* 58–75.

Krosnick, J. A., Betz, A. L., Jussim, L. J., Lynn, A. R., & Stephens, L. (1992). Subliminal conditioning of attitudes. *Personality and Social Psychology Bulletin, 18,* 152–162.

Krosnick, J. A., Boninger, D. S., Chuang, Y. C., Berent, M. K., & Carnot, C. G. (1993). Attitude strength: One construct or many related constructs? *Journal of Personality and Social Psychology, 65,* 1132–1151.

Kruglanski, A. W. (1989). *Lay epistemics and human knowledge: Cognitive and motivational bases.* New York: Plenum Press.

Kruglanski, A. W. (1996). Motivated social cognition: Principles of the interface. In E. T. Higgins & A. W. Kruglanski (Eds.), *Social psychology: Handbook of basic principles* (pp. 493–520). New York: Guilford Press.

Leippe, M. R., & Elkin, R. A. (1987). When motives clash: Issue involvement and response involvement as determinants of persuasion. *Journal of Personality and Social Psychology, 52,* 269–278.

Lord, C. G., & Lepper, M. R. (1999). Attitude representation theory. In M. P. Zanna (Ed.), *Advances in experimental social psychology* (Vol. 31, pp. 265–343). San Diego, CA: Academic Press.

Lord, C. G., Ross, L., & Lepper, M. R. (1979). Biased assimilation and attitude polarization: The effects of prior theories on subsequently considered evidence. *Journal of Personality and Social Psychology, 37,* 2098–2109.

MacDonald, T. K., & Zanna, M. P. (1998). Cross-dimension ambivalence toward social groups: Can ambivalence affect intentions to hire feminists? *Personality and Social Psychology Bulletin, 24,* 427–441.

Maio, G. R., Bell, D. W., & Esses, V. M. (1996). Ambivalence and persuasion: The processing of messages about immigrant groups. *Journal of Experimental Social Psychology, 32,* 513–536.

Maio, G. R., Fincham, F. D., & Lycett, E. J. (2000). Attitudinal ambivalence toward parents and attachment style. *Personality and Social Psychology Bulletin, 26,* 1451–1464.

Maio, G. R., & Olson, J. M. (1995). Relations between values, attitudes, and behavioral intentions: The moderating role of attitude function. *Journal of Experimental Social Psychology, 31*, 266–285.

Maio, G. R., & Olson, J. M. (1998). Values as truisms: Evidence and implications. *Journal of Personality and Social Psychology, 74*, 294–311.

Maio, G. R., & Olson, J. M. (2000). What *is* a value-expressive attitude? In G. R. Maio & J. M. Olson (Eds.), *Why we evaluate: Functions of attitudes* (pp. 249–269). Mahwah, NJ: Lawrence Erlbaum Associates, Inc.

Maio, G. R., Roese, N. J., Seligman, C., & Katz, A. (1996). Ratings, rankings, and the measurement of values: Evidence for the superior validity of ratings. *Basic and Applied Social Psychology, 18*, 171–181.

McClelland, J. L., Rumelhart, D. E., & Hinton, G. E. (1986). The appeal of parallel distributed processing. In D. E. Rumelhart, J. L. McClelland, & PDP Research Group (Eds.), *Parallel distributed processing* (Vol. 1, pp. 3–44). Cambridge, MA: MIT Press.

Millar, M. G., & Millar, K. U. (1990). Attitude change as a function of attitude type and argument type. *Journal of Personality and Social Psychology, 59*, 217–228.

Moreland, R. L., & Beach, S. R. (1992). Exposure effects in the classroom: The development of affinity among students. *Journal of Experimental Social Psychology, 28*, 255–276.

Newby-Clark, I. R., McGregor, I., & Zanna, M. P. (2002). Thinking and caring about cognitive inconsistency: When and for whom does attitudinal ambivalence feel uncomfortable? *Journal of Personality and Social Psychology, 82*, 157–166.

Ohira, H., Winton, W. M., & Oyama, M. (1998). Effects of stimulus valence on recognition memory and endogenous eyeblinks: Further evidence for positive–negative asymmetry. *Personality and Social Psychology Bulletin, 24*, 986–993.

Olson, J. M., & Maio, G. R. (in press). Attitudes in social behavior. In T. Millon & M. Lerner (Eds.), *Comprehensive handbook of psychology: Vol. 4. Personality and social psychology*, London: Wylie Press.

Olson, J. M., & Zanna, M. P. (1979). A new look at selective exposure. *Journal of Experimental Social Psychology, 15*, 1–15.

Olson, J. M., & Zanna, M. P. (1993). Attitudes and attitude change. *Annual Review of Psychology, 44*, 117–154.

Olson, M. A., & Fazio, R. H. (2001). Implicit attitude formation through classical conditioning. *Psychological Science, 12*, 413–417.

Osgood, C. E., & Tannenbaum, P. H. (1955). The principle of congruity in the prediction of attitude change. *Psychological Review, 62*, 42–55.

Paulhus, D. L. (1991). Measurement and control of response bias. In J. P. Robinson, P. R. Shaver, & L. S. Wrightsman (Eds.), *Measures of personality and social psychological attitudes* (Vol. 1, pp. 17–59). San Diego, CA: Academic Press.

Petersen, K. K., & Dutton, J. E. (1975). Certainty, extremity, intensity: Neglected variables in research on attitude–behavior consistency. *Social Forces, 54*, 393–414.

Petty, R. E., & Cacioppo, J. T. (1983). The role of bodily responses in attitude measurement and change. In J. T. Cacioppo & R. E. Petty (Eds.), *Social psycho-physiology: A sourcebook* (pp. 51–101). New York: Guilford Press.

Petty, R. E., & Cacioppo, J. T. (1986). The elaboration likelihood model of persuasion. In L. Berkowitz (Ed.), *Advances in experimental social psychology* (Vol. 19, pp. 123–205). San Diego, CA: Academic Press.

Petty, R. E., & Cacioppo, J. T. (1990). Involvement and persuasion: Tradition versus integration. *Psychological Bulletin, 107*, 367–374.

Petty, R. E., & Krosnick, J. A. (Eds.) (1995). *Attitude strength: Antecedents and consequences.* Mahwah, NJ: Lawrence Erlbaum Associates, Inc.

Petty, R. E., & Wegener, D. T. (1998). Matching versus mismatching attitude functions: Implications for scrutiny of persuasive messages. *Personality and Social Psychology Bulletin, 24*, 227–240.

Petty, R. E., Wegener, D. T., & Fabrigar, L. R. (1997). Attitudes and attitude change. *Annual Review of Psychology, 48*, 609–647.

Petty, R. E., Wheeler, S. C., & Bizer, G. Y. (2000). Attitude functions and persuasion: An elaboration likelihood approach to matched versus mismatched messages. In G. R. Maio & J. M. Olson, (Eds.), *Why we evaluate: Functions of attitude.* Mahwah, NJ: Lawrence Erlbaum Associates, Inc.

Priester, J. R., & Petty, R. E. (1996). The gradual threshold model of ambivalence: Relating the positive and negative bases of attitudes to subjective ambivalence. *Journal of Personality and Social Psychologyr, 71*, 431–449.

Reeder, G. D., & Pryor, J. B. (2000). Attitudes toward persons with HIV/AIDS: Linking a functional approach with underlying process. In G. R. Maio & J. M. Olson (Eds.), *Why we evaluate: Functions of attitudes* (pp. 295–323). Mahwah, NJ: Lawrence Erlbaum Associates, Inc.

Rohan, M. (2000). A rose by any name? The values construct. *Personality and Social Psychological Review, 4*, 255–277.

Rokeach, M. (1973). *The nature of human values.* New York: Free Press.

Rosenberg, M. J. (1960). An analysis of affective-cognitive consistency. In C. I. Hovland & M. J. Rosenberg (Eds.), *Attitude organization and change: An analysis of consistency among attitude components* (pp. 15–64). New Haven, CT: Yale University Press.

Rosenberg, M. J. (1968). Hedonism, inauthenticity, and other goals toward expansion of a consistency theory. In R. P. Abelson, E. Aronson, W. J. McGuire, T. M. Newcomb, M. J. Rosenberg, & P. H. Tannenbaum (Eds.), *Theories of cognitive consistency: A sourcebook* (pp. 827–833). Chicago: Rand McNally.

Roskos-Ewoldsen, D. R., & Fazio, R. H. (1992). The accessibility of source likability as a determinant of persuasion. *Personality and Social Psychology Bulletin, 18*, 19–25.

Russell-McCloud, P. (1999). *A is for attitude: An alphabet for living.* New York: HarperCollins.

Ryan, M. J. (1999). *Attitudes of gratitude: How to give and receive joy every day of your life.* Berkeley, CA: Conari Press.

Sanbonmatsu, D. M., & Fazio, R. H. (1990). The role of attitudes in memory-based decision making. *Journal of Personality and Social Psychology, 59*, 614–622.

Schwartz, S. H. (1992). Universals in the content and structure of values: Theoretical advances and empirical tests in 20 countries. In M. P. Zanna (Ed.), *Advances in experimental social psychology* (Vol. 25, pp. 1–65). San Diego, CA: Academic Press.

Shavitt, S. (1990). The role of attitude objects in attitude functions. *Journal of Experimental Social Psychology, 26*, 124–148.

Smith, M. B., Bruner, J. S., & White, R. W. (1956). *Opinions and personality.* New York: Wiley.

Staats, A. W., & Staats, C. K. (1958). Attitudes established by classical conditioning. *Journal of Abnormal and Social Psychology, 57*, 37–40.

Sweeney, P. D., & Gruber, K. L. (1984). Selective exposure: Voter information preferences and the Watergate affair. *Journal of Personality and Social Psychology*, *46*, 1208–1221.

Tesser, A. (1978). Self-generated attitude change. In L. Berkowitz (Ed.), *Advances in experimental social psychology* (Vol. 11, pp. 289–338). San Diego, CA: Academic Press.

Tesser, A., & Leone, C. (1977). Cognitive schemas and thought as determinants of attitude change. *Journal of Experimental Social Psychology*, *13*, 340–356.

Thompson, D. (1996). *The pocket Oxford dictionary of current English*. Oxford: Oxford University Press.

Thompson, E. P., Kruglanski, A. W., & Spiegel, S. (2000). Attitudes as knowledge structures and persuasion as a specific case of subjective knowledge acquisition. In G. R. Maio & J. M. Olson (Eds.), *Why we evaluate: Functions of attitudes* (pp. 59–95). Mahwah, NJ: Lawrence Erlbaum Associates, Inc.

Thompson, M. M., Zanna, M. P., & Griffin, D. W. (1995). Let's not be indifferent about (attitudinal) ambivalence. In R. E. Petty & J. A. Krosnick (Eds.), *Attitude strength: Antecedents and consequences* (pp. 361–386). Mahwah, NJ: Lawrence Erlbaum Associates, Inc.

Thomsen, C. J., Lavine, H., & Kounios, J. (1996). Social value and attitude concepts in semantic memory: Relational structure, concept strength, and the fan effect. *Social Cognition*, *14*, 191–225.

Trafimow, D., & Sheeran, P. (1998). Some tests of the distinction between cognitive and affective beliefs. *Journal of Experimental Social Psychology*, *34*, 378–397.

Vallone, R. P., Ross, L., & Lepper, M. R. (1985). The hostile media phenomenon: Biased perception and perceptions of media bias in coverage of the Beirut massacre. *Journal of Personality and Social Psychology*, *49*, 577–585.

van der Pligt, J., & de Vries, N. (1998). Belief importance in expectancy-value models of attitudes. *Journal of Applied Social Psychology*, *28*, 1339–1354.

Verplanken, B., Hofstee, G., & Janssen, H. J. W. (1998). Accessibility of affective versus cognitive components of attitudes. *European Journal of Social Psychology*, *28*, 23–35.

Wal-Mart Canada (1997). *Meeting of Wal-Mart Canada employees, Toronto, ON*. Toronto: Wal-Mart Canada.

Wicker, A. W. (1969). Attitude versus actions: The relationship of verbal and overt behavioral responses to attitude objects. *Journal of Social Issues*, *25*, 41–78.

Wittenbrink, B., Judd, C., & Park, B. (1997). Evidence for racial prejudice at the implicit level and its relationship with questionnaire measures. *Journal of Personality and Social Psychology*, *72*, 262–274.

Wood, W., Rhodes, N., & Biek, M. (1995). Working knowledge and attitude strength: An information processing analysis. In R. E. Petty & J. A. Krosnick (Eds.), *Attitude strength: Antecedents and consequences* (pp. 455–487). Mahwah, NJ: Lawrence Erlbaum Associates, Inc.

Zajonc, R. B. (1968). Attitudinal effects of mere exposure. *Journal of Personality and Social Psychology*, *9* (Monograph suppl. No. 2, Pt. 2), 1–27.

Zanna, M. P., & Rempel, J. K. (1988). Attitudes: A new look at an old concept. In D. Bar-Tal & A. W. Kruglanski (Eds.), *The social psychology of knowledge* (pp. 315–334). Cambridge: Cambridge University Press.

# Author index

# Subject index